Gorazd Meško
Eszter Sárik
Anna-Maria Getoš Kalac (eds.)

Mapping the Victimological Landscape of the Balkans

Research Series of the Max Planck Institute
for Foreign and International Criminal Law

Publications of the Max Planck Partner Group for Balkan Criminology

Edited by Hans-Jörg Albrecht
& Anna-Maria Getoš Kalac

Volume BC 4

Max-Planck-Institut für ausländisches
und internationales Strafrecht

Gorazd Meško
Eszter Sárik
Anna-Maria Getoš Kalac (eds.)

Mapping the Victimological Landscape of the Balkans

A Regional Study on Victimology and Victim Protection with a Critical Analysis of Current Victim Policies

Duncker & Humblot · Berlin

Bibliographic information published by the Deutsche Nationalbibliothek

The Deutsche Nationalbibliothek lists this publication in the Deutsche Nationalbibliografie; detailed bibliographic data are available on the in-ternet at http://dnb.d-nb.de

c/o Max Planck Institute for Foreign and International Criminal Law
Günterstalstr. 73, 79100 Freiburg i.Br., Germany
www.mpicc.de
Sales and distribution together with Duncker & Humblot GmbH, Berlin, Germany
www.duncker-humblot.de
University of Zagreb – Faculty of Law, Trg Republike Hrvatske 14, 10000 Zagreb, Croatia
www.pravo.unizg.hr

Cover picture: Harut Movsisyan/Pixabay

Printing: Stückle Druck und Verlag, Stücklestr. 1, 77955 Ettenheim, Germany
Printed in Germany

ISSN 2199-658X
ISBN 978-3-86113-279-0 (Max Planck Institute)
ISBN 978-3-428-15993-2 (Duncker & Humblot)
ISBN 978-953-270-136-4 (Zagreb Faculty of Law)

DOI: https://doi.org/10.30709/978-3-86113-279-0

Preface

The Max Planck Institute for Foreign and International Criminal Law in Freiburg (MPI) and the Faculty of Law at the University of Zagreb started a series of books on criminology in the Balkans in 2012. This book series has been co-founded and co-edited by Prof. Dr. Dr. h.c. mult. *Hans-Jörg Albrecht*, the acting director of the Max Planck Institute for Foreign and International Criminal Law and Head of its Department of Criminology, and Assoc. Prof. *Anna-Maria Getoš Kalac*, PhD, Head of the Max Planck Partner Group for Balkan Criminology (2012–2019) and Head of the Institute of Criminal Law Sciences, Criminology and Victimology at the Faculty of Law, University of Zagreb, Croatia.

After the first volume of the series that successfully mapped the criminological landscape of the Balkans (2014), the next step entailed aspiring to conduct a comparative victimological study focusing on victimisation, victim protection policies, legal perspectives and practice of victim protection in the Balkans and neighbouring countries.

The second volume, covering the Balkan's 'victimological landscape', is based on a comparative victimological survey of the Max Planck Partner Group for Balkan Criminology (MPPG) entitled "Mapping the Victimological Landscape of the Balkans: A Regional Survey on Victimology, Victimisation and Victim Protection Policies with a Critical Analysis of Current Victim Policies".

Gorazd Meško, Eszter Sárik, Anna-Maria Getoš Kalac

Ljubljana, Budapest and Zagreb, July 2020

Acknowledgements

We would like to express our gratitude to everyone who has actively contributed to the successful publishing of this volume. Our gratitude first goes to the authors of the papers included in this book who have worked for more than two years to complete their manuscripts for publishing. The authors' zeal and dedication have been present during the entire editing process, from the first peer reviews, paper revisions to copyediting. The authors' work greatly contributed to the recognition of victimology in their respective countries.

Our thanks also go to the peer reviewers who helped us improve the drafts. Without the active support and thoughtful advice of *Michael Kilchling,* PhD, we probably never would have successfully tackled the complex publishing process at the Max Planck Institute for Foreign and International Criminal Law. We are particularly grateful to him and much obliged for his significant contribution, as well as for the book's cover design.

Not less valuable is the technical editing in order to prepare, proofread, layout and typeset this book. The editors especially thank *Katharina John*, Assist. Prof. *Rok Hacin*, PhD, and *Dalia Pribisalić* for their excellent proofreading and typesetting. Similarly demanding was the language and writing style editing managed by *Chris Murphy*, PhD, *Jan Ruk,* and *Sandra Belko Leović*. We are grateful for their great efforts in improving the English, and occasionally even the contents, of the texts that were written by non-native English authors. Special thanks go to Prof. Dr. Dr. h.c. mult. *Hans-Jörg Albrecht,* the former acting director of the Max Planck Institute for Foreign and International Criminal Law and Head of its Department of Criminology, as well as Prof. *Igor Gliha,* PhD, Dean of the University of Zagreb Faculty of Law, for continuously supporting our effort to publish this valuable victimological volume. Their sincere commitment and strong encouragement over the past few years have been, and in many regards still are, an inexhaustible source of inspiration and motivation. It is also necessary to mention the University of Maribor Faculty of Criminal Justice and Security and the Hungarian National Institute of Criminology (OKRI) and to thank them for their support to the editors.

During the process of finalising the volume at hand, the Max Planck Partner Group for Balkan Criminology has reached its goal and therefore formally ceased to exist in spring 2019. However, the Balkan Criminology Initiative, as founded back in 2012 by Prof. Dr. Dr. h.c. mult. *Hans-Jörg Albrecht* and Assoc. Prof. *Anna-Maria Getoš Kalac,* PhD, continues its work and overall mission to increase the visibility and presentation of comparative criminological research in the Balkans and beyond. Through the Balkan Criminology Network, a core group of highly committed and genuinely enthusiastic researchers from the Balkan countries and those from other regions of Europe interested in the Balkans has emerged, developed, persevered to the present time, and is looking forward to new research challenges. Their active engagement has ensured that the current volume is not just another book. It is a significant milestone in achieving the overall mission of the Balkan Criminology Initiative to ambitiously explore state of the art in current criminological, victimological, and penological practice, policies, and research. We believe that the core group members of the Balkan Criminology Network have developed into relevant contributors to the European and global criminological research community. Therefore, we thank all the members and supporters of the Balkan Criminology Initiative and its Network.

The Editors, Ljubljana, Budapest and Zagreb, July 2020

Contents

Introduction to "Balkan Victimology"

Gorazd Meško, Anna-Maria Getoš Kalac & Michael Kilchling

I.

Far too long has the Balkan region been a 'terra incognita' in the European criminological and victimological research area. This deficit can be explained mainly by the lack of publications in English (with a small number of exceptions). We are convinced that this volume is a milestone of utmost importance for the development of victimological research and victim-oriented policies and practices in the Balkan countries. It should provide for the first point of departure to anyone's journey into victimological research in the Balkans.

The results of this regional comparative victimological survey originate from the 4th Annual Conference of the Max Planck Partner Group for Balkan Criminology, hosted by the Hungarian National Institute of Criminology (OKRI) in Budapest in 2017, aiming to provide an attempt to write a comprehensive victimological overview of the Balkans. The papers presented at the Budapest conference have been peer-reviewed, revised, and edited. Some authors joined the project later on.

Part One of this volume presents an overall picture of victimology in the Balkans from a wider (Western) European and cultural perspective, followed by country-specific chapters on the situation and status of victims and victimisers, formal and informal responses to victimisation, victim protection, and an overview of victimological research in *Part Two*. In *Part One*, *Antony Pemberton* elaborates on the cultural perspectives of victimology in different regions in Europe and the influence of Western victimology on other 'victimologies'. *Zoran Kanduč* addresses postmodern perspectives on crime victims and victimisation in the region, putting victimisation into a cultural, social and economic context, featuring structural, group-related and individual patterns of victimisation, victimisation in times of neo-liberal capitalism and thereby significantly expands the understanding of the complexity of victimisation. *Part One* concludes with short abstracts of the individual country reports, which will follow in full length in *Part Two*.

The magnitude and importance of such victimological research venture comprising fifteen contributions from thirteen countries of the region and beyond turned into an ambitious project. We provided all authors with a tentative structure for their contributions (mainly for comparative reasons). Still, as was to be expected, the final papers occasionally deviate from these guidelines due to country-specific contexts. Besides its content-related implications, the title of this book – *Victimology, Victimisation and Victim Protection Policies* – also suggests a basic structure of the chapters, so we expected to learn about the development of and current state of victimology, data on victimisation, and an introduction into national victim protection policies, including legislative reforms/initiatives/changes and their implementation in practice. To continue with the subtitle, emphasising *the critical analysis of current victim protection policies*, the following summary of contributors' key arguments provides insights into specific foci of each country's contribution of *Part Two*.

II.

Evisa Kambellari from **Albania** states that, despite the slight progress in victim policies and victim protection in the books, there are still challenges for the delivery of victim protection services in practice. Especially, supportive programmes to ensure medical, psychological and social assistance for victims of crime as well as of compensatory schemes for victims of organised crime need to be developed. Capacity building is essential to protect victims and safeguard fair treatment throughout the criminal proceedings. The author also emphasises the need for the establishment of an official system for the registration of victims of crime in this country.

Monika Stempkowski and *Barbara Kraml* critically assess problems of inconsistency in **Austria** regarding the legal entitlement to receive psycho-social and legal support. These benefits, provided in the Austrian Victims of Crime Act, are currently available only for victims who have suffered immediate physical injury or damage to their health. It would be desirable to include all victims traumatised by a severe felony as well. In practice, it would also be important to remove bureaucratic barriers. Austria does not provide enough places in women's shelters to comply with the requirements established by the Council of Europe. Furthermore, the necessity of educating professionals from various fields who may come into contact with victims in their everyday work, including police officers, prosecutors and judges as well as medical staff in hospitals and educators in kindergartens is emphasised in this paper. Finally, the authors claim that effective victim protection and support requires sufficient funding. The organisations which provide these services need to have a long-term perspective and the security of legally binding warranties regarding the money they receive from public authorities.

Azra Adžajlić-Dedović and *Miodrag Simović* discuss the challenges for victim-oriented policies against the background of the complexity of a post-conflict society such as **Bosnia and Herzegovina.** They put emphasis on the need for a better understanding of victims and their protection. The country is still struggling with a lot of tensions originating from the war in the territories of the former Yugoslavia and is now facing additional social, political and economic challenges, including the relatively new international demands such as the introduction of enhanced standards for victim protection.

Kamen Lyubomirov Novikov argues that, despite considerable progress in victim-related legislation, **Bulgaria** is in fact still far from the point of providing adequate victim support. On the one hand, state bodies are not doing enough for the victims. This reluctance can be explained by financial constraints, poor facilities and low levels of staff motivation. On the other hand, victims themselves often remain passive; they do not want to make use of the legal system to seek protection for their rights, and they do not trust the state authorities at all.

Anna-Maria Getoš Kalac, Sunčana Roksandić Vidlička and *Zoran Burić* from **Croatia** put particular emphasis on the importance of the Directive 2012/29 of the European Union that has not yet been fully implemented in their country. The need for the setting-up of adequate restorative justice measures and systematic training for professionals involved in victim support and victim protection, especially in the context of hate crime, continues to exist. Moreover, under-staffing and under-financing of victim protection programmes are further obstacles to the successful implementation of effective victim protection policies. In addition, victimisation from economic crime requires special attention in light of the processes of privatisation and ownership transformation.

There are two papers from **Hungary** in this volume. *Andrea Tünde Barabás* wrote the first one which introduces the situation of victimological research, policymaking and practice-oriented activities related to victims and their protection. The author emphasises the role of prevention of victimisation and the need of data from victimisation surveys to learn about the dark figure of crime and fear of crime. She suggests the strengthening of restorative justice to fill the gap between the unconditional demand for the exercise of the state's penal authority and the attainment of 'victims' rights. *Ákos Kara, Anna Kiss, Eszter Sárik* and *Viktória Szentmihályi-Soós* co-authored the second paper on Hungary. They discuss a contradicting role of victimology in a postmodern perspective. It is forced to be a practical and useful discipline, vital in the development of effective criminal policy. In addition, victimology and victims' rights are also critically assessed as a kind of service in a consumer society.

Velimir Rakočević and *Aleksandra Jovanović* write about the development of victimology, and victim protection policies and practices in **Montenegro**. They mainly focus on the victims of organised crime, especially killings ordered by organised crime groups, smuggling and money laundering. They take two perspectives – individual victimisation through violent and property crimes, and victimisation of the state through criminal activities related to organised crime and economic crime.

Gordana Lažetić and *Aleksandra Gruevska-Drakulevski* note that, even though there have been many efforts to better protect victims in **North Macedonia**, a successful implementation of victim protection policies still faces many challenges. In accordance with Directive 2012/29/EU the definition of "victim of crime" should be extended to encompass the family members as indirect victims: the spouse or the person who is living with the victim in a marriage-like relationship in a joint household and on a stable and continuous basis, the relatives in direct line, the siblings and the dependants of the victim as well as other family members of a person whose death was directly caused by a criminal offence and who have suffered harm as a result of that person's death. There is also a need to provide state compensation to victims of violence. Currently, such a scheme does not exist, although North Macedonia has ratified all the relevant international instruments and has already accepted the obligation to implement this form of compensation domestically. In the course of forthcoming amendments of the Law on Justice of Children, there is a necessity to reintroduce the legislative basis for the establishment of a fund to compensate child victims of violent crime. In light of the international trend of strengthening the position of victims during the criminal procedure, there is also a need for providing the procedural framework that would allow representatives from specialised NGOs to accompany victimised minors – be they specialised in providing help and support for victims in general, or (at least) for victims of particular offences such as trafficking, domestic violence, paedophilia, etc.

Andra-Roxana Trandafir and *Flaviu Ciopec* of **Romania** use figurative speech in their conclusion, calling victims "the new stars of the criminal arena" and addressing criminologists as nothing less than "research angels". A lack of domestic victimisation surveys, a rigid understanding of victims and concept of their role, as well as insufficient activities of non-governmental organisations require a substantial reconsideration of the compliance or non-compliance of their country with the minimum standards of victim protection as provided in the EU's Victims' Rights Directive 2012/29. They also identify a need to search for a concept that goes beyond a pure formalistic approach with its limited focus on criminal legislation; in addition to the activities carried out by the public authorities or institutions involved in this sector, economic, social and sometimes even religious aspects should be taken into consideration.

Vesna Nikolić Ristanović and *Sanja Ćopić* have spearheaded efforts to contribute to the development of victimology and the victim movement in **Serbia**. They follow the broadest notion of the subject of victimology, arguing for a science that deals with all victims of suffering, regardless of whether or not they are considered victims of crime in any sense. They also warn that missionary care for victims can be seen as a means to achieve repression, although such a goal is not necessarily requisite for the victims. Such an approach is particularly apparent in relation to victims of human rights violations and war crimes. It can be very dangerous since it stimulates victims to become vengeful and unrealistic about punishment, but it does not help them cope with trauma. One driving factor behind the increase in public victim awareness is the work of the women's movement to expose male violence against women and, in parallel, against children. In recent years, the focus of attention has shifted to other particularly vulnerable groups of victims such as victims of homophobic crimes, human trafficking, and war crimes. Future challenges that will come up in the course of Serbia's EU accession process lie in the strengthening of the rule of law and fundamental rights, which explicitly include 'victims' rights. In this respect, the transposition of the EU Directive 2012/29 into national law and its implementation in practice have been recognised as a key objective, as defined in the accession action plan for Chapter 23 (Judiciary and fundamental rights). The accession action plan states that the legal framework will be aligned with the standards of the EU Directive, requiring the establishment of victim support services and the building-up of the necessary capacities for the full implementation of minimum standards on the rights, support, and protection of victims of crime.

Gorazd Meško, Katja Eman, Rok Hacin and *Urška Pirnat* discuss structural, group-related and individual victimisation as well as future efforts needed to better protect victims, especially victims of medical negligence and normalised violence in **Slovenia**. Violence (especially domestic violence, crimes against the elderly and hate speech), mobbing (violence at the workplace), victimisation related to migration, victimisation of consumers, environmental crime, and cybercrime deserve special attention by politics, legislation and practice in order to increase public awareness and enhance victim protection.

Tuba Topçuoğlu and *Selman Dursun* contributed a paper on victimological reality in **Turkey**. The general interest in victims and victim rights is relatively new in the country. Although no special law on victims exists to date, various provisions spread over different laws – such as the penal code, penal procedure code, child protection law, the law on protection of the family and prevention of violence against women, the law on probation services, and the law on combating terrorism – relate to victim rights and victim protection. Recently, the government proposed a draft law on victim rights. Several governmental and state-related institutions in cooperation with various NGOs deal with issues of victim support and victim protection, and they play a key role in victimology in Turkey. Turkey also does not conduct regular victimisation surveys that cover the various types of crime at the national level. Although such crimes differ from case to case and not every victimisation is considered as equally serious, violent offences, particularly when committed against women and children, attract enormous public and media attention in Turkey. Nonetheless, reliable national statistical data do not exist in Turkey, neither on the number nor on the characteristics of victims, not to speak of profound empirical data on the extent of the dark figure of crime.

III.

The critical analysis of victim-oriented policies can begin by understanding the position of the victim from the societal perspective, followed by an individual's experience with criminal victimisation, secondary victimisation and coping strategies to survive victimisation, not only for the victim but also all people in his or her proximity. Informal and formal support is of vital importance, but it significantly depends on the nature and consequences of victimisation. The countries from the studied region (with some exceptions) are poor (on the bottom of the economic power in Europe) (World Bank, 2017). The Global Peace Index (2018) shows the lowest scores in Europe with regard to ongoing domestic/international conflicts and low societal safety. Regarding the so-called Fragile State Index, risk factors such as refugee status, including internally displaced people, factionalised elites, group grievance, economic decline, human flight and brain drain, as well as the high need for international intervention and support (e.g., military, police, humanitarian, economic) are present in the Balkan countries. The UN reports call for investments in the Balkan countries (e.g., empowerment of state institutions, development of local democracy, empowerment of governments) with the purpose to improve the protection of children and families. Activities of the OSCE – Organisation for Security and Co-operation in Europe – offering awareness-raising programmes, education and training have been present in the region in the past two decades trying to contribute to the development of the rule of law, policing in a democratic society, and victim protection with the emphasis on preventing secondary victimisation by police officers.

It is difficult to discuss the position of victims, victimisation and protection of victims outside the social-economic perspective. As some of the studied countries belong to a group of the poorest European countries, it is necessary to say that any effort to help victims should be appreciated and supported. Another perspective is the humanistic one. Without humanity and protection of the human rights of individuals in weak (fragile) states, victimisation continues and sometimes even perpetuates. Too often, victims are blamed for their victimisation. Victims of crime are often marginalised and stigmatised in the same manner as other "deviants". Therefore, victims' needs require respectful treatment and recognition; protection from intimidation, retaliation and further harm inflicted by the accused or suspected victimiser or his (or her) environment, and from (collateral) harm/distress arising from criminal investigations and court proceedings; support, including immediate assistance following a crime, longer-term physical and psychological assistance and practical assistance; access to justice to ensure that victims are aware of their rights and understand them, and possibilities to participate in proceedings; and compensation and restoration, whether through financial damages paid by the state or by the offender or through mediation or other forms of restorative justice as prescribed by the EU Directive 2012/29 on minimum standards on the rights, support and protection of victims of crime.

Effective prevention of secondary victimisation is still a challenge in the majority of the studied countries. It requires proper training of professionals, especially police officers, prosecutors and judges. Despite considerable changes and amendments in legislation, the victim is too often instrumentally exploited only for proving the guilt of the offender, but victims' needs and rights are neglected for various reasons.

We also hope that the voice of this book will be loud enough to reach those responsible for developing good practice of support and protection for the victims – the vulnerable and often too exposed individuals who, despite the recent efforts of politics and legislature, get support only from their families, peers, and not least from the non-governmental organisations but also get a better service and protection in formal (criminal) proceedings. There is a need to build, reinforce and maintain the trust between state institutions and non-governmental organisations. The development of such joint victim-related activities differs between the countries. Moreover, the cooperation of researchers in the field of victimological research and the provision of proper funding of research can contribute to more evidence-based policy-making in the future. Victimisation surveys can help learn about victimisation risk factors, hidden victimisation, fear of crime, willingness to report crimes to the police, experience with the criminal justice system and coping strategies for the victims, to mention a few.

IV.

This volume is not just a collection of country surveys, but an essential reading about the specific victimisation and victim protection policies in each of the studied countries. There are also papers from relevant neighbouring countries in the volume which are meant to enrich specific Balkan perspectives. A transfer of ideas, research results, practices, policies and legislative models/solutions/examples can contribute to the understanding of the situation and needs of victims and the development of effective victim protection schemes. As mentioned at the beginning of this introduction, our contribution is just a small stone in a mosaic of victimology. We hope that we have succeeded to open the main topics for further discussion and development in this field of research.

Last but not least, we would like to emphasise that none of the authors and editors are native English-speaking persons. The victimological research presented in this volume is mainly based on the authors' ambition and dedication to develop victimology, develop policies and practices of victim protection in their respective countries. It is the authors' zeal and belief that victimological perspectives deserve scientific grounding, theoretical as well as empirical studies, either as a part of criminology or as an independent scientific discipline, victimology. We appreciate the effort of all those who contributed to this volume to let the readers know about the development of victimology, victimological research, as well as policies and practices of victim protection and victim support in their respective countries.

PART I

INTRODUCTION AND ABSTRACTS

Balkan Victimology as an Important Contribution to Cultural Victimology

Antony Pemberton

1. Introduction

In the past decades, victimology has shown a remarkable growth, co-occurring with the rising stature of the plight of victims in policy and practice in Europe. Where in the 1970s it was safe to say that victims were the "forgotten party" of criminal justice, this cannot be said to be true in 2019. The same can be said of academic research into victimisation and its consequences. In the same period, victimology has moved from being a "wayward sub-discipline of criminology" to being a full-fledged academic endeavour.

Nevertheless, the rise of victimology is skewed methodologically, topically and geographically. Available victimological knowledge is largely based upon analysis of large and quantitative datasets.[1] This has offered important insights, revealing the phenomena of repeat and secondary victimisation, and providing compelling evidence of the existence of a "dark number" of victims who do not report their crimes to the authorities. These data nevertheless cannot go into depth as to the specific features of victim groups in varying contexts, to interrogate mechanisms within key phenomena and/or to fully understand the perspectives of victims and practitioners on victims' needs and experiences. These large-scale surveys therefore need to be supplemented by innovative qualitative and experimental research designs, which can query these issues in more detail.

Second research has largely focused on a small number of subjects: the prevalence and incidence of victimisation, the impact on mental health and related psychological phenomena and victim's experiences with certain features of justice processes, for instance victim impact statements or victim-offender mediation.[2] No qualms with the attention afforded to these phenomena, but there is a widespread need to complement this with research that embeds victimological phenomena in the relevant

---

1 *McGarry & Walklate* 2015.

2 *Green & Pemberton* 2017.

societal, historical, religious, institutional and political context. Questions relating to how victimisation is experienced first-hand, the existence and variance of norms concerning appropriate reactions to and from victims and the manner in which wider society understands and views victimhood are culturally embedded and constructed. In particular, the transplant of constructs and findings, policies and practices from one context is in need of being examined, moderated and mediated by cultural conditions and sensitivities.

Finally, and most relevant to the current volume, empirical research concerning the experience of victimisation, analysis of victimisation as a social phenomenon and the historical development of victims' rights have all concentrated on the experience in the English speaking world and a small group of countries in the north-west of Europe. The availability of basic victimological research for many other areas of Europe and the globe more generally is in doubt.

It is to this end that victimologists have highlighted the need for a cultural victimology.[3] Like its counterpart, cultural criminology, this entails placing victimisation and the reaction to victimisation in the context of culture, i.e., seeing victimisation and the reaction to victimisation as at least partly cultural products. The current volume presents a highly significant contribution to this new development. The contributions unlock a wealth of data and knowledge concerning the countries under study, of which undoubtedly the victimological commonwealth was previously unaware. That at once assuages some of the worries of cultural victimologists that there is decidedly more material already available, meaning that we might have more eyes on the blind spots of the victimological map than we were previously aware. But at the same time it emphasizes the importance of taking up the challenge that cultural victimology poses. The contributions to the volume make clear how important it is to review victimological phenomena in their own cultural habitat, be that societal, institutional or etymological, to be able to weigh the breadth and depth of victimological findings. In this short epilogue I will not revisit the many interesting findings presented by the authors, or repeat their conclusions. Instead I will offer my reflections on the lessons I learned from being offered the opportunity to review their chapters, which can apply to victimology more generally.

2. Widening the Evidence Base beyond the Anglophone Scope

Much of the work of the researchers upon which the chapters are based, reported their findings in their own language, rather than in English. It speaks to the error of equating the victimological evidence base, with its availability in the academic lingua franca. Indeed it is apparent from this volume that the extent to which English dominates the victimological research landscape can be questioned. In turn this

3 *Pemberton* 2018.

makes it clear that overviews of research in which a requirement is the use of the English language, will present an incomplete and biased picture.[4]

It is true that in general the use of the native tongue for scientific communication is more prevalent in the social sciences than it is in the natural sciences.[5] And it is particularly so for research in law and in other law-related disciplines, including criminology, and, we can assume, victimology.[6] That is undoubtedly due to the fact that the law – and in particular the criminal law – is bounded by national borders, with empirical findings tracing these national legal systems. For legal scholars, it is often questionable whether findings will hold elsewhere, which has also influenced the extent to which findings are reported in other languages. The publication tradition in the study of law often resists the tendency of many areas of social science to become increasingly biased in favour of English publications, although criminology is starting to follow the example of other social sciences in this regard.[7]

Much of the work on scientific communication emphasizes the importance of the lingua franca in knowledge production, as this harbours the potential that researchers from different linguistic backgrounds will be able to draw on each other.[8] However, a move to English – particularly if it is primarily guided by motives relating to one's standing in the academic community and career advancement for researchers – also comes with significant costs. As the former director of UNESCO, *Bokova* emphasized such a move would present a

> missed opportunity to explore perspectives and paradigms that are embedded in other cultural and linguistic traditions. A more culturally and linguistically diverse approach by the social sciences would be of tremendous value to organizations such as UNESCO in our efforts to foster mutual understanding and intercultural dialogue.[9]

This is also true for victimological phenomena, for which central concepts and terms might lose meaning once translated to English. Perhaps the clearest example of this is the word "victim" itself that in languages based in Latin, comes equipped with particular etymological root.[10] This "vitima"-label carries with it connotations of sacrifice that in other languages of the world are absent. *Van Dijk* has argued that this meaning – perhaps more obscure to native English language speakers, than to those in the country I call home, where "slacht-offer" literally translates as butchered

---

4 *Faraldo-Cabana* 2018.

5 *Tardy* 2004.

6 *Faraldo-Cabana* 2018.

7 *Faraldo-Cabana* 2018.

8 *Tardy* 2004.

9 *Albarillo* 2014, p. 79.

10 *Van Dijk* 2009.

sacrifice – is not innocent, but for instance influences the position victims may or may not have in criminal justice processes. Maintaining a publication tradition in a native language is therefore not only a handicap but also has advantages, and I would welcome work that translates research from different languages into English, with comparative research in which this comparison is made without the Anglophone side-step.[11]

Another issue is the audience of research. As I will emphasize below, victimological research can have real, tangible, emancipatory value. For this, however, it is important that societal actors within countries have sufficient access to this research. An all too eager emphasis on English language journal publications neglects that most policy officials, practitioners and other relevant actors have neither access nor inclination to read such publications. They are instead more likely to take stock of findings published in their native language, and indeed of so-called grey research, research that is not primarily targeting an academic audience. At my own university, I have had the strange experience that a 200-page report for our department of Security and Justice on an academically relevant subject, and conducted at the highest scientific standards, was *not* counted as academic output. However, a subsequent 10-page journal article was, even though it only reported a small part of the findings. We could expand the lament of UNESCO director *Bokova* to argue that such an emphasis also applies to other societal institutions, including those of the country themselves.

3. The Necessity of Culturally Sensitive Victimology

The aforementioned issues already reinforce the necessity of a more culturally sensitive victimology. The meaning of key terms and constructs might differ relevantly. As noted this is true for the term victim itself, and applies to many others as well. A good example is the mental health construct "post traumatic stress disorder" (hereinafter PTSD). The largest body of empirical research in the area of victimology concerns this phenomenon, with the volume of studies concerning PTSD or traumatic stress outnumbering research under the heading of victimology by ten to one. In his book "Crazy Like Us", *Watters* pointed to PTSD as an example of a more general translation of Western and in particular American diagnoses of psychological problems to other areas and situations around the globe.[12] PTSD is defined by a particular event and the interpretation of that event by the person experiencing it, but it is only recently waking up to the importance of the interpersonal and cultural environment of the victim in question that this definition implies.[13] In turn, this means that di-

---

11 *Van Dijk* 2009.

12 *Watters* 2011.

13 *Hinton & Good* 2016.

agnoses, assumed mechanisms and remedies need to be applied with much more caution than is now often the case: indeed this observation not only holds true for its transport outside the American borders, but also applies to particular areas of and conditions in the United States itself.[14] The importance of such a cultural sensitive approach to key terms and constructs only increases when it concerns victimological phenomena in and around justice processes - given the importance of justice processes in meaning-making and normative issues.[15]

In many chapters, the role of particular academics and institutions is highlighted in bringing victimology and/or victims' rights forward. They do this against the backdrop of diverse political climates, in which the national mood, public opinion and institutional and governmental support together determine the receptiveness for policy changes.[16] A crucial element in the development of victim policy moreover is often a so-called focusing event, such as mass-victimisation or an eye-catching case of victimisation, which can be parlayed by media organizations and/ or political entrepreneurs into political capital. This not only influences the importance of victimisation as a political phenomenon, but also the particular shape that victim policy might take. Different countries across Europe have for instance instituted victim-oriented policies in a reaction to large-scale acts of terror or political violence, resulting in a particular emphasis on these groups.[17] The recent historical and present societal context therefore also differentiates the development of victim policy, and perhaps to a lesser extent victimology. In turn the development has to be situated in this context to be understood.

What applies to society in general, also applies to the more immediate surrounding of victim policy and victimology. In this societal ecology,[18] a particular emphasis could be placed in the actors and institutions in criminal justice. The way they function and the manner in which they are organized differ from one jurisdiction to the next and the same applies to the way they are perceived across society. For instance many countries have seen fit to afford the police and the prosecution service important gateway functions in victim services, and this is also a staple of international legal instruments. But performance of such a function is intimately interconnected with the manner in which the police force is and has been perceived in society. That varies between societies, but as is, for instance, apparent from the Black Lives Matter movement in the United States, also varies within societies.[19] The stance of criminal justice agencies towards victims' issues moreover largely determines the

---

14 *Jenkins & Haas* 2016.

15 *Pemberton* 2019.

16 *Kingdon* 1984.

17 *Letschert, Staiger & Pemberton* 2010.

18 *Biffi et al.* 2016; *Bolivar, Pelikan & Lemonne* 2015.

19 *Mutsaers* 2018.

effectiveness of victim policies, while resistance on either organizational or cultural grounds can undo potentially well-meaning legislation.[20]

4. Emancipatory Potential of Victimological Research

Beyond the occurrence of high profile events, the scope of victimological phenomena can also be highlighted by research. Much of the current profile of victimological issues can be traced to the emergence of research that emphasized the prevalence and incidence of the problem, like the victimisation surveys;[21] to research that revealed the primary impact of victimisation[22] and to (feminist) research that revealed the deleterious effects of criminal justice processes.[23] Research into victimological issues has the potential to highlight the difficulties faced by victims and makes it more difficult for governments to ignore the scope and impact of victimisation. The different contributions to this volume all bear witness to this, even though the impact this has had is markedly different from one jurisdiction to the next. Moreover I would also not be the first to note that the focus and perspective adopted in research can and will also influence the type of policies that be enacted. For instance much victimological research has a decidedly therapeutic bent, also when it concerns justice processes.[24] That is not without its merits, but does include the danger, which *Furedi* highlighted in his "Therapy Culture"; that problems are perceived as individual and psychological issues, rather than structural and sociological.[25]

The emancipatory potential of victim research also depends on the extent to which an actual victim perspective is included. Elsewhere my colleagues and I, for instance, have made an argument for a "narrative victimology".[26] One of the advantages that we see for this approach is that it would move "from defining victimological experience in the terms of justice institutions, to understanding (criminal) justice processes in the way they are encountered by victims as an element of their unfolding narrative." Rather than imposing a particular vision of what the experience of injustice of victims entails and the options that may or may not be open to victims, the point of departure for research and reflection would be the view of the victim him or herself. This can also be argued for cross-cultural settings, in which the difficulties of applying perspectives and a vernacular derived from the formal criminal justice

---

20 *Pemberton & Groenhuijsen* 2012.

21 *Van Dijk* 2007.

22 *Herman* 1997.

23 *Brownmiller* 1975.

24 *Pemberton & Reynaers* 2011.

25 *Furedi* 2004.

26 *Pemberton, Mulder & Aarten* 2018.

process to victim experience, come supplied with the additional complexity of doing so from a different cultural and linguistic background.

Finally research might be adopted by societal organizations to further the plight of victims and/ or they may interact with victimological academics in doing so. The experience in different European jurisdictions as well as of international bodies like Victim Support Europe or the World Society of Victimology speaks to the interaction between policy-makers and practitioners and academics, using research as a means to further the case of victims at the national and international level.[27] Such a combination can also serve to distinguish earnest attempts to improve the position of victims of crime from often more disingenuous attempts to shoehorn victim misery into law and order campaigns.[28] Many proposals for victim policy are victimological in name only, instead seeking to diminish the rights of suspects or offenders.

5. The Ambivalent Nature of International Legal Instruments

In developing the position of victims in national legal orders, much might be expected from the developments at the international level.[29] International bodies like the United Nations and the Council of Europe have been active in the field of victimology since halfway through the 1980's. In the past twenty years the European Union has also leapt into the fray. Ensuring that sufficient support and aid is available, as well as tools to navigate the intricacies of the justice processes that follow victimisation, contained in the "EU victims directive", or the "Directive 2012/29/EU of the European parliament and of the council of 25 October 2012 establishing minimum standards on the rights, support and protection of victims of crime" in full.[30]

However, a key variable missing in the European legislative equation is that of culture. Diversity in cultures of national compliance to EU law, cultures of legislative enforcement and administrative prowess, police and prosecutorial culture.[31] Such diversity also applies to the political and institutional climate in which victim policy will need to be grounded. This made even more pertinent due to the fact that what matters in victim policy is not "law on the books", but "law in practice". Merely harmonizing and/ or improving legal texts will not as such harmonize and/ or improve the position of victims. That is largely up to the actors working in the practice of victimology and their ability to navigate the distance and – at least to a degree – close

---

27 *Groenhuijsen* 2014.

28 *Goodey* 2005.

29 *Groenhuijsen* 2014.

30 Directive No. 2012/29/EU, 14.11.2012, Official Journal of the European Union 315/57; https://eur-lex.europa.eu/legal-content/EN/TXT/PDF/?uri=CELEX:32012L0029&from=en [09.09.2019].

31 *Biffi et al.* 2016; *Pemberton & Groenhuijsen* 2012.

the gap between the supranational, top-down aspirations of the Brussels behemoth and the lived reality across the 27 member states. That is an endeavour to which cultural victimology can have much to offer.

That is also true beyond the confines of the European Union. Previous work in comparative victimology has already suggested the porous borders between hard law and soft law at the international level, for instance.[32] But the move from international legal instruments, to national legal orders, to governance and implementation has yet to receive the attention and culturally sensitive answer it deserves. This would not only serve to offer insight into the interplay between international and supranational law and practice on the ground, but also provide much needed knowledge of the ways to overcome the difficulties inherent to victims rights in criminal justice. How can they be sufficiently armed, to actually make them enforceable rights? What kind of remedies are possible and (how) can they be implemented in criminal justice processes? How can we sensibly learn from the experience in other jurisdictions?

6. Final Remarks

The type of comparative work contained in this volume can offer valuable points of departure for the aforementioned questions. As is apparent, I believe this to be true for all the aspects of cultural victimology covered in this brief epilogue. The wealth of the material contained in this volume will enrich the victimological community, unlocking bodies of research that in part due to linguistic reasons had yet to find a larger audience. As a stand-alone piece of work this would already be highly worthwhile.

But I would like to express the hope that this volume is a starting point or a stepping stone on a longer voyage, in which the work of the collaborators here can provide further impetus to cultural victimology, not only in the Balkans, but through what is learned and may serve as an example to other areas of the globe as well. It can enrich our understanding of the linguistic issues in victimology, of the cultural differences and similarities across countries, of manners in which research can interact with practice to further the cause of victims, and of the ways in which international law can stimulate activity on the ground.

Each of these issues is not only worthwhile as an academic pursuit but also stands a real chance of contributing to the lived experiences of victims. The latter might not be as forgotten as they were in the 1970s, but that does not mean they are now particularly well understood. And this lack of culturally sensitive understanding has real – negative – consequences for the victims in question, as well as hampering our ability to exact real change in their circumstances. So let me finally express the hope

---

32 *Groenhuijsen & Pemberton* 2009.

that the material contained in this volume does not only find its way to a Dutch-British academic, but also, and perhaps primarily to those who are in a position to see to such changes.

Literature

Albarillo, F. (2014): Language in social science databases: English versus non-English articles in JSTOR and Scopus. Behavioral & Social Sciences Librarian 33, pp. 77–90.

Biffi, E., Mulder, E., Pemberton, A., Santos, M., Valério, M., Vanfraechem, I. & van der Vorm, B. (2016): Project IVOR Report: Implementing victim-oriented reform of the criminal justice system in the European Union. Lisbon.

Bolivar, D., Pelikan, C. & Lemonne, A. (2015): Victims and restorative justice: towards a comparison, in: I. Vanfraechem, D. Bolivar & I. Aertsen (eds.), Victims and restorative justice. Oxon, pp. 172–200.

Brownmiller, S. (1975): Against our will: Men, women, and rape. New York.

Faraldo-Cabana, C. (2018): Research excellence and Anglophone dominance: The case of law, criminology and social science, in: K. Carrington, R. Hogg, J. Scott, M. Sozzo (eds.), The Palgrave handbook of criminology and the global south. Cham, pp. 163–181.

Furedi, F. (2004): Therapy culture: Cultivating vulnerability in an uncertain age. London.

Goodey, J. (2005): Victims and victimology. Research, policy, practice. Harlow.

Green, S. & Pemberton, A. (2017): The impact of crime: Victimisation, harm and resilience, in: S. Walklate (ed.), Handbook of victims and victimology. 2nd ed. Oxon, pp. 77–102.

Groenhuijsen, M.S. (2014): The development of international policy in relation to victims of crime. International Review of Victimology 20, pp. 31–48.

Groenhuijsen, M.S. & Pemberton, A. (2009): The EU Framework Decision. Does hard law make a difference? European Journal of Crime, Criminal Law and Criminal Justice 17, pp. 43–59.

Herman, J. (1997): Trauma and recovery. New York.

Hinton, D.E. & Good, B.J. (eds.). (2016): Culture and PTSD: Trauma in global and historical perspective. Philadelphia.

Jenkins, J.H. & Haas, B.M. (2016): Trauma in the lifeworlds of adolescents: Hard luck and trouble in the land of enchantment, in: D.E. Hinton & B.J. Good (eds.), Culture and PTSD: Trauma in global and historical perspective. Philadelphia, pp. 179–201.

Kingdon, J.W. (1984): Agendas, alternatives and public policies. New York.

Letschert, R.M., Staiger, I. & Pemberton, A. (eds.). (2010): Assisting victims of terrorism. Dordrecht.

McGarry, R. & Walklate, S. (2015): Victims: Trauma, testimony and justice. London.

Mutsaers, P. (2018): #BlackLivesMatter: Understanding anti-police protest as a cultural practice, in: M. Hoondert, P. Mutsaers, & W. Arfman (eds.), Cultural practices of victimhood. Oxon, pp. 167–192.

Pemberton, A. (2019): Time for a rethink: Victims and restorative justice: Annual Lecture in Restorative Justice. International Journal of Restorative Justice 2, pp. 13–33.

Pemberton, A. (2018): Imagining cultural victimology, in: M. Hoondert, P. Mutsaers & W. Arfman (eds.), Cultural practices of victimhood. Oxon, pp. 234–247.

Pemberton, A. & Groenhuijsen, M. (2012): Developing victim's rights within the European Union: Past, present and future, in: H. Morosawa, J. Dussich & G. Kirchhoff (eds.), Victimology and human security: New horizons. Nijmegen, pp. 538–559.

Pemberton, A. & Reynaers, S. (2011): The controversial nature of victim participation: Therapeutic benefits in victim impact statements, in: E. Erez, J.A. Wemmers & M. Kilchling (eds.), *Therapeutic jurisprudence and procedural justice for victims of crime: International perspectives*. Durham, pp. 229–248.

Pemberton, A., Mulder, E. & Aarten, P.G.M. (2019): Stories of injustice towards a narrative victimology. European Journal of Criminology 16, pp. 391–412.

Tardy, C. (2004): The role of English in scientific communication: Lingua franca or Tyrannosaurus rex? Journal of English for Academic Purposes 3, pp. 247–269.

Van Dijk, J.J.M. (2009): Free the victim: a critique of the Western conception of victimhood. International Review of Victimology 16, pp. 1–33.

Van Dijk, J.J.M. (2007): World of crime. Thousand Oaks.

Watters, E. (2011): Crazy like us: The globalization of the American psyche. New York.

Victims, Victimisers, Postmodern Culture, Neoliberal Capitalism, and the Case of Slovenia as a Transitional Society

Zoran Kanduč

> *O Zeus, what can I say?*
> *That you look on man and care?*
> *Or do we, holding that the gods exist,*
> *deceive ourselves with unsubstantial dreams*
> *and lies, while random careless chance and change*
> *alone control the world?*
> *(Euripides, Hecuba)*[1]

1. Introductory Remarks

We do not want to suffer, do we? Well, of course not. To be sure, as a rule, we do not like to be (or become) involuntarily the object of some harmful action, omission, misadventure, or ill-fortune. On the other hand, there are a considerable amount of people wanting to be (recognized as) "victims", even trying energetically to get this label or status, and, if possible, some (moral or pecuniary) compensation for the damage, violation of the legally valid right, or downtrodden dignity. Needless to say, there are a lot of situations in which it is extremely important who is formally or informally defined as a (potential or actual) victim and thus not being a victimiser (e.g., bad guy, aggressor, performer of illegitimate violence, oppressor, exploiter, usurer, blackmailer, predator, or simply criminal), particularly in serious political and military conflicts causing enormous human, social, and material destruction, and involving a myriad of subjects, driven not necessarily or solely by clear evil intentions (such as the wish to eliminate the hated or despised enemy), but also by a more trivial or "banal" motivation (for instance, by firmly consolidated conformism, blind patriotism, readiness to follow orders even in striking contrast to one's own moral convictions, fear of negative sanction, or desire for personal advancement and other petty gains). Just think of the bloody wars on the territory of the ex-Yugoslavia. Every ethnicity that engaged in armed conflicts perceived itself as a (or

1 Quoted in *Kekes* 2008, p. 255.

rather the) victim, threatened and aggressed by guilty victimisers. In Slovenia, for example, there was unanimous consensus that the freshly-born independent state was attacked and afterwards victimised by the Yugoslav "unpopular" and "communist" army ("we were thoroughly innocent", "our nationalism was merely defensive, an altogether understandable reaction to the Serbian one", "our political aims were immaculate", "the decomposition of federal state was in no way our fault", "we were good guys and girls just striving for democracy, human rights, peace, and prosperity, not to mention more elegant, faster, or otherwise better cars").[2]

Furedi argues that we are living in "the culture of victimhood and complaint" (being an outgrowth or maybe even an essential by-product of "the culture of fear"), i.e., in an era in which "a key symbol" is the victim.[3] He explains this trend by the generalised experience that we are usually more the object than the subject of our busy lives, propelled and directed by mysterious (impersonal) forces beyond our own control. Positively, this impression is indeed quite accurate. Namely, many contemporary fears (e.g., those regarding unemployment, redundancy, poverty, status degradation, or dark future perspectives) are quite well founded (and, besides, very useful for the ruling classes, particularly for private and public employers).[4] Also, capitalist social formation does not and, as a matter of fact, cannot control itself. It is headless (and, unfortunately, increasingly braindead), governed by objective, quasi-natural (anonymous) economic laws maintained (and reproduced) by market competition and the imperative of endless accumulation.[5] Consequently, we can rightly experience ourselves as "victims", but it is very difficult to be acknowledged and recognized as such socially, politically, or ideologically. Simply put, almost everyone cannot and, more precisely, must not be a (so to say *a priori*) victim. What is more, it is not an easy task to find out who are our principal victimisers, first of all because a lot of more or less annoying

2 The "war" in Slovenia was quite modest in terms of its duration, intensity, and victims involved, particularly in comparison with the bloodshed that takes place regularly on Slovenian roads and highways. Yet, it was followed by the huge ethnic cleansing, albeit performed in an administrative, cyber, red-tape, "civilized" manner. In February 1992, the Ministry of Interior expunged more than 18,000 "undesired" persons from the register of permanent residence. Their principal "sin" was that they did not belong to the Slovene ethnicity. Also, they were perceived (by the ruling elite and by a large part of the populace) as an alien threat, some sort of insidious "fifth column" (being potentially or actually disloyal to the new political regime), and therefore unsuitable for living in the new-born nation state. Although the "erasure" in question caused enormous (albeit publicly mostly "invisible") suffering, it was not officially recognized as mass victimisation. According to the prevailing opinion, what happened to the erased persons was the consequence of their own fault or, put more briefly, they got what they deserved (or looked for).

3 *Furedi* 2002, pp. 95–103.

4 For an analysis of the widespread fears associated with generalized economic insecurity, see *Gorz* 1999, pp. 52–54.

5 *Heinrich* 2013, pp. 71–74.

problems we are facing on an almost daily basis are structurally (and increasingly globally) driven. *Boutellier* connects "the victimological twist" (or "rediscovery of the victim") with secularization, moral fragmentation, atomization (accompanied by rampant – and more often than not stupid – "individualism"), and decay of "positive" solidarity (based on common values and shared views of how "a good society" should look like in some better or brighter future).[6] He is of the opinion that in "an ideologically weak era", it is the victim (real or metaphorical) who can serve as the most appropriate basis (or criterion) of at least "pragmatic morality", especially the unambiguously victimised person (e.g., the one being the target of some cruel or abject crime) whose victimhood is crystal clear due to the suffering that is easy to perceive and identify with. But why should primarily the victims of crimes (treated regularly by criminal justice systems) function as a paradigm of victimhood? Besides, the question of what is or should be interpreted as "criminal" is extremely (traditionally and almost proverbially) controversial. As a rule, the greatest atrocities in human history were not sanctioned as "the crime", and their innumerable anonymous "victims" were soon forgotten. Just think of the enormous amount of violence (e.g., in the form of genocide,[7] military aggression, mass killing, assassination, torture, imprisonment, terrorist attack, sabotage, overthrowing of legitimate governments, extortion, and various economic sanctions) that has been associated with the building and maintenance of the empire made by USA, and with its merciless fight against "the red enemy" (threatening the global or national capitalist rule), for instance in Indochina, Latin America, Iran, Indonesia, Afghanistan, Iraqi, Libya, or Syria.[8]

Let us now turn to the topics to be dealt with in this text. They are divided in two sections (followed by some brief concluding remarks). At first, we address the relationship between victimhood and the human condition in general. After that, our attention is focused on problems concerning human suffering in the context of postmodern culture and repercussions on crimes and victimisations. The second section highlights more specifically the position of victims and victimisers in Slovene (post)transitional (post-socialist) society. So, this is the plan. Will we manage to realize it? Doubtless, the final judgment belongs to the reader. Nevertheless, we can reveal our basic thesis in advance. Slovene society, seen and analysed from the perspective of victimology (and criminology), shows characteristics and trends that are more or less typical for a contemporary, neoliberal capitalist system. Nothing to write home about? Well, hopefully not.

---

6 *Boutellier* 2000, pp. 47–54.

7 *Stannard* 2017, pp. 211–266.

8 *Anderson* 2017, pp. 78–111.

2. Victimhood, the Human Condition, Culture, and Crime

Let us begin with an elementary question. Who is or should be (recognized, labelled, and treated as) a victim? In other words, is there something like the essence of victimhood shared by all concrete victims and perhaps even by the abstract or rather fictive ones, such as state, nation, law, morality, currency (or money), corporation, God, church, or any other intersubjective reality (existing solely in the collective imagination and communication)? As it seems, one possible common denominator is suffering (in its manifold forms), that is to say some sort of painful subjective experience, trauma, or unpleasant sensations (e.g., feelings, thoughts, memories, or emotions). In that case, the definition excludes all merely imagined entities (although they have extremely important functions in our personal lives and in predominant social – economic, financial, political, and cultural – activities),[9] for they cannot feel anything at all (obviously enough, they are not sensitive, conscious beings). Of course, suffering as such may have various causes or reasons. Nevertheless, we are usually tempted to say that what constitutes a legitimate (although not necessarily legally acknowledged or socially recognized) victim is the suffering which is imposed to a thoroughly innocent person against her or his will. Unfortunately, it is this very conception that generates some curious (or even bizarre) problems. First of all, it apparently turns every (or at least almost every) human being into a victim.

Do we exaggerate? Well, not really (to my mind at least). Certainly, suffering is an entirely normal, intrinsic, unescapable, and therefore also expected part of human existence (needless to say, the specifically human affliction in question, appearing in its kaleidoscopic forms, is finished solely by the death, our inexorable and absolute master, on condition of course that there is no hell waiting for us also in the after world, i.e., no never ending torture as the – just or sadistic? – punishment for sinful immortal souls). Moreover, suffering is an important or, as a pessimist philosopher and Buddhist would gladly add,[10] even essential part of our undoubtedly difficult lives. The list of physical, psychic, intersubjective (or relational), social and "existential" troubles, pains or inconveniences is long, large, and (qualitatively and quan-

---

9 *Harari* (2017, pp. 181–203) points out that it is advisable to stop from to time and look at things from the perspective of some objectively reals entity, i.e., the one that can indeed suffer: When the euro loses its value, the euro doesn't suffer. When a bank goes bankrupt, the bank doesn't suffer. When a country suffers a defeat in war, the country doesn't really suffer. It is just a metaphor. In contrast, when a soldier is wounded in battle, he really does suffer. When a cow is separated from her new-born calf, she suffers. This is reality. Of course suffering might well be caused by our belief in fictions. For example, belief in national and religious myths might cause the outbreak of war, in which millions lose their homes, their limbs and even their lives. The cause of war is fictional, but the suffering is 100 per cent real. This is exactly why we should strive to distinguish fiction from reality" (*Harari* 2017, p. 206).

10 For a succinct description of *Buddha's* "truth of suffering" *(dukkha)*, see *Keown* 2013, pp. 50–53.

titatively) diversified enough to diagnose the human condition as a more or less bad thing. For instance, it includes (corporal and psychical) suffering associated with birth, growing, aging, dying, ill health, sickness, accidents, craving, frustrations, diverse emotional forms of distress (e.g., grief, lamentation, sorrow, despair, or depression), boredom, disappointment, disillusionment, confusion, unrest, betrayal, misery, unsatisfactory relationships with subjectively important persons, unfulfilling way of living, alienation, self-deception, humiliation, unjust, violent, unfair, hateful, inhumane, or cruel treatments by others, and so on. Clearly, there are normally also bright episodes in human lives that contain active or passive pleasures, sensual and spiritual enjoinments, relative wellbeing, contentment based upon finding the appropriate "meaning" of life (i.e., some valuable idea that justifies the painful, tiresome, dull, and unfortunate aspects of one's existence), and many other pleasant feelings (connected, for instance, with some desirable activity or realisation of personal projects and aims). Yet, alas, pleasures usually do not last very long. All too often one gets quickly used to an achievement that he or she longed for. Desirable (intrinsically enjoyable) activity may become dull or tedious (and also accompanied by the fear that it will be lost or endangered).The so much cherished meaning of life is (in the pernicious last analysis at least) just a subjective illusion (although it is usually very effective, in particular when it is shared or compatible with the similar imaginary constructions of many other persons).

Needless to say, there is nothing new in the gloomy insights of innumerable kinds of suffering ingrained into the very fabric of each and every human being (and also into his or her individual and social existence). By looking at some selected classic examples, we can detect their echo as early as in the famous (albeit quite bitter) accords in *Sophocles*' last tragedy (entitled "Oedipus at Colonnus") that can be paraphrased as follows: the best (or the most valuable) thing for a human is not to be born, period.[11] In this sense, life seems to be a failure of one's own non-birth or, what is more, the fiasco that one has to live and endure (the very body, i.e., its urge for self-preservation, and the society demand that a living being respects the duty not to pass away too soon).[12] On the other hand, *Sophocles* insisted that for a person who has nevertheless caught the sight of light, the second best thing is to return (preferably as soon as possible) to where he or she came from. *Kant* also estimated that life's evils, miseries, and misfortunes evidently outweigh its fragile satisfactions. Moreover, he thought that, considering solely hedonistic criteria, virtually no

11 *Sophocles* 401BC/2010.

12 In the light of contemporary culture, one has an inexorable duty to fight for his or her life as long as one can, and by using all possible means, including painful medical remedies, treatments, and operations (which, in many regards, bear strong resemblance to medieval torture), solely in order to prolong his or her life (or to avoid the imminent end) for some time. In other words, even our death has to be deserved, all too often by previous torments, sufferance, pains, or anguish of mind. Nevertheless, we do not live in sadomasochistic culture, do we?

rational human being would prefer to continue to be alive, particularly when one feels deep despair or weariness with an "empty" or hopelessly painful existence (that is why *Kant* insisted that suicide should be strictly prohibited by the categorical imperative, i.e., by moral duty imagined as a "universal law of nature" ensuring the continued existence of the human species).[13] *Neiman* emphasises that such an opinion was not at all unusual or bizarre in the eighteenth century, regardless of the blossoming optimism associated with the Enlightenment's hopes concerning the possibilities of human, cultural, and social progress: namely, the belief that human life contains less good than evil was sheer common sense.[14] Indeed, *Schopenhauer* made of this his central philosophical point. For him, it is impossible to imagine the human existence being free of suffering which is, thus, its very essence (only the form of pains is a matter of contingency or accident).[15] *Schopenhauer* described life as a continual deception (we are deluded either by the hope or by what is or was the object of our desire), as a struggle for existence destined to fail, as a long and slow torment preceding the death (that of course we should not fear, for to someone who does not exist the non-existence cannot really matter). Of course, that does not mean that human lives generally are completely without joy, contentment, pleasure, and satisfaction (defined, for instance, as an absence of pain or as a state of mind in which one feels no deficiency). Nevertheless, *Schopenhauer* was surely of the opinion that every kind of happiness is necessarily bound up with different types of unavoidable suffering.[16] Yet, humans normally try to carefully hide their own misery, usually in order to save face and avoid other people's schadenfreude. Finally, *Freud,* the immortal founding father of psychanalysis, also held that "life, as we find it, is too hard for us", for it contains "too many pains, disappointments and impossible tasks".[17] Indeed, misery threatens us from three directions, i.e., from our own vulnerable bodies (condemned, so to speak, to inescapable debilitating, ugliness, decay, and dissolution), from the external world, and from other people causing suffering

---

13 *Kant* 1785/2005, pp. 44–46. For a more precise presentation of *Kant*'s perspective on suicide, see *Neiman* 2015, pp. 76–81; *Wood* 2008, pp. 172–173.

14 *Neiman* 2015, p. 77.

15 *Schopenhauer* 1819/2008, pp. 329–345. For a brief commentary of *Schopenhauer*'s pessimistic view of human existence, see *Janaway* 2002, pp. 103–115.

16 *Goethe* was, perhaps somewhat surprisingly, a supporter of *Schopenhauer*'s depressing view of human life: "In all times and all countries things have been miserable. Men have always been in fear and trouble, they have pained and tortured each other, what little life they had, they made sour one to the other. The beauty of the world and the sweetness of existence which the beauty of the world offered them, they were not able to esteem or enjoy. Only to a few life become comfortable and enjoyable. Most people, after having played the game of life for a time, preferred to depart rather than to begin anew. That which perhaps gave or gives them some degree of attachment to life was and is the fear of death. Thus life is; thus it always was; thus it will always remain. That is the lot of man" (quoted from *Neiman* 2015, pp. 209–210).

17 *Freud* 1916–17/1977, p. 22.

that is more often than not the most painful because of its experienced gratuitousness (or, in the worst case, even cruelty). For *Freud*, the main purpose of human life is no secret. Namely, we presumably want to be and remain happy (mainly according to the pleasure principle), but, unfortunately, this is generally not possible (or is at least extremely difficult), for almost everything is opposed to or runs counter to this purpose (of which realization is apparently not included in "the design of creation"). On the other hand, human beings, can nevertheless obtain some sort of limited happiness (or at least diminish painful sensations or unpleasant feelings to palliate their miserable realities). How? For instance, by intoxicating (psychoactive) substances (illegal, legal, and medical drugs), by withdrawal into some form of madness, by creative, intellectual work, or otherwise meaningful activity (for instance by cultivating one's own garden, as *Voltaire* suggests in the end of "Candide"), or by love.[18] Yet, these remedies are of restricted efficiency: they are risky, quite rare, or reserved just for the few (e.g., for extremely gifted or simply lucky individuals). In short, more or less good lives (depending to a great extent on increasing our control over the small segments of the world that could be in our power or under efficient control) are not principally impossible, but they are, as a rule, deviations from the otherwise generally grim normality.

By summing up the arguments articulated briefly in this section, could we conclude that to exist as a human being equals being a victim (an object of existential "primary victimisation")? The answer seems to be an affirmative one. Yes, life necessarily includes suffering. One suffers against his or her will, for no one comes into this world according to his or her own decision or choice. Moreover, the new born child is obviously innocent: birth (and further existence) is not due to the fault of the child. Then, is there anyone to be blamed? Should we, perhaps, reprimand the child's parents who decided to produce a new human being, often in order to give meaning (or reason) to their own lives or to stabilize their own personalities (troubled inner worlds)? Well, sometimes parents really should be scorned, particularly when they can control their reproduction and foresee more or less clearly that the future of their offspring will be, in all likelihood, very or even unbearably dark. Although, parents normally want (and try to provide) the best for their children (regardless of the fact that too many adults neglect or physically, psychically, or sexually abuse these extremely vulnerable and dependent victims). Nowadays, in the context of the "culture of fear" and in "a world of risky strangers", parental care for their child's safety and prosperity is often even exaggerated (we can easily detect this trend in Slovene society). Namely, parents want to protect their offspring from all kinds of dangers, threats, and victimisations. Unfortunately, the price of their overprotection is very high, for instance in terms of restriction of a child's mobility (resulting in sedentary lives accompanied by increased obesity),

---

18 *Voltaire* 1762/1988. For a Lacanian commentary of *Freud*'s remedies addressing human suffering, see *Dolar* 2010, pp. 75–79.

reduction of activities which are not supervised by responsible and trustworthy adults (e.g., opportunities for free play, adventure, making mistakes, learning from them, and acquiring various social skills in peer-group and other unstructured or unregulated situations), and generalized reorganization of childhood according to the principle of extreme caution (coupled by anxiety), often associated with prolonged states of helplessness or dependent immaturity.[19] But postmodern parental care (and guidance) does not stop just at providing a safe environment for their offspring, who are placed in the very centre of their family or even personal lives. The child must not be or become a loser. On the contrary, he or she must become a winner, enjoying a successful and happy life. Therefore, the child must be prepared, preferably as soon as possible, for the merciless competition (increasingly resembling a rat race), for excellent marks in school, for employment or other acquisitive opportunities, e.g., by accumulating diverse forms of human (cultural, social, symbolic, and personal) "capital". However, these expectations also have a high price, not only for the (increasingly burdened) children (who are obliged, so to speak, to fulfil their parents' expectations, hopes, dreams, and ambitions), but also for adults who are compelled (directly or indirectly, implicitly or explicitly) to sacrifice a lot of their time and energy (not to mention money and nerves) by functioning as, for instance, a child's bodyguards, drivers, supervisors, counsellors, animators, guides, coaches, mentors, additional teachers, therapists, motivators, advertisers, public relations agents, or advocates. On the other hand, there are numerous adults who reject procreation consciously, wilfully, and on explicit ethical grounds (of course not by sexual abstinence, but by means of contraception, sterilization, or, *in extremis*, abortion). They simply do not want to increase (e.g., in order to realize some egoistic wish or motive) the already enormous amount of human (and, let us not forget, also animal) suffering in our overpopulated world, i.e., suffering due either the human condition "as such", or to unfavourable (and victimising) conditions associated with capitalist economy, culture, and society (or both). They act according to the following principle: the human being who does not exist does not suffer (for an average life presumably contains more bad than good things). It should also be mentioned that members of the so-called antinatalist movement even believe that the (possibly voluntary) extinction of the human species would be the best option for the planet, for people have done and keep doing too much harm to each other, to animals, and to nature (yet, antinatalists do know all too well that this is a utopian, utterly unrealistic end).

Let us anticipate at least some possible objections to the ideas developed above. First, one could say, together with *Nietzsche* and *Voltaire* (who were well aware of our propensity for complaining, alongside our pleasure for exaggerating and

---

19 *Furedi* 2002, pp. 115–121.

projecting subjective moods onto the world),[20] that the pessimist view of human life (described as a bad or even worthless thing) reveals primarily the melancholia, sorrow, decadence, sickness (or poisoning) of the soul, or perhaps the impotence of its author.[21] Moreover, one could add that we should not judge, slander, or despise human existence (and, perhaps *a fortiori*, the world generally), especially not in light of some transcendental (purely rational) values or moral ideals (prescribing how it ought to be, although it is evidently not such).[22] Yes, life assuredly includes various forms of meaningless misery (meaningful suffering – due to its good cause or good consequences – is, as a rule, not problematic for human beings), but every mature adult, freed from childish fantasies and fears, has to accept and cope with them, possibly in constructive ways (what is much more, *Nietzsche* recommended that we should even love our fate, with all its troubles, pains, and inconveniences – *amor fati*), even if one does not believe that suffering ennobles the human soul. Doubtless, such a conception of human existence (stressing, presumably more realistically, the mixture of good and bad experiences accompanying it) seems much more acceptable and attractive to the majority (who have already got used to live as they can and have to), particularly for young people who are unmarked by the inevitable scars of ageing and still full of energy, and whose future appears relatively open, unoccupied by straining, wearying, or stressful tasks and obligations associated with heteronomous work and conventional family life. However, the "realistic" point of view (or attitude) runs somehow counter to the prevailing mood of postmodern culture that shows, on the one hand, increasing intolerance towards all negative (painful and unpleasant) sensations and, on the other hand, intensified pursuit of or craving for happiness (understood mainly in biological terms, i.e., as (a possibly everlasting) experience of pleasurable or pleasant sensations), fuelled by ballooning expectations of what (and how) one could and should enjoy life, especially by consuming all kinds of goods and services offered by the capitalist economy and promoted by the omnipresent advertising industry (that is to say, by economic propaganda being the most important message of both public and private media). In our present cultural atmosphere, it is just not enough that you are not affected by some moral or natural evil (or victimisation). You have to be happy.[23] Moreover, you presumably have a right to happiness (so that you may be unhappy solely because you are not happy enough).

This trend has important victimological and criminological implications and repercussions. For one thing, people in general have become very (and much more so than in the past) self-conscious about avoiding and preventing all sorts of risks

20 *Voltaire* 1762/1988. For a comprehensive presentation of *Voltaire*'s views on the human condition, see *Neiman* 2015, pp. 128–148.

21 *Nietzsche* 1889/1989, pp. 16–29.

22 *Nietzsche* 1889/1989, pp. 30–35.

23 *Bruckner* 2004, pp. 17–22.

(i.e., probabilities of damage, ill health, injury, and other misfortunates understood as "something that must not happen"), and consequently prone to various fears, free-floating anxieties, and panic, i.e., various negative emotions which are additionally incited by the private security industry.[24] But how can one avoid victimisations, when dangers (particularly hidden or invisible ones) seem to be almost everywhere, for example in the form of paedophiles, cyber-stalkers, sexual predators, molesters, junkies, drug dealers, thieves, fraudsters, violent youngsters, refugees, terrorists, tobacco smokers, vandals, drunken drivers, hooligans, graffiti drawers, toxic pollutants, global warming (and other natural catastrophes), abusing or bullying peers, risky vaccines, unhealthy food, poisoned water, "work-saving" technologies, foreign workers stealing "our" jobs, diminishing wages, internet pornography, video games, and smartphone addiction, etc.? Conversely, there is growing demand for legal and illegal drugs designed to alleviate (or, preferably, kill) pain, produce euphoria (or at least temporary bliss), sharpen concentration, drive away depression, worries, fears, tensions, boredom, stress, or tiredness; such drugs can make the user insensible to the intolerably meaningless of life and boost productivity, self-confidence, communication, and/or creativity.[25] Obviously, people nowadays have great interest in the biochemical way of dealing with the pressing problems concerning their happiness and unhappiness. That comes as no surprise. Drugs, old and new, offer an easy, quick, and relatively certain solution (despite their manifold risks), unlike, for instance, the Buddhist method for the elimination of human suffering.[26] Yet, the widespread use of drugs creates serious problems for postmodern criminal justice systems[27] and for the state itself which tries (nor very successfully, as experiences have demonstrated) to regulate the biochemical pursuit of happiness, mostly by separating "bad" manipulations (e.g., those which endanger social stability and economic growth) from the supposedly "good" ones (e.g., those which are compatible with or even promote social order, market competitiveness, and capitalist accumulation). But there is yet another

---

24 For a detailed and critical discussion of »the explosion of risk« in postmodern society, see *Furedi* 2002, pp. 15–42.

25 For an analysis of the principal reasons for the attractiveness of psychoactive substances (in their widespread use), see *Galimberti* 2010, pp. 57–74. For a critique of the "new economy" propelled by Prozac (and other stimulant psychoactive drugs), see *Berardi* 2013, pp. 108–114.

26 For a brief description of *Buddha*'s "noble truth off cessation" *(nirodha)* by the liberation from the endless process of craving and gratification, see *Keown* 2013, pp. 56–58.

27 *Harari* estimates that the biochemical pursuit of happiness (or, alternatively, fight against unhappiness) has become the number one cause of crime in the world: "In 2009 half of the inmates in US federal prisons got there because of drugs; 38 per cent of Italian prisoners were convicted of drug-related offences; 55 per cent of inmates in the UK reported that they committed their crimes in connection with either consuming or trading drugs. A 2001 report found that 62 per cent of Australian convicts were under the influence of drugs when committing the crime for which they were incarcerated" (*Harari* 2017, p. 46).

phenomenon tightly connected to the contemporary problem of crime: namely, following the recommendations of postmodern culture (and concomitant "consumerist ethos"), to be happy equals buying and consuming commercial goods and services, preferably "romanticized" (or "dream like") commodities. Thus, consumption becomes an alluring symbol of personal identity, life-style, success, excitement, adventure, or new (possibly extravagant) experiences. In order to satisfy new needs, wants, or desires (and to achieve material or symbolic goals that, according to the dominant ideology, can and are to be attainable by everyone), or at least to compensate everyday alienation (and accompanying inconveniences) in work time (increasingly invading also "leisure" or "free" time), one needs money, the good (or rather the God) of all goods. Of course, it is preferable that you earn it by legal ("hard and honest") work, but, as we know all too well, the "king's road" leading to this "holy" thing (the object of meta-desire *par excellence*) is crime.[28] Therefore, it is no surprise that, to take the nearest historical example, Slovene society, immersed (or rather "pushed") into the fast and turbulent transition from "socialism" to capitalism (coupled with bourgeois law and the "democratic" state), has quickly become a veritable hotbed for systematic corruption and unprecedented criminal activities (predominately acquisitive ones), a veritable heaven on earth for all sorts of scoundrels, plunderers, thieves, and fraudsters, operating alone or in *ad hoc* coalitions, informally organized networks, and new born political parties (providing immunity from apparatuses of formal control, access to legal, semi-legal, and illegal business opportunities, well paid and pleasant jobs, and generous loans from state-owned banks – thus resembling mafia-like structures). The attractiveness of illegal, deviant, or "merely" illegitimate paths to material wealth (pecuniary strength) has also been associated with the fact that the risks (perceived and also "objective" ones) of serious negative—formal and informal—sanctions have apparently been very low or even negligible.[29]

---

28 *Scheerer & Hess* 1997, pp. 119–120. The authors point out that endless creation of desires and material goals (being the driving power of "opiatized" type of pro-active social control as the key characteristic of contemporary "consumer society") produces, at the same time, endless dissatisfaction, and thus also the motivation to do away with legal restrictions (and moral barriers) and to take criminal, deviant, or illegitimate short cuts. Yet, are there truly moral or legitimate methods for enrichment? In our opinion, this question should be best understood as a rhetorical one, for the right answer is so clearly the negative one (*Scheerer & Hess* 1997, loc. cit.).

29 It must be emphasised that the impotence of repressive state apparatuses in relation to powerful, influential, and respectable criminals has been, in many respects, intentionally ("politically") created, maintained, and reproduced. Therefore, it is not just the deplorable consequence of deficient material and human resources, purges of politically unsuitable employees, corruption, or exodus of many capable and experienced cadres to better paid jobs in the private sector. Clearly, the ineffectiveness of formal (and also informal) control fits well with the interests of the greedy ("money hungry") individuals, groups, networks, and lobbies.

We can easily understand various doubts one can have with regard to the inclusion of human life into the concept (theoretical construct, to be sure) of "primary victimhood" (or rather victimisation). Nevertheless, even the one who completely rejects judgment in question has to take into consideration the sad and brute fact that human life can – and indeed all too often does – become utterly intolerable or unbearable for its "possessor" (or "captive", so to speak), due to various, albeit essentially subjective or existential reasons. When this is the case, suicide presents itself as an ultimate option, solution, or hope, usually not because the person has lost the will to live, but because the will's very object (i.e., life itself) has become too meaningless, "empty", bleak, painful, terrible, hopeless, or unworthy. However, suicide is an act (or omission of life-maintaining activities resulting in its definitive end) that is rather difficult to realize, not just because of the fear of death, possible failure ("what if I survive, perhaps in an even worse condition?"), or moral hindrances ("in all likeliness, members of my family will be sad, angry, put in shame, or materially victimised"), but also due to the purely technical reasons. Namely, access to the means ensuring a (subjectively preferred) "beautiful" death (e.g., one which is quick, without pain, and certain) is very restricted. A human being wanting to die has to improvise or even choose the form of death that is ugly and painful. In other words, the would-be suicidal person is usually obliged to leave this world in secret like a deserter or criminal. The key problem is that we still do not have an effective (legally recognized) right to euthanasia ("good" – i.e., self-determined or meaningful – death), in spite of much pompous talk of human dignity and individual liberties, and this weird (or rather scandalous) fact could and should be probably conceived as the most important existential "secondary victimisation". Clearly, liberal criminal law does not treat suicide as a crime anymore. But helping someone to die is still a punishable act (the Slovene penal code also incriminates assisting a suicide).[30] Crazy, but true. And what is more, it seems that this anachronistic and cruel regulation will not be abolished in the next future, as if humans have to be a victim (i.e., unwillingly forced to undergo suffering) for as long as possible, as if suicide (as an act of autonomously preferred redemption) is something sinful, wrong, or pathological (some sort of *de iure* decriminalized, but *de facto* "criminal" act against humankind, being the only truly holy value in the perspective of modern humanism, i.e., the dominant religion of the secularized society that has killed – or rather sentenced to death – the old transcendental God).

---

30 Helping someone who wants to die embraces various activities ranging from providing a desirable means (causing the chosen death) to killing the person who cannot finish his/her life by himself or herself (e.g., because of a paralysis).

3. Victims, Victimisers, and Neoliberal Capitalism

Let us now focus more directly on Slovene society, dramatically and radically transformed during the so-called (post-socialist) transition into a, more or less, typical postmodern and capitalist formation, designed according to the neoliberal model, as propagated and enforced by the cadres of trans-national power apparatuses (e.g., European Union,[31] NATO, WTO, IMF, World bank, and OECD),[32] enviably well-paid "priests" and "soldiers" of the global (and national) rule of capital.[33] How does it look like from the victimological (and criminological) perspective? "Not very good", one would rightly remark, although the situation could be of course much worse. To begin with, during the turbulent period in question, various ideas and topics have been (not so rarely in a great hurry) imported from the Western victimology and victims' movements (many of them were also put into practice), for example victim surveys (examining the quantity and experiences of victims of crime) and other forms of empirical and theoretical studies, victim support facilities (such as shelters for battered and otherwise abused women and children), non-governmental organizations and voluntary groups counselling, helping, advocating, empowering, or trying to improve the normative and factual condition of specific categories of victims, "discoveries" of socially invisible or silenced forms of victimhood (for instance bullying in schools, mobbing associated with the work place, hate speech, sexual harassment, family violence, discrimination and maltreatment of some par-

---

31 For a critical analysis of the prevailing Slovenian perceptions of "Europe", see *Mastnak* 2001, pp. 10–15. The author is of the opinion that the membership of the EU transformed the Slovenian (formally "sovereign" and "independent") state into a "province" or "region", servile to the "dictatorship of European bureaucracy". Referring to "Europe" (as a sort of metaphor) has indeed functioned as a ready-made justification for implementing "unpopular" (but presumably "necessary") political, legal, economic, monetary, and fiscal measures. Anyway, when we put into parenthesis the EU's icy institutional architecture, ideologically correct discourse, and the impenetrable fog created by unreadable (indigestible) normative provisions, the key message of its managing elites appears quite unambiguously: "You must work more, better, faster, cheaper, and without complaints!" (*Mastnak* 2001, loc. cit).

32 Clearly, the fundamental "transitional" processes were orchestrated according to the Western "Ich-Ideal" in the manner that we might describe them as results of hyper-mimicry, i.e., the slavish (or at least apish) imitation and mindless (or possibly merely naïve) acceptance of the suggestions, advices, expectations, and imperatives delivered by foreign experts, politicians, diplomats, functionaries, and other representatives of the "Great Other". However, this attitude – reflecting the deeply rooted feeling of inferiority towards the West (core economies of the capitalist world system) – cannot be explained as something completely new, say as a peculiar emotional disposition that emerged suddenly after the painful death of "socialism". On the contrary, it could be observed much earlier in the souls of both "ordinary" working people and members of the ideological and political avant-garde.

33 For a critical view of the capital as "the sole possessor of sovereignty", see *Gorz* 1999, pp. 14–16.

ticularly vulnerable minorities, e.g., same-sex oriented individuals, patients in psychiatric institutions, elders, and the Roma population), debates concerning "victimless crimes" (such as prostitution, use of marihuana, gambling, and even abortion which, at least in the austere eyes of many clerics, believers, and members of the neo-conservative political right, should be forbidden or even sanctioned as a crime), institutionalized schemes for mediation of conflicts, official protectors of human rights ("ombudsman"), etc. However, in comparison with the socialist past, people (as the potential sufferers or objects of some harmful event) are much more concerned about their safety, interpreted and dealt with as the value which responsible, self-sufficient, "active", and independent citizens have to protect primarily by themselves, for example by cautiously performing everyday activities, by fortifying their homes, carefully assessing and managing risks, acquiring self-defence skills, installing anti-burglary doors, fences, techno-preventive devices, and other "useful stuff" of this kind, or, if they can afford it, by employing private security services. Yet, this is generally not an easy task. Apparently, offenders are everywhere, they can victimise (e.g., attack, defraud, or rob) you at any time, and many "new" criminals have become horribly fearless, audacious, cruel, self-confident, professional, or powerful, not only in relation to actual or potential victims, but also in their capacity to threaten or endanger the agents of criminal justice system, shirk their own responsibilities, and evade formal punishment.[34] Doubtless, the increased fear of crime is probably, to a quite great extent, also the side effect of the massive and spectacular entrance of criminal events into the "liberated" media space, i.e., into newspapers, radio, and television broadcasts. Of course, victims (describing the harmful event they have been forced to undergo, showing its emotional repercussions, or claiming justice) are also included in crime-related bad news, but, all in all, individuals suspected, prosecuted, indicted, or condemned of criminal offences, and their self-asserting lawyers, are regularly given more attention by both public and private media (and consequently by their audiences), so that they can proclaim (often in an offended or even outraged manner) their innocence, accuse the accusers, complain about illegal police work, poke fun at agents of the criminal justice system, or boldly affirm that they are scapegoats or innocent victims of a politically motivated plot.

The most typical (and harmful) transitional criminals, causing enormous material (and also moral) damage, particularly in comparison with their conventional colleagues who operate in more or less traditional and old fashioned ways, do not inspire fear. They are mostly "kind" or at least nonaggressive, nicely dressed, intelligent, articulated, formally educated, normally socialized and relatively cultivated persons, well off, vocationally successful, belonging to respected and influential families, occupying high positions in the hierarchies of the state apparatus, private

---

34 For an instructive analysis of the increasing power of criminal offenders, blurring identities, and the progressive "normalisation" of crime (being no longer an unexpected, abnormal, marginal, or exogenous event), see *Lea* 2002, pp. 135–143.

firms, and civil society's organisations. Just take a look at the following list of criminal "new comers". It includes prime and other ministers, leaders and important members of new (obligatory "democratic") political parties, diplomats, judges, public prosecutors, lawyers, notaries, elected representatives of the "people", army officers, police and secret service officials, ordinary bureaucrats, directors, managers, businessmen, bankers, stock-exchange brokers and speculators, financial "magicians", various counsellors, tax optimization and public relations experts, mayors, medical doctors, academics, scientists, artists, journalists, popular show-business figures, professional sportsmen, clerics, leaders of humanitarian organisations, lobbyists, functionaries of sport clubs, and so forth. Obviously, this "new breed" of (post)transitional criminal offenders is indeed very special. Namely, the individuals in question are in general not marked or affected by deficits (or prior victimisations) which in the perspective of the modern criminological (biological, psychological, or sociological) theories are to be understood as the causes, reasons, factors, or roots of criminal behaviour, such as deficient self-control, low IQ, being abused or neglected during childhood, growing up in a dysfunctional family, living in a disorganized community, performing poorly in school, associating with delinquent peers, interiorizing subcultural values, being unemployed and without money, and so on. On the contrary, they are more often than not enviably privileged, for they can enjoy a wide range of opportunities for both legal and illegal enrichment, huge amounts of "negative" freedom, various forms of "capital" and, not to be forgotten, great immunity from the sanctioning mechanisms of formal and informal (re-active) social control. Furthermore, the motivation for their criminal activities seems utterly normal, namely the desire for the relatively quick, easy, effortless acquisition of money, following the fundamental "categorical imperative" of "eroticized" capitalist culture: catch the cash,[35] steal as much as you can (preferably from public resources or from what in the past was – and what also in the present is or at least in the future should be – social, collective, or common property),[36] for when the theft (or plunder) is big

---

35 The ultimate attraction of money (as the only quasi-religious authority in the secularized, "rationalized", fragmented, and disenchanted world) has been enormously intensified by the irresistible (but warmly welcomed) invasion of foreign commodities, luxury and branded goods (with Western cars taking the honour for first place), glittering images of seductive role models and paragons (the exemplars of undeniable success stories, breath-taking beauty, or madding sex-appeal), i.e., idols ready made for imitation encouraged by the explosion of commercial media and its glorification of the glamorous lives of famous personalities, focusing on contemporary hedonistic "aristocracy", and showing precious symbols of individual distinction ("you have to be different, not like the others, possibly the special one").

36 *Žižek* (2009, pp. 428–439) defines "the commons" as "the shared substance of our social being whose privatization is a violent act which should be resisted with violence, if necessary". Moreover, he insists that precisely this reference to "the commons" (i.e., "the substance of productivity" which is neither private nor public) justifies the resuscitation of the notion of communism.

enough (and its protagonists "weighty" enough) it becomes – almost prodigiously, so to say – "just" business or politics "as usual" (or "a job well done"). In addition, it should be emphasized that the victims of the crime in question are often dispersed, unconscious of being victimised, unknown, invisible, hardly identifiable, or somehow abstract (e.g., tax-payers, citizens, consumers, or workers).

Typically transitional crime did not incite fear, but it provoked many other reactive emotions, such as anger, outrage, indignation, a sense of unfairness, injustice and powerlessness, bitterness, envy, resentment, generalized dissatisfaction, and extensive distrust of new economic elites, key institutions of the "democratic" state, political parties (and politicians being supposedly "all the same", i.e., equally corrupted or at least disposed to corruption),[37] the church, and many other organizations of the "civil" society. This inflammable (Molotov-cocktail-like) cocktail finally exploded on 21 November 2012 in Maribor, popularly dubbed "the city of ghosts", because of the high rate of unemployment, ruined industry, relative poverty, and abandoned public places. The utterly unexpected and therefore quite shocking uprising (also due to the violent, even brutal police reaction) was triggered by a seemingly trivial reason: radar traps the mayor set up (in cooperation with a private company) in the streets in order to fine speeding drivers. Yet, it was almost immediately followed by other mass uprisings, protests, civil initiatives, and demonstrations that took place not only in Maribor, but also in Ljubljana (the capital of Slovenia) and, to a much lesser extent, in some other smaller towns. What did the protestors want to achieve (apart from venting their emotional distress)? What did they try to communicate to bewildered politicians, media, and the public in general? Well, it is somewhat hard to say, even retrospectively. Namely, you could hear various voices and read diversified messages (albeit the most frequent slogan was "They are finished"). That came as no surprise. For one thing, the protestors were not organized or guided from one command centre.

---

37 Clearly, corruption is by no means a phenomenon which is exclusively characteristic of (post)transitional, post-socialist societies. *Wallerstein* points out that political corruption is an altogether normal and, unfortunately, also indestructible attribute of the capitalist world economy; see *Wallerstein* 2004, pp. 150–151. *Badiou* argues that corruption is to be understood as the essence of "democracy" representing first of all the key interests (or "functional imperatives") of the capitalist economy, or indeed of any political system whose central goals are private and collective enrichments, permanent economic growth, endless and limitless accumulation, and the untouchability of the private property of super-rich owners; see *Badiou* 2008, pp. 89–91. On the other hand, *Hardt* and *Negri* define corruption as the capital's expropriation, segmentation, control, and privatization of what is socially produced by common work, action, and thinking (in their opinion, corrupted forms of "the common" can be detected in the central institutions of capitalist social formations, e.g., in the family, corporation, and nation); see *Hardt & Negri* 2010, pp. 151–155.

The uprising movement was in no way ideologically or politically unified.[38] Differences (and also disagreements leading to conflicts) among various groups and individuals soon emerged, alongside the growing role of cultural events during the demonstrations (transforming them in some sort of improvised spectacle), and the gap between the intellectual minorities ("elites") and the ordinary ("screaming") crowd. However, the chief targets of anger (or rage) were the publicly most exposed members of the predatory political and economic "elites" (on a national and local level). In this regard, the protest movements can also be criticized because of the over-personalization of manifold problems caused by the completion of primary accumulation of capital, by the global financial crises (followed by unpopular "austerity policies"), and of course by the introduction of capitalist rule, although this orientation could be easily understood (and excused) if we take into consideration the fact that the extremely accelerated transition appeared to the public as a more or less continuous procession of mostly unsanctioned "scandals" and "affairs", revealed by the media and widely known either by personal experience or informal hearsay. Yet, at least the minority of protestors tried to (re)direct the attention to the structural violence[39] and its systemic generators, such as market competition, profit oriented economy, class based inequalities (e.g., the condition of radical material heteronomy as the key characteristic of the subordinated sellers of their own "labour power" which, unfortunately, cannot be separated from the workers themselves, i.e., from their "bodies, souls and hearts"), and private property of the means of production. Be that as it may, we can also interpret the uprisings in question as a spontaneous reaction to the spectacular "theft of the century" and its subsequent harmful effects, i.e., as the most important (although politically unsuccessful and perhaps even the historically very last) protest of direct and indirect victims (or losers) of the turbulent transitional processes and radical structural transformations.[40]

---

38 For a detailed description, sociological analysis, and critical commentary of the uprisings in Maribor and the following protest movement in Slovenia, see *Koršič* 2013, pp. 93–101; *Kurnik* 2013, pp. 11–20; *Trček* 2013, pp. 60–71.

39 *Žižek* (2009, p. 481) points out that structural violence is an inherent characteristic of the completely normal functioning of capitalist economy: "Systemic violence is thus something like the notorious 'dark matter' of physics, the counterpart to an all-too-visible subjective violence. It may be invisible, but it has to be taken into account if one is to make sense of what otherwise seem to be 'irrational' explosions of subjective violence. Benjaminian 'divine violence' is precisely the direct subjectivization of (or, rather, the direct subjective reaction to) this objective violence."

40 It should be remembered that the expression "theft of the century" does not refer only to the criminal or unlawful (illegal) acquisition of material wealth, e.g., to the drainage of enterprises by their managers, various forms of "wild" privatization of formerly social or state property, planned bankruptcies, creation of by-passing firms, and the like. Moreover, it cannot be attributed merely to the so-called tycoons (as the postmodern version of feudal robber barons and baronesses). Namely, the historically unprecedented "theft

Interestingly (or rather paradoxically), what appeared as the (socially, economically, and culturally devastating) "crime of the century" can be also interpreted as the "punishment of the century" (and not just as, say, a historical tragedy or an irreparable political mistake). Punishment for exactly what crime? Well, the only imaginable candidate is the socialist (economic and political) system, established after the bloody Second World War through the revolution ("expropriation of expropriators" in the form of nationalization or socialisation of the key economic resources). Although the majority of people living and working under the socialism did not experience it as something criminal, it has been unanimously condemned as such by the victorious contra-revolutionary "democratic" (neo-liberal and neo-conservative) forces defining it as a "totalitarian" regime (somehow equal to the fascist and Nazi ones), based on "illegitimate" revolution (i.e., nationalization of industrial, natural, and other basic economic resources) as "the crime of all crimes" (accompanied also by mass killings of quislings after the end of the National Liberation War, oppression of dissidents (being otherwise quite rare in Slovenia), denial of political "human rights", favouring state and social property over private property, restricting the freedom of expression, and so on). Even if you do not accept the severe judgement in question, you probably have to admit that the post-socialist transition could be described as a historically unique and, to a great extent, self-imposed collective chastisement to pursue and realise many purposes, such as:

(a) material compensation (in the form of restitution in nature and pecuniary indemnification), given to the principal sufferers, the most victimised (objective and fictive) persons, i.e., one-time owners of nationalized property and their often very remote heirs;

(b) retribution (in terms of exploitation, extortion, oppression, humiliation, and subjection of workers to their new bosses, job insecurity, social incertitude, and acceptance of the growing material inequalities);

(c) deterrence (generated by implicit and explicit warnings that can be summarized roughly as follows: You have to get accustomed to the constraints of the capitalist mode of production, if you want to avoid even worse evils, e.g., pov-

---

of the century" – mostly in the form of denationalization and privatization – has been perpetrated to the great extent in accordance with the ill-omened letters and spirits of law (in this regard, the law itself could be estimated as somehow "criminal"). In other words, the crime in question was a collective, politically orchestrated project (indeed the very "heart" of post-socialist transition), based upon widespread consensus and indispensable support of the public and private media, "democratic" politicians, ex-members and leaders of the communist party, "critical" intellectuals, and experts, particularly lawyers and economists. For instance, privatization certificates were warmly accepted (like a sort of gift from heaven inviting everyone's soul to transmigrate into the capitalist body), not to mention an exceptional opportunity to buy state-owned or social apartments at extremely low prices.

erty, unemployment, individual insignificance, status degradation, excommunication, or, in the worst case, even a huge and pernicious societal catastrophe);

(d) incapacitation (for example by "freely" sacrificing the majority of one's time, energy, and freedom to heteronomous, alienating economic activities determined by instrumental rationality);

(e) re-socialization and rehabilitation (for instance by means of intensive work therapy to create a new – active, productive, competitive, self-disciplined, self-motivated, creative, healthy, and self-sufficient – person internalizing the ideology of "work as value", being proud of selling "labour power", and functioning obediently, eagerly and efficiently as a grateful "liberal slave" of some temporary private or public master);

(f) preventive control performed by the new breed of democratic and liberal politicians, "organic" intellectuals (employed in the media apparatuses and educational system), and institutions of global governance (e.g., EU, NATO, WTO, IMF, OECD, and WB);

(g) lustration (i.e., removal of all potentially dangerous elements involved in the "criminal" theory and practice of the defunct "totalitarian" regime).[41]

Let us conclude this section by observing that fear of crime (and criminals) is not the principal worry of people in Slovenia. Speaking of this particular emotion (often anxiety), we may argue that it has other more important roots, for instance, more or less generalized economic insecurities (accompanied by social status insecurities) that are associated with the increase of poverty (nowadays probably the crucial

---

41 In this regard, *Žižek* (2009, p. 404) offers an interesting example (albeit not from the Slovenian context): "A few days before the Czech municipal and Senate elections, on October 16, 2006, the Ministry of the Interior of the Czech Republic banned the organisation the Communist Youth League (KSM). What was its 'criminal idea' on account of which, according to the Ministry of the Interior, the KSM deserved to be banned? The fact that its program advocates the transformation of private ownership of the means of production into social property, thereby contradicting the Czech constitution … To claim that demand for social ownership of the means of production is a crime is to say that modern left-wing thought has criminal roots." It goes without saying that Slovene society has also been affected by the huge explosion of rugged (post-communist) anti-communism, in spite of the fact that there had been no real communist threat left (ex-communists – or rather once loyal members of the bygone ruling party – evaporated almost overnight or converted somehow miraculously into new democrats, liberals, conservatives, nationalists (or rather quasi patriotic lovers of Slovene ethnicity), defenders of human rights, ruthless managers, money-hunger private owners of once *de iure* social firms, bold entrepreneurs, innovative businessmen, successful traffickers in arms, influential lobbyists, value-free academics, public relations experts, tireless propagandists of free-market economy, and so on). Conversely, the new initiatives for "democratic socialism" that emerged from the Slovene uprisings surely do not justify the die-hard anti-communism, for these initiatives are politically too weak and culturally too marginal.

form of meta-humiliation),[42] unemployment, unjust (and unjustifiable) inequalities in material wealth (and income), deterioration of work conditions, and expansions of so-called a-typical work (e.g., flexible, project, precarious, or short-term jobs), not to mention "ontological" insecurities associated with identity crises, eroded (formal and informal) social solidarity, weakening of normative restraints, blurring and shifting moral boundaries separating good and evil, marriage and family instability, changing gender roles, fluidity of "existential" reference points, and heightened individualism (propagating "free choice", spontaneity, authenticity, personal success, expressivity, immediacy, consumeristic hedonism, life-style, happiness, and achievement of self-actualization).[43] Moreover, crimes and accidents (or, to use the old concepts, moral and natural evils), as the object *par excellence* of mainstream victimology,[44] can scarcely be viewed as the key sources of victimisation. Apparently, taking into account the harm done to values, such as human time, energy, freedom, autonomy, health, dignity, and opportunities for self-determined activities, it certainly could be argued that humans are victimised mostly by utterly normal social and economic processes and conditions, for instance by long working hours, stressful or meaningless work, poverty, ecological damage, mindless competition, endless accumulation of capital, culturally imposed stupidity, and the like. But are we allowed to interpret these harmful phenomena as "victimisations"? The "right" (i.e., politically correct) answer is of course a negative one, at least in the perspective of the dominant ideology assuring us that everything is just fine (or rather just and fine): the things are as they ought to be.[45] Of course there are (and, unfortunately, will always be) winners and losers. Yet, as a rule, everybody deserves his or her good or bad fate. Namely, it is the market – functioning infallibly according to its objective (quasi natural) laws determined by the invisible hand of Providence – that guarantees the smooth reproduction of the right (and probably the best possible) social order. Instead of complaining or even asking to be recognized as a victim of the capitalist economy, one has to blame her- or himself. It is the lack of talents, competences, competitiveness, enterprising spirit, diligence, initiative, boldness,

---

42 For a more detailed elaboration of this point, see *Young* 2007, pp. 76–77.

43 For a more precise analysis of the nature (and causes) of postmodern ontological insecurity, see *Young* 1999, pp. 98–102.

44 *Šeparović* 1985, pp. 15–17.

45 Before complaining, one should pay regard to many advantages associated with the inauguration of the new social formation: not only democracy (free election and party pluralism), admission to EU & NATO, legal state (treating and protecting all citizens as formally free and equal private owners of their property), and officially uncensored media, but also innumerable hastily purchased glittering cars (worshiped objects of popular longing and day-dreaming), spacious parking places, underground garages, highways, mushrooming shopping-centres, prestigious designer stores, family-friendly amusement parks, enticing casinos, reality-shows, multiplex motion-picture theatres (replacing uncompromisingly the old-fashioned ones), all sorts of electronic devices and digital gadgets, vividly painted or otherwise embellished public and private buildings, and so on.

knowledge, self-discipline, inventiveness, adaptability, ambitiousness, creativeness, perseverance, flexibility, assiduity, far-sightedness, or some other important personal characteristic and disposition that explains and justifies one's failure, low pay, poor work conditions, unemployment, poverty or relative deprivation, and other inconveniences. As a matter of fact, considering the Slovene situation, we can see that it is extremely difficult to be acknowledged as a victim who has a justified or valid right to complain, to attract public compassion, or to get some sort of material or symbolic compensation. Namely, mere suffering, albeit occurring against one's will, does not suffice. If you want that your personal troubles, grief, sufferance, and subjectively experienced (perceived and estimated) harm be (socially and preferably officially) recognized, you must fulfil severe criteria regarding the quality and the quantity of human misery, wretchedness, distress, penury, or squalor. The would-be victim can be quickly told that his or her troubles are not serious enough, for there are a lot of other sufferers (both in Slovenia and abroad) who undergo a much worse (or painful) fate, for instance hapless children starving to death, honourable women gang raped, feeble old people cruelly beaten by violent youngsters, babies burnt alive, utterly innocent people tortured, workers toiling silently from morning till night in some invisible sweatshop, have-nots who lose everything due to some social or natural catastrophe. In other words, in comparison with the true sufferers (or veritable victims), the would-be (or "self-styled") victim is still a somewhat privileged – or maybe merely pretentious, impatient, touchy, lazy, coddled, exploitative, parasitic, or corrupt – person (not to be taken seriously at all). In short, there is always someone to be found who suffers more and whose innocence is more impeccable.

On the other hand, we can detect, also in Slovenia, a category of privileged postmodern victims, although they, paradoxically, consist mainly of imagined entities, such as the state, the (conventional) family, the Catholic Church, the economy, the nation, the law, and the corporation. What is the nature of their victimhood? To begin with, the neoliberal state is supposedly victimised by influential social groups (e.g., trade unions, lobbies, monopolistic enterprises, and also by its own citizens or voters)[46] trying to realize their particular interests to the detriment of "free market" and "unbound competition". The "traditional" family is victimised by the denaturalization of its basic structure, by frequency of divorce, by radical feminists

46 According to the neoliberal creed, the "good" state must be strong enough to discipline and de-politicize itself in order to enable and protect the "spontaneous market order" – and its "iron laws", incomprehensible for the ordinary or layperson who, mistakenly and driven by "atavistic emotions" *(Hayek* 1983, pp. 197–1989*)*, interpret their effects as unjust, irrational, or immoral – from the noxious influences of politics, democracy, and opposing movements advocating (social and economic) human rights and fair redistribution of wealth. For a critical analysis of neoliberal fundamental dogmas (such as infallibility of the market "logic", advantages of generalised competition, privatization of public services, deregulation of work, and free circulation of capital and commodities), see *Supiot* 2013, pp. 21–26.

denouncing patriarchy (in its modern or renewed forms), by emancipated women renouncing marriage, male authority, and even motherhood, by relaxed postmodern sexual morality, by cyber pornography tempting men to commit adultery or spend money on prostitutes, and by same-sex oriented persons wanting to marry and adopt children. The Catholic Church is presumably victimised because it still does not have enough rights, privileges, political and cultural influence, and material wealth. The economy is victimised by the striking workers, rigidity of the valid "rules of the game", administrative constraints ("unfit for life"), high taxes and wages, low or deficient subsidies, and unnecessary ("obsolete") workers' rights. The nation (or rather the dominant ethnicity) is victimised by non-patriotic cosmopolitans, undesired foreigners threatening "our way of living", safety and "sacred cultural values" (as the chief pillars of "our common" identity), and pacifists suggesting the abolition of the professionalized army and withdrawal from NATO. The law is victimised by deviant and illegal activities, especially by unsanctioned ones (because of the inefficient, corrupt, or incompetent agents of formal social control). Finally, the corporation is victimised by workers' laziness, scrimshanking, high wages, and other forms of stealing employer's money. In distinction from all these imagined entities human ("flesh and blood") beings indeed can, and all too often do, suffer, i.e., experience painful or unpleasant sensations and emotions, such as sadness, bitterness, anger, injustice and powerlessness, frustration, chronic fatigue, fear, anxiety, depression, guilt, despair, grievance, or unhappiness. Cleary, various forms of dissatisfaction are nowadays widespread and tightly connected with the need to find the culprits responsible for the miseries experienced. Consequently, an important moral and political question arises: who and where are the key victimisers ("suitable enemies") of the proverbial "little people", i.e., honest and hard-working members of both the silent and moral majority? In Slovenia, it is right-wing and populist politicians who have been particularly eager to publicly identify candidates for that ominous social role. Since the very beginning of the post-socialist transition, many of them have pointed their accusing finger at the "udbomafija", i.e., supposedly mafia-like structures or informal networks of the "old boys" (embracing influential ex-communists, ex-members of National security agency, and "red" managers still in function), dubbed also "uncles from the backstage" or "operators of the deep state". However, this suggestion has been accepted mainly by their most faithful followers, supporters, and sympathizers, not solely because the victimisers in question seem too abstract and somehow mysterious, but primarily because it soon turned out that there were too many greedy newcomers who had also chosen the royal road of acquisitive crime as the principal means for personal or family enrichment. Finally, running parallel with the progressive neo-liberalization of Slovene society, a more widely accepted category of victimisers – called "social parasites" – has appeared in quite a stabilized form. Doubtless, the kaleidoscope of "social parasites" includes various groups of supposedly unworthy (or inferior) human creatures, for instance the unemployed, unemployable, work-shy, lazy, sick, mentally disturbed, disabled, homeless, and other marginal persons, pensioners (living too long to the detriment of younger generations and their relatives who have to care for them), welfare "scroungers" (enjoying their "happy-go-lucky" lives thanks to the tax-payers' money), immigrants, refugees, and asylum seekers (praying on the scarce resources of the social state), junkies, beggars, ordinary or "conventional" criminals (stealing, robbing, and attacking honest and loyal citizens), irresponsible youths studying too long or studying the "wrong things" (which the productive capitalist economy does not really need), "useless" artists and intellectuals, etc. In the neoliberal perspective, the common denominator of all these various bad guys and girls ("the new idlers" or "demons of postmodernity") is "passivity".[47] They are not productive participants in the capitalist economy and society. Therefore, they are without "legitimate income", being merely a heavy burden for the state and economy (because they diminish global competitiveness); they are direct or indirect victimisers of the "active" population, i.e., capitalists and productive wage earners. In addition, the sellers of "labour power" are divided into two categories: those working in the private (competitive) sector are seemingly superior to those employed in the public (non-competitive) sector, for the former work harder, under more stressful conditions, and in more or less permanent fear. They do suffer, but that should mean that the "social parasites" must suffer even more. Although this kind of "negative solidarity" (and accompanying morality) leads to the lowering (or worsening) of the general standard of life (and its diminished quality), it has become widely accepted by normal, straight, decent, self-restrained, hard-working, and law-abiding people (being all too often just one step above relative poverty).

4. By Way of Conclusion

Victimology is a relatively young social science, but the topics it deals with are very old and all too human. In the past, these topics were interpreted as the "problem of evil".[48] It can be expressed in many ways. For instance: Why is there evil rather than good? Why is the world full of innocent suffering (the question is especially puzzling if we assume that the universe has been created by an omnipotent, omniscient, and benevolent God, and not by some malicious demon)? Why is wrongdoing rewarded, while good deeds are, all too often, punished? Why do bad things happen to decent people? Why does life as such (or at least heteronomous work by which so many people routinely ruin their bodies and souls) all too often look like a more or less continuous torture or chastisement? Why is there a stubbornly persevering gap between the real and the rational, between life and justice, between nature and morality, between virtue and happiness, between "is" and "ought"? In the context of the capitalist system, we can formulate the perennial "problem of evil" even more

---

47 For a more precise commentary of this phenomenon, see *Tamás* 2016, pp. 246–253.

48 *Neiman* 2015, pp. 314–328.

specifically. Why are grotesque and evidently unjustified inequalities in wealth and income tolerated? Why are accidents of birth (e.g., one's talents, beauty, intelligence, creativity, or other socially appreciated dispositions, including one's personality or character[49]) still interpreted and treated as an individual's just deserts? Why do we not abolish the anachronistic law of inheritance (permitting that the legally or illegally stolen or pillaged resources can be passed – as some kind of "original sin" – to subsequent generations)? Why does the enormous increase of productivity (due to the scientific and technologic progress) function as a curse, and not as a blessing for employed workers? How can we accept the social world being morally[50] "turned upside down"?

By focusing mainly on the victims of crimes and also, to a lesser extent, on those of accidents, mainstream victimology shrinks the traditional "problem of evil", leaving much of human misery unexplored, unrecognized, or even overlooked. But people normally need to justify or make sense of their own suffering (e.g., by finding some meaning to it and thus making it more bearable), and it is the dominant capitalist ideology (accompanied by systematic economic propaganda) which helps in so doing.[51] In its perspective, the painful social reality is repaint-

---

49 *Baggini* and *Fosl* (2007, p. 223) point out that one's moral standing is in many aspects a consequence of "constitutive luck": "How good or bad one is depends a great deal on one's personality or character. But character is formed through both nature and nurture, and by the time one becomes mature enough to be considered a morally responsible adult, these character traits are more or less set. So, for example, a kind person hasn't fully chosen to be kind: that's how she grew up. Certainly many cruel and nasty people were themselves mistreated as children; that abuse almost certainly affected the way their personalities developed. Since people don't choose their genes, or their parents, or their culture of origin, or a lot of the other factors that affect moral development, there therefore seems to be another important element of luck in morality."

50 *Galeano* 2011, pp. 3–5.

51 From the Marxist perspective, it is first of all ideology (much more than repression) that explains the die-hard class domination, at least in fully developed, self-reproducing capitalism (which is able to produce its own structural presuppositions by itself), looking like an "organic system" in which each part presupposes all others. *Heinrich* points out that capitalist ideology is not the result of intentional manipulation by the economic and political elites, or their intellectual apologists, e.g., those responsible for the indoctrination of cadres (particularly lawyers and managers); see *Heinrich* 2013, pp. 195–202. By contrast, it springs "naturally" from the basic structures of the capitalist economy and society (and from innumerable human actions that continuously reproduce and internalise these structures). Ideological representations – i.e., mystifications and fetishes (linked to capital, money, and commodities) – are something that spontaneously comes to mind (or appears) if one has to function normally in capitalist social relations (or "forms"). As a result of this "religion of everyday life", members of capitalist society live in a "bewitched world turned upside-down", i.e., in a reality that is fundamentally non-transparent, regardless of growing quantities of contemporary data and an information overabundance; see *Marx* 1894/1973, p. 925. For example, due to ideological distortions, one perceives one's wage as (usually too low) payment for work (or "a job well done"). Profit

ed in brighter colours. For instance, the "free" market is described as an earthly deity, wisely directing human decisions and actions, providently allocating fundamental economic resources, and generously rewarding all competent subjects, whilst severely punishing the non-competent ones. Work is presented as superior to non-work, "passivity", or "non-activity", usually interpreted as "laziness" (the principal human vice), even if the acquisitive activity in question is poorly paid, undoubtedly meaningless, alienating,[52] or even (in)directly destructive (e.g., for humans, society, culture, or nature), performed in degrading, unhealthy, or dehumanising conditions, in great hurry, or under torturing pressure. Economic uncertainty and precariousness of employment are said to be good because they encourage workers to work more, faster, and better, to obediently and productively serve their private or public masters, and, moreover, to mobilise their whole personality under the command of the Other (i.e., not only their technical knowledge and professional skills, but also unlimited openness to be adjustable, imaginative, co-operative, creative, predictive, analytical, linguistic, communicative, etc., and to display a passion for and devotion to heteronomous work). To sum up, capitalism, based firmly on human (contractual) freedom (free will and choice), does not victimise people. On the contrary, it provides them with desirable goods and services (preferably at the lowest prices), it encourages them to enjoy their lives as much as possible, and it stimulates vertiginous scientific and technological progress (eliminating many sources of human misery and, thus, replacing an old idea of Providence). Moreover, its basic morality is admirably simple and easy to follow: the rich (in the economic role as capitalists) must accumulate (i.e., reinvest their profits in order to make more money) and the rest must shop (and of course work in order to earn legitimate income). In other words, greed is good (whilst the

---

seems like the achievement of a particular company, obtained in market competition with others. Capital, land (natural resources), and "work" appear to be "productive factors" whose owners are remunerated according to the portion of value their factors have created or "added". And so on. Yet, even if we are deeply immersed in the ideological (objectively or socially valid) mental forms, we do have more than enough information for a revolt. But this does not happen very often. Why? Our suggestion is that we should also take into account the emotional dimensions of class control, e.g., the notorious fact that capitalist masters manage, extremely successfully, to capture, attract, seduce, shape, and create the desires of subordinated people in a manner that maintains their domination. That is why economic propaganda, as the chief function (or message) of mass media, is so important for the perpetuation of the capitalist *status quo*. It endlessly celebrates the cult of material wealth (presented as accessible to all, at least "in principle"), the cult of buying and consuming commercial goods and experiences, and the cult of the rich; see *Canfora* 2006, pp. 321–324.

52 *Baggini* and *Fosl* (2007, p. 161) emphasize that alienation need not only be from others for one can also be alienated from one's true self: "To be thus alienated is to be estranged, to be at a distance from oneself, to be somehow not where it's natural to be, where one fits or is at home, where one can truly be oneself." For a critical analysis of alienating wage work in postmodern capitalism, see also *Tamás* 2016, pp. 169–171.

incessant economic growth is the supreme value), and egoism is, in fact, altruism, because the individual desire for private enrichment works best for the interests of all. The rich, being the most useful and benevolent members of society, are to be treated (doubtless with due respect) as humanity's superior avant-garde (for they are the chief motor of material growth and social progress), as paragons to be admired and (if possible) imitated, or at least as "holy cows" to be left in peace so that they can safely enjoy their deserved successes. As regards the undisputable forms of unjust human suffering, criminals have to be punished, terrorist must be eliminated, and innocent victims are to be pitied, helped, cured, compensated, and empowered. The majority of all other contemporary problems will be soon resolved by means of further economic growth and technological development.[53] That's all, folks!

Indeed, we cannot blame capitalism for what one would call "evils", individual and social "harms", or "injustices" (e.g., absurdly increased economic inequalities, ecological destruction, unemployment, exploitation, oppression, or extortion of workers, governments, and debtors). Namely, its chief purpose is not to promote social welfare, individual freedom, human rights, economic justice, equality, or democracy, nor to provide enough wage work for all. Its fundamental (or even sole) purpose is the valorisation of capital, production of surplus value, infinitive and limitless accumulation. Therefore, the capitalist economy is inherently irrational and destructive, particularly when its development is not limited "from the outside", i.e., by firm political opposition, collective resistance of workers, and the power of the nation state. Yet, due to the victorious neoliberal counter-revolution, almost every form of opposition has become extremely weak. As a depressing consequence, capitalists can use (and abuse) "happily" employed human workers and natural resources as (primarily) means for their "never ending" race for profits much more unimpeded-

---

53 *Baggini* and *Fosl* (2007, p. 217) point out that even the predominant liberal political beliefs with which people understand and justify the social relations they do observe can be interpreted as "instruments of false consciousness": "Talk of 'free' markets blinds people to the coercion and manipulation that are endemic to them. Talk of 'freedom of speech' obscures how speech only actually matters politically if one has access to the media. Talk of 'property rights' masks how the ideology of private property makes it possible for vast concentrations of it to deprive others of their holdings and degrade the natural world with impunity." Furthermore, the authors remark that it is perhaps not false that people who say they have earned what they have got have worked very hard for it, and maybe exercised remarkable intelligence, creativity, and sacrifice: "There is, however, no divine or natural law about what sort of return or reward someone is to receive for hard work, intelligence, creativity, sacrifice, or anything else. It's only the peculiar social arrangements of our society (as well as, in many cases, a fair measure of good fortune) that have distributed to any particular individual the precise amount he or she claims to have earned. Other social arrangements might have distributed far less or far more" (*Baggini & Fosl* 2007, p. 216).

ly than in the period (so-called "golden age") of the Keynesian political project,[54] founded upon the "historical class compromise" reached by organized labour, private employers and chief (right- and left-wing) political parties, and characterized by almost full employment, rising material standard, a solid welfare state, and constant growth (stimulated by governmental monetary and fiscal policies). However, it should not be forgotten that capitalists are forced to act in such a way, if they want to stay (i.e., avoid economic ruin) and prosper in the market "game". In addition, they are compelled – primarily by the inexorable (impersonal or anonymous) "law of competition" – to constantly increase the productivity of labour (for instance by co-operation, division of work, and use of machines), preferably to gain some extra profit, at least temporarily (before the technological or organisational innovation become an obligatory standard or average condition of production). In that regard, capitalism can be described as a system of mutual pressures and threats. Each capitalist is (and operates) under constraints, while he or she, at the same time, constrains all other competitors. Consequently, everyone has to follow the "blind force of things", as *Heinrich* puts it, in the system that looks like a gigantic machine, running without some ruling or directing individual or collective mastermind,[55] and energised by countless human "machinists" functioning as personifications of specific economic categories (e.g., capital, money, labour power, and consumer power) and following the prevailing type of rationality imposed on them by the dominant social relationships and structures (existing in the form of personal dispositions, attitudes, opinions, desires, rationalizations, beliefs, and aspirations). So how can we draw a clear-cut dividing line between guilty victimisers and innocent victims? Only by scapegoating or, what is even worse, by demonising some arbitrarily chosen category of "evil-doers" (e.g., bankers, monopolist corporations, or financial speculators)? Should the "would-be victims" of the capitalist economy blame themselves

---

54 *Beck* remarks that postmodern entrepreneurs (especially transnational corporations) have discovered "the philosopher's stone" for accumulating wealth and, consequently, also social, political, and legal power: capitalism without work and without taxes. Employers can select workers from the vast ocean of eager candidates competing for their favours. Economic masters, as the indisputable winners in the class war over structurally subordinated workers, can hire labour power "just in time", only when they need it (and dismiss it after profitable use). In other words, they can pass the burden (or "violence") of intensified competition on to economically dependent "partners", i.e., to their workers and subcontracting companies. "Happily" employed staff have no other option than to increase or maintain productivity at the demanded (global) level or to accept longer working hours, lower payment, and fewer traditional (nowadays apparently obsolete) rights; see *Beck* 2003, pp. 15–20.

55 See *Heinrich* 2013, p. 110. Therefore, the term "social control" appears quite misleading, for members of the capitalist society are under the firm control of things, and not *vice versa*. It is the movement of commodities (and their market prices) that determines the actions and reactions of capitalists, workers, and consumers. Neither society nor state (as its political "organ" or representation) controls production, exchange, and consumption (for instance according to autonomously defined needs); see *Marx* 1876/2012, p. 60.

or, preferably, stop seeing themselves as "victims"? Is there really no one whom we could consider responsible for the enormous human, social, cultural, political, and ecological damage (or destruction) caused by the routine and legally anonymous capitalist "automaton"? Should we assume that dominant (social, economic, and legal) structures – i.e., precisely those social "forms" that agents (in various roles and position) obey and in such manner reproduce in their everyday lives – annul or erase human responsibility and altogether justify the otherwise harmful activities of capitalists (and of course also those of workers and consumers)? Are we to conclude that, unfortunately, "shit just happens"? Regardless of how one answers these questions, what we can see quite clearly is that the grip of capitalist power is generally taken for granted, or accepted with apathy, cynicism, resignation, despair, and a sense of impotency (for "there is in fact no alternative" and, furthermore, history does not seem to be *a priori* on the side of the exploited, oppressed, or otherwise damned human beings).

At the very end, let us return to the mass victimisations and sacrifices associated with the construction of new "independent" states on the territory of the ex-Yugoslavia. Was the terrifying bloodbath, material destruction, and human suffering justified by what has followed the Balkan wars, i.e., by the introduction of the neoliberal capitalist system? Well, to be sure, it would be a great surprise if those who victimised (e.g., killed, tortured, raped, destroyed, or drove away) others and also those who sacrificed themselves (e.g., in order to protect the ethnicity or religious community they belonged to) admit that all that was somewhat "pointless", without acceptable meaning, value, or purpose, the result of deplorable mistakes due to some illusion or naïve belief in an imaginary story, fantasy, fiction, or myth. As *Harari* points out, people usually desperately want to give meaning to the suffering they have caused to others and also to the sacrifices they (or their loved ones) have made.[56] Paradoxically, the more painful sacrifices they make, or the more harm they cause to others for an imaginary story or entity, the more tenaciously they hold on to the fiction in question (and the more they believe in its existence). What is even more, *Harari* argues that, all too often, our narrating self "would much prefer to continue suffering in the future, just so it won't have to admit that the past suffering was devoid of all meaning".[57] Doubtless, it is a bizarre, but nevertheless "all too human" way

---

56 *Harari* 2017, p. 349.

57 *Harari* 2017, p. 353. The author insists that our self too is an imaginary story, just like nations, corporations, gods, and money: "Each of us has a sophisticated system that throws away most of our experiences, keeps only few choice samples, mixes them up with bits from movies we've seen, novels we've read, speeches we've heard, and daydreams we've savoured, and out of all that jumble it weaves a seemingly coherent story about who I am, where I came from and where I am going. This story tells me what to love, whom to hate and what to do with myself. This story may even cause me to sacrifice my life, if that's what the plot requires" (*Harari* 2017, loc. cit.). *Broks* too holds that the most typical human activity is constructing a story about oneself: "From

of addressing our inevitable suffering. Also, in this light we can see more clearly why the "will to meaning" is so vitally important for human beings. For *Frankl* it is even more important than the will to pleasure and the will to power.[58] Besides, the powerful need to make sense of one's own life (by means of some ideals, values, or imaginary stories) shows, among other things, how difficult (and so often miserable) it is to exist as a human subject.

On the other hand, we must emphasize that ex-socialist men and women have quickly learned all the key rules of the new capitalist "game". They know all too well that capitalism has to be accepted in spite of its many deficiencies (and even totalitarian tendencies[59]). Of course, we can still detect some fading fragments of nostalgia for the expired and interred socialist system (remembered – in somehow idealized form – as the workers' "paradise lost", e.g., due to enviable living standard, economic and social security, solidarity, plenty of leisure time, and tolerable work burdens). In any case, people in general experienced its political destruction with enthusiasm and relief. It was the capitalist system that they preferred. Why? Probably because it looks "so sexy", especially in advertising messages, virtual reality, fiction, shopping malls, and, let us not forget, in the real lives of the rich and famous (winners and celebrities), and also because it offers plenty of cheap "luxury", vulgar fun, and colourful trash.[60] It is an imagined (and craved for) earthly heaven of joyful consumption that justifies the (ideologically strictly separated) hell of (stressful and stupefying) work

---

a neuroscience perspective we are all divided and discontinuous. The mental processes underlying our sense of self – feelings, thoughts, and memories – are scattered through different zones of the brain. There is no special point of convergence. No cockpit of the soul. No soul-pilot. They come together as a work of fiction. A human being is a story-telling machine. The self is a story" (*Broks* 2003, p. 41). The post-socialist "transition" also functions retrospectively as a narrative with its own cast of heroes and villains, good and bad guys, angels and demons, victimisers and victims, winners and losers, leaders and followers, saints, prophets, priests, believers, and dissidents. As a matter of fact, there are several stories dealing with "our" (socialist and transitional) past, present and future (of course, some are dominant, whilst others are ignored or ex-communicated). However, they should not be underestimated, for they do have real consequences (personal and collective ones).

58 *Frankl* 2013, pp. 128–131.

59 Capitalist system tends to invade, occupy, and subdue the totality of an individual's life, i.e., one's "labour" and "leisure" (or other disposable) time; see *Kurz* 2000, pp. 111–112. In other words, capitalist power moulds people's motives, opinions, attitudes, desires, dreams, vital energies, personalities, and modes of behaviour in a way that maximises its control over them. It tends to reduce the individual to a target, a mere consumer, and a human resource for the production of wealth, information, or might; see *Gorz* 1999, pp. 128–143.

60 No wonder that the first thing done in the new regime of "democracy, human rights, and freedom" was a type of mechanical lustration, i.e., the acquisition of beautifully designed Western cars. Logically, that was followed by the accelerated construction of highways ("fast roads") and comfortable "homes" for the holy vehicles.

and the capitalist domination that reproduces itself smoothly, for there is no serious opposition to it (in clear distinction from the "old regime"). Apparently, people possess more than enough commodities (and other opportunities created by capitalist economy) to be happy or at least to endure the difficulties of life until its more or less happy end. And *nota bene*: there are no victims of capitalism (nor of life as such), for hapless sufferers are now (in the light of dominant neoliberal mentality) to be interpreted as pure losers. There can be solely victims of some crime or accident, if the persons in question are really innocent and if they did all they could in order to prevent their victimisation.

5. Summary in Slovene

Po kratki analizi razlogov za pomembnost "statusa" (ali etikete) žrtve v sodobni "kulturi strahu" (Furedi) prvi razdelek poglavja obravnava človeško življenje kot obliko "eksistencialne" primarne viktimiziranost, saj je že "kot tako" neizogibno povezano z različnimi vrstami trpljenja. Nato so večni problem človeške (ne)srečnosti in njegove povezave s sodobnimi oblikami kriminalitete (in viktimizacij) interpretirani v kontekstu postmoderne potrošniško usmerjene kulture. Drugi razdelek se ukvarja s temeljnimi značilnostmi žrtev in viktimizatorjev v slovenski postsocialistični družbi. Posebna pozornost je namenjena tranzicijskemu ekonomskemu in političnemu kriminalu (npr. plenilskim, prevarantskim in korupcijskih pridobitniškim aktivnostim), ki je bil v tem turbulentnem obdobju večinoma nesankcioniran, in še prav posebej "kraji stoletja" (v obliki privatizacije in denacionalizacije), ki pa jo je mogoče, na nek način paradoksno, razumeti tudi kot kolektivno kazen za zločine socialističnega "totalitarizma". V zadnjem delu so osvetljeni značilnosti izbranih privilegiranih (čeravno zvečine fiktivnih) žrtev, narava "družbenih parazitov" (ki so čedalje bolj dojeti kot poglavitni viktimizatorji produktivnih članov družbe) in problem viktimizacij (npr. izkoriščanja, zatiranja, zastraševanja, izsiljevanja in poniževanja prodajalcev delovne sile), ki so povezane s sicer popolnoma normalnim delovanjem neoliberalne kapitalistične ekonomije, podprte z veljavnim meščanskim pravom in državnim represivnim aparatom (seveda pa tudi z vladajočo ideologijo in jedrnimi kulturnimi vrednotami).

Literature

Anderson, P. (2017): Ameriška zunanja politika in njeni snovalci [American foreign policy and its thinkers]. Ljubljana.

Badiou, A. (2008): Ime česa je Sarakozy? [What is the name Sarakozy?]. Ljubljana.

Baggini, J., & Fosl, P.S. (2007): A compendium of ethical concepts and methods. Oxford.

Beck, U. (2003): Kaj je globalizacija? Zmote globalizma – odgovori na globalizacijo [What is globalisation? The mistakes of globalisation – Answers to the globalisation]. Ljubljana.

Berardi, F. (2013): Duša na delu [Soul at work]. Ljubljana.

Boutellier, H. (2000): Crime and morality. The significance of criminal justice in post-modern culture. Dordrecht.

Broks, P. (2003): Into the silent land. New York.

Bruckner, P. (2004): Nenehna vzhičenost. Esej o prisilni sreči [Continuous excitement. An essay on forcible happiness]. Ljubljana.

Canfora, L. (2006): Demokracija. Zgodovina neke ideologije [Democracy. The history of some ideology]. Ljubljana.

Dolar, M. (2010): Oficirji, služkinje in dimnikarji [Officers, chambermaids and chimney-sweepers]. Ljubljana.

Frankl, V.E. (2013): Kljub vsemu reči življenju da [Despite everything say yes to life]. Celje.

Freud, S. (1916–17/1977): Predavanja za uvod v psihoanalizo [Lectures for the introduction to psychoanalysis]. Ljubljana.

Furedi, F. (2002): Culture of fear. Risk-taking and the morality of law expectation. London.

Galeano, E. (2011): Narobe. Šola narobe sveta [Wrong. School of the wrong world]. Ljubljana.

Galimberti, U. (2010): Grozljvi gost: nihilizem in mladi [Horrible guest: Nihilism and young people]. Ljubljana.

Gorz, A. (1999): Reclaiming work. Beyond the wage-based society. Cambridge.

Harari, Y.N. (2017): Homo deus. A brief history of tomorrow. London.

Hardt, M., & Negri, A. (2003): Imperij [Empire]. Ljubljana.

Hayek, F.A. (1983): L'Ordre politique d'un people libre [The political order of the free people]. Paris.

Heinrich, M. (2013): Kritika politične ekonomije. Uvod [Criticism of political economy. Introduction]. Ljubljana.

Janaway, C. (2002): Schopenhauer. A very short introduction. Oxford.

Kant, I. (1785/2005): Utemeljitev metafizike nravi [Groundwork of the metaphysics of morals]. Ljubljana.

Kekes, J. (2008): Enjoyment. The moral significance of styles of life. Oxford.

Keown, D. (2013): Buddhism. A very short introduction. Oxford.

Koršič, I. (2013): Druga faza vstaj [Second phase of uprising]. Časopis za kritiko znanosti [Journal for the Critique of Science] 41, pp. 93–101.

Kurnik, A. (2013): Artikulacije potrebujejo neartikuliran bes [Articulations require inarticulate rage]. Časopis za kritiko znanosti [Journal for the Critique of Science] 41, pp. 11–20.

Kurz, R. (2000): Svet kot volja in dizajn. Postmoderna levica in estetizacija krize [The world as will and design. Postmodern left and aestheticization of the crisis]. Ljubljana.

Lea, J. (2002): Crime & modernity. Continuities in left realis criminology. London.

Marx, K. (1894/1973): Kapital, 3. knjiga [Capital, third book]. Ljubljana.

Marx, K. (1867/2012): Kapital, 1. knjiga [Capital, first book]. Ljubljana.

Mastnak, T. (2001): Naša Evropa [Our Europe], in: A. Drolc & M. Pajnik (eds.), Obrazi naše Evrope [The faces of our Europe]. Ljubljana, pp. 9–22.

Neiman, S. (2015): Evil in modern thought. An alternative history of philosophy. Princeton.

Nietzsche, F. (1889/1989): Somrak malikov [Twilight of idols]. Ljubljana.

Scheerer, S., & Hess, H. (1997): Social control: A defence and reformulation, in: R. Bergalli & C. Sumner (eds.), Social control and political order. European perspectives at the end of the century. London, pp. 96–131.

Schopenhauer, A. (1819/2008): Svet kot volja in predstava [The world as will and performance]. Ljubljana.

Šeparović, Z.P. (1985): Victimology. Studies of victims. Zagreb.

Sophocles (401BC/2010): Ojdip v Kolonu [Oedipus in Kolon]. Celje.

Stannard, D.E. (2017): Ameriški holokavst. Osvajanje novega sveta [American holocaust. The conquest of the new world]. Ljubljana.

Supiot, A. (2013): Duh Filadelfije. Socialna pravičnost proti totalitarnemu trgu [Spirit of Philadelphia. Social justice against the totalitarian market]. Ljubljana.

Tamás, G.M. (2016): Komunizem po letu 1989. Razprave o razredni teoriji, realsocializmu in Vzhodni Evropi [Communism after 1989. Debates on class theory, realsocialism and Eastern Europe]. Ljubljana.

Trček, F. (2013): Ugasnimo Facebook – premislek o mariborski vstaji [Let's shut down Facebook – A reflection on the Maribor uprising], Časopis za kritiko znanosti [Journal for the Critique of Science] 41, pp. 60–71.

Voltaire (1762/1988): Kandid ali optimizem [Candide, or optimism]. Ljubljana.

Wallerstein, I. (2004): Zaton ameriške moči [The decline of American power]. Ljubljana.

Wood, A.W. (2008): Kantian ethics. Cambridge.

Young, J. (2007): The vertigo of late modernity. Los Angeles.

Žižek, S. (2009): In defence of lost causes. London.

Abstracts

Mapping the Victimological Landscape of the Balkans

Evisa Kambellari

Albania 65–102

The paper provides a general picture of the status of victims in the Albanian criminal legislation, as well as victim policies and the current situation of victim support and victim protection in Albania. It also focuses on the legal regulation of restorative justice, on the features of civil actions within the criminal proceedings, and on the forms of compensation available to victims of crime. Part of the focus of the study is on the practical implementation of victim protection measures. The aim is to critically review current protective measures and determine whether they are working. It will also assess practical problems and challenges, and offer possible solutions. Further, the paper discusses the procedural status of victims, especially in light of the recent amendments to the Criminal Procedure Code of the Republic of Albania, which were highly influenced by the EU Directive 2012/29. The new provisions adopted under Law no. 35/2017 recognise the right of victims to receive information on their legal rights, access to legal aid, the right to professional support when needed, the right to the protection of privacy, and an overall right to actively participate in the criminal proceedings. The idea is to analyse the practical implications that such changes will have on expanding the role of victims in criminal trials and the proper administration of justice in general. The author discusses the evolution of criminal policy for the protection of victims in Albania over the years, including the role that main international instruments have had in this regard. Civil society's role in providing victim support is also addressed. Lastly, the author focuses on various issues that remain unimplemented. These include lack of funds for compensatory schemes, lack of training among law enforcement officers and practitioners, inability to assess victim-specific protection needs that can lead to repeat victimisation, lack of official figures on victims of crime, problems on providing free legal aid and integrated social services, and the lack of holistic empirical research on victims of crime. The paper concludes that practical and conceptual obstacles still prevent proper protection of victims. It provides several recommendations on matters that need to be addressed by relevant stakeholders and policymakers to emancipate the legal and social status of victims in Albania.

Monika Stempkowski & Barbara Kraml

Austria 103–146

Looking at the support system for victims of crime in Austria, victims can rely on comprehensive and detailed instruments to obtain their rights during a trial as well as crucial protections measures to prevent crimes and harm from happening in the first place. While Austria still lacks institutionalized victimological research as well as complete victimisation surveys, a wide-ranging system of victim support was established in the past decades. General support organizations such as the local branch of the White Circle, as well as specialized institutions, protect victims from impending harm and support them before and during criminal proceedings. In practice, the instrument of the psycho-social and legal support for the proceedings is of great importance. Professional psycho-social caregivers prepare the victim for the strains of the criminal trial and accompany them during this challenging time. Attorneys exercise the victim's rights during the trial and make sure the victim understands the proceedings as well as the results of the trial. The Federal Ministry of Justice pays the caregivers and attorneys, thereby providing the victims with this support free of charge. Additionally, the interests of victims are considered extensively in other areas of the criminal justice system; a victim-offender mediation can be conducted only if the victim consents. Professional mediators support the victim and the offender during mediation and try to find a sustainable solution, with a focus on the victim's needs of recognizing the harm inflicted onto them by the crime as well as the need for compensation. Thus, although diverse support options are available for victims, there is still room for improvement in certain aspects. For example, the group of victims entitled to receiving support for the proceedings should be expanded. Further, on, Austria needs to establish more spaces in women's shelters to comply with the requirements established by the Council of Europe and make sure that the professionals potentially dealing with victims in their daily work are prepared to recognise victimisation and the specific needs of victims of crime.

Azra Adžajlić-Dedović & Miodrag Simović

Bosnia and Herzegovina 147–176

In this paper, we present the development of victimology as a scientific discipline in Bosnia and Herzegovina. Based on new knowledge on victimology and victimological studies and scientific papers, we will try to illustrate the legal position, assistance, support and protection of victims in Bosnia and Herzegovina. This will be done through a comparison between the above mentioned and the European legal norms, standards and international obligations, which we have taken over in order to recognise the most significant issues regarding the protection of victims in Bosnia and Herzegovina. In addition, this paper will present an approximate scope and specific case studies that reflect the legal position of victims of a gross violation of the international humanitarian law, victims of human trafficking, victims of domestic violence, victims of power and authorities abuse in Bosnia and Herzegovina, etc. In the end, we will also tackle the protection of victims of natural disasters and ecological crime and propose the best and most effective measures that should be implemented in Bosnia Herzegovina as a special Strategy on the reform of the victim protection system. In this regard, we propose *de lege ferenda* measures that will enable the harmonisation of the B&H legislation in terms of minimum assistance, support and protection of the victims in line with the 2012 European Directive, which is our obligation if we want to become a member of the European Union. We also propose the drafting of the Law on Compensation to Criminal Offences Victims and the establishment of the Victims' Compensation Fund (or the Law and Funds in Bosnia and Herzegovina in accordance with the organization of authorities under the Constitution of Bosnia and Herzegovina [Annex 4, General Framework Agreement for Peace in Bosnia and Herzegovina, Dayton, 1995]). In conclusion, we specifically point out the need to establish centres for women and children victims of sexual violence, domestic violence and other forms of violence in accordance with the Istanbul Convention, which is also our international obligation (victims of human trafficking for the purpose of sexual exploitation) that we took over in 2014.

Kamen Lyubomirov Novikov

Bulgaria 177–218

The majority of experts consider the accused "The Central Figure" in criminal procedures. However, the focus on the accused should not lead to underestimating the figure of the victim. The present article contains a detailed analysis of the legal position of victims in all relevant Bulgarian legislation: the Penal Code, the Penal Procedure Code, the Crime Victims Assistance and Financial Compensation Act, and the Combating Trafficking in Human Beings Act. The goal of the author is to reveal the big picture and to be helpful to anybody who might need legal help as a victim in Bulgaria. The point of this study is to not only present the country's legal framework but also see how the laws work in practice and look at possible measures of optimisation. Moreover, this article contains actual information on criminology and victimology in Bulgaria. Statistics are used to provide information and give the reader a realistic picture of social life in Bulgaria and the challenges its citizens face. Finally, the author presents his review of the media discourses about victimisation and victim protection in Bulgaria. This question is very interesting because, in the age of electronic media, social networks, and fake news, it is very easy to manipulate public opinion (or at least guide it into wrong and dangerous directions). It is evident that victims are one of the most vulnerable and sensitive parts of our society. When victims suffer a crime, they need total public support, and of course, they need to feel protected by the state institutions. Unfortunately, at present in Bulgaria, the victims often do not receive the necessary support and protection. We hope that this research will show them that they are not abandoned in their fight for justice.

Anna-Maria Getoš Kalac, Sunčana Roksandić Vidlička & Zoran Burić

Croatia

219–272

The paper offers a comprehensive insight into the current status and future prospects of victimology in Croatia. When discussing 'victimology' in the framework of this paper, the term relates to the scientific study of the how and why of criminal victimisation, including its individual and societal reactions. In this regard, victimology is almost non-existent in Croatia, or at least not recognisable as a specialised and developed area of research (within or closely related to Croatian criminology). In Croatia, the overall crime rates, as well as murder rates, are generally low and below the European average. However, there is a rather stable trend detectable when it comes to the total of adults convicted of criminal offences. Just as in the rest of the SEE region, the challenge in Croatia is not crime in general, but rather specific types of non-conventional crime (e.g., corruption and trade in influence, organised crime, etc.) and the conditions acting as their facilitators (e.g., the crime-conflict and the crime-politics nexus). Here, research conducted within the Balkan Criminology Group contributed to developing new legal solutions that adequately deal with transitional economic crimes, thus contributing to the research of crimes of the powerful and white-collar crimes. Still, being a post-conflict and war-affected country, as well as one still heavily affected by the social, economic and political transition, Croatia faces an ongoing struggle with the rule of law and good governance, which is naturally also reflected in its criminal justice system. During the past decade, the Croatian criminal justice system had to face several huge reforms, covering both significant areas of society's basic repressive mechanisms dealing with crime, criminals and their victims – the criminal procedure as well as the penal reaction. This requires further research, as well. When one looks at the Croatian criminal justice system, one of the lines of its development in the last two decades has been dedicated to the improvement of the position of victims of crime. Many changes in the national legislation have been enacted to recognise specific rights and legitimate interests of victims of crime and to give those rights and legitimate interest a clear and strong legislative basis. Different, completely new rights for victims of crime have been introduced. Some of these are connected with the participation of victims in criminal proceedings, while others have an independent, extra-procedural character. This process has been followed and supported by the process of establishment of a victim support system in Croatia. Despite the existence of comprehensive victimology research, victimology started developing in Croatia at the same time as its development began at the international level. However, this development did not lead to the establishment of victimology as an independent scientific discipline.

This paper, therefore, tries to fill the void detected in Croatian victimology and presents the first typology of victims of crime in Croatia. Furthermore, it provides an analysis of criminal offences and concludes what type of further research is needed and in which areas.

Andrea Tünde Barabás

Hungary 273–302

The first part of the paper describes the situation of victims of crime in Hungary and its main associated issues. In addition to discussing the relevant legislation, it outlines the results of research projects carried out under the leadership or with the participation of the National Institute of Criminology (OKRI) over the past 15 years. This is necessary because it is important to 'look behind the facts' and examine the various phenomena empirically, in addition to analysing official documents and statistical data. This way, it becomes possible to gain an in-depth knowledge of a specific phenomenon – in this case, victimisation – in a given country. The conducted research projects have shown that, although the regulations and the institutional system established for supporting victims fully comply with European standards, in reality, victims of crime are still at risk of secondary victimisation induced by the authorities, and latency is high due to victims' countless previous bad experiences. This means that criminal offences remain hidden and that this happens mainly because those concerned do not report the crime. Because of this, the fear of victimisation is much greater among the population, especially when compared to the levels of actual criminal activity. This corresponds to the international results produced by OKRI's collaborative research projects and its other international research projects (for example, the International Crime Victims Survey [ICVS]). Moreover, the issue of compensating victims is also unresolved, despite the existence of fully EU-compliant legal regulations. This is why the second part of the paper discusses the regulation of and the possibilities inherent in restorative justice, as well as the relevant Hungarian and international research that outlines the possibilities for expanding the range of restorative methods.

Ákos Kara, Anna Kiss, Eszter Sárik & Viktória Szentmihályi-Soós

Hungary 303–340

The paper provides the reader with a general overview of victimology in Hungary. The article intends to reflect on the basic theoretical and scientific dilemmas of victimology, on some aspects of victim's morphology, and on the position of the victim in the legal context (the procedural rights of victims), mostly with regards to the new Criminal Procedure Law. The paper intends to describe not only how the victim is treated but to also enquire about several other important points:

What do crime statistics say about victims? Can we develop a valid picture about them in view of statistics? What kind of victimology research is conducted in Hungary?

Velimir Rakočević & Aleksandra Jovanović

Montenegro 341–364

This paper focuses on the state of victimology, victimological research and protection of victims in criminal proceedings in Montenegro. Victimological perspectives need to be taken into consideration more seriously in Montenegro as victimology is still under the umbrella of criminology and needs to develop into an independent discipline. Montenegro still suffers from insufficient victimological research that would provide a substantial basis for the development of victim protection from specific crimes. Progress has been made on the legislative front with new victim-protection laws following the European Union models of victim protection. It is still challenging to apply good legal solutions in practice, and there is still room for improvement. Approaching the systematic investigation of victims of criminal offences is still pending. Support and assistance schemes to protect crime victims and develop preventive strategies to reduce victimisation are in progress. The paper analyses the normative basis for the protection of victims of crime, as well as the trends of victimisation of various forms of crime.

Gordana Lažetić & Aleksandra Gruevska Drakulevski

North Macedonia 365–400

The article provides a general picture of the state of victimology, victim policies, victim-related legislation and the current situation of victim support and victim protection in the Republic of North Macedonia. The authors of the paper refer to victim-related data from official statistics on victimisation as well as data from victim surveys and an analysis of relevant legal regulations related to the rights of victims, their support and their protection related to victimisation and victim protection within and outside the scope of criminal procedure. The authors primarily analyse the data from the State Statistical Office of the North Macedonia, the centres for social affairs, the police, the prosecution and the courts, as well as the relevant ciliv society organisations whose primary activity is the support and protection of victims. The analysis includes the assessment of media coverage of crime. The authors offer a brief overview of the legislation related to the rights and protection of victims, as the legal regulation of restorative justice and the feature of civil actions (within criminal trials) to obtain compensation. The article refers to several issues, such as the general country background, the current state of victimology, criminal policy, data and research findings and public and/or media discourses. The authors of the article conclude that the study of victimology is currently not sufficiently developed since victimology is a relatively neglected area of criminology in the country. There is a need for improvements to be made, especially in terms of conducting surveys on victims, their rights, support and protection.

Andra-Roxana Trandafir & Flaviu Ciopec

Romania 401–444

When it comes to victimology, Romania shows a paradox: although the country gave the world the "founding father" of the concept of victimology, Benjamin Mendelsohn, he and his research are barely known and victimology is not really being taught at any University as a separate discipline. However, this does not mean that there is no interest in victims or victim protection. Statistics contain some data about the victims and their status, especially at the level of the General Prosecutors Office. Also, several entities fight for the rights and the protection of specific categories of victims (i.e., former political convicted persons, victims of the 1989 events, etc.). Even more recent associations speak about current problems in Romania (i.e., road traffic accidents, as the country leads the statistics in terms of number of victims in this field; domestic violence – a social problem possibly specific to the Balkan region; victims of a devastating fire in a night club in Bucharest; victims of abuses committed within judicial procedures; bullying in schools, etc.). One must not forget that victimisation is always influenced by a country's history, meaning that people do not always perceive themselves as victims of certain crimes (i.e., women in case of domestic violence) or cannot perceive someone as a victim in other cases (i.e., offering money to medical doctors in order to thank them for their services). Thus, the paper covers the most important aspects in this field and examines the particularities of victimology, victim protection and victimisation in Romania, showing the gaps and the main problems arising from both legislation and policies set in motion in this field.

Vesna Nikolić-Ristanović & Sanja Ćopić

Serbia 445–488

In recent decades, the situation of victims in Serbia has received increasing attention from researchers and society at large. The first systematised scientific papers and empirical research efforts in the field of victimology, as well as first initiatives for the improvement of the position of victims in Serbia, occurred in the 1980s, with the feminist movement playing an important role. During the 1990s, other factors influenced victim-related developments as well as initiatives from human rights organisations, the development of victimology as an academic discipline, an increase of crime in Serbia, ethnic conflicts on the territory of the former Yugoslavia, and war-related humanitarian initiatives. Civil society advocacy in the 2000s also contributed to changes in the relationship between the state and victims. Since 2012, in the context of the EU accession process and harmonisation of Serbian legislation and policy with the EU acquis, a more favourable climate for the wider social acceptance of a holistic approach to the rights of all victims and their support and assistance has been created. In addition, in recent years, a number of reforms and improvements have been carried out to improve the availability of assistance and support for victims. Nevertheless, there are still numerous shortages, gaps, and inconsistencies that prevent the adequate implementation of laws in practice as well as equal access to victim support and protection. This paper provides an overview of victim-related developments in Serbia, including the development of victimology and the victim rights movement.

Zoran Kanduč

Slovenia 21–52

After a brief analysis of the reasons for the importance of the "victim status" (or etiquette) in the contemporary "culture of fear" *(Furedi)*, the article's first section addresses human life as a form of "existential" victimhood, for it is inevitably associated with suffering. After that, the perennial problem of human (un)happiness and its connection to actual forms of crime (and victimisation) are interpreted in the context of postmodern consumer culture. The second section deals with the basic characteristics of victims and victimisers in Slovene post-socialist society. Special attention is paid to transitional economic and political crimes (e.g., predatory, fraudulent, and corruptive activities) that went mostly unsanctioned in the turbulent period often characterized as the "theft of the century" (in the form of privatization and denationalization). These crimes could be, somehow paradoxically, understood as a form of collective punishment for the evil(s) of socialist "totalitarianism". The final part highlights the specific victimhood of the selected privileged (although mostly fictive) victims, the nature of various "social parasites" (being increasingly perceived as the principal victimisers of productive members of society), and the problem of victimhood (e.g., in terms of exploitation, oppression, intimidation, extortion, and humiliation of the sellers of work power) associated with the altogether normal functioning of the neoliberal capitalist economy, supported by bourgeois law and the state's repressive apparatus (and, of course, by dominant ideological and cultural values).

Gorazd Meško, Katja Eman, Rok Hacin & Urška Pirnat

Slovenia 489–530

This paper focuses on victimology, which can be defined as a science dealing with the study of victims, the causes and different types of victimisation, the processes and consequences of victimisation, as well as the study of social reactions to victimisation. In Slovenia, the following laws define the role of victims in criminal proceedings:

1) the Crime Victim Compensation Act,
2) the Criminal Code, and
3) the Criminal Procedure Act.

A literature review shows that during the past 50 years, more than 70 studies regarding victims were conducted in Slovenia. The studies focused on

1) victimisation surveys,
2) different types of victimisation,
3) provision of assistance to victims,
4) satisfaction of victims of crime with the police,
5) fear of crime, and
6) implementation of restorative justice.

In Slovenia, there are two major sources of statistical data on crime victims: official crime statistics from the Ministry of the Interior and data on crime victims from victimisation surveys. Official crime statistics show that the number of victims has decreased over the past 15 years. In the future, victimology in Slovenia should also focus on new types of crime (cybercrime, environmental crime, etc.), as these crimes are leading to new forms of victimisation.

Tuba Topçuoğlu & Selman Dursun

Turkey 531–572

This paper presents a general picture of the current state of victimology, victim policies, victim-related legislation and victim support in Turkey. The first part provides basic background information on Turkey. The second part describes the status of victimology as a scientific discipline and extant victimological research in Turkey, as well as the key governmental and NGO actors involved in victim support and protection. The third part provides a brief discussion of national legal provisions on victim rights and protection, with an evaluation of the recently proposed draft law on victim rights. The fourth part presents the reality of victimisation in Turkey, based on available official data and empirical research findings. The fifth part describes the media discourse and perception of victims and victimisation in Turkey. The sixth part presents an assessment of Turkey´s standing with regards to victimology, victim protection policies, regulations and practice as well as suggestions for further improvement. The seventh part concludes with a summary of the main findings and the position of victimology and victim protection in Turkey.

PART II

COUNTRY CHAPTERS

Albania

Victimology and Victim Protection

Evisa Kambellari

1. General Country Background

Albania is a country in South-Eastern Europe, positioned in the West of the Balkan Peninsula. The Republic of Albania is a parliamentary democracy. The country's administrative division consists of 12 counties and 61 municipal entities. The official language of Albania is Albanian. According to official statistics, the total population of the country is 2,870,324: 50.1% male and 49.9% female.[1] Islam is the predominant religious affiliation in Albania. Muslims make up 56.7% of the total population, followed by Catholics (10%) and Orthodox Christians (6.75%).[2] The population's structure consists of Albanian nationals (82.6%) and some ethnic groups: Greek (0.87%), Macedonian (0.20%), Montenegrin (0.01%), Aromanian (0.30%), Roma (0.30%), and Egyptian (0.12%).[3] The last population census was conducted in 2011.

More recent data on the demographic structure of the country was also procured by the National Statistical Institute (INSTAT) in 2017. Accordingly, the medium age among the Albanian population was 35 years. Average life expectancy at birth was 77.1 years for males and 80 years for females. The population growth rate was 8,637 persons (which represented a decrease of 16.5% compared to 2016), and the net migration rate was –14,902 persons. The major populated administrative units are Tirana county with a population of 883,996 inhabitants (which is 30.8% of the total population of the country), followed by the counties of Fier (298,144 inhabitants), Durres (289,628), and Elbasan (278,547). The population in 9 out of 12 counties is predominantly rural. The rural population rates in the respective counties vary from 51% to 79% of each county's total population.

---

1 StatOffice 2019.

2 The figures are based on the 2011 census entitled "Resident population by religious affiliation"; see StatOffice 2012.

3 StatOffice 2012.

The unemployment rate for specific age groups is as follows: 15–29 years (25.9%), and 30–64 years (10.8%).[4] There are no notable gender-based differences in the unemployment rates for each age group.

In 2017, the total labour force of the country consisted of 1,122,130 persons: 163,885 (14.6%) were employed in the public sector, 501,431 (44.7%) in the non-agricultural private sector, and 456,814 (40.7%) in the agricultural private sector.[5]

Concerning education, data on the number of students/graduates for the school/academic year 2015–2016 show the following composition: 43,084 completed secondary education, 37,721 completed high school, 4,507 received vocational education only, and 31,530 are university graduates, of which, 18,652 have a bachelor's degree.[6] The gross domestic product (GDP) in 2015 amounted to 1,427,799 million Albanian Lek (ALL), or 10.2 billion EUR and the GDP per capita amounted 490,000 ALL or 377 EUR.[7]

The criminal justice system of the Republic of Albania consists of four main parts:

1) Law enforcement (the state police),
2) Prosecution,
3) Courts, and
4) Corrections (prisons and pre-trial detention facilities).

The state police, the prosecution, and the courts ordinarily work with victims, who can act both as complainants and witnesses in criminal cases.

Judicial power in the Republic of Albania is exercised by 22 courts of first instance, six courts of appeal, and the Albanian Supreme Court. Prosecutors and/or the police are made aware of criminal offences through their own initiative,[8] by citizens,[9] by medical staff,[10] or by civil employees.[11] Information about possible criminal offences can also be forwarded by the international counterparts, for example, through mutual legal assistance or international arrest warrants.[12] The police or the prosecutors register the offence, entering specific data such as the name of the defendant,

---

4 StatOffice 2018b.

5 StatOffice 2018a.

6 StatOffice 2016.

7 StatOffice 2017.

8 Article 280 (becoming aware of the criminal offence) of the Criminal Procedure Code of the Republic of Albania, Law. No. 7905, 21.03.1995, Official Gazette 79/1995.

9 See Article 283 (indictment from citizens) of the Law No. 7905.

10 See Article 282 (indictment from the medical personnel) of the Law No. 7905.

11 See Article 281 (indictment by public officials) of the Law No. 7905.

12 See Article 495 (the arrest by the judicial police) of the Law No. 7905.

the date and time of the alleged offence, the alleged criminal offence, etc.[13] Judicial police officers and prosecutors conduct, within their respective competences, the necessary investigations in relation to the criminal prosecution.[14] If the prosecutor decides to send the case to court, the case will be adjudicated by the court of first instance. The decision of the court can be appealed. The appellate decision is generally final, however, if matters of law are involved (such as possible misinterpretation of law or failure to guarantee procedural rights), then the Supreme Court can review the decision.[15]

Before the constitutional changes of 2016, judicial power in Albania was also exercised by the First Instance Court for Serious Crimes and the Court of Appeals for Serious Crimes, both of which ceased to exist after the entry into force of the constitutional changes approved by the legislative assembly on 22.07.2016 and by decree of the President on 26.07.2016.[16] In addition, the constitutional changes in 2016 provided for a new Special Prosecution Office,[17] independent from the Prosecutor General as well as an independent investigative unit (SPAK), subordinate to the Special Prosecution Office, to investigate and prosecute corruption and organised crime.

Victimology remains an unexplored area of study in Albania, which significantly affects the general awareness among law enforcement officials and practitioners on the relevance of protecting victims' rights. As of today, only a few occasional studies have focused on specific trends or legislative changes regarding victims of crime: this is insufficient to provide a holistic research approach. Being a state–driven prosecutorial system, Albanian criminal proceedings tend to focus on punishing the perpetrator of the criminal offence rather than making the victim whole again. This paper tries to enrich the line of contributions dedicated to the study of the victims' status in the Albanian criminal justice system and of criminal policies that relate to the protection of victims. By so doing, it tries to open new perspectives and lines of

---

13 See Article 287 (the registration of the notification of the criminal offences) of the Law No. 7905.

14 The term judicial police officer refers to police officers that are primarily engaged to assist the prosecution in the investigation of criminal cases; see Article 18 (on state police) of the Criminal Procedure Code of the Republic of Albania, Law. No. 21/2014, 31.07.2014, Official Gazette 108/2014.

15 Decisions of the Supreme Court can be subject to constitutional review by the Constitutional Court of Albania. The Court will decide whether the constitutional rights of the defendant were guaranteed during trial, appeal, or the Supreme Court review.

16 Albania went through a major justice reform in 2016. These efforts started in 2014 in an attempt to strengthen the rule of law and place the country on a European path. Reforms included amendments to the Constitution, changes to the prosecution and judicial system, and changes to numerous laws including the Criminal and Criminal Procedure Code, Civil and Civil Procedure Code, Code of Criminal Justice for Minors, Customs Code, etc.

17 Article 148 (the office of the prosecutor) of the Constitution of the Republic of Albania, Law No. 76/2016, 21.07.2016, Official Gazette 76/2016.

thought regarding the perception of victims, the potential that exists (through resent reforms) to involve victims in criminal proceedings, the limitations of restorative justice in compensating victims of crime, and the relevance of evidence-based approaches to make informed policy decisions on protecting victims of crime.

2. Current State of Victimology

2.1 Professional Perception of Victims

There is no definition of the term “victim” in Albanian criminal legislation. The only reference for a legal definition can be made in relation to international instruments adopted by the Republic of Albania. In this respect, the United Nations Declaration of Basic Principles of Justice for Victims of Crime and Abuse of Power of 1985 defines victims as

> persons who, individually or collectively, have suffered harm, including physical or mental injury, emotional suffering, economic loss or substantial impairment of their fundamental rights, through acts or omissions that are in violation of criminal laws… [I]t also includes, where appropriate, the immediate family or dependants of the direct victim and persons who have suffered harm in intervening to assist victims.[18]

Council of Europe Directive 2012/29/EU,[19] which was the point of reference for the 2017 changes to the Albanian Criminal Procedure Code, notes that

> victim means a natural person who has suffered harm, including physical, mental or emotional harm or economic loss which was directly caused by a criminal offence; (ii) family members of a person whose death was directly caused by a criminal offence and who have suffered harm as a result of that person’s death.

Among scholars and practitioners, there is a founded opinion that procedurally, both natural persons and legal entities can be regarded as victims of criminal offences and invoke the rights recognised by law. However, if we were to support the position that the Criminal Procedure Code takes the same line adopted by Directive 2012/29/EU, the broader definition of the term “victim” does no longer find a grounded explanation.

---

18 Declaration of Basic Principles of Justice for Victims of Crime and Abuse of Power, No. A/RES/40/34, 29.11.1985; https://www.un.org/documents/ga/res/40/a40r034.htm [20.05.2019].

19 Directive 2012/29/EU of the European Parliament and of the Council of 25 October 2012 establishing minimum standards on the rights, support and protection of victims of crime, and replacing Council Framework Decision 2001/220/JHA., Directive No. 32012L0029, 14.11.2012, Official Journal of the European Union 315/57; https://eur-lex.europa.eu/legal-content/EN/TXT/PDF/?uri=CELEX:32012L0029&from=EN [20.05.2019].

Among criminal justice professionals, the term victim is closely related to a person who is primarily injured by a criminal offence. So, a victim of crime is one who has been exposed to a certain criminal act sanctioned as a specific offence under the Criminal Code of the Republic of Albania. However, it is worth noting that the police might have a broader perception on victims of human trafficking. This is because there is a difference between the indicators used by the police to identify trafficked persons and those used for the classification of a criminal act as trafficking in human beings. Relevant police manuals note that the identification process should be independent of any criminal proceedings against the perpetrators.[20] A criminal conviction must therefore have no impact, either for starting or for completing a victim's identification process.[21] The identification of trafficked persons is targeted, first and foremost, to the provision of assistance to trafficked persons: "[I]t should be a simplified procedure. Information obtained for purposes of victim identification should be subject only to general verification; conclusive proof is not necessary at this stage. For this reason, the set of indicators for the identification of trafficked persons should be flexible and adaptable to new challenges and emerging trends in the human trafficking phenomenon."[22]

Criminological literature provides a broader definition of victims as it tries to unfold aspects of victims' perception of crime and aspects of victims' experiences with the criminal justice system as well.[23] Criminological victim surveys concern not only actual crime victims, but also experiences with victimisation. Victimisation is referred to as the process of interaction that takes place between people, which results in the victimisation of a person or persons who subsequently acquire the status of victim.[24] While the agenda of penal victimology is primarily set by criminal legislation, there are a number of instances when victimology concerns also morally wrong conduct that is not addressed by the law, which results in victimisation. For example, abuses of power by the state may not constitute crimes in the legal sense but would clearly be considered immoral.[25] Criminological textbooks used in Albanian universities embrace the general definition of victimology. So, victimology is defined as the science that studies the exposure, causes, and conditions of becoming a victim of crime, the consequences of crime on people involved, the social attitude, and especially the criminal justice system's response (and the response of related professionals) to victims of crime.[26] Social victim surveys of crime pay attention to

---

20 Ariadne Network 2012.

21 Ariadne Network 2012.

22 Ariadne Network 2012.

23 *McLaughlin & Muncle* 2013, p. 449.

24 *Goldson* 2008, p. 361.

25 *Wemmers* 2010.

26 *Hysi* 2005, pp. 193–194.

the experience of crime from the viewpoint of victims. They also seek to examine victim's experiences of being processed by the criminal justice system, for example by the police and courts.[27]

Given the political history of Albania, a legally recognised category of victims are those who were politically convicted and prosecuted by the communist regime. For almost half a century (1945–1991), Albania experienced a severe dictatorship. It represented a communist country that preserved the totalitarian dictatorship until the end of 1980s. The country was subjected to a long–lasting period of repression where political opponents were imprisoned, exiled, or executed.

The status of politically persecuted victims is regulated by the Law on the Status of Politically Ex-Convicted and Persecuted People by the Communist Regime.[28] The law recognises the specific status to these categories of people:

1) persons that lost their lives or are psychologically unstable due to persecution;
2) persons imprisoned or exiled due to persecution;
3) persons interned or banished due to persecution;
4) persons who lost their civil rights, village kulaks,[29] the déclassé, and those that suffered deprivations of all sorts due to persecution; and
5) persons that although they meet the conditions to be categorised in one of the above categories, do not enjoy the right of this status.

2.2 Governmental and NGO Actors Involved in Victim Protection

The main domestic instruments addressing matters of victim criminal policy are the cross-sectoral and sectoral strategies on crime. There are two main governmental documents that develop the main lines of action with regards to specific victims of crime: The Cross-Sectoral Strategy on the Fight against Organised Crime, Illegal Trafficking, and Terrorism, 2013–2020 and The national strategy on the Fight against Human Trafficking 2014–2017.[30] These are the only documents that present the Albanian government's lines of action in relation to adult victims. Both strategies

---

27 *McLaughlin & Muncle* 2013, p. 449.

28 Law on the Status of Politically Ex-Convicted and Persecuted People by the Communist Regime, Law No. 7748, 29.07.1993, Official Gazette 7748/1993.

29 The term kulak was used under the communist regime to refer to landowners targeted as rich peasants under the regime whose land and fortune was taken away from them.

30 *Gjebrea* 2016; The 2013–2020 Cross-Sectoral Strategy on the Fight against Organised Crime, Illegal Trafficking and Terrorism, Decision No. 814, 26.11.2014; https://www.unodc.org/res/human-trafficking/2012/strategy-on-human-trafficking-and-migrant-smuggling_html/Thematic_Programme_on_Transitional_Threats.pdf [20.05.2019].

are focused on specific victims and there is no general strategy to address problems of victims and of preventing victimisation.

The Cross-Sectoral Strategy provides some guidelines on the support for victims of crime, especially, victims of human trafficking. Protection of victims of human trafficking is presented as one of the main priorities of state action. The strategy highlights the importance of early detection of victims/potential victims of human trafficking for the purpose of their referral for services and their effective protection, the design of comprehensive awareness campaigns (including both state actors and private sector), and completion of studies/research in order to prevent early new forms of trafficking and other types of exploitation. Among the specific objectives listed in the document are: improvement of legislation to fight against human trafficking and the implementation of standardised procedures for the identification, referral, and protection of victims of trafficking, with a special focus on children; the proactive monitoring of standard operative procedures for the identification and referral of victims of trafficking to ensure their effective implementation; early awareness raising among children on the rights they enjoy and strengthening of children through protective systems, through education, motivation, and prioritisation.[31]

The National Strategy on the Fight against Human Trafficking 2014-2017 sets objectives in line with the Cross-Sectoral Strategy and further specifies the main areas of work with victims of human trafficking. The main goals of the strategy are: strengthening the rights of victims of trafficking (VT) and ensuring their fair, non-discriminatory treatment by law enforcement and judicial authorities; mandatory and specific staff training on the standards of treatment of minors in contact with the criminal justice system; ensuring that VT are informed about their rights as well as about potential risks and benefits over the course of the criminal proceeding; guaranteeing mechanisms of early detection and referral of VT and potential VT; promoting re-integration and social inclusion of minor victims of human trafficking; and decreasing the risk of re-victimisation and re-trafficking by providing specialised support for re-integration, focused on the family and supported by the community.[32]

The main governmental actors involved in the protection of victims of trafficking are: the police (the anti-trafficking department), the National Anti-Trafficking Coordinator, the National Anti-Trafficking Committee at the Ministry of Interior, the Ministry of Social Health and Social Welfare (psychological assistance and health care services), the Ministry of Justice (coordination of free legal aid service). The main anti-trafficking structures currently in place in Albania are:

1) the State Committee for Combating Trafficking in Human Beings;
2) the National Anti-Trafficking Task-Force;

31 See Decision No. 814.

32 *Gjebrea* 2016.

3) the Office of the National Coordinator for the Fight against Trafficking in Persons;
4) the Responsible Authority for the National Referral Mechanism for Victims of Trafficking; and
5) the Regional Anti-Trafficking Committees.[33]

Three specialised NGO-operated shelters and one state-run shelter provide assistance to trafficking victims, including food, counselling, legal advice, medical care, educational services, employment services, assistance to victims' children, financial support, long-term accommodation, social activities, vocational training, and post-reintegration follow-up. NGO-run shelters supported 75 trafficking victims and potential victims and the state-run shelter supported 30, of which 10 were from 2015.[34]

In terms of the fight against domestic violence, the Ministry of Health and Social Protection (MoHSP) is the authority in charge of addressing gender equality issues and drafting policies against domestic violence. The MoHSP is also responsible for policy development to address the abuse of children and women (as well as other groups), gender equality, protection of children's rights, non-discrimination based on sexual orientation, disability, ethnicity, and minority.[35]

In relation to support for child victims of crime, by the end of 2017 the Ministry of Justice launched the Draft Strategy on National Justice for Children 2017–2020.[36] The strategy will serve as the main document on the design and implementation of juvenile crime prevention mechanisms and the protection of juvenile victims. The strategy has an interdisciplinary approach that ensures alignment with all other existing national documents and contains concrete activities. Some of the main innovative aspects of the strategy are as follows:

- guaranteeing the physical accessibility and standards of protection for child victims and building the capacities of professionals working with them;
- provision of free legal aid to child victims, as well as to children who seek remedies for violations of their rights in various areas of law by lawyers/attorneys specialised and licensed to handle child cases;

---

33 *Gjebrea* 2016.

34 U.S. Department of State, Office to Monitor and Combat Trafficking in Persons 2017.

35 Albania's comments on GREVIO's draft final report on the implementation of the Istanbul Convention 2017; https://rm.coe.int/final-comments-of-the-albanian-government-on-the-first-report/16807688aa [20.05.2019].

36 The Draft Strategy was launched on 20.11.2017 in a round table meeting with the presence of all actors involved in the field of administration of Juvenile Justice and representatives of the civil society; see Ministry of Justice 2017.

- development of specific treatment and rehabilitation programmes for child victims of torture, human trafficking, sexual violence, and domestic violence, in collaboration with non-profit organisations experienced in the relevant are of work; and
- implementation of pilot counselling and rehabilitation (support) programmes for parents of child victims.

UNICEF Albania was extensively involved in the drafting and consultation stages of the strategy to ensure that child protective mechanisms satisfy international standards on child treatment and assistance. UNICEF Albania is actively engaged in studies on the Situation of Children's Rights in Albania and in the implementation of campaigns to protect children from abuse.

In terms of victimisation prevention policies, the Ministry of Education (MoE) has supported the implementation of a program on prevention of bullying and extremism in the Albanian educational system (target group: pupils in secondary schools). Also, the MoE recently launched a campaign on avoiding discrimination against LGBTs, which consists in promoting dialogue among high school students and secondary school pupils over the rights of people belonging to the LGBT community and the available mechanism for their protection. Nationally, some of the main civil society organisations engaged in offering support to victims are: the Albanian Helsinki Committee (AHC), the Albanian Rehabilitation Centre for Trauma and Torture (ARCT), the National Centre for the Treatment of Victims of Domestic Violence (QKTDHF), Terre des hommes Albania (TdhA), and the Centre for Legal Civic Initiatives (CLCI).[37]

The AHC_is primarily engaged in strengthening the rule of law and promoting respect for human rights. Its main contributions to support crime victims and prevent victimisation are: the provision of free legal aid in the context of strategic litigation, to assist victims whose human rights have been violated (legal representation is offered both in domestic courts and at the ECrHR), monitoring, advocating for and protecting, in a proactive manner, respect for fundamental human rights and freedoms in Albania and beyond, preparation of reports for the implementation of human rights in Albania, etc.[38]

The ARCT has been operating in Albania since 1995, designing and implementing programmes on the rehabilitation of victims of torture and providing related services (combined with scrupulous documentation of violation practices and human suffering) as well as Prevention of Torture programmes (reporting periodically to International agencies/organisations on the situation of torture in the country, training for police and health staff in prison, pre-detention places, psychiatric hospitals,

---

37 Council of Europe 2019.

38 Albanian Helsinki Committee 2019.

educational system), providing assistance and a window of opportunities for this target group.[39] Main areas of activity of ARCT are rehabilitation of torture survivors (direct assistance and rehabilitation to victims (mainly, medical, social, and psychological services) supported by the UN Voluntary Fund for Victims of Torture), providing access to justice to victims of torture, advocacy against torture, monitoring compliance with the UNCAT Convention standards in prisons and pre-trial detention facilities.[40] ARCT has been engaged in the domestic court system, as well as at the ECrHR to provide legal assistance and services in the field of human rights to vulnerable detainees in prisons, especially chronically ill inmates, juvenile offenders, and the poor.[41]

The CLCI operates as a legal and psycho-social service centre for violated and poor women. All services are provided for free.[42]Some of the main objectives of the Centre are: building female access to the legal and judicial system by offering legal services, accompanied by free psycho-social support for the poor and/or violated women and girls, participation in the drafting of laws and of state policies concerning gender equality, etc. The CLCI was one of the main partners in the implementation of the project "Promoting a Victim-Centred Approach in Trafficking Cases in Albania and Bosnia-Herzegovina" (June 2013 – July 2017).[43] The main goal of the project was to support judges, prosecutors, and judicial academies in making sure the rights of victims of human trafficking are guaranteed during judicial procedures.

The QKTDHF's activities consist of offering rehabilitation programmes for women, girls, and children who are victims of domestic violence. It offers regular social and professional services to victims of domestic violence that aim to promote their independence and social inclusion within communities.[44]

Terre des hommes Albania has established a network of professionals and dedicated activists to protect children from various abusive situations that might lead to

---

39 Albanian Rehabilitation Centre for Trauma and Torture 2019. Additional information on ARCT activities is available online at http://www.arct.org/index.php/about-us.

40 Albanian Rehabilitation Centre for Trauma and Torture 2016, pp. 13–18.

41 Albanian Rehabilitation Centre for Trauma and Torture 2016, pp. 25–26.

42 Center for Legal Civic Initiatives 2019. Additional information on the CLCI activities is available online at http://www.qag-al.org/ang/html/about.htm.

43 Partners of the project were: Centre for Legal and Civic Initiatives (Albania), International Forum of Solidarity – Emmaus (Bosnia-Herzegovina), Dutch Judicial Academy and Council for the Judiciary (The Netherlands). Additional information on the project is available online at https://www.nhc.nl/themes/building-up-rule-of-law/promoting-rights-trafficked-persons/promoting-victim-centered-approach-trafficking-cases-albania-bosnia-herzegovina/.

44 Center for Legal Civic Initiatives 2019.

vulnerability. Its direct interventions aim to consolidate a national system of child protection.[45]

2.3 The Study of Victimology in Albania

At a university level, victimology is studied as part of the criminology curricula in the bachelor and master's programmes. A certain number of topics are dedicated to victimology in the general curricula of criminology, and there is no scientific discipline exclusively dedicated to the study of victims of crime. Criminology courses are offered to law students and to students of sociology in the Faculty of Social Sciences, University of Tirana. Special topics on victimology are also integrated in the curricula of the "Criminal Policy" course, which is taught to master's students at the Faculty of Law, University of Tirana. There are several recent studies on victims of crime that deserve mentioning:

1) Social services for victims of trafficking in Albania;[46]
2) Victims of mines and munitions in Albania: An overview of the state of the art and needs;[47]
3) Promotion of the rights of trafficked persons in Albania – A legal analysis of the current situation in regard to the rights of victims of trafficking;[48]
4) Bullying in secondary education schools in Tirana;[49]
5) Study on the cooperation between victims of trafficking and law enforcement authorities;[50]
6) Study on the social and economic reintegration of victims of trafficking in Albania;[51] and
7) Criminology.[52]

2.4 Research on Victimology

The last crime victim survey was conducted in 2000. The sample city was Tirana, the capital of Albania. Other recent surveys conducted were as follows:[53]

45 Terre des Hommes in Albania 2019.

46 *Biçoku, Kuri & Luniku* 2017.

47 *Kola & Nela* 2016.

48 Center for Legal Civic Initiatives 2015.

49 *Ismaili* 2015.

50 OSCE Presence in Albania 2014.

51 *Meshi, Picari & Pinderi* 2009.

52 *Hysi* 2005.

53 HEUNI 2014, p. 343.

- The International Crime Business Survey in 2000,
- a National Survey on Children Violence in 2006, and
- a National Survey on Domestic Violence in 2008.

A lack of countrywide (national representative) surveys on victimisation makes it impossible to draw any valid and reliable estimates concerning the situation of victimisation in Albania. Police statistics are not a sufficient basis to obtain a general representative picture on the situation of victimisation in the country because of two main limitations: first, they provide data on reported crimes only; and second, police data cannot provide information on a broader aspect of victimisation which is that of victimisation noticed/perceived in victims' interaction with the criminal justice system. Also, there are some new trends of victimisation that remain quite unexplored, such as victimisation of Albanian illegal immigrants, and of the LGBT community, especially when discriminatory practices occur in prisons.

Civil society organisations conduct specific surveys mainly focused on prisoners and juvenile delinquents. The AHC publishes annual reports on the situation and conditions of treatment of prisoners and pre-trial detainees. In 2017, the AHC published the manual "On the monitoring of respect of the rights of asylum seekers and immigrants in Albania".[54] With this document, the AHC confirmed its commitment to consider the respect of human rights for these groups as a matter of priority. The ARCT performs fact finding missions and monitoring visits to police cells and prisons with a focus on the implementation of international accepted standards on torture prevention.[55] Monitored aspects include: prisoner and detainee treatment, protection measures, material (living) conditions, access to medical services, prisons staff conduct and relevant training. A 2016 study conducted by the Albanian Rehabilitation Centre for Trauma and Torture addressed matters of child access to justice and potential discrimination.[56] The analysis of 45 criminal cases involving children, reviewed by the Supreme Court during the monitoring period, showed that none of them concerned any children involved in the process in the capacity of the victim/injured of criminal offence or witness.[57] The analysis of cases of lower courts shows that the access to justice mechanisms is not always adequate for the children from marginalised social groups or people with special needs. In cases of victimisation, special institutions and structures show a lack of management, poor analysis, or superficial assessment of the dynamics and trends of crime against children. Conse-

---

54 Albanian Helsinki Committee 2017.

55 Albanian Rehabilitation Centre for Trauma and Torture 2016, p. 28.

56 Albanian Rehabilitation Centre for Trauma and Torture 2016; UNICEF 2016.

57 Albanian Rehabilitation Centre for Trauma and Torture 2016, p. 41.

quently, due to a lack of professionalism or because of scarce capacity, they cause secondary victimisation of children and other vulnerable social groups.[58]

3. Relevant Legal Framework and Criminal Policy

The criminal policy for protection of victims in Albania has been developed under the influence of the main international instruments related to victims of crime. Some of the most influential documents in this area are the UN Declaration of Basic Principles of Justice for Victims of Crime and Abuse of Power of 1985, the Council of Europe adopted Recommendation no. r (85) 11 of the Committee of Ministers of the CE on the position of the victim in the framework of criminal law and procedure, [59] and Recommendation no. r (87) 21 of the Committee of Ministers of the CE on assistance to victims and the prevention of victimisation.[60] As regards victims of violent crimes, a specific regulation on issues of their compensation is made by the European Convention on the Compensation of Victims of Violent Crimes of 1983.[61] The Convention was ratified by the Republic of Albania in 2004.[62] In this respect, the obligation imposed on member states to introduce or develop schemes for the compensation of these victims is to be fulfilled by the Albanian government. Lately, one of the most influential instruments on protection of victims of crime at a national level has been Directive 2012/29/EU establishing minimum standards on the rights, support, and protection of victims of crime.[63] The recommendations coming from this Directive were highly reflected in the amendments made to the Albanian Criminal Procedure Code. Approximation of standards for the treatment of victims in Albania with the EU standards was a necessary commitment resulting from Albanian's candidate status to EU membership. Systematic and adequate statistical data

---

58 Albanian Rehabilitation Centre for Trauma and Torture 2016, pp. 41–42.

59 Recommendation no. r (85) 11 of the Committee of Ministers of the CE on the position of the victim in the framework of criminal law and procedure, 28.06.1985; https://www.barobirlik.org.tr/dosyalar/duyurular/hsykkanunteklifi/recR(85)11e.pdf [20.05.2019].

60 Recommendation no. r (87) 21. of the Committee of Ministers of the CE on assistance to victims and the prevention of victimisation, 17.09.2019; https://www.barobirlik.org.tr/dosyalar/duyurular/hsykkanunteklifi/recR(87)21e.pdf [20.05.2019].

61 European Convention on the Compensation of Victims of Violent Crimes, ETS No. 116, 24.11.1983; https://www.coe.int/en/web/conventions/full-list/-/conventions/treaty/116 [20. 05.2019].

62 Law on the Ratification of the Convention on Compensation of Violent Crimes, Law No. 9265, 29.07.2004, Official Gazette 9265/2004.

63 According to the Directive 2012/29/EU, victims shall have the right to: receive information, access legal aid, specialised/professional help when needed, protection of privacy, actively participate in the criminal proceedings, appeal the decision not to prosecute, and be compensated for the harm/injury suffered; see Directive No. 32012L0029.

collection is recognised as an essential component of effective policy-making (as set out in the Directive).

3.1 Victim Protection in Accordance with the Material Criminal Law

In the Criminal Code of the Republic of Albania there are a number of provisions dedicated to the protection of special categories of victims. So, the commission of murder against minors, physically/mentally disabled persons, or pregnant women must be sentenced for no less than 20 years of imprisonment/life and for no less than 30 years of imprisonment/life imprisonment when the offence is committed against a judge, prosecutor, lawyer, or other public official.[64] Specific provisions criminalise racist and xenophobic activities such as intimidation or incitement of hatred/disputes on grounds of race, nationality, ethnicity, religion, or sexual orientation committed personally or through computer systems.[65] Special attention is paid to the protection of minors from any kind of criminal behaviour that impinges on their physical and psychological integrity as well as their normal sexual development and freedom. Harsh sanctions are applied for criminal acts such as pornography and obscene acts with minors, kidnapping or stalking a minor, rape, exploitation for prostitution, or trafficking of minors.[66] In addition, section IX of Chapter II of the Criminal Code is totally dedicated to the protection of children, marriage, and family from any offences that endangers the normal well-being of a child, acts of non-performance of parental responsibilities, and acts that violate marital freedom of choice. Other categories of victims that are given special protection under the criminal legislation are public officials on duty and witnesses and justice collaborators when the criminal offence is committed because of their special role within the criminal justice system.[67] In addition, in 2009 the Albanian Parliament passed the special law on

---

64 Articles 79 (murder committed under other qualifying circumstances) and 79/b (murder of the state police officers) of the Criminal Code of the Republic of Albania, Law No. 7895, 27.01.1995, Official Gazette 7895/1995.

65 See Articles 84/a (threat due to racist and xenophobic motives through the computer system), 119/a (dissemination of racist or xenophobic materials through the computer system), and 265 (incitement of hatred or disputes) of the Law No. 7895.

66 See Articles 100 (sexual or homosexual relations with minors), 101 (violent sexual or homosexual intercourse with a minor who is fourteen to eighteen years old), 108 (immoral acts), 109 (kidnapping or holding a person hostage), 114 (exploitation of prostitution), 117 (pornography), 121/a (stalking), and 128/b (trafficking of minors) of the Law No. 7895.

67 See Articles 237 (assault because of duty), 238 (intimidation because of duty), 295/a (disclosure of secret documents or data), and 311 (intimidation not to report) of the Law No. 7895.

"Collaborators of Justice and Witness Protection".[68] The law provides for special and temporary protective measures and protection procedures for witnesses and collaborators of justice who have knowledge or are part of a criminal organisation in order to prevent and detect criminal acts and terrorist acts.

The criminal legislation can also serve as a tool to ensure offender's compliance to the obligation to compensate the victim of crime for the civil damage caused by the offence. Under Article 60 of the Criminal Code, the court is authorised to oblige a convicted person to compensate for the civil damage incurred by the victim.[69] If the convict, during the probation term, violates the conditions or obligations set by the court, the probation services shall report immediately to the prosecutor. For minor violations, the prosecutor has the right to give a warning, which is registered in the personal file of the convict, while for severe and repeated violations, the prosecutor shall request the court to change the imposed obligation, add up other obligations, replace them with other sanctions, or revoke the decision for the suspension of the sentence.[70]

3.2 Procedural Status of Victims Under the Criminal Procedure Code

The Criminal Procedure Code is the main body of law offering effective procedural tools for victims of crime to exercise their rights. It also provides for real guaranties in the case victim's rights are not properly addressed over the course of criminal proceedings. Amendments in 2017 introduced very significant changes to the Criminal Procedure Code, and notably expanded the active participation of victims of crime in criminal proceedings.[71] Such changes were highly influenced by the Directive 2012/29/EU, which calls for minimum standards on the rights, support, and protection of victims of crime.

3.2.1 Guaranteeing the Dignity of Victims

The commitment of lawmakers to recognise the status of victims and to protect their dignity can be noted in the very conceptual change brought by the amendments in 2017, which replaces the words "person injured from the criminal offence" with the word "victim". This marked the first time that the notion of the victim of crime

---

68 Collaborators of Justice and Witness Protection, Law No. 10173, 22.10.2009, Official Gazette 10173/2009.

69 See Article 60 (obligations of the sentenced person in probationary) of the Law No. 7895.

70 See Article 62 (violation of the conditions and obligations during the probationary period) of the Law No. 7895.

71 Criminal Procedure Code of the Republic of Albania, Law No. 35/2017, 30.03.2017, Official Gazette 35/2017.

was introduced in the Albanian legal system. Special provisions in the Code require public bodies to guarantee that victims of criminal offences be treated with respect for their human dignity in the exercise of the rights provided for by the Criminal Procedure Code.[72] A very important development of the new piece of legislation is that of prohibiting confrontation between an adult defendant and a minor victim.[73] This regulation is primarily designed to protect minor victims from further trauma and embarrassment, which often results from testifying in an offender's presence.

3.2.2 Active Participation of Victims in Criminal Proceedings

A number of provisions in the Criminal Procedure Code are concerned with providing extended rights to victims to actively participate in every stage of the criminal proceeding. Victims' access to information on the handling of their case is generally recognised in each stage of the criminal proceedings. They have the right to request information on the state of the proceedings, and to have access to evidence contained in the prosecutor's file.[74] The right to information also includes the right to be informed about the arrest of the accused person and/or his/her release, non-initiation of the proceeding, the dismissal of the case, and the initiation/completion of the trial.[75] The recent amendments to the Code have recognised victim's rights to receive specialised care and legal support throughout the criminal process. Crime victims have the right to seek medical care, psychological assistance, and counselling and to receive free legal aid if they are unable to afford a lawyer.[76] The proceeding authority has to inform victims about their rights *ex officio* and not wait for their invocation by the victim.

The provision of various sources of support to victims is a very good step to expand victims' effective participation in the criminal process and to ensure their competent standing during the course of the process. However, the implementation of such provisions represents an open challenge when it comes to bringing together state agencies and civil society in a common framework of cooperation to support crime victims. At present, there is a notable lack of coordination between agencies and insufficient resources to establish permanent schemes of integrated social services.

Other provisions in the Criminal Procedure Code recognise the accusing victim's rights to take part in the trial as a party to prove the charge against the defendant and claim the reimbursement of damages for a number of criminal offences.[77] These

---

72 See Article 9a (the right of the victim of the criminal offence) of the Law No. 35/2017.

73 See Article 169 (grounds for confrontation) of the Law No. 35/2017.

74 See Article 279/a (information on the state of the proceedings) Law No. 35/2017.

75 See Article 58 (the rights of the victim of the criminal offence) of the Law No. 35/2017.

76 See Article 58 (the rights of the victim of the criminal offence) of the Law No. 35/2017.

77 See: Article 59 (the accusing victim) of the Law No. 35/2017.

offences include such criminal acts as reckless serious injury, non-serious intentional injury, trespassing, defamation, slander, breach of privacy, spreading of personal secrets, etc.[78] These criminal acts primarily affect close personal interests as opposed to state interests; therefore, participation of the victim as a party in the trial is indispensable to highlight the very private nature of the dispute. The same logic applies to provisions that regulate the victim's right to control the commencement of prosecution for certain criminal offences,[79] which impinge on private interests in the first place. Such offences include: intimidation, non-serious intentional injury, forced sexual intercourse with adult females, sexual intercourse by abuse of power or between persons in lineal consanguinity, violation of the marital freedom of choice, violation of intellectual property rights, trespassing committed by public officials, malicious use of phone calls, and violation of road traffic regulations resulting in *minor injuries*.[80] The prosecution of the given offences shall commence only upon complaint of the victim, who may withdraw it at any stage of the proceedings.

3.2.3 Additional Guarantees to Challenge Prosecutorial Discretion

The victim or their heirs can file a complaint against a prosecutor's decision to not initiate proceedings.[81] If the complaint is found to be grounded, the court orders the prosecutor to register the proceeding and to carry out the necessary investigations, indicating also the further direction of the investigation.[82] The related provision of the Code has undergone substantial change as compared to the earlier version. Before the legislative amendments of 2017, there was no indication on the court's authority to order the prosecution to register the case, and moreover, to indicate the investigation's direction. The new regulation seems to limit prosecutorial discretion and expand judicial control during the investigative stage. In addition, if the prosecutor of a case concludes that the charge or the case should be dismissed, s/he has to get the court's approval in deciding the matter. The prosecutor's request is notified to the defendant, their defence lawyer, and the victim (or their identified heirs who have the right to access acts and evidence).[83] Moreover, the victim of a criminal offence has the right to make an appeal in the court against the prosecutor's decision

---

78 See Law No. 7895.

79 See Article 284 (the criminal complaint) of the Law No. 35/2017.

80 See Law No. 7895.

81 Article 291 (decision not to initiate proceedings) of the Law No. 35/2017 states: "When the circumstances that do not allow the initiation of proceedings exist, the prosecutor issues a reasoned decision not to initiate the proceedings, within 15 days of the filing of the criminal report [...] Notice of the decision is served promptly to those who have lodged a criminal report or a complaint, to the victim or the victim's heirs, who may file a complaint with the court, within 10 days of the notification of the decision."

82 See Article 291 (decision not to initiate proceedings) of the Law No. 35/2017.

83 See Law No. 7895.

for the non-initiation of the proceeding and the decision of the prosecutor/judge of the preliminary hearing to dismiss the charge or the case.[84] In order to ensure compliance with legal provisions that ask for the consideration of victims' rights, an absolute invalidity follows any procedural act performed without summoning the victim when it is mandatory to do so.

3.2.4 Special Protection of Vulnerable Victims

The 2017 amendments to the Criminal Procedure Code introduced a number of rights and guaranties to expand the protection of minor victims and of sexually abused/human trafficking victims. The new provisions are in line with the with the recommendations of Directive 2012/29/EU on the standards of treatment of these special categories of victims. Some of the main requirements on proceedings involving minor victims are:

1) the mandatory presence of a person of trust;
2) protection of confidentiality of his/her personal data;
3) the right to ask that the hearing takes place without the presence of the public;
4) the questioning only by specialised professionals;
5) the requirement for the questioning to be recorded with audio-visual recording tools, when possible; and
6) the obligation to do the questioning in at minors' premises for minors under 14 years of age.[85]

The victims of sexual abuse and human trafficking are entitled to the same rights as regards the confidentiality of data, the non-publicity of hearing sessions, and the questioning by specialised staff (through audio-visual tools, if requested). In addition, they have the right to:

1) be heard without delay by a judicial police officer or prosecutor of the same gender; and
2) refuse to answer questions regarding their private life obviously not related to the criminal offence.[86]

The last provision reflects the prohibition to use character evidence as regards victims' lifestyle, which might prejudicial to the case.

---

84 See Law No. 35/2017.

85 See Article 58a (the rights of the minor victim) of the Law No. 35/2017.

86 See Article 58/b (the rights of the sexually abused victim and human trafficking victim) of the Law No. 7895.

The audio recording of the questioning for both minors and victims of sexual abuse are designed as a tool for protecting their psychological integrity from embarrassment and trauma that is often experienced by repeated questioning. It can also have a facilitating effect in smoothing the procedures.

As regards the standards of treatment of minor victims, the new Code of Criminal Justice for Children[87] offers a complete framework of integrated services and specialised assistance. One of the aims of this Code is to protect the rights of minors who are witnesses or victims of a criminal offence. The Code requires that proceeding involving juveniles (as offenders, victims, or witnesses) be dealt with as high priority.[88] Other relevant provisions call for the mandatory presence of a psychologist during the questioning of both juvenile offenders and juvenile victims, and their right to free psychological and legal assistance.[89] Of particular practical importance is the obligation for any person involved in the administration of juvenile justice to receive mandatory specialised training regarding the techniques and methods of protection and support to juvenile victims and witnesses of a criminal offence. Chapter V of the Juvenile Justice Code is totally dedicated to the protection of the minor who is a victim or a witness. It provides for special professional support to protect privacy and ensure minor victims are informed during the proceeding. Since the Juvenile Justice Code is a new piece of legislation, the main challenge seems to be the establishment of the necessary structures that will coordinate and implement the requisite reforms. [90]

3.3 Compensation for Victims of Crime

Specific measures in relation to financial and social services support for victims of organised crime and human trafficking are provided by the so-called Anti-Mafia Law.[91] Accordingly, funds gained from the confiscation of organised crime and human trafficking assets are to be used to fund assistance programs for victims of organised crime and trafficking and to provide compensation for the victims of organised crime and trafficking (to the extent determined by a judicial decision).

The above-mentioned laws provide for the support for victims of organised crime and human trafficking. Questions of support to victims of conventional crime and

---

87 Code of Criminal Justice for Children of the Republic of Albania, Law No. 37, 30.03.2017, Official Gazette 37/2017.

88 See Law No. 37/2017.

89 See Law No. 37/2017.

90 See Law No. 37/2017.

91 Law on Preventing and Striking at Organised Crime, Trafficking, Corruption and other Crimes through Preventive Measures against Assets, Law No. 10 192, 03.12.2009, Official Gazette, 10192/2009.

its prevention remain mostly unaddressed, which leaves relevant crime vulnerabilities for victims of conventional acts of murder, assault, or rape open. However, there seems to be some awareness on the part of the legislature that victim support programmes need to be more comprehensive and target various victim groups. In the Anti-Mafia Law there is a provision stating that, in addition to central state institutions, the beneficiaries of the financing of projects may also be: non-profit organisations that have within the scope of their activity the social, cultural, and health rehabilitation of vulnerable categories of people, especially those affected or endangered by crime, including therapeutic centres and organisations, centres for rehabilitation of users of narcotic substances, as well as centres for the assistance and rehabilitation of the victims of human trafficking.[92] Here, the reference is not only to victims of organised crime, but also to victims of crime in general.

The right to compensation for those persecuted under the communist regime is regulated in accordance with the Law on the Compensation of the Former Politically Persecuted People of the Communist Regime.[93] According to the law, compensation can consist of: instant remuneration in cash, life pension, salary compensation, land, premises or any other form of material profit, which will be given without return to the persecuted person or his family if he is dead, to compensate for the loss of life, loss of freedom, or unpaid work and sufferings. The aim of the law is to create the conditions and possibilities for his or his family's quicker integration into the normal economical-social life of Albania. In 2007, the government passed the Law on the Compensation of the Former Politically Persecuted People of the Communist Regime, which provided specific rules for the compensation procedures of this category of victims.[94] Over the years, there have been significant problems with the operation of the compensatory scheme prejudicing the rights of this class. In September 2012, the politically persecuted started a strike in Tirana to influence the government to address their claims for compensation according to the law. One of the protesters self-immolated himself to protest the government's silence to their claims.[95] As of 2018, the members of the social class persecuted politically during the communist era are still struggling to receive attention and understanding from state.

In 2004, Albania ratified the European Convention on Compensation of Victims of Violent Crimes.[96] The scope of the Convention is to elaborate state funded compensation schemes for victims of intentional violent offences where the perpetrator of the offence is not identified or has no sources to pay compensation. If compensation

---

92 See Law No. 10 192.

93 Law on the Compensation of the Former Politically Persecuted People of the Communist Regime, Law No. 9831, 12.11.2007, Official Gazette 9831/2007.

94 See Law No. 9381.

95 *Pustina* 2012.

96 See Law No. 9265.

cannot be provided by other sources, the victim can be paid by state funds provided that the harm suffered was the direct cause of serious bodily injury or damage to health. The dependants of persons who have died as a result of a violent crime are also eligible for compensation. Compensation covers at least the following categories: loss of earnings, medical expenses (which may include prescription charges and the cost of dental treatment), hospital fees, funeral expenses, and, in the case of dependants (children, spouse, etc.), loss of maintenance. Though the Convention represents a good tool to address the question of compensation for victims of violent crime, it has a notable limitation: it fails to design a financing mechanism to achieve the compensation goals in the member states, including Albania. No indication is made concerning how compensation schemes are to be established and operate in the member states. Another limitation of the Convention is that it cannot be used as a redress tool for losses suffered by business entities. The problem does not seem to be the terminology used to define the potential recipients of compensation (since the convention uses broadly inclusive terms such as "nationals" or "applicants"), but rather the type of loss eligible to receive compensation. Compensation is limited to those who have suffered serious bodily injury or impairment of health attributable to a crime of violence and to dependants of a dead victim of a violent crime. Therefore, property damage or pure financial lose cannot form a ground for compensation.

3.4 Civil Lawsuits in Criminal Proceedings

The purpose of the civil lawsuit in criminal proceedings is that victims of criminal offences can claim for restitution of the property damage or the reimbursement of the injury suffered in the same action as the criminal case against the offender. It is primarily motivated to save the victim's financial resources. Under criminal procedural law, one who has suffered injury by the criminal offence (or his/her heirs) may file a civil lawsuit in the criminal proceedings against the defendant or the person liable to pay for damages (defendant), claiming the restitution of the property and reimbursement of the injury.[97] Traditionally, victims of crime could claim for reimbursement of the injury suffered only if the injury resulted in manifest physical consequences. Amendments to the Criminal Procedure Code in 2017 brought a radical change by introducing the non-material aspect of an injury resulting from a criminal offence. In order for the victim to bring a civil lawsuit in criminal proceedings, the injury to the victim does not need to be material. As regards the time-line for presenting the civil claim to the criminal court, it is necessary that the request be submitted before the commencement of the trial.[98]

97 See Article 61 (civil lawsuit in criminal proceedings) of the Law No. 35/2017.

98 Article 62 (time limit for the legal standing of the civil plaintiff) of the Law No. 35/2017, states that "Legal standing of the plaintiff may be decided by the proceeding authority prior to commencing of the trial [... T]his time limit may not be extended".

Moreover, such a request cannot be presented on appeal if not submitted originally to the First Instance Court.[99] Another positive development worth mentioning is the introduction of the institution of judgement upon agreement in the Criminal Procedure Code. Accordingly, the prosecutor, the defendant, or his/her special representative may propose to reach an agreement on the conditions of admission of guilt and of setting the punishment for criminal offences for which the law provides for a maximum punishment of not more than seven years of imprisonment.[100] The respective provisions offer additional guarantees on the victims' right to receive compensation by declaring the invalidity of any agreement reached in absence of the civil plaintiff's (who is legitimated) consent concerning the amount of damages to be paid by the defendant.

Although in theory the victim can obtain satisfaction through the civil lawsuit in criminal proceedings, effective compensation is seldom in practice. First of all, crime victims are not excluded from court fees. Second, the practice shows that there are notable problems when it comes to the execution of criminal court decisions recognising a victim's right to receive compensation from the offender. Bailiff services have high fees, which victims have to pay in advance. Moreover, the assets designed for the compensation of the victim are often already confiscated by the state.[101]

3.5 Civil Lawsuit for Compensation of Harm Caused by an Illegal Act

Victims of criminal offences might claim compensation by bringing a civil lawsuit in the civil court. The right to civil compensation legitimates the victim to ask for indemnification of any personal injury and property damage caused by the offender.[102] These injuries can be physical and/or emotional/psychological.

Compensation for physical harm might consist of, but it is not limited to, costs of medical and psychological treatment, physical care, rehabilitation costs, profession-

[99] The Supreme Court held that the submission of the civil action request to the Appellate Court handling the criminal case would "violate the principle of respect for each instance of trial as provided in article 135 of the Albanian Constitution" (Supreme Court, Unifying Decision No. 284, 06.10.2000).

[100] See Article 406/d (content of the agreement) of the Law No. 35/2017.

[101] Center for Legal Civic Initiatives 2015.

[102] The right to civil compensation derives from Article 608 (liability for causing the damage) of the Civil Code of the Republic of Albania, Law No. 7850, 29.07.1994, Official Gazette 7850/1994, which states that "The person culpably and illegally causing damage to another in person or in rem shall be obliged to indemnify the caused damage… The damage shall be illegal where ever it emerges out of the breach of impairment of the interests of rights of others, being protected by the legal order or good customs".

al costs, lost income, legal fees and other technical costs afforded by the victim, and any other cost the victim suffered because of the crime. In case of death of the victim, his/her family members are entitled to indemnification for the living expenses of their minor children, spouse, and parents being incapable of working, having been dependants of the deceased, as well as of the persons having lived with the family of the deceased and being entitled to the right of alimony.[103]

Emotional harm[104] can refer to:

1) psychological harm and emotional disturbance that is related to the crime,
2) reputational harm or harm resulting from impairment of privacy, and
3) pain suffered due to lose of consortium (company and affection) of a family member, and lose of potential care toward the plaintiff.

As regards the estimation of the emotional harm suffered, the court shall take into account the relevant values specified by a compensation table issued by the Ministry of Finances. If such guidelines are missing, the court decides as it deems fair under the circumstances. In order to avoid that the compensation should be symbolic or not to allow the plaintiff (victim) to get a windfall, the compensation for the emotional harm is to be set within the limits of one-quarter to half of the amount of compensation assigned by the court for the permanent physical harm or in the same amount of compensation assigned for the temporary physical harm in the specific case. If family members of the deceased victim ask for compensation for emotional harm, the court shall refer to a "terminal" physical harm to assign the amount of compensation, which in the case of a victim's survival, would have been a compensation in the amount of 100%.[105]

4. The Reality of Victimisation

The only official figures on victims of crime are those produced by the Albanian State Police. The prosecution and the courts do not produce any statistical data on victims of crime. *Table 1* presents the number of victims registered by the Albanian State Police according to the main crime categories that are provided under the Criminal Code of the Republic of Albania. Crimes against the person, domestic violence, and violation of road traffic rules are the categories that represent the largest number of victims.

Table 2 is more specific as it presents the number of victims for each specific criminal offence, enabling a better understanding of the victims' situation. The

---

[103] See Article 643 (damage compensation) of the Law No. 7850.

[104] Supreme Court, Unifying Decision No. 12, 14.09.2007.

[105] See Unifying Decision No. 12.

Table 1 Number of Victims Registered by the Albanian State Police per 100,000 Inhabitants (2014–2016)

	2014	2015	2016
Total number of victims	781.70	698.80	663.40
Crimes against the person	17.49	15.17	14.46
Crimes against property	5.63	5.09	3.19
Acts for terrorist purposes	0.13	0.03	0.00
Illegal trafficking*	8.98	4.01	3.79
Domestic violence	142.40	122.70	128.60
Violation of road traffic accidents	92.40	111.90	116.70
Other	787.40	439.80	396.50

Source: Data Taken From the General Directorate of Albanian State Police 2018 (unpublished).

* The data provided in this category refer to the offences of trafficking of persons, trafficking of minors, trafficking of narcotic substances, of motor vehicles, and of arms and military munitions.

difference between the total numbers of victims presented in *Table 1* and those presented in *Table 2* are explained with the fact that over 10,000 victims declared in the final statistics refer to the number of victims as identified by the police in the exercise of its investigative and crime prevention powers. These categories of victims do not qualify as victims of a specific criminal offence provided under the Criminal Code.

Data presented in *Table 2* show that the majority of victims are victims of murder (attempted murder), robbery, fraud, and domestic violence. It is worth noting that sometimes there are notable differences in the official figures produced by the Albanian State Police as compared to the same figures produced by the Ministry of Justice. This is because of the change of the legal qualification of the offence at the moment of investigation. In lieu of statistics from the prosecution or courts, it is impossible to estimate the variation in the number of victims that might result from the change of the qualification of the offence.

To illustrate this point, a judge at the Court for Serious Crimes noted that sometimes there are notable differences in the official figures on minor victims of trafficking produced by the Albanian State Police and same figures produced by the Ministry of Justice. This is because of the change of the legal qualification of the offence at the moment of investigation. For example, police have standard check-lists to identify victims of trafficking and they list a person as a victim of human trafficking based on these indicators. But a number of trafficking offences are not registered as such by the prosecution, but as exploitation of prostitution since the prosecutors consider that not all the elements of trafficking in human beings are present. The statistics produced by the police provide

Table 2 Number of Victims of Specific Offences per 100,000 Inhabitants (2014–2017)

Type of offence	2014*	2015		2016		2017	
	Total	Total	Dead victims	Total	Dead victims	Total	Dead victims
Murder	5.01	2.14	2.14	1.98	2.70	1.87	1.46
Attempted murder	6.32	5.37	–	5.84	–	5.70	–
Homicide	0.20	0.17	0.17	0.13	0.13	0.10	0.10
Domestic murder	–	0.69	0.69	0.66	0.59	0.48	0.48
Grievous bodily harm (intentional)	5.04	6.34	0.06	4.38	0.00	4.90	0.10
Grievous bodily harm (unintentional)	–	0.24	0.00	0.38	0.00	0.20	0.00
Kidnapping/unlawful deprivation of freedom	0.06	0.10	0.00	0.17	0.03	0.06	0.00
Robbery	8.78	6.48	0.00	4.86	0.00	5.63	0.00
Armed robbery	2.03	2.00	0.00	0.59	0.00	0.62	0.00
Robbery resulting in death of the victim	0.13	0.13	0.13	0.24	0.20	0.03	0.03
Fraud	–	22.90	–	28.20	–	27.30	–
Document forgery	–	9.14	–	9.42	0.03	10.50	–
Sexual crimes	–	5.05	–	4.2	0.03	3.96	0.00
Domestic violence	142.40	47.70	0.00	56.1	0.03	53.84	0.00
Trafficking of adult persons	1.69	1.38	0.00	0.93	0.1	0.73	0.00
Trafficking of minors	0.34	0.55	0.00	0.62	0.03	0.62	0.00
Other	0.13	5.47	–	5.14	–	0.03	–
Total	172.20	110.5	8.59	119.7	3.79	116.70	2.19

Source: Data Taken From the General Directorate of Albanian State Police 2018 (unpublished).

* There are no data available as to the share of dead victims in 2014.

information on the age, gender, and nationality of the victims of crime. *Table 3* provides information on these characteristics for the victims of criminal offences registered by the police.

As can be seen, there is not a great deal of information available on the victims and no specific information to enable further analysis on the conditions of victimisation. There is no information on time of the accident, place (urban/non-urban area), distribution of crime victims in various cities in the country, victim's relationship with the author of the offence, the tools/weapons used to inflict injuries on the victim, etc.

Table 3 Socio-Demographic Characteristics of Victims of Crime per 100,000 Inhabitants

<table>
<tr><th></th><th>2014</th><th>2015</th><th>2016</th><th>2017</th></tr>
<tr><td>Total number of victims</td><td>172.20</td><td>110.50</td><td>119.70</td><td>116.70</td></tr>
<tr><td>< 14 years</td><td rowspan="2">9.50</td><td>3.39</td><td>3.23</td><td>3.50</td></tr>
<tr><td>14–18 years</td><td>4.43</td><td>4.70</td><td>4.80</td></tr>
<tr><td>> 18 years</td><td>162.70</td><td>102.70</td><td>111.80</td><td>108.40</td></tr>
<tr><td>Females</td><td>111.70</td><td>50.10</td><td>58.50</td><td>56.30</td></tr>
<tr><td>Males</td><td>60.50</td><td>60.60</td><td>61.10</td><td>60.50</td></tr>
<tr><td>Foreign citizens</td><td>1.27</td><td>0.90</td><td>0.73</td><td>1.46*</td></tr>
</table>

Source: Data Taken From the General Directorate of Albanian State Police (unpublished) 2018.

* Foreign citizens are mostly victims of robbery and fraud.

A lack of situational characteristics of victimisation make it impossible to undertake comprehensive studies.

Table 4 provides information on the distribution of crime victims according to gender. The data show that females are more frequently victims of domestic murder, domestic violence, sexual crimes, trafficking of persons, and trafficking of minors. On the other hand, males are more frequently victims of murder, grievous bodily injuries, robbery, fraud, and document forgery.

Table 5 presents national data on victims of road traffic accidents. The number has remained significantly high over the years despite the government's efforts to increase criminal sentences and administrative sanctions for violations of road traffic rules.

The statistics produced by the Regional Road Traffic Directorates in each district provide information on a number of characteristics regarding the victims and the conditions of the accident such as: victim's sex, the injuries caused by the accident, the attitude of the victim in relation to the accident, the attitude of the driver, age and experience of the driver, the time of the accident, the relevant road conditions, weather conditions, etc. These data enable further analysis. However, there is no integrated document presenting all the specific indicators in national statistics for a complete year. To have a certain view on the situation of the victims of road traffic accidents, we are referring to the statistics prepared by the Regional Road Traffic Directorate of Tirana since the larger number of victims of road traffic accidents is noticed in Tirana County. *Table 6* provides the data on the number of victims of traffic accidents over the period 2014–2017.

Table 7 provides specific information on the conditions of victimisation. Referring to these data, it can be noted that the larger number of victims of road traffic accidents

Table 4 Crime Victims According to Gender per 100,000 Inhabitants

Type of offence	2014			2015			2016			2017		
	Total	**F**	**M**	**Total**	**F**	**M**	**Total**	**F**	**M**	**Total**	**F**	**M**
Murder	5.01	0.40	4.60	2.10	0.20	1.90	0.86	0.13	0.73	1.90	0.06	1.84
Attempted murder	6.30	0.44	5.80	5.40	0.27	5.13	5.80	0.34	5.46	5.70	0.50	5.20
Homicide	0.20	0.07	0.13	0.17	0.03	0.14	0.13	0.00	0.13	0.10	0.03	0.07
Domestic murder	–	–	–	0.70	0.34	0.36	0.66	0.45	0.21	0.50	0.30	0.20
Grievous bodily harm (intentional)	5.04	0.24	4.80	6.34	0.30	6.04	4.38	0.17	4.21	4.90	0.30	4.60
Grievous bodily harm (unintentional)	–	–	–	0.24	0.03	0.21	0.38	0.03	0.35	0.24	0.00	0.24
Kidnapping/unlawful deprivation of freedom	0.07	0.00	0.07	0.10	0.06	0.04	0.17	0.03	0.14	0.06	0.00	0.06
Robbery	8.8	2.00	6.80	6.50	1.30	5.20	4.70	1.25	3.35	5.63	1.30	4.30
Armed robbery	2.03	0.20	1.80	2.00	0.27	1.73	0.60	0.03	0.57	0.62	0.03	0.59
Robbery/ death of the victim	0.13	0.10	0.03	0.13	0.06	0.07	0.25	0.03	0.22	0.03	0.03	0.00
Fraud	–	–	–	22.90	5.40	17.50	28.20	8.60	19.60	27.40	7.80	19.60
Document forgery	–	–	–	9.10	1.80	7.30	9.40	2.30	7.10	10.50	2.70	7.80
Sexual crimes	–	–	–	5.00	4.10	0.90	4.20	3.75	0.45	4.00	3.50	0.50
Domestic violence	142.50	106.80	35.70	47.70	34.40	13.30	56.10	40.00	16.10	53.80	38.50	15.30
Trafficking of adult persons	1.70	1.24	0.46	1.38	1.14	0.24	0.90	0.80	0.10	0.70	0.60	0.10
Trafficking of minors	0.30	0.20	0.10	0.55	0.34	0.21	0.62	0.45	0.17	0.60	0.40	0.20
Other	0.13	–	–	5.47	–	–	5.10	–	–	0.03	–	–
Total	172.20	–	–	110.50	–	–	119.80	–	–	116.70	–	–

Source: Data Taken From the General Directorate of Albanian State Police 2018 (unpublished)

Table 5 Victims of Road Traffic Accidents per 100,000 Inhabitants

Number of victims	2014	2015	2016	2017
Total	90.40	93.20	96.60	90.80
Injured	66.20	69.00	70.70	68.70
Dead	9.10	9.30	9.35	7.70

Source: Data Taken From the Tirana Regional Road Traffic Directory 2018 (unpublished).

Table 6 Number of Road Traffic Victims in Tirana County per 100,000 Inhabitants

Number of victims	2014	2015	2016	2017
Total	95.70	85.70	99.30	104.40
Dead	5.02	5.03	6.16	4.98
Serious injuries	9.40	13.00	15.20	11.50
Non-serious injuries	81.20	67.80	77.90	87.90

Source: Data Taken From the Tirana Regional Road Traffic Directory 2018 (unpublished).

for the year 2017 were males (570 male and 330 female victims). More frequent car accidents are registered in the time-frame from 8.00 am to 5.00 pm and from 7.00 pm to 12.00 am. Most of the accidents are not caused by bad road conditions or by a vehicle defect. Also, there is no significant number of registered accidents on days of bad weather. Most of the accidents occur during the daytime, in normal light conditions. The most frequent traffic violations leading to car accidents are: not respecting other vehicle's priority in passing, too close driving distance between the cars, fast change of the driving lane, exceeding speed limits, driving under the influence of alcohol/drugs. Most of the accidents are caused by drivers who 3–6 years' experience in driving, belonging to the group aged 25–35 years old. From a total of 734 accidents in the year 2017, 565 accidents were caused by the driver's conduct, and 169 by the pedestrian's conduct.

5. Public Discourses about Victims: Their Rights, Protection, and Victimisation

Among the main concerns shared in public discourses and various victims' studies are those related to capacity building, limitation of human and material resources to offer supportive services to victims of crime, problems of inter-agency coordination, and inefficiencies in the identification of victims of human-trafficking. In relation to victims of human trafficking, experts note that high staff turnover among police

Table 7 Figures on Road Traffic Accidents in the Region of Tirana per100,000 Inhabitants in 2017

		Vehicle involved		Dead		Serious injuries		Non-serious injuries	
Description	**Number of accidents**	**Insured car**	**Uninsured car**	**Males**	**Females**	**Males**	**Females**	**Males**	**Females**
Total	734	875	103	27	16	65	34	478	280
Day of accident	734	874	103	27	16	65	34	478	280
Monday	115	149	18	5	2	11	11	76	32
Tuesday	112	129	13	5	3	12	3	73	41
Wednesday	100	126	15	5	3	12	4	68	36
Thursday	108	124	18	4	0	9	5	67	40
Friday	100	112	10	2	2	3	4	64	49
Saturday	108	129	14	2	1	8	6	68	43
Sunday	91	105	15	4	5	10	1	62	39
Time of accident	734	874	103	27	16	65	34	478	280
00.00–06.00 am	51	65	7	3	2	4	1	44	16
06.00–08.00 am	45	55	5	3	0	3	4	28	20
08.00–12.00 am	191	227	24	7	3	19	5	116	77
12.00–2.00 pm	103	115	14	0	3	10	6	61	40
2.00–5.00 pm	121	154	21	6	1	7	5	91	36
5.00–7.00 pm	79	99	13	2	4	8	5	48	27
7.00–12.00 am	144	159	19	6	3	14	8	90	64
Classification of the road	734	874	103	27	16	65	34	478	280
Highway	2	1	0	0	0	0	0	2	1
Primary interurban road	74	115	3	5	4	4	2	60	43

Table 7 cont. Figures on Road Traffic Accidents in the Region of Tirana per100,000 Inhabitants in 2017

Description	Number of accidents	Vehicle involved		Dead		Serious injuries		Non-serious injuries	
		Insured car	Uninsured car	Males	Females	Males	Females	Males	Females
Secondary interurban road	84	110	12	9	2	9	9	59	24
Primary urban road	327	382	42	8	7	29	16	188	136
Secondary urban road	222	242	39	5	3	16	5	156	68
Local road	24	23	7	0	0	7	2	13	7
Other (car park, ports, airports)	1	1	0	0	0	0	0	0	1
Road conditions	734	874	103	27	16	65	34	478	280
Good	724	867	99	26	16	65	34	473	275
Road with holes	3	0	3	0	0	0	0	2	2
Waving road	1	0	1	0	0	0	0	1	0
Slippery road	5	6	0	1	0	0	0	2	2
Dusty road	1	1	0	0	0	0	0	0	1
Weather	734	874	103	27	16	65	34	478	280
Dry weather	656	779	89	20	12	55	32	437	245
Wet weather	74	91	13	7	4	9	2	38	34
Snow/frost	4	4	1	0	0	1	0	3	1
Foggy weather	0	0	0	0	0	0	0	0	0
Light conditions	734	874	103	27	16	65	34	478	280
Day	522	633	75	16	9	49	27	333	197
Night	185	215	24	9	6	15	6	129	71
Sunrise/sunset	27	26	4	2	1	1	1	16	12

Age of the driver	734	874	103	27	16	65	34	478	280
0–16 years	1	0	1	0	0	0	0	0	1
16–25 years	152	205	16	5	4	22	7	100	59
25–35 years	231	296	40	10	9	19	15	155	81
35–45 years	121	158	14	6	1	10	5	71	51
45–60 years	127	157	18	4	0	11	6	84	51
> 60 years	43	47	11	1	0	3	1	32	15
Driver leaving the scene of the accident	**59**	**11**	**3**	**1**	**2**	**0**	**0**	**36**	**22**
Experience in driving	734	874	103	27	16	65	34	478	280
No driving license	38	23	19	1	0	5	2	25	12
0–3 years	74	96	5	2	6	12	3	47	29
3–6 years	278	382	29	10	5	28	13	189	103
6–9 years	138	170	25	6	3	9	7	88	49
> 9 years	147	192	22	7	0	11	9	93	65
Conduct of the users of the road as a cause of the accident	734	874	103	27	16	65	34	478	280
Driver's conduct	565	725	96	16	9	52	20	414	204
Close distance between cars	38	62	4	0	0	6	0	33	12
Unexpected braking	16	27	5	0	0	1	0	11	11
Ignoring traffic signs	15	23	2	0	0	0	0	13	8
Driving a car back without care and attention	0	0	0	0	0	0	0	0	0

Table 7 cont. Figures on Road Traffic Accidents in the Region of Tirana per100,000 Inhabitants in 2017

		Vehicle involved		Dead		Serious injuries		Non-serious injuries	
Description	**Number of accidents**	**Insured car**	**Uninsured car**	**Males**	**Females**	**Males**	**Females**	**Males**	**Females**
Non-respecting the lanes	0	0	0	0	0	0	0	0	0
Exceeding speed limits	54	65	9	2	1	10	3	39	11
Inappropriate stop/parking	6	7	0	0	0	0	1	5	2
Fast change of the driving lane	73	91	15	2	0	4	4	51	28
Not respecting a "Stop" sign	4	6	0	0	1	0	0	2	4
Not respecting another vehicle's priority in passing	182	211	24	4	4	12	6	110	73
Incorrect passing of another car	19	31	3	0	0	2	0	20	6
Use of alcohol/drugs	38	47	12	3	2	5	3	28	13
Other	120	155	22	5	1	12	3	102	36
Pedestrian's conduct	169	149	7	11	7	13	14	64	76
Incorrectly crossing the road	51	48	0	5	2	1	1	22	25
Crossing across an uninterrupted line	10	9	1	0	0	0	2	2	8
Other	108	92	6	6	5	12	11	40	43

Source: Data Taken From the Tirana Regional Road Traffic Directory 2018 (unpublished).

officers and prosecutors leads to serious gaps in the referral mechanism because anti-trafficking knowledge and expertise is not handed over to new colleagues.[106] The 2017 US Department of State Report on Trafficking in Persons noted that the Government of Albania does not fully meet the minimum standards for the elimination of trafficking.[107] The government demonstrated increasing efforts by prosecuting and convicting more traffickers and using, for the first time, its "special fund" towards victim protection from assets seized from traffickers.[108] However, the government did not meet minimum standards in several key areas (i.e., police reflected problems of a limited understanding of human trafficking and failed, in some cases, to identify victims of trafficking).

The report recommended the implementation of training programmes for the police, labour inspectors, border police, and other front-line officials on proactive identification of victims; the establishment of a sustainable funding mechanisms for mobile units operated by law enforcement and civil society groups to identify victims; increased protection for victims from threats and intimidation during court proceedings by facilitating participation in the witness protection program; increased funding of NGO-run shelters for trafficking victims and providing funding on a regular basis.[109]

Other reports emphasise the need for the government to take necessary measures to effectively eliminate the worst forms of child labour and economic exploitation of minors. Special attention should be paid to the situation of street children in the context of the country's policy on providing adequate protection for children.[110]

A very worrisome problem for Albanian society remains the phenomenon of domestic violence. Official statistics show that this is one the most widespread crimes affecting Albanian women. NGOs made a public call with a letter to the government to take action to effectively prevent and fight violence against women, particularly victims of domestic violence. The public letter stated that

> Domestic violence has been treated more as an individual problem belonging only to family members and not the society, while it is both a government and individual responsibility to undertake efficient steps in protecting women and children as well as preventing violence.[111]

---

106 International Centre for Migration Policy Development 2015.

107 U.S. Department of State, Office to Monitor and Combat Trafficking in Persons 2017.

108 U.S. Department of State, Office to Monitor and Combat Trafficking in Persons 2017.

109 U.S. Department of State, Office to Monitor and Combat Trafficking in Persons 2017.

110 United Nation Human Rights Council 2017.

111 Tirana Times of 11.11.2016; Only one out of seven women report domestic violence cases; http://www.tiranatimes.com/?p=129869 [29.05.2019].

In its 2015 EU Enlargement Strategy Report on Albania, the European Commission highlighted that, in terms of protection of fundamental rights, there is "poor functioning of mechanisms to address gender equality and gender-based violence".[112]

In the fight against domestic violence it is also crucial to address the factors which may still prevent women from filing complaints regarding episodes of violence. There is a national government-run shelter for victims of domestic violence located in Tirana, which opened in 2011.The 2015 EU commission report noted that the number of shelters and reintegration services needs to be increased, and existing volunteer-run shelters have yet to be supported by the authorities. Due to poor administrative and financial resources, the national referral mechanism for preventing domestic violence is operational in very few municipalities, and it applies unnecessarily restrictive admission criteria for victims.[113]

6. Conclusions

International regulations relating to victims of crime and domestic legislation and strategic documents adopted in their response establish a complete regulatory framework on the rights, support, and protection of victims of crime. They provide for a variety of rights that victims enjoy over the course of criminal proceedings and beyond, and describe the related tools and procedures necessary for the effective implementation of these rights. Even though the Albanian government has made significant progress on passing legislation that meets international standards on the status and treatment of crime victims, there are many challenges at the implementation level.

First, there is a significant lack of supportive programmes to ensure medical, psychological, and social assistance to victims of crime. There is a relative low number of actors (public or private actors) involved in offering such services and there is no integrated system of victim support services. Besides state action, it is necessary to further promote the involvement of non-profit organisations with experience in supporting victims and offer funding opportunities to sustain their engagement. Also, a monitoring system needs to be designed in order to measure the performance of all actors involved in victim support programmes. Concerning victims of violent and serious crime, a promising solution would be the adoption of an integrated strategy to support and protect victims rather than narrow sectorial strategies. Such an alternative seems to be more adequate because it allows for concentration of capacities and resources by engaging staff and structures in some common supportive frames, rather than engaging them in different, and sometimes, inconsistent lines of action. Another issue that needs to be addressed is the effective implementation of free le-

112 European Commission 2015.

113 European Commission 2015.

gal aid for victims of crime. It is necessary that the State Commission on Legal Aid drafts guidelines to specify the responsibilities of the actors involved. In addition, specific funds of the Commission's budget need to be designed to support the legal aid system for victims of crime.

Second, there is an urgent need to establish a compensatory scheme for victims of organised crime and avoid the technical obstacles that complicate compensation for victims of crime in general. The purpose of any effort to emancipate victims is undermined when their financial stability is at question. In relation to compensation of victims of organised crime and human trafficking, the specific legislation[114] provides for the creation of a state body that would administer the process. So far, this structure has not been created and no regulation has been made concerning the specific rules and practices according to which the compensation mechanism will operate. It is worth mentioning that such a compensation scheme would still not satisfy the obligation imposed by the Convention on Compensation of Victims of Violent Crimes to create a state compensation scheme to support all victims of violent crime.[115]

Third, capacity building is essential to protect victims and ensure their fair treatment throughout the criminal proceedings. In this respect, there is a need for the special training of judges, prosecutors, lawyers, and law enforcement officers to enhance their knowledge on the instruments and mechanisms available to protect victims, especially in the light of the new amendments made to the Criminal Procedure Code in 2017. Specific training programmes need to be designed and conducted by the School of Magistrates, the Academy of Security, the Faculty of Social Sciences (Department of Psychology and Social Sciences), the Bar Association, the Association of Mediators, the Probation Service, and the State Agency for the Rights and Protection of Minors. It is important that such training courses do not include only legal and technical terms, but also the human and communication components that dominate in the professional interaction with victims of crime.

Last but not least, it is very important to establish an official system for the registration of crime victims. Adequate statistical data collection is an essential component of evidence-based policy decisions. So far, the only information recorded is the one provided in the register of criminal offences which shows the victim's name, age, and whether he/she is Albanian or not. It is clear that this is insufficient for the mapping of the victimological landscape of the country. The very limited data about victims of crime seriously limit the opportunities to identify the most vulnerable groups and their demographic characteristics, as well as the ability to decide on the most adequate lines of intervention and determine the expected outcomes.

---

114 See Law No. 10 192

115 OSCE 2008, p. 66.

7. Summary in Albanian

Punimi paraqet një panoramë të përgjithshme mbi statusin e viktimave në legjislacionin penal shqiptar, të politikave penale për mbrojtjen e viktimave të krimit dhe parandalimin e viktimizimit, si dhe një analizë të situatës aktuale të vikitimizimit në Shqipëri, dhe të programmeve e mekanizmave të ngritura në mbështetje të viktimave të krimit. Punimi paraqet gjithashtu aspekte të drejtësisë restauruese, ta padisë civile në procesin penal dhe të formave të kompensimit për viktimat e krimit. Nje pjesë e studimit analizon parashikimet specifike të legjislacionit penal material dhe procedural në mbrojtje të viktimave dhe efektivitetin e zbatimit të tyre. Në mënyrë të vecantë punimi studion statusin procedural të viktimave pas ndryshimeve që pësoi Kodi i Procedurës Penale me ligjin 35/2017 me qëllim përafrimin e ligjit tonë procedural me standartet e vendosura nga Direktiva 2012/29 e Bashkimit Evropian lidhur me trajtimin e viktimave të krimit. Punimi synon gjithashtu të paraqesë një panoramë të situatës aktuiale të viktimizimit në Shqipëri, duke analizuar statistikat zyrtare mbi viktimat e krimit në vend. Së fundmi, trajtesa synon të evidentojë disa probleme që kërkojnë adresim të mëtejshëm në nivelin e zbatimit të masave për mbrojtjen e viktimave të tilla si: mungesa e fondeve për zbatimin e skemës për kompensimin e viktimave të krimit, mungesa e trajnimit në radhët e punonjësve ligjzbatues, paaftësia për të identifikuar nevojat specifike për mbrojtje për kategori të caktuara viktimash, mungesa e statistikave të integruara për viktimat e krimit, probleme në sigurimin e ndihmës ligjore falas dhe të shërbimeve të integruara sociale, si dhe mungesa e studimeve gjithëpërfshirëse mbi situatën e viktimizimit në vend.

Literature

Biçoku, A., Kuri, V. & Luniku, R. (2017): Shërbimet sociale me viktimat e trafikuara në Shqipëri [Social services for victims of trafficking in Albania]. Tirana.

Gjebrea, L. (ed.) (2016): The national strategy on the fight against trafficking of human beings and the trafficking of children 2014–2017. Tirana.

Goldson, B. (2008): Dictionary of youth justice. Oregon.

Hysi, V. (2005): Kriminologija [Criminology]. Tirana.

Ismaili, E. (2015): Bullizmi tek shkollat 9-vjeçare të Tiranës [Bullying in secondary education schools in Tirana]. Tirana.

Kola, J. & Nela, A. (2016): Viktimat e minave dhe municioneve në Shqipëri: vështrim i përgjithshëm i gjendjes dhe nevojave [Victims of mines and munitions in Albania: An overview of the state of the art and needs]. Tirana.

McLaughlin, E. & Muncle, J. (2013): The Sage dictionary of criminology. London.

Meshi, M., Picari, B. & Pinderi, R. (2009): Studim mbi riintegrimin social-ekonomik të viktimave të trafikimit në Shqipëri [Study on the social and economic reintegration of victims of trafficking in Albania]. Tirana.

Pustina, H. (2012): Ish i perndjekuri politik Ndreca digjet me benzine [Former political persecution of Ndreca burns with gasoline], in: Panorama online, 8.10.2012; http://www.panorama.com.al/ish-i-burgosuri-politik-ndreca-i-ve-flaken-vetes/.

Wemmers, J.A. (2010): A short history of victimology, published, in: O. Hagemann, P. Schäfer & S. Schmidt (eds.), Victimology, victim assistance and criminal justice: Perspectives shared by international experts at the Inter-University Centre of Dubrovnik; https://papers.ssrn.com/sol3/papers.cfm?abstract_id=2482627 [20.05.2019].

Documents

Albanian Helsinki Committee (2019): Kreu [Home]; http://www.ahc.org.al/?lang=en [29.05.2019] [in Albanian and English].

Albanian Helsinki Committee (2017): Manual 2017 [Manual 2017]; http://www.ahc.org.al/wp-content/uploads/2018/02/MANUAL-1-2017.pdf [20.05.2019] [in Albanian only].

Albanian Rehabilitation Centre for Trauma and Torture (2019): About ARCT 20-years history; http://www.arct.org/index.php/about-us [20.05.2019] [in English only].

Albanian Rehabilitation Centre for Trauma and Torture (2016): Annual report; http://www.arct.org/index.php/publications/human-right-and-justice [20.05.2019] [in English only].

Ariadne Network (2012): Regional guidelines on the identification of trafficked persons: A manual for South-Eastern and Eastern Europe]; http://www.arct.org/media/attachments/2017/11/22/ariadne-brochure-embeded-links-web.pdf [20.050.2019] [in English only].

Center for Legal Civic Initiatives (2019): Rreth nesh [About us]; http://www.qag-al.org/ang/html/about.htm [20.05.2019] [in Albanian and English].

Center for Legal Civic Initiatives (2015): Promovimi i të Drejtave të Personave të Trafikuar në Shqipëri – Analizë ligjore e situatës aktuale lidhur me të drejtat e viktimave të trafikimit të qënieve njerëzore [Promotion of the Rights of Trafficked Persons in Albania – A legal analysis of the current situation in regard to the rights of victims of trafficking]. Tirana.

Council of Europe (2019): Lufta Kundër Bullizmit dhe Ekstremizmit në Sistemin Arsimor në Shqipëri [Fighting bullying and extremism in the education system in Albania]; https://www.coe.int/sq/web/tirana/fighting-bullying-and-extremism-in-the-education-system-in-albania1 [29.05.2019] [in Albanian and English].

European Commission (2015): Commission staff working document Albania 2015 report SWD(2015) 213 final. Brussels; https://ec.europa.eu/neighbourhood-enlargement/sites/near/files/pdf/key_documents/2015/20151110_report_albania.pdf [21.05.2019] [in Albanian and English].

HEUNI: see The European Institute for Crime Prevention and Control, affiliated with the United Nations.

Institute of Statistics (StatOffice) (2019): Statistikat sipas temave [Statistics by theme]; http://www.instat.gov.al/ [10.03.2019] [in Albanian and English]; cited as: StatOffice 2019.

Institute of Statistics (StatOffice) (2018a): Bujqësia [Agriculture]; http://www.instat.gov.al/al/temat/bujq%C3%ABsia-dhe-peshkimi/bujq%C3%ABsia/ [10.03.2018] [in Albanian and English]; cited as: StatOffice 2018a.

Institute of Statistics (StatOffice) (2018b): Punësimi dhe papunësia [Labour force survey 2017]; http://www.instat.gov.al/en/themes/labour-market-and-education/employment-and-unemployment-from-lfs/#tab3 [10.03.2018] [in Albanian and English]; cited as: StatOffice 2018b.

Institute of Statistics (StatOffice) (2017): Produkti i brendshëm bruto, 2015 [Gross domestic product, 2015]; http://www.instat.gov.al/en/themes/labour-market-and-education/education/ [29.05.2019] [in Albanian only]; cited as: StatOffice 2017.

Institute of Statistics (StatOffice) (2016): Nxënësit dhe studentët e diplomuar në kuadër të programeve të veçanta të studimit 2015–2016 [Graduated pupils and students under specific programs of study 2015–2016]; http://www.instat.gov.al/media/2093/produkti-i-brendsh%C3%ABm-bruto-final-2014-gjys%C3%ABm-final-2015.pdf [29.05.2019] [in Albanian and English]; cited as: StatOffice 2016.

Institute of Statistics (StatOffice) (2012): Censusi i Popullsisë dge banesave [Census of population and housing]; http://www.instat.gov.al/en/themes/censuses/census-of-population-and-housing/#tab1 [10.03.2018] [in Albanian and English]; cited as: StatOffice 2012.

International Centre for Migration Policy Development (2015): Fight against trafficking in human beings and organised crime – Phase 2 (Assessment of the national and transnational referral mechanism for victims of trafficking in Albania). Tirana.

Ministry of Justice (2017): Strategjia e drejtësisë për të mitur [National justice for children strategy 2017–2020]; https://drejtesia.gov.al/wp-content/uploads/2017/11/02_Strategjia_e_Drejtesise_per_te_Mitur_2017-2020_English.pdf [20.05.2019] [in Albanian and English].

OSCE (2008): Dëmshpërblimi për personat e trafikuar dhe të shfrytëzuar në rajonin e OSBE-së [Compensation for victims of trafficking and exploitation in the OSCE region]; http://www.osce.org/sq/odihr/75930?download=true [21.05.2019] [in Albanian only].

OSCE Presence in Albania (2014): Studim mbi çështjet e bashkëpunimit të viktimave të trafikimit me autoritetet e zbatimit të ligjit [Study on the cooperation between victims of trafficking and law enforcement authorities]. [in Albanian and English].

StatOffice: see Institute of Statistics.

Terre des Hommes in Albania (2019): Shqipëri [Albania]; https://www.tdh.ch/en/our-interventions/albania [29.05.2019] [in Albanian and English].

The European Institute for Crime Prevention and Control, affiliated with the United Nations (HEUNI) (2014): European Sourcebook of Crime and Criminal Justice Statistics 2014; https://www.heuni.fi/en/index/tiedotteet/2014/09/europeansourcebookofcrimeandcriminaljusticestatistics2014published.html [29.05.2019] [in English only]; cited as: HEUNI 2014.

U.S. Department of State, Office to Monitor and Combat Trafficking in Persons (2017): Trafficking of persons report; https://www.state.gov/j/tip/rls/tiprpt/countries/2017/271130.htm [20.05.2019] [in English only].

UNICEF (2016): Children, access to justice and discrimination. An overview of judicial decisions in relation to children from the point of view of discrimination and equality; https://www.unicef.org/albania/2016-Access_to_Justice.pdf [20.05.2019] [in English only].

United Nation Human Rights Council (2017): Mid-term report of Albania on the implementation of the recommendations received during the second cycle of Universal Periodic Review (UPR); https://www.upr-info.org/sites/default/files/document/albania/session_19_-_april_2014/albania-midterm-2017.pdf [21.05.2019] [in English only].

Austria

Monika Stempkowski & Barbara Kraml

1. Introduction and General Country Background

At the end of the Second World War, in 1945, Austria became a democratic republic. The constitution dates back to 1920 and was reinstated after the war. However, it was not until 1955 that Austria regained its independence. For ten years, the country was occupied by the four allies, the United States of America, the United Kingdom, France and the Soviet Union, until a State Treaty was signed, establishing Austria as an independent country. In 1958, Austria joined the European Convention of Human Rights, which is, since then, being enforced on a constitutional level within the Austrian legal system. Since 1995, Austria is a Member State of the European Union.

In 2017, Austria had a population of 8,795,073 people, 51% being female. In total, 1,395,880 inhabitants (15.9%) were of foreign nationality. 19.5% were children and juveniles up to 19 years, 61.8% were adults between 20 and 64 years of age and senior citizens aged 65 or older made up 18.7%. The mean age of the population was 42.6 years, the life expectancy of people born in 2017 amounted to 79.3 years for men and 83.9 years for women.[1] Regarding the highest level of education people had received, 18.3% of the population had only completed compulsory schooling up until the age of 15. 34.4% completed an education in the form of an apprenticeship mainly for craftsmanship. 30.2% finished secondary school, whereas 17.1% completed their education with an academic degree.[2] In 2018, the GDP per capita stood at 43,680 EUR, placing Austria on rank four within the European Union.[3]

Important entities within the Austrian criminal justice system are the federal police, the prosecution authorities and the judiciary. The Federal Criminal Police Office (Bundeskriminalamt) is heading nine State Criminal Police Offices (Landeskriminalämter), while it is subordinated to the Directorate General of Public Safety (Generaldirektion für die öffentliche Sicherheit), a department of the Federal Ministry of the Interior.

---

1 StatOffice 2019c.

2 StatOffice 2019b, p. 470.

3 StatOffice 2019d.

The main legal framework for the work of the police is the National Security Police Act (hereinafter NSPA; Sicherheitspolizeigesetz [SPG])[4]. Head of the investigation proceedings are the public prosecutors. This agency is not independent but subject to directives of the Senior Public Prosecutor's Office and subsequently the Federal Minister of Justice. The Public Prosecutor's Act regulates the organization of the agency. The judiciary is an independent agency, organized within the Federal Ministry of Justice. From the district courts to the Supreme Court, there are four levels of jurisdiction: 115 district courts, 20 courts of first instance, 4 higher regional courts and one Supreme Court. Important sources of law for the organization of the courts are the Court Organization Act (Gerichtsorganisationsgesetz [GOG])[5] and the Supreme Court Act (Gesetz über den Obersten Gerichtshof [OGH-Gesetz])[6]. The prison system is centrally organized by the Directorate General for the Administration of Custodial Sanctions and Measures Involving Deprivation of Liberty, a department of the Federal Ministry of Justice.[7]

In 2017, a total of 510,536 crimes were reported to the police.[8] Compared with the Austrian population, this results in 5,842 reported crimes per 100,000 inhabitants.[9] In Germany, which has a similar population structure and criminal justice system, this number was 6,982 in 2017.[10]

2. Current State of Victimology

2.1 Victimology as an Academic Discipline and Victimisation Surveys

Currently, victimology is not established as an academic discipline in Austria. There is no chair at an Austrian university dedicated to victimology. Academics engaged in the subject mostly teach criminal law and criminal procedure. The subject is mainly taught as part of the penal law education students receive within their legal studies. However, at most universities courses about victimological issues are not mandatory, but can be chosen by interested students as an optional subject. Thus, not everybody who receives a degree from a law faculty is automatically trained in victimology. Likewise, no aca-

4 National Security Police Act, Austrian Federal Law Gazette No. 566/1991, 31.10.1991, last amended by Austrian Federal Law Gazette I No. 55/2018, 14.08.2018.

5 Court Organisation Act, Official Gazette 217/1896, 27.11.1896, last amended by Austrian Federal Law Gazette No. 760/1996, 30.12.1996.

6 Supreme Court Act, Austrian Federal Law Gazette No. 328/1968, 28.08.1968, last amended by Austrian Federal Law Gazette I No. 112/2007, 28.12.2007.

7 Ministry of Justice 2016.

8 Federal Ministry of Internal Affairs 2018a.

9 Federal Ministry of Internal Affairs 2018b, p. 22.

10 Federal Ministry of the Interior, Construction and Homeland 2019, p. 12.

demic journal solely deals with victimological issues; corresponding articles are mainly published in general legal journals as well as journals covering criminal law. Currently, there is one textbook on victimology written by an Austrian professor, which covers victimology as a scientific discipline, main results of victimological research as well as the relevant legal framework within the Austrian criminal law system.[11]

Until this day, no general victimisation survey has been conducted in Austria. The country did participate in some international surveys, for example, the International Crime Victim Survey 1996 and 2004/2005.[12] On a national level, victimisation surveys were carried out on specific types of victimisation. For example, in 2011, the Austrian Institute for Family Studies (Österreichisches Institut für Familienforschung) published a study representative for the Austria population between 16 and 60 years of age concerning violence within the family and the close social environment.[13] Another example is a recent survey by the Research Centre for Human Rights (University of Vienna) in cooperation with the White Ring Austria studying victimisation experiences of a representative sample of women above the age of 15 in the field of online hate speech.[14]

2.2 Victim Support in Austria

There is room for improvement when it comes to the scientific institutionalisation of victimology. However, concerning victim protection, Austria has an elaborate system of supporting victims before and during criminal trials. Criminal procedure legislation has focused strongly on victims' needs throughout the proceedings in recent years. The danger of secondary victimisation because of the harmful treatment of victims by the police or judiciary are known, and various precautions are taken to prevent this kind of harm. Different public authorities are involved in developing and executing legislation aimed at protecting and supporting victims, e.g., the Federal Ministries of Justice, of the Interior and of Labour, Social Affairs, Health and Consumer Protection. A variety of NGOs are engaged in providing assistance on a legal as well as emotional level.[15] While procedural provisions will be explained in *section 3,* an overview of the most important governmental entities as well as NGOs is laid out in the following paragraphs.

2.2.1 General Victim Support

The most prominent victim support organization in Austria is the local branch of the White Ring Austria, which was founded in 1978, thereby celebrating its 40th

---

11 *Sautner* 2014.

12 *Van Dijk, van Manchin, Kesteren & van Hideg* 2007.

13 *Kapella, Baierl, Rille-Pfeiffer, Geserick & Schmid* 2011.

14 Research Centre for Human Rights/White Ring Austria 2018.

15 For an overview of organizations and the respective web pages, see *Sautner* 2014, p. 191.

founding year in 2018. Run as a private NGO, the organization is mainly funded by donations as well as the financing of services by public authorities like the Federal Ministry of Justice.[16] Victims receive counselling and psychological support as well as legal advice. The White Ring Austria also offers psycho-social and legal assistance for the proceedings (see *Section 3.2.4* and *4.3*). Should the situation of the victim require immediate financial support, the White Ring Austria is able to assist by providing shopping vouchers, interest-free loans or direct financial support. Apart from these individual services for victims of crime, the White Ring Austria also plays an important role when it comes to lobbying for the institutionalization and funding of victims' rights. In 2018, 2,061 victims received extensive personal support; the White Ring Austria had already supported 81% of them in 2017. Individual counselling, therefore, often stretches over a period of more than a year. In 43.5% crimes against life or physical integrity had been committed, 20.5% had been crimes against freedom, and 18% concerned offences against personal property.[17]

Additionally to personal counselling, the White Ring Austria runs a victim support hotline (Opfer-Notruf), reachable around the clock every day of the year.[18] Counselling on the phone is free of charge and anonymous, offering first aid concerning psychological harm as well as primary legal advice. Should further support be necessary, the victim is referred to a competent expert. The service is paid for by the Federal Ministry of Justice.[19] In 2018, the support hotline registered 13,209 calls, resulting in 31 calls on average every day. The distribution based on the type of offence was similar to the one found in the personal support service of the White Ring Austria; most cases referred to offences against life or physical integrity, followed by offences against freedom and personal property. In 61%, the caller was female.[20]

Other than this form of general victim support, a variety of organizations can be found engaged in supporting specific groups of victims. In order to coordinate those organizations as well as the involved federal ministries, the police and the judiciary, the Management Centre for Victim Support (Managementzentrum Opferhilfe) was installed in 2011.[21] The centre is financed by the Federal Ministry of Justice and is also concerned with the development of educational standards for people engaged in the field of victim support.[22] The organization is run by the Centre of Legal Competence – Forschung und Consulting GmbH.[23]

---

16 White Ring 2018.

17 White Ring 2019, p. 9.

18 Victim Emergency Call 2019.

19 *Nachbaur* 2017, p. 226.

20 White Ring 2019, p. 9.

21 Federal Ministry of Justice 2011.

22 Federal Ministry of Constitution, Reforms, Deregulation and Justice 2019a.

23 Centre of legal competence 2019.

2.2.2 Specialized Victim Support: Women as Victims of Domestic Violence

As one important example of areas in which different organizations are engaging in helping victims, the support network for women who have become victims of domestic violence shall be explained in detail: women's shelters, domestic abuse intervention centres and the women's helpline against violence.

In order to ensure the immediate safety of women exposed to domestic violence, a network of women's shelters, organized in two associations, offers a safe space for the women and their children all over Austria. The shelters provide temporary accommodation as well as counselling and support in dealing with the authorities and organizing a safe environment for the time after the women leave the shelter. For safety reasons, the addresses of the shelters are kept secret and are only given to the women calling in for help. The nine regional governments mainly fund the women's shelters[24]. In 2018, 30 houses all over Austria provided a total of 766 places for victims to stay. In the same year, 3,284 people (1,664 women and 1,620 children) received help in one of those shelters.[25] On average, a woman stayed in the shelter for 63 days.[26] Apart from their work with women and children as victims, the employees of the women's shelter engage in education, prevention, networking with other organizations and media information. Unfortunately, the number of places provided is not enough to accommodate every victim requiring shelter. In an emergency, extra beds can be set up, so that no endangered woman has to be sent away. Nevertheless, the Council of Europe suggests providing one place in a women's shelter for 10,000 inhabitants.[27] Given the Austria population of about 8.8 million inhabitants, 880 places would be needed to fulfil this requirement.

The women's helpline against violence serves as a first contact point for victims experiencing or threatened by violence, offering counselling, information concerning legal questions and support systems as well as information about possibilities for women's shelters. Additionally, the helpline also informs girls about questions concerning puberty, sexuality and pregnancy and offers information for women concerning depression, divorce, or coping with critical life events. While the information in German and English is available 24 hours every day, the information in Bosnian-Croatian-Serbian, Romanian, Turkish, Arabic and Hungarian is offered at certain times every week.[28] Like the other support systems, the helpline is free of

---

24 Association of Austrian Autonomous Women's Shelters/Vienna Intervention Centre against Domestic Violence 2016, p. 76.

25 Association of Austrian Women's Shelters 2019; Autonomous Austrian Women's Shelters 2018b, p. 63.

26 Autonomous Austrian Women's Shelters 2018a, p. 2; 2018b, p. 63.

27 Council of Europe 2008, p. 51.

28 Women's Helpline against Violence 2019a.

charge for the callers and is financed by the Federal Ministry of Women, Families and Youth. In 2018, the helpline received a total of 8,581 calls, 86.4% coming from women and girls. If men are calling the helpline, it is mainly to receive information about how to support a female relative or friend exposed to violence. 61% of the female callers contacted the hotline because of experiences with violence.[29]

Finally, the Domestic Abuse Intervention Centres also play an important part within the support system for women as victims of domestic violence.[30] If the victim is exposed to domestic violence, the police can enact a barring order, prohibiting the perpetrator from entering the home of the victim or their joint home respectively for a period of two weeks. The ownership of the home is irrelevant, thereby providing the victim with a safe space after an immediate danger. Should the victim wish to extend the length of the barring order, an application for a temporary injunction can be filed before a civil court, which can extend the period of time up to six months.[31] Whenever a barring order is issued, the police informs the regional Domestic Abuse Intervention Centre, providing it with the personal data of the victim. The employees of the Intervention then contact the victim pro-actively and offer their services. They provide the victim with information about legal as well as psychological support options and they also offer psycho-social and legal assistance for the proceedings (see *Section 3.2.4* and *4.3)*. Since victims are under immense personal stress and often experience feelings of intense fear, they sometimes do not find the strength to reach out for help. This danger can be intercepted by the Intervention Centres contacting the victim pro-actively.[32] In 2017, 18,860 people received help and information from one of the Intervention Centres, which are spread all over Austria. 83% of the victims were female.[33] The Intervention Centres are funded by the Federal Ministries of the Interior as well as Labor, Social Affairs, Health and Consumer Protection. Additionally, centres receive remuneration for their work within the system of psycho-social and legal assistance for the proceedings.[34]

3. Legal Framework

This section gives an overview of the legal framework regarding victim rights and victim protection in criminal proceedings.[35] There are, indeed, other legal fields

---

29 Women's Helpline against Violence 2019b, p. 13.

30 *Sorgo* 2005, p. 197.

31 Domestic Abuse Intervention Centre Vienna/Association of Austrian Autonomous Women's Shelters 2019, p. 2.

32 *Hojas* 2014, p. 386.

33 Domestic Abuse Intervention Centre Vienna 2018, p. 34.

34 *Nachbaur* 2017, p. 228.

35 Cited legislation refers to the version of the legislation applicable on 31st October 2019 as specified upon first mention of the legal provision.

which contain regulations concerning victims as well. The Austrian civil procedure law contains an option to extend psycho-social support for victims, originally granted for the criminal proceedings, to a trial before a civil court (see *Section 4.3.1*) and to seek a temporary injunction before a civil court in order to secure provisional protection of the victim (see *Section 2.2.2*). In cases of domestic violence, the Austrian security police law offers the legal opportunity to enact a barring order, prohibiting the perpetrator from entering the home of the victim or their joint home respectively for a period of two weeks (see *Section 2.2.2*). Due to space constraints, the following subsections deal only with legal provisions concerning criminal proceedings.[36]

3.1 Historical Development

Up until the 1970's, victims appeared in Austrian criminal procedural law primarily in conjunction with their claims for compensation; other necessities remained largely unconsidered. Starting with an amendment in 1987,[37] the legislative attention has shifted more and more from monetary to non-pecuniary interests and needs of victims, which has led to several subsequent amendments to the Austrian Code of Criminal Procedure (hereinafter CCP; Strafprozessordnung [StPO])[38] up until now. This development has been characterized by conflicting interests between strengthening victims' procedural rights and, at the same time, safeguarding the rights of defendants.[39]

In the course of this development, important impulses have been provided by legal requirements stemming from European Union level, in particular, the Council Framework Decision of 15 March 2001 on the standing of victims in criminal proceedings (2001/220/JHA)[40] and, succeeding the latter, the Directive 2012/29/EU of the European Parliament and of the Council of 25 October 2012 establishing minimum standards on the rights, support and protection of victims of crime, and replacing Council Framework Decision 2001/220/JHA.[41] These legal requirements are binding for the

---

36 The English translations of the legal provisions cited in this article stem from *Schloenhardt & Höpfel* (2016) regarding the Austrian Criminal Code (ACC) and from *Schloenhardt, Eder & Höpfel* (2019) regarding the Austrian Code of Criminal Procedure (CCP), complemented by translations of recent legislative changes by the authors of this article.

37 Strafrechtsänderungsgesetz 1987 (amendment of the Code of Criminal Procedure), Austrian Federal Law Gazette (Bundesgesetzblatt) No. 605/1987, 22.12.1987.

38 Code of Criminal Procedure (CCP), Austrian Federal Law Gazette No. 631/1975, 30.12.1975, last amended by Strafrechtsänderungsgesetz 2018, Austrian Federal Law Gazette I No. 70/2018, 25.10.2018.

39 *Kier* 2017a point 2 et seq with further references.

40 Council framework Decision of 15 March 2001 on the standing of victims in criminal proceedings, Decision No. 2001/220/JHA, Official Journal of the European Communities L-82/2001, 22.03.2001, p. 1.

41 Directive 2012/29/EU of the European Parliament and of the Council of 25 October 2012 establishing minimum standards on the rights, support and protection of victims of crime,

member states and had to be implemented as minimum standards regarding victims' rights, support and protection in national procedural law. Due to the implementation[42] of the Council Framework Decision 2001/220/JHA, the legal term "victim" has been adopted into domestic law and has been introduced to the CCP in 2008.[43] The subsequent Victims' Rights Directive 2012/29/EU was implemented in 2016.[44]

3.2 Victim Rights in Criminal Proceedings

Victim participation, victim rights and victim protection form an important part of the legal provisions regarding criminal proceedings in Austria. The principle of victim participation in criminal proceedings as laid down in Article 10 of the CCP states that, as a general rule, victims of criminal offences are entitled to participate in criminal proceedings subject to the provisions in Chapter 4 of the CCP (Article 10 paragraph 1 CCP). According to Article 10 paragraph 2 of the CCP, criminal investigation and prosecution authorities and the courts have a duty to give reasonable consideration to the rights, interests, and special protection needs of victims of criminal offences; additionally, they have to inform all victims about the fundamental rights during the proceedings and about the possibility to obtain compensation or assistance.

Article 10 paragraph 3 of the CCP refers to protection needs of crime victims on the one hand and their reparation interests on the other. All authorities, institutions and persons engaged in criminal proceedings have the duty to treat victims with due regard for their personal dignity and respect their interest to keep their personal sphere protected during the proceedings, specifically concerning the transfer of photographs and the communication of personal information that may lead to their identity being released to a larger number of people without this being warranted for criminal justice purposes. The prosecution authority and the court have to examine the victims' reparation interests in any decision about the conclusion of the proceedings and have to support these interests to the greatest possible extent.

3.2.1 Definition of "Victim"

The fourth chapter of the Austrian CCP, which puts the principles mentioned above (Article 10 of the CCP) in concrete terms, starts with definitions of the legal term "victim". As some of the legal provisions regarding victim rights and victim protec-

and replacing Council Framework Decision 2001/220/JHA, Directive No. 2012/29/EU, Official Journal of the European Union L-315/2012, 14.11.2012, p. 57.

42 Strafprozessreformgesetz (amendment of the Code of Criminal Procedure), Austrian Federal Law Gazette I No. 19/2004, 23.03.2004.

43 *Pühringer* 2011, p. 25.

44 Strafprozessrechtsänderungsgesetz I 2016 (amendment of the Code of Criminal Procedure), Austrian Federal Law Gazette I No. 26/2016, 20.05.2016.

tion apply only to specific groups of victims, the definitions laid down in Article 65 subparagraph 1 litera a to c of the CCP are crucial in view of the actual claiming of these rights in practice.

According to Article 65 subparagraph 1 litera a of the CCP, the first group of victims defined are persons who, through an intentionally committed criminal offence, might have been exposed to violence or dangerous threats, or might have been violated in their sexual integrity or sexual self-determination, or whose personal dependency might have been exploited by such an offence. The second category of victims stipulated in Article 65 subparagraph 1 litera b of the CCP includes the spouse, registered partner, domestic partner, relatives in a direct ancestral line, siblings, and other dependants of a person, whose death might have been caused by a criminal offence, or other relatives[45] who were witnesses of the crime. These two categories of victims are perceived as particularly affected by the crime in question, which is why specific additional rights and protection are due to these victims (see *Sections 3.2.3* and *3.2.4*). The third definition of victim is worded much more generally and the broadest of all three definitions; Article 65 subparagraph 1 litera c of the CCP determines any other person a victim who might have suffered damage or whose legal interests protected by criminal law might have been violated through a criminal offence.

In order to gain compensation and to avoid further civil proceedings to seek restitution for damages suffered by the criminal offence, victims have the possibility to join the criminal proceedings as the so-called "private party" (Articles 67 and 69 of the CCP; see *Section 3.2.5.1*). Therefore, private party refers to any victim stating that she or he will participate in the proceedings in order to receive compensation for damages or violations suffered (Article 65 subparagraph 2 of the CCP). It is necessary to formally distinguish the role of the victim from a private party in proceedings, although in practice both roles frequently coincide, because private parties enjoy additional rights in proceedings compared to victims (Article 67 paragraph 6 of the CCP).

3.2.2 Victim Rights in General

According to Article 66 paragraph 1 of the CCP, all victims within the meaning of Article 65 subparagraph 1 of the CCP have a set of procedural rights they might em-

---

45 According to Article 72 paragraph 1 of the ACC, relatives of a person include all relatives and in-laws in direct ancestral line of that person; the person's spouse or registered partner, the siblings of the spouse or registered partner; the person's siblings and their spouses or registered partners, children and grandchildren; the siblings of the person's parents and grandparents; the person's cousins; the other parent of the person's child; the person's adoptive and foster parents; the parent's adoptive and foster children; as well as other persons for whom the person is a guardian or under whose guardianship the person is. Additionally, persons in a domestic relationship are treated as relatives; children and grandchildren of one of the domestic partners are treated as relatives of either partner (Article 72 paragraph 2 of the ACC).

ploy in the course of the proceedings. These general victim rights mainly encompass the rights of information and participation in criminal proceedings, but also the right to interpretation and translation, and the right to have their special protection needs assessed as soon as possible (Article 66 paragraph 1 litera 1b and Article 66a of the CCP; see *Section 3.2.3*).

3.2.2.1 Informational rights

Regarding informational rights, victims have the right to obtain information about the subject matter of the proceedings and their principal rights before being questioned as a witness (Article 66 paragraph 1 subparagraph 3 of the CCP). The right to obtain information is specified in greater detail in Article 70 paragraph 1 of the CCP. As a general rule, the criminal investigation authority or the prosecution authority has to inform the victims about their fundamental rights as laid down in Articles 66 to 67 of the CCP as soon as investigation proceedings are conducted against a particular accused person. This information of a victim may only be omitted so long as this would jeopardize the purpose of the investigations and needs to take place before their first interview as a witness at the latest. Additionally, victims within the meaning of Article 65 subparagraph 1 litera a or b of the CCP are to be informed about the conditions for support for the proceedings and victims with special protection needs about their rights under Article 66a of the CCP no later than before their first interview. At that time, all victims under Article 65 subparagraph 1 of the CCP are to be informed about their right to be notified, upon request, about specific incidents regarding the remand of the accused and the imprisonment of the convicted (escape and re-arrest, first unsupervised exit, discharge; Article 70 paragraph 1 of the CCP).

There are also informational rights of victims in cases of withdrawal of the prosecution (diversion; Chapter 11 of the CCP). In any case, victims must immediately be notified about their rights, especially their right to obtain support for the proceedings, and about any relevant victim support organisation (Article 206 paragraph 1 of the CCP, referring to Article 70 paragraph 1 of the CCP). Additionally, and insofar as this appears necessary to protect the interests and rights of victims, especially their right to compensation, victims and their representatives have to be given sufficient time to make a statement prior to withdrawal from the prosecution (see *Section 3.2.5.2*).

In order for informational rights to be effective, the information about rights needs to be given in a language that the victim can understand and in a comprehensible manner, taking into account any special personal needs of the victim (Article 70 paragraph 1 last sentence in conjunction with Article 50 paragraph 2 of the CCP). But victims of crime shall not be kept informed against their will; once a victim has been informed, she or he may at any stage during the proceedings declare that she or he refrains from receiving further notifications and summons, in which case any further participation of the victim will cease (Article 70 paragraph 2 of the CCP).

Not only private parties are entitled to access files; insofar as their interests are concerned, this right is also open to victims who do not participate in the proceedings as private parties (Article 68 paragraph 2 of the CCP). Access to files may only be refused or limited insofar as such access would jeopardize the purpose of the investigations or the uninfluenced witness testimony. Concerning practical aspects of granting access to files, Article 68 paragraph 1 of the CCP refers to most of the provisions regarding access to files for the accused (Article 51; Article 52 paragraph 1, paragraph 2 subparagraphs 1 and 3; Article 53 of the CCP) which apply *mutatis mutandis*. Likewise, the prohibition against publishing applies *mutatis mutandis* to victims and private parties (Article 68 paragraph 3 in conjunction with Article 54 of the CCP).[46]

According to Article 66 paragraph 1 subparagraph 4 of the CCP, victims have the right to be notified about the progression of the proceedings. This concerns, first of all, the lifting of remand; if the accused is released, the court has to immediately notify the victim (if the victim so requested; Article 70 paragraph 2 of the CCP) of the release and by stating the grounds for release and the more menial means imposed on the accused. However, victims within the meaning of Article 65 subparagraph 1 litera a of the CCP and victims with special protection needs (Article 66a of the CCP) must be informed *ex officio* without delay (Article 177 paragraph 5 in conjunction with Article 172 paragraph 4 first and second sentence of the CCP).

Investigation proceedings might be closed in different ways. First, a discontinuation of investigation proceedings comes into question insofar as the conduct is not punishable by criminal law or if the prosecution of the accused is not permissible for reasons of law, or no factual grounds exist to pursue the prosecution of the accused (Article 190 of the CCP). Furthermore, they are to be discontinued because of trifling nature of the criminal offence in question (Article 191 of the CCP), and they may be discontinued under certain conditions if multiple criminal offences are prosecuted (Article 192 of the CCP). Second, the prosecution authority has to abort investigation proceedings against absentee and unknown perpetrators (Article 197 of the CCP). Third, the prosecution authority has to decide to withdraw from the prosecution (diversion) under the general conditions set out in Article 198 of the

---

46 The prohibition concerns any information which they obtained, *inter alia*, through access to files; victims and private parties are not authorized to publish, in a media piece or in any other way that would render the information available to the broader public, any information containing personal details of other participants in the proceedings or of third parties that did not feature in public hearings or that otherwise became known publicly, if this would infringe on the interests of confidentiality (Article 1 paragraph 1 Data Protection Act [Datenschutzgesetz (DSG), Austrian Federal Law Gazette I No. 165/1999, 17.08.1999, last amended by Austrian Federal Law Gazette I No. 14/2019, 15.01.2019]) of other participants in the proceedings or of third parties that are worthy of protection and that prevail over the interest to inform the public.

CCP, and fourth, it can file the indictment for the commission of an offence that is to be prosecuted *ex officio* (Article 210 of the CCP).

If the prosecution authority decides to discontinue the investigation proceedings, it has to notify the victim about the discontinuation and provide reasoning. Furthermore, the prosecution authority has to inform the victim about the option to file a motion for the continuation of proceedings (Article 195 paragraph 1 of the CCP), about the requirements for filing it, and about the fact that within 14 days she or he may request an explanation in which the material facts and considerations on which the discontinuation are summarized. The victim must also be informed in case of the subsequent continuation of proceedings (Article 194 of the CCP).

According to Article 66 paragraph 1 subparagraph 8 of the CCP, victims have – independent of their role as private parties – the right to demand continuation of proceedings that were discontinued by the prosecution authority. Such a motion for continuation of investigation proceedings has to be filed with the prosecution authority within 14 days of the discontinuation or of the service of the explanation of the discontinuation (Article 194 paragraph 2 of the CCP); if, however, the victim was not notified of the discontinuation, within three months of the discontinuation of proceedings (Article 195 paragraph 2 of the CCP). The motion must specify the proceedings for which continuation is sought and must contain all the information required to assess the on-time lodgement. Furthermore, the reasons from which the violation or wrong application of the law or the serious concerns derive need to be stated individually and definitively. If liability for the crime has not passed the statute of limitations, the court has to order the continuation by the prosecution authority of investigation proceedings that were discontinued under Articles 190 to 192 of the CCP if, according to Article 195 paragraph 1 of the CCP,

1) the law was violated or applied incorrectly;
2) there are serious concerns regarding the accuracy of the material facts on which the decision to close the proceedings was based; or
3) new material facts or pieces of evidence are provided, which, by themselves or in conjunction with the other outcomes of the proceedings, appear to be capable of sufficiently ascertaining the facts of the case in order to proceed pursuant to Chapters 11 (diversion) or 12 (indictment) of the CCP (Article 195 paragraph 1 of the CCP).

If the prosecution authority decides to abort investigation proceedings against a known, but absentee perpetrator, it has to notify the victim about aborting the proceedings as well as about the subsequent resumption or commencement of proceedings (Article 197 paragraph 3 of the CCP).

The provisions concerning the withdrawal of the prosecution (diversion) entail further specifications of the right to notification about the progression of the proceedings as well. Article 206 paragraph 2 of the CCP states that, in any case, victims must be notified if the accused agrees to compensate any damage caused by the crime or to contribute to remedying the consequences of the crime. The same applies in cases in which the accused accepts a duty that directly affects the interests of the aggrieved party. Additionally, the prosecution authority or, after the prosecution authority has filed the indictment to the court, the court (if it has discontinued the proceedings pursuant to Article 199 of the CCP) must notify the victim about the withdrawal from the prosecution, whereby the notification has to contain the circumstances relevant for the resolution in keywords (Article 208 paragraph 3 of the CCP).

3.2.2.2 Rights of participation

First of all, any person who becomes aware of the commission of a criminal offence – and therefore any victim of crime – has the right to report this matter to any criminal investigation authority or prosecution authority (Article 80 paragraph 1 of the CCP). In this regard, victims under Article 65 subparagraph 1 of the CCP who file a report must be furnished with a written confirmation of their report (Article 66 paragraph 1 subparagraph 1a in conjunction with Article 80 paragraph 1 of the CCP).

Regarding rights of participation in pre-trial investigation proceedings (Article 66 paragraph 1 subparagraph 6 of the CCP), victims have on the one hand the right to participate in the adversarial examination of witnesses and accused, *in concreto* to participate in adversarial questioning and to pose questions (Article 165 paragraph 2 of the CCP). On the other hand, victims have the right to participate in a re-enactment of the crime and, in doing so, the right to ask questions and to request additional investigations and determinations (Article 150 paragraph 1 of the CCP).

Concerning rights of participation in the main trial (Article 66 paragraph 1 subparagraph 7 of the CCP), victims have the right to be present during the main trial, to question the defendant, witnesses and expert witnesses, and to be heard concerning their claims. It is, however, important to stress that victims who do not declare to join the criminal proceedings as a private party are not entitled to formally request the taking of evidence (Article 55 of the CCP; see *Section 3.2.5.1*).

Thereby, victims do not have to exercise their rights of participation themselves; they also have the right to be represented. In this regard, Article 66 paragraph 1 subparagraph 1 of the CCP refers to Article 73 of the CCP, which states that representatives assist victims (as well as private parties; see below) with advice and support and, in principle,[47] exercise the same rights as those who they represent. Any person admitted to exercise the function of an attorney, any institution for victim protection

---

47 Unless provided otherwise by the CCP, see Article 73 of the CCP.

recognised under Article 25 of the NSPA (National Security Police Act[48]), or any other suitable person may be authorized to act as a representative.

3.2.2.3 Right to interpretation and translation

Article 66 paragraph 1 subparagraph 5 of the CCP states that victims also have the right to obtain interpretation aid through an interpretation service and refers to Article 66 paragraph 3 of the CCP for further details. Victims who do not speak or cannot understand the language in which the proceedings are conducted, interpretation aid is to be provided by applying *mutatis mutandis* the provisions under Article 56 of the CCP. Interpretation aid encompasses, on the one hand, the right to receive interpretation assistance which is to be provided orally and, in particular, for the hearing of evidence and for court hearings where the victim is present (Article 66 paragraph 3 in conjunction with Article 56 paragraph 2 of the CCP).

On the other hand, interpretation aid includes the right to obtain written translations of essential documents, insofar as this is necessary to preserve the rights and interests of the victim (Article 66 paragraph 3 in conjunction with Article 56 paragraphs 1, 3, 4 and 5 of the CCP). Essential files that have to be translated at the request of the victim include the written confirmation of the report of the crime (Article 80 paragraph 1 of the CCP), notification of and the reasons for discontinuation of investigation proceedings (Article 194 paragraph 2 of the CCP) as well as copies of the verdict and the penal order. Other documents, which need to be precisely specified, are to be translated in writing at the request of the victim if reasons for the need of translation in order to preserve the rights and interests of the victim (Article 10 of the CCP) are given or if the need is obvious. The translation of essential documents may be limited to any part of the document relevant to the victim, and written translations may be substituted by oral translations or oral summaries so long as such substitution does not prevent a fair trial.

Eventually, the right to obtain interpretation aid is also due to victims who are deaf or mute (Article 66 paragraph 3 in conjunction with Article 56 paragraph 7 of the CCP). In that case, an interpreter using sign language is to be employed, if the victim is able to communicate in sign language. Otherwise, the victim has to be engaged in writing or in another suitable way in which she or he can communicate.

3.2.3 Victims in Special Need of Protection

As mentioned above, victims under Article 65 subparagraph 1 of the CCP have the right to have their special protection needs assessed as soon as possible (Article 66 paragraph 1 subparagraph 1b, Article 66a CCP). Article 66a of the CCP has been

48 See *Footnote 4.*

included only in 2016[49] to transpose Community provisions of the Victim Rights Directive 2012/29/EU (hereinafter VRD) regarding individual assessment of victims to identify specific protection needs (Article 22 VRD), the right to protection of victims with specific protection needs (Article 23 VRD) and the right to protection of child victims during criminal proceedings (Article 24 VRD) into domestic law. A set of additional rights (Article 66a paragraph 2 of the CCP; see *below*) is linked to the status of being a victim with special protection needs, and a victim who, upon request, is not afforded these rights must be informed about the reasons (Article 66a paragraph 4 of the CCP).

According to Article 66a paragraph 1 of the CCP, victims have the right to have their special protection needs assessed and determined as soon as possible, whereby their age, their psychological and health condition and the type and specific circumstances of the criminal offence have to be taken into account. Specific categories of victims are considered as victims with special protection needs in any case: victims whose sexual integrity and self-determination might have been violated, who might have been exposed to domestic violence (Article 38a of the NSPA), and victims who are minors (Article 74 paragraph 1 subparagraph 3 of the ACC (Strafgesetzbuch [StGB][50]).

Victims with special protection needs have additional rights consequent from these needs, mainly concerning interviews, stated in Article 66a paragraph 2 of the CCP. First, they may demand to be interviewed in investigation proceedings by a person of the same gender if possible, which is especially important in cases of sexual offences and of violence in the close social surrounding. Second, these victims have the right to refuse to answer questions concerning details of the criminal offence, if they consider giving their account to be unreasonable, or questions concerning details of most personal private sphere (for further details, see Article 158 paragraph 1 subparagraphs 2 and 3, paragraph 2 of the CCP).

Third, victims with special protection needs are entitled to demand to be interviewed in a considerate manner in investigation proceedings (Article 165 of the CCP) and in the main trial (Article 250 paragraph 3 of the CCP). A victim who is a minor and whose sexual sphere might have been violated by the accused through the offence he or she is accused of has to be, in any case, interviewed in the considerate manner described in Article 165 paragraph 3 of the CCP; if necessary, the interview is conducted by an expert witness.

---

49 Strafprozessrechtsänderungsgesetz I 2016 (amendment of the Code of Criminal Procedure), Austrian Federal Law Gazette I No. 26/2016, 20.05.2016.

50 Austrian Criminal Code (ACC), Austrian Federal Law Gazette No. 60/1974, 29.01.1974, last amended by Strafrechtsänderungsgesetz 2018 (amendment of the Austrian Criminal Code), Austrian Federal Law Gazette I No. 70/2018, 25.10.2018; according to Article 74 paragraph 1 subparagraph 3 of the ACC, a “minor“ is a person under the age of 18 years.

Adversarial questioning of witnesses in pre-trial investigation proceedings is a very important procedural instrument to avoid re-traumatisation caused by repeated questioning. Adversarial questioning must be carried out by the court at the request of the prosecution authority, and the court has to afford the prosecution authority, the accused, the victim, private parties, and their representatives the opportunity to participate in adversarial questioning of a victim-witness and to pose questions (Article 165 paragraph 2 of the CCP). The opportunity to participate must be restricted, upon request by the prosecution authority or ex officio, in a manner that these participants in the proceedings and their representatives can follow the questioning using technical audio and video transmission equipment and to exercise their right to pose questions without being present at the questioning (Article 165 paragraph 3 of the CCP). An audio and video recording of the adversarial questioning is to be done, and the recording must in every case be transcribed in full without delay and must be added to the file as a transcript (Article 165 paragraphs 1 and 5a CCP). With the right of victims with special protection needs to be interviewed in a considerate manner in investigation proceedings corresponds their exemption from the duty to answer questions: According to Article 156 paragraph 1 subparagraph 2 CCP, victims with special protection needs under Article 66a of the CCP are exempted from the duty to answer questions if the parties had the opportunity to participate in a prior adversarial questioning in the main trial. Instead, the transcript and/or audio and video recordings of the questioning of the respective witness may be read out or presented if the witness rightfully refuses to give testimony (Article 156 paragraph 1 subparagraph 2 of the CCP) and the prosecution authority and the defendant had the opportunity to participate in the questioning by the court under Article 165 of the CCP (Article 252 paragraph 1 subparagraph 2a of the CCP).

Furthermore, victims with special protection needs have the right to demand to exclude the public from the main trial (Article 229 paragraph 1 of the CCP) and to consult a person who they trust if questioned (Article 160 paragraph 2 of the CCP). Finally, regarding the rights to be notified according to Article 172 paragraph 4, Article 177 paragraph 5 and Article 181a of the CCP mentioned above, victims with special protection needs have the right to be informed ex officio immediately.

Article 66a paragraph 3 of the CCP provides for problematic constellations regarding the legal representation of victims who are minors in criminal proceedings. If the legal guardian of a victim who is a minor is suspected or found guilty of the criminal offence, if there is any other risk of a conflict of interests between the victim who is a minor and his or her legal guardian, or if no legal guardian can assist the victim who is a minor in criminal proceedings, it must be suggested to the Guardianship Court to assign a legal representative.

3.2.4 Psycho-Social and Legal Support

At the very heart of victim support is psycho-social and legal assistance in criminal proceedings for victims particularly affected by the crime in question. Originally started as a pilot project on 1st January 2006,[51] psycho-social and legal support for victims has been established as a regular part of criminal proceedings, together with a fundamental reform of investigation proceedings[52] having entered into force, in 2008.[53]

Victims within the meaning of Article 65 subparagraph 1 litera a or b of the CCP and, since 1st November 2018,[54] also all victims under Article 65 subparagraph 1 of the CCP of terrorist offences as defined in Article 278c of the ACC are to be afforded psycho-social and legal support for the proceedings, insofar as this is necessary to preserve the rights of the victim, taking into account their personal concerns (Article 66 paragraph 2 of the CCP). The decision upon whether psycho-social and/or legal support is necessary in a specific case is taken by victim support institutions authorized by the Federal Minister for Justice; criminal investigation and prosecution authorities and the courts are not involved in this decision.[55] In principle, psycho-social and legal support is only provided upon request, with one exception: victims whose sexual integrity might have been violated and who are under the age of 14 are provided with psycho-social support for the proceedings in any case.

Psycho-social support for the proceedings aims at emotional stabilization of the victim and at avoiding (additional) traumatisation. According to Article 66 paragraph 2 of the CCP, psycho-social assistance encompasses the preparation of the victim concerned for the proceedings and for the emotional stress associated with the proceedings, as well as accompanying the victim to questioning during investigation proceedings and the main proceedings. It is important to stress that it is not the purpose of psycho-social support to train the victim for the questioning (in the sense of memorizing a preferably coherent witness statement), as it is not the task to translate legal terms and questions.[56] Psycho-social support is provided by suitable institutions[57] authorized by the Federal Minister for Justice.

---

51 Änderung der Strafprozessordnung 1975, des Staatsanwaltschaftsgesetzes und des Tilgungsgesetzes (amendment of the Code of Criminal Procedure), Austrian Federal Law Gazette I No. 119/2005, 27.10.2005.

52 Strafprozessreformgesetz (amendment of the Code of Criminal Procedure), Austrian Federal Law Gazette I No. 19/2004, 23.03.2004.

53 *Kier* 2017b point 17 with further references.

54 Strafrechtsänderungsgesetz 2018 (amendment of the Code of Criminal Procedure), Austrian Federal Law Gazette I No. 70/2018, 25.10.2018.

55 *Kier* 2017b point 30.

56 *Kier* 2017b point 26.

57 According to the last sentence in Article 66 paragraph 2 of the CCP, the Federal Minister of Justice is authorized to enter into agreements with established, suitable institutions so that they, after assessing the statutory requirements, provide support for the proceedings to victims within the meaning of Article 65 subparagraph 1 litera a or b of the CCP. The Federal Minister of Justice is also authorized to issue further regulations concerning the requirements to commission an institution under Article 66 paragraph 2 of the CCP and,

Legal support for the proceedings includes legal advice and representation by an attorney (Article 66 paragraph 2 of the CCP). Legal assistance may only be performed by attorneys[58], and is mainly concerned with the enforcement of all the victim rights mentioned above as well as with the assertion of claims regarding compensation.[59]

3.2.5 Compensation

3.2.5.1 Civil law claims of private parties in criminal proceedings

In order to avoid extra civil proceedings to gain compensation, victims have the right to join criminal proceedings as a private party (Article 65 subparagraph 2 of the CCP; see *Section 3.2.1*) and to seek restitution for any damages suffered by the criminal offence or compensation for infringements of their legal interests protected by criminal law (Article 67 paragraph 1 of the CCP).[60] There are actually two options to gain compensation in the course of the criminal proceedings: The first option is to reach a settlement *(Vergleich)*. In the main proceedings, the court must at any time record any settlement of private law claims, and upon request or ex officio, the court may also summon the private parties and the accused to attempt reaching a settlement and present proposals for a settlement (Article 69 paragraph 2 of the CCP). The second option is a formal decision of the criminal court upon civil law claims of a private party that forms part of the conviction (Article 260 paragraph 1 subparagraph 5 of the CCP).[61] A conviction, as far as it concerns awarded compensation, as well as a court settlement constitutes an executory title under Article 1 subparagraph 5 of the Execution Act (Exekutionsordnung[62]).

In case of a court decision regarding civil law claims of private parties, the extent of the damages or infringements has to be determined ex officio insofar as this

---

in consultation with the Federal Minister for Education and Women and the Federal Minister for Family and Youth, issue regulations concerning the quality standards of support for the proceedings, especially concerning the training of persons providing such support (Article 66 paragraph 4 CCP).

58 *Kier* 2017b point 28.

59 *Kier* 2017b point 27.

60 Private parties may assert claims against the accused deriving from a criminal offence, concerning delivery, determination, or constitutive action; see Article 69 paragraph 1 of the CCP.

61 If the defendant is convicted, a decision about any private law claims of the private parties has to be made in the judgement; in cases in which the outcomes of the criminal proceedings do not provide a sufficient basis even partly to assess the raised private law claims, the private parties have to be referred to the civil law proceedings (Article 366 paragraph 2 of the CCP). If the defendant is acquitted, private parties also have to be referred to the civil law proceedings for their claims (Article 366 paragraph 1 of the CCP).

62 Execution Act, Official Gazette No. 79/1896, 27.05.1896, last amended by Austrian Federal Law Gazette I No. 68/2005, 05.07.2005.

is possible on the basis of the outcome of the criminal proceedings or further simple inquiries; if an expert witness is appointed to assess a bodily injury or any damage to the health of the victim, the expert witness also has to be asked to determine the periods of suffering (which are relevant for determining pain and suffering awards). If further taking of evidence to determine the extent of the damages would considerably delay the proceedings, such evidence shall not be taken, especially in respect to the right to a fair trial (Article 6 of the European Convention of Human Rights[63]).[64]

From a procedural point of view, victims become private parties by way of declaration, in which they have to give reasons for their entitlement to participate in the criminal proceedings and for their claims to restitution or compensation. The declaration must be submitted prior to the conclusion of evidential proceedings; by this time, the amount of restitution or compensation also has to be specified (Article 67 paragraphs 2 and 3 of the CCP). A declaration must be rejected by the prosecution authority or, once the indictment has been filed, by the court if it is evidently unfounded, if it was submitted too late, or if the amount of restitution or compensation was not specified in time (Article 67 paragraphs 4 and 5 of the CCP). Furthermore, the victim may withdraw the declaration at any time.

Concerning their role in proceedings, private parties have additional rights exceeding the rights of victims (Article 66 of the CCP; see *Section 3.2.2*). According to Article 67 paragraph 6 of the CCP, a private party is entitled to request the taking of evidence (Article 55 of the CCP), and to uphold the indictment pursuant to Article 72 of the CCP if the prosecution authority withdraws it; additionally, a private party has the right to raise an objection against the decision by the court to discontinue proceedings (Article 87 of the CCP). Private parties also have the right to be invited to attend the main trial and, after the closing statement by the prosecution authority, be given the opportunity to state and give reasons for their claims. Finally, private parties are entitled to lodge an appeal because of their private law claims under Article 366 of the CCP.

According to Article 67 paragraph 7 of the CCP, private parties are entitled to legal aid for the proceedings under specific conditions, unless they must be afforded legal support under Article 66 paragraph 2 of the CCP. Private parties are to be granted legal aid, on the one hand, insofar as their representation by an attorney is in the interest of justice, in particular if this is necessary for a purposeful assertion of their claims in order to avoid further civil proceedings (legal requirement). Additionally, on the other hand, legal aid must be granted to private parties if they are unable to

---

63 European Convention on Human Rights (2010); https://www.echr.coe.int/Documents/Convention_ENG.pdf [02.10.2019] [in English only].

64 *Korn & Zöchbauer* 2017 point 3 with further references.

meet the costs for legal representation without compromising their basic livelihood[65] (economic requirement). Legal aid encompasses providing private parties with an attorney free of charge.[66]

3.2.5.2 Compensation in case of abatement of action

Concerning the withdrawal of the prosecution (diversion), there are also provisions regarding the compensation of victims. Regardless of the form of diversion chosen, which might be payment of a sum of money (Article 200 of the CCP), community service (Articles 201 and 202 of the CCP), probation (Article 203 of the CCP) or victim–offender mediation (Article 204 of the CCP), it is paramount to take into consideration the interests of victims and to support these to the greatest extent possible, especially their interests concerning reparation (Article 206 paragraph 1 of the CCP). Insofar as this appears necessary to protect their interests and rights, especially their right to compensation, victims and their representatives, in any case in instances of domestic violence (Article 38a of the NSPA), and victims within the meaning of Article 65 subparagraph 1 litera a of the CCP, have to be given sufficient time to make a statement prior to a withdrawal from the prosecution. In any case, victims must be notified if the accused agrees to compensate for any damage caused by the crime or to contribute to remedying the consequences of the crime (Article 206 paragraph 2 of the CCP).

Victim–offender mediation (Article 204 of the CCP) is the form of diversion that focuses in particular on victims and their legally protected interests directly affected by the crime in question, including reparation. Under the general conditions set out for diversion in Article 198 of the CCP, the prosecution authority may withdraw from the prosecution if the crime may have directly affected legally protected interests of a person and if the accused agrees to accept responsibility for the crime and confront the cause of the crime, if the accused rectifies the consequences of the crime in a manner appropriate to the circumstances, especially by rectifying any damages or contributing to the compensation for the consequences of the crime, and if the accused, where necessary, accepts duties that demonstrate the accused's willingness to henceforth avoid the kind of behaviour that led to the crime (Article 204 paragraph 1 CCP). According to Article 204 paragraph 2 of the CCP, victims and their representatives, insofar as they agree, must be included in the mediation efforts. The victim's consent is required to achieve conciliation unless the victim does not consent for reasons that are not worthy of consideration in the criminal justice process. The legitimate interests of the victim under Article 206 of the CCP must be considered in any case (see *Section 4.4*).

---

65 The basic livelihood refers to the alimentation needed to maintain a simple livelihood by the person for herself or himself and for her or his family in her or his care; see Article 67 paragraph 7 of the CCP.

66 Article 61 paragraph 4, Article 62 paragraphs 1, 2 and 4 as well as Article 63 paragraph 1 of the CCP (regarding the assignment and appointment of defence counsel for the accused) apply *mutatis mutandis* to the assignment and appointment of such a representative.

3.2.5.3 Benefits pursuant to the Victims of Crime Act

The Victims of Crime Act (hereinafter VCA; Verbrechensopfergesetz [VOG])[67] entitles victims of specific crimes to apply for support measures listed in Article 2 of the VCA, which are funded by federal resources (Article 15 of the VCA). Victims have to meet several criteria in order to be entitled to these support measures. First, they have to be citizens of the European Union and the European Economic Area, or persons legally resident in Austria who are harmed in that country; second, they have to have suffered physical injury or damage to her or his health; and third, the crime in question has to carry a penalty of more than six months of imprisonment (Article 1 paragraphs 1 and 6 of the VCA). If the crime caused the death of the victim, surviving dependants are entitled to benefits as well, specifically regarding the loss of maintenance (Article 3 of the VCA) and funeral expenses (Article 7 of the VCA).

According to the list in Article 2 of the VCA, support measures available are compensation in respect of a loss of earnings or maintenance (Article 3 of the VCA), therapeutic care (Article 4 of the VCA), coverage of costs for crisis intervention (Article 4a of the VCA), orthopaedic care (Article 5 of the VCA), medical, job-related and social rehabilitation (Article 5a of the VCA), supplementary payments for recipients of care allowance or blind person's allowance (Article 6 of the VCA), the reimbursement of funeral expenses (Article 7 of the VCA), means-tested additional benefits (Article 3a of the VCA) and flat-rates of damages for pain and suffering (Article 6a of the VCA). Concerning the latter, a system of blanket sums was put in place, so that a victim can obtain a minimum of 2,000 EUR as compensation for their suffering; should the incident result in permanent damages and the necessity for long-term care, up to 12,000 EUR can be disbursed. From 2011 to 2016, the costs have constantly risen from 2.9 million EUR in 2011 to 4.9 million in 2016, before decreasing slightly in 2017 to 4.2 million EUR.[68] Article 8 of the VCA contains exclusionary clauses, according to which benefits are not awarded, inter alia, if the victim or surviving dependant was involved in the crime, provoked the perpetrator, or was guilty of not helping to solve the case.

From a procedural point of view, safety authorities, the prosecution authority and the criminal courts have to inform victims about the support measures available under the Article 14 of the VCA. The application must be submitted within two years of the crime (Article 10 paragraph 1 of the VCA). The Federal Office for Social Affairs and Disabled Persons (Bundesamt für Soziales und Behindertenwesen) decides upon such an application at first instance (Article 9 of the VCA), and the applicant has the possibility to appeal against this decision with the Federal Administrative Tribunal (Article 9c of the VCA).

---

67 Victims of Crime Act, Austrian Federal Law Gazette No. 288/1972, 28.07.1972, last amended by Austrian Federal Law Gazette I No. 100/2018, 22.12.2018.

68 Federal Ministry of Constitution, Reforms, Deregulation and Justice 2018d, p. 223 et seq.

4. Victimisation in Austria

4.1 Official Prevalence Data Concerning Victims Published by the Federal Police Authority and the Federal Ministry of Justice

In the course of their investigation, the Austrian Federal Police collects information about the victims as well as about the perpetrators. This information is further passed on to the judicial authority and, as such, published in the yearly security report by the Federal Ministry of Justice. In 2017, a total number of 286,793 victims were registered with the judicial authority.[69] Comparing this number to the number of inhabitants, 3281.5 people per 100.000 inhabitants were registered as victims. Since the criminal proceedings may last for over a year, not all of the corresponding crimes were necessarily committed in 2017. Furthermore, this number does not automatically correspond with the number of victimised persons because a victim of two offenders whose cases are conducted separately is listed twice within the available data set.

59% of the registered victims were male, 41% were female. The majority (81%) were Austrian, whereas every fifth victim (19%) was of a different nationality. Of those registered cases, 127,739 victims were affected by crimes against life or physical integrity, the majority (61%) again being male, while 39% were female. 78% of these registered persons were Austrian, 22% were of a different nationality. Concerning sexual offences, 6.966 victims were registered in 2017. As can be expected, the majority were women (77%), 23% were men. Concerning their nationality, four out of five victims (82%) were Austrian, whereas 18% were of a different nationality.[70]

Additionally, the police publishes yearly reports, including certain victim-related information, such as the age of the victims as well as the victim–offender relationship concerning specific crimes.[71] No data are available for other types of crime, e.g., crimes against personal property, which account for the majority of offences (60.5%) reported to the police in 2017. This fact constitutes one of the reasons why the numbers published by the police differ strongly from the figures reported by the Ministry of Justice (*Table 1* and *Figure 1*).

Looking at the data, the over-representation of children and juveniles as victims of sexual offences is notable. While the distribution of each of the other reported types of crimes is similar to the total number, almost 50% of the reported victims of sexual offences were below the age of 21. Additionally, information is availa-

---

69 Federal Ministry of Constitution, Reforms, Deregulation and Justice 2018d, p. 218.

70 Federal Ministry of Constitution, Reforms, Deregulation and Justice 2018d.

71 The numbers published by the police only display information about crimes against life and physical integrity, freedom, robbery and sexual offences.

Table 1 Age Distribution of Victims of Specific Crimes in 2017

		Years of age			
		0–13	**14–20**	**21–64**	**65+**
Crimes against life or physical integrity		2,422	8,300	32,363	1,286
	%	5.5	18.7	72.9	2.9
Crimes against freedom		965	4,246	21,723	1,082
	%	3.4	15	76.9	3.8
Robbery		156	840	3,545	362
	%	3.2	17.1	72.3	7.4
Sexual offences		923	1,277	2,091	77
	%	21.1	29.2	47.9	1.8
Total		4.695	14,663	59,722	2,807
	%	5.7	17.9	72.9	3.4

Source: Federal Ministry of Internal Affairs 2018a.

Figure 1 Age Distribution of Victims of Specific Crimes in 2017

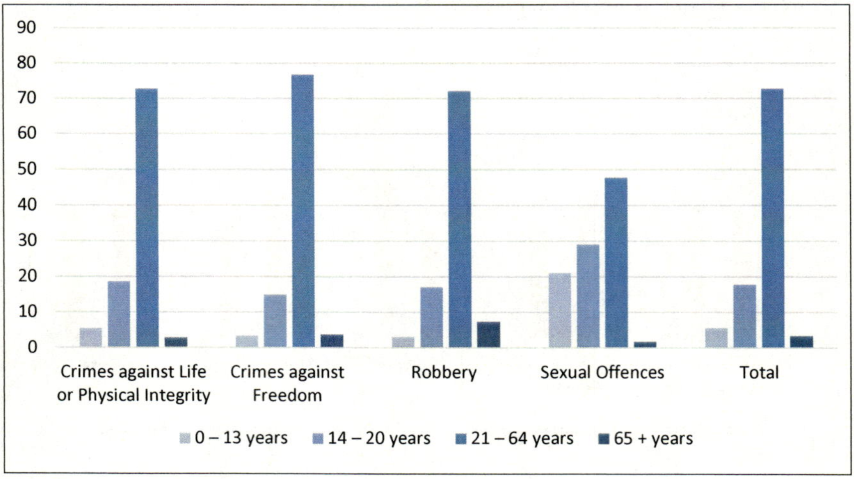

Source: Federal Ministry of Internal Affairs 2018a.

ble concerning victim-offender relationships with regard to the aformentioned types of crime (*Table 2* and *Figure 2*).

Whereas the victim–offender relationship concerning offences against life and bodily integrity as well as against freedom distributes similarly as the total amounts of crime, that is not the case for all kinds of offences. Robbery is seldom committed within the family, in most cases the perpetrator is unknown. Concerning sexual of-

Table 2 Victim–Offender-Relationship Concerning Specific Crimes in 2017

		Relationship				
		Related	**Acquainted**	**Acquainted by chance**	**Stranger**	**Unknown**
Crimes against Life or Physical Integrity		9,334	9,642	1,906	12,143	734
	%	27.6	28.6	5.6	36	2.2
Crimes against Freedom		8,157	8,518	1,180	7,058	374
	%	32.2	33.7	4.7	27.9	1.5
Robbery		99	458	102	1.101	35
	%	5.5	25.5	5.7	61.3	1.9
Sexual Offences		641	1,121	269	982	95
	%	20.6	36.1	8.7	31.6	3.1
Total		18,231	19,736	3,457	21,284	1,238
	%	28.5	30.9	5.4	33.3	1.9

Source: Federal Ministry of Internal Affairs 2018a.

Figure 2 Victim–Offender-Relationship Concerning Specific Crimes in 2017

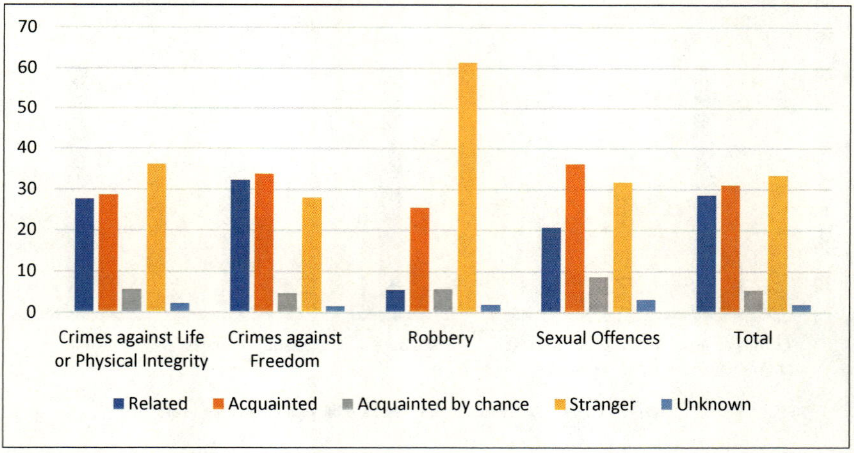

Source: Federal Ministry of Internal Affairs 2018a.

fences, the reported crimes within the family occur slightly less often than in the overall number of crimes, whereas acquaintances appear to be perpetrators more often. One has to bear in mind though that the relationship between victim and offender is an important reason for victims to report a crime or to abstain from doing so. Specifically, in cases of sexual and bodily abuses, the victim might be reluctant to report an offender who is a relative or a friend.

4.2 Specific Victimisation Surveys

As mentioned above, no general victimisation surveys are conducted in Austria. Therefore, no estimates exist about the dark figure of offences not reported to the police. There are however, some data available concerning specific forms of victimisation. Two studies, one concerning experienced violence in the close social surrounding, one concerning online hate speech, will be presented in the following paragraphs.

4.2.1 Violence within the Family and the Close Social Environment

In 2011, a study was published by the Austrian Institute for Family Studies concerning violence within the family and the close social environment.[72] Combining an online questionnaire and face-to-face interviews, a representative sample of the Austrian population between 16 and 60 years (n = 2,343) was asked about their experiences with violence:

1) at any point in their lifetime,
2) within the last three years before the study, and
3) during their childhood up until the age of 16.

By choosing this study design, changes over time, specifically concerning children and juveniles as victims of violence, could be detected. Four different kinds of violence were studied: psychological violence, physical violence, sexual harassment and sexual violence. For each of those types, a variety of examples were presented to the interviewees, asking them to comment on whether they had experienced this kind of behaviour. While some of the examples clearly described criminal offences (e.g., "Somebody punched me with their fists" or "Somebody penetrated me with a penis or an object against my will"), others concerned behaviour that was unquestionably troublesome for the victim, but not necessarily a criminal offence (e.g., "I have suffered discrimination because of my age, gender, looks or place of birth").

The results showed that only 7% of the women and 15% of the men had no experience with any of the described behaviours. Except for physical violence, which was more often experienced by men, the prevalence of all kinds of violence was higher for women. During their adult life, 86% of the women and 78% of the men had experienced psychological violence. 40% of the women and 30% of the men regarded these situations as threatening. Experiences with physical violence were the only ones slightly more common among men; 61% of the male and 57% of the female participants reported having experienced this kind of assaults. Nearly 30% of both sexes assessed those situations as threatening. Considerable differences were detected concerning the surrounding in which physical violence was experienced:

---

72 *Kapella et al.* 2011.

while men were mostly assaulted in public places, women were mostly exposed to physical violence in their homes and their partnerships. Stark differences between the sexes were detected concerning sexual harassment. 74% of the women had experiences with this kind of behaviour, compared to 27% of the men. 30% of the women and 6% of the men did consider their experiences as threatening. 30% of the women and 9% of the men had endured sexual violence in their adult life. Since the described behaviours all constituted serious violations, the participants were not asked whether they experienced them as threatening.

Apart from studying the participants' experiences with violent behaviour, the consequences and reactions of the affected persons were examined as well. Psychological consequences of these experiences, such as "pondering over what happened", "feeling humiliated", "feelings of anger or revenge" or "feeling crestfallen or depressed", were described by almost 90% of the women and 80% of the men. Concerning physical and sexual violence, physical reactions like bruises, injuries or pain were reported by two thirds of the men and women affected by bodily assault. Sexual violence resulted in physical consequences for almost 40% of the women and 20% of the men. Finally, the study examined the victims' long-term psychosocial consequences, such as "discontinuation of contact to friends/family" or "changing the workplace". Psychological violence caused these kinds of reactions stronger than physical or sexual violence, with 66% of the women and 56% of the men reporting this kind of response. Concerning sexual violence, 42% of the female and 22% of the male participants reacted with this kind of behaviour. Women presumably react this way more often than men because the victimisation experiences of women more often emerge from situations in their families and partnerships. Ending these relationships can be a way of escaping the violent surroundings.

When asked about violence experienced during childhood, an interesting trend appeared among the participants: while more than 80% of the 51 to 60 year old participants had experienced physical violence in their youth, while this number declined to 55% in the group of 16 to 20 year old participants. Regarding sexual violence, the change was even stronger, decreasing from 41% of the women and 20% of the men to 20% of the women and 6% of the men. These results indicate that the attitude towards violence against children has changed dramatically within the last 40 years. While this is undoubtedly a welcome development, there is still much room for improvement, since more than 50% of the young people still report violent experiences during their childhood.

4.2.2 Online Hate Speech

In 2018, a research group consisting of the Austrian White Ring Austria and the Research Centre for Human Rights (University of Vienna) conducted a survey on the victimisation experiences of girls and women concerning online hate speech.[73] Although

73 Research Centre Human Rights/White Ring Austria 2018.

not all reported kinds of behaviour (ranging from disparaging or insulting the victim to circulating intimate pictures of the victim, extortion or threats) did necessarily meet the criteria for a criminal offence, the results are nevertheless interesting since they are the first to shed light onto this new and emerging phenomenon. Apart from expert interviews and focus groups, a representative sample of girls and women over the age of 14 (n = 1.021) was asked about their experiences with online hate speech. One in three women (32.4%) reported having experienced this kind of behaviour within the last 12 months. The most common behaviour referred to insults aiming at personal believes of the victim, followed by sexually offensive messages and insults aiming at the sex of the victim. In the majority of cases, the offenders were unknown to the victim; every fifth perpetrator acted anonymously. Age turned out to be the most important predictor of whether a person had already experienced this kind of victimisation; the group of girls between 15 and 18 years were significantly more affected than any other group, with the prevalence declining with every following age group. The majority of offences occurred via Facebook, followed my messenger systems like WhatsApp and email services. Victims were further asked to specify the effects stemming from the experiences. Almost 40% said they were 'angry and furious' about what happened, 20% felt 'sad and depressed', whereas 28% declared that they did not have an emotional reaction to the offences. One out of five women reacted to the experiences by reducing their participation in online discussions or retreating from the forum altogether. 18% felt threatened by the experiences they had made.

4.3 Victim Support: A Closer Look at the System of Psycho-Social and Legal Assistance for Victims in Austria

Enduring a criminal trial is challenging and stressful for the victims, especially in situations where the perpetrator is a relative or (ex)partner. The dangers of re-traumatisation, as well as secondary victimisation, derive from the exposed role as a witness, which might include the obligation to testify and in some cases the questioning of the victim's credibility by attorneys or judges. In order to mitigate these burdens, psycho-social and legal support for the proceedings, as described in *Section 3.2.5*, were introduced into the CCP in 2006. As outlined above, the aim of the support system is neither to increase the conviction rate nor to prepare the victim to be a "good" witness. Instead, the support system broadly addresses the emotional burden of the victim during the challenging period of the trial. Ideally, the support should start before the victim files criminal charges against the offender and continue throughout the criminal proceedings.

The requirements, as well as the practical implementation and the extent to which this support is used, are described in the following paragraphs. In 2014, Austria received the "Silver Award" of the Future Policy Award for this support system.[74]

---

[74] FuturePolicy.org 2019.

4.3.1 Psycho-Social Support During Proceedings

Pertinent education and experience is mandatory for any individual who is to offer psycho-social support during the proceedings. Apart from obtaining a university (or similar) degree in psychology, social work or a similar field, each caregiver has to complete specific training. Until 2015, training for psycho-social caregivers was divided depending on which group of victims they will later on work with: children and young adults, women as victims of gender-based violence or victims of situational violence. Between 2012 and 2015, a group of experts developed a curriculum for all psycho-social caregivers that includes some specific parts for the three groups of victims as described above.[75]

Caregivers need to have specific knowledge about issues such as child development, gender-based power imbalances and violence. Furthermore, they need experience in the field of counselling as well as the capacity to work together with other stakeholders such as representatives of the judiciary system. Caregivers need to be resilient, flexible and able to deal with conflicts. Finally, it is necessary for them to have basic knowledge and understanding of the legal framework and the criminal proceedings.[76]

The main task of the psycho-social caregiver is providing the victim with the emotional support throughout the criminal proceedings. Filing criminal charges as well as testifying at court against the perpetrator entails intense distress, possibly deriving from traumatization, ambivalence towards the offender as well as fear and uncertainty about the outcome. In order to ease these burdens for the victim, the caregiver supports him or her from the decision on whether to file criminal charges up until the end of the proceedings. Caregivers accompany the victims to all the important procedural steps such as filing the charges at the police, testifying before a public prosecutor, a judge or in some cases an expert. Beforehand they explain the procedures in detail since many victims do not have experience with the judiciary system before and often are intimidated by it. The caregivers describe the roles and functions of the different stakeholders involved, clarify what is expected of the victim during the trial and take care of certain security measures, such as the avoidance of a meeting between the victim and the offender outside of the courtroom.[77] Victimisation is often accompanied by feelings of helplessness and loss of control. Caregivers ensure that the victim understands the procedural steps taken in order to avoid re-traumatisation.[78] After every procedural step, they make sure that the victim understood the

---

75 Federal Ministry of Justice/Federal Ministry of Education and Women/Federal Ministry for Families and Youth 2015, p. 8.

76 Federal Ministry of Constitution, Reforms, Deregulation and Justice 2018a; 2018b; 2018c.

77 *Amesberger & Haller* 2016b, p. 25.

78 *Riezler* 2018, p. 1307.

outcome as well as the implications and they pay attention to potential disappointments and frustrations of the victim. If necessary, they refer the victim to support organisations. Furthermore, it is the caregiver's responsibility to make sure that all parties involved in supporting the victim (attorneys, support organizations, etc.) are well connected and that they exchange information on a regular basis.

Unlike the legal support for the proceedings, psycho-social support can be extended to a trial before a civil court, ensuing the criminal proceedings; such an extension presupposes that the psycho-social support was granted during the criminal procedure, the civil trial deals with the same incident as the criminal procedures did, and the support by the psycho-social caregiver is necessary in order for the victim to pursue his or her rights.[79] Before a civil court, only the victim can be supported, not her or his relatives.

The Federal Ministry of Justice finances the work of the caregiver.[80] This financial support is granted to the victims disregarding their financial situation; the victim does not have to be financially dependent on this contribution to receive the support.

4.3.2 Legal Support During Proceedings

In addition to the psycho-social caregivers, attorneys constitute the second element of victim support provided by Article 66 paragraph 2 of the CCP. By combining these two crucial groups of stakeholders, a holistic set of support for the victim is ensured. Unlike the psycho-social caregivers, the attorneys do not have to go through specific training. It is the victim support organisations' responsibility to ensure that only the capable attorneys are entrusted with this task.

The attorneys are responsible for preserving all of the victim's rights. They can also accompany the victim to hearings and counsel him or her on the questions such as whether to file charges. An important task for the attorney is to translate the legal proceedings to the victim since the language used by the judiciary often is too complicated and technical for laypersons to understand. Due to their legal expertise and their prestige, attorneys are generally better accepted by public prosecutors and judges than social workers and psychologists.[81] As with the psycho-social support, the Federal Ministry of Justice finances the work of the attorneys.[82]

---

79 Article 73 of the Code of Civil Procedure (Zivilprozessordnung [ZPO], Official Gazette No. 113/1895, 01.08.1895, last amended by Austrian Federal Law Gazette I No. 109/2018, 28.12.2018.

80 Federal Ministry of Justice 2017, p. 31.

81 *Amesberger & Haller* 2016b, p. 25.

82 Federal Ministry of Justice 2017, p. 63.

4.3.3 Development of the Psycho-Social and Legal Support During Proceedings 2011–2018

Before psycho-social and legal support during proceedings were implemented into the Austrian Criminal Proceedings Act in 2006, a pilot project took place, supporting children and adolescents who had become victims of sexual violence. In 2000, a total of 52 victims received this kind of support, facilitated at the time by four victim support organizations and funded by the Federal Ministry of Justice.[83] Since then, the numbers of supported victims have constantly been rising. In 2011, the Federal Ministry of Justice installed a database in order to facilitate the billing of the victim support organisations. The following information derives from this database.[84] Unfortunately, no data are available concerning the offences committed as well as the relationship between the victim and the offender.

In 2011, 6,137 persons received psycho-social and legal support for the proceedings, costing 4.5 million Euro. Rising almost constantly, a total of 8.331 persons received support in 2018, resulting in more than 7 million EUR paid by the Federal Ministry of Justice *(Figure 3)*.

Figure 3 Victims Receiving Support During Proceedings and Costs, 2011–2018

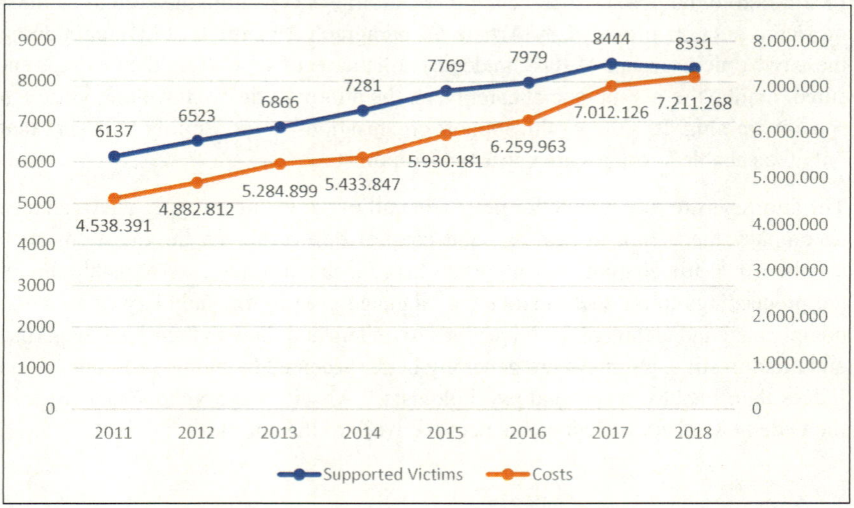

Source: Federal Ministry of Constitution, Reforms, Deregulation and Justice, 2019b.

---

[83] *Haller & Hofinger* 2008, p. 19.

[84] We would particularly like to thank *Franz Riegler* and the Federal Ministry of Justice for providing us with the information from the internal database.

Under specific circumstances, a relative of the victim may be entitled to this kind of support during the trial. This is the case if the victim, who is also directly receiving support, is under 18 years and is strengthened by the presence of her or his relative during the proceedings.[85] However, the majority of support goes to the victims. Of the 8,444 persons supported in 2017, 7,629 (90.4%) were victims, while the remaining 815 (9.6%) were relatives or in another way affected.

Over the course of the years, the majority of the supported victims and relatives were female; specifically 82.1%, whereas the remaining 17.9% were male. Compared with the overall ratio of registered female and male victims in Austria, an interesting picture emerges. In 2017, 286,793 people were registered as victims of crime, of which 40.6% were female, while 59.4% were male (see *Figure 4*).[86] Of the 7,629 victims who received psycho-social and legal support for the proceedings in 2017, 6,061 or 79.4% were female and 1,568 or 20.6% were male (see *Figure 5*). These numbers illustrate that women are disproportionately affected by the corresponding crimes. Correspondingly, the majority of all victims of sexual offences in Austria are female (77.1% in 2017).

Figure 4 Gender Distribution of Victims of all Crimes in 2017

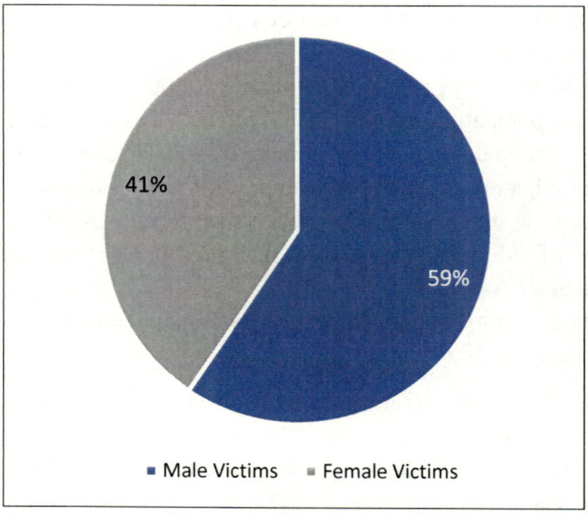

Source: Federal Ministry of Constitution, Reforms, Deregulation and Justice 2018d.

85 Federal Ministry of Justice 2017, p. 10.

86 Federal Ministry of Constitution, Reforms, Deregulation and Justice 2018d, p. 218.

Figure 5 Victims Receiving Support in 2017

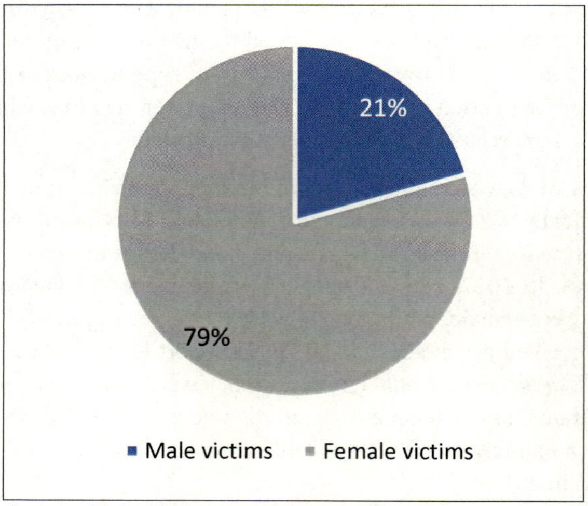

Source: Federal Ministry of Constitution, Reforms, Deregulation and Justice 2018d.

Looking at the age distribution of victims who received social and legal support for the proceedings, the data show that, between 2011 and 2017, the majority (76.7%) were adults over the age of 21 years. The second largest group of supported victims were between 14 and 17 years old. Compared with the age distribution within the general Austrian population, an over-representation of juveniles can be detected, whereas the age group 0-3 is under-represented.[87] This distribution can partly be attributed to the obligatory psycho-social support for victims of sexual assaults under the age of 14 years as described above.[88] A chi-square-test was conducted comparing the two groups of individuals. It revealed that the difference between the distributions was statistically significant, $\chi^2(6)=1271.07$, $p=.000$. *Table 3* and *Figure 6* show the distribution of victims compared to the general population between the age of 0 and 20 years in 2017.

Specific gender differences also become evident when looking at the age distribution of male and female victims. Between 2011 and 2017, 20% of the female victims were minors, whereas 37% of the supported male victims had not reached the age of 18. These numbers demonstrate mainly that adult men are the least likely to receive psycho-social and legal support for the proceedings compared to adult women and minors of both sexes. One reason for this phenomenon can be seen in the above described mechanism of the police giving the personal data of a victim of domestic

87 StatOffice 2019a.

88 Legal support is not mandatory.

Table 3 Age Distribution of Victims and the General Population in 2017

Age	Victims	Victims (%)	Population	Population (%)
0–3	70	0.92	347,969	3.94
4–6	188	2.46	252,248	2.86
7–9	238	3.21	250,694	2.84
10–13	445	5.89	337,553	3.83
14–17	811	10.63	345,105	3.91
18–20	491	6.44	286,994	3.25
21 and older	5,877	77.03	7,001,704	79.36

Source: StatOffice 2019a.

Figure 6 Age Distribution of Victims and the General Population in 2017 (0–20 years)

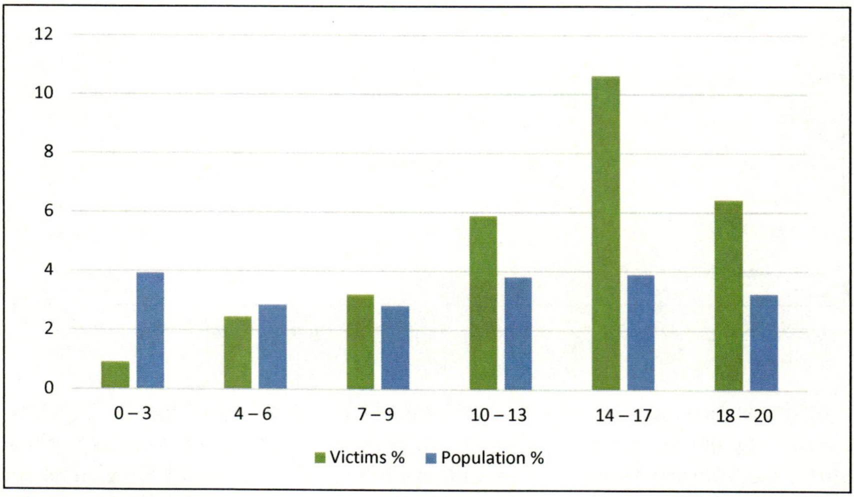

Source: StatOffice 2019a.

violence to the local Domestic Violence Intervention Centre (see *Section 2.2.2*). The Intervention Centre then approaches the victim and, in many cases, pro-actively offers support for the proceedings. Since men are significantly less affected by domestic violence, this kind of support is rather seldom offered to them by a support organization.

Not in all cases are psycho-social caregivers and attorneys both assigned as support for the proceedings. The available data show that until 2014, the majority of victims received only psycho-social support. In almost equally as many cases, the two forms of support were applied together. A smaller number of victims was solely supported by an attorney. This number has been declining steadily since 2011, whereas the application of solely psycho-social support, as well as the combination of the two types, has increased, although a slight decline can be observed starting in 2015 concerning psycho-social support. Since 2015, the majority of victims received psycho-social as well as legal support. The following figure illustrates the development *(Figure 7)*.

Figure 7 Form of Support During Proceedings, 2011–2018

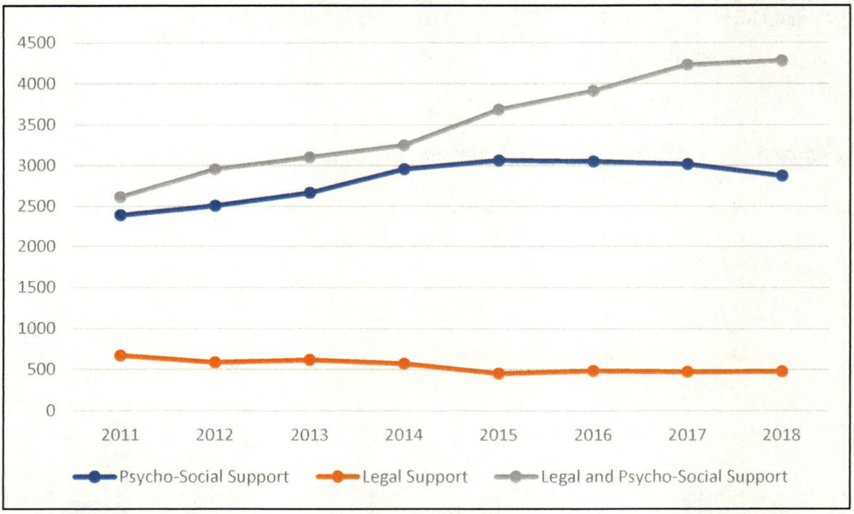

Source: Federal Ministry of Constitution, Reforms, Deregulation and Justice, 2019b.

Looking at the amount of money spent by the Federal Ministry of Justice, a comprehensive picture of the actions taken by the caregivers and attorneys emerges. Since 2011, the Ministry has spent 44.8 million EUR for the support of the victims and their relatives. The most substantial amount (8.2 million) was spent on coordination between the stakeholders involved, followed by 6.3 million for counselling sessions for the victim and 5.5 million, which were needed because the victim was accompanied during the trial. These three elements – emotional encouragement and counselling, support during proceedings and well-conducted coordination of the aiding systems at hand – constitute the key components of the institutionalized support for the proceedings. Studies show that this system of assistance for the victim is perceived as an important and helpful instrument in order to alleviate the strains borne by the victims.[89]

---

89 *Amesberger & Haller* 2016a, p. 112.

4.4 An Example of Restorative Justice: Victim–Offender Mediation in Austria

The CCP stipulates the possibility for a victim–offender mediation in certain cases. If the facts of the case are sufficiently clear, and a punishment does not appear to be warranted, in order to prevent the accused from committing criminal offences or to deter others from committing criminal offences, the prosecution authority has to withdraw from the prosecution of a criminal offence. Additionally, the following requirements have to be fulfilled: the offence is not punishable by more than five years imprisonment and the culpability of the accused would not be considered serious[90]. Also, the crime did not result in the death of a person, unless a relative of the accused was killed negligently and punishment does not appear to be warranted given serious mental distress was caused by the death of the relative to the accused (Article 198 of the CCP). Instead of proceeding with the prosecution, one of several possibilities is offering a victim–offender mediation (Article 204 of the CCP).[91] If legally protected interests of the victim have been affected, the accused must agree to accept responsibility for the crime and rectify any damages or contribute to the consequences of the misconduct. The victim has to agree to this procedure and must be included in the process. The victim's consent is required to achieve conciliation unless the victim does not consent for reasons that are not worthy of consideration in the criminal justice process. The prosecution authority may request the services of a mediator to provide the victim and the accused and their representatives with information about the possibility of victim–offender mediation, to notify them about their rights and to guide and support them in their conciliation efforts. Mediation is often used as the method of choice if the victim and the accused are related and if it is likely that this relationship will continue in the future.

The NEUSTART association, the organization in charge of probation services, is usually commissioned to conduct the mediation. If both the victim and the accused have consented to this proceeding, the mediator holds preliminary talks with the involved parties. Then the victim, the accused and the mediator meet in person to discuss the incident, thereby offering the victim the possibility to explain her or his experience, the damages and feelings deriving from the crime. The mediation aims at providing the victim with an apology by the perpetrator as well as with an arrangement concerning the material compensation.

The possibility for such a mediative procedure exists since 1985. Since then, a total of 157,533 victims, as well as 186,394 accused persons, have been involved

---

90 See Article 32 of the ACC.

91 Alternatively, the prosecution can proceed by offering the payment of a sum of money (Article 200 of the CCP), community service (Articles 201 and 202 of the CCP) or a set probation period in conjunction with probation assistance and the fulfilment of duties (Article 203 of the CCP).

in the procedure. In 2017, 5,845 accused persons were offered mediation by the prosecution authorities. Due to mutual accusations of experienced damages, 2,052 of those people also participated in the role of the victim. NEUSTART offers the possibility for the accused to pay the sum agreed upon in the mediation over an account controlled by NEUSTART. In 2017, 549,000 EUR were paid to victims as material compensation. In total, the mediation was successful in 73% of the cases, thereby leading to the discontinuation of the proceedings.[92] Concerning recidivism, the mediation shows particularly good results: 87% of the perpetrators participating in a victim–offender mediation do not re-offend within a period of 2.5 to 3.5 years.[93]

5. Conclusion

Looking at the described support system for victims of crime, a clear picture emerges: victims can rely on comprehensive and detailed instruments to obtain their rights during a trial as well as crucial protection measures in order to prevent crimes and harm from happening in the first place. However, concerning certain aspects, improvement is mandatory.

First, there are inconsistencies regarding the legal entitlement to psycho-social and legal support (Article 66 paragraph 2 of the CCP). This entitlement has been extended to all victims (Article 65 subparagraph 1 of the CCP) of terrorist offences (Article 278c of the ACC) in 2018,[94] but there are still emotionally strongly affected victims of crime who are not entitled to psycho-social and legal assistance in criminal proceedings. Witnesses of attempted murder or excessive violence against their relatives – especially children who witness domestic violence against a parent or another reference person without themselves being the direct target of violence – do not have the legal opportunity to make use of psycho-social and legal support. This leads to the following paradox; for example, a victim under Article 65 subparagraph 1 litera c of the CCP who suffers (solely) financial damage because her or his parked car has been damaged by a terrorist attack is (in principle) entitled to support under Article 66 paragraph 2 of the CCP, whereas a child who witnesses the father beating the mother constantly over the years is by no means entitled to task this support in the criminal proceedings against the father.[95]

Regarding benefits under the VCA, these benefits are only available for victims who have suffered physical injury or damage to their health at the moment. It would be desirable to include other victims traumatized by severe felonies as well. In practice,

---

92 Federal Ministry of Constitution, Reforms, Deregulation and Justice 2018d, p. 69.

93 *Hofinger & Peschak* 2018, p. 18.

94 Strafrechtsänderungsgesetz 2018 (amendment of the Code of Criminal Procedure), Austrian Federal Law Gazette I No. 70/2018, 25.10.2018.

95 *Kraml & Lehner* 2019, p. 252.

it would also be important to break down bureaucratic barriers in order to simplify access to the benefits under the VCA. This is especially true for victims of sexual violence who face difficulties and further psychological stress due to the necessity to provide sufficient evidence of severe physical injury or damage to their health in order to access the higher flat-rates of damages for pain and suffering (Article 6a of the VCA).

As mentioned above (see *Section 2.2.2*), Austria does not provide enough places in women's shelters to fulfil the requirements established by the Council of Europe.[96] To comply with the country's duty of providing 880 places, a total of 114 places is currently missing. Looking at the number of women as victims of murder, it becomes evident that those safe spaces in women's shelters are imperatively needed. From 2014 to 2017, the number of female murder victims has doubled, from 19 victims in 2014 to 41 in 2017.[97] Although these numbers are too low to draw statistically significant conclusions, this considerable rise nevertheless demonstrates the need for efficient protection measures.

Another point of criticism concerns the education of professionals from various fields who may encounter victims in their everyday work, including police officers, prosecutors and judges as well as medical staff in hospitals and educators in kindergartens and schools. These professionals need to be trained to recognize violence and subsequently to deal with their observations. They need to be informed about the danger of secondary victimisation as well as the often inadvertently happening mechanism of victim-blaming. When it comes to medical staff, injuries from bodily harm have to be detected and properly documented, as they can be of vital importance in an ensuing criminal trial. Additionally, the psychological consequences of assaults need to be recognized and documented as well. Concerning this important part of victim protection and support, there is undoubtedly room for improvement in Austria.

Finally, it must be stressed that effective victim protection and support requires sufficient funding. The organizations involved need to have a long-term perspective and the security of legally binding warranties that the money they receive from public authorities such as the Federal Ministry of Justice will also be at their disposal in the future.

6. Summary in German

Während die viktimologische Forschung bis heute nur unzureichend im österreichischen Wissenschaftsbetrieb institutionalisiert ist und weitreichende

96 Council of Europe 2008, p. 51.

97 Autonomous Austrian Women's Shelters 2019.

Opferbefragungen fehlen, verfügt Österreich über ein umfassendes Netz an Unterstützungsmöglichkeiten für Opfer von Straftaten. Neben allgemeinen Opferhilfeeinrichtungen wie dem Weissen Ring finden sich eine Reihe spezialisierter Organisationen, die unterschiedlichen Gruppen von Opfern Schutz vor Übergriffen sowie Beratung und Begleitung vor und während eines Strafverfahrens zukommen lassen. Von großer praktischer Bedeutung ist das System der juristischen und psychosozialen Prozessbegleitung. Hierbei werden bestimmte Opfer von professionellen Unterstützer*innen aus dem psychosozialen Bereich auf das Strafverfahren vorbereitet sowie währenddessen emotional und organisatorisch unterstützt. Anwält*innen nehmen die Rechte der Opfer im Verfahren wahr und achten darauf, dass die Opfer die Vorgänge während des Verfahrens sowie dessen Ausgang verstehen. Diese Unterstützung ist für die Opfer kostenfrei, da die Begleiter*innen durch das Bundesministerium für Justiz bezahlt werden. Andere Instrumente stellen ebenfalls stark auf die Interessen der Opfer ab: Stimmt das Opfer diesem Vorgehen zu, kann in gewissen Fällen an Stelle eines Strafverfahrens ein Tatausgleich durchgeführt werden. Hierbei begleiten professionelle Konfliktregler*innen Täter*innen und Opfer durch einen mediativen Prozess und erarbeiten gemeinsam mit den Betroffenen eine tragfähige und zukunftsträchtige Lösung, welche die Bedürfnisse der Opfer im Hinblick auf Wahrnehmung ihrer Verletzungen sowie Entschädigung umfassend berücksichtigt. Obgleich somit im Bereich des Opferschutzes vielfältige Unterstützungsmöglichkeiten zur Verfügung stehen, zeigt sich dennoch in manchen Bereichen Verbesserungspotenzial. So sollte beispielsweise die Gruppe der Personen, die Anspruch auf Prozessbegleitung haben, erweitert werden. Ferner sollten künftig mehr Plätze in Frauenhäusern zur Verfügung stehen und es sollte darauf geachtet werden, dass Personen, die im Rahmen ihrer täglichen beruflichen Arbeit mit Opfern von Straftaten zu tun haben, mit Blick auf die Wahrnehmung von Viktimisierung(en) sowie die Bedürfnisse der Betroffenen ausreichend geschult werden.

Addendum due to Legislative Changes

The descriptions within in this chapter represent the state of legislation at the end of October 2019. Entering into force on 1st January 2021, the Code of Criminal Procedure was amended by regulations combating hatred in all online media (Hass-im-Netz-Bekämpfungs-Gesetz, Austrian Federal Law Gazette I No. 148/2020, 23.12.2020). Following the results from the study described in chapter 4.2.2., this amendment has also aimed at improving support and protection for victims of online hate speech.

Regarding provisions outlined in this chapter, the regulations concerning the psycho-social and legal support for victims have been amended and extended. Firstly, these regulations have been moved from Article 66 paragraphs 2 and 4 of the CCP to a newly implemented Article 66b of the CCP, dealing solely with psycho-social and legal support for victims. Additionally, to the victim groups already eligible for psycho-social and legal support for victims before this amendment, three other groups have been added in Article 66b paragraph 1 litera c to e of the CCP. On the one hand, victims mainly affected by online hate speech have been included, so that victims of the following offences may now also access this kind of support: persistent stalking (Article 107a of the ACC), persistent harassment involving telecommunication or computer systems (Article 107c of the ACC) and hate speech (Article 283 of the ACC). Furthermore, victims of the following offences are now eligible for psycho-social and legal support, if it can be assumed that the offence has at least partly been committed involving telecommunication or computer systems: criminal defamation (Article 111 of the ACC), accusation of prior offences that have been served or waived (Article 113 of the ACC), insult (Article 115 of the ACC), and false accusation (Article 297 of the ACC). On the other hand, another group of victims has been added, for whom the lack of psycho-social and legal support has long been criticized by victim support organisations: minors who have become witnesses of violence within their close social surrounding, e.g. within their family.

Prosecuting online hate speech is regularly impeded by the obstacle of identifying the perpetrators, who often act anonymously. Therefore, the amendment stipulates improved measures for identifying the offenders of online hate speech. Further amendments concern regulations within other laws such as the ACC or the Media Act (Mediengesetz, Austrian Federal Law Gazette No. 314/1981, 07.07.1981, last amended by Austrian Federal Law Gazette I No. 148/2020, 23.12.2020), all aiming at improving support and protection for victims of online hate speech. However, due to space constraints it is not possible to describe and discuss these provisions in detail.

Literature

Amesberger, H. & Haller, B. (2016a): Rights and needs of victims of intimate partner violence in criminal proceedings in Austria. Vienna.

Amesberger, H. & Haller, B. (2016b): The protection of IPV victims: Legal framework and criminal procedures. Vienna.

Haller, B. & Hofinger, V. (2008): Die Begleitung von Gewaltopfern durch das Strafverfahren – das österreichische Modell der Prozessbegleitung [The accompaniment of victims of violence through criminal proceedings – The Austrian model of process monitoring]. Neue Kriminalpolitik [New Crime Policy] 8, pp. 19–22.

Hofinger, V. & Peschak, J. (2018): Legalbiografien von NEUSTART KlientInnen II [Legal biographies of NEUSTART clients II]. Vienna; https://www.irks.at/assets/irks/Legalbiografien_Endbericht_final_Feb2018.pdf [in German only] [13.07.2019].

Hojas, R. (2014): Opferschutz im Fokus oder am Rande der Justiz [Victim protection in focus or on the edge of justice]. Juridikum 3, pp. 386–390.

Kapella, O., Baierl, A., Rille-Pfeiffer, C., Geserick, C. & Schmid, E. (2011): Gewalt in der Familie und im nahen sozialen Umfeld [Violence in the family and in the close social environment]. Vienna; https://www.oif.ac.at/fileadmin/user_upload/p_oif/andere_Publikationen/gewaltpraevalenz_2011.pdf [in German only] [21.06.2019].

Kier, R. (2017a): §10 StPO [Article 10 StPO]; in: H. Fuchs & E. Ratz (eds.), Wiener Kommentar zur Strafprozessordnung [Vienna Commentary on the Code of Criminal Procedure]. Vienna.

Kier, R. (2017b): §66 StPO [Article 66 StPO]; in: H. Fuchs & E. Ratz (eds.), Wiener Kommentar zur Strafprozessordnung [Vienna Commentary on the Code of Criminal Procedure]. Vienna.

Korn, G. & Zöchbauer, P. (2017): §67 StPO [Article 47 StPO]; in: H. Fuchs & E. Ratz (eds.), Wiener Kommentar zur Strafprozessordnung [Vienna Commentary on the Code of Criminal Procedure]. Vienna.

Kraml, B. & Lehner, A. (2019): Terrorismusbekämpfung neu [Counterterrorism]. Journal für Strafrecht [Journal of Criminal Law] 3, pp. 248–256.

Nachbaur, D. (2017): Die richtige Linie – Gesetzliche Grundlagen und praktische Umsetzung der Unterstützungsleistungen für Opfer in Österreich [The right line – Legal foundations and practical implementation of support services for victims in Austria]; in: L. Sautner & U. Jesionek (eds.), Opferrechte in europäischer, rechtsvergleichender und österreichischer Perspektive [Victim rights in European, comparative and Austrian perspectives]. Vienna, pp. 215–236.

Nachbaur, D. (2012): Opferschutz als Kinderschutz – Kinder und Jugendliche als Opfer im Strafverfahren – zwei Praxisfelder auf dem Prüfstand internationaler Standards [Victim protection as child protection – Children and adolescents as victims in criminal proceedings – Two practice fields on the test bench of international standards]. Interdisziplinäre Zeitschrift für Familienrecht [Interdisciplinary Journal for Family Law] 5, pp. 228–230.

Pühringer, L. (2011): Die Rechte von Opfern im österreichischen Strafverfahren [The rights of victims in Austrian criminal proceedings]. Frankfurt.

Riezler, C. (2018). Prozessbegleitung [Process support]; in: A. Deixler-Hübner, R. Fucik & M. Mayrhofer (eds.), Gewaltschutz und familiäre Krisen [Violence protection and family crises]. Vienna, pp. 1304–1308.

Sautner, L. (2014): Viktimologie [Victimology]. Vienna.

Schloenhardt, A., Eder, J. & Höpfel, F. (2019): Strafprozessordnung [Austrian Code of Criminal Procedure]. Vienna.

Schloenhardt, A. & Höpfel, F. (2016): Strafgesetzbuch [Austrian Criminal Code]. Vienna.

Sorgo, M. (2005): Was sind Interventionsstellen? [What are intervention agencies?]; in: A. Dearing & B. Haller (eds.), Schutz vor Gewalt in der Familie [Protection against domestic violence]. Vienna, pp. 197–230.

Van Dijk, J.J.M., van Manchin, R., Kesteren, J.N. & van Hideg, G. (2007): The burden of crime in the EU. Research report: A comparative analysis of the EU International Crime Survey (EU-ICS) 2005. Brussels.

Documents

Association of Austrian Autonomous Women's Shelters/Vienna Intervention Centre against Domestic Violence (2016): Österreichischer NGO-Schattenbericht für GREVIO [Austrian NGO shadow report for GREVIO]; https://www.interventionsstelle-wien.at/download/GREVIO-Schattenbericht_2016_de.pdf [10.07.2019] [in German only].

Association of Austrian Women's Shelters (2019): Statistik ZÖF 2018 [Statistics ZÖF 2018]; http://www.frauenhaeuser-zoef.at/statistik.htm [14.07.2019] [in German only].

Autonomous Austrian Women's Shelters (2019): Gewalt an Frauen in Österreich [Violence against women in Austria]; https://www.aoef.at/index.php/zahlen-und-daten [14.07.2019] [in German only].

Autonomous Austrian Women's Shelters (2018a): Statistik AÖF 2018 [Statistics AÖF 2018]; https://www.aoef.at/images/04a_zahlen-und-daten/AOEF-Statistik_2018_barrierefrei.pdf [14.07.2019] [in German only].

Autonomous Austrian Women's Shelters (2018b): Tätigkeitsbericht AÖF 2018 [Activity report AÖF 2018]; https://www.aoef.at/images/06_infoshop/6-2_infomaterial_zum_down loaden/taetigkeitsberichte/AOEF-Taetigkeitsbericht_2018_barrierefrei.pdf [14.07.2019] [in German only].

Centre of legal competence (2019): Über uns [About us]; https://www.clc.or.at/ [24.06.2019] [in German and English].

Council of Europe (2008): Council of Europe task force to combat violence against women, including domestic violence (EG-TFV). Final Activity Report. Strasbourg.

Domestic Abuse Intervention Centre Vienna (2018): Statistics 2017. Vienna.

Domestic Abuse Intervention Centre Vienna/Association of Austrian Autonomous Women's Shelters (2019): Victim's rights to support and protection from violence – Legislation for the protection from violence in Austria. Vienna.

Federal Ministry of Constitution, Reforms, Deregulation and Justice (2019a): Managementzentrum Opferhilfe (MZ.O) [Management Centre Victim Assistance (MZ.O)]; https://www.justiz.gv.at/web2013/home/buergerservice/opferhilfe-und-prozessbegleitung/managementzentrum-opferhilfe-mzo~2c94848535a081cf0135a49e31aa001d.de.html [26.06.2019] [in German only].

Federal Ministry of Constitution, Reforms, Deregulation and Justice (2019b): Tätigkeitsbericht Prozessbegleitung [Activity Report Psycho-Social and Legal Support for the Proceedings]; https://www.justiz.gv.at/file/2c94848535a081cf0135bdec5753010a.de.0/pb_t %C3%A4tigkeitsbericht_2011-2018.pdf [22.10.2019] [in German only].

Federal Ministry of Constitution, Reforms, Deregulation and Justice (2018a): Qualitätsstandards für Prozessbegleitung bei Gewalt gegen Kinder und Jugendliche [Quality standards for process support in violence against children and adolescents]; https://www.justiz.gv.at/web2013/file/2c94848535a081cf0135a49ef4880021.de.0/qualitätsstandards_pb_kind er_und_jugendliche.pdf [14.07.2019] [in German only].

Federal Ministry of Constitution, Reforms, Deregulation and Justice (2018b): Qualitätsstandards für Prozessbegleitung für Frauen als Betroffene von Männergewalt und Frauenhandel [Quality standards for process support for women as victims of male violence and trafficking in women]; https://www.justiz.gv.at/web2013/file/2c94848535a081cf01 35a49ef4880021.de.0/qualitätsstandards_pb_frauen.pdf [14.07.2019] [in German only].

Federal Ministry of Constitution, Reforms, Deregulation and Justice (2018c): Qualitätsstandards für Prozessbegleitung für Opfer situativer Gewalt [Quality standards for process support for victims of situational violence]; https://www.justiz.gv.at/web2013/file/2c94848535a081cf0135a49ef4880021.de.0/qualitätsstandards_pb_opfer_situativer_gewalt.pdf [14.07.2019] [in German only].

Federal Ministry of Constitution, Reforms, Deregulation and Justice (2018d): Sicherheitsbericht 2017 [Security report 2017]; https://www.justiz.gv.at/web2013/file/2c94848525

f84a630132fdbd2cc85c91.de.0/sicherheitsbericht%202017%20bmvrdj.pdf?forcedownload=true [24.06.2019] [in German only].

Federal Ministry of Internal Affairs (2018a): Kriminalitätsbericht – Statistik und Analyse 2017 [Crime report – Statistics and analysis 2017]; https://www.bmi.gv.at/508/files/SIB_2017/03_SIB_2017-Kriminalitasetsbericht_web.pdf [21.06.2019] [in German only].

Federal Ministry of Internal Affairs (2018b): Sicherheitsbericht 2017 – Kriminalität – Vorbeugung und Bekämpfung – Anhang [Security Report 2017 – Crime – Prevention and control – Annex]; https://www.parlament.gv.at/PAKT/VHG/XXVI/III/III_00211/imfname_715994.pdf [21.06.2019] [in German only].

Federal Ministry of Justice (2017): Handbuch Prozessbegleitung – Leitfaden für die Abrechnung von Leistungen nach dem Leistungskatalog für Prozessbegleitung [Handbook process monitoring – Guideline for the billing of services according to the service catalog for process support]. Vienna Federal Ministry of Justice (2016): Correctional Services in Austria; https://www.justiz.gv.at/web2013/file/2c9484853e44f8f9013ef9d9e2b928dd.de.0/correctional_services_2016_download.pdf [02.07.2019] [in English only].

Federal Ministry of Justice (2011): Erlass BMJ-V306.200/0029-III 4/2010 [Decree BMJ-V306.200 / 0029-III 4/2010]; https://www.justiz.gv.at/web2013/home/buergerservice/opferhilfe-und-prozessbegleitung/managementzentrum-opferhilfe-mzo~2c94848535a081cf0135a49e31aa001d.de.html [26.06.2019] [in German only].

Federal Ministry of Justice/Federal Ministry of Education and Women/Federal Ministry for Families and Youth (2015): Psychosozioale Prozessbegleitung – Allgemeine Grundausbildung zur Ausübung von psychosozialer Prozessbegleitung [Psychosocio process accompaniment – General basic training for the exercise of psychosocial process monitoring]. Vienna.

Federal Ministry of the Interior, Construction and Homeland (2019): Polizeiliche Kriminalstatistik 2018 – Ausgewählte Zahlen im Überblick [Police crime statistics 2018 – Selected figures at a glance]; https://www.bmi.bund.de/SharedDocs/downloads/DE/publikationen/themen/sicherheit/pks-2018.pdf?__blob=publicationFile&v=3 [22.06.2019] [in German only].

FuturePolicy.org (2019): Austria's support for victims of violence in court procedures; https://www.futurepolicy.org/rights-and-responsibilities/austrias-support-for-victims-of-violence/ [21.06.2019] [in English only].

Research Centre Human Rights/White Ring Austria (2018): Gewalt im Netz gegen Frauen und Mädchen in Österreich [Violence in the net against women and girls in Austria]; www.frauen-familien-jugend.bka.gv.at/dam/jcr:05f7a42d-e9f3-4d67-b3eb-06b1fe1f1d05/Bestandsaufnahme_Gewalt_im_Netz_gegen_Frauen_und_Mädchen_in_Österreich.pdf [21.06.2019] [in German only].

Statistics Austria (2019a): Bevölkerung nach Alter und Geschlecht [Population by age and sex]; https://www.statistik.at/web_de/statistiken/menschen_und_gesellschaft/bevoelkerung/bevoelkerungsstruktur/bevoelkerung_nach_alter_geschlecht/index.html [30.09.2019] [in German and English]; cited as StatOffice 2019a.

Statistics Austria (2019b): Bildung in Zahlen 2017/18 – Tabellenband [Education in numbers 2017/18 – Table book]. Vienna; cited as StatOffice 2019b.

Statistics Austria (2019c): Demografisches Jahrbuch 2018 [Demographic Yearbook 2018]. Vienna; cited as StatOffice 2019c.

Statistics Austria (2019d): Statistics Brief – Jänner 2019 [Statistics letter – January 2019]; https://www.statistik.at/web_de/statistiken/wirtschaft/volkswirtschaftliche_gesamtrech

nungen/bruttoinlandsprodukt_und_hauptaggregate/index.html [22.06.2019] [in German only]; cited as StatOffice 2019d.

StatOffice: see Statistics Austria.

Victim Emergency Call (2019): Home; https://www.opfer-notruf.at/ [21.06.2019] [in German only].

White Ring (2019): Jahresbericht 2018 [Annual report 2018]; http://www.weisser-ring.at/2019/06/14/jahresbericht-2018/ [22.06.2019] [in German only].

White Ring (2018): Spendenbilanz 2017 [Donations 2017]: http://www.weisser-ring.at/wp-content/uploads/2018/10/Spendenbilanz2017.pdf [22.06.2019] [in German only].

Women's Helpline against Violence (2019a): Frauenhelpline gegen Gewalt [Women helpline against violence]; http://frauenhelpline.at/sites/default/files/frauenhelpline_en_17031.pdf [14.07.2019] [in English only].

Women's Helpline against Violence (2019b): Jahresbericht 2018 [Annual report 2018]; http://www.frauenhelpline.at/sites/default/files/jahresbericht-_frauenhelpline__2018.pdf [14.07.2019] [in German only].

Bosnia and Herzegovina

The Development of Victimology and Victim Protection in Bosnia and Herzegovina

Azra Adžajlić-Dedović & Miodrag Simović

1. Background

According to the Census of Population, Households and Dwellings, which was conducted in Bosnia and Herzegovina in the period 1–15 October 2013, 3,531,159 people lived in Bosnia and Herzegovina, out of which 1,798,889 are women and 1,732,270 are men.[1] Bosnia and Herzegovina has an area of 51,129 km². Per capita GDP in 2017 was 4,880 USD, with a total nominal GDP of approximately 16.8 billion USD according to the World Bank. The World Bank affirmed Bosnia and Herzegovina an economic growth forecast of 3.2% in 2018, up from 3% in 2017. The European Bank for Reconstruction and Development (EBRD) also increased its 2018 GDP growth forecast for Bosnia and Herzegovina to 3.3% and projected a growth of about 3.5% in 2019.[2] Bosnia and Herzegovina has been a potential candidate country for the accession to the European Union (EU) since 2003. The Government formally applied for EU membership in February 2016. The Commission adopted its Opinion (Avis) on the membership application in May 2019, identifying 14 key priorities for the country to fulfill in view of opening the accession negotiations. The European Council endorsed the Opinion and key priorities in December 2019. The Opinion constitutes a comprehensive roadmap for deep reforms in the areas of democracy/functionality, rule of law, fundamental rights, and public administration reform. In addition, the EC released the Strategy for the Western Balkans in February 2018.[3]

Out of the total number of inhabitants, 46% live in urban, and 54% live in rural areas. The average number of members of the households is 3.04.[4] More than 50%

---

1 StatOffice 2018, p. 12.

2 Securities Commission of Federation of Bosnia and Herzegovina 2019.

3 Securities Commission of Federation of Bosnia and Herzegovina 2019.

4 StatOffice 2018, p. 15.

of the population older than 15 years in Bosnia and Herzegovina have completed a secondary school. A higher proportion of the female population is without any education or has incomplete basic education, as well as completed elementary school, while the proportion of men with completed secondary and higher education levels is slightly higher compared to women.[5] By accepting quite a number of international acts, Bosnia and Herzegovina does not always accept its commitments. By observing the current trends in exercising and protecting, based on the knowledge that might be relevant to some criteria, the impression is that the gap of politics and rights yet remains, but it is reduced to the benefit of the law.[6]

There are a total of 80 regular courts and 20 prosecutors' offices in Bosnia and Herzegovina. According to the 2011 Bosnia and Herzegovina Council of Ministers' Report, the total number of judges in Bosnia and Herzegovina was 952 with 4 international judges, while 115 additional judges were in the courts. The total number of prosecutors in Bosnia and Herzegovina was 305, and 4 international prosecutors. Data from HJPC in 2015 indicate that 983 judges and 368 prosecutors were in the judicial system of Bosnia and Herzegovina.[7]

The police in Bosnia and Herzegovina, organised from the lowest to the highest authority, operates through police departments, stations, ministries of internal affairs (10 in the Federation and 1 in Republika Srpska), the State Investigation and Protection Agency of Bosnia and Herzegovina (SIPA), the Border Police of Bosnia and Herzegovina and the Judicial Police in Bosnia and Herzegovina. Researching the number of staff in the Ministry of Security of Bosnia and Herzegovina and seven organizations at the state level, we have come to the conclusion that 4,255 persons are employed at this organizational level. When it comes to the numerical situation of the employees in the complete organizational police structure in Bosnia and Herzegovina, the data show that, within the above three organizational levels, 22,738 employees were engaged.

2. The Development of Victimology in Bosnia and Herzegovina

The development of victimology is strongly related to the development of a study programme in the Department of Criminology of the University of Sarajevo (1994) in Bosnia and Herzegovina. Victimology has been a subject at the Faculty of crime sciences since 1994. The faculty later changed its name to the Faculty of Criminalistics, Criminology and Security Studies. Victimology is no longer a subject of bewilderment or curiosity but is slowly becoming a household name. This is being

5 StatOffice 2018, p. 22.

6 *Simović* 2001.

7 *Hadžović & Kržalić* 2015, p. 34.

facilitated by the extensive coverage that crime news and victim issues are receiving in the mass media; by the wide publicity that programmes for victims are getting and by the proliferation of victim services and programmes of victim assistance in many countries.[8]

2.1 Theoretical Aspects of Victimology Development in Bosnia and Herzegovina

The first curriculum and textbook titled "Theoretical or Victimology 1" (2004), "Restorative Justice or Victimology 2" (2010), and "Special or Victimology 3" (2010) by *Azra Adžajlić-Dedović* of the Department of Criminology of the Faculty of Criminalistics, Criminology and Security Studies of the University of Sarajevo in Bosnia and Herzegovina. The concept about the development of Victimology was published by *Gerd Ferdinand Kirchhoff* of Graduate School of Victimology, Tokiwa University Mito Japan as a lecture to the 29th Postgraduate Course in Victimology held at Inter-University Centar Dubrovnik from 13 to 26 May 2013. Professors *Alija Ramljak*,[9] *Petrović Borislav*,[10] and *Miodrag Simović*[11] gave a strong contribution to the development of victimology in Bosnia and Herzegovina. The first victimology study on fear of victimisation[12] and the first manual for teaching victimology in Bosnia and Herzegovina was made on the Department of Criminology of the Faculty of Criminalistics, Criminology and Security Studies of the University of Sarajevo[13].

The second study was about fear of victimisation that was initiated by *Azra Ažajlić-Dedović* and *Saša Mijalković* from the Criminal Police Academy in Belgrade, under the title "Prevention of Ethnic, Religious and Racial Intolerance and Conflicts", as a regional project with the participation of all universities from the region (a written consent and financial participation have been provided by the partners and co-authors *Metodije Angelovski* of the University of Skopje, *Ilir Tafa* of the University of Priština, *Duško Modly* of the University of Zagreb, *Saša Mijalković* of the University of Belgrade, *Gorazd Meško* of the University of Maribor, and *Ramo Masleša* of the University of Sarajevo). They offered measures for the prevention of conflict and peacebuilding in the Balkans, but their study paper was not published because their further engagement in the development of this multidisciplinary victimological research was suspended in 2009.

---

8 *Kirchhoff* 2013.

9 *Ramljak & Halilović* 2004.

10 *Petrović* 2005.

11 *Ramljak & Simović* 2006.

12 *Adžajlić-Dedović* 2003.

13 *Adžajlić-Dedović & Balić* 2004.

2.2 The Study on Fear of Victimisation in Bosnia and Herzegovina

"The Influence of the Victim on the Phenomenon of Crime" and "Women as Crime Victims" are two seminal books in the development of Serbian victimology. Both dealt with issues such as domestic violence, marital rape, inadequate legislation about victims, the position of rape victim before the police, the prosecutor and the court, shelters and hotlines for battered women, etc. Moreover, the books served as important platforms for advocacy on legal changes.[14] The Study on Fear of Victimisation in Bosnia and Herzegovina or victimological research are: "Prostitution in Bosnia and Herzegovina" (2003), "Long roads of justice" (2004), "Domestic violence – Developmental study in Bosnia and Herzegovina" (2005), "Police and domestic violence in the Federation of Bosnia and Herzegovina" (2007), "The betrayal of Bosnia and Herzegovina" (2018), and "Peace study in Bosnia and Herzegovina" (2019).

2.3 Restorative Justice in Bosnia and Herzegovina

Restorative justice as a special scientific discipline has been developed and separated as an individual subject since 2010[15] on the Faculty of Criminalistics, Criminology and Security Studies of the University of Sarajevo. Bosnia and Herzegovina has selected the mediation as a model for the realisation of restorative justice. Pursuant to the Law on Mediation Procedure in Bosnia and Herzegovina, the Association of Mediators of Bosnia and Herzegovina has been entrusted with the mediation. The Association of Mediators of Bosnia and Herzegovina is in charge to conduct mediation under the Law on Mediation Procedure in Bosnia and Herzegovina,[16] as one of the out-of-court models alternative for achieving restorative justice.[17] There have been 590 mediations done by the end of 2006 in Bosnia and Herzegovina, out of which 330 have been solved with consent or 56%.

The economic cases, debts, and annulment of contracts are leading cases, whereas there are no cases of peer violence and domestic violence because judiciary bodies not instruct parties to mediations.[18] Thus, mediation at the same time seeks to achieve a dialogue between the perpetrator and the victim, satisfy the needs of the victim, encourage and develop empathy among the perpetrators, and their overall growth and development in terms of reduction of recidivism in the future.

---

14 *Nikolić-Ristanović* 2012.

15 *Adžajlić-Dedović* 2011.

16 Act on Mediation Procedure, Law No. 2004-L-99950, 29.06.2004, Official Gazette 37/2004.

17 *Adžajlić-Dedović* 2014.

18 *Adžajlić-Dedović* 2011.

It is interesting to observe how the citizens of Bosnia and Herzegovina see an agreement that ended the war in Bosnia and Herzegovina, with a time distance of 20 years. Compared to the international mediator, the national mediator has no mandate to propose a part of the solution or a solution of the subject dispute.[19] Frozen justice is a timely, critical account of the challenges to dealing with the past more than a quarter of a century after ethnic conflict and subsequent human rights violations devastated Bosnia and Herzegovina in the 1990s. *Jared Bell* provides an in–depth analysis of transitional justice mechanisms in the post–Dayton Peace era, including retributive and restorative justice strategies, to foster accountability and reconciliation. Despite the decades that have passed, the author soberly demonstrates that the international policy strategies implemented on the ground have only resulted in partial success to promote peace and security.[20]

Retributive justice further reduces the risk of revenge, prevents a return to power by the perpetrators of war crimes and crimes against humanity, and leads to the individualization of accountability, thus removing the stigma of collective guilt from communities.[21] The above mentioned is confirmed, in other words, by a textbook for the execution of the victimological course as a lifelong learning titled "Preventing and Combating Domestic Violence through the Application of Mediation in Churches and Religious Communities in Bosnia and Herzegovina", which served to educate citizens on the best measures and models of prevention of the violence in the family within the church and religious communities.[22]

2.4 The other Scientific Research with a Victimological View on the Crime Prevention in Bosnia and Herzegovina

The "Fear of Crime in Urban Neighbourhoods: A Comparative Analysis of Six Capitals" is the first criminology study about fear of crime research in Western Europe. The research presented in this article is the first comparative research using the socio-demographic and social psychological model in the region of South Eastern Europe.[23]

---

19 Criminal Procedure Code of Bosnia and Herzegovina, Law No. 3/03, 24.01.2003, Official Gazette 3/2003; Law on Changes and Amendments to the Criminal Procedure Code of Bosnia and Herzegovina, Law No. 65/18, 21.09.2018, Official Gazette 65/2018.

20 *Bell* 2018.

21 *Bejtić* 2015, p. 59.

22 *Adžajlić-Dedović, Sofradžija, Deljkić,* Čamo, Šabani, *Martinović, Humačkić, Topić, Stočanin-Hrustemović, Pandžo & Gavrić* 2015.

23 *Meško & Areh* 2003; *Meško & Kovčo* 1999; *Meško & Pavlović* 1998; *Meško & Umek* 1999; *Pavlović* 1998; *Zvekić* 1998.

The socio-demographic model focuses on demographic characteristics of potentially fearful people, people at risk, or victimised people.[24] The situation in Bosnia and Herzegovina looks like the following: in the Federation of Bosnia and Herzegovina, the crime rate for the observed Republika Srpska the property crime rate is 471.6 for theft, 13.7 for frauds and 16.6 for robberies and robbery theft; finally for the Brčko District of Bosnia and Herzegovina it is 701.2 for theft, 11.1 for frauds and 17.2 for robberies and robbery theft. The exposed items that give average rates for thefts, armed robberies and robbery theft in Europe are 3–4 times higher than in Bosnia and Herzegovina and are 10 times higher and more for fraud rates.[25] Bosnia and Herzegovina is well-positioned country finding itself in a group of countries in the pre-last quartile, being the country below an average rate of armed robberies.[26]

Fight against juvenile delinquency in the Federation of Bosnia and Herzegovina requires a coordinated action of all social subjects starting from the Federal Ministry of Justice, Cantonal and Municipal Courts, prosecutors, guardianship bodies and all the subjects having "an active" role, both in the criminal proceedings and in implementation of the criminal sanctions against juveniles.[27]

The goal of the part of the procedure, in which the juvenile offender does not enter the area of initiation of criminal proceedings, is not to initiate a criminal proceedings in the cases where the law permits or ensures proper development of the juvenile and strengthens their responsibility, so they would not commit criminal offences in the future.[28] The above mentioned is confirmed, in other words, by a textbook for the execution of the victimological course as a lifelong learning with the title "Preventing and combating domestic violence through the application of mediation in churches and religious communities in Bosnia and Herzegovina", which served to educate citizens on the best measures and models of prevention of the violence in the family within the church and religious communities.[29]

Accordingly, most children know who they should address in case they are victims or testify to violence within the school, but they say that they would rarely have decided on such a step. The reason is the shattered confidence that children have in adults in the school environment, who, according to the children's testimony, often failed earn their trust, discovered the identity of the one who reported violence and failed to protect them from possible violent consequences.[30]

---

24 *Meško, Fallshore, Muratbegović & Fields* 2008.

25 *Mujanović, Datzer & Budimlić* 2012.

26 *Mujanović et al.* 2012.

27 *Simović & Simović* 2018.

28 *Simović & Simović* 2018.

29 *Adžajlić-Dedović et al.* 2015.

30 *Muratbegović, Bulić & Budimlić* 2017.

The national strategy for dealing with drug abuse must be based on a multidisciplinary approach where two dimensions must be stressed – first, one needs enough qualified people and second, they need to be coordinated and work together. The multidisciplinary approach may be achieved by the constant striving of various social institutions – the holders of programs for drug-related problems – and here the national coordinating body has an important role.[31] The research results show that newspapers influence public perception of crime in society because the majority of people learn about crime and criminals from the mass media. Sensationalism often contributes to more "picturesque" reporting of "ordinary" crime and marginalized people who are considered to be guilty of all crucial problems in society.[32]

It is also important to mention that in addition to research and teaching our colleagues have had some impact on policymaking, especially *Elmedin Muratbegović*. He researched the protection of children in Bosnia and Herzegovina. *Maljević, Datzer, Muratbegović*, and *Budimlić* published a book on police and corruption, featuring an impressive collection of papers showing challenges for the development of policing, especially about the improvement of police integrity and governance in general.[33] This theory attaches all the social problems to the fact that in society there is poor social control, poor individuality and loose social connections in groups, and weaker socialization of members of problem groups.[34]

Improvement of a formal system of social control of criminality relies upon findings that are derived from scientific research used to improve the knowledge about phenomenology and aetiology of criminal behaviour, as well as mechanisms and effects of reaction to criminality. Criminology and other related disciplines, by using theoretical concepts of natural, social and technical sciences, are constantly striving not only after innovations in the area of analysis but also after more efficient and effective crime control.[35] Unfortunately, it should be emphasised that the system is primarily focused on the rights of the suspect or defendant, while witnesses and victims are mostly treated as objects within the process rather than subjects whose fundamental rights should be respected and adhered to.

3. The Relevant Legal Framework in Terms of Criminal Policy

Victims do not exercise the right to effective forms of assistance and support, including access to specialised victim's support services with the view of reduction

31 *Petrović* 2002.

32 *Meško* 2002.

33 *Maljević, Datzer, Muratbegović & Budimlić* 2006.

34 *Šabani* 2013.

35 *Budimlić, Kavazović, Puharić & Kobajica* 2017.

of the possibility of secondary victimisation.[36] After more than 16 years since the adoption of the Law on Criminal Procedure of Bosnia and Herzegovina, the issue of the offended in the capacity of the prosecutor (subsidiary) did not lose that form in the theory and practice of the Criminal Procedure Law of Bosnia and Herzegovina.[37]

The earlier legal solution defined the injured party as one of the parties authorised for prosecutions in a situation when the public prosecutor concludes that there are no grounds for initiation or continuation of the criminal proceeding. Currently, only the prosecutor, representative of the State Prosecutor's Office, is defined to be an authorised prosecutor in terms of all criminal offences under the applicable legal solution. The restitution of the previous legal arrangement, referring to the injured party to be a prosecutor, would be a control mechanism for the work of a public prosecutor in terms of correction of his work by the injured party, regardless of whether a property claim was filed in the criminal proceedings or not. Most of the new provisions of the aforesaid Law refer to the harmonisation of the domestic crime proceedings system with the European system for the protection of basic human rights and freedoms. Other things are noticeable when arranging the main trial.[38]

The injured party, as a person whose personal or property right was violated or endangered by a criminal offence, in accordance with the applicable legal regulations in Bosnia and Herzegovina, is entitled to the following rights in the criminal procedure:

1) the right to report an executed crime,
2) the right to submit a proposal for realization of a property right claim, including the right to refer, in the closing statement, on evidence that substantiates the property right claim, and the right to submit a proposal for directing to mediation,
3) the right to be informed of the failure to carry out the investigation and the reasons for it, in case of which, they have the right to file a complaint to the prosecutor's office within eight days,
4) the right to be informed of the suspension of the investigation, as well as the reasons for that, in which case also they have the right to file a complaint to the prosecutor's office within eight days,
5) the right to be informed of the results of the guilty plea,
6) the right to be informed on the withdrawal of the indictment, and the termination of criminal proceedings;

36 *Gracin & Butorac* 2017.

37 *Simović & Šikman* 2018.

38 *Simović & Simović* 2014.

7) the right to attend the hearing of witnesses or professional expert outside the courtroom, as well as the reconstruction of events,

8) the right to be heard in the capacity of witness during the course of the investigation and at the main hearing,

9) the right to attend the main hearing,

10) the right to appeal against the court's decision on the costs of criminal proceedings and property claim, but not on the punishment sentence, and

11) the right to be informed of the waiver of prosecution in the juvenile proceedings.[39]

Finally, the injured party may also appear in the role of a passive means of proof in circumstances where they are subjected to certain actions against their will, such as, for example, mental health examination, the examination of body injuries, physical examination, taking blood tests and other medical procedures.[40] A special category of witnesses are witnesses – the offended, i.e. victims of criminal offences who, with their statement, present the direct information on the criminal offence.

4. Image of the Victimisation Reality Based on Data and Research Findings

4.1 The Victims of the War in Bosnia and Herzegovina (1992–1995)

The state of Bosnia and Herzegovina must have designing policies and measures of reparation for the victims of international crimes. The United Nations Declaration on the Right to Victims of Crime and Abuse, together with the acts of the Council of Europe and the European Union, contains the essence of the rights of victims in democratic states in which we have the rule of law. The reparation programmes are vital in the transitional justice process but many female victims have more problems with the attempt to access reparations. The restitution, compensation, rehabilitation and punishment are the formal categories of reparations in the Basic Principles and Guidelines on the Right to a Remedy and Reparation for Victims of Gross Violations of International Human Rights Law and Serious Violations of International Humanitarian Law *(Table 1)*.[41]

---

39 *Halilović, Adžajlić-Dedović, Budimlić* 2019.

40 *Sijerčić-Čolić* 2003.

41 Basic Principles and Guidelines on the Right to a Remedy and Reperation for Victims of Gross Violations of International Human Rights Law and Serious Violations of International Humanitarian Law, Resolution No. A/RES/60/147, 16.12.2005; https://documents-dds-ny.un.org/doc/UNDOC/GEN/N05/496/42/PDF/N0549642.pdf?OpenElement [10.06.2019].

Table 1 The Cases of Sexual Violence in the War in Bosnia and Herzegovina (1992–1995)

Case: Sexual Violence	Defendants	Punishment ITCY
(IT-94-2) Vlasenica (VRS)	Dragan Nikolic "Jenki"	20 years of imprisonment
(IT-95-9) Bosanski Šamac (VRS)	Simo Zaric	6 years of imprisonment
(IT-95-10/1) Brčko (VRS)	Ranko Cesic	18 years of imprisonment
(IT-95-17/1) Vitez (HVO)	Anto Furundzija	10 years of imprisonment
(IT-96-21) Čelebić (HVO)	Hazim Delic	18 years of imprisonment
(IT-96-23, IT-96-23/1) Foča (VRS)	Dragoljub Kunarac	28 years of imprisonment
(IT-96-23, IT-96-23/1) Foča (VRS)	Radomir Kovac	20 years of imprisonment
(IT-96-23, IT-96-23/1) Foča (VRS)	Zoran Vukovic	12 years of imprisonment
(IT-97-24) Prijedor (VRS)	Milomir Stakic	40 years of imprisonment
(IT-95-12) Vareš (HVO)	Ivica Rajic	12 years of imprisonment
(IT-95-17) Lašvanjska dolina (HVO)	Bralo Miroslav	20 years of imprisonment
(IT-96-23/2) Foča (VRS)	Dragan Zelenovic	15 years of imprisonment
(IT-99-36) Krajina (VRS)	Radoslav Brdanin	32 years of imprisonment
(IT-04-74) Herceg-Bosna (HVO)	Jadranko Prlic	25 years of imprisonment
(IT-04-74) Herceg-Bosna (HVO)	Brune Stojica	20 years of imprisonment
(IT-04-74) Herceg-Bosna (HVO)	Praljak Slobodan	20 years of imprisonment
(IT-04-74) Herceg-Bosna (HVO)	Milivoja Petkovica	20 years of imprisonment
(IT-04-83) El Mudžahid (ARBiH)	Rasima Delica	3 years of imprisonment
(IT-95-5/18) BiH i Srebrenica (VRS)	Ratka Mladica	40 years of imprisonment

Source: Adžajlić-Dedović 2010.

VRS: Army of Republika Srpska; HVO: Croatian Defense Council; ARBiH: Army of Bosnia and Herzegovina.

Since 2004, the Witness Protection Department has become operative until 2015, and has provided protection and support measures for the benefit of 1,017 witnesses and 1,027 protection measures against them. By 2012, this number was about 700 witnesses. The state's failure to implement the 2004 Law on Missing Persons led to problems for the families of the disappeared, including the denial of their rights to justice and reparation. The Fund for Providing Assistance to the Families of Missing Persons envisaged by the 2004 Law had still not been established. Many judgments of the Constitutional Court of Bosnia and Herzegovina in cases involving enforced disappearances remained unimplemented. On 1 June 2016, the Special War Crimes Chamber has indicted a total of 606 people charged with war crimes and serious violations of international humanitarian law, making Bosnia and Herzegovina's Prosecutor's Office the institution with the highest number of the accused internationally, after the Second World War and the tribunal in Nuremberg and Tokyo. As of July

2009, the State Court of Bosnia and Herzegovina had delivered final judgments in 12 cases against 15 persons accused in relation to war crimes of sexual violence.[42] The jurisprudence of the international tribunals favours the notion of "coercive circumstances" as well as direct force or the threat of force as an element of rape. This approach was also taken by the Trial Chamber of the International Criminal Tribunal for Rwanda (ICTR) in the Akayesu case.[43] The judgment states that "coercive circumstances need not be evidenced by a show of physical force. Threats, intimidation, extortion and other forms of duress which prey on fear or desperation may constitute coercion, and coercion may be inherent in certain circumstances, such as armed conflict." The relevance of this reasoning to the context of the war in Bosnia and Herzegovina was confirmed by the Trial Chamber of the ICTY in its judgment in the Delalic case.[44]

Narratives about reconciliation, implacability and terms for reconciliation are not only formed in relation to the war as whole, but also in relation to other victims of different ethnics or religions in Bosnia and Herzegovina like the result of analysis presented on the experiences by former concentration camp detainees who were placed in concentration camps where they experienced sexual violence at the beginning of the Bosnian war in the 1990s.[45] Since its creation, the ICTY has prosecuted and concluded 18 cases which included charges of rape and other forms of sexual violence related to the war. The focus lies on the description of how the interviewees portray the phenomenon of a "victimhood" and construct the "victim of sexual violence in the war" as a special category of the victims of war.[46] The fact that an additional 120 case files were transferred to the entity prosecutors' offices did not automatically facilitate the investigations.

There was no training and there is no training currently being done by the experts (supervisors), who would work with clients assisting displaced persons, refugees, and returnees (supervision).[47] Referring to the needs of this group of beneficiaries, we discovered information *ad hoc* through a history, diagnosis and individual dossiers kept with the individual experts.[48] A general observation about this type of psychosocial problems is such that after the war trauma, the people from displaced-refugee population-RIP are constantly exposed to various types of post-war stressful

---

42 *Wood* 2006.

43 *Prosecutor v. Akayesu,* ICTR-96-4-T, International Criminal Tribunal for Rwanda (1998).

44 *Prosecutor v. Delalic, Delic, Mucic and Landzo,* IT-96-21, International Criminal Tribunal for Yugoslavia (1998).

45 *Bašić* 2017.

46 *Adžajlić-Dedović, Rizvo & Hasković* 2018.

47 *Petrović* 2016.

48 *Petrović* 2016.

Table 2 The Victims of War in the Bosnian Krajina – A Review of Selected Cities (1992-1995)

Municipality	Men			Women			Total
	Civilians	Soldiers	Total	Civilians	Soldiers	Total	
Bihać	220	1,288	1,508	80	10	90	1,598
Bos. Dubica	32	238	270	18	5	23	293
Bos. Krupa	125	1,157	1,282	54	1	55	1,337
Bosanski Novi	229	388	617	66	0	66	683
Bos. Petrovac	136	186	322	69	1	70	392
Bos. Grahovo	47	119	166	22	4	26	192
Cazin	88	812	900	28	2	30	930
Drvar	35	106	141	19	0	19	160
Ključ	518	582	1,100	113	2	115	1,215
Prijedor	3,428	1,045	4,473	391	4	395	4,868
Sanski Most	899	514	1,347	231	2	233	1,580
Velika Kladuša	174	885	1,059	50	2	52	1,111
Total	5,865	7,320	13,185	1,141	33	1,174	14,359

Source: Kurtović 2013.

events. The main stressors are the loss of relatives, unresolved housing issues, unemployment, and poverty. In some areas, floods were a new traumatic experience.[49]

4.2 Victims of Human Trafficking and Sexual Violence

According to police reports, the number of identified victims of human trafficking in 2005 was 54, and 43 in 2006. At the same time, it has been noticed that there were more investigations in 2006, precisely 90 in total (42 new investigations were launched with 48 unresolved results from the previous period, which is an increase compared to 2005 when a total of 68 investigations were conducted; 37 investigations were launched in 2005, and 31 investigations have continued from 2004), and 14 orders were issued on non-conducting the investigation, while 13 investigations were suspended (*Tables 3, 4* and *5*).[50]

Also, 31 indictments were filed in 2006 and 33 were confirmed in court (two indictments that had been filed in 2005, have been confirmed in 2006), and 24 indictments were filed in 2005, while courts confirmed 26 indictment.[51]

49 *Petrović* 2016.

50 *Topić* 2011.

51 *Topić* 2011.

Table 3 Reported Cases of Trafficking in Human Beings in Bosnia and Herzegovina (2005–2008)

	2005	2006	2007	2008
Criminal offences	36	34	34	23
Perpetrators	59	77	56	55
Victims	54	43	41	59

Source: Topić 2012.

Table 4 Numbers of Reported Criminal Offences of Trafficking in Human Beings (2009–2012)

	2009	2010	2011	2012
Criminal offences	69	94	4	17
Perpetrators	25	99	6	25
Victims	35	52	0	30

Source: Topić 2012.

Table 5 Numbers of Victims of Human Trafficking and Sexual Violence (2012–2014)

	2012	2013	2014
Number of victims	39	16	49

Source: Topić 2012.

The Ministry of Security of Bosnia and Herzegovina has specific authorities dealing with the fight against human trafficking and illegal migration in Bosnia and Herzegovina, determined by the Decision of the Council of Ministers of Bosnia and Herzegovina on Procedures and Methods for Coordinating the Activities in the Prevention of Trafficking in Human Beings and Illegal Migrations in Bosnia and Herzegovina.[52]

Although these victim assistance programmes vary in their goals, the types of victims they address, service delivery systems, and the size and levels of resources, they have a common core task: treating victims and witnesses with dignity, compassion and respect while at the same time striving for the prevention of secondary victimisation.[53]

52 *Rizvo, Hunček & Muratbegović* 2018.

53 The Victimological Society of Bosnia and Herzegovina 2005, p. 153.

The most widespread prejudice about the perpetrators of sexual offences is a story of persons with mental health conditions and intellectual or developmental disabilities. The truth is much more complex, and it indicates that very few people with mental health conditions are committing criminal offences.[54] The legislation is not fully in compliance with the international standards, but as we have seen throughout legislative analysis and compliance with conventions, it is still being done, and progressive steps are being taken towards the adoption of these standards in our area. In order to provide an adequate support and protection for the victims, it is also necessary to provide a continuous education with the aim of raising the awareness of employees in the judicial and other competent authorities of the county participating in the process of solution and investigation of cases relating to sexual abuse and trafficking in human beings. Education is necessary, both in terms of an easier identification of a criminal offence and perpetrators and from the aspect of the position and rights of the victims of sexual violence and human being trafficking.[55] "The unspecified legal beings" of the criminal offences and generally unspecified regulations pose a great danger to the principle of legal certainty and safety. If the beings of the criminal offences are unspecified, diffuse, if it is not seen what is punished, we open the possibility that the principle of legality is sidestepped in practice.[56]

The victims are subjected to a continuous re-traumatization due to multiple interrogations and the perpetrators do not receive adequate punishment, which prevents the achievement of moral satisfaction even after long and exhausting processes.[57]The truth is much more complex, and it indicates that very few people with mental health problems are committing criminal offences.[58] The legislation is not fully in compliance with the international standards, but as we have seen throughout legislative analysis and compliance with conventions, it is still being done, and progressive steps are being taken towards the adoption of these standards in our area.

4.3 The Victims of Conventional Crime

There are also traces of the means of execution on the victim, which can be different depending on which particular asset is being used.[59] Victims have the experience of multiple secondary victimisations within the judicial system because the process of proving and pronouncing the verdict lasts too long. Statistics on crime include the Banja Luka area and the period from 2013 to 2015 since only those data are available on the website of the Ministry of Internal Affairs of RS.

---

[54] *Adžajlić-Dedović et al.* 2018.

[55] *Adžajlić-Dedović et al.* 2018.

[56] *Simović & Simović* 2013.

[57] *Šarić* 2015.

[58] *Adžajlić-Dedović et al.* 2018.

[59] *Korajlić & Muharremi* 2011.

Within the statistical data, data from the area of property crime, crime against life and body, gender identity hate crime and other criminal offences from the area of conventional crime are included (*Tables 6* and *7*).[60]

Table 6 The Victims of Conventional Crime: Crime of Murder in the Banja Luka Area (2014–2016)

2014	5
2015	7
2016	4

Source: Antić 2017.

Table 7 The Victims of Conventional Crime: Property Crimes in the Banja Luka Area (2013–2015)

	2013	**2014**	**2015**
Theft	1,207	829	774
Heavy theft	1372	921	912
Robbery theft	3	1	–
Robbery	52	49	30
Scams/Frauds	79	78	74
Extortion	14	16	8
Blackmail	8	6	1
Concealing	64	49	47
Evasion	–	56	65
Damaging other's property	–	164	169
Deprivation of a vehicle	–	29	35
Arson	–	11	13
Other criminal offences	392	45	50
Total	3,191	2,254	2,178

Source: Gavrić 2017.

Statistics on crime include the Banja Luka area and the period from 2013 to 2015 since only those data are available on the website of the Ministry of Internal Affairs of Republika Srpska. Within the statistical data, data from the area of property crime, crime against life and body, gender identity hate crime and other criminal offences from the area of general crime are included.[61] The highest number of murders in the

60 *Gavrić* 2017.

61 *Gavrić* 2017.

Banja Luka area was recorded in 2015 when there were seven murders. This number in 2014 amounted to five. During 2016, four murders were committed.

During 2015, three murder cases were resolved, while one murder was resolved during 2014. A minor was involved in one criminal offence in 2014. The total number of reported persons in 2014 was five, as it was the number of crimes committed at the same time. Out of seven criminal offences in 2015, four persons were reported, while in 2016 five persons were reported.[62] Given the overall data in the area of crime against life and body, the largest number was recorded in 2013 with 231 cases, while this number in 2015 amounted to 179.[63]

In regards to criminal offences in the area of general crime, the largest number of criminal offences was recorded in 2013, when it amounted to incredible 1,160 criminal offences. The largest numbers of criminal offences were recorded in the following categories: unauthorized production and trafficking of weapons, domestic violence, forgery of documents and forest wood theft. This number was 784 in 2014, while it was slightly increased to 794 in 2015.[64]

The highest number of murders in the Banja Luka area was recorded in 2015, when there were 7 murders. This number in 2014 amounted to five. During 2016, four murders were committed. During 2015, three murder cases were resolved, while one murder was resolved during 2014. A minor was involved in one criminal offence in 2014.

The total number of reported persons in 2014 was five, as it was the number of crimes committed at the same time. Out of sewven criminal offences in 2015, four persons were reported, while in 2016 five persons were reported.[65]

4.4 The Victims of Natural Disasters

Environmental protection implies all actions taken to prevent the causes of degradation, pollution or destruction of the environment and excessive consumption of natural resources and space, which are the only way to provide clean air, sufficient quantities of quality and hygienically proper drinking water, unpolluted agricultural land and healthy food, and therefore the survival of man and the development of human civilization (*Table 8*).

The Ministry of Security of Bosnia and Herzegovina coordinates jobs and tasks of protection and rescue. The data exchange, information, reports on undertaken measures of protection and rescue among holders of the tasks, and jobs of protection and

62 *Antić* 2017.

63 *Gavrić* 2017.

64 *Gavrić* 2017.

65 *Antić* 2017.

Table 8 Fires in the Federation of Bosnia and Herzegovina – Victims and Damage (2008–2012)

	2008	2009	2010	2011	2012
Total number of fires	1,219	1,151	1,413	3,379	5,975
Burnt area (ha)	1,288.64	405.24	390.35	1,796.29	41,717.81
Death casualties	9	35	16	25	18
Evacuated	0	27	7	0	0

Source: Cicović 2016.

rescue are within the authority of the bodies and services of civil protection of the Bosnia and Herzegovina Entities and the Brčko District of BiH. The safety report should contain at least the following, pursuant to Article 3 of the Rulebook: plan of major accidents prevention, description of plants and facilities' sites; description of plants and facilities; identification and analysis of potential risks and measures of the prevention, protection measures and intervention plans that prevent the spread of the consequences of an accident.

The Ministry of Foreign Trade and Economic Relations is responsible for environmental protection, but only to a very limited extent. Current developments suggest that this could be broadened in the near future. Within the Ministry, there is the Sector of Natural Resources, Energy and Environmental Protection, which includes the understaffed Department for Environmental Protection and the Department for Coordination of the Management of Natural Resources.

There are no state institutions dealing with or responsible for environmental health issues, such as monitoring, inspection or reporting. These responsibilities are dealt with by the two entities. In the Federation, responsibilities for environmental protection policy, health care, communication and transport infrastructure, tourism and the use of natural resources are divided between the Federation and the cantons. The Ministry of Foreign Trade and Economic Relations is responsible for environmental protection, but only to a very limited extent. Current developments suggest that this could be broadened in the near future. Within the Ministry, there is a Sector of Natural Resources, Energy and Environmental Protection, which includes the Department for Environmental Protection, small in size, and the Department for Coordination of the Management of Natural Resources. There are no state institutions dealing with or responsible for environmental health issues, such as monitoring, inspection or reporting. These responsibilities are dealt with by the two entities. In the Federation, responsibilities for environmental protection policy, health care, communication and transport infrastructure, tourism and the use of natural resources are divided between the Federation and the cantons.

There are other institutions dealing with environmental health, such as the Institute of Environmental Care and Ecology, the Institute of Veterinary Medicine, the

Agropedological Institute, the School of Chemical Engineering, the School of Agriculture, the School of Forestry, the public company "Srpske Sume", the Faculty of Science and Mathematics, the Institute for Urbanism, the Hydro-Meteorology Institute, and the Directorate for Water. The Ministry of Health and Social Welfare has a health inspectorate, which is part of RS surveillance system, together with the veterinary, agricultural and market inspectorates. Local inspections are organized by the municipalities. However, the health statistics system has difficulties in defining the size of the population and other basic demographic indicators. Underreporting and under diagnosis of diseases and incomplete registration of demographic indicators influence the quality of health statistics. There is a lack of studies investigating the influence of environmental conditions on the health of the population.

4.5 The Victims of Discrimination

The European Code on the Police Ethics emphasises that the police shall carry out the tasks in a fair manner, especially guided by the principles of impartiality and non-discrimination. Also, the Council of Europe Declaration on the Police emphasises the prohibition of action against persons based on racial, religious or political convictions (Article 8).

Also, as long as Bosnia and Herzegovina is a devided society, the constitutional reform will not be able to significantly exceed the existing constitutional model based on the dominance of the ethnic principle and on one-dimensional man, who is primarily and almost exclusively a member of a nation, and only after that, a member of other social groups or an abstract citizen.[66] Out of a total number of registered 230 cases of discrimination, 118 were registered in the Sarajevo regional office, 72 in the Banja Luka head office, 22 in the Regional office of Brčko District, 12 in the Mostar regional office and 6 in the Livno branch office (*Table 9*).[67] A total of 230 complaints were registered in the Department for the Elimination of All Forms of Discrimination in 2014. The largest number of complaints relates to mobbing as a special form of discrimination at the workplace (69), followed by complaints of discrimination based on social status and gender (25), discrimination based on ethnicity (22), discrimination based on national or social origin (19) and discrimination based on education (12).[68] According to studies conducted in the period from 1 January 2014 to 1 January 2015, the police intervened in 2,865 cases of domestic violence in 15 towns in Bosnia and Herzegovina in total. Out of 2,865 cases of domestic violence, 1,233 cases have been prosecuted and completed in court proceedings.[69]

---

66 *Marković* 2014.

67 *Bijeljanjić* 2016.

68 *Bijeljanjić* 2016.

69 *Adžajlić-Dedović, Deljkic, Ćatić-Lučić, Bojanić & Hasković* 2007.

Table 9 The Victims of Discrimination in Bosnia and Herzegovina in 2013

	Saraje-vo	**Banja Luka**	**Brčko**	**Mostar**	**Livno**	**Total**
Mobbing	42	16	7	3	1	69
Segregation	0	1	0	0	0	1
Supporting	0	0	0	0	0	0
Encouraging	0	0	2	0	0	2
Based on race	0	0	0	0	0	0
Based on skin colour	0	0	0	0	0	0
Based on the language	3	1	0	0	1	4
Based on religion	1	1	0	0	0	2
Based on ethnicity	11	11	0	0	0	22
Based on social origin	11	5	3	0	0	19
Connection with a minority	0	0	2	1	0	3
Based on political conviction	1	2	0	1	1	5
Trade union membership	1	4	0	0	1	6
Based on education	5	5	2	0	0	12
Based on social position and gender	7	10	7	0	1	25
Based on sexual orientation	3	8	0	0	0	11
Other	32	3	0	6	1	42

Source: Bijeljanjić 2016.

4.6 The Victims of Corruption and Victims of Abuse of Power

In this regard, the 1985 UN Declaration of Basic Principles of Justice for Victims of Crime and Abuse of Power should be primarily referred to, as it reflects the collective will of the international community to establish a balance between basic rights of suspects and offenders on the one hand, and victims' rights and interests on the other.[70] In terms of advocating for justice for victims, as against the existing documents about victims to that date, this Declaration made one step further by establishing two definitions of victims: victims of conventional crimes and power abuse victims, and relevant standards of support and protection of these victims. In accordance with point 18 of the Declaration, a power abuse victim is defined as a person who, independently or collectively, suffered damage, including physical or mental injuries, emotional suffering, economic loss or significant violation of own basic rights, due to actions or failure to take action, which still does not pose vio-

70 *Mehić* 2013.

lation of any national criminal code, but is against internationally recognized human rights norms. The Declaration implies a conclusion that one does not become a victim only in criminally relevant situations but in other difficult situations as well, which created extensive possibilities and ways of suffering. A result of power abuse can thus be any degree in a wide range of possibilities of human rights violations: from murders, tortures, persecutions, detention to frequent violations of political, labor and social rights. Therefore, modern victimology largely deals with human rights violations that are unfortunately prevailing in contemporary society.[71]

The Victims of abuse of power are persons who, individually or collectively, have suffered harm, including physical or mental injury, emotional suffering, economic loss or substantial impairment of their fundamental rights, through acts or omissions not yet being the violations of national criminal laws, but violating internationally recognized norms related to human rights.[72]

The research has shown that the biggest problems in the content of the judicial acts refer to precisely the most important aspect of adjudication – argumentation and reasoning of judgments, and in particular imposed criminal sanctions. By comparing the collected data on the processing of corruption in 2015 with the findings of Transparency International in 2014, there is a marked decline in the number of inquiries by 53.32%, which in itself represents a negative trend. However, the growing number of reports that result in investigations, as well as the number of investigations based on which the indictment charges, still indicate a slightly positive trend, which is necessary to follow in the coming years.

On the other of the first-instance verdicts to which the appeal was lodged, 33.34% of them were altered or returned to a re-trial.[73] In 2014, based on 32.22% of applications, investigations were initiated, while in 2015, this was the case with 40.51% of applications. This is probably also about improving quality reports coming to the prosecutor's offices. Then, in 2015 there is an increase in the number of investigations that ended with the indictment in relation to 2014, when 27.99% the investigation resulted in the indictment, while the following year this was the case with 46.18% of the investigation.[74] The effectiveness of the criminal proceedings is, first of all, determined by the application of the simplified forms of treatment in criminal matters, and available statistical data show that more than half of the indictments in the Republika Srpska were filed in the period from 2004–2015, raised in a simplified criminal procedure, or with the aim of leading summary criminal proceedings. Namely, in the period from 2004–2015. In total, 78,895 indictments were filed, out of which in regular criminal proceedings 37,555 or 47.60% of indictments, and in simplified criminal proceedings

---

71 *Mehić* 2013.

72 *Adžajlić-Dedović* 2017.

73 *Burzić, Dodik, Hodžić, Korlat, Kurtović, Mehmedić & Sarajlija* 2017.

74 *Burzić et al.* 2017.

41,340 or 52.40% of the indictments.[75] Special problems arise when the victims refuse to cooperate with organs formal social controls, when a country does not allow enjoyment or "period reflections".[76]

5. Public and/or Media Discourses on Victims, Rights and Protection of Victims, and Victimisation

Thus, within the scope of its appellate jurisdiction, the Constitutional Court deals solely with the question of a possible violation of constitutional rights or rights under the European Convention on the proceedings before the ordinary courts, and whether the application of the law was eventually discretional or discriminatory. The main mission of the television or the media, in general, to objectively inform, educate and entertain the huge mass of people, under the pressure of the consumer society's demand, is often sacrificed on behalf of sensationalism, commercialism, disinformation and imposition of influence. Freedom of the media may be restricted when it is necessary to protect national security, the public order or the rights of others, and especially the rights of the child. Unfortunately, there are often examples of violations of the journalists' code of ethics that threatened the protection of children and young people (especially the identity of juvenile victims of trafficking), and this unprofessional behaviour of journalists, as well as of staff in judicial bodies, causes serious consequences. The Convention for the Protection of Human Rights and Fundamental Freedoms provides a starting point for victims to encourage the media to protect the privacy and identity through relevant measures, prevent secondary victimisation of victims of trafficking, protect their safety, and enable the protection of victims' privacy reputation and rights. The Convention stipulates the terms on the protection of children who would be particularly damaged if their identity would be disclosed. The Convention obliged each party to adopt measures to ensure that the identity or data enabling the identification of a child, a victim of trafficking, are not publicly disclosed throughout the media or in any other way, except under exceptional defined circumstances in order to find and recognise the victim. The Secondary victimisation is a way of re-exposing children to violence, caused by unprofessional and unethical media reporting. Article 10, paragraph 2 of the ECHR is the basis for taking appropriate measures to prevent the secondary victimisation, in the context of the protection of safety, privacy, reputation, rights, and integrity of the child.[77]

---

75 *Kostić* 2017.

76 *Mijalković* 2009.

77 The Communications Regulatory Agency is an independent Bosnia and Herzegovina institution that operates pursuant to Bosnia and Herzegovina's Communications Law, in accordance with the general principles of objectivity, transparency and non-discrimination. By doing so, the CRA continuously monitors the television content in order to eliminate the one that could negatively affect the population of children and juveniles, thus protecting their integrity and rights.

6. Discussion

In accordance with European legal norms, the legislator in Bosnia and Herzegovina should urgently set the definition of a victim with a clear differentiation between primary and secondary victims, as well as differentiate between the rights of the offended victims. In addition, the victims must be allowed to state their opinion on the potential exclusion of the public from the main hearing, and they must not be punished when they refuse to testify. When the hearing of witnesses and expert witnesses outside the courtroom is concerned, as well as the reconstruction of the event, the offended is always summoned to attend the above-mentioned processing events, which is certainly a secondary victimisation of a victim, if the victim does not give their consent or does not want to attend it.

On the other hand, the criminal offence of abuse of job position is defined in the Criminal Code of the Federation of Bosnia and Herzegovina, within the group of criminal offences against freedom and human and citizen's rights, in the provision of Article 182. The act is done by a person who, in the performance of their work, abuses another person causing them heavier physical and mental suffering, intimidates or insults them.

Related to this, it should be emphasized that Bosnia and Herzegovina has ratified the Optional Protocol to the Convention against Torture and Other Cruel, Inhuman or Degrading Treatment or Punishment in October 2008, thus committing to implement standards specified in the Protocol, and one of them is the establishment of the preventive mechanism.

The Victims Protection Council must be established as a spokesperson for the victims, with the participation of the representatives of the academic community (victimologists and criminologists), NGOs and the judiciary. The opinions of this panel should oblige state authorities to develop short-term strategies and action plans that will respond appropriately to the failure of the repressive organ authorities. Those responsible for preventing the rule of law in state and public services should be punished, and laws should be harmonised with international legally binding documents so that rights become available to citizens through clear and precise procedures. The powers of the Office of the Ombudsman should be increased in such a way that his opinions and recommendations are obliges all, and each case should be notified to the competent prosecutor's offices.

The protection of victims must not be conditional upon the victim's consent to testify because all crimes must be proven without the victim's statement or only with material evidence. It is imperative to establish centres for victims of gender-based and sexual violence in both entities and the Brčko District in Bosnia and Herzegovina, and within the Centre of Victims, to enable physical examination, documenting bodily injuries, psychological expertise, toxicological expertise, as well as all other expert evaluations that can be carried out because the state is obliged to enable its citizens to take advantage of the rights guaranteed by the constitutions and laws.

The Victim's report on criminal offence does not necessarily initiate the criminal prosecution of the suspects but only the prosecutorial investigation, which may last from six months to one year.

The protection and support of victims are provided only for victims of crimes within the jurisdiction of the Court of Bosnia and Herzegovina. After the victim's report of the criminal offence to the police, they must obtain a signed record and a certificate and must be informed in writing about the course and the results of the investigation. The police does not have victimology-based training and knowledge, nor the obligation to inform and instruct the victims or to collect on their behalf the evidence of the consequences suffered in the context of the damage caused to them by the criminal offence during the investigation (such as a victim impact statement in the USA), nor has it an obligation to take the collected evidence from the victim (if the victim has collected it himself/herself), and to present it to the prosecutor. This is often abused in practice in such a way that the information on the right to submit a property claim is denied to victims out of ignorance or deliberately all the time until the criminal proceedings are concluded. Only afterwards, the victim is informed about the possibility of realisation of their claims for damages in a civil lawsuit, which represents the denial of the victim's right on information and the right to legal aid, and an increased risk of secondary victimisation of victims.

The right to free legal aid through the agency "Your Rights" does not imply the free-of-charge legal representation of Bosnian citizens, victims of crimes, in any rkcase, but it is reduced to legal counselling and representation of citizens only in exceptionacases. In addition, the "right to legal assistance" is the obligation of all government services that contact victims, but this obligation is not strictly stipulated in the secondary legislation, and its application is left to the conscience and responsibility of civil servants. The victim gives a statement to the police, in the prosecutor's office, and in the court on the circumstances under which a criminal offence was committed and about the perpetrator, which is why the statement does not have any impact on the verdict, but only helps the police and the judiciary system to prosecute the perpetrators of crimes. Thus the victim is reduced to a passive participant in criminal proceedings with denied rights, resulting ultimately in unfair judgments for victims.

In some countries, there are mechanisms providing that the confiscated unlawfully acquired property gains are allocated to the witness protection budget. On the other hand, one of the biggest problems in the implementation of the witness protection measures and programs is the lack of financial resources and permanent sources of funding for very complex protection programs that relate to the change of identity and the relocation of protected witnesses under the protection program.[78] We need a crime victims' compensation programme and victim impact statements on the consequences of crime or pain, suffering and prejudice suffered by victims. Crime vic-

---

[78] *Simović, Simović & Simović* 2019.

tims and their families may need information, resources, or financial assistance. The Crime Victims' Compensation (CVC) Programme helps crime victims and their immediate families with the financial costs of crime. CVC covers crime-related costs such as counselling, medical treatment, funerals, and loss of income not paid by other sources.

One of the most important and basic rights of victims during prosecution is the right to participate.[79]

The Victims' services have not been established in order to provide adequate assistance, support and protection to victims of domestic violence, as still there is no adequate professional staff for the implementation of protective measures of compulsory psychosocial treatment and mandatory treatment of alcoholism and the illness of addicts in the family. Therefore, we did not make progress, despite the adoption of new international standards and obligations, nor did we provide effective and expeditious justice for the victims of domestic violence. In addition, the law did not define specific provisions relating to the possession and purchase of weapons for the persons who have had a history of domestic violence and violence against women, nor did we agree and decide to bind records of imposed protective measures and penalties for domestic violence, with the obligation to create a victim's profile and a criminological profile in the police in order to propose more effective measures to prevent domestic violence in the future. We have not succeeded to effectively implement the Council of Europe Convention on the Prevention and Suppression of Domestic Violence and Violence against Women, as we have not established a methodology for monitoring the fulfilment of obligations under international documents concerning domestic violence, violence against women and gender discrimination.

The country must have policies and measures of reparation for the victims of international crimes defined. The reparation programs are vital in the transitional justice process, but many female victims have more problems with an attempt to access reparations. The restitution, compensation, rehabilitation and punishment are the formal categories of reparations in the Basic Principles and Guidelines on the Right to a Remedy and Reparation for Victims of Gross Violations of International Human Rights Law and Serious Violations of International Humanitarian Law.[80] Bosnia and Herzegovina is not efficient in paying compensations for primary and secondary victims of terrorism and human trafficking.

Criminal legislation must define the victim and extend the scope of their rights in accordance with international legally binding documents. This is not done in order to protect victims, it is only guaranteed for victims of crimes within the jurisdiction

---

79 Department of Commerce 2019.

80 Resolution No. A/RES/60/147, 16.12.2005; https://documents-dds-ny.un.org/doc/UNDOC/GEN/N05/496/42/PDF/N0549642.pdf?OpenElement [10.06.2019].

of the Court of Bosnia and Herzegovina, which has the Victims Support Unit, and through the SIPA Victim Protection Department, which provides an extra-procedural and procedural safeguards in compliance with the Law on Protection of Witness Under Threat and Vulnerable Witnesses, while all other victims are discriminated against or disabled. Unfortunately, the protection of victims under the aforesaid law is conditioned by the obligation to testify, which is certainly secondary victimisation of victims in Bosnia and Herzegovina.

Finally, it is necessary to prevent the shortening of criminal trials dealing with certain criminal offences, and in particular to determine the criteria for pronouncing a suspended sentence, as well as the amnesty of the perpetrators of the criminal offence, but also because in practice these institutes are abused to the detriment of victims and produce victims. The statute of limitations in committed criminal offences and at the detriment of minors is not regulated in accordance with European law and practice, which is why it should be changed in the "de lege ferenda" provisions in Bosnia and Herzegovina.

The Law on Compensation for Victims of Criminal Acts should be adopted and establish funds and criteria for the realization of this Law. It is necessary to adopt specific Environmental Protection Strategies and Laws, as well as the Law on the Law of the Sea, and the Law on the Protection of Victims of Crimes, and in addition to urgently amend the Criminal Procedure Code and by-laws or the Regulations on the treatment of victims of war, sexual violence, domestic violence, migrants and especially vulnerable social groups in Bosnia and Herzegovina. All civil servants are obliged to ensure and all citizens of the state to comply with the rule of law or effective and prompt justice for victims. The establishment, strengthening and expansion of national funds for compensation to victims should be encouraged. Where appropriate, other funds may also be established for this purpose, including those cases where the state of which the victim is a national is not in a position to compensate the victim for the harm. When compensation is not fully available from the offender or other sources, states should endeavour to provide state compensation payments for at least the following direct and indirect victims:

1) victims who have sustained significant bodily injury or impairment of physical or mental health as a result of serious crimes; and
2) the family, in particular dependants of persons who have died or become physically or mentally incapacitated as a result of such victimisation.

The state should provide social welfare, including mental health, educational, economic and specific crime prevention policies to reduce victimisation, and encourage assistance to victims in distress. It should also promote community efforts and public participation in crime prevention, periodically review their existing legislation and practices in order to ensure responsiveness to changing circumstances, and enact and enforce legislation proscribing acts that violate internationally recognized norms relating to human rights, corporate conduct and other abuses of power, establish and strengthen the means of detecting, prosecuting and sentencing those guilty of crimes, and promote the observance of codes of conduct and ethical norms – in particular international standards – by public servants, including law enforcement, correctional, medical and social service, and military personnel.

7. Summary in Bosnian

U ovom radu predstavit ćemo razvoj viktimologije kao nauke u Bosni i Hercegovini. Kroz nova znanja viktimologije i viktimološke studije i naučne radove nastojat ćemo da oslikamo pravni položaj, pomoć, podršku i zaštitu žrtava u Bosni i Hercegovini, da bi smo kroz komparaciju sa evropskim pravnim normativima i standardima i međunarodnim obavezama koje smo preuzeli uočili najveće probleme u vezi sa zaštitom žrtava u Bosni i Hercegovini. Pored toga, u ovom radu biti će prezentiran aproksimativan obim i specifične studije slučaja koji oslikavaju pravni položaj žrtava grubog kršenja međunarodnog humanitarnog prava, žrtava trgovine ljudima, žrtava nasilja u porodici, žrtavama zloupotrebe moći i vlasti u Bosni i Hercegovini. Na kraju još osvrnut ćemo se na zaštitu žrtava prirodnih katastrofa i ekološkog kriminaliteta i predložiti po nama najbolje i najefikasnije mjere koje bi trebale biti implementirane u Bosni Hercegovini kao posebna Strategija o reformi sistema zaštite žrtava. S tim u vezi u zaključku predlažemo mjere de lege ferenda koje će omogućiti usklađivanje bosanskohercegovačkog zakonodavstva u vezi sa minimumom pomoći, podrške i zaštite žrtava u skladu sa Evropskom direktivom iz 2012. godine, a što je naša obaveza ako želimo postati članicom Evropske Unije. Također, predlažemo izradu Zakona o naknadi štete za žrtve krivičnih djela i formiranje Fonda za osvarivanje ove naknade (ili Zakona i Fondova u Bosni i Hercegovini u skladu sa organizacijom vlasti prema Ustavu Bosne i Hercegovine (Anex 4, Opći okvirni sporazum za mir u Bosni i Hercegovini, Dayton, 1995). U zaključku također posebno ističemo potrebu formiranja Centara za žene i djecu žrtve seksualnog nasilja, nasilja u porodici i drugih oblika nasilja u skladu sa Istambulskom konvencijom, što je također naša međunarodna obaveza (žrtve trgovine ljudima radi sekusualne eksplatacije) koju smo preuzeli 2014. godine.

Literature

Adžajlić-Dedović, A. (2017): The Womens Rights in Bosnia and Herzegovina, Proceedings from international scientific and professional victimological conferences entitled "Ambassadors of Peace in Bosnia and Herzegovina". Sarajevo, p. 16.

Adžajlić-Dedović, A. (2014): Restorativna Pravda [Restorative justice]. Sarajevo.

Adžajlić-Dedović, A. (2011): Viktimologija [Victimology]. Sarajevo.

Adžajlić-Dedović, A. (2010): Pravni položaj žrtve u Ustavu i Međunarodnom pravu – bosanskohercegovačka paradigma [The legal position of the victim in the Constitution and international law – The Bosnian Herzegovinian paradigm]. Bihać.

Adžajlić-Dedović, A. (2003): Prostitucija u Bosni I Hercegovini [Prostitution in Bosnia and Herzegovinag. Sarajevo.

Adžajlić-Dedović A., & Balić H. (2004): Handbook for victimology. Sarajevo.

Adžajlić-Dedović, A., Deljkic, I., Ćatić-Lučić, M., Bojanić, N., & Hasković, E. (2007): Family and police in the Federation of Bosnia and Herzegovina. Sarajevo.

Adžajlić-Dedović, A., Drpljanin, Š., Ninković, O.L., Topić, B., & Bajramović, M. (2018): Handbook for dealing with cases of gender-based and sexual violence against women and children for police, prosecutors and judges. Sarajevo.

Adžajlić-Dedović, A., Rizvo, S., & Hasković, E. (2018): The international law and rights of victims of sexual violence in war – Case study Bosnia and Herzegovina (1992–1995). Paper presented at IPRA general conference 2018 – Innovation for sustainable global peace. Ahmedabad.

Adžajlić-Dedović, A., Sofradžija, H., Deljkić, I., Čamo, M., Šabani A., Martinović, D., Humačkić, T., Topić, Ž, Stočanin-Hrustemović, Pandžo A., & Gavrić, S. (2015): Priručnik za viktimološki kurs: Prevencija i suzbijanje nasilja u porodici kroz primjenu medijacije u crkvama i vjerskim zajednicama u Bosni i Hercegovini [Handbook for victimological course: Preventing and combating domestic violence through the application of mediation in churches and religious communities in Bosnia and Herzegovina]. Sarajevo.

Antić, A. (2017): Victimization study on blood and sexual crimes: Case study Banja. Sarajevo.

Bašić, G. (2017): Definicija počinitelja ratnog nasilja i žrtve. Analitički model za analizu rituala ratnog nasilja u koncentracionim logorima tokom rata [Definition of perpetrators of war violence and victims. An analytical model for analysing the rituals of war violence in concentration camps during the war]. Paper presented at The Second international scientific victimology conference "Ambassadors of peace in Bosnia and Herzegovina". Sarajevo.

Bejtić, N. (2015): Transitional justice in Bosnia and Herzegovina: Examining the effects of post-conflict statebuilding, transnational justice and reconciliation. Ontario.

Bell, J.O. (2018): Frozen Justice: Lessons from Bosnia and Herzegovina's failed transitional justice strategy. Delaware.

Bijeljanjić, M. (2016): 'The sexual discrimination in Bosnia and Herzegovina. Sarajevo.

Budimlić, M., Kavazović, M., Puharić, P., & Kobajica, S. (2017): Mapiranje kriminaliteta u Bosni i Hercegovini – stanje i perspective [Crime mapping in Bosnia and Herzegovina – Current situation and prospects for the future]. Kriminalističke teme [Criminal Justice Issues] 3, pp. 11–30.

Burzić, D., Dodik, B., Hodžić, E., Korlat, S., Kurtović, A., Mehmedić, A., & Sarajlija, E. (2017): Monitoring the judicial response to corruption in Bosnia and Herzegovina: Pilot Report. Sarajevo.

Cicović, A. (2016): Assistance, support and protection of fire in Bosnia and Herzegovina. Sarajevo.

Gavrić, T. (2017): Victimization study on fear of victimization: Case study of Banja Luka. Sarajevo.

Gracin, D., & Butorac, K. (2017): Rights, status and support to the criminal offences' victims in modern European criminal law and practice, in terms of adopting the Directive 2012/29 EU; in: A. Adžajlić-Dedović (ed.), Proceedings from international scientific and professional victimological conferences entitled "Ambassadors of Peace in Bosnia and Herzegovina". Sarajevo, p. 54–67.

Hadžović, D., & Kržalić, A. (2015): Procjena rizika korupcije u sigurnosnom sektoru u Bosni i Hercegovini [Assessment of the risk of corruption in the security sector in Bosnia and Herzegovina]. Sarajevo.

Halilović, H., Adžajlić-Dedović, A., & Budimlić, M. (2019): Krivični postupak u Bosni i Hercegovini: osvrt na procesni položaj oštećenog krivičnim djelom [Criminal proceeding in Bosnia and Herzegovina: View on the process position of the offended by criminal deed]. Criminalistic Theory and Practice 6, pp. 77–94.

Kirchhoff, G. (2013): Presentation: Theoretical victimology. Lecture to the 29th postgraduate course in victimology. Dubrovnik.

Korajlić, N., & Muharremi, D. (2011): Heuristic Criminalistic. Sarajevo.

Kostić, D. (2017): Criminal law of Bosnia and Herzegovina as a normative presumption of efficiency of criminal proceedings things. Annial Faculty of Legal Sciences 7, pp. 260–275.

Kurtović, K. (2013): Tipologija žrtava rata u Bosni i Hercegovini: studija slučaja Bihać [Typology of victims of war in Bosnia and Herzegovina: Case study of Bihać]. Sarajevo.

Maljević, A., Datzer, D., Muratbegović, E., & Budmlić, M. (2006): Overtly about police and corruption. Sarajevo.

Marković, G. (2014): Problems of removing the discrimination from the Constitution of Bosnia and Herzegovina; Collection of papers - International scientific conference "Public and private aspects of necessary legal reforms in Bosnia and Herzegovina: How far can we go?" Tuzla, pp. 511–531.

Mehić, A. (2013): Assistance and protection of victims of abuse of power by criminal regulatory member state of the European Union. Sarajevo.

Meško, G. (2002): Osnove preprečevnaja kriminalitete [Basics of crime prevention]. Ljubljana.

Meško, G., & Areh, I. (2003): Strah pred kriminaliteto v urbanih okoljih [Fear of crime in urban environment]. Revija za kriminalistiko in kriminologijo [Journal of Criminal Investigation and Criminology] 54, pp. 144–152.

Meško, G., & Kovčo, I. (1999): Strah pred kriminaliteto v Sloveniji in Hrvaško [Fear of crime in Slovenia and Croatia]. Varstvoslovje [Journal of Criminal Justice and Security] 1, pp. 26–30.

Meško, G., & Pavlović, Z. (1998): Strah pred kriminaliteto – izzivi za raziskovanje [Fear of crime – A challenge to research]. Revija za kriminalistiko in kriminologijo [Journal of Criminal Investigation and Criminology] 49, pp. 346–353.

Meško, G., & Umek, P. (1999): Značilnosti socialnopsihološkega in demografskega modela strahu pred kriminaliteto [Characteristics of sociopsychological and demographic model of fear of crime]. Revija za kriminalistiko in kriminologijo [Journal of Criminal Investigation and Criminology] 50, pp. 131–137.

Meško, G., Fallshore, F., Muratbegović, E., & Fields, C.B. (2008): Fear of crime in two post-socialist capital cities – Ljubljana, Slovenia and Sarajevo, Bosnia and Herzegovina. Journal of Criminal Justice 36, pp. 546–553.

Mujanović, E., Datzer, D., & Budimlić, M. (2012): Imovinski kriminalitet u Bosni I Hercegovini prema zvaničnim statistikama [Property crime in Bosnia and Herzegovina according to official statistics]. Kriminalističke teme [Criminal Justice Issues] 12, p. 1–27.

Muratbegović, E., Bulić, D., & Budimlić, M. (2017): Nasilje nad djecom i među djecom u domovima za djecu bez roditeljskoh staranja u Bosni i Hercegovini [Violence against children and among children in homes for children without parental care in Bosnia and Herzegovina]. Kriminalističke teme [Criminal Justice Issues] 5, pp. 140–168.

Mijalković, S. (2009): Supporting human trafficking and migrants of charge – Opportunities for improvement security-criminal practices national security system. Belgrade.

Nikolić-Ristanović, V. (2012): Victimology and victim support in Serbia: A descriptive review. Newsletter of the European Society of Criminology. Criminology in Europe 13, pp. 4–5.

Pavlović, Z. (1998): Mednarodni anketi o kriminaliteti oz. viktimizaciji Slovenija (Ljubljana) 1992–1997 (1. del) [International (crime) victimization survey – Slovenia (Ljubljana) 1992–1997 (part 1)]. Revija za kriminalistiko in kriminologijo 49, pp. 257–265.

Petrović, B. (2016): Psychosocial support to forced woman migrants – A review of work done so far and recommendations for further work; in: S. Porobić (ed.), Gender study of forced migration and psychosocial well-being in Bosnia and Herzegovina. Sarajevo, p. 114.

Petrović, B. (2005): Victimological glossary. Sarajevo.

Petrović, B. (2002): The national strategy for drug related problems: The case of Bisnia and Herzegovina, in: G. Meško, B. Dobovšek, M. Jager & D. Petrovec (eds.), Challenges of Slovenian criminology. Conference proceedings: Abstracts. Ljubljana, p. 26.

Ramljak, A., & Halilović, H. (2004): Viktimologija [Victimology]. Sarajevo.

Ramljak, A., & Simović, M.N. (2006): Viktimologija [Victimology]. Sarajevo.

Rizvo, S., Hunček S., & Muratbegović, E. (2018): Guidelines for the conduct of regional monitoring teams for the fight against human trafficking in Bosnia and Herzegovina. Sarajevo.

Sijerčić-Čolić, H. (2003): Discussion on criminal justice reform and criminal legislation of Bosnia and Herzegovina, with special emphasis on new Criminal procedural law. Croatian Yearbook on Criminal Law and Practice 10, pp. 181–208.

Simović, M.N. (2001): Judge of the Constitutional court of the RS freedom of spirit and freedom of communication from the European convention on the protection of human rights and their applications in the legal system of the RS. Practice of the Constitutional court of Bosnia and Herzegovina of entities courts and courts Brčko district. Sarajevo.

Simović, M.N., & Simović, M.M. (2018): Legal frame for criminal proceedings against juveniles in the Federation of Bosnia and Herzegovina. Sociology Study 8, pp. 123–137.

Simović, M.N., & Simović, V. (2014): Evidence in criminal proceedings in Bosnia and Herzegovina and their importance in detecting and providing criminal offenses. Yearbook of the Faculty of Law in East Saray 5, pp. 31–52.

Simović, M., & Simović, V. (2013): Term and the meaning of the principle of legality in criminal law, in Proceedings from International scientific conference "Public and private aspects of necessary legislation reforms in BIH. How far can we go?" Tuzla, pp. 23–33.

Simović, M.N., & Šikman, M. (2018): Efficiency of criminal proceedings – Between expectations and reality. Journal of Criminology and Criminal Law 1, pp. 9–31.

Simović, M., Simović, V., & Simović, M. (2019): Protection of witnesses in criminal proceedings before the Court of Bosnia and Herzegovina; in Proceedings of the International Scientific Conference entitled "Harmonization of legal regulations with the acquis communautaire of the European Union – Situation in Bosnia and Herzegovina and the experiences of others". Banja Luka, pp. 66–89.

Šabani, A. (2013): The social control: Meaning and function. Journal of Criminalistics, Criminology and Security Studies Special Edition, pp. 65–77.

Šarić, K. (2015): Sexual abuse – Victimization study. Sarajevo.

Topić, Ž. (2012): Special investigative actions and protection of victims of human trafficking in Bosnia and Herzegovina. Sarajevo.

Topić, Ž. (2011): Voluntary and forced victims of prostitution in Bosnia and Herzegovina from 2006 to 2008. Sarajevo.

Zvekić, U. (1998): Criminal victimisation in countries in transition. Rome.

Wood, E.J. (2006): Variation in sexual violence during war. Politics & Society 34, pp. 307–341.

Documents

Agency for Statistics of Bosnia and Herzegovina (StatOffice) (2018): Žene i muškarci u Bosni i Hercegovini [Women and men in Bosnia and Herzegovina]. Sarajevo [in Bosnian and English].

StatOffice: see Agency for Statistics of Bosnia and Herzegovina.

Criminal Justice Degree Schools (2019): Criminal Rights: Laws and Protections; https://www.criminaljusticedegreeschools.com/criminal-justice-resources/criminal-rights-laws-and-protections/ [21.05.2019] [in English only].

Department of Commerce (2019): Office of crime victim advocacy – Washington state department of commerce; https://www.commerce.wa.gov/serving-communities/crime-victims-public-safety/office-of-crime-victims-advocacy/ [21.05.2019] [in English only].

Securities Commission of Federation of Bosnia and Herzegovina (2019): Početna [Home]; http://www.komvp.gov.ba/site/index.php [31.05.2019] [in Bosnian and English].

The Victimological Society of Bosnia and Herzegovina (2005): International handbook on the justice for victims and the use and application of the United Nations Declaration on basic principles of justice for victims of crime and abuse of power. Sarajevo.

Bulgaria

Kamen Lyubomirov Novikov

1. Introduction

Since the fall of the socialist regime in 1989, the Republic of Bulgaria has been in a state of permanent reform in all areas, including politics, economics, legislation, and culture. Several sociologists and political scientists have claimed that the Bulgarian transition ended when the country joined the European Union in 2007. But in fact after 2007, the reform process has gained even more momentum. To develop into a democratic European country is a goal that is very difficult to reach and this is still the greatest challenge facing Bulgarian society today.

In the last 25–30 years, the crime situation in Bulgaria has changed. The total number of crimes has increased significantly, offenders are increasingly "innovative", and Bulgarian law enforcement authorities are fighting against various types of modern crimes which were unknown in the past. Located strategically as a gateway between the Middle East, North Africa, and Europe, Bulgaria lies at one of the key exterior borders of the EU and is an important transit country regarding international crime.

Of course, the central figure in the criminal procedure always has been the offender, but in recent years, Bulgarian legal theory and practice has focused on victims and victim protection as well. In order to analyse the current situation of victimology in the Republic of Bulgaria, we will present a short general country background, the current state of victimology, the relevant legal framework, statistical data and research findings, public and media discourses about victims, victim rights and protection, the main problems with suggestions for improvement and some general conclusions.

2. General Country Background

The Republic of Bulgaria is located in the eastern part of the Balkan Peninsula in South-Eastern Europe. It borders on Romania to the north, Serbia and Macedonia to the west, Greece and Turkey to the south, and the Black Sea to the east. With a territory of 110,994 square kilometres, Bulgaria is Europe's 16th largest country (11th in the EU).

The population of Bulgaria according to the data provided by the National Statistical Institute was 7,050,034 on 31.12.2017,[1] which is equal to 1,4% of the population of the EU. Compared to 2010, the population has decreased by 319,397 people. According to data from the National Statistical Institute in 2017, the gender mix was 3,422,409 men and 3,627,625 women.[2] The population decrease in Bulgaria has been a consistent trend for the last 25–30 years; according to a 1992 census, the population was 8,487,317.[3] The main reasons for this trend are the economic migration after the fall of the socialist regime, high mortality rates, low fertility rates, a general drop in quality of life, problems in health care, in education, and social care, for example. The last population census in Bulgaria occurred in February 2011. According to its results, the population of Bulgaria was 7,364,570.[4]

The Republic of Bulgaria is divided into 28 provinces, which are the first level administrative divisions of the country. The provinces are further subdivided into 265 municipalities. The capital of Bulgaria is Sofia, which is situated in the western part of the country. Other major cities are Veliko Tarnovo (with a population of 239,132 on 31.12.2017), Varna (472,120), Burgas (411,579), Stara Zagora (319,067), and Plovdiv (669,796).[5] Sofia is the largest city in the country with a population of 1,291,591.[6] According to the data provided by the National Statistical Institute as at 31.12.2017, the population of the capita was 1,325,429.

The above-mentioned numbers for Sofia, although provided by state institutions, are not precise and do not give the real picture at all. The reason is that thousands of people live and work in the capital without making the mandatory address registration. As a result nobody can give the real number of the population of Sofia, but according to unofficial data and media information, nearly 2,000,000 people live in Sofia at the moment, or almost 25% of the Bulgarian population. The capital city is so attractive due to its labor market, higher incomes and quality of life, large supply of residential accommodation and better social environment in comparison to the other regions of the country. This great concentration of the population with different social, ethnic, economic and educational characteristics attracts criminals and major criminal activities and increases the number of victims of crimes. This is also the case for the other large cities in the country. Only major urban areas can offer

---

1 StatOffice 2019a.

2 StatOffice 2019b.

3 LogoInfograf 2019.

4 StatOffice 2011.

5 StatOffice 2019c.

6 StatOffice 2011.

Bulgarians the necessary opportunities for education, careers, family, and a better life, and that is why they are so attractive to young people. Coupled with the general decreasing trend of the population, this urbanisation means that large regions of the country are now desolate. The north-west part of Bulgaria (which includes the provinces Vratsa, Montana, and Vidin) is considered the poorest region of the country with a very low quality of life, low incomes and practically no perspectives for the future. The demographic problems in the rural areas all over Bulgaria are even more serious than in urban regions. Young people are leaving rural areas for the big cities or migrating abroad. Rural areas are mainly populated by pensioners, who are financially dependent on their children. According to the data of the National Statistical Institute, the population growth per 1,000 inhabitants is negative for all the regions of Bulgaria. With regards to the above-mentioned in the north-west parts of the country, the growth rate is in terminal decline: –9,463 in 2017.[7]

The traditional religion in Bulgaria is Orthodox Christianity, and according to the census results from 2011, more than 4,300,000 Bulgarians follow Eastern Orthodoxy. The second largest religious group are Muslims (around 600,000). Other religious groups are Roman Catholics and Jews, but their numbers are considerably lower (not more than 5% of the population). Bulgaria is a country with constitutionally guaranteed religious freedom. As a geographical crossroad between Europe and Asia, and due to historical reasons, Bulgarians are used to living together with people of other religions and cultures. Of course there have been some exceptions over the years, but Christians and Muslims generally live peacefully together in Bulgaria, with mutual respect and understanding. The possible conflicts between these large ethnic groups are more often economic, than religious.

The ethnic structure of the Bulgarian population consist of three main groups – Bulgarians, Turks and Roma. According to the data of the National Statistical Institute, only the population of the Roma group is increasing. According to the census results from 2011 there were more than 320,000 Roma living in Bulgaria. The provinces with the largest Roma population in Bulgaria are Montana, Dobrich, Sliven and Shumen, where Roma account for approx. 10–14% of the population. The data about this ethnic group are very imprecise. Roma often do not register births and deaths and children do not go to kindergartens and schools, so nobody can calculate their exact number. According to unofficial data, the Roma population at this moment is more than 450,000.[8] In Bulgaria there are permanent discussions and proposed measures for the education and integration of the Roma population, but unfortunately most of them remain only on paper. There is also a big problem with Roma criminality, which has constantly grown over the last years.

---

7 StatOffice 2019c.

8 StatOffice 2011.

The Republic of Bulgaria successfully joined the EU on 1 January 2007, which is considered the greatest political, economic and social achievement. Bulgaria is also a member of NATO (joining on 29 March 2004). A currency board exchange rate regime was introduced in Bulgaria in 1997. The Bulgarian Lev was fixed first to the Deutsche Mark and later to the Euro. This board gives stability to the Bulgarian currency and will remain until Bulgaria adopts the Euro and enters the Eurozone.[9] According to Bulgarian financial experts this will happen in the next 4–5 years. Joining the EU was a very important step for Bulgaria because Bulgarians now have full access to a free European labour market and the import and export with EU countries has increased immensely. Moreover, Bulgaria can now utilise EU funds, which has helped to develop and modernise infrastructure all over the country. Bulgaria is waiting to join the Schengen Agreement, but there are still requirements, which must be fulfilled in order to achieve this. In recent years, the macroeconomic indicators of Bulgaria have been very good, and the country is used as a good example among EU countries for financial discipline and stable growth. This success is publicly acknowledged by the European Commission.[10] However, on a microeconomic level the situation is far from satisfactory. The incomes in both public and private sectors are considerably lower in comparison with other EU countries, although the living standard in Bulgarian big cities is almost equal to European cities. A big financial and property disproportion exists between different parts of Bulgarian society. This is a serious social problem in Bulgaria and of course a strong criminal and victimological factor.

3. Current State of Victimology

Victimology in Bulgaria does not exist as a separate legal discipline but only as a part of criminology. The beginning of victimological research in Bulgaria is set in the 1960s. In the beginning of the 1970s it became more systematic, complete, and precise, because the criminology in general was developing very strongly. The goal was to study crime phenomena with a complex approach and to take long term measures for its control and prevention. At present there are nine law faculties in Bulgaria. Some experts consider this far too many for a country the size of Bulgaria and, as a consequence of this oversupply, the standard has dropped enormously. The biggest and oldest law faculty in Bulgaria (founded in 1892) is Sofia University's "St. Kliment Ohridsky".[11] Before the fall of the Curtain in 1989, this was the only law faculty in the country. The current curriculum sees criminology as an elective, third-year discipline. It is obvious that in this picture, the place of victimology is very insignificant.

---

9 *Stojanov* 2017.

10 European Commission 2018.

11 Faculty of Law of the University of Sofia 2019.

A key author in the field of victimology is *Boyan Stankov*. He has published several books and monographs in recent years: "Victimology",[12] and "Criminology, Theoretical basis".[13] He has also researched crime and victim protection in the period of Bulgaria's transition (after the fall of the socialist regime in 1989) – "Bulgaria: Crime victims in the transition period. Problems of the victimisation in the countries of Balkan region,[14] and "The transition, crime and victims of crimes".[15] Other important authors from the past who must also be mentioned are – *Yulia Miteva* – "Victimological problems of the murders",[16] "Victimological researches and crime prevention"[17] and *Baycho Panev* – "Legal protection of crime victims",[18] and "Criminology".[19]

Apart from the universities, the most important centre of criminological science and victimology is the Ministry of Interior's Research Institute for Criminalistics and Criminology (hereinafter RICC).[20] The RICC performs highly professional programs and studies in criminalistics, criminology, and forensic medicine, educates experts needed in the different structures of the Ministry of Interior, and implements new methods for discovering and examining evidence. It was founded on 11 March 1968 with Directive No. 89 of the Bulgarian government as a scientific centre for performing expert research activity. The research centre developed into an institute due to the objective necessity of the operational police work and due to the need to have precise, modern, and complete analysis of evidence, collected not only in criminal cases, but in civil cases too. Another reason for this development was that it was very important for the police and the judiciary to examine and know the current status, the structure, and the dynamics of the crime situation in the country. These two trends resulted in the two main directions of the RICC: criminalistics and criminology.

There are three main periods in the history of RICC.[21] In the first one (1968–1975) the first technical devices were acquired and the first employees were recruited. The second period (1976–1985) saw the staff being further educated and conducting scientific research. In this period, different scientific labs were opened; they were supplied with modern physical, chemical, audio, and video equipment as well as

---

12 *Stankov* 2001b.

13 *Stankov* 2012.

14 *Stankov* 1998.

15 *Stankov* 2001a.

16 *Miteva* 1979.

17 *Miteva* 1980.

18 *Panev* 1983.

19 *Panev* 1993.

20 Ministry of the Interior, Forensics Research Institute 2019a.

21 Ministry of the Interior, Forensics Research Institute 2019b.

computers. This development made it possible to implement new working methods. It was during this second period that significant scientific research into the topics of criminology and victimology occurred. The third period of the RICC began after 1986, when the Institute had already collected rich theoretical and practical experience. The RICC provided reports which contained not only statistical data but also analyses, trends, and suggested measures to be taken. Although in this brief historical review the RICC marks only the three above-mentioned periods on its website, we can say that there is a fourth one – after 2013. Due to financial and human resource problems, the activity of the Institute has decreased significantly. Its work is limited mostly to criminalistics and forensic examinations. In comparison to past periods, neither criminological nor victimological researches have been made, nor has statistical information about rates of crime or victimisation been collected and presented. This is a serious problem, because the RICC, with his rich scientific and technical potential, must show the course of the penal politics of the state and propose measures for fighting modern crime.

A significant function of the RICC has been its published works. The RICC has published hundreds of research articles, monographs, and books on criminalistics, criminology, victimology, investigation and expertise, and national security, for example. The RICC has been a member of the European Network of Forensic Science Institutes (ENFSI) since 2002. Concerning the state bodies, the Bulgarian court system is directly responsible for victims and victim protection. The leading roles in the pre-trial phase (the preliminary investigation) are performed by the prosecution and the investigative organs. Investigative organs in Bulgaria are investigators, who are part of the judicial branch and investigating police officers, who are employed by the Ministry of Interior and are part of the executive branch.

The Prosecution Office of the Republic of Bulgaria is a centralised institution, and its structure is correspondent to the structure of the courts, which means that each penal court operates the relevant prosecutor's office. The pre-trial phase of the penal procedure has preliminary/preparatory functions in order to ensure that the court phase (the central phase of the penal procedure) occurs in full accordance with the law.[22]

The courts in the Republic of Bulgaria (which are in charge of criminal matters) are the District, Regional, Appeal, Military, Supreme Cassation, Specialised Penal, and the Appeal Specialised Penal Courts.[23] The district courts are the main courts of the first instance. There are 113 in Bulgaria. There are 28 regional courts, and they are located in each of the 28 municipal centres of the country. In the capital Sofia, the Sofia City Court operates with the statute of a regional court. In each regional court's area there are several district courts (depending on the size of the territory and the population). There are five appeal courts in Bulgaria and they are located in

22 Penal Procedure Code, Law No. 8605 of 28.10.2005, Official Gazette 86/28.10.2005.

23 Supreme Judicial Council 2019.

Sofia, Plovdiv, Burgas, Varna, and Veliko Tarnovo. The Supreme Cassation Court is the highest instance on penal and civil cases. Its seat is in Sofia but its jurisdiction is the whole of Bulgaria. Apart from the work on individual cases, when the Supreme Court discovers contradictory or incorrect practice of courts all over the country, interpretative decisions are also drafted. These interpretative decisions are absolutely mandatory for all judicial and government bodies. The Specialised Penal Court and the Appeal Specialised Penal Court are located in Sofia, with countrywide jurisdiction. They primarily deal with organised criminal groups. According to information of the Supreme Judicial Council, on 1 January 2018, there were 2,443 judges (penal, civil, and administrative) engaged in the Bulgarian courts. All the above-mentioned authorities have the legal duty to find, accuse, take to trial, and convict criminal offenders in Bulgaria. They must also guarantee the rights and legal interests of victims.[24]

In addition to the courts, another state body that should be mentioned is the National Commission for Combating Traffic in Human Beings.[25] Combating human trafficking is an important national priority, not only in Bulgaria, but in all EU countries. Because of this, the Combating Trafficking in Human Beings Act was published in the State Journal on 07.05.2003 and became law on the 20.05.2003.[26] The National Commission was founded in accordance with Article 4 of this Act.[27] The National Commission determines and administers the implementation of national policy and strategy in the area of combating trafficking in human beings. It organises and coordinates the interaction between separate institutions, helps to prevent human trafficking, and protects, assists, and reintegrates victims. The National Commission prepares an annual National Program for the Prevention and Counteraction of Trafficking in Human Beings and Protection of Victims, which is approved by the Council of Ministers. This National Program researches, analyses, and provides statistical data on human trafficking, and highlights information, awareness and education campaigns, aimed at potential victims of trafficking. It manages and supervises the activities of the Local Commissions for Combating Trafficking in Human Beings and the centres for the protection and support of victims of trafficking. It also facilitates international cooperation to prevent and counteract of human trafficking. The chairman of the National Commission is one of the deputy prime ministers of Bulgaria.[28]

24 Supreme Judicial Council 2019.

25 National Commission for Combating Trafficking in Human Beings 2019.

26 Combating Trafficking in Human Beings Act, Law No. 4603 of 20.05.2003, Official Gazette 4/20.05.2003.

27 See Article 4 (commissions for combating trafficking) of the Law No. 4603.

28 See Law No. 4603

In Bulgaria there are many NGOs, active in the area of victim protection. The participation of such organisations in penal procedure is not regulated by law. We can point out several cases of NGO involvement in criminal proceedings: NGO representatives support victims in their contact with the police or with the court, and accommodate victims in crisis centre, so that victims are not taken into shelters; NGOs may also help the psychological or health recovery of victims. In addition NGOs provide legal assistance and legal representation to victims. Civil organisations support victims of crime substantially through their involvement in the identification process and by providing psychological, social, and health services. Other important activities are connected with shelters and crisis centres for temporary accommodation for victims of trafficking and violence. In September 2008, eleven of the most prominent NGOs combating gender based violence, established the Alliance for Protection against Gender-based Violence. The Alliance's mission is to coordinate and provide sustainability for actions and legislative reforms that offer protection against domestic and gender-based violence, human trafficking, and which strive for equality between women and men, and the cooperation between the civil sector and state institutions. The most important NGOs, active in victim support and anti-trafficking policies are: Association of Victim Support Organisations, "Animus Association" Foundation, Bulgarian Fund for Women, Women's Association Ekaterina Karavelova, Nadia Foundation, Bulgarian Gender Research Foundation, Open Door Centre Association, Foundation SOS Families at Risk, Demetra Association, Dinamika Center Association, A21, Social Activities and Practice Institute, H&D Gender Perspectives Foundation, Association Naia, PULSE Foundation, Association "Knowledge, Success, Change", Gender Alternatives Foundation.[29]

The Center for the Study of Democracy (hereinafter CSD),[30] is highly appreciated amongst those NGOs active in the area of victimology due to its scientific and survey activity. Founded in 1989, the CSD is an interdisciplinary public policy institute dedicated to the values of democracy and market economy. It is an independent organisation fostering reform process in Europe through policy and civil society. The successful prevention and fight against crime requires an effective and functioning criminal justice system. The efforts of the Law Program of the CSD in the area of criminal justice reform covers a great variety of issues, from the structure and operation of the prosecution service and the investigating authorities to the rights of defendants and victims of crime. Other areas of interest focus on specific types of criminal behaviour, such as organised crime, corruption, human trafficking, cybercrime, racist violence, and hate crime. The role of prisons and the reform of the penal system are also part of the Law Program's scope of activities as is the use of public confidence indicators for the development and assessment of criminal justice policies. Victims of Crime – New Trends in Identifying Victims of Crime, Needs

---

29 *Berbec, Ilcheva, Nordstrom, Heinonen, Feito & Freudenberg* 2018.

30 Center for the Study of Democracy 2019.

Assessment, and Referral in Bulgaria and the EU is one of the important topics of the Law Program of the CSD.[31] The CSD also provides its own National Crime Survey (NCS). The NCS is a survey of victims of crime, based on the methodology of the international Crime Victims Survey, originally developed by the United Nations Institute on Criminal Justice (UNICRI).

In February 2014, the Bulgarian Association for Criminology, Criminalistics, and Psychology was officially registered.[32] The Association is a not-for-profit organisation. Its main aim is to assist in the collaboration between students, professionals, and interested parties in the fields of criminology, forensics, psychology, and the social sciences. Its mission is to contribute to the development and dissemination of knowledge and experience. The Association promotes research, publishes and distributes information, organises workshops and events, and contributes to public debates on issues affecting society via a multidisciplinary focus.

4. Relevant Legal Framework in Terms of Criminal Policy

The most important legal act on the topic of criminal policy in Bulgaria is the Penal Procedure Code (hereinafter PPC). The current version of the PPC was published in the State Journal No. 86/28.10.2005, and entered into force on 29.04.2006.[33] Since 2006, more than 40 amendments have been made to the PPC. The most substantial amendments are those from 04.08.2017 (State Journal No 63/2017),[34] which entered into force on 05.11.2017.

The victim (the injured party) and his/her basic rights and duties are regulated in Chapter 8 of the PPC.[35] Because the "victim" was incorporated into the PPC as a participant in the penal procedure for the first time in 2005, the relevant legislation has been modified several times in order for the optimal formulation to be found. The goal of the legislature is to regulate the rights of the injured party in the pre-trial and court phases with the relevant guarantees for its exercising. With the amendments to the PPC, for the first time in Bulgaria the requirements of Directive 2012/29/EU of the European Parliament and of the Council of 25 October 2012,[36] have been

31 Center for the Study of Democracy 2019.

32 The Bulgarian Association of Criminology, Forensics and Psychology 2019.

33 See Law No. 8605.

34 Amendment to the Penal Procedure Code, Law No. 6317 of 04.08.2017, Official Gazette 63/04.08.2017.

35 See Law No. 6317.

36 Directive 2012/29/EU of the European Parliament and of the Council of 25 October 2012 establishing minimum standards on the rights, support and protection of victims of crime, and replacing Council Framework Decision 2001/220/JHA, Official Journal of the European Union 315/57.

implemented. This included establishing the minimum standards of the rights, support, and protection of victims of crime, and replacing Council Framework Decision 2001/220/JHA. In the former version of the Bulgarian PPC, which was in force until the end of 2005, the procedural figure of the victim was not regulated at all. As a result of several theoretical and practical disputes, caused by this obvious and unacceptable gap in the law, the criminal chamber of the Supreme Cassation Court made interpretative decision No. 2/07.10.2002.[37] In this decision, the judges declared that the penal procedure in Bulgaria does not accept the procedural figure of the injured party. The injured party is only a material legal concept, used by the legislature to determine who has the right to become a private prosecutor or a civil claimant in front of the court. The victim of the crime was not included in the participants in the criminal procedure, exhaustively listed in Chapter 7 of the old PPC.

As a conclusion, we can say that in the former version of the Bulgarian PPC, the injured party did not have any rights as a separate participant in the pre-trial phase. The victim had the opportunity to defend his/her rights only in the court phase. This concept was heavily criticised and led to numerous theoretical and practical problems. These problems were finally solved with the current version of the PPC, in force since 29.04.2006.[38] The latest PPC has resolved the dispute in the Bulgarian law doctrine and court practice about victims in penal procedure. The "victim" is legally defined as the person who has suffered material or non-material damage by the crime.[39] The first important practical question is whether this definition only covers a natural person or whether it extends to legal entities. The arguments that a "victim" can be only a natural person are to be found firstly in the letter of the law. The PPC[40] provides that if the person who has suffered damage by the crime dies, the procedural rights of the victim are transferred to his/her inheritors. Of course only a natural person can die and have inheritors. When a legal entity is aborted we are speaking about successors, not about inheritors. In accordance with this Bulgarian penal legislation uses a specific name when a legal entity obtains rights for damage, suffered by a crime: "damaged legal entity". The "victim", respectively the "damaged legal entity" are procedural attributes only of the pre-trial phase. In the court phase, the legal entity can participate only as a civil claimant, and the victim as a private prosecutor, as a civil claimant, or in both roles simultaneously.

Directive 2012/29/EU of the European Parliament and European Council, establishing minimum standards on the rights, support and protection of victims of crime, gives a definition of "victim" as a natural person who has suffered harm, including physical, mental, or emotional harm or economic loss which was directly caused by

---

37 Supreme Cassation Court, Judgement No. 2/07.10.2002.

38 See Law No. 8605.

39 See Article 74 (person who can participate as injured party) of the Law No. 8605.

40 See Article 74 (person who can participate as injured party) of the Law No. 8605.

a criminal offence.[41] That means that the Bulgarian penal legislation even enlarges this standard, by giving procedural rights and guarantees in the pre-trial and in the court phase to natural and legal persons, who have suffered as a result of a criminal offence.

The procedural conditions for participating as an injured party or as a damaged legal entity in the pre-trial phase (according to the current version of the PPC) are the following:[42]

- An investigation must have started. The victim can participate and execute his/her rights even when the proceeding is against an unknown offender and nobody is accused at this stage. This legal solution of the PPC is more than justified. We cannot deny the participation in the proceedings of the person who has suffered by the crime simply because the authorities have not collected enough evidence against the offender. The absence of an accused person does not mean that there is no injured party.
- The damage must be a direct result of the criminal offence. Of course, the natural person can suffer both material or non-material damage as a result of a crime. Concerning legal entities, the damage can be only material, because according Bulgarian legislation legal entities cannot suffer pain, harm, and other non-material disadvantages.
- In order to have a legitimate injured party, the crime must contain a specific harmful result directed against a specific person. This restrictive approach is heavily criticised, but is still dominant in the relevant decisions of the Supreme Court in recent years.
- The suffered damages must be real and objective. A claim for an eventual loss of profit is unacceptable.[43]

From a theoretical and practical view point, it is important to make a detailed analysis of the victim's rights in the pre-trial phase according to the Bulgarian penal procedure. Firstly, we must clarify the basic legislative idea, that the injured party has always the right and never the obligation to participate in the procedure. If he/she wants to exercise his/her rights, a specific request in front of the state authorities should be made.[44]

---

41 See Law No. 8605.

42 See Law No. 8605.

43 *Chinova* 2013.

44 See Article 75 (rights of the injured party in the preliminary investigation) of the Law No. 8605.

According to the PPC, the injured party has the following substantial rights in the penal procedure:[45]

- To be notified about his/her procedural rights. The PPC does not provide the time and form for this notification, but the proper interpretation of the legislation requires this to happen in writing and without delay after the start of the investigation. This notification includes not only the rights in the pre-trial phase, but the rights in the central (court) phase as well. Of course the notification must not include only listing of rights, mentioned in the PPC. The authorities are obliged to give all the necessary explanations, especially when it is required by the age, education level, health, or some other personal features of the victim.
- To receive protection for his/her security and the security of his/her relatives. At the victim's request or with his/her acceptance, the Ministry of Interior should provide the victim with physical security. When the victim is being interrogated his/her identity can be kept secret to protect the life and well-being of the victim and any close family members or partners. The PPC provides specific "measures to protect the victim".[46] Upon the victim's request or the prosecutor's suggestion, the court can forbid the offender to approach the victim, to establish any contact with him/her, including by phone, email, etc., and to enter specified places, which the victim usually visits. The problems with the above-mentioned measures are the lack of legislative conditions for their practical implementation and the lack of effective controls. Directive 2012/29/EU, which requests an individual assessment of the victim (to identify specific protection needs), is still not being applied in Bulgaria.
- To receive information about the criminal proceedings. Of course this right shall not be interpreted literally as an obligation for the authorities to inform the injured party concerning each step or measure in the investigation. Of importance for the victim is to be aware of the development of the procedure in general in order to be able to protect their legitimate interests. The injured party should be informed without delay about starting, suspending, or aborting an investigation as well as about the end of the pre-trial phase and the beginning of court proceedings. The Bulgarian PPC still does not include an obligation to inform the victim about final judgments in a trial, contrary to Article 6 of Directive 2012/29/EU.

---

45 See Article 75 (rights of the injured party in the preliminary investigation) of the Law No. 8605.

46 See Article 67 (measures to protect the injured party) of the Law No. 8605.

- To participate in the proceedings according to the PPC. With this formulation the legislature wants to make it clear that the victim's rights in the pre-trial phase are not unlimited, but strictly defined. Typical examples include the presence of the victim during investigation measures,[47] and at the disclosure of the investigation file,[48] the right to appeal against legal acts of prosecutors or investigators,[49] the right for interim measures connected with the future civil claim,[50] and the collection of costs.[51]
- To make requests, notes, and objections. In this context we must mention the most important right of the victim: the right to request that evidence be collected. This right has no time limit, which is very helpful not only for the victim, but also for state authorities which are trying to uncover the truth. Obviously, the offender and the victim are the persons most connected to the crime and who can provide the most substantial information.
- To appeal against a prosecutor's decision to suspend or abort the penal procedure. The main guarantee for exercising this right is the obligation of the state authorities to send to the injured party a copy of the relevant prosecutor's decision.[52] The procedure for appeal is described in the PPC and includes a two-staged court control when the investigation has been aborted, and a one-staged court control when it is only temporary suspended. In both cases, the appeal is examined by the court in a closed hearing in the absence of the parties involved. This means that the victim does not have the right to appear personally in front of the court. This solution causes many practical problems in Bulgaria and leads to a lot of incorrect and unmotivated court decisions, although it is not contrary to Directive 2012/29/EU.
- To have a lawyer in the procedure. Of course the injured party has the unlimited right to choose, authorise, or change his representatives. A lawyer can be named by the court if the private prosecutor and the civil claimant request legal aid and provide evidence that they are not able to pay the lawyer fees.

---

47 See Article 224 (presence of the injured party during the investigation) of the Law No. 8605.

48 See Article 227 (disclosure of the investigation) of the Law No. 8605.

49 See Article 200 (appeal against the prosecutor's acts) of the Law No. 8605.

50 See Article 73 (measures for securing the civil claim) of the Law No. 8605.

51 See Article 73a (measures to guarantee the costs) of the Law No. 8605.

52 See Articles 243 (discontinuation of the penal procedure by the prosecutor) and 244 (suspending the penal procedure by the prosecutor) of the Law No. 8605.

- To obtain written translation of the acts for suspending or aborting penal procedure, if he/she does not understand or speak the Bulgarian language. This right was included in the PPC with the last amendments and is in accordance with Article 7 of Directive 2012/29/EU. The translation is provided upon request and free of charge.[53]

We can conclude that Bulgarian legislation uses the words "victim" and "damaged legal entity" in order to define the persons who have suffered harm by a criminal offence and who have certain legal rights in the pre-trial phase.

The rights of the victim during the trial phase are even more detailed. Moreover, in a criminal court the victim can participate in the procedural role of a private prosecutor and/or a civil claimant. The private prosecutor is the person who has suffered material or non-material damage by a criminal offence that is being investigated by the state.[54] The private prosecutor is always an additional (associated) court party. The reasons for this position are that he/she can enter only in a court case already opened by the state prosecutor; his/her personal intention to start or abort a court procedure are irrelevant. The participation of the private prosecutor in the trial is always a right and never an obligation. The private prosecutor can maintain the charge parallel with the state prosecutor,[55] but of course both parties cannot replace each other in their duties. The state prosecutor is a mandatory participant who represents the state's interests; only the state prosecutor can initiate a court procedure against the offender. By contrast, the private prosecutor represents only himself/herself and determines alone which legal instruments to use in order to protect his/her rights. At the same time, the private prosecutor is an absolutely separate court party fully independent of the state prosecutor. To prove this independence, the Bulgarian legislature has given the private prosecutor the opportunity to maintain the charge even in cases when the state prosecutor resigns from the charge and claims that the defendant is not guilty.[56] The PPC provides the private prosecutor with specific rights in the court proceeding: to receive information about the case, to provide and collect evidence, to make requests, notes and objections, and to appeal all court acts which are against his rights and legitimate interests.[57]

The victim or his/her inheritors, or the damaged legal entity who has suffered harm by a crime, can submit a civil claim to get compensation. This procedural figure is called "civil claimant".[58] Participating in the criminal court procedure, the civil

---

53 *Chinova* 2013.

54 See Article 76 (person who can participate as private prosecutor) of the Law No. 8605.

55 See Article 78 (procedural functions of the private prosecutor) of the Law No. 8605.

56 See Article 78 (procedural functions of the private prosecutor) of the Law No. 8605.

57 See Article 79 (rights of the private prosecutor) of the Law No. 8605.

58 See Article 84 (person, who can participate as civil claimant) of the Law No. 8605.

claimant has the serious advantage of being supported by the state prosecutor in proving the claim and receiving compensation.

A court procedure, which includes a criminal charge against the offender and a civil claim against him/her, is called a "mixed" procedure. Although the main legal relations are penal and not civil, this mixture helps the parties avoid leading double proceedings between the same persons, with the same subject and of course the proving of the same facts for the second time. The mixed procedure also spares the injured party a lot of time and costs, which is very important, especially in Bulgaria, with its slow judicial system. The civil claimant participates in the penal court proceedings only in order to receive compensation for the damage caused to him/her by the criminal offence. He/she is not responsible for the criminal charge against the offender. This is why the PPC legally restricts the procedural activity of civil claimants to proving the legal basis and the amount of compensation.[59]

The legal frame examined above concerns so-called "state" criminal offences and the procedural rights and obligations of the victim. In order to be fully precise we must mention that the Bulgarian Penal Code regulates also the so-called "private" criminal offences (such as insult, defamation, and minor injuries). In these type of cases a pre-trial investigation is not carried out.[60]

Private prosecution/ plaintiff cases start with a petition, submitted by the victim directly to the court. The victim of a private criminal offence is called the "private plaintiff". In a private prosecution, a public prosecutor does not usually participate at all, as the private plaintiff alone is fully responsible for the charge. In comparison with the public prosecutor, the private plaintiff is not a public body, which has the obligation to maintain the charge in front of the court. He/she is a citizen, defending his/her own rights and legitimate interests and he/she is fully independent. Even when he/she is absolutely sure about the guilt of the offender, he/she can resign from the case and abort it. The private plaintiff is a main court party with the following substantial rights:[61] to receive information about the case, to collect evidence, to make requests, notes, and objections, to appeal all the court acts, which are against his/her rights and legitimate interests, and to withdraw the petition and close the case.[62]

Apart from the PPC, there are some other important legal acts in the areas of victims and victim protection in Bulgaria, such as the Crime Victim Assistance and Financial Compensation Act[63] and the Combating Trafficking in Human Beings

---

59 See Article 87 (rights of the civil claimant) of the Law No. 8605.

60 See Article 80 (person, who can participate as private plaintiff) of the Law No. 8605.

61 See Article 82 (rights of the private plaintiff) of the Law No. 8605.

62 *Ilkova* 2005.

63 Crime Victim Assistance and Financial Compensation Act, Law No. 105/2017.

Act.[64] The Crime Victim Assistance and Financial Compensation Act[65] regulates "public compensation by the state to victims of crime". This institute is established in accordance with several international contracts, framework decisions and recommendations – the European Convention on the Compensation of Victims of Violent Crimes (Council of Europe, 1983);[66] Declaration of Basic Principles of Justice for Victims of Crime and Abuse of Power (1985);[67] Recommendation No. R/85/11 of the Committee of Ministers to member states on the position of the victim in the framework of criminal law and procedure;[68] Recommendation No. R/87/21 of the Committee of Ministers to member states on assistance to victims and prevention of victimisation;[69] Convention of 29 May 2000 on Mutual Assistance in Criminal Matters between the Member States of the European Union;[70] Council Directive 2004/80/EC relating to compensation to crime victims.[71]

According the general standards, set by the aforementioned acts, when adequate compensation cannot be provided, including due to the insolvency of the offender, the state must pay the compensation. The subject of the Crime Victim Assistance and Financial Compensation Act is to set the terms and procedures for assistance and financial compensation from the state to victims of crime who are Bulgarian nationals or nationals of the European Union's member states. Assistance and financial compensation may also be provided to foreign nationals in cases envisaged by international agreements to which the Republic of Bulgaria is a party. This Act shall apply when a criminal offence has been committed in the Republic of Bulgaria, or when such a crime has been committed outside the country and the victim is a Bulgarian national.

Assistance may be provided to victims who have suffered material and non-material damages as a result of state crimes.[72] Financial compensation can be awarded to victims who have suffered material damages as a result of the following crimes: terror-

---

64 See Law No. 4603

65 See Law No. 105.

66 Council of Europe 1983.

67 Declaration of Basic Principles of Justice for Victims of Crime and Abuse of Power, Resolution No. 40/34 of 29.11.1985.

68 Recommendation No. R(85)11 of the Committee of Ministers to member states on the position of the victim in the framework of criminal law and procedure of 28.06.1985.

69 Recommendation No. R(97)13 of the Committee of ministers to member states concerning intimidation of witnesses and the rights of the defence of 10.09.1997. .

70 Convention of 29 May 2000 on Mutual Assistance in Criminal Matters between the Member States of the European Union, Convention No. 197, Official Journal of the European Communities 197/3.

71 Council Directive 2004/80/EC relating to compensation to crime victims of 06.08.2004, Official Journal of the European Union 261/15.

72 See Article 3 (general provisions) of the Law No. 105.

ism; intentional murder; attempted murder; intentional grievous bodily harm; sexual abuse; rape; trafficking in people; crime committed by order or under a decision of an organised criminal group or another serious premeditated crime resulting in death or grievous bodily harm, as consequences of an offence defined by Bulgarian law. Chapter 2 of the Act regulates the obligation to notify the victims about their rights. Responsibility for this lies with the Ministry of Interior, investigators, and victim support organisations, the representative offices of the Republic of Bulgaria in the member states of the European Union and a special body, set up under the Ministry of Justice: the National Council for Assistance and Compensation to Victims of Crime. The forms of assistance to victims of crime are listed in Article 8 of the Act: medical treatment in emergency situations according to the procedures established by the Health Act;[73] psychological counselling; free legal assistance under the Legal Aid Act;[74] practical help. Financial compensation shall cover the provision of an amount by the state at the maximum level for an individual not exceeding 10,000 Bulgarian Lev (approximately 5,000 EUR). It covers, jointly or separately, material damages directly caused by a crime and consisting of: medical expenses, except for expenses covered by the budget of the National Health Insurance Fund; lost income; legal fees and litigation costs; lost support to dependants; funeral expenses; other material damages.[75]

The Combating Trafficking in Human Beings Act regulates measures to prevent the trafficking of human beings, the measures aimed at protecting and supporting the victims of human trafficking, especially women and children and the powers and objectives of the state authorities involved in combating trafficking in human beings in general.[76] The Act also provides for the formation of special state units responsible for the prevention and protection of victims of human trafficking: national and local commissions for combating trafficking in human beings, shelters for temporary housing of victims of trafficking, and centres for the protection and support of victims of trafficking.[77]

As a conclusion we can say that the legal framework in connection with victims and victim protection in Bulgaria is constantly improving and has successfully implemented the relevant European legislation and recommendations. The basic problems appear on a practical level when the legislation must be enforced in reality. This will be the greatest challenge facing state authorities in Bulgaria over the next years.

---

73 Health Act, Law No. 70/10.08.2004, Official Gazette 70/04.

74 Legal Aid Act, Law No. 2105/21.09.2005, Official Gazette 21/05.

75 See Article 14 (forms of financial compensation) of the Law No. 105.

76 See Article 1 (general provisions) of the Law No. 4603.

77 See Article 2 (general provisions) of the Law No. 4603.

5. The Reality of Victimisation in Bulgaria, Based on Data and Research Findings

At the present moment in the Republic of Bulgaria there is little representative criminological and victimological research being conducted. Moreover, state institutions are not providing official criminal statistics that focus on the number and socio-demographic characteristics of victims. Research is only occasionally carried out by NGOs, though this is usually of a regional and crime-specific nature. Firstly we must mention the official criminal statistics, provided by the National Statistical Institute. We can say that the statistical information is focused on the crimes and the criminal offenders and less on the victims. But from the data available we can deduct some general information about the victims as well. On the website of the National Statistical Institute, official statistical information is available on the following: crimes, accused persons, convicted persons. There is very detailed information about crimes committed, penalties inflicted, and convictions by statistical regions, districts, and municipalities. Also there is detailed information about anti-social acts and crimes of minor and juvenile persons.[78]

On 14.07.2017, the National Statistical Institute published the official data for 2016 (data for 2017 are not yet available). From the available data, we can see that in 2016 there was a total amount of 28,119 convictions by the courts for crimes committed in Bulgaria.[79] The convictions for 2011 were 36,707, for 2012 – 34,249, for 2013 – 31,301, for 2014 – 28,880 and for 2015 – 26,423. The National Statistical Institute provides statistical information about the total number of intentional homicides, rapes, and thefts recorded by the police in Bulgaria, in other EU countries, and in 11 more countries outside the EU. In *Table 1* information for the period 2010–2015 is displayed.

Table 1 Total Number of Selected Recorded Crimes (2010–2015)

	2010	2011	2012	2013	2014	2015
Homicide	148	128	141	109	116	129
Rape	211	157	187	164	148	119
Theft	50,479	47,323	44,462	45,256	41,246	38,315

Source: StatOffice 2019d.

When we calculate these numbers per 100,000 persons of the population, we get the following results *(Table 2)*:

78 StatOffice 2019d.

79 StatOffice 2019e.

Table 2 Number of Selected Recorded Crimes per 100,000 Persons (2010–2015)

	2010	2011	2012	2013	2014	2015
Homicide	1.99	1.74	1.92	1.5	1.6	1.79
Rape	2.84	2.13	2.55	2.25	2.04	1.65
Theft	680.15	642.15	606.81	621.26	569.25	531.99

Source: Source: StatOffice 2019d.

Table 3 shows a general comparison with the data available for homicide, rape, and theft per 100.000 people in 12 other randomly chosen EU countries for 2015.[80]

Table 3 Number of Recorded Crimes per 100.000 Persons in Selected EU Countries for 2015

	Homicide	Rape	Theft
Austria	0.49	13.18	1586.92
Belgium	1.96	25.5	1660.42
Germany	0.81	8.65	1646.84
Greece	0.79	1.12	923.72
Estonia	3.19	12.24	863.51
Slovakia	0.89	1.6	444.37
Slovenia	0.97	2.04	1105.16
Lithuania	5.75	5.31	688.78
Latvia	4.08	3.02	976.14
Poland	0.75	3.24	363.54
Romania	1.46	5.11	545.72
Hungary	1	3.84	1031.67

Source: StatOffice 2019d.

The above-mentioned data show a slight decreasing trend in Bulgaria for all three crimes in the period from 2010 to 2015, especially for rape and theft. When we make a general comparison with the 12 EU countries, shown in *Table 3*. We can see that the number of homicides recorded by the police in Bulgaria per 100.000 persons are less than those in Belgium. Estonia. Latvia, and Lithuania, but more than in the other EU countries. Violent crimes are still a serious problem in Bulgaria. Regarding the number of recorded rapes and thefts per 100.000 persons for 2015, we can see

80 The data source for the other countries is EUROSTAT.

that the picture for Bulgaria is definitely better. In most of the other EU countries the numbers are considerably higher.

The National Statistical Institute provides detailed victimisation data on minors and juveniles. The picture for 2017 is the following *(Table 4)*:

Table 4 Number of Minor and Juvenile Victims (2017)

Total number of minor and juvenile victims	1,463
8–13 years	605 (332 boys and 273 girls)
14–17 years	858 (514 boys and 344 girls)

Source: StatOffice 2018.

It becomes obvious that boys are more likely to become victims that girls. This can primarily be explained by the Bulgarian family tradition: often, young aged boys are more independent and active compared to girls who are better protected by their parents. Three types of crimes were common against minors and juveniles in 2017: crimes against property (830), physical violence (240), and sexual offences (106). Of course victims of sexual crimes were most commonly girls.[81]

All the district and regional courts in the Republic of Bulgaria provide annual reports on their activities. These reports are public and are available on the websites of the courts. From the reports we can see the number of criminal cases submitted by the prosecution and decided by the court in the relevant period. There is also an indication of the cases by type of crime (the crimes are grouped by chapters of the Penal Code). The information from the annual reports of the courts can provide (to some extent) a picture of crime rates in Bulgaria by regions, but it cannot be precise and representative, because it contains only cases that have gone to trial. As regards the number of victims, and their rights and protection measures, the annual reports of the courts in Bulgaria do not provide any substantial information at all, which can be considered a serious problem. The accused persons and the victims are the main participants in the penal procedure and have equal rights in front of the state bodies. We cannot understand why the Bulgarian courts underestimate the work with victims and focus only on the offenders. *Table 5* provides information about the total number of criminal cases in 2016 and 2017, submitted by the prosecution in the 5 biggest and most important district courts in Bulgaria – Sofia, Plovdiv, Varna, Burgas, and Veliko Tarnovo.

From these data, we can deduct some basic information about the crime and victimisation situation in the biggest regions of the country. It is clear there is a great

81 StatOffice 2018.

Table 5 Total Number of Criminal Cases Submitted by the Prosecution to a Relevant Court

	2016	2017
Sofia	22,346	21,934
Plovdiv	8,419	8,491
Varna	6,670	/
Burgas	7,359	6,330
Veliko Tarnovo	2,535	2,313

Source: Burgas Regional Court 2017; Plovdiv Regional Court 2017; Sofia Regional Court 2017; Varna Regional Court 2016; Veliko Tarnovo Regional Court 2017.

imbalance between the capital and the other big cities in Bulgaria, mainly due to the big difference in the sizes of the respective population.

The Research Institute for Criminalistics and Criminology (RICC) used to be the main state body to provide detailed and precise information about criminal offences and victims in Bulgaria. But after 2013[82] the activities of the Institute have been practically aborted. If any statistical surveys have been made by the RICC in the last few years, they have not been made public, but are regarded as classified and only for internal use. One of the last public research effort of the RICC, regarding criminalisation and victimisation, is from 2013 and entitled "Criminalisation and victimisation of persons aged 18–30"[83]. The sources of the data of this research are very interesting – police statistics from 2007–2011, criminal cases against persons between 18–30 years, reports from police officers, interviews with specialised investigators on child crime, with school pedagogues, with members of local commissions against anti-social acts of minors and juveniles, and with young people themselves. According to data provided by police sources, 22.6% of the victims of crime in Bulgaria are between 18 and 30 years old. People aged between 18 and 30 in Bulgaria are most commonly affected by personal crime (36.7% of the victims). Typical crimes include sexual abuse of young women. They are also victims of trafficking for sexual exploitation. The quota of juvenile victims of crimes against property (20.2%) and of dangerous crimes (25.3%) is significantly lower. According to this research, the number of juvenile victims between 2007 and 2011 constantly decreased (with the slight exception of 2009) and at the end of this period the drop was almost 25%. The number of young victims of personal crime decreased by one third.

Victimisation risk factors can be found in different spheres of social and personal life. They include: economic factors like poverty and unemployment as well as

82 *Belova* 2013.

83 Ministry of the Interior 2013.

domestic violence. In addition taking money from loan sharks can lead to violent crimes and extortion.

Another important victimisation factor is migration, which has increased in Bulgaria and elsewhere. It is well known that migration has an intense criminological aspect, but the transfer from one region to another often leads to victimisation as well. Legal migration is risky because of the separation from home, family and relatives. Physical discomfort communication with unknown people with different languages and cultures, and walking into unknown social and economic situations are factors that also play a role. Consequently, illegal migration has an even stronger victimisation factor. Illegal emigrants are vulnerable and susceptible to persuasion because, apart from the above-mentioned difficulties, they cannot rely on local state authorities for support. Additional problems include lack of employment or abode, meaning they are more often involved in crime situations. In addition they often have a rudimentary level of education, are naïve, and have no social skills. Very often illegal migrating young women are at risk, especially when they are raising children alone.

An important social and psychological factor for the victimisation of juveniles is the justification of violence, especially within the family. Domestic violence against young women and children is seldom reported due to shame and prejudices. That leads to acceptance and toleration of this type of crime. The family often blames the victim, and not the offender. Young people, especially Roma, use blood revenge as an instrument for keeping their personal and family dignity. As a consequence pride, jealousy, and other emotions are strong criminalisation and victimisation factors among juveniles. Of course very important personal factors for victimisation among juveniles are alcohol and drug abuse. Victims of homicide, physical abuse, and sexual violence are often young people under the influence of alcohol. They have lower self-control and unrealistic judgment of the situation. The addiction to drugs and the pain of abstinence are reasons for walking into extremely risky situations. Police officers with experience in victimisation also note that some drugs have a relaxant effect, meaning that victims are not able to protect themselves. In connection with prevention we must consider that drug and alcohol addiction often begin during early adolescence and are thus hard to overcome.

A very important conclusion of this research is that the victimisation of young people can lead to their later criminalisation. State bodies must take effective measures to prevent this. As mentioned above, since 2002, the National Commission for Combating Trafficking in Human Beings has been operating in Bulgaria. It determines and administers the implementation of the national policy and strategy in the area of combating trafficking in human beings. The National Commission provides annual reports, which contain detailed, very precise and professionally processed information about the victims of trafficking, data about their sex and age, the actual trends in internal and external trafficking, the measures already taken by the state for victim protection, and the necessary future steps in this direction. In the reports, there are international comparisons with other EU countries.[84]

Nowadays, Bulgaria is still a country where victims of trafficking originate from; it is also a transit country. The registered victims of trafficking are mainly Bulgarian citizens. According to the official statistics of the preliminary investigations, provided by the prosecution, there is a continuing tendency that the victims of this crime are girls and women (in about 90% of all cases). Worldwide and in Europe (including Bulgaria), most of the registered cases of trafficking tare for sexual exploitation. At the same time, the number of people forced into organised begging and labour exploitation has been rising in recent years. Many professionals consider that the reason why trafficking for sexual exploitation is still the most common form of this crime lies in the fact that victims of other types of trafficking (especially for labour exploitation) often do not recognise themselves as victims and do not seek legal protection.

The Republic of Bulgaria has developed a full institutional framework for the prevention and protection of victims. In 2016, a National mechanism for the referral and support of trafficked persons in Bulgaria was adopted. The purpose of this mechanism is to provide different institutions to work with victims, to determine their formal and informal identification, and to give victims necessary safeguards for their rights and provide opportunities for support. In the beginning of 2017, after several consultations at local and international level, the national strategy for combating trafficking in human beings and protection of victims was produced. This is a strategic document, approved by the government, which determines policy over a long period.

In Bulgaria, ten local Commissions for Combatting Trafficking in Human Beings (LCCTHB) – Blagoevgrad, Burgas, Varna, Veliko Tarnovo, Montana, Pazardjik, Pleven, Plovdiv, Ruse and Sliven – are operating at present. Their main purpose is not only to work on signals for trafficking, prevention, and the protection of victims, but also the training of specialists at a local level. In its capacity as the leading state institution engaged with the formal identification of victims, the Bulgarian prosecution is the main data source for information on trafficking in human beings. *Table 6* lists the statistical information, provided by the prosecution in 2017 on trafficking in human beings.[85]

According to the data in *Table 7*, the Bulgarian prosecution has made the following conclusions for the period 2015–2017:

1) sexual exploitation is still the main purpose for trafficking in Bulgaria, although the number of victims for labour exploitation is increasing;

---

[84] The data source for the other countries is EUROSTAT.

[85] National Commission for Combating Trafficking in Human Beings 2017.

2) the largest percentage of victims are women;
3) there is an increasing number of identified cases of trafficked pregnant women for the sale of their unborns.

Table 6 Total Number of Victims of Human Trafficking, by Age and Gender Structure (2015–2017)

Number of Victims	**2015**	**2016**	**2017**
Total number	409	447	508
Women (total)	381	409	444
Minors (14–18 years old)	27	20	36
Girls (under 14 years old)	1	1	1
Men (total)	28	38	64
Minors (14–8 years old)	0	1	0
Boys (under 14 years old)	5	3	5

Source: National Commission for Combating Trafficking in Human Beings 2017.

Table 7 Victims of Trafficking Grouped by Purpose of Trafficking (2015–2017)

Purpose of trafficking	**2015**	**2016**	**2017**
Sexual exploitation	314	329	323
Women (total)	311	318	316
Minors (14–18 years old)	24	19	32
Girls (under 14 years old)	2	1	0
Men (total)	3	11	7
Minors (14–18 years old)	0	1	0
Boys (under 14 years old)	1	0	0
Labour exploitation	26	31	67
Women	4	8	16
Men	22	23	51
Removing of organs	1	1	1
Women	0	0	0
Men	1	1	1
Forced servitude	6	5	17
Women	6	3	14
Men	0	2	3
Baby selling (before delivery)	59	80	97

Source: National Commission for Combating Trafficking in Human Beings 2017.

Table 8 Sex and Age Structure of Victims of Trafficking for 2013 and 2014

	2013	2014
Total number of victims	538	491
Women (total)	475	462
Under 18 years old	48	29
Over 18 years old	427	433
Men (total)	63	29
Under 18 years old	17	12
Over 18 years old	46	17

Source: National Commission for Combating Trafficking in Human Beings 2016.

Comparing the data from previous periods about the sex and age of the victims of trafficking, we can see that the trends are still the same and women are the ones affected most. *Table 8* provides statistical information for 2013 and 2014.

At present, the Center for the Study of Democracy (hereinafter CSD) is one of the most important data sources for criminalisation and victimisation processes in Bulgaria, although it is not a state body. The National Crime Survey is an instrument, implemented by the CSD which gives a detailed analysis of crime rates and trends. The CSD and its subsidiary social research company (Vitosha Research) have been conducting the National Crime Survey annually since 2005.[86] It collects data on reported and unreported crimes. From a positive point of view, the survey focuses on victims. From negative point of view, respondents are only questioned if they have fallen victim to nine specific types of crime, mainly against property (stolen vehicles, burglary, robbery). In recent years there have been additional questions about sexual offences. The reason for this type of questions is that in Bulgaria crimes against property are the most common, making up about 65–70% of the total number of crimes committed. However, the National Crime Survey index does not include homicide and other crimes against the persons, transport offences, and drug offences, for example. *Table 9* shows the results of the National Crime Survey for 2008, 2009, and 2010.

It is obvious that there is a downward trend in the total number of victims recorded in the survey, but the levels in general are still relatively high.[87] On 30.07.2015, the CSD organised a public discussion, entitled Dynamics of Conventional Crime in Bulgaria 2014–2015.[88] At the discussion the results of the last National Crime Sur-

---

86 Center for the Study of Democracy 2019.

87 Vitosha Research 2010.

88 Center for the Study of Democracy 2019.

Table 9 Results of the National Crime Survey

	2008	2009	2010
Victimisation rate*	10.6%	10.54%	9.63%

Source: Vitosha Research 2010.

* Prevalence rate of the Bulgarian population: at least one of the nine crime types surveyed.

vey in 2015 were presented to the Minister of Interior and senior police officers. The general conclusions of the discussion, with focus on the victims, were the following: Crime rates in 2014 decreased compared to the record high levels of 2012 and the total number of victims dropped from 17.2% in 2012 to 13.3% in 2014. Nevertheless, conventional crime rates are still at a high level. Confidence in the police increased, because in 2014 more victims reported crimes. The participants in the public discussion detected a continuing discrepancy between data of the victimisation surveys and official police statistics. For instance in 2014, police reported the lowest crime rate since 1990. However, the results of the National Crime Survey in 2015 clearly showed that the decrease in the numbers of crimes committed is not as large as the police data claim. As a confirmation of this trend, in *Table 10* we can see statistics from the emergency calls (112) for four types of crime in the period 2012–2014 and the registered crimes of the same type by the police.

The discrepancy is huge and the main reason for this is that the official statistics obviously recorded a smaller number of crimes than were actually committed. This can be due to several factors: for instance, the so-called "latency" (victims of crimes choose, for various reasons. not to report a crime to the police); another factor is the existence of "police filters" (crimes get reported, but are not registered by the police). According to the survey results, in Bulgaria only one out of three reported crimes is registered.

To deal with this problem, a variety of measures were proposed: performing regular regional comparisons to detect discrepancies between registered and committed crimes; comparing police statistics with 112 (emergency calls) statistics; deploying "mystery clients" in the regional police departments (who report uncommitted crimes); and carrying out spot checks. On 08.12.2017, a national round table was held by the CSD. The subject was "Victims of crime – new trends in the identifi-

Table 10 Total Number of Emergency Calls and Crimes, Registered by the Police (2012–2014)

	2012	2013	2014
Emergency calls reported	90,468	97,382	96,170
Recorded crimes by the police	71,446	73,623	67,260

Source: Ministry of the Interior 2017.

cation, needs assessment and guidance in Bulgaria and in the EU". The round table was attended by magistrates, high ranking police officers, social workers, and NGOs. The general conclusion was that although most of the relevant legal frameworks in victim protection are successfully transposed. Bulgaria is still far from providing real and adequate support to victims. The main problems at the present moment are connected with the participation of victims in both phases of the criminal procedure, the absence of good conditions for professional work with them, and the lack of financial resources for protection measures and for compensation by the state. The Ministry of Interior provides monthly and annual statistical reports about the crime situation in Bulgaria. These reports are very detailed, especially in the capital city of Sofia, where 25% of the country's population lives. From police reports we can collect data about the number of registered crimes and the number of resolved crimes. There is available information about the offenders: sex, age, and citizenship. But these reports do not include any substantial information about victims, which is a big disadvantage. When we look at *Table 11,* we can see the data for 2017 and 2016, provided by the directorate "Analysis and policies" of the Ministry of Interior.[89]

Table 11 Total Number of Registered and Resolved Crimes

	2016	**2017**
Total number of registered crimes	99,941	96,125
Total number of resolved crimes by the police	41,135	42,634
Percentage of resolved crimes	41.2%	44.4%

Source: Ministry of the Interior 2017.

As mentioned, the official statistical data of the Ministry of Interior are not completely precise. In Bulgaria, a big difference between the number of crimes committed and the number of crimes registered has been detected. As a conclusion at the present moment, little attention is paid to victims in Bulgaria, especially in officially gathered data. Some NGOs occasionally initiate research with a focus on victimisation, but unfortunately they do not have the capacity to be representative for the whole country and to give a real picture.

6. Public and Media Discourses about Victims. Victims' Rights, Protection, and Victimisation

Crime is a theme that has been discussed very often in the Bulgarian media over the last 25 years. The reasons for this interest are different: before 1989 – during the socialist regime – violence and offences against persons and property were not

89 Ministry of the Interior 2017.

discussed in public and only experts had detailed information about the real crime situation in the country. That said, crime (as a social phenomenon) has always been an interesting topic for all members of society. At present, the crime situation in the country has become significantly more complicated: the number of crimes has increased, the types of offences have changed, and there are new challenges for state institutions, such as international crimes, terrorism, and migration, for example.

In the global fight against crime at all levels, the role of the media is, of course, not only informative. The media have become "the fourth power" with its powerful instruments to influence society. Of course, we must put electronic media first. Of late, social networks have had a great impact on building and controlling public opinion too. Nowadays, journalists are reporting each day of different crimes seeking sensations and public attention. Car crashes and other incidents resulting in injured people are constantly shown on TV and internet sites. In fact. Bulgarian news is predominantly negative. A professional survey, named "Inside the News", was carried out in 2017 by experts from Sofia University.[90] They concluded that a "catastrophic" agenda was being built by the media. The people, especially in smaller towns and villages, feel fear and insecurity. The same media outlets also constantly report on corruption in the judicial system, legal absurdities, and the slow pace of courts. While such reports are very often justified, they are sometimes based on suspicions and unknown sources rather than real evidence. We must say that the last case of a Bulgarian magistrate being convicted for corruption was in 2016.[91]

The result of this media campaign are devastating for Bulgarian society. First of all, potential offenders have no fear of committing a crime. They have a strong belief that. if they eventually get caught, they will escape the punishment by paying a bribe. Lots of media reports about corruption appear daily and society is very sensitive to this problem. Unfortunately, criminal cases for corruption and convictions are relatively seldom. There was a very popular case in the summer of 2017, when a drunk Swedish tourist intentionally kicked and injured a Bulgarian maid in his hotel at the Black Sea.[92] The tourist was immediately sent to trial and convicted with the maximum punishment for this type of crime according to the Penal Code – a fine of 4.500 Lev.[93] A very strong media campaign began the same day to send the offender to prison for years and to convict the judge, who only fined the tourist. It was

---

90 Union of Bulgarian Journalists of 27.07.2017, Černite novini preobladavat v b″lgarskite medii [Black news is prevalent in the Bulgarian media]; https://www.sbj-bg.eu/index.php?t=36335 [18.09.2019] [in Bulgarian only].

91 Pravni svet of 25.05.2016; Čudo! S″dija i prokuror vljazoha v zatvora [Wonder! A judge and prosecutor went to jail]; http://legalworld.bg/53217.chudo!-sydiia-i-prokuror-vliazoha-v-zatvora.html [18.09.2019] [in Bulgarian only].

92 *Burgas* 2017.

93 Pravni svet of 26.09.2017; S″d″t globi s 4500 leva šveda, kojto ritna kamerierka v Sl″nčev brjag [Court fines 4500 Levs for Swede who kicks maid in Sunny Beach]; http://legal-

insinuated that the judge (probably) took a bribe. Even members of the Bulgarian parliament criticised the court without legal arguments contradictory to the principle of the separation of powers.[94] Experts and other magistrates tried several times to explain that the judge made a decision in full accordance with the law and there is nothing illegal: these calls were made in vain. Manipulated by the media, most Bulgarians still think that the Swedish tourist paid for a milder punishment. From the victim's point of view, this picture has serious consequences. Victims believe that they cannot receive adequate help and protection from state authorities. In their opinion. a visit to the police may even increase their problems. Thus, many crimes remain unreported. This is s dangerous situation as victims are left alone without the support of state institutions. Victims may even turn into offenders. For example in 2018, a doctor in Plovdiv saw a thief in his courtyard and shot him dead.[95] This case started a big public discussion about the limits of self-defence; a discussion that was unfortunately led by the media and social networks, rather than by legal experts. This case has not yet been ruled on.

Finally, we want to mention a very interesting crime phenomenon, called "telephone fraud".[96] Investigators and prosecutors consider this a Bulgarian "invention", which over the last few years has been rapidly spreading across the whole of Europe (Romania, Greece, Germany, Austria, etc.). The mechanism of these frauds is very simple: an old man receives a telephone call from his "relative" who needs money for urgent medical treatment or to "fix things" after a car accident he was involved in. Recently there has been a new variation: victims receive calls from fake police officers, who ask for money as bait to catch dangerous criminal offenders. After the offender is caught, the money will be returned. Amazingly, every month hundreds of Bulgarians fall victim to these frauds. According to police data, in 2017 alone, over 5,000,000 Lev were stolen from Bulgarians,[97] but the media reports that amounts of up to four times higher were actually stolen. Recently, in the beginning of June 2018, a 65-year-old woman from Sofia gave fraudsters 420.000 Lev (210.000 EUR); another 76-year-old man lost over 600.000 EUR within several months.[98] It is important to clarify that even in the cases where the offenders are caught and convicted, the money is never returned to the victims. There are lots of media campaigns for combating telephone fraud, but the effect is still far from satisfactory.

world.bg/65751.sydyt-globi-s-4500-leva-shveda-kojto-ritna-kamerierka-v-slynchev-briag.html [18.09.2019] [in Bulgarian only].

94 *Ivanova* 2017.

95 *Stoev* 2018.

96 Bulgarian National Television of 19.09.2019; Telefonni izmami [Telephone fraud]; http://news.bnt.bg/bg/e/telefonni-izmami [19.09.2019] [in Bulgarian only].

97 *Martinov* 2018b.

98 *Martinov* 2018a.

We believe that the Bulgarian media has to change the negative discourse and use its social instruments to find reliable information sources about crimes and victims, to be precise and objective, to give the public a real picture without manipulations, to build trust in the state authorities, to respect basic human rights, and to refuse to tolerate violence of any kind.

Professional publications in the Bulgarian media which focus on victims, victimisation, and victim protection are rare to find. These topics are considered as (probably) not interesting to the public. We think that the Bulgarian media should start organised campaigns for promotion of programs for victims' support in cooperation with the state authorities in charge. Victims must be aware of their rights and must be encouraged to seek justice without fear.

7. Expert Assessment and Constructive Criticism with Suggestions for Improvement

Although Bulgarian legislation has implemented the basic European acts on victims and victim protection, lots of improvements still have to be made at many different levels. One can begin with the main Act – PPC – and analyse the very popular use of "differentiated procedures". The differentiated procedures are a derivation from the standard model of penal practice. Their main benefit is the significant acceleration of the pre-trial and court phases in accordance with the requirements of Article 6 Paragraph 1 of the European Convention for the Protection of Human Rights and Fundamental Freedoms[99] and Recommendation No. R(86)12 of the Committee of Ministers to Member States concerning Measures to Prevent and Reduce the Excessive Workload in the Courts.[100] These procedures enable the judicial system to work more effectively, saving costs and time. From the offender's point of view, they can result in important advantages and benefits, including a lighter sentence and milder punishment. The picture is significantly different from the victim's point of view, because in these cases, he/she cannot execute basic rights and instruments. Many law specialists and human rights defenders believe that the accused is substantively favoured to the disadvantage of the victim.

Below we will analyse the four differentiated procedures (quick investigation; brief inquiry in front of the court of first instance; replacement of the penal liability with an administrative sanction; and concluding the criminal case with a settlement) with a focus on the victim and his/her procedural position.

---

99 European Court of Human Rights 2019.

100 Recommendation No. R(86)12 of the Committee of Ministers to Member States concerning Measures to Prevent and Reduce the Excessive Workload in the Courts of 16.09.1986.

The quick investigation is regulated in Chapter 24 of the PPC.[101] In the pre-trial phase, when a quick investigation is deployed, the victim does not have the right to participate in the collection of evidence and to make requests, notes, and objections as in the general procedure.[102] Later, in front of the court, the person who has suffered material or non-material damage by the criminal offence, does not have the legal option to participate as a private prosecutor or to submit a civil claim. This is another significant difference in comparison to general procedural rules that and has some very important consequences. Theoretically, in this case the victim does not lose the option to claim and receive financial compensation for damages. When the penal court issues its final sentence, the victim can go to a civil court to claim compensation. This civil procedure is free of state fees and charges.[103] Besides. Article 300 of the Civil Procedure Code[104] stipulates that the sentence of the penal court is mandatory for the civil court in regards to the fact that a criminal offence has been committed, and the offender has been found guilty. Therefore, the victim does not need to prove these basic facts again, and can concentrate on the claim for compensation. But practically, when the victim does not have the legal option to submit a civil claim in front of the penal court, in order to receive compensation, the victim must conclude two separate procedures (first penal and then civil). Taking into consideration the extremely high workload of the Bulgarian courts (especially in Sofia and the other big cities)[105] this can take 4 to 5 years, which is far from reasonable and justified. And this is not the end, because after the civil decision begins the enforcement procedure, which is expensive and slow as well. Due to the above-mentioned reasons, the victims always prefer to submit a civil claim in front of the penal court in order to receive compensation in the same court act with the conviction. When a quick investigation is deployed it is obvious that this is not legally possible.

While, the victim can nonetheless receive compensation during a subsequent civil case, the victim's procedural role as a private prosecutor is different. During the quick investigation the victim has no legal instruments to influence important questions about the liability and punishment of the offender. This is a very serious problem and the only possible way to resolve it is at legislative level by giving the victim the legal option to participate in the court phase as a private prosecutor. This resolution may be defined as a slight retreat in the legislature's idea to accelerate the penal procedure. But when the rights of the victim are concerned, this is more than reasonable. The acceleration of the procedure should not happen at the disadvantage

---

101 Law No. 8605.

102 See Article 356 (Application of the quick investigation) of the Law No. 8605.

103 Article 83 (Exemption from fees and expenses) of the Civil Procedure Code, Law No. 01/08 of 01.03.2008, Official Gazette 01/08.

104 See Article 300 (Obligatory effect of a sentence) of the Law No. 01/08.

105 According to information of the Supreme Judicial Council, a civil judge from the Sofia District Court decides more than 1,000 cases per year.

of the victim.[106] The brief inquiry in front of the court of first instance is regulated in Chapter 27 of the PPC.[107] Currently, the brief inquiry is probably the most used differentiated procedure in Bulgaria. The brief inquiry gives the accused the legal option in front of the court to accept all the facts, referred in the charge act, or accept only part of them. As a consequence, the court will not collect evidence concerning facts that have been accepted. In this case, the pre-trial phase follows the general rules. The injured party has all the rights and legal instruments given by the PPC.[108] In the court phase this differentiated procedure is applied only when the offender personally initiates it. It is more than obvious that neither the court, nor the prosecutor, can force the offender to accept facts. From the victim's point of view, he/she has the legal option to participate as a private prosecutor and/or submit a civil claim. This resolution comes from the mandatory law practice of the Supreme Cassation Court – interpretative decision No. 1/2009.[109] Of course the most important question is whether the victim has the right to influence the decision of the accused to accept the facts in the charge and to initiate this differentiated procedure. In the above-mentioned interpretative decision, the Supreme Cassation Court determined that the injured party has the right to participate in the court hearing and to express its opinion at the defendant's request. This opinion, however, is only informative and the court cannot refuse to apply the brief inquiry due to the victim's disagreement. The brief inquiry is under heavy criticism due to the resolution that, if the accused decides to accept all the facts, referred in the charge act, the court determines the period of imprisonment and automatically reduces it by one third.[110] Thus dangerous offenders receive disproportionately mild sentences. We will illustrate this procedure with an example: the sanction for intentional homicide according to the Penal Code[111] is imprisonment from 10 to 20 years. The defendant accepts all the facts from the charge and requests a brief inquiry to be applied. The court must accept this request and the other parties cannot interfere. After the offender is found guilty, the sentence is determined – for instance 15 years imprisonment. This sentence is immediately reduced by one third. As a result, the offender convicted of intentional homicide (one of the most serious crimes) will go to prison for only 10 years, a sentence that may be additionally reduced and result in eventual early release. It is clear that a great number offenders accept all the facts to receive a more mild punishment and get out from jail as soon as possible. We are not speaking about regret or guilt at all. The victims, however, are left with the impression that they are not supported

---

106 *Milev* 2011.

107 Law No. 8605.

108 Law No. 8605.

109 Supreme Cassation Court, Judgement No. 1/2009 of 06.04.2009.

110 See Article 58a (determining of the penalty) of the Penal Code, Law No. 261968 of 01.05.1968, Official Gazette 26/1968.

111 See Article 115 (homicide) of the Law No. 261968.

and defended by the state. Until 2010, Article 369a of the PPC was in force, which did not allow the brief inquiry in front of the court of first instance to be applied if the crime was a homicide, a serious bodily harm, or if the offender was drunk when committing the crime. This provision legally stopped the practice of the accused making formal confessions in front of the court in order to receive disproportionally mild sentences. Art. 369a was publicly discussed and repealed in 2010. Since then, there are absolutely no limitations to apply for a brief inquiry in front of the court. We believe that the Bulgarian PPC should not allow the brief inquiry to be applied in all cases. This legal resolution is definitely in favour of the offender and does not give the victim necessary protection. As a result there are comments in Bulgarian society that it is better to be an offender than a victim and that a lot of people are enjoying impunity for their unlawful actions.[112]

Replacement of the penal liability with an administrative sanction is regulated in Chapter 28 of the PPC.[113] The court sets as a sanction a fine of up to 5.000 Bulgarian Lev according to the cumulative existence of certain legal conditions.[114] In these type of cases the pre-trial phase follows general procedural rules and the accused and the victim have all their regular rights. The differences to the general procedural rules appear in the court phase. Concerning the victim in particular, there is a legal prohibition to participate as a private prosecutor and/or to submit a civil claim.[115] In this situation the victim, who has taken part in the pre-trial phase with all his procedural rights, suddenly is legally dismissed from the court phase and does not have the possibility to continue defending himself/herself. In the court hearing, the victim can appear only as a witness. The consequence of the victim not participating as a private prosecutor or submitting a civil claim were explained in detail above. In connection with this differentiated procedure, we must mention the existence of one very important guarantee for the rights of the victim: the offender can receive an administrative fine instead of a penal sanction only if he/she has compensated all material damage caused by the crime to the victim or to the state. The resolution motivates the offender to pay for the damage caused and is the easiest and quickest way for the victim to be compensated.

The last differentiated procedure is the option to conclude the criminal case with a settlement with the Prosecution.[116] First we must clarify that the PPC legally excludes the possibility of a settlement for a special list of intentional crimes, including

---

112 *Chinova & Gatev* 2012.

113 Law No. 8605.

114 See Article 78a (replacement of the penal liability with an administrative sanction) of the Law No. 8605.

115 See Article 376 (court procedure) of the Law No. 261968.

116 Law No. 8605.

all cases where death is caused.[117] With this regulation, the legislature has created a safety mechanism against unlimited use of settlements and. at the same time, has sought to relay to the public that criminals in Bulgaria do not escape the punishment they deserve. This is also an important instrument for protecting the legal interests of the victim, who is interested in seeing the offender receive the right sentence for the crime committed. There are two possible options to conclude a case via settlement. If the defendant and the prosecution arrange the settlement in the pre-trial phase, the victim cannot participate in this procedure at all.[118] In this case, the settlement is signed by the parties and approved by the court not only irrespective of the victim's opinion, but very often against the victim's will. It is a different situation when the settlement is made in front of the court of first instance. In this case, if eventually the defendant proposes a settlement, it can be approved by the court only after all other parties (including the victim) agree. If for any reason the victim, acting as private prosecutor and/or civil claimant, does not accept the settlement, the criminal case can continue only according to the general procedure.[119] In concluding, the application of the differentiated procedures has had an extremely positive influence on penal procedure in Bulgaria, particularly concerning acceleration of cases and the saving of sources. However, we must also note that the procedures often give more rights to offenders and less rights to victims. In fact, in some cases the victim is legally dismissed from participating in the procedure. This has been heavily criticised. The biggest challenge for the legislature is to find a proper balance between the victim and the offender. Of course, this will happen only with the strong support of the magistrates, lawyers, and Bulgarian society as a whole.

The next step is to make a critical analysis of the Crime Victims Assistance and Financial Compensation Act. Currently, most of the measures provided in this Act do not exist in practice. Although it was published in 2006, it has only been in the past few years that investigative bodies have begun to provide victims with declarations that list their procedural rights. However, despite these tentative inroads it can still be argued that the legislation has a mainly formal character, because many investigators are not prepared to provide victims with detailed explanations concerning of their rights. This statement can be substantiated with numbers. On the internet site of the National Council for Assistance and Compensation to Victims of Crime (Ministry of Justice), under the section "Decision/Protocols" the protocols of the hearings of the Council from 02.07.2015, 09.03.2015, 09.10.2015, and 14.03.2016 (we do not know why more actual information is not provided) are available.[120] From these protocols we can see that on the mentioned hearings, and 18 requests by citizens for

---

117 See Article 381 (settlement during the preliminary investigation) of the Law No. 8605.

118 See Article 381 (settlement during the preliminary investigation) of the Law No. 8605.

119 *Marinova* 2017.

120 National Council for Assistance and Compensation to Victims of Crime 2019.

financial compensation have been examined. In almost one third of the cases the Council rejected the payment of compensation mostly because the claims do not respond to the legal requirements. Irrespective of this a total number of 56 submitted and examined requests within a year and a half is highly inadequate, especially with regard to the complicated criminalisation and victimisation situation in Bulgaria.

The Bulgarian media have requested and received data about the implementation of the Crime Victims Assistance and Financial Compensation Act from the Ministry of Justice according to the Public Information Access Act. For the whole of 2016, the state paid compensation to only 23 victims of crime (or their inheritors), the total amount of 47.514 Bulgarian Lev. That gives an average amount of 2,065 Bulgarian Lev (1,056 EUR) per person. Between January and May 2017, 36,702 Bulgarian Lev were paid to 16 victims, which makes 2,293 Lev (1,172 EUR) per person. In the period from the beginning of 2016 until May 2017, in the National Council for Assistance and Compensation to Victims of Crime, 88 requests for compensation were submitted, and more than a half of them were rejected.[121] The above-cited numbers are so insignificant that it is clear that the compensation procedures in Bulgaria do not work properly.

In 2016, the Ministry of Justice paid 27,692 Bulgarian Lev to two organisations for offering and providing free psychological aid to 22 victims of crime. These are foundation are "Nadia" and "For Crime Victim Assistance and Fight against Corruption". Psychological aid from only two organisations is highly ineffective. There is a proposal to establish at least one organisation throughout the five regions in the country with an appeal court (Sofia, Plovdiv, Burgas, Varna, and Veliko Tarnovo), though at present this has not yet happened.

Finally, we do not think that the limit of financial compensation should be capped at 10.000 Bulgarian Lev. It is clear that the state budget does not dispose of big amounts of money, but each case has its individual characteristics and it can often happen that even the highest amount will not be enough for the proper compensation of a victim. Moreover, the list of crimes for which compensation can be paid should be extended; this would automatically enlarge the number of victims who can claim and receive financial compensation.

Based on all these findings, whilst the appropriate legislation concerning victims and victim protection exists in Bulgaria, its practical implementation remains problematic. In addition this problem is multiplied by low trust of the population in the judicial system, a lack of substantial information for victims about their rights, a lack of well prepared and highly motivated employees in state bodies, insufficient research efforts at universities and institutes on the topics of criminology and victimology, and a dearth of available statistical information sources and data. The Bulgarian state

---

121 *Dachkova* 2017.

must start work on all these issues simultaneously in order to achieve better results in victim protection over the next years.

8. Conclusion

Although Bulgaria has been a member of the EU since the beginning of 2007, there is still a long way to go until the goal of its membership is reached: to become a modern, prosperous country with high standard of living. People in Bulgaria face many challenges, including low incomes, unemployment, unnecessary bureaucracy, and insecurity. A large number of young and educated people have left the country in search of a better standard of living. While state and municipal institutions have been transformed and reorganised several times, they are still criticised for displaying inefficiency, non-transparency, and corruption.

The first victimological research in Bulgaria occurred during the 1960s. Over the years, research has become more systematic, complete, and precise. Of particular importance has been the role played by the Research Institute for Criminalistics and Criminology (Ministry of Interior) and the law faculty of Sofia University "St. Kliment Ohridsky" (the only law school in Bulgaria before 1989). While state-based research on victimology has declined, of late NGOs have stepped in to fill this gap not just at theoretical, but also at practical level (e.g., by providing psychological,social, and health services).

Over the last 20 years, the Bulgarian government has made big steps in the right direction to give victims of crime adequate support. In the repealed version of the Bulgarian PPC (before 2006), the procedural figure of the injured party was not regulated at all. However, as of now, the current PPC protects the procedural position of the victim in the preliminary investigation and in the court phase. Victim have numerous rights and protections. Moreover, the general legal principle in Bulgaria is that the injured party participates in the proceedings always by choice and never by obligation.[122]

At present, all the significant European Regulations, Directives, and other Acts have been successfully transposed into Bulgarian legislation (including Directive 2012/29/EU of the European Parliament and of the Council of 25 October 2012, establishing minimum standards on the rights, support, and protection of victims of crime). Apart from the PPC, other important Bulgarian laws concerning the rights of the victim are: the Crime Victims Assistance and Financial Compensation Act, the Combating Trafficking in Human Beings Act, and the Legal Aid Act. The legislature has tried to find the proper balance between the rights of the accused and the rights of the victim. Of course, some criticism can be applied, but in general, we can say

---

122 See Law No. 8605.

that the Bulgarian legislation (regarding victims) corresponds with European standards.[123]

Unfortunately, in reality, Bulgaria is still far from the point where adequate victims support is provided. On the one hand, state bodies are not doing enough for the victims (due to financial constraints, poor facilities, and low levels of staff motivation). On the other hand, victims themselves often remain passive, they do not want to use the legal system to protect their rights, and they have no trust in state authorities. These are very fundamental problems of Bulgarian society in general, and the solution cannot be found with a single measure.

The idea of "public compensation by the state to victims of crime" is relatively new for the Bulgarian legislation. This scheme has been established in accordance with standards to provide victims with adequate compensation when the offender cannot pay. However, the scheme is a very good example of the poor implementation of a good mechanism. A brief review of the activity of the National Council for Assistance and Compensation to Victims of Crime (Ministry of Justice) shows that improvement is more than necessary. For the whole of 2016, the state paid compensation to only 23 victims of crime (amounting to 47.514 Bulgarian Lev). It is out of the question that this number is absolutely negligible when one looks at the statistics on victimisation in Bulgaria. Moreover, the average compensation of 1.056 EUR per person does not appear adequate. Public compensation scheme must be significantly improved, starting with the legislation.

Victims of crime are one of the most vulnerable and sensitive social groups. We consider that their position has improved in the last years, but there are lots of additional measures that still need to be taken. This will prove a significant challenge not only for Bulgarian state authorities, but also NGOs, media outlets and all public institutions.

We consider that the necessary steps for improvement must occur in four basic directions:

- increasing the trust in the Bulgarian police and judicial system in general. This will give people a feeling that they are protected by the state and will encourage them to report crimes;
- preparation of highly educated and motivated staff to work with victims;
- better communication with the victims and the provision of information about their rights;
- more qualitative theoretical work in universities and institutes on the topics of criminology and victimology.

---

123 See Directive No. 31557; Law No. 2105; Law No. 105; Law No. 4603.

9. Summary in Bulgarian

Povecheto experti narichat obvinjaemia "centralna figura" v nakazatelnia proces. I verojatno nie bi trjabvalo da se suglasim s podobno mnenie. Sustevremenno obache tova ne sledva po nikakuv nachin da vodi do podcenjavane na figurata na postradalia ot prestupnoto posegatelstvo. Nastojasteto izsledvane sudurja na purvo mjasto podroben analiz na pravnoto polojenie na postradalia suglasno aktualnoto bulgarsko zakonodatelstvo. Vkljucheni sa vsichki relevantni normativni aktove – Nakazatelen kodex, Nakazatelnoprocesualen kodex, Zakon za podpomagane i finansova kompensacia na postradali ot prestuplenia, Zakon za borba s trafika na hora. Mojem da kajem che procesualnite prava i zaduljenia na postradalia sa podrobno i obektivno izjasneni, kato celta na avtora e bila ne samo mehanichno da gi izbroi, no i da razkrie tochnoto im sudurjanie i nachina za naj-efektivnoto im uprajnjavane. V tozi smisal nastojasteto izsledvane bi imalo seriozna prakticheska polza za vseki, koito eventualno bi imal nujda ot pravna pomost v kachestvoto si na postradal v Republika Bulgaria. Celta na nastojasteto izsledvane obache ne se ogranichava samo s izjasnjavane na sustestvuvastata pravna uredba.Normite sa podlojeni na analiz ot teoreticheska i prakticheska gledna tochka, avtorut e posochil sustestvuvastite spored nego problemi i e napravil predljenia za optimiziraneto im. Nastojasteto izsledvane na vtoro mjasto vkljuchva informacia za aktualnata kriminogenna i viktimogenna obstanovka v Republika Bulgaria. Predstavjaneto na nalichnata statisticheska informacia e suchetano s analizi i izvodi na specialisti ot razlichni nauchni oblasti, kato celta e chitateljat da pridobie realna predstava za obstestvenia jivot v Republika Bulgaria, za postijeniata i predizvikatelstvata, s koito se sresta suvremenniat bulgarin. Nakraja avtorut e napravil i svoj pregled na medijnia diskurs na temata za jertvite ot prestuplenia v Republika Bulgaria. Tozi vupros susto e osobeno interesen, zastoto vuv vremeto na elektronnite medii, socialnite mreji i falshivite novivi e mnogo lesno obstestvenoto mnenie da bude manipulirano ili tlasnato v nepravilna posoka. Vseizvesten fakt e che postradalite ot prestuplenia sa edni ot naj-ujazvimite i chuvstvitelni chlenove na obstestvoto. V momenta kogato te sa se srestnali po edin ili drug nachin s prestupnoto dejanie i sa preturpeli vredi te imat nujda ot obstestvena podkrepa, kakto i razbira se da usetjat v pulna stepen, che durjavata stoi zad gurba im. Za sujalenie v nashi dni chesto postradalite v Republika Bulgaria se chuvstvat napulno izostaveni i ne znajat kum kogo da se obarnat. Nadjavame se, che nastojasteto izsledvane ste dade svoja skromen prinos tova da se promeni.

Literature

Belova, N. (2013): Criminalizacia i victimizacia na lica na vuzrast 18–30 [Criminalization and victimization of persons aged 18–30]. Sofia.

Berbec, S., Ilcheva, M., Nordstrom, R., Heinonen, H., Feito, P. & Freudenberg, D. (2018): Victims of crimes rights, competent stakeholders in Romania, Bulgaria, Germany, Sweden. Bucharest.

Burgas, D. (2017): Šokiraŝo napadenie: Šved rita v glavata kamerierka v Sl"nčev brjag (VIDEO) [Shocking attack: Swede kicks in maid's head in Sunny Beach (VIDEO)], in Daik News, 06.06.2017; https://dariknews.bg/novini/bylgariia/shokirashto-napadenie-shved-rita-v-glavata-kamerierka-v-slynchev-briag-video-2028604 [18.09.2019] [in Bulgarian only].

Chinova, M. (2013): Dosadebnoto proizvodstvo po NPK [The preliminary investigation according to the Penal Procedure Code]. Sofia.

Chinova, M. & Gatev, G. (2012): Sakratenoto sudebno sledstvie po NPK [The shortened inquiry according to the Penal Procedure Code]. Ciela.

Dachkova, D. (2017): Samo 23 žertvi na prest"plenija sa kompensirani ot d"ržavata za godina [Only 23 victims of offenses have been compensated by the state for the year], in Sega, 16.10.2017; http://old.segabg.com/article.php?id=876654 [18.09.2019] [in Bulgarian only].

Ilkova, R. (2005): Nakazatelni dela ot chasten harakter [Private criminal cases]. Ciela.

Ivanova, A. (2017): Ninova za kamerierkata: Koj s"dija uniži dostojnstvoto j? [Ninova for the maid: Which judge humiliates her dignity?], in Dnes.bg, 27.09.2017; https://www.dnes.bg/obshtestvo/2017/09/27/ninova-za-kamerierkata-koi-sydiia-uniji-dostoinstvoto-i.354563 [18.09.2019] [in Bulgarian only].

Marinova, G. (2017): Sporazumenieto v bulgarskia nakazatelen proces [The deal in the Bulgarian Penal Procedure]. Sibi.

Martinov, D. (2018a): 5 mln. leva zadignati pri telefonni izmami za 2017 g. [5 million BGN raised in telephone fraud for 2017], in 24chasa.bg, 27.02.2018; https://www.24chasa.bg/novini/article/6738206 [18.09.2019] [in Bulgarian only].

Martinov, D. (2018b): Djade dodк 600 000 кvpe no tкlкfenni izmomnici. o žкno no 65 g. - 420 000 lv. (Obzep) [Old Man looses 600.000 Lev and 65-year-old woman 420.000 Lev in telephone fraud (Obsep)], in 24chasa.bg, 08.06.2018; https://www.24chasa.bg/novini/article/6903903 [18.09.2019] [in Bulgarian only].

Milev, S. (2011): Barzoto proizvodstvo po NPK [The fast investigation according to the Penal Procedure Code]. Ciela.

Miteva, Y. (1980): Viktimologichnite izsledvania i prevenciata na prestupnostta [Victimological researches and crime prevention]. Sofia.

Miteva, Y. (1979): Viktimologichni problemi na umishlenite ubiistva [Victimological problems in the case of murder]. Sofia.

Panev, B. (1993): Criminologia [Criminology]. Burgas.

Panev, B. (1983): Pravna zastita na jertvite na prestuplenia [Legal protection of crime victims]. Sofia.

Stankov, B. (2012): Kriminologia: teoretichni osnovi [Criminology: Theoretical basis].

Stankov, B. (2003): Kriminologia [Criminology]. Varna.

Stankov, B. (2001a): Prehodut, prestupnostta, jertvite na prestupnostta [The transition, crime, and victims of crimes]. Varna.

Stankov, B. (2001b): Viktimologia [Victimology]. Varna.

Stankov, B. (1998): Problemi na viktimizaciata v strani ot balkanskia region [Bulgaria: Crime victims in the transition period. Problems of the victimisation in the countries of the Balkan region]. Sofia.

Stoev, V. (2018): Povdignaha obvinenie za ubijstvo na plovdivskija lekar. zastreljal kradec [They have charged a Plovdiv doctor who shot a thief with murder], in trafficnews.bg,

03.03.2018; https://trafficnews.bg/krimi/povdignaha-obvinenie-ubiistvo-plovdivskiia-lekar-ubiistvoto-97770/ [18.09.2019] [in Bulgarian only].

Stojanov, N. (2017): Valutnijat bord: 20 godini ne stigat [Currency board: 20 years will not suffice], in: Kapital [Capital], 30.06.2017; https://www.capital.bg/politika_i_ikonomika/bulgaria/2017/06/30/2998415_valutniiat_bord_20_godini_ne_stigat/ [16.09.2019].

Documents

Burgas Regional Court (2017): Doklad za dejnostta na rajonen s″d – Burgas prez 2017 g. [Activity report of the Burgas Regional Court in 2017]; http://www.bourgasrc.court-bg.org/index.php?im=131 [19.09.2019] [in Bulgarian only].

Centre for the Study of Democracy (2019): Za nas [About us]; http://old.csd.bg/index.php?id=2 [16.09.2019] [in Bulgarian and English].

Council of Europe (1983): European Convention on the Compensation of Victims of Violent Crimes; https://www.coe.int/en/web/conventions/full-list/-/conventions/rms/0900001680079751 [in English only].

European Commission (2018): Evropejski semest″r: B″lgarija namaljava stepenta na makroikonomičeskite si disbalansi [European Semester: Bulgaria reduces its macroeconomic imbalances]; https://ec.europa.eu/bulgaria/news/european-semester-reviewing-member-states-progress-on-economic-and-social-priorities_bg [16.09.2019] [in Bulgarian and English].

European Court of Human Rights (2019): European Convention on Human Rights; https://www.echr.coe.int/Documents/Convention_ENG.pdf [in English only].

Faculty of Law of the University of Sofia (2019): Doma [Home]; http://www.law.uni-sofia.bg/default.aspx [16.09.2019] [in Bulgarian only].

LogoInfograf (2019): Naselenieto na B″lgarija (1946–2011) [The population of Bulgaria (1946–2011)]; https://www.infograf.bg/article/1496042439000 [16.09.2019] [in Bulgarian only].

Ministry of the Interior (2017): Statističeski analiz [Statistical analysis]; https://www.mvr.bg/docs/librariesprovider55/статистически-анализи/analiz_november.pdf?sfvrsn=-30fa3935_2 [19.09.2019] [in Bulgarian only].

Ministry of the Interior (2013): Kriminalizacija i viktimizacija na lica na v″zrast 18–30 g. [Criminalization and victimization persons 18–30.]; https://www.mvr.bg/docs/librariesprovider62/default-document-library/d73e321c-04_2013_tema_belova_bg_18pdf.pdf [19.09.2019] [in Bulgarian only].

Ministry of the Interior, Forensics Research Institute (2019a): Dejnosti izv″ršvani ot sektorite na NIK – MVR [Activities carried out by the NIC - MoI sectors]; https://www.mvr.bg/nik [16.09.2019] [in Bulgarian only].

Ministry of the Interior, Forensics Research Institute (2019b): Za nas [About us]; www.mvr.bg/nik [16.09.2019] [in Bulgarian only].

National Commission for Combating Trafficking in Human Beings (2019): Za nas [About]; https://antitraffic.government.bg/ [16.09.2019] [in Bulgarian and English].

National Commission for Combating Trafficking in Human Beings (2017): Godišen doklad [Annual Report]; https://antitraffic.government.bg/ [18.09.2019] [in Bulgarian and English].

National Commission for Combating Trafficking in Human Beings (2016): Godišen doklad [Annual Report]; https://antitraffic.government.bg/en/about [18.09.2019] [in Bulgarian and English].

National Council for Assistance and Compensation to Vicims of Crime (2019): Decisions/Protocols; http://www.compensation.bg/en/node/23 [18.09.2019] [in Bulgarian and English].

National Statistical Institute (StatOffice) (2019a): Demografska i socialna statistika [Demographic and social statistics]; https://www.nsi.bg/en/content/11224/demographic-and-so cial-statistics [16.09.2019] [in Bulgarian and English]; cited as StatOffice 2019a.

National Statistical Institute (StatOffice) (2019b): Estestven prirast na 1000 duši ot naselenieto po statističeski rajoni: oblasti i mestoživeene [Natural increase per 1000 persons of the population by statistical regions: districts and place of residents]; https://www.nsi.bg/en/content/6718/natural-increase-1-000-persons-population-statistical-regions-dis tricts-and-place [16.09.2019] [in Bulgarian and English]; cited as StatOffice 2019b.

National Statistical Institute (StatOffice) (2019c): Naselenie po oblasti. obŝini. mestoživeene i pol [Population by districts, municipalities, place of residence, and sex]; http://www.nsi.bg/en/content/6704/population-districts-municipalities-place-residence-and-sex [16.09.2019] [in Bulgarian and English]; cited as StatOffice 2019c.

National Statistical Institute (StatOffice) (2019d): Pravos″die i prest″pnost [Justice and Crime]; https://www.nsi.bg/en/content/6210/justice-and-crime [19.09.2019] [in Bulgarian and English]; cited as StatOffice 2019d.

National Statistical Institute (StatOffice) (2019e): Prest″plenija, zav″ršili s os″ždane po glavi ot nakazatelnija kodeks i po oblasti [Crimes and penalties inflicted by chapters of penal code and by districts]; https://www.nsi.bg/en/content/14342/crimes-penalty-inflicted-and-persons-convicted-place-commitment-crimes [16.09.2019] [in Bulgarian and English]; cited as StatOffice 2019e.

National Statistical Institute (StatOffice) (2018): Maloletni i nep″lnoletni lica, postradali ot prest″plenija, po pol, v″zrast, njakoi vidove prest″plenija i po statističeski zoni, statističeski rajoni i oblasti [Minor and juvenile persons, victims of crimes by sex, age, type of crime and by statistical zones, statistical regions and districts]; https://www.nsi.bg/en/content/6305/minor-and-juvenile-persons-victims-crimes-sex-age-kinds-crimes-and-statistical-zones [16.09.2019] [in Bulgarian and English]; cited as StatOffice 2018.

National Statistical Institute (StatOffice) (2011): Grid na naselenieto. 1 kv.km. Prebrojavane 2011 [Population grid. 1 sq.km. Census 2011]; https://www.nsi.bg/en/content/12309/population-grid-1-sqkm-census-2011 [16.09.2019] [in Bulgarian and English]; cited as StatOffice 2011.

StatOffice: see National Statistical Institute.

Plovdiv Regional Court (2017): Doklad za dejnostta na Plovdijski rajonen s″d prez 2017 [Activity report of the Plovdiv Regional Court in 2017]; http://www.rs-plovdiv.com [19.09.2019] [in Bulgarian only].

Sofia Regional Court (2017): Doklad za dejnostta na Sofijski rajonen s″d prez 2017 g. [Activity report of the Sofia Regional Court in 2017]; http://srs.justice.bg/srs/uploaded_files1//Godishen_otcheten_doklad-2017.pdf [19.09.2019] [in Bulgarian only].

Supreme Juducial Council (2019): S″debni rajoni [Judicial districts]; http://www.vss.justice.bg/page/view/1999 [16.09.2019] [in Bulgarian and English].

Bulgarian Association of Criminology, Forensics and Psychology (2019): Za nas [About us]; https://www.linkedin.com/company/bulgarian-association-of-criminology-forensics-and-psychology [16.09.2019] [in English only].

Varna Regional Court (2016): Doklad za dejnostta na rajonen s″d - Varna prez 2016 g. [Activity report of the Varna Regional Court in 2016]; http://www.vrc.bg/upload/DOKUMENTI/Godi6ni_dokladi/doklad_2016.pdf [19.09.2019] [in Bulgarian only].

Veliko Tarnovo Regional Court (2017): Doklad za dejnostta na rajonen s″d – Veliko Tarnovo prez 2017 g. [Activity report of the Veliko Tarnovo Regional Court in 2017]; https://vtarnovo-rs.justice.bg/bg/5677 [19.09.2019] [in Bulgarian only].

Vitosha Research (2010): Nacionalno proučvane na prest″pnostta 2010 [National Crime Survey 2010]; http://old.csd.bg/fileadmin/user_upload/EURPRReport__crime_2010_f.pdf [19.09.2019] [in Bulgarian only].

Croatia[1]

Victimology, Victimisation (Typology) & Victim Protection

Anna-Maria Getoš Kalac, Sunčana Roksandić Vidlička & Zoran Burić

1. Introduction

Victimology, just like criminology,[2] has a long history but a rather poor tradition in terms of the substantial scientific content in Croatia. As far back as 1985, Croatia/Zagreb hosted the World Society of Victimology's 2nd Symposia on Victimology,[3] and *Zvonimir Paul Šeparović* of the Zagreb Faculty of Law was one of its founders and a true pioneer in victimology, both internationally and at home. He was the 2nd President of the World Society of Victimology (WSV) from 1985 until 1988 and holds the WSV's Hans von Hentig Award (2000).[4] In terms of substantial scientific victimological content, and among many of his other relevant publications, *Šeparović*'s monograph "Victimology" has to be pointed out.[5] Unfortunately, even in this introductory section it has to be noted that there was little if any reception of *Šeparović*'s rich victimological work in Croatia among the relevant scientific community that would result in following the path he set for a fruitful Croatian victimology, or even broadening its scope to a full-fledged stand-alone discipline outside

---

1 The research for this publication has been conducted within the framework of the Installation Research Project titled "Croatian Violence Monitor: A Study of the Phenomenology, Etiology, and Prosecution of Delinquent Violence with Focus on Protecting Particularly Vulnerable Groups of Victims", funded by the Croatian Science Foundation (UIP-05-2017-8876). Additional information is available online at www.violence-lab.eu.

2 For a complete analysis and review of history and development with current state of art and new lines of research in Croatian criminology; see *Getoš* 2009; 2011; *Getoš Kalac & Bezić* 2017; *Getoš Kalac & Karlović* 2014.

3 World Society of Victimology 2019b. Additional information is available online at www.worldsocietyofvictimology.org/about-us/history-and-overview.

4 World Society of Victimology 2019c. Additional information is available online at www.worldsocietyofvictimology.org/about-us/wsv-honors-list.

5 *Šeparović* 1985.

the framework of criminology and criminal law. Like in many other countries of the Balkan region, and very similar to the history and development as well as current state of art in criminology, frequently it all comes down to one or two pioneering scholars that try to innovate and advance the field. And these few scholars per country are predominantly rooted at law faculties with a primary (but not exclusive) interest in criminal law.[6] With the exception of a few Balkan countries, like Slovenia or Serbia, both victimology as well as criminology in more general terms, still have to develop in terms of a critical mass of scholars, scientific content and institutionalisation in order to be regarded as nationally established disciplines. Croatia is no exception in this regard.

There are, however, continuous victimological efforts in Croatia to be mentioned, especially the Postgraduate Course on Victimology, Victim Assistance and Criminal Justice held annually at the Inter-University Centre in Dubrovnik/Croatia.[7] With its 34th edition, the course has proven to have become a tradition. However, the involvement of Croatian scholars (and students), although well documented, is still far from "significant" and again reflects a weak scholarly interest in victimology in Croatia. So, in spite of early on involvement and contribution to victimology's overall development, only a handful of victimological studies have been conducted in Croatia, and even today victimological research is lacking in Croatia. There are, however, some key players, projects and victimologically relevant findings to be presented in more detail throughout this paper.

Looking at victimisation in Croatia and available data in this regard, the overall situation is highly unsatisfactory. However, based on police statistics on victims and injured/damaged persons of criminal offences from 2010 until 2018, it will be possible to provide basic insights into criminal victimisation in Croatia. This includes major findings on the prevalence, incidence and trends in crime victimisation, distribution by gender, age and type of offence, as well as a first victim typology for Croatia. The paper will also use alternative sources of data to official victimisation statistics (interviews with key players from criminal justice and victim protection) with the aim of assessing the practical aspects of victim protection. Eventually, based on these analyses, it will be possible to highlight further avenues of future research, as well as identify normative and practical challenges.

In the last decade, a lot has been done in terms of improving the position of victims of crime in the Croatian criminal justice system regarding the normative level. Victims have, for the first time, entered the provisions of the Croatian Criminal

---

6 Balkan Criminology 2019. Additional information is available online at http://balkan-criminology.eu/en/network/.

7 World Society of Victimology 2019a. Additional information is available online at www.worldsocietyofvictimology.org/wsv-events/victimology-courses/europe-dubrovnik-croatia.

Procedure Act (hereinafter CPA)[8] as separate procedural subjects with specific procedural and extra-procedural rights. The victims of intentionally committed crime with elements of violence have the right to compensation based on the Crime Victim Compensation Act (hereinafter CVCA).[9] The Croatian Criminal Code (hereinafter CC)[10] has defined the term victim as a physical person (not a legal person) who by an unlawful act has been inflicted physical or mental pain, emotional suffering, has suffered damage to his/her property or against whom a serious violation of human rights and fundamental freedoms has been committed. Regarding the provisions of the CC, when determining the type and range of punishment, the court shall take into account the offender's relationship to the victim and efforts to compensate for the damage. This relationship is also very relevant, at least on the normative level, for imposing more lenient punishment, suspended sentence, conditional release and remission of punishment. The process of normative recognition of specific interests of victims of crime in the Croatian criminal justice system has been strongly influenced by the process of Croatian accession to the EU. At the same time, the process of establishing the Croatian victim-support system has also begun. Although the system is established, a lot still needs to be done for its services to be accessible to all victims of crime in Croatia. Despite extensive reforms undertaken on the normative level, recognition of victims of crime and their rights is still challenging in everyday practice. The whole process requires not only normative changes, but even more fundamental changes in the attitudes of major criminal justice actors in Croatia, namely police officers, prosecutors, defence attorneys, and judges.

2. About Croatia – Victimologically Relevant Facts and Figures

In order to place the victimological analysis in its overall crime and criminal justice context, it is necessary to first provide some basic facts and figures. Croatia does not fit the profile of a European high crime country, nor does it have a conventional crime problem, just as the rest of the countries of Southeast Europe (hereinafter SEE).[11] Overall, crime rates are generally low and below the European average, as are murder rates,[12] whereas there is a rather stable trend detectable when it comes to the total of adults convicted for criminal offences (exception: war-time-drop), as *Figure 1* shows.[13] And just as in the rest of the SEE region, the challenge in

---

8 Criminal Procedure Act, Law No. 7609, 03.07.2009, Official Gazette 76/09.

9 Crime Victim Compensation Act, Law No. 8008, 07.01.2008, Official Gazette 80/08.

10 Criminal Code, Law No. 12511, 01.01.2013, Official Gazette 125/11.

11 United Nations Office on Drugs and Crime 2008.

12 *Aebi et al.* 2017, p. 33.

13 *Getoš & Bezić* 2017.

Croatia is not crime in general, but rather specific types of non-conventional crime (e.g., corruption and trade in influence,[14] organised crime, etc.) and the conditions acting as their facilitators (e.g., the crime-conflict and the crime-politics nexus).[15] This indirectly gives a first sense of the victimisation in Croatia when compared to other European countries, especially when it comes to violent street crime, which as such is moderate, as is the likeliness of becoming the victim of a robbery, assault or murder in Croatia.

Figure 1 Reported and Convicted Adults for Criminal Offences in the Period 1953–2016

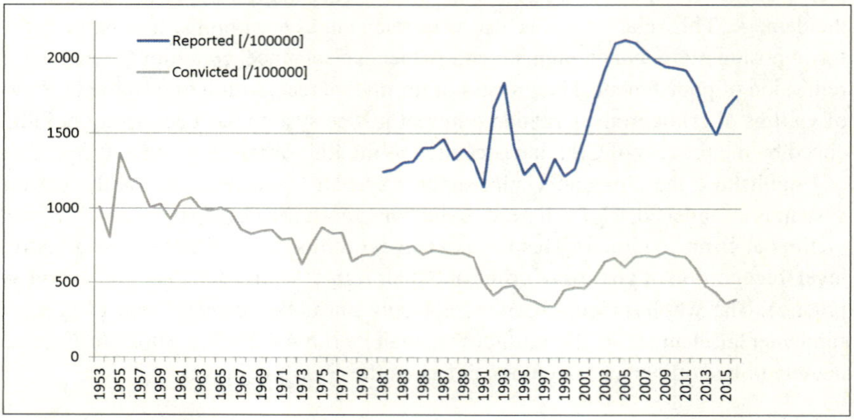

Source: Croatian Bureau of Statistics 2019.

So far, Croatia has not been a country attracting significant immigration and has mainly been a country of transition in the context of the migration crises, whereas the immigration occurring relates to immigrants from Croatia's SEE neighbouring countries. A far bigger issue is the high and rising trend in emigration from Croatia towards other EU countries, mainly Germany, amounting up to a total of approximately 200,000 emigrants in the past four years only (that is approximately a 5% loss in population).[16] This might also be connected to the increase in persons of Croatian (and regional) citizenship suspected for organised crime in Germany.[17] This emigration trend from Croatia towards the EU, taken together with other demographic factors (especially negative natural population growth trends), as well as low levels of urbanisation (outside the big cities) with most of Croatia's territory being loosely populated and more rural than urbanised, might not only explain Croatia's low lev-

---

14 *Roksandić Vidlička* 2017a; 2017c.

15 *Tarantini* 2016.

16 *Podgornik* 2017.

17 Bundeskriminalamt 2016, pp. 16–17.

els of street crime and related victimisation, but also dramatically change the crime structure and related victimisation in forthcoming decades.

The crime picture in Croatia, when analysed not based on the offences' legal, but their criminalistic qualification, used by police to typologies crime, is presented in *Figure 2*.

Figure 2 Recorded Criminal Offences According to Criminalistic Classification in 2016

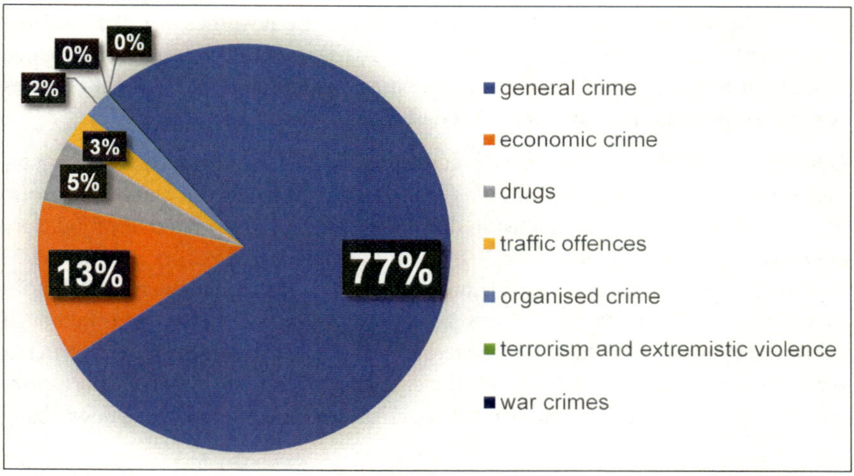

Source: Ministry of the Interior 2017.

Being a post-conflict and war-affected country, as well as still heavily affected by the social, economic and political transition, Croatia faces an ongoing struggle with rule of law and good governance, which is naturally also reflected in its criminal justice system. Although clearly positioned as one of the countries that are advancing well in its SEE context, Croatia still lags behind its western EU neighbours and the EU in general (see for example the Fragile State Index's comparative analysis of indicators on human rights and rule of law, state legitimacy, factionalised elites, group grievances or public services).[18] During the past decade, the Croatian criminal justice system had to face several huge reforms, or more accurately complete novelties, covering both big areas of society's basic repressive mechanisms for dealing with crime, criminals and their victims – the criminal procedure as well as the penal reaction. In 2008, a new CPA[19] came into force, but then the Croatian Constitutional Court assessed a rather large share of its

---

18 Fund for Peace 2019.

19 See Law No. 12511.

provisions to be unconstitutional[20] in 2013. Year 2013 brought numerous changes to the CPA.[21] Again, as of December 1st 2017, major changes have been applied.[22] In short – from having an investigative judge as the main actor in the investigation phase (prior to 2008), Croatia moved to having a public prosecutor as the master of the investigation (2008 until 2017), and finally now ended up at transmitting the greater role to the police, which were given a new mandate to formally interrogate suspects (post 2017). Given the provisions have only recently been adopted, it is yet to be seen how this will work in practice. Since police informal interrogation of a suspect has been abolished, there is a fear that the efficiency of the prosecution will be reduced.[23] Almost overlapping with these novelties was the enacting of a completely new CC[24] as of January 1st 2013, and the confusion this created in relation to the question of applying the more lenient law for criminal offences committed prior to the enactment of the new CC.[25]

Other major justice system reforms also relevant for the criminal justice sector have rather recently taken place. The most notable of all in this context is surely the reform of the judiciary in 2015. It resulted in drastically decreasing the number of judiciary bodies (mainly courts) so that as of 2015 there are now 'only' 15 county courts and 22 municipal courts (criminal and misdemeanour) left in Croatia,[26] compared to the prior 21 county, 115 municipal and 27 misdemeanour courts.[27] The main goal (although many more goals are proclaimed in the relevant strategic documents) of the reform has surely been to rationalise and upgrade the efficiency of the justice system's organisation. In light of Croatia's current population (slightly over 4 million)[28] this downsizing

---

20 *Burić* 2014; *Đurđević* 2012; U-I-448/2009, Constitutional Court of the Republic of Croatia (2012).

21 Criminal Procedure Act, Law No. 14513, 01.01.2013, Official Gazette 145/2013; *Đurđević* 2013.

22 Criminal Procedure Act, Law No. 7017, 01.12.2017, Official Gazette 70/2017; *Đurđević* 2013. An important part of these changes refers to the position of victims of crime, not only in the criminal procedure but in the Croatian legal system in general; see *Burić* 2015.

23 There has been no analysis of the results of the prosecutor's investigation, but it has to be mentioned that a working group for the new CPA is in the process of establishing and that one of the ideas is to revert to the old system of investigative judges; see Law No. 7017.

24 See Law No. 12511.

25 In terms of crime statistics, it has to be noted that the new CC has excluded drug offences from the chapter of crimes against vales protected by international law and included them in the chapter of crimes against peoples' health, and thus combined the drugs offence with substances prohibited in sport. The change in positioning drug offence in the health chapter results in a large shift in crimes from one to the other chapter; see Law No. 12511.

26 Ministry of Justice of the Republic of Croatia 2019b.

27 United Nations Office on Drugs and Crime 2010, p. 101.

28 According to the most recent population estimate: 4,174,300; see Croatian Bureau of Statistics 2017.

of the courts seems reasonable, especially when taking into account that the majority of people live in large and mid-sized cities. However, due to Croatia's rather particular geographical shape, it is challenging to rationalise judiciary bodies without leaving whole regions of the country simply 'cut-off'.

On a last contextual note, it has to be pointed out that Croatia, compared to the rest of the EU, is rather worse off when it comes to employment, economy, population trends, etc. Croatia has one of the lowest employment rates in EU28 (61.4% in 2016) – only Greece, and non-EU member states Turkey and Macedonia are worse off.[29] When looking at the 2016 list of European countries by GDP per capita, Croatia is at the very bottom as well.[30] Most problematic factors for doing business in Croatia and thus undermining economic development and growth are inefficient government bureaucracy, policy instability, tax regulations, corruption, and tax rates.[31] These socio-economic factors thus have a notable impact on illegal markets as well as the shadow economy, especially since the indicated problematic factors reveal that in order to do business in Croatia one has to either work within corrupt practices or move along with one's business rather slowly (or not at all).

These conditions, together with the current situation in the criminal justice sector, are only some of the most relevant contextual settings, which have to be taken into account when analysing and assessing crime and victimisation in Croatia, especially when mentally or actually trying to compare findings with those from other countries, where the contextual setting might be significantly different.

3. Croatian Victimology

As already briefly touched upon in the introductory part, Croatian victimology has yet to arrive at the level of a nationally recognisable scientific discipline. Currently, it may best be described as an integral part of Croatian criminology, which in itself has witnessed a revival and meaningful development only a few years back. Although the accomplishments in this regard, as well as Croatian criminology's impact on the national, but even more regional scientific setting through its "Balkan Criminology",[32] are truly astonishing (given the short time span), it is still far away from a nationally recognisable scientific discipline. When it comes to victimology, such a scientific "take-off" is not even in sight (yet). Before analysing the current state of art in Croatian victimology, it has to be stressed that there is obviously a huge difference between victims' rights movements, victim

29 Eurostat 2017.

30 International Monetary Fund World Economic Outlook 2016.

31 According to the Global Competitiveness Index 2017–2018, Croatia has been ranked 74th out of 137; see World Economic Forum 2017.

32 Balkan Criminology 2019.

organisations, victim policies and legislation, victim programs and victimology as a scholarly discipline, characterised first and foremost by sound methodology and scientific approach to the subject of interest: the victim and the process of victimisation, as well as individual and societal coping mechanisms and strategies. When discussing "victimology" in the framework of this paper, the term relates to the scientific study of the how and why of criminal victimisation, including its individual and societal reactions. In this regard, victimology is almost non-existent in Croatia, or at least not recognisable as a specialised and developed area of research (within or closely related to Croatian criminology). However, there are traces of victimological research scattered throughout the Croatian research scene, but their occurrence and quality vary largely, whereas many of the works are primarily focused on crime or offending or even totally different disciplines (e.g., stomatology and identification of victims of war crimes), whereas victimological aspects are not their focus.

When it comes to the Croatian victims' rights movement, it is worth mentioning the Croatian Society of Victimology (hereinafter CSV), founded in 1991. As a non-profit NGO, in a scientifically and application-oriented manner, it aims at studying and following occurrences and causes of human victimisation, strives to provide victims' legal protection, assistance and support to victims of crime and abuse of power; particularly follows and investigates the problems of victims of war, violence and human rights breaches, domestic violence, ecology, traffic, work-related, natural and other disasters, victims in the legal system, administration, health-sector, schools and other public services; investigates the vicwtimisation of children, women, elderly, minorities and other victims.[33] A review of the CSV's aims shows that it has taken a broad approach to victimology, that does not limit itself 'only' to victims of crime, but covers the whole spectrum of human victimisation/suffering, regardless of its man-made origin and (criminal) causation. Although also aimed at the scientific study of victimisation, in practice the CSV predominantly acts as a victim organisation, focusing mainly on victims of war and the abuse of power.

Besides the CSV, which has at least a proclaimed aim of scientifically investigating victimisation, there are no comparable nation-wide players following such goals. Numerous governmental and non-governmental organisations assist victims (of crime) in general but they also sub-specialise according to the age or gender of victims or the type of victimisation. There is also a national free phone-hotline for victims of crime and misdemeanours aimed at providing them with information and advice in Croatian and English. Victims' organisations acting on the national level are listed on the Croatian Government's web page (with contacts), which also provides a listing of all victim and victim rights' organisations according to the geo-

---

33 Croatian Society of Victimology 2019.

graphical distribution by county. *Table 1* shows the main national victim assistance organisations/programs with working hours (implicitly pointing towards funds and relevance in national context), whereas *Table 2* (see *next page*) provides for a count of organisations/programs by county.

Table 1 List of National Victim Assistance Organisations and/or Programs Provided Publicly by the Croatian Government

Name of organisation	**Working hours**
National Call Centre for Victims of Crimes and Misdemeanours	Working days: 08.00–20.00
National Call Centre for Missing Child Reporting	Every day: 00.00–24.00
Brave Phone for Children	Working days: 09.00–20.00
Brave Phone for Parents	Working days: 09.00–20.00
SOS Hotline for the Suppression of Trafficking in Human Beings	Every day: 10.00–18.00
Female Counseling Centre for Victims of Violence Autonomous Women's House Zagreb	Every day: 11.00–17.00
SOS Phone for Women and Children ictims of Violence Women's Help Now	Every day: 00.00–24.00
Free Legal Aid for Victims of Domestic Violence B.a.B.e.	Working days: 09.00–15.00
Centre for Victims of Sexual Violence – Women's Room	Working days: 10.00–17.00
Psychological Help Psychological Centre TESA	Working days: 10.00–22.00
Blue Phone	Working days: 09.00–21.00
Free Legal Aid – Law Clinic of the University of Zagreb Faculty of Law	Working days: 10.00–12.00, Wednesdays and Thursdays: 17.00–19.00
Centre for States of Crisis and the Prevention of Suicides at the Hospital of Zagreb	Every day: 00.00–24.00

Source: Ministry of Justice of the Republic of Croatia 2019a.

The data presented in *Tables 1* and *2* demonstrate that there is in fact a very strong, i.e., impressively well-numbered victims' rights movement in Croatia, as well as broad national and local assistance-coverage provided by numerous NGOs and governmental agencies (primary social services and health institutions) that are addressing a broad range of victim profiles, from mobbing all the way to domestic violence and war crimes. When looking at the basic indicators of the geographical distribution of victim assistance organisations throughout Croatia, it immediately becomes clear that there is an even distribution that follows the relative size of the main cities in the different counties, with Zagreb City and County clearly dominating. This makes sense since Croatia is rather centralised in terms of government institutions so that many of the organisations seated in Zagreb are also acting as

Table 2 *Count of Victim Assistance Organisations and/or Programmes by County Provided Publicly by the Croatian Government*

County	Number of victim assistance organisations and/or programmes
Grad Zagreb i Zagrebačka županija	85
Primorsko-goranska županija	39
Splitsko-dalmatinska županija	36
Sisačko-moslavačka županija	23
Istarska županija	21
Osječko-baranjska županija	20
Dubrovačko-neretvanska županija	16
Zadarska županija	16
Varaždinska županija	13
Vukovarsko-srijemska županija	13
Bjelovarsko-bilogorska županija	12
Ličko-senjska županija	12
Karlovačka županija	11
Krapinsko-zagorska županija	11
Šibensko-kninska županija	11
Međimurska županija	10
Virovitičko-podravska županija	10
Brodsko-posavskažupanija	8
Koprivničko-križevačka županija	8
Požeško-slavonska županija	7
Total	**382**

Source: Ministry of Justice of the Republic of Croatia 2019a.

national organisations. However, most of the national organisations/programs (*Table 1*) provide for little if any meaningful data about the incidence, prevalence or types of victimisation in their annual reports, let alone analytical investigations into victimisation in Croatia.

Obliging all of the approximately 400 victims' rights organisations and agencies to a uniform data collection mechanism when they deal with victims of crime and misdemeanours should be considered. The value of such a database would be considerable, whereas its scientific and application-oriented feasibility should provide for the basic empirics to start developing victimology as a scientific discipline, as well as creating the preconditions for an evidence-based victim protection policy.

Specific national research projects dealing with or at least partially focusing on victims of crime and victimisation are scarce. The Croatian components of the Balkan Epidemiological Study on Child Abuse & Neglect (BECAN study)[34] and the International Self-Reported Delinquency Study (ISRD3)[35] are definitely worth mentioning with regards to their findings on self-reported victimisation. Both research projects have been conducted within the framework of the University of Zagreb's Faculty of Law scientific research activities. In line with this academic research, a project funded by the Croatian Science Foundation has started in 2018 and should provide empirical data and sound knowledge about violent victimisation in Croatia.[36] A study into the protection of rights and support to victims/witnesses of domestic violence conducted by the 'Women's Room' in cooperation with the Governmental Office for Gender Equality in 2010 is also of interest to our analysis.[37] On the governmental level, the Ministry for demographics, family, youth and social policy has started to become proactively engaged when it comes to domestic violence and violence against women and children. It has recently published the (far overdue) guidelines for media reporting on domestic violence,[38] but also seems to collect and occasionally provide for basic facts and figures about domestic violence-related victimisation.[39] In its annual reports (summaries available in English), the Ombudsman for Children regularly provides data on child victimisation as well as protection of the rights of children as victims and witnesses in criminal procedures.[40] On its webpage, the Ombudsman for Children also hosts all the relevant protocols of procedure in cases where children are victims of domestic violence, youth violence, abuse and neglect, and sexual violence.[41] The aforementioned Ministry also provides for a collection of relevant legal sources as well as the national strategy for the protection from domestic violence 2017–2022.[42] The strategy also includes basic data on victimisation (e.g., victims of homicides 2013–2017 by gender and victim-offender relationship; victims of assault; victims of family violence, etc.).[43] The data will

---

34 Institute of Child Health 2019.

35 Northeastern University 2019.

36 Violence Research Lab 2019.

37 *Mamula & Dijanić Plašć* 2014.

38 Ministry of Demographics, Family, Youth and Social Policy 2018.

39 Dnevnik.hr of 20.04.2018; Obiteljsko nasilje: Svakih 15 minuta netko u Hrvatskoj trpi neki oblik nasilja, uloga skloništa presudna [Domestic violence: Every 15 minutes someone in Croatia suffers some form of violence, the role of shelter is crucial]; https://dnevnik.hr/vijesti/hrvatska/skup-o-zrtvama-obiteljskog-nasilja-presudna-uloga-sklonista---514411.html [12.09.2019].

40 Ombudsperson for Children 2019b.

41 Ombudsperson for Children 2019a.

42 Ministry of Demographics, Family, Youth and Social Policy 2019.

43 Ministry of Demographics, Family, Youth and Social Policy 2017.

be presented in *Section 4.2,* together with data from the previously listed projects/reports. However, even at this early point it has to be stressed that the poor quality of the "analysis" provided in the Strategy, aimed at detecting the "current victimisation situation", is probably the best indicator of the poor state of art in Croatian victimology and lack of empirically-based (or at least well informed) victim protection policy creation. Basically, data are presented out of the overall context, lacking at least the appearance of an objective analysis, but rather serving as a numerical justification of past policy decisions.

Authors worth mentioning in the context of Croatian victimology, besides *Zvonimir Šeparović*, include, but are not limited to, *Mladen Singer*,[44] *Marina Ajduković*,[45] *Ksenija Turković*,[46] *Velinka Grozdanić*,[47] *Irma Kovčo Vukadin*,[48] *Dalida Ritossa*,[49] *Vesna Bilić*,[50] and *Mirjana Radetić-Paić*.[51] However, none of the above, besides *Zvonimir Šeparović*, might be understood as actual victimologists or even criminologists *stricto sensu.*

4. Victim Protection Through Criminal Justice with Special Focus on Procedural and Material Criminal Law

Until recently, the term "victim" *(žrtva)* has been almost unknown in the two most important pieces of criminal justice legislation in Croatia: the CC and the CPA. The term used to identify the person against whom a criminal offence has been committed and who has suffered harm as a result of a criminal offence was "the injured person" *(oštećenik)*. These two terms have a lot in common, as they both relate to the person who has suffered harm as a result of a criminal offence.[52] During the last decade, the situation in the Croatian criminal justice legislation changed. Now, both the CC and the CPA use both terms: the victim and the injured person.

The CC only provides the definition of the victim by determining that it is a natural person who has suffered physical and mental health consequences, pecuniary damage or a substantial violation of his/her fundamental rights and freedoms as a

44 *Singer* 2005.

45 *Ajduković & Marohnić* 2011.

46 *Turković* 2002.

47 *Grozdanić* 2015.

48 *Kovčo Vukadin* 2014.

49 *Rittossa* 2016.

50 *Bilić* 2013.

51 *Radetić-Paić* 2010.

52 *Burić* 2011, pp. 495–497.

direct consequence of the criminal offence. The victim of a criminal offence shall also mean the spouse, common-law spouse, life partner or informal life partner, descendant, and if there are no, ancestor and sibling of the person whose death is the direct consequence of the criminal offence and the person whom the latter was required by law to maintain.[53] This definition follows, although not completely, the definition of victims as defined in the Art. 1.1. Recommendation Rec(2006)8,[54] but with one important addition. It is broader with the following wording "serious violation of human rights and fundamental freedoms."[55] On the other side, the CPA provides for a definition of both terms – the injured party and the victim. A term victim is defined with the same wording as in the CC.[56] The injured person, pursuant to CPA, is a victim of a criminal offence and the legal person to whose detriment the criminal offence was committed, which participate as the injured person in the proceeding.[57] If we analyse the definitions provided by the CPA, we can conclude that the legislator wanted to draw a line between these two terms. Pursuant to that delineation, the term victim is primarily an extra-procedural term, while the term injured person is connected with the willingness of the victim to play a more active role in criminal procedure, and thus this term, unlike "victim" also includes legal persons.

Legal persons are excluded from the definition of victims, both in the CC and in the CPA.[58] However, it is clear that legal persons can also 'suffer' harm as a result of a criminal offence. In limiting the concept of victims to natural persons, Croatia followed the opinion of Court of Justice of EU (hereinafter: CJEU)[59] that repeatedly confirmed, when addressing the preliminary ruling questions on the interpretation of the Framework Decision 2001/220/JHA (FD),[60] that the concept of a victim for the purposes of the FD does not include legal persons who have suffered direct harm by violations of the criminal law in a Member State. However, it must be noted that the

---

53 See Article 87 (The meaning of terms is the Criminal Code) of the Law No. 12511.

54 Victim means a natural person who has suffered harm, including physical or mental injury, emotional suffering or economic loss, caused by acts or omissions that are in violation of the criminal law of a member state. The term victim also includes, where appropriate, the immediate family or dependents of the direct victim; see Article 1 (Definitions) of the Recommendation Rec(2006)8 of the Committee of Ministers to member states of assistance to crime victims, Recommendation no. 20068, 14.06.2006.

55 *Turković et al.* 2013, p. 128.

56 See Article 87 (The meaning of terms is the Criminal Code) of the Law No. 12511.

57 See Article 202 (The meaning of legal terms) of the Law No. 7017.

58 *Burić* 2011, pp. 392–393.

59 CJEU, C-467/05, Court of Justice of European Union (2010).

60 Directive 2012/29/EU of the European Parliament and of the Council of 25 October 2012 establishing minimum standards on the rights, support and protection of victims of crime, and replacing Council Framework Decision 2001/220/JHA, Directive No. 2012/29/EU, 14.11.2012, Official Journal of the European Union 315/57.

EU Member States may choose to apply the standards of victim protection also to legal persons.[61]

Although the term victim, as previously stated, has been unknown to the CPA, this does not mean that the victim was completely left out of the criminal justice processes. Quite the contrary. In the Croatian criminal justice system, a victim of crime, through the institution of an injured person, traditionally enjoyed a very strong procedural position. As underlined by *Krapac*,[62] former Yugoslavia's rather liberal CPA of 1976 contained a whole array of provisions concerning the victim's role in the criminal process and these provisions were later taken over by the Croatian legislation.[63] The victim of a criminal offence has, therefore, been present in the Croatian criminal legislation and in the criminal justice system in general, even long before it became recognised "verbatim", about a decade ago.

The process, which has been ongoing in the last two decades, and which resulted in the inauguration of the victim as a separate procedural subject in criminal proceedings in Croatia, could be described as the result of two factors. The first one was the Homeland War and the need to establish mechanisms for the effective prosecution of war crimes. In order to do this, it was necessary to devote more attention to the protection of needs and legitimate interests of victims of crime, since it was impossible to effectively prosecute these grave offences without the participation of victims as witnesses in the criminal procedure. The second process was the harmonisation of Croatian legislation with European standards in the area of victims' protection. Besides the standards established in the Council of Europe, standards developed in the law of the European Union were a primary consideration. The current position of victims of crime in the Croatian criminal justice legislation reflects the standards deriving from the Directive 2012/29/EU of the European Parliament and of the Council of 25 October 2012 establishing minimum standards on the rights, support and protection of victims of crime, and replacing Council Framework Decision 2001/220/JHA. Furthermore, the provisions of CC, the purpose of which is to grant special protection to victims of certain crimes, followed the provisions of the Council of Europe Convention on

---

61 European Commission 2013, p. 9.

62 *Krapac* 2002, p. 156.

63 For example, a victim, acting as the injured person in the criminal proceedings, had the right to ask for compensation of damages from the accused, and, in most cases where the public prosecutor decided not to institute or to discontinue the procedure, the injured person had the right to act as prosecutor in the case. In those cases, where the public prosecutor was representing the case, an injured person had the right to act next to the public prosecutor and to undertake various procedural actions in order to promote his/her procedural interests. There were also measures in place used to safeguard victims from secondary victimisation during the criminal procedure. However, these measures were primarily construed as measures for vulnerable witnesses and not as measures for victims; see *Tomašević & Pajčić* 2008.

preventing and comba ting violence against women and domestic violence, even before the later was ratified by the Croatian parliament.

Looking at the misdemeanour legislation in Croatia, namely the provisions of the Misdemeanour Act,[64] it becomes apparent that it does not use the term victim. It still only uses the term injured person. The inauguration and the promotion of the term victim in the criminal justice legislation has not been followed by the same development in the misdemeanour legislation. However, this does not mean that a victim of a misdemeanour does not enjoy the same rights as a victim of a criminal offence. On the contrary, to the extent to which misdemeanour proceedings can be considered criminal proceedings within the meaning of the standards developed in the jurisprudence of the European Court for Human Rights, victims of misdemeanours should enjoy the same rights as the victims of criminal offences. This is further confirmed by the rule, which requires that the rules of criminal procedure should be applied, *mutatis mutandis*, in misdemeanour procedure, as well as by the possibility to apply the provisions of the Directive on the victims of crime directly in misdemeanour proceedings in Croatia. Special legislation, which regulates the position of domestic violence within the framework of misdemeanour justice, grants specific rights to victims of such offences. These rights are comparable to the rights of victims of crime in criminal proceedings to a very high degree.

4.1 General Overview of Victim Protection Through Criminal Policy

The main piece of national legislation that regulates the position of victims of crime is the CPA. The first Croatian CPA that specifically referred to victims of crime (and not to injured persons) and that contained a specific list of rights for victims of crime was the CPA from 2008. The biggest novelty of this Act with regard to the position of victims of crime was that it did not only regulate the rights in connection with their participation in criminal procedure (in the role of an injured person or a witness) but also extra-procedural rights of victims of crime, such as the right to access victim support services, notwithstanding the fact whether the victim participates in the criminal procedure or not.[65] Besides general rights for all victims of crime, special rights were introduced for vulnerable categories of victims of crime: victims of offences punishable by five years of imprisonment or more, children victims of crime and victims of sexual offences. Further development of the CPA led to stronger recognition and protection of victims of crime. This is especially true for amendments that were introduced in the Act in 2017. The amendments introduced were significant and they related to victims of crime to a large extent, due to Croatia's need to transpose the provisions of the Directive

---

64 Misdemeanour Act, Law No. 107/07, 24.04.2009, Official Gazette 107/07.

65 *Burić* 2011, pp. 495–497.

establishing minimum standards on the rights, support and protection of victims of crime into its national legal order. By those amendments, Croatia has transposed the Directive and it could be stated that the conformity with the provisions of Directive is largely achieved.

Earlier the same year, 2008, another piece of legislation important for victims of crime was adopted in the national parliament: the Act on Monetary Compensation to Victims of Criminal Offences.[66] Its application was postponed until the day of Croatian accession to the European Union. This Act was the result of the harmonisation of Croatian law with the demands arising out of European Union law, more specifically from the provisions of the Council Directive 2004/80/EC of 29 April 2004 relating to compensation to crime victims. This Act regulated the right of victims of violent offences to gain monetary compensation for the harm suffered by the criminal offence, not from the offender, but the State.[67]

The new Croatian CC, which was adopted in 2011, and entered into force on 1st January 2013, also represented a shift in the legislative treatment of victims of crime. It is the first Croatian CC that gives primacy to the term "victim" over the term "injured person", and it is also the first Croatian CC that defines the victim of crime.[68]

Besides these pieces of national legislation, which generally regulate the position of victims of crime, some statutes give special rights to certain categories of victims of crime. Two statutes need to be mentioned here: the Act on Protection from Domestic Violence[69] and the Act on Rights of Victims of Sexual Violence during Armed Aggression on Republic of Croatia in Homeland War.[70]

Moreover, there are many other laws and by-laws that regulate the position of victims, like the Juvenile Courts Act[71] and Act on the Police Powers and Duties.[72] As underlined, Croatia has mostly transposed the Directive and it could be stated that the conformity with the provisions of Directive is largely achieved, if not directly by the CPA or CC, then at least by implementing these acts. However,

---

66 Act on Monetary Compensation to Victims of Criminal Offences, Law No. 702-01/08-01/02, 02.07.2008, Official Gazette 80/08.

67 Council Directive 2004/80/EC of 29 April 2004 relating to compensation to crime victims, Directive No. 2004/80/EC, 06.08.2004, Official Gazette 261/15.

68 See Article 89 (The meaning of terms is the Criminal Code) of the Law No. 12511.

69 Act on Protection from Domestic Violence, Law No. 022-03/16-01/134, 07.07.2017, Official Gazette 70/17.

70 Act on Rights of Victims of Sexual Violence during Armed Aggression on Republic of Croatia in Homeland War, Law No. 022-03/14-01/88, 18.06.2015, Official Gazette 64/15.

71 Juvenile Courts Act, Law No. 740-02/96-01/02, 01.01.1998, Official Gazette 111/1997.

72 Act on Police Powers and Duties, Law No. 7019, 01.08.2019, Official Gazette 70/19.

the implementation of certain rights is not achieved as will be explained in this article.

4.2 Protecting and Empowering Victims Through Criminal Procedure

As already stated, the CPA is a statute that regulates not only the position of victims in criminal procedure but their status in the Croatian legal system generally. Article 43, in general fashion, defines rights of victims of crime. The following rights are: access to victim support services; efficient psychological and other professional assistance and support of the victim support system; protection from intimidation and retaliation; protection of the dignity of the victim when testifying; to be heard without unjustified delay after the complaint with regard to a criminal offence has been made and to be further heard only insofar as this is necessary for the purposes of the criminal proceeding; to be accompanied by a person enjoying his/her confidence when taking part in any acts; to be subject to a minimum number of medical interventions and only where strictly necessary for the purposes of the criminal proceedings; to file a motion for prosecution and a private action pursuant to the provisions of the Criminal Act; the right to participate in the criminal proceeding as an injured party; the right to be informed of the dismissal of the criminal complaint and of the state attorney dropping the criminal charge, and the right to take over criminal prosecution in lieu of the state attorney; to be informed by the state attorney of the acts performed as a result of his/her complaint and the right to complain to a senior state attorney; to be informed without unjustified delay, at his/her request, of the release from custody or the investigative prison, the defendant having fled or the convicted person having been released, and of the measures taken for the purposes of his/her protection; to be informed, at his/her request, of any decision finally terminating a criminal proceeding and any other rights provided for by law.[73]

Besides general rights for all victims of crime, the CPA also regulates rights of specific categories of victims of crime: victim of a criminal offence punishable by imprisonment for more than five years who has suffered severe harm as a result of a criminal offence,[74] victim of an intentional violent crime,[75] children victims of crime,[76] victims

73 Law No. 7017.

74 He/she is entitled to the professional assistance of an advisor appointed at government expense when bringing a civil claim; see Law No. 7017.

75 He/she is entitled under a special act to compensation from the state budget; see Law No. 7017; Law No. 702-01/08-01/02.

76 Child victim of a criminal offence is, in addition to the rights enjoyed by all victims, entitled to: an attorney-in-fact appointed at government expense, the confidentiality of personal information and the exclusion of the public; see Law No. 7017.

of sexual criminal offences and human trafficking,[77] and victims with special protection needs.[78]

Recent changes to the CPA have introduced a mandatory procedure of individual assessment of every victim. The purpose of this procedure is to enable the application of mechanisms that safeguard that all victims and especially the most vulnerable ones are not exposed to secondary victimisation through their participation in criminal proceedings. Such procedure is foreseen by the provisions of the Directive establishing minimum standards on the rights, support and protection of victims of crime. The biggest challenge Croatian authorities encountered in transposing those provisions of the Directive into the national legal system was the determination of the authority competent to conduct the individual assessment procedure. In the end, it was decided that this procedure should be conducted by the authority that is interrogating the victim (police officer, public prosecutor or a judge) in cooperation with authorities, services and institutions of the victim support system.[79]

4.3 Victim Protection by the Croatian Criminal Code

As underlined above, the CC contains provisions throughout the whole Code that are oriented toward special protection of vulnerable victims. The CC devotes special protection of victims through the construction of its criminal offences, e.g., already following the recent, not yet ratified Council of Europe's Convention on preventing and combating violence against women and domestic violence (hereinafter: Istanbul Convention).[80] The CC introduced a new qualifying circumstance for aggravated murder that is in line with the concept of protecting all victims: the murder of a person who is especially vulnerable due to his/her age, a severe physical or mental

---

77 He/she is, in addition to the rights enjoyed by all the victims, entitled to: counseling services at government expense before being interrogated, an attorney-in-fact appointed at government expense, be interrogated at the police and the state attorney's by a person of the same sex and that in case of any further interrogation he/she be interrogated, where possible, by that same person, refuse to answer any strictly private questions not related to the criminal offence, demand to be questioned via an audio-video link, confidentiality of personal information and demand that the hearing be closed to the public; see Law No. 7017.

78 He/she is, in addition to the rights enjoyed by all the victims, entitled to: counseling services at government expense before being interrogated, be questioned at the police and the state attorney's by a person of the same sex and that in case of any further questioning he/she be questioned, where possible, by that same person, refuse to answer any strictly private questions not related to the criminal offence, demand to be questioned via an audio-video link, confidentiality of personal information and demand that the hearing be closed to the public; see Law No. 7017.

79 Law No. 7017.

80 Council of Europe Convention on preventing and combating violence against women and domestic violence, 11.05.2011; https://www.coe.int/en/web/conventions/full-list/-/conventions/rms/090000168008482e.

disorder or pregnancy.[81] This provision, unlike what was prescribed before the CC, enhanced protection to all particularly vulnerable victims, not only to children and pregnant women, but to all other persons who are vulnerable due to their age (seniors), or because of illness or severe physical or mental disruption. This trend, providing enhanced protection to all victims that are particularly vulnerable because of special characteristics, which has been present in European legislation, and Croatia, after 2013, when this Code came into force, is no exception to this rule.[82]

The CC also introduced a number of new criminal offences that are protecting vulnerable victims. Based on the provisions of the Istanbul Convention, namely Article 34, *stalking* became a criminal offence, as did sexual intercourse without consent. By that, *rape* became an aggravated offence. As proscribed in Article 36 of the Istanbul Convention, Croatia took, in drafting the CC in 2011, the necessary legislative measures to ensure that the offence is aggravated when committed against a vulnerable victim or against a close person.[83] Moreover, forced marriage is a criminal offence under the criminal offence *trafficking in person* (Article 106). Even *female genital mutilation* became a separate offence, defined in Article 116. *Forced abortion* (Article 117) and *forced sterilisation* are also punishable (later *explicite* if committed as a war crime or under bodily injury or medical malpractice). *Sexual harassment* became a new offence, regulated in Article 156 of the CC.[84]

Regarding sentencing, the Article 47 of CC regulates that, when deciding on the type and extent of the punishment, the court, based on the degree of guilt and the purpose of the punishment, shall assess all the circumstances that affect the type and scope of the sentence being more lenient or more severe (mitigating and aggravating circumstances), including the conduct after the perpetration of the criminal offence and compensation for damage. That also refers to provisions regulating the reduction of the penalty.[85] The punishment provided for a particular criminal offence may be exempted, or the sentence reduced if there are particular mitigating circumstances, in particular if the perpetrator is reconciled to the victim, if he/she has fully or partially compensated for the damage caused by the offence, or seriously attempted to compensate for that damage, and the purpose of punishment can be achieved with

---

81 See Article 111 (Aggravated murder) of the Law No. 12511.

82 This is also characteristic for the recent Council of Europe instruments, like the Convention on the Protection of Children from Sexual Exploitation and the Convention on the Prevention and Combating of Violence against Women and Family Violence that both the vulnerability of the victim due to the specific circumstances as a qualifying circumstance.

83 The term is defined, as a family member, former marital or extra-marital partner or same sex partner and person living in the same household; see Article 87 (The meaning of terms in the Criminal Code) of the Law No. 12511.

84 Law No. 12511.

85 See Article 47 (Sentencing) of the Law No. 12511.

such a mild punishment.[86] The court may therefore exempt from the punishment a perpetrator if the perpetrator attempted to eliminate or reduce the consequences of an offence committed by negligence and to compensate for the damage caused to him, and when the perpetrator of the criminal offence punishable by imprisonment for one year was reconciled with the victim and reimbursed the damage. Regarding the conditional release, when deciding on a proposal to grant conditional release, the court will assess the relation of the perpetrator to the perpetrated crime and assess the behaviour toward the victim.[87]

Based on the aforementioned, three cases of sentence mitigation are foreseen in the CC: When the law explicitly stipulates so; when there are relevant mitigating circumstances, particularly if the perpetrator has reconciled with the victim, and compensation has been paid or the perpetrator gave serious effort to reduce the suffered harm; or upon procedural settlement between the state attorney and the perpetrator (similar provisions are found in foreign laws, e.g., in Germany [88] or Poland[89]).

Furthermore, additional victims' protection is given by prescribing different types of special obligations that enhance the protection of victims, including repairing the damage caused by the criminal offence and paying a certain amount of money into an account of a public institution, to support humanitarian or charitable causes, or into a fund for compensation to victims of criminal offences, if this is appropriate in view of the offence committed and the personality of the perpetrator.[90] As common in criminal codes, the Croatian CC contains security measures deemed to directly protect victims, such as prohibition of approaching a person and removal from a shared household.[91]

4.4 Protecting Victims Through Other Normative Frameworks

4.4.1 Victim Support System in Croatia

Croatia is still in the process of establishing its Victim Support System (hereinafter VSS). Although major cities do have effective VSS, it is clear that the system is not equally effective throughout the country. The VSS in Croatia is composed of state bodies and non-governmental actors. With regard to the state-part of the VSS in

86 See Articles 48 (Mitigation of sentence) and 50 (Remission of punishment) of the Law No. 12511.

87 See Article 61 (Parole revocation) of the Law No. 12511.

88 German Criminal Code, Articles 46/46a; German Criminal Procedure Code, Art. 153a.

89 Polish Criminal Code, Law No. 6101997, 06.06.1997, Official Gazette 06/97.

90 See Article 62 (Types of special obligations) of the Law No. 12511.

91 See Articles 73 (Prohibition of approaching a person, harassing or stalking) and 74 (Removal from shared household) of the Law No. 12511.

Croatia, it is headed by a special body within the Ministry of Justice, the Independent Office for Support to Victims and Witnesses, that is in charge of coordination, harmonisation and supervision of the work of departments for support to victims and witnesses that operate in courts. Besides that, the independent Office has a leading role in the institutionalisation of VSS in Croatia, it promotes inter-institutional cooperation in the field and it governs the strategic development of VSS. Departments for Support to Victims and Witnesses exist in seven county courts (Zagreb, Rijeka, Split, Osijek, Vukovar, Sisak, Zadar). The role of the department is to provide emotional support, practical information and information on rights to victims and witnesses.[92]

NGOs are a very important part of Croatian VSS, especially in the following areas: victims of war, victims of sexual and family violence, victims of human trafficking, children victims of crime. NGOs establish and run shelters for victims of domestic violence, primarily women and children. Here, it is possible to see the difference depending on the area of the Republic of Croatia. During the interviews, it was confirmed that, for instance, the Split-Dalmatia County has less than 10 available beds for victims of violence.[93]

Recent research has shown that there are a lot of problems with regard to the regional coverage of the VSS in Croatia.[94] This refers both to those parts of VSS that belong to the governmental sector, as well to those that belong to the non-governmental sector. At this moment, Departments for Support to Victims and Witnesses exist only in seven county courts and the majority of work is done by Zagreb's Department. There are none on municipal or misdemeanour courts. However, in some areas, the departments established at county courts also provide their services to municipal and misdemeanour courts established on the territory of their jurisdiction. The presence of non-governmental organizations that are a part of VSS in non-urban areas is also scarce.[95] Although scarce, it is still very important, as they are the only carriers of VSS in the areas where there are no county courts.

4.4.2 Compensation for Crime Victims

Victims have different avenues in order to accomplish compensation of damages caused by a criminal offence. They can ask for compensation of damages from the offender either in the framework of criminal proceedings or in the framework of civil proceedings. The first avenue is regulated by the provisions of Articles 153–162 of the CPA. In order to file a motion for compensation of damages in the criminal procedure, the victim needs to take over the role of an injured party in criminal

92 *Burić & Lučić* 2017.

93 *Burić & Lučić* 2017.

94 *Burić & Lučić* 2017.

95 *Burić & Lučić* 2017.

proceedings. Furthermore, such a motion shall be decided upon in criminal proceedings, unless deciding on it would significantly protract the criminal procedure. Such a motion can relate to any demand that can be made in a civil action.[96] Such a motion can be decided only if the defendant has been found guilty. In that situation, the motion can be fully or partially awarded, or the victim (injured party) can be referred to make such a motion in a civil action. If the court does not find the defendant guilty at the end of the proceedings, the victim (injured party) shall be referred to make such a motion in a civil action.[97] The victim can always decide to ask for compensation of damages in the framework of civil proceedings, and thereby use the second avenue for compensation of damages from the offender.

The victim can ask for compensation of damages not only from the offender but also from the state. This procedure is regulated by the Act on Monetary Compensation to Victims of Criminal Offences.[98] Pursuant to that Act, victims of intentional violent offences committed on the territory of the Republic of Croatia after July 1, 2013, can ask for compensation of damages caused by the criminal offence directly from the state. This possibility is reserved only for victims who are citizens of Croatia or the other Member States of the European Union.[99] Special situation with regard to the compensation of damages exists in relation to victims of sexual offences committed during the Homeland War and is regulated in the special act – Act on Rights of Victims of Sexual Violence during Armed Aggression on Republic of Croatia in Homeland War.[100]

4.4.3 Victim-Offender Settlements

The CPA foresees two situations where the approval of the victim is necessary in order to dispose of a criminal case. One of those situations is where the public prosecutor has the possibility not to start criminal proceedings or to drop criminal charges in relation to minor offences, if the defendant is willing to fulfil a certain obligation. It is an out of court settlement between the public prosecutor and the defendant. However, approval of the victim is a necessary precondition in order to reach such a settlement. Among various obligations that the defendant may fulfil as a condition for settlement, a number of them are oriented towards the victim and offer the possibility to remedy the situation caused by the criminal offence or to compensate the damages.[101] Another situation is foreseen within the procedure for the rendering of a judgement that is based on an agreement between the parties. For certain criminal

---

96 Law No. 7017.

97 Law No. 7017.

98 See Law No. 702-01/08-01/02.

99 *Bukovac-Puvača* 2013.

100 See Law No. 022-03/14-01/88.

101 Law No. 7017.

offences (against life and limb, and against sexual freedom, punishable by more than 5 years imprisonment), such a judgment can only be rendered where the public prosecutor has also gained the approval of the victim.[102]

4.4.4 Restorative Justice Services

Restorative justice services are not well developed in Croatia. However, there are two procedures that can be regarded as restorative justice schemes. The first one is in the CPA and it refers to the peace councils. This procedure is foreseen only for criminal offences for which criminal prosecution is undertaken not by the public prosecutor *ex officio*, but by the victim of the criminal offence – in this situation called the private prosecutor. Therefore, this situation only applies to a very small number of criminal offences, mainly criminal offences against the honour and reputation of a person or minor bodily injury. A judge may, after a private indictment has been raised and received at the court, decide to refer the victim and the accused to a peace council, if such a council exists at the territory of the court and if both parties reside at that territory. The purpose of the referral is to try to reach a reconciliation. The judge also determines a deadline within which such a reconciliation needs to take place. If no reconciliation has been achieved, the criminal procedure resumes.[103] The second procedure, which is more developed in practice, is foreseen by the Juvenile Courts Act.[104] It is the procedure of mediation through an out of court settlement, where the offender and the victim meat in order to remedy or compensate consequences of the criminal offence, with the mediation of a third, neutral, person. This procedure is applicable only in relation to criminal offences committed by juvenile offenders.[105]

Although usually not considered as part of the restorative justice service in Croatia, one must underline that the CC contains an important provision that, in the opinion of the authors, should be more frequently used in the Croatian criminal justice system. As stipulated earlier, the court may exempt a perpetrator from the punishment if the perpetrator attempted to eliminate or reduce the consequences of an offence committed by negligence and to compensate for the damage caused to victim, or when the perpetrator of the criminal offence punishable by imprisonment for one year was reconciled with the victim and reimbursed the damage.[106]

In any case, further research is necessary on the need to include and develop the most adequate restorative justice measures in the Croatian criminal justice system.

---

102 Law No. 7017.

103 Law No. 7017.

104 See Law No. 740-02/96-01/02.

105 *Mirosavljević, Koller-Trbović & Lalić-Lukač* 2009.

106 See Article 50 (Remission of punishment) of the Law No. 12511.

Therefore, one can conclude that, except for the two above mentioned procedures, Croatia has not yet developed restorative justice models.

5. Croatian Victimisation Reality and Preliminary Typology

This section will first provide an overview of the data sources on victimisation in Croatia with an assessment of their actual and potential usefulness in terms of victimological research. The analysis focuses on publicly available official statistics, reports and data collection mechanisms. It also takes into account the sources of existing victimological research. The second part focuses on (officially) registered victimisation (mainly police statistics, but also a victimisation survey) and analyses the data in terms of prevalence, incidence and trends in crime victimisation, as well as distribution by gender, age and type of offence. In the next step, the third part of this section, the prior quantitative descriptions and analysis will be supplemented using a more qualitative approach to determining victimisation. Here, findings from interviews with key actors from the criminal justice system will enable to deepen the understanding of victimisation. The findings based on using both these approaches, the quantitative and the qualitative, will be the grounds for delivering a preliminary victim typology.

5.1 Data Sources on Victimisation in Croatia

When analysing crime in general and based on publicly available official crime and criminal justice statistics in Croatia, the Croatian Bureau of Statistics (hereinafter CBS) is a highly valuable source of data. Their annual statistical reports on adult, juvenile and legal persons reported, accused and convicted for criminal offences and misdemeanours are extremely detailed in terms of breakdowns and very timely, as they are usually published on-line within less than one year (even 6 months) after the year of coverage. In addition to these regular publications, the CBS also provides thematic analyses (e.g., domestic violence, corruption, criminal victimisation of children and juveniles, drug abuse) and is currently also participating in the pilot for the new EU-wide survey on gender based violence, interviewing women and men about their experiences of violence. The current version of the survey questionnaire contains a wide range on victimologically relevant items, covering socio-demographics, as well as sexual harassment at work, (non) partner violence, former and current partner violence and background, stalking, violence in childhood, awareness about victim protection rights and services, as well as general victimisation (non-violent).[107] Croatia has also participated in the 2012 EU Agency

[107] Additional information is available online at https://circabc.europa.eu/sd/a/5ffc3f71-38ae-4b7f-a998-73a1dfeff8ed/Questionnaire%20for%20pilot%20%20survey%20VER2(0).pdf.

for Fundamental Rights' (hereinafter FRA) survey on the violence against women, which asked 42,000 women in EU-28 about their experiences of physical, sexual and psychological violence, sexual harassment, stalking and violence in childhood, the findings of which will be presented in *Section 5.2*.[108] There is also a CBS thematic study into "potentially lost years of life" that contains basic data on violent deaths during 2000–2004 (see *Section 5.2* for findings). However, when it comes to victimisation data, the CBS does not regularly publish any data or conduct definite victimisation surveys. The idea of conducting a Crime Victimisation Survey appeared on the CBS's publication agenda even back in 2008 but was never realised. So far, no victimological study has ever been conducted and published by the CBS, whereas the two studies that might appear to provide some victimological insights (domestic violence 2007–2010; criminal victimisation of children and juveniles 2001–2006) also focus on the perpetrators, rather than the victims, while covering the situation from over a decade ago. CBS statistics on beneficiaries and services of social care regarding the domestic violence victimisation are also worth mentioning as they provide basic figures on numbers of children and youth as beneficiaries of social services related to cases of domestic violence. Overall, in Croatia, there are no comprehensive and publicly available official (criminal) statistics, which focus on the number and socio-demographic characteristics of victims and situational characteristics of victimisation.

The most comprehensive and publicly available official statistics, which contain at least basic victimisation data and are thus up-to-date, are the police statistics. The police collect statistical data on all reported perpetrators, victims and the offences as such. The Ministry of Interior's Department for strategical planning, analytics and development compiles annual reports on basic security indicators that contain victimisation data useful for analysing the incidence, type and basic variables of victimisation in Croatia (the data covering 2010–2018 are analysed and presented in *Section 5.2*).

Finally, there are scientific papers and monographs or PhDs that also deal with victimologically relevant subtopics in Croatia (victims of war, domestic violence, violence in schools, intimate partner violence, etc.), with some of them containing analyses of original empirical victimisation data. However, their quality varies tremendously and, due to the strong publication focus on victims of war (World War I and II, as well as the Homeland War in Croatia) and the former state repression, useful victimological research publications are difficult to identify (at least on the general topic-level and without searching for all the different sub-topics).

---

[108] FRA European Union Agency for Fundamental Rights 2014.

5.2 Victimisation Realities – Prevalence, Incidence, and Trends

5.2.1 Victimisation in General and by Type of Offence (Groups)

Based on official police statistics,[109] which are currently the only publicly available source of basic victimisation data, it is clear that the number of victims in Croatia has been slightly, but steadily decreasing during the past 8 years *(Figure 3)*.[110] Whereas this slight decrease is well reflected when it comes to male victims, the situation is not as clear when looking at female victims. In this regard, there even seems to be a slight increase. The noticeable one-time increase in female victims in 2013 is the result of the new CC, which includes a new criminal offence, failure to reimburse wage. Only in 2013, a total of 1,182 female victims had been reported as victims of this offence (compared to 44 male victims). In the following years, the number of female victims for this single offence decreased considerably, while the male-female victimisation ratio clearly shifted towards male victims.[111]

Figure 3 Victimisation Trends Overall and by Gender 2010–2018

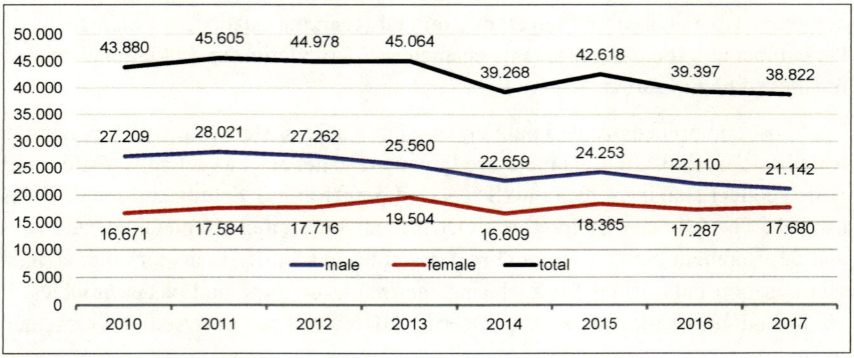

Source: Ministry of the Interior 2011–2018.

Looking at victims by offence type, the majority of victims are victims of property crime (*Figures 4* and *5*), as expected. This is a constant feature of victimisation with a share of property crime victimisation in overall victimisation by type of offence rather constantly around 60% during 2010–2018. This applies for male, as well as female victims *(Figure 4)*.

The two predominant property offences (2010–2018), amounting to more than 4/5 of all offences, are aggravated theft and theft. Aggravated theft, although more

---

109 Ministry of the Interior 2010–2018.

110 The police statistics on victimisation contain data on natural as well as legal persons.

111 Victims of failure to reimburse wage in 2016: 292 males, 102 females; 2017: 212 males, 118 females; see Ministry of the Interior 2017; 2018.

Figure 4 Share of Property Crime Victimisation (Dark) in Total Victimisation (Light) by Gender 2010–2018

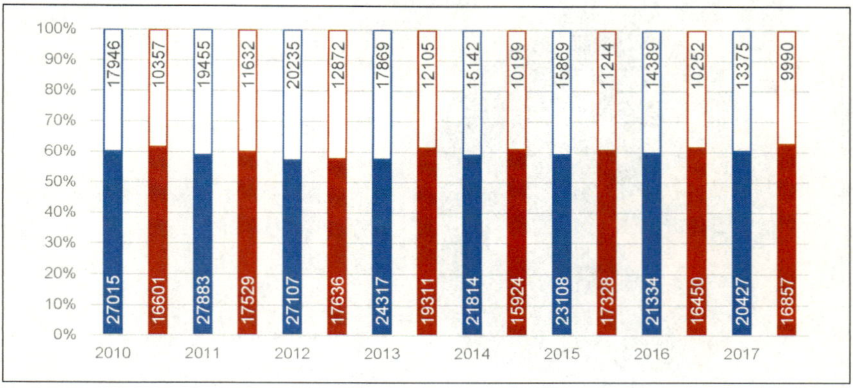

Source: Ministry of the Interior 2011–2018.

* Blue colour – male; Red colour – female.

frequent than theft during 2010–2016, slowly started dropping whereas theft remained rather constant, until the two changed places in 2016–2018, making theft the leading offence for victimisation (for both males and females). There is a notable declining trend not only when it comes to the severity of property crime related victimisation, but also to its frequency (especially in the past few years). The overall victimisation drop in 2014 *(Figure 3)* is also attributed to a drop in property crime victimisation. In 2014, there were almost 5,000 fewer victims of property crime than in the previous year(s), or to be more exact, 25,341 in 2014 compared to 29,974 in 2013. The numbers of adults and juveniles reported for offences against property crime where analysed, in order to exclude as a potential cause of this huge decrease in recorded victims of property crime a change in "counting/registering" victims of crime by the police or a simple error. Indeed, the number of reported perpetrators of property crime also significantly decreased (from 39,503 in 2013 to 34,802 in 2014), whereas the share of unknown perpetrators remained around 75% and the share of juveniles between 4–5% so that none of these factors might explain the drop. Further investigation into the drop in property crime should be of general criminological but also victimological interest since it affects approximately 60% of victims in Croatia.

Shifting the focus away from property crime as a cause of victimisation, in 2017 the next big group concerns victims of criminal offences against personal freedom (12%). The single leading offence in this group is threat (over 90% in 2017), with an almost equal distribution amongst male and female victims (*Figures 4* and *5*). In the group of victims of offences against traffic safety (7%) the most common single offence leading to victimisation is causing an accident in road traffic (97% in 2017), with the majority of victims being male (60%). Interestingly, when looking

Figure 5 Victims by Offence type in 2017 (Without "Other")

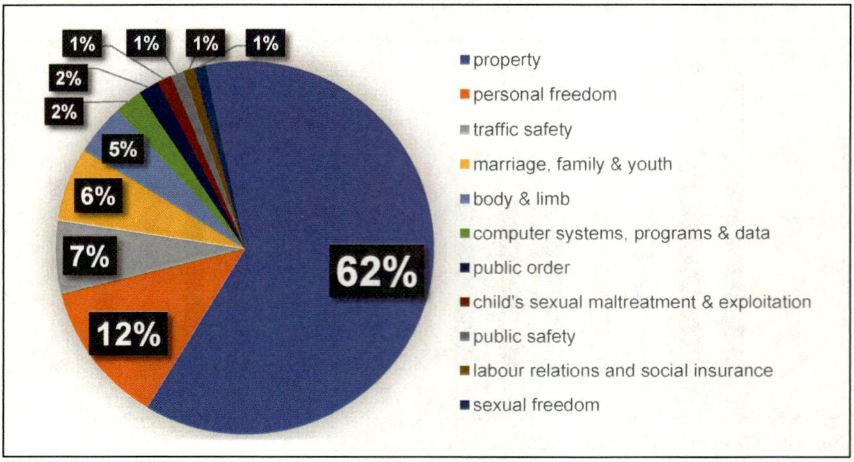

Source: Ministry of the Interior 2018.

at reported adult persons[112] for this offence in 2017 (total without unknown perpetrators: 1,302), the gender distribution also favours male perpetrators, but with a far more obvious ratio of 80:20. The stereotype of women being worse drivers than men might still be true but, at least in Croatia, women cause fewer criminal traffic accidents, with their share in victims of traffic accidents being twice as high as their share in perpetrators of this offence.

The next big group of victims owes their victimisation to an offence against marriage, family and youth (6%). Here the majority of victims, as one might expect, are females (almost 60%). The most frequent offence in this group is the violation of child's rights (almost 50%), followed by failure to provide maintenance (25%), and family violence (almost 25%). Whereas the gender distribution of victims is rather equal for the violation of child's rights and the failure to provide maintenance, when it comes to family violence the vast majority of victims (over 80%) are female. Since a large share of family/domestic violence in Croatia is not 'handled' through criminal law procedure, but rather through misdemeanour proceedings, as these proceedings are far more convenient for the police and provide for a lower level of suspects' rights, making it far easier to immediately remove the perpetrator from the domestic environment, the victimisation as appearing in the police crime statistics is undoubtedly only a smaller part of the whole phenomenon of victimisation by domestic violence. Only in 2017, there were 10,592 registered misdemeanours against the Act on protection against domestic violence, compared

112 In 2017, only 17 juveniles had been reported for committing the offence of causing an accident in road traffic; see Ministry of the Interior 2018.

to only 94 registered perpetrators of the criminal offence of domestic violence (90 of them male). A more thorough investigation into the issue of delineation between domestic violence criminal offences and misdemeanours is desperately needed, especially when taking into account that 94 perpetrators are responsible for the victimisation of 554 victims. The fact that the police uses misdemeanour proceedings extremely frequently when it comes to domestic violence indicates that there might be much room for improvements in the criminal procedures related to domestic violence.

Figure 6 Victims by Gender Distribution within Most Frequent Offence Types in 2017 (Without "Other")

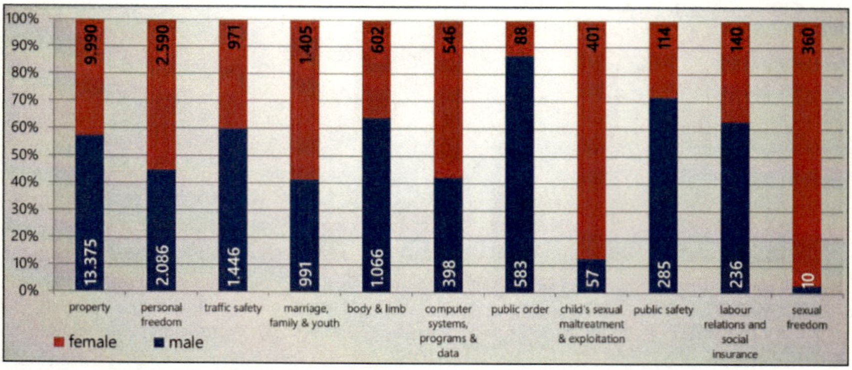

Source: Ministry of the Interior 2018.

The remaining groups of victims in 2017 by type of offence are related to offences against body and limb (5% share in overall victimisation, most frequent single offences: 45% bodily injury and 40% grave bodily injury), computer systems, programs and data (2%, most frequent single offence: 99% computer fraud), public order (2%, most frequent single offences: 34% coercion against an official person and 23% attacking an official person), child's sexual maltreatment and sexual exploitation (1%, most frequent single offences: 40% sexual maltreatment of a child younger than fifteen years of age and 33% abuse of children in pornography), public safety (1%, most frequent single offence: 97% endangering life and property by dangerous public acts or means), labour relations and social insurance (1%, most frequent single offence: 88% failure to reimburse wage), and sexual freedom (1%,most frequent single offences: 30% lewd acts, 27% prostitution, 18% sexual intercourse without consent and 18% rape) *(Figure 6)*.

5.2.2 Victimisation and Gender

The magnitude of victimisation by different types of offence groups (without property crime), as well as by gender distribution, shall be presented in order to get a sense of the overall victimisation during 2010–2018. This is done separately in *Figures 7* and *8*, for the periods 2010–2013 and 2015–2018 respectively. One should keep in mind that the new CC also introduced new headings, creating the need to differentiate between the "Old CC" and the current "New CC" when analysing crime and victimisation statistics prior to 2013. The single figures are provided for both 3-year periods by type of offence and by gender.

Figure 7 Total Victims 2010–2013 by Offence Types Based on "Old CC" and Gender (Without Property Crime and "Other")

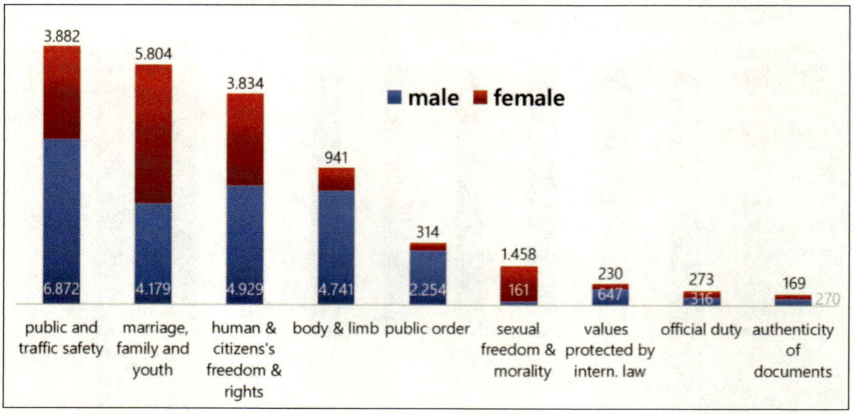

Source: Ministry of the Interior 2011–2014.

Figure 8 Total Victims 2015–2018 by Offence Types Based on "New CC" and Gender (Without Property Crime and "Other")

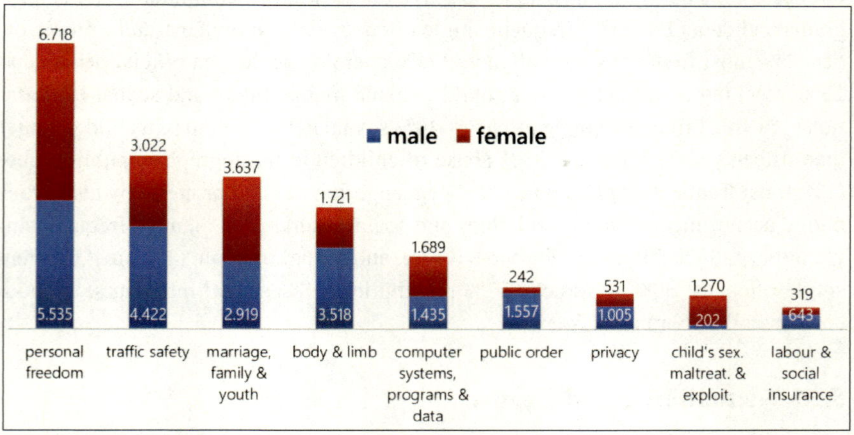

Source: Ministry of the Interior 2016–2019.

When looking for continuities and changes in the victimisation data due to the enactment of the new CC offence, significant normatively induced changes become apparent with the changes in offence groupings (*Figures 7* and *8*). Before briefly discussing these, it has to be noted that there are also obvious continuities, especially when it comes to victimisation by offences against body and limb (assault), against public order (obstruction), against marriage, family and youth (violation of child's rights; failure to provide maintenance; family violence) and against traffic safety (causing a traffic accident). Here the normative change had little if any impact on the victimisation data. However, the situation is far more complex when looking at those chapters of the CC that are completely new or considerably revised compared to the previous CC. To start with the easier ones: the offence group "against human and citizen's freedom and rights" in essence (and in terms of interpreting victimisation data) became the new offence group "against personal freedom", where the continuity is established through the offence of threat. Threat remains the single most frequent offence and cause of victimisation in both CCs. A sort of 'novelty' in the CC refers to the group of offences against computer systems, programs & data (leading offence: computer fraud), which as such did not exist in the "Old CC", although computer fraud was, of cause, punishable even before the enactment of the "New CC". This change follows new technical developments and causes of victimisation, without breaking continuity with prior victimisation data, but rather pointing towards the growing incidence of computer fraud as a source of victimisation in Croatia. The situation is quite similar regarding the new offence groups against privacy (the leading offence is the unauthorised use of personal data) and against labour relations and social insurance (the leading offence is the failure to reimburse wage). The interpretation of changes in victimisation data due to normatively induced changes is most complex when it comes to the "old" chapter of offences against sexual freedom and morality and the "new" chapter of offences against child's sexual maltreatment and exploitation. Put far too simplistically, but probably making it most easy to comprehend, the old chapter of offences against sexual freedom and morality was 'split up' by the new CC into the chapters of offences against sexual freedom and against child's sexual maltreatment and exploitation. This means that sexual offences against children have now not only legally, but also victimologically, become a separate and easily detectable (statistical) category, whereas sexual offences against all other persons (adults as well as helpless persons, etc.) continue to exist. Comparing the data presented in *Figures 7* and *8*, it becomes obvious that the majority of offences in the "old" group of offences against sexual freedom and morality were in fact committed against children, now in the 9th place on the list of the top 10 leading offence types causing victimisation in Croatia.

Finally, when it comes to the impact of gender on victimisation, then the incidence of victimisation by type of offence group (and without the impact of property crime) displays itself very unequally among men and women, as was already presented. However, the difference in gender-related victimisation becomes much more obvious when looking at the 10 most frequent offence groups separately for men and women *(Figure 9)*. While men are most likely to become victims of threats, traffic accidents and assaults, followed by offences against marriage, family and youth (most likely boys), women are most likely to become victims of threats, domestic violence and traffic accidents, only then followed by assaults, computer frauds and sexual victimisation.

Figure 9 Male (Blue) and Female Victims (Pink) by 10 Most Frequent Offence Types in 2017 (Without Property Crime and "Other")

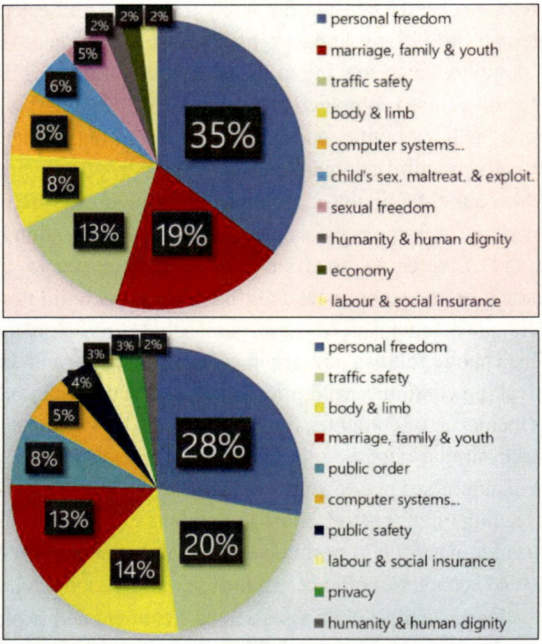

Source: Ministry of the Interior 2018.

5.2.3 Victimisation and Age

In the framework of analysing the age distribution among registered victims in Croatia, data are presented using the 'source age groups', as defined within the police statistics, as well as "adjusted age groups". The "source groups" are used since they contain a much more detailed insight into the prevalence of children and young people as victims, whereas the "adjusted groups" are used for comparing the prevalence and trends of victimisation among different age groups, but without the misleading visual impact of the source groups' unequal age intervals *(Figure 10)*.[113]

---

113 Although the age groups have been adjusted, the intervals are not equal, since the source intervals allowed only for an approximate, not a complete adjustment.

Figure 10 Total Number of Victims by Age Distribution within Different Age Groups 2010–2018 (1. Source Age Groups; 2. Adjusted Age Groups)

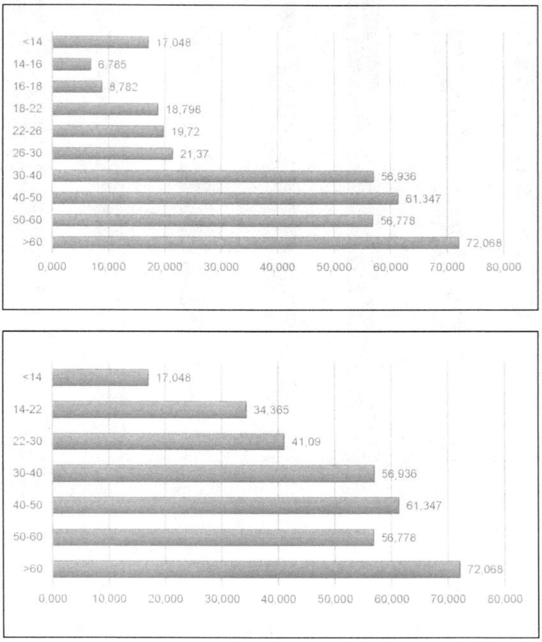

Source: Ministry of the Interior 2011–2019.

Analysing the structure of victimisation in Croatia based on age, it immediately becomes clear that there are no unexpected anomalies of fluctuations, neither in movements of trends nor in the share of different age groups in total *(Figure 11)*. Basically, there is a clear, slowly, but steadily moving rise in the share of older victims (over 60 years of age), whereas the majority of victims in Croatia (more than 50%) is well over 40 years old. Young people (16–26 years of age) participate in victimisation with less than 15% and children (less than 16 years of age) with a share of well below 10%.

Looking at the same data, but now distributed in adjusted age groups *(Figure 12)*, we see a slight declining trend in all age categories and a noticeable rise in the number of elderly victims above the age of 60. These trends are closely interlinked with Croatia's demographics (natural ageing-out of the population in combination with work-emigration of the younger and mid-aged population) and well reflected in a declining trend in crime in Croatia.

Focusing on victimisation trends of children and young people *(Figure 13)*, the same slightly declining trend appears again. However, interestingly the age group of young adults (between 18 and 22 years of age) displays more of a stable

Figure 11 Victims by Age Distribution 2010–2018 (Source Age Groups)

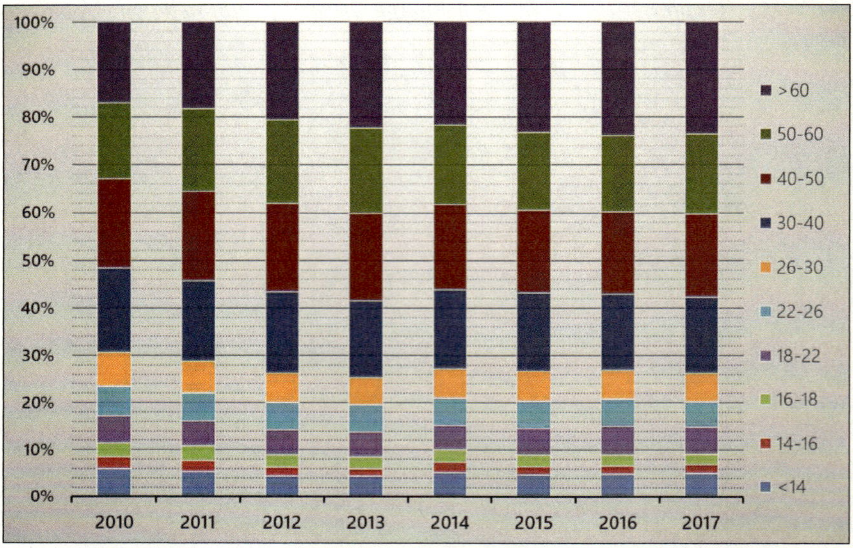

Source: Ministry of the Interior 2011–2019.

Figure 12 Victims by Age Distribution 2010–2018 (Adjusted Age Groups with Linear Trends)

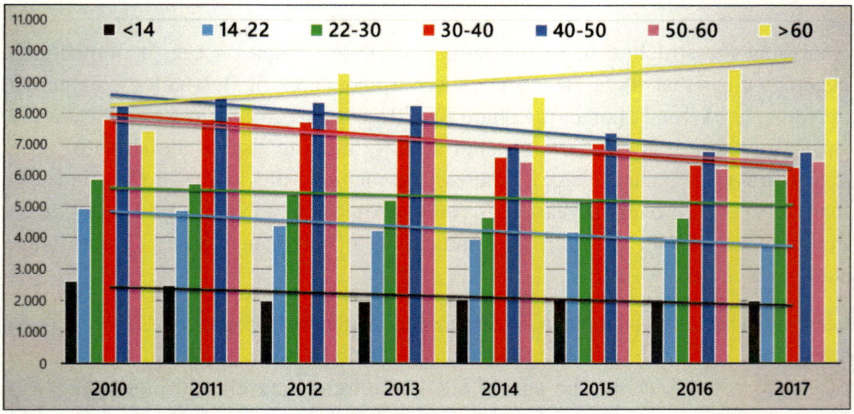

Source: Ministry of the Interior 2011–2019.

trend with an almost unnoticeable decline that does not fit the other age groups' decline. A further and more detailed investigation into this anomaly would be needed in order to determine the causes of rather persistent and unchanging vic-

Figure 13 Victimisation Trends of Children and Young People 2010–2018 (Adjusted Age Groups with Linear Trends)

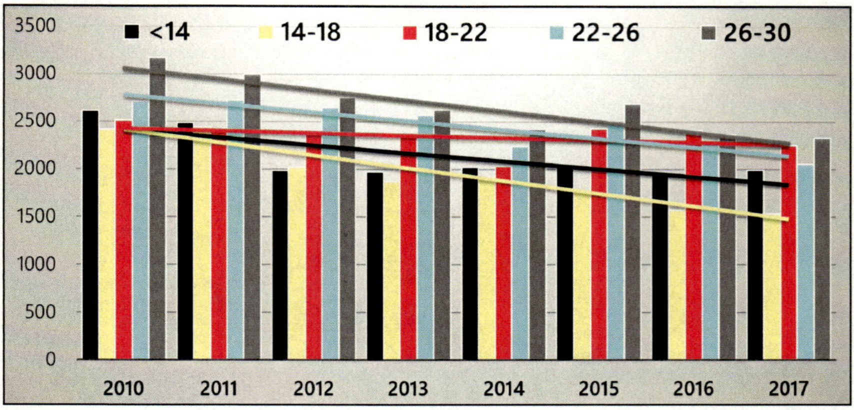

Source: Ministry of the Interior 2011–2019.

timisation of the group of young adults. Since the only drop in victimisation incidents in this age group appears in 2014, it is very unlikely that any of it can be explained by impacts of the new CC. Looking at data on the victimisation by type of offences and age groups might potentially provide for first hints on the probable causes.

5.2.4 Violent Victimisation by Police and Against Police

The last point of discussion, relevant in terms of violent victimisation in Croatia, deals with the issue of police victimisation and victimisation by police (*Figure 14,* see *next page*). Although the incidence of such types of victimisation appears not to be too dramatic, it should be noted that, when it comes to police-related victimisation, the number of citizens injured by the police is almost twice as high as the number of police officers injured by citizens. There is also a detectable drastic rise in the incidence of both types owf victimisation in 2012. It is very unlikely that in 2012 the police, as well as citizens, simply started attacking each other much more frequently than in 2010 or 2011. The only plausible explanation for the drastic increase seems to be the enactment of a new Act on the Police.[114] But exactly how and why these normatively induced changes to victimisation data, due to the new Act on the Police, occurred remains a mystery (for now).

[114] Act on the Police, Law. No. 011-01/11-01/41, 23.03.2011, Official Gazette 34/11.

Figure 14 Policing-Related Injuries and Deaths among Citizens and Police Officers 2010–2018

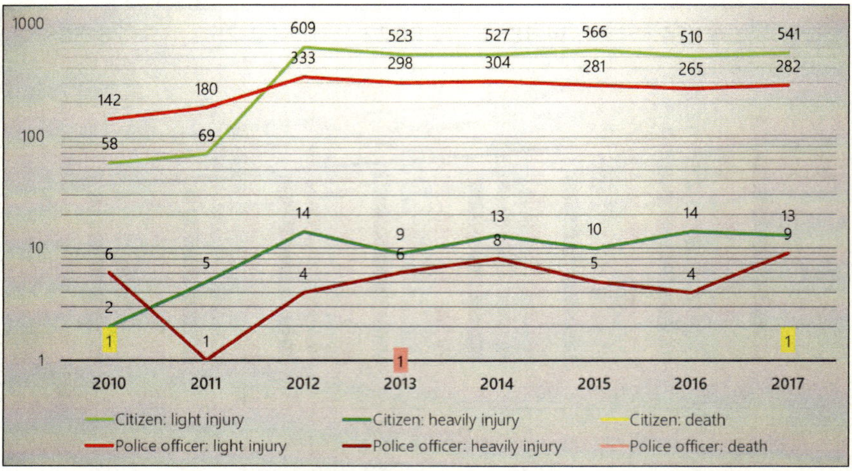

Source: Ministry of the Interior 2011–2019.

5.2.5 Violent and Sexual Victimisation of Women

Shifting our focus away from the official police statistics and towards victimisation surveys, the incidence of violence against women in Croatia shall be analysed. Croatia successfully participated in the 2012 FRA gender-based violence against women survey (1,505 completed interviews).[115] Some of the more interesting findings (in the EU comparative perspective) shall be presented and briefly discussed. When looking at childhood violent victimisation of women in Croatia (see *Figure 13*), it is highly interesting to see that, compared to other countries, the majority of perpetrators were not male, but female (72%), with mothers accounting for as much as 64% of the perpetrators.[116] Looking at the data of respondents by age groups and using it to determine the trend in violent physical childhood victimisation by mothers and female perpetrators, it becomes clear that this is a fairly stable "Croatian tradition", rather than a past or more recent trend. Overall, in terms of violent physical childhood victimisation, Croatia finds itself among the few countries that are above the EU average *(Figure 15)*.

---

115 FRA European Union Agency for Fundamental Rights 2014, p. 24.

116 Ireland also shows a rather unique pattern in terms of gender and type of perpetrator when compared to other EU countries; see FRA European Union Agency for Fundamental Rights 2014.

*Figure 15 Physical Violence before the Age of 15 by an Adult Perpetrator, by Gender and Type of Perpetrator**

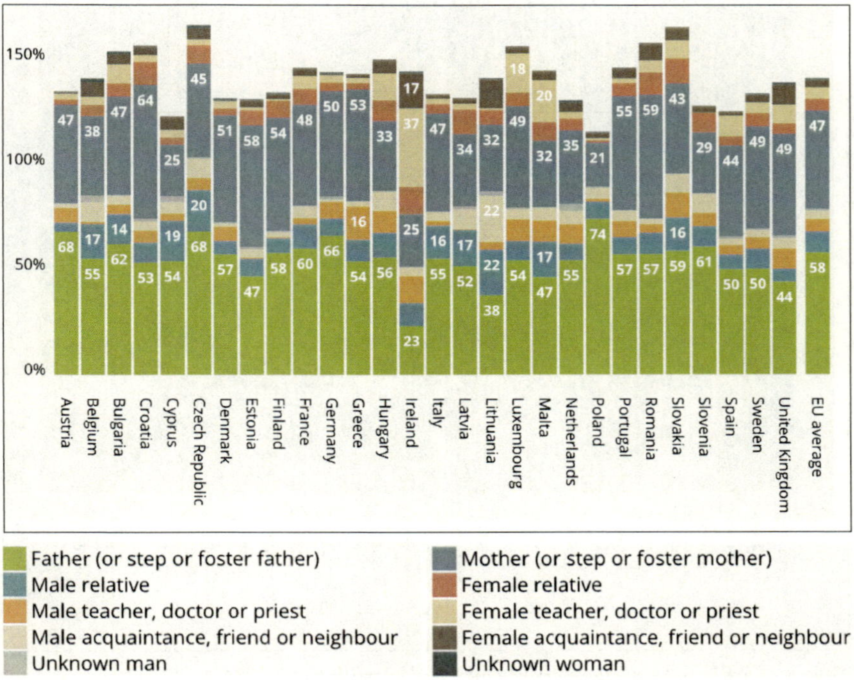

Source: FRA European Union Agency for Fundamental Rights 2014.

* In the FRA survey, physical violence before the age of 15 was asked about as follows: Before the age of 15 how often did an adult who was 18 years or over the following to you: 1) Slap or pull you by the hair so that it hurt, 2) Hit you very hard so that it hurt, 3) Kicked you very hard so that it hurt, 4) Beat you very hard with an object like a stick, cane or belt, and 5) Stabbed or cut you with something? For each type of violence women could indicate whether this had taken place "never", "once" or "more than once". In the FRA data explorer, the results are presented in two categories which correspond to women who had experienced any of the listed forms of physical violence (category "yes") and women who had never experienced any of them (category "no"), see FRA European Union Agency for Fundamental Rights 2014.

Croatian high levels in violent physical childhood victimisation of women initially point towards generally higher levels of violent physical victimisation after the age of 15. Although this would be a logical assumption, the data in *Figure 16* show that this is clearly not the case *(Figure 16)*. On the contrary. Croatia displays rather low levels of violent physical victimisation after the age of 15, and with 19% is positioned well beneath the EU average (31%). The issue of whether the perpetrator is a partner or non-partner does not play a significant role (partners: 12%, EU average: 20%; non-partners: 11%, EU average: 20%).

Figure 16 Physical Violence by a Partner or a Non-Partner after the Age of 15

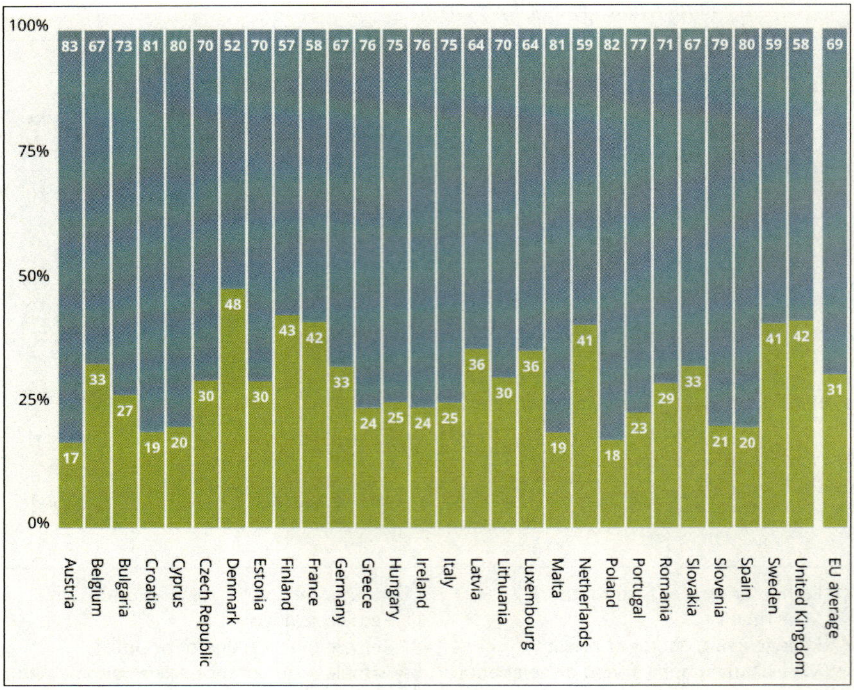

Source: FRA European Union Agency for Fundamental Rights 2014.

Looking at sexual violence against women,[117] Croatian victimisation levels are again well beneath the EU average. The same goes for levels of fear of violent and/

---

[117] In the FRA survey, concerning sexual violence, women were asked a set of questions: Since you were 15 years old / In the past 12 months, how often has someone:

1) Forced you into sexual intercourse by holding you down or hurting you in some way,
2) Apart from this, attempted to force you into sexual intercourse by holding you down or hurting you in some way,
3) Apart from this, made you take part in any form of sexual activity when you did not want to or were unable to refuse,
4) Or have you consented to sexual activity because you were afraid of what might happen if you refused?

With regard to each form of sexual violence, women could indicate that they had experienced this "never", "once", "2–5 times" or "6 or more times". In the FRA data explorer, the results are presented for respondents who have experienced these forms of violence at least once (category "yes" – combination of "once", "2–5 times" and "6 or more times") and respondents who have never experienced them; see FRA European Union Agency for Fundamental Rights 2014.

or sexual victimisation, avoiding places or situations due to fear of being physically or sexually assaulted, stalking victimisation or victimisation through sexual harassment. In sum, based on the data (and especially in EU comparison), women in Croatia display low levels of violent physical and/or sexual victimisation, fear of such victimisation, avoiding behaviour, etc. In light of all the data and analyses, the only detected anomaly relating to high levels of violent physical childhood victimisation with predominantly female (same-sex) perpetrators becomes even more interesting and should be further explored, especially by taking a close look at Croatian methodology, e.g., in terms of questionnaire translation, and survey implementation, in order to exclude these as plausible causes of the detected anomaly.

5.3 Actual Victimisation – Key Actors' Assessments

As stated earlier, in July 2017, the Croatian Parliament voted on changes in the CPA, the main instrument for transposing the Directive 2012/29/EU into national law. Another measure relevant for the transposition of this Directive is the Act on Domestic Violence, prescribing the rights of victims of domestic violence, which came into force on 1st January 2018. Supporting the victims of crime, or the institutionalisation of support activities, is rather new to Croatian society. There has been an intense development during the last ten years. Currently, the system is a combination of services provided by various institutions and organisations, general and specialised, governmental and non-governmental, dedicated to protecting the rights and interests of victims of crime. To obtain comprehensive information on the implementation of victims' rights in practice, interviews were conducted with a specialised judge on juveniles at the municipality court in Zagreb, representatives of the police in Zagreb, a representative of the Victim Support Department at the County Court in Zagreb, a representative of the NGO providing support to victims of crime in Split and the Dalmatian area, a representative of the NGO specialised in protection of victims of domestic violence. According to the interviews, stakeholders noted that the geographical availability of victim support services varies greatly in Croatia. Another major issue that became apparent after the interviews is the lack of systematic training provided to practitioners dealing with victims. Moreover, the training is principally voluntary and, according to the stakeholders, the practitioners have not shown a strong interest in it. This potentially affects the overall compliance with the Directive. Additionally, based on the interviews but also based on the available reports of the NGOs and the provided materials (leaflets on victim's rights) that are aimed to help the victims understand their rights, it could be noted that just providing the victims with the leaflets is not enough for the victims to fully understand their rights. This is even more present when, e.g., the police neither recognise the crime that has been committed toward the victims nor the special rights victims have due to specific crimes that entitle them to have special rights based on their status of vulnerability. It has been reported that the police often do not recognise that a victim is, for example, the victim of hate crime. Due to the inability to recognise and acknowledge the elements of hate crime, the victim is often not assessed as such and, therefore, special rights are not given to this victim.[118] Consequently, the data gathered on the actual victimisation in Croatia cannot be deemed as complete.

5.4 Preliminary Croatian Victim Typology

The question of victim typologies has been an integral part of victimology since its very start, dating back to 1948 and *Hans von Hentig*'s typology of victims based on the degree to which victims contribute to causing the criminal act,[119] or *Benjamin Mendelsohn*'s 1956 typology of criminal victims,[120] as well as *Stephen Schafer*'s 1968 typology, focusing on both social characteristics *(von Hentig)* and behaviours *(Mendelsohn)*, placing victims in groups based on how responsible they are for their own victimisation.[121] The basic idea behind these and the more recent victim typologies is to better understand and investigate crime-related victimisation with the ultimate goal of identifying type-specific, as well as type-overarching predictors of victimisation. In light of the apparent lack of victimologically relevant empirical data needed for constructing such a country-specific victim typology, a promising first approach to victimisation in Croatia is to focus on victims' vulnerabilities to criminal victimisation in Croatia's socioeconomic, historical and geographic context. This obviously includes the following groups:

1) women and girls;
2) children;
3) refugees, internally displaced persons and immigrants;
4) national, ethnic and religious minorities;
5) disabled persons;
6) elderly persons;
7) lesbian, gay and transgender people;

---

118 V-START 2018.

119 *Von Hentig* classified victims into 13 categories depending on their propensity for victimisation: 1) young; 2) females; 3) old; 4) immigrants; 5) depressed; 6) mentally defective/deranged; 7) the acquisitive; 8) dull normal; 9) minorities; 10) wanton; 11) the lonesome and heartbroken; 12) tormentor; and 13) the blocked, exempted, and fighting; see *Daigle* 2011.

120 *Mendelsohn*'s typology consists of six categories: 1) completely innocent victims; 2) victims with minor guilt; 3) voluntary victims; 4) victims guiltier than the offender; 5) victims who alone are guilty; and 6) the imaginary victims; see *Mendelsohn* 1956.

121 *Schafer* identified seven categories and labelled their levels of responsibility as follows: 1) unrelated victims – no responsibility; 2) provocative victims – shared responsibility; 3) precipitative victims – some degree of responsibility; 4) biologically weak victims – no responsibility; 5) socially weak victims – no responsibility; 6) self-victimising – total responsibility; and 7) political victims – no responsibility; see *Schafer* 1968.

8) institutionalised persons
(children and youth; elderly; mentally ill; detainees and prisoners; suspects);
9) war veterans' family members; and
10) men and boys.

Clearly, the typology is preliminary and not exhaustive, awaiting for an empirical testing and further adjustment to the phenomenology of victimisation in Croatia.[122] The typology's categories shall be briefly discussed in light of victimisation incidences, trends and types as presented earlier.

Women and girls as a special type of victims owe their vulnerability to their gender, which is particularly relevant when it comes to sexual violence, sexual abuse and harassment or stalking, but also forced prostitution or begging in relation to organised crime and trafficking in human beings. Croatia is a rather conservative and very patriarchal society in many aspects, which still very much determines the role women and girls play and are expected to play. Especially when looking at domestic violence, where female victims are over-represented, it is interesting to note that, despite an existing criminal law framework, the overwhelming majority of cases is dealt with through misdemeanour proceedings, rather than criminal ones. There is obviously a strong impact of practical issues related to police work and prosecution, but such frequent use of a far more lenient prosecution framework (and sanctions) is very likely also linked to the perceived 'normality' of a certain degree of domestic violence in Croatia by the relevant authorities, basically the police. It would be interesting to compare typical cases of domestic violence prosecuted through the misdemeanour as well as the criminal procedure in Croatia and then conduct a comparative analysis with similar cases from other European countries with similar double-track systems, but a less conservative and patriarchal societal setting. Currently, the frequent usage of the misdemeanour system is almost exclusively explained using the "practicality" argument when it comes to prosecuting domestic violence.

Children under the age of 14 (and, when it comes to the CC, also under the age of 15)[123] are more vulnerable due to their dependence on adult persons and their lack of the ability to ensure respect and fulfilment of their rights themselves. Thus, more often than not, those who victimise them are in fact their guardians. In many

---

[122] The design of a full-fledged typology of criminal victimisation together with its empirical testing and further development is an integral and prominent part of the research project "Croatian Violence Monitor: A Study of the Phenomenology, Etiology, and Prosecution of Delinquent Violence with Focus on Protecting Particularly Vulnerable Groups of Victims", funded by the Croatian Science Foundation (UIP-05-2017-8876). Additional information available online at www.violence-lab.eu.

[123] CC protects children under age of 15 proscribing their special protection by criminal offences of sexual abuse and exploitation of the child where the age limit of 15 years was set as the threshold; see Law No. 12511.

ways, their particular vulnerability comes close to that of disabled and elderly persons, as well as institutionalised persons, with the difference being the degree of awareness of their rights and ability to enforce these rights independently of their "guardians". However, children are obviously also a special group in terms of violent and sexual victimisation, as well as neglect, since a whole group of criminal offences and misdemeanours specifically regulates their criminal victimisation. A special topic, which has received little if any scholarly attention in Croatia, relates to (sexual) abuse and harassment of children perpetrated by members of the clergy. While in many countries the Catholic Church has initiated self-lead or outsourced independent investigations into (sexual) abuse and harassment of children perpetrated by members of their clergy in the past decade,[124] there has been no such initiative by the Croatian Catholic Church. The issue remains a total taboo, still waiting to be addressed by Croatian researches as well as the Church.

Refugees, internally displaced persons and immigrants as a particularly vulnerable group of victims have been present in Croatia long before the ongoing European migration crisis and date back to the armed conflicts following the violent breakup of Yugoslavia. Since then, Croatia, as well as other countries in the region, had to face huge waves of refugees and internally displaced persons who, more often than not, were also the victims of (war) crimes. This group has not only experienced victimisation in past times, but continues to be particularly vulnerable to future victimisation, e.g., when resettling to their places of pre-conflict origin, or within the framework of still ongoing and prospective criminal investigations and proceedings related to war crimes.

National, ethnic and religious minorities owe their vulnerability to their individual and group affiliation to certain national, ethnic and religious entities, which may have a minority or majority status, depending on the local, regional and national context. The Sinti and Roma, who are particularly vulnerable to victimisation, represent a special case. The particular vulnerability of this groups has been recognised in Croatia and is (among other activities) given special attention within data collection and assessment activities of the Government's Office for Human Rights and Rights of National Minorities through the activities of the Working Group for the Monitoring of Hate Crimes. The Working Group is comprised of experts from the non-governmental sector (academia and NGOs), as well as representatives from the police, prosecution, courts and the Office of the Croatian Ombudsman. Based on participation in the Working Group's meetings,[125] especially based on the insights into data collected on hate crime cases on the grounds of nationality, ethnicity, gender, sexual orientation, etc., it appears that the incidence, as well as the severity of

---

[124] Additional information available online at https://www.ebfr.de/html/content/praevention_und_hilfe_bei_missbrauch.html?t=qk54v542jfbb2jnj9m2vus7v17&tto=a78702f9&&.

[125] *Getoš Kalac* has been appointed a member of the respective working group for the past several years.

such hate crimes that have come to the attention of the authorities, is rather low. However, it is safe to assume that the issue of dark figure plays an important role here and that the officially recorded incidents most likely are merely a fraction of criminal victimisation.

Disabled persons and elderly persons have briefly been mentioned, but it is safe to assume that their position and related vulnerability in Croatia is particularly concerning. The assessments on their victimisation are almost impossible due to the lack of normative safeguards and, even in cases, these are in place, due to practical difficulties in effective oversight of institutions and natural persons providing care to these groups. Social work experts have characterised the sector as a ruthless "business" that is largely left without actual oversight and control, little mechanisms for sanctions, and virtually no chance to detect harassment and abuse by social workers. With the growing share of elderly persons in Croatia's population, this is definitely one of the areas where thorough investigation and normative,[126] as well as practical improvements, are urgently needed. The situation is very similar when it comes to institutionalised persons, where the challenge is even greater, due to the difficulties in access to these persons and insight on their living conditions and treatment from outside the institutions in charge of "caring" for them.

The group of lesbian, gay and transgender people has been recognised as a particularly vulnerable group, subject to discrimination, as well as instances of violent victimisation. In contrast to many of the other mentioned vulnerable groups, these have meanwhile managed to form a strong interest group in Croatia with supporting and promoting activities. This vulnerable group is also at the attention of the aforementioned work of the Government's Office for Human Rights and Rights of National Minorities.

A group that is rather neglected in terms of vulnerability to victimisation in Croatia is comprised out of war veterans' family members. Although much attention has been given to former military personnel that participated in Croatia's Homeland War, especially with respect to the post-traumatic stress disorder, extremely high incidence of suicides, and frequent substance abuse, little is known about how these and other long-term impacts of military engagement have affected their families. Over the years there have been several cases of severe violence with war veterans as perpetrators (most frequently ending in their suicides), indicating that treatment and care might be suboptimal, with many problematic aspects, such as many of the veterans still in possession of registered as well as illegal firearms. It would be highly interesting to get a closer look at domestic violence with a particular focus on the victimisation of war veterans' family members.

---

126 *Roksandić Vidlička & Šikoronja* 2017.

The last group, which is usually excluded from any listings of particularly vulnerable victim groups, but which is, however, the predominantly victimised one, concerns men, and, based on gender, also boys. Their specific vulnerability can be found in risk-prone behaviour, which makes them appear much more frequently not only on the victimising but also on the victimised side. Based on this phenomenological frequency, this group constitutes a separate victimological group and, as such, deserves special attention.

6. Public Discourses About Victims and Victimisation, Victim Rights and Protection

In the last couple of years, public and media discourse on victims and victimisation in Croatia has been strongly oriented towards victims of domestic violence, especially women. It may be argued that society has become more susceptible to violence in general, although the incidence and severity of (violent) victimisation are clearly dropping, as in most other European countries. This leads to a situation where domestic violence is no longer considered, not only legally but also from the point of view of the general public, a private family matter, but an important social, legal and political matter. The society often, especially in cases of hideous crimes, views the position of the victim of a crime and its family as unsatisfactory in the framework of the national criminal justice system. In that context, public and media discourse becomes dominated by voices of those who ask for a more efficient, severe and victim-oriented criminal justice. Croatia has also been experiencing a very interesting social development in the last couple of months with regard to the ratification of the Council of Europe Convention on preventing and combating violence against women and domestic violence (Istanbul Convention). The ratification of this Convention has become a major political battlefield between those interest groups who saw the Convention as a Trojan horse of gender ideology and those who saw it as an instrument whose ratification is necessary in order to improve prevention and suppression of violence against women and domestic violence. The Convention was finally ratified, despite strong opposition from the Catholic Church, which has a very prominent role in Croatian society. This also raises a concern about the general awareness and attitudes towards a sincere implementation of the provisions of the Istanbul Convention. As previously explained, many of the Convention's provisions have already been incorporated in the CC back in 2011, long before the discussion about its ratification escalated.[127]

Until recently, special protection of victims of war-related sexual violence represented a very present topic in Croatia's victim-narratives, especially given the fact that this category of war victims never got special recognition of their status, contrary

127 See the Law No. 12511.

to other victims of war. Only after conducting the UNDP's Study on the assessment of the number of sexual violence victims during the Homeland War on the territory of the Republic of Croatia, and publishing a special policy paper on optimal forms of compensation and support to victims,[128] which led to a new law, this topic is no longer considered as one of the main topics in the area of victim protection in Croatia's social arena. However, the implementation of this law does require further research.

The public might have become more aware of the problem of hate crime, especially against the LGBT (Lesbian, Gay, Bisexual and Transgender) community and other minorities, as public discourse intensified during the last decade or two. However, it is difficult to assess whether the public discourse simply reflects the heightened sensitivity of relevant NGOs, governmental bodies and the media on the topic of hate crimes, or if it really reflects a changed awareness in society. The question is rather interesting and should be further investigated but, based on expert opinion, it seems to be much more likely that the media discourse is not an accurate reflection of the public discourse or even societal attitudes towards minority rights and their protection.

7. Expert Assessment and Constructive Criticism with Suggestions for Improvement

Croatia has transposed the Directive 2012/29/EU to a large extent but there are still some important issues that are affecting the complete implementation of the Directive on victim protection. When analysing legislation, we have noticed that there is practically no restorative justice mechanism in Croatia and it is, in our opinion, long needed. Furthermore, the lack of systematic training provided to practitioners dealing with victims points to the need for implementing training in a more systematic way. This would lead to a broader understanding of the importance of individual assessment of victim's rights in criminal proceedings. This would also help the police identify the crimes better, which would have repercussions on the rights that victims have. This is especially visible in the identification of committed hate crimes. On the level of implementation, it is important to have enough staff and funds to effectively implement Victim Support Services, The Victim Support Service, as established at the Zagreb's County Court, could serve as a role model for all institutions established with the aim to enhance victims' rights. Although this Service is helping all stakeholders, they are simply not able to serve as the main centre for the whole of Croatia since they were established for a much narrower jurisdiction. Moreover, special attention to victims of economic violence is needed in Croatia.[129] This is

---

[128] United Nations Development Programme 2013.

[129] *Roksandić Vidlička* 2017b.

especially true due to the fact that the criminal offences resulting from privatisation and ownership transformation are not yet resolved. The same occurs with victims of war profiteering. This being underlined, the Balkan Criminology Group plans to further engage in researching the identified weak points in the area of victim protection in Croatia. Moreover, further research is necessary on the need to include and develop the most adequate restorative justice measures in the Croatian criminal justice system.

8. Conclusions

Victimology has a long history, but a rather poor tradition in terms of the substantial scientific content in Croatia. Croatian victimology has yet to rise to the level of a nationally recognisable scientific discipline. However, there is a strong presence of victim rights movements, organisations, victim protection policies and legislation. Under the influence of international law and especially criminal law of the EU, the legal position of victims of crime has been gradually becoming stronger. The peak of this development has been characterised by the adoption of an EU Directive-conform legislation on victim protection, which came into force in December 2017. When looking at the development of victim-centred legislation in Croatia, one can identify two tendencies influencing this process. The first one relates to the strengthening of mechanisms, which enable the victim to cope with the consequences of a criminal offence more easily. It is the basis for the recognition of victimisation – recognition of a status of a victim of a criminal offence, followed by the establishment of different extra-procedural and procedural rights that protect the victim from repeated and secondary victimisation. Moreover, access to the compensation of damages caused by criminal offences is guaranteed, as well as access to victim support services. The second tendency relates to the strengthening of the legal position of the victim in criminal proceedings. This position guarantees the transformation of a victim from a passive participant in criminal proceedings, most often as a witness, to an active procedural participant who is given different procedural rights that enables the victim to promote his/her own interests in criminal proceedings. Croatian CC puts an emphasis on victim protection by introducing new offences and aggravated circumstances when the victims are vulnerable. Regarding victimisation in Croatia and in light of the apparent lack of victimologically relevant empirical data needed for constructing such a country-specific victim typology, a promising first approach, used in this article, was to focus on victims' vulnerabilities to criminal victimisation in Croatia's socioeconomic, historical and geographic context. Police statistics are the most comprehensive and publicly available official statistics that contain at least the basic victimisation data and are thus up-to-date. Based on these statistics, the following groups of victims were identified: 1) women and girls; 2) children; 3) refugees, internally displaced persons and immigrants; 4) national, ethnic and religious minorities; 5) disabled persons; 6) elderly persons; 7) lesbian, gay and transgender people; 8) institutionalised persons (children & youth; elderly; persons with mental disabilities; detainees and prisoners; suspects); 9) war veterans' family members; and 10) men and boys.

Moreover, special attention should be given to victims of economic violence in Croatia especially due to the fact that the criminal offences resulting from privatisation and ownership transformation are not yet resolved. Therefore, a special typology should be created to analyse victims of those crimes. The same occurs with victims of war profiteering. Taking all the above mentioned into consideration, additional endeavours will be necessary in order to establish victimology as an independent scientific discipline in Croatia. The focus of this discipline might be on those categories of victims, which may be considered the most vulnerable, having in mind the specific Croatian context. Besides victims of violent crimes, women and children victims of crime, minority groups that are most likely to become victims of crime, special attention should also be devoted to elderly people since Croatian population is becoming older.[130] In addition, victims of economic crime deserve more attention. Due to the transition from one economic system to the other in the 1990s, Croatian society is still struggling with the consequences of economic crimes that occurred during the process of privatisation and ownership transformation. Croatia has still not found an appropriate way to efficiently address those violations and compensate the victims of those crimes (transitional economic crimes).[131]

9. Summary in Croatian

Viktimologija ima dugu povijest, ali nedovoljno razvijenu tradiciju u pogledu sistematiziranih znanstvenih sadržaja u Hrvatskoj. Hrvatska se viktimologija još nije podigla na razinu nacionalno prepoznatljive znanstvene discipline iako su hrvatski znanstvenici stvarali Svjetsko viktimološko društvo. Međutim, prisutna je snažan pokret za jačanje prava žrtava, organizacija, politika i zakona o zaštiti žrtava. Pod utjecajem međunarodnog prava, a posebno kaznenog prava EU, pravni položaj žrtava kaznenih djela postupno jača. Vrhunac tog razvoja obilježilo je donošenje svobuhvatnog zakonodavstva o zaštiti žrtava u skladu s Direktivom EU, koje je stupilo na snagu u prosincu 2017., iako su i brojni zakoni daleko prije toga vremena sadržavali odrebe o zaštiti prava žrtava. Kada se razmatra razvoj zakonodavstva usmjerenog na zaštitu žrtava u Hrvatskoj, uočavaju se dvije tendencije. Prva se odnosi na jačanje mehanizama koji omogućuju žrtvi da se lakše suoči sa posljedicama kaznenog djela. Temelj za to je priznavanje činjenice viktimizacije – priznanje statusa žrtve kaznenog djela, nakon čega slijedi uspostava različitih izvanpostupovnih i postupovnih prava koja žrtvu štite od ponovljene i sekundarne viktimizacije. Štoviše, zajamčen

---

130 *Roksandić Vidlička & Šikoronja* 2017.

131 *Roksandić Vidlička* 2017.

je pristup naknadi štete prouzročene kaznenim djelima, kao i pristup službama za podršku žrtvama. Druga tendencija odnosi se na jačanje pravnog položaja žrtve u kaznenom postupku. Ova pozicija jamči transformaciju žrtve iz pasivnog sudionika u kaznenom postupku, najčešće kao svjedoka, u aktivnog procesnog sudionika kojem se pružaju različita procesna prava koja omogućuju žrtvi da promiče svoje interese u kaznenom postupku. Hrvatski kazneni zakon stavlja naglasak na zaštitu žrtava uvođenjem novih kaznenih djela, često kvalificiranih, kada su žrtve ranjive. Što se tiče viktimizacije u Hrvatskoj i s obzirom na očigledan nedostatak viktimološki relevantnih empirijskih podataka potrebnih za izgradnju specifične tipologije žrtava, novi pristup, korišten u ovom članku, bio je usmjeravanje na ranjivost žrtava na kaznenu viktimizaciju u hrvatskom socioekonomskom smislu te povijesnom i zemljopisnom kontekstu. Kako je policijska statistika najopsežnija i javno dostupna službena statistika koja sadrži barem osnovne podatke o viktimizaciji i ažurna je, služila je kao temelj za utvrđivanje sljedećih skupina žrtava: 1) žene i djevojke; 2) djeca; 3) izbjeglice, interno raseljene osobe i imigranti; 4) nacionalne, etničke i vjerske manjine; 5) osobe s invaliditetom; 6) starije osobe; 7) lezbijske, gej i transrodne osobe; 8) institucionalizirane osobe (djeca i mladi; starije osobe; osobe s duševnim smetnjama; zatočenici i zatvorenici; osumnjičeni); 9) članovi obitelji branitelja; i 10) muškarci i dječaci. Nadalje, posebnu pozornost hrvatski stručnjaci i znanstvenici trebaju posvetiti žrtvama gospodarskog kriminala u Hrvatskoj, posebice zbog činjenice da kaznena djela proizašla iz pretvorbe i privatizacije još nisu riješena. Stoga bi trebalo stvoriti posebnu tipologiju za analizu žrtava tih zločina. Isto se događa i sa žrtvama ratnog profiterstva. Osim žrtava nasilnih zločina, žena i djece žrtava zločina, manjinskih skupina koje najvjerojatnije postaju žrtve zločina, posebnu pažnju treba posvetiti i starijim osobama s obzirom na činjenicu da hrvatsko stanovništvo postaje sve starije. Pored toga, žrtve gospodarskog kriminala zaslužuju više pozornosti. Zbog prelaska s jednog gospodarskog sustava na drugi tijekom 1990-ih, hrvatsko se društvo još uvijek bori s posljedicama gospodarskih zločina koji su se dogodili tijekom procesa privatizacije i vlasničke transformacije. Hrvatska još uvijek nije pronašla odgovarajući način za učinkovito rješavanje tih kršenja i naknadu žrtava tih zločina (tranzicijska gospodarska kaznena djela). Uzimajući u obzir sve gore spomenuto, bit će potrebni dodatni napori za uspostavu viktimologije kao neovisne znanstvene discipline u Hrvatskoj. Fokus ove discipline mogao bi biti na onim kategorijama žrtava, koje se mogu smatrati najugroženijima, imajući u vidu specifični hrvatski kontekst. Ovo poglavlje predstavlja korak u tom smjeru.

Literature

Aebi et al. (2017): European sourcebook of crime and criminal justice statistics 2014. Helsinki; http://wp.unil.ch/europeansourcebook/files/2018/03/Sourcebook2014_2nd_revised_printing_edition_20180308.pdf [in English only] [12.09.2019].

Ajduković, M. & Marohnić, S. (2011): Smjernice za planiranje, provedbu i evaluaciju prevencijskih i tretamanskih programa zaštite djece od nasilja [Guidelines for the planning, implementation and evaluation of prevention and treatment programmes for the protection of children against violence]. Zagreb.

Bilić, V. (2013): Nasilje među vršnjacima: uloga branitelja žrtava, pomoćnika i pristaša počinitelja nasilja te pasivnih promatrača [Peer violence: The role of victims' advocates, helpers and supporters of perpetrators of violence and passive bystanders]. Život i škola [Life and School], 59, pp. 193–209.

Bukovac-Puvača, M. (2013): Državne naknade žrtvama kaznenih djela u Republici Hrvatskoj [State compensation to victims of crime in the Republic of Croatia]. Zbornik Pravnog fakulteta Sveučilišta u Rijeci [Proceedings of the Law Faculty of the University of Rijeka], 34, pp. 333–357.

Burić, Z. (2015): Novi položaj žrtve u kaznenom postupku – u povodu obveze transponiranja odredaba Direktive 2012/29/EU u hrvatski kaznenopravni sustav [New position of victim in criminal proceedings – Regarding the obligation to transpose the provisions of Directive 2012/29/EU into the Croatian criminal justice system]. Hrvatski ljetopis za kazneno pravo i praksu [Croatian Annual of Criminal Law and Practice], 22, pp. 383–410.

Burić, Z. (2014): New Croatian Criminal Procedure Act: Europe Says "Yes", Constitutional Court Says "No". Justice Report 29, pp. 23–24.

Burić, Z. (2011): Položaj žrtve u hrvatskom i makedonskom kaznenom procesnom pravu kroz prizmu Okvirne odluke o položaju žrtava u kaznenom postupku [The position of the victim in Croatian and Macedonian criminal procedural law through the prism of the Framework Decision on the Status of Victims in Criminal Procedure]. Zbornik Pravnog fakulteta u Zagrebu [Proceedings of the Law Faculty in Zagreb], 61, pp. 491–517.

Burić, Z. & Lučić, B. (2017): Pravni i institucionalni aspekti položaja žrtve kaznenog djela u RH [Legal and institutional aspects of the position of victims of crime in the Republic of Croatia]. Zagreb.

Daigle, L.E. (2011): Victimology: The essentials, 2nd ed. Sage.

Đurđević, Z. (2013): Rekonstrukcija, judicijalizacija, konstitucionalizacija, europeizacija hrvatskog kaznenog postupka V. novelom ZKP/08: prvi dio? [Reconstruction, judicialisation, constitutionalisation, Europeanisation of the Croatian Criminal Procedure Act V of the CPC/08: First part?]. Hrvatski ljetopis za kazneno pravo i praksu [Croatian Annual of Criminal Law and Practice], 20, pp. 315–362.

Đurđević, Z. (2012): Odluka Ustavnog suda RH o suglasnosti Zakona o kaznenom postupku s Ustavom [Decision of the Constitutional court of the Republic of Croatia on the conformity of the Criminal Procedure Act with the Constitution]. Hrvatski ljetopis za kazneno pravo i praksu [Croatian Annual of Criminal Law and Practice], 19, pp. 409–438.

Getoš, A.M. (2011): Kriminologie in Kroatien – Institutionalisierung und Entwicklungen von 1906 bis zur Gegenwart [Criminology in Croatia – Institutionalisation and developments from 1906 to the present]. Monatsschrift für Kriminologie und Strafrechtsreform [Monthly Journal of Criminology and Criminal Law Reform], 94, 213–221.

Getoš, A.M. (2009): Mjesto i uloga kriminologije i viktimologije u Hrvatskoj i u međunarodnom kontekstu [The position and role of criminology and victimology in Croatia and in the international context]; in: K. Turković, A. Maršavelski & S. Roksandić Vidlička (eds.), Liber Amicorum Zvonimir Šeparović: Od kaznenog prava do viktimologije. Zbornik radova u čast 80. rođendana profesora emeritusa Zvonimira Šeparovića [Liber Amicorum Zvonimir Separovic: From Criminal Law to Victimology. Proceedings commemorating the 80th birthday of Professor Emeritus Zvonimir Separovic]. Zagreb, pp. 119–140.

Getoš Kalac, A.M. & Bezić, R. (2017): Criminology, crime and criminal justice in Croatia. European Journal of Criminology, 14, pp. 242–266.

Getoš Kalac, A.M. & Karlović, R. (2014): Criminology and Crime in Croatia; in: A.M. Getoš Kalac, H.J. Albrecht, & M. Kilchling (eds.), Mapping the criminological landscape of the Balkans. A Survey on criminology and crime with an expedition into the criminal landscape of the Balkans. Berlin, pp. 139–174.

Grozdanić, V. (ur.) (2015): Komentar zakona o zaštiti osoba s duševnim smetnjama: s provedbenim propisima, primjerima sudskih odluka, međunarodnim dokumentimai presudama Europskog suda za ljudska prava [Commentary on the Law on the Protection of People with Mental Disorders: With implementing regulations, examples of court decisions, international documents and judgments of the European Court of Human Rights]. Rijeka.

Kovčo Vukadin, I. (2014): Prevencija nasilja u zatvorima: restorativni pristup; in: Zbornik radova Međunarodna naučno-stručna konferencija: Izgradnja modernog pravnog sistema [Conference proceedings of the International scientific conference: Building of the modern legal system]. Sarajevo, pp. 129–150.

Krapac, D. (2002): The victim's procedural role in the Croatian criminal procedure. Revue Internationale de Droit Pénal [International Journal of Criminal Law], 73, pp. 155–166.

Mamula, M., & Dijanić Plašć, I. (2014): Tipična žrtva obiteljskoh nasilja u RH – sociodemografski profil [Typical victims of family violence in the Republic of Croatia – Sociodemographic profile]. Život i škola [Life and School], 60, pp. 111–128.

Mendelsohn, B. (1956): The victimology. Paris.

Mirosavljević, A., Koller-Trbović, N. & Lalić-Lukač, D. (2009): Evaluacija uspješnosti izvansudske nagodbe u stručnoj službi za izvansudsku nagodbu Zagreb [Performance evaluation of out-of-court settlement in the Professional Out-of-court settlement service Zagreb]. Kriminologija i socijalna integracija [Criminology and Social Integration], 18, pp. 77–95.

Podgornik, B. (2017): Podaci OECD-a: Ubrzava se iseljavanje iz lijepe naše – u dvije godine iz Hrvatske odselilo 138 tisuća ljudi [OECD figures: Emigration from our beautiful country is accelerating – 138,000 people emigrated from Croatia in two years], in: Novi List, 13.08.2017; http://www.novilist.hr/novilist_public/Vijesti/Hrvatska/UBRZAVA-SE-ISELJAVANJE-IZ-LIJEPE-NASE-U-dvije-godine-iz-Hrvatske-odselilo-138-tisuca-ljudi [12.09.2019].

Radetić-Paić, M. (2010): Izloženost romskoga i ostalog stanovništva u Istri viktimizaciji kaznenim djelima [Exposure of Roma and other population in Istria to crime victimisation]. Migracijske i etničke teme [Migration and Ethical Themes], 26, pp. 49–65.

Rittossa, D. (2016): Kaznenopravna zaštita djece od seksualnog zlostavljanja u Republici Hrvatskoj – potreba za daljnjom reformom? [Criminal justice protection of children against sexual abuse in the Republic of Croatia – need for further reform?]; in S. Popović (ed.), Zaštita prava djece i mladih na seksualno zdravlje. Zbornik radova s interdisciplinarnog znanstveno-stručnog skupa [Protection of the rights of children and young people concerning sexual health. Proceedings of an interdisciplinary scientific-professional conference]. Rijeka, pp. 37–60.

Roksandić Vidlička, S. (2017a): Filling the void: The case for international economic criminal law. Zeitschrift für die gesamte Strafrechtswissenschaft [Journal for All Criminal Science], 129, pp. 581–884.

Roksandić Vidlička, S. (2017b): Prosecuting serious economic crimes as international crimes. A new mandate for the ICC? Berlin.

Roksandić Vidlička, S. (2017c): Transitional justice measures and application of Law for economic crimes in Croatia: What can Macedonia and Balkan countries learn out of them? Makedonska revija za kazneno pravo i kriminologija [Macedonian Journal for Criminal Law & Criminology], 24, pp. 343–362.

Roksandić Vidlička, S. & Šikoronja, S. (2017): Pravna zaštita starijih osoba, osobito sduševnim smetnjama, iz hrvatske perspektive: zašto nam je potrebna Konvencija UN-a o pravima starijih osoba [Legal protection of the elderly, especially those with disabilities, from a Croatian perspective: why we need the UN Convention on the Rights of the Elderly]. Zbornik Pravnog fakulteta Sveučilišta u Rijeci [Proceedings of the Law Faculty of the University Rijeka], 38, pp. 1101–1132.

Šeparović, Z. (1985): Viktimologija: studije o žrtvama [Victimology: Studies of victims]. Zagreb & Samobor.

Singer, M. (2005): Kriminologija delikata nasilja: nasilje nad djecom i ženama, maloljetničko nasilje [Criminology of violence: Violence against children and women, juvenile violence]. Zagreb.

Tarantini, G. (2016): The Balkan route: Organized crime in South-Eastern Europe – Root causes, current developments and future prospects. Bruges.

Tomašević, G. & Pajčić, M. (2008): Subjekti u kaznenom postupku: pravni položaj žrtve i oštećenika u novom hrvatskom kaznenom postupku [Subjects in criminal proceedings: The legal position of the victim and the injured person in the new Croatian criminal proceedings]. Hrvatski ljetopis za kazneno pravo i praksu [Croatian Annual of Criminal Law and Practice], 15, pp. 817–857.

Turković, K. (2002): Overview of the victimological data related to war in Croatia. European Journal of Crime, Criminal Law and Criminal Justice, 10, pp. 202–215.

Turković, K., Novoselec, P., Grozdanić, V., Kurtović Mišić, A., Derenčinović, D., Bojanić, I., Munivrana Vajda, M., Mrčela, M., Nola, S., Roksandić Vidlička, S., Tripalo, D. & Maršavelski, A. (2013): Komentar Kaznenog zakona [Commentary of the Criminal Code]. Zagreb.

Documents

Balkan Criminology (2019): Mapping the criminological landscape of the Balkans ("Balkan Criminology" Network – BCNet); https://www.balkan-criminology.eu/network/ [in English only] [12.09.2019].

Bundeskriminalamt (2016): Organisierte Kriminalität [Organised crime]. Wiesbaden; https://www.bka.de/SharedDocs/Downloads/DE/Publikationen/JahresberichteUndLagebilder/OrganisierteKriminalitaet/organisierteKriminalitaetBundeslagebild2016.html [in German only] [12.09.2019].

Croatian Bureau of Statistics (2019): Pravosuđe [Criminal justice]; https://www.dzs.hr/default_e.htm [in Croatian and English] [16.09.2019].

Croatian Bureau of Statistics (2017): Procjena ukupnog broja stanovnika sredinom godine [Estimate of total population in mid-year]; https://www.dzs.hr/Hrv_Eng/Pokazatelji/Procjene%20stanovnistva.xlsx [in Croatian and English] [16.09.2019].

Croatian Society of Victimology (2019): O nama [About us]; http://viktimologija.com.hr/wp/ [in Croatian only] [12.09.2019].

European Commission (2013): DG justice guidance document related to the transposition and implementation of Directive 2012/29/EU of the European Parliament and of the Council of 25 October 2012 establishing minimum standards on the rights, support and protection of victims of crime, and replacing Council Framework Decision 2001/220/JHA; https://www.legal-tools.org/en/browse/record/daaee5/ [in English only] [12.09.2019].

Eurostat (2017): Employment rate by sex, age group 20–64; https://ec.europa.eu/eurostat/web/products-datasets/-/t2020_10&lang=en [in English only] [12.09.2019].

FRA European Union Agency for Fundamental Rights (2014): Violence against women: An EU-wide survey. Main results report; http://fra.europa.eu/en/publication/2014/violence-against-women-eu-wide-survey-main-results-report [in English only] [12.09.2019].

Fund for Peace (2019): What we do; http://fundforpeace.org/fsi/comparative-analysis/ [in English only] [12.09.2019].

Institute of Child Health (2019): Balkan Epidemiological Study on Child Abuse & Neglect; http://www.becan.eu/ [in English only] [12.09.2019].

International Monetary Fund World Economic Outlook (2016): Subdued Demand: Symptoms and remedies; https://www.imf.org/en/Publications/WEO/Issues/2016/12/31/Sub dued-Demand-Symptoms-and-Remedies [in English only] [12.09.2019].

Ministry of Demographics, Family, Youth and Social Policy (2019): Nasilje u obitelji [Family violence]; https://mdomsp.gov.hr/istaknute-teme/djeca-i-obitelj/nasilje-u-obitelji/1847 [in Croatian only] [12.09.2019].

Ministry of Demographics, Family, Youth and Social Policy (2018): Priručnik sa smjernicama za medijsko izvještavanje o nasilju u obitelji [Handbook on media reporting on domestic violence]. Zagreb; https://mdomsp.gov.hr/UserDocsImages/Publikacije/PRIRUC NIK%20SA%20SMJERNICAMA%20ZA%20MEDIJSKO%20IZVJESTAVANJE%20 O%20%20NASILJU%20U%20OBITELJI.pdf [in Croatian only] [12.09.2019].

Ministry of Demographics, Family, Youth and Social Policy (2017): Nacionalna strategija zaštite od nasilja u obitelji za razdoblje od 2017. do 2022. Godine [National Strategy for the protection against domestic violence for the period from 2017 to 2022]; https://mdom sp.gov.hr/UserDocsImages//Vijesti2017//Nacionalna%20strategija%20zastite%20od%20 nasilja%20u%20obitelji%20za%20razdoblje%20do%202017.%20do%202022.%20go dine.pdf [in Croatian only] [12.09.2019].

Ministry of Justice of the Republic of Croatia (2019a): Podrška žrtvama i svjedocima [Support for victims and witnesses]; https://pravosudje.gov.hr/o-ministarstvu/djelokrug-6366/ iz-pravosudnog-sustava-6372/podrska-zrtvama-i-svjedocima/6156 [in Croatian only] [12. 09.2019].

Ministry of Justice of the Republic of Croatia (2019b): Sudovi [Courts]; https://pravosud je.gov.hr/pravosudni-sustav-11207/sudovi/pravosudna-podrucja-opcinskih-zupani jskih-i-prekrsajnih-sudova/11724 [in Croatian only] [12.09.2019].

Ministry of the Interior (2019): Statistički pregled temeljnih sigurnosnih pokazatelja i rezultata rada u 2018. godini [Statistical review of basic safety indicators and performance in 2018]. Zagreb; 2017: http://stari.mup.hr/UserDocsImages/statistika/2018/Statisticki%20 pregled_2017.pdf [in Croatian only] [13.09.2019].

Ministry of the Interior (2018): Statistički pregled temeljnih sigurnosnih pokazatelja i rezultata rada u 2017. godini [Statistical review of basic safety indicators and performance in 2017]. Zagreb; 2017: 2016:http://stari.mup.hr/UserDocsImages/statistika/2016/Pre gled%20sigurnosnih%20pokazatelja%20u%202016.%20godini.pdf [in Croatian only] [13.09.2019].

Ministry of the Interior (2017): Statistički pregled temeljnih sigurnosnih pokazatelja i rezultata rada u 2016. godini [Statistical review of basic safety indicators and performance in 2016]. Zagreb; 2017: 2015:https://www.mup.hr/public/documents/Statistika/Pregl ed %20 sigurnosnih%20pokazatelja%20u%202015.%20godini.pdf [in Croatian only] [13.09.2019].

Ministry of the Interior (2016): Statistički pregled temeljnih sigurnosnih pokazatelja i rezultata rada u 2015. godini [Statistical review of basic safety indicators and performance in 2015]. Zagreb; 2014:https://www.mup.hr/UserDocsImages/statistika/2015/Statisticki_ pregled_2014.pdf [in Croatian only] [13.09.2019].

Ministry of the Interior (2015): Statistički pregled temeljnih sigurnosnih pokazatelja i rezultata rada u 2014. godini [Statistical review of basic safety indicators and performance in 2014]. Zagreb; 2013: https://www.mup.hr/UserDocsImages/statistika/2014/Statisticki%20pregled2013.pdf [in Croatian only] [13.09.2019].

Ministry of the Interior (2014): Statistički pregled temeljnih sigurnosnih pokazatelja i rezultata rada u 2013. godini [Statistical review of basic safety indicators and performance in 2013]. Zagreb; 2012: https://www.mup.hr/UserDocsImages/statistika/2013/statistika_2012_3.pdf [in Croatian only] [13.09.2019].

Ministry of the Interior (2013): Statistički pregled temeljnih sigurnosnih pokazatelja i rezultata rada u 2012. godini [Statistical review of basic safety indicators and performance in 2012]. Zagreb; 2011: https://www.mup.hr/UserDocsImages/statistika/2012/pregled%20 2011.pdf [in Croatian only] [13.09.2019].

Ministry of the Interior (2012): Statistički pregled temeljnih sigurnosnih pokazatelja i rezultata rada u 2011. godini [Statistical review of basic safety indicators and performance in 2011]. Zagreb; 2010: https://www.mup.hr/UserDocsImages/statistika/2011/statistika2010.pdf [in Croatian only] [13.09.2019].

Ministry of the Interior (2011): Statistički pregled temeljnih sigurnosnih pokazatelja i rezultata rada u 2010. godini [Statistical review of basic safety indicators and performance in 2010]. Zagreb; https://mup.gov.hr/UserDocsImages/statistika/2011/statistika2010.pdf [in Croatian only] [13.09.2019].

Northeastern University (2019): International Self-Report Delinquency Study – Croatia; https://web.northeastern.edu/isrd/croatia/ [in English only] [12.09.2019].

Ombudsperson for Children (2019a): Protokoli postupanja u zaštiti djece [Child protection treatment protocols]; http://dijete.hr/en/dokumenti/domaci-propisi/protokoli-postupanja-u-zastiti-djece/# [in Croatian only] [12.09.2019].

Ombudsperson for Children (2019b): Reports of the Ombudsperson for children; http://dijete.hr/en/reports-of-the-ombudsperson-for-children/# [in Croatian and English] [12.09.2019].

United Nations Development Programme (2013): Assessment of the number of sexual violence victims during the Homeland War on the territory of the Republic of Croatia and optimal forms of compensation and support to victims. Zagreb; https://www.undp.org/content/dam/croatia/docs/Research%20and%20publications/socialinclusion/UNDP-HR-SEXUAL%20-VIOLENCE%20-IN%20-CONFLICT-RESEARCH-ENG-2014.pdf [in English only] [12.09.2019].

United Nations Office on Drugs and Crime (2010): Development of monitoring instruments for judicial and law enforcement institutions in the Western Balkans 2009–2011; https://www.bib.irb.hr/513417 [in Croatian and English] [12.09.2019].

United Nations Office on Drugs and Crime (2008): Crime and its impact on the Balkans and affected countries; https://www.unodc.org/documents/Balkan_study.pdf [in English only] [12.09.2019].

V-START (2018): Sustav podrške žrtvama zločina u Hrvatskoj [Report V-start on victims of hate crimes in Croatia]; http://www.vstart.eu/wp-content/uploads/2018/11/Sustav-podrs%CC%8Cke-z%CC%8Crtvama-zloc%CC%8Cina-iz-mrz%CC%8Cnje-u-Hrvatskoj_launching.docx.pdf [in Croatian and English] [12.09.2019].

Violence Research Lab (2019): About us; https://www.violence-lab.eu/ [in English only] [12.09.2019].

World Economic Forum (2017): The Global Competitiveness Report 2017–2018. Geneva; http://www3.weforum.org/docs/GCR2017-2018/05FullReport/TheGlobalCompetitivenessReport2017%E2%80%932018.pdf [in English only] [12.09.2019].

World Society of Victimology (2019a): Europe – Dubrovnik, Croatia; http://www.worldsocietyofvictimology.org/wsv-events/victimology-courses/europe-dubrovnik-croatia/ [in English only] [12.09.2019].

World Society of Victimology (2019b): History and overview; http://www.worldsocietyofvictimology.org/about-us/history-and-overview/ [in English only] [12.09.2019].

World Society of Victimology (2019c): WSV awards and honors list; http://www.worldsocietyofvictimology.org/about-us/wsv-honors-list/ [in English only] [12.09.2019].

Hungary

Victimisation and Victim-Related Questions of Restorative Justice

Andrea Tünde Barabás

1. Introduction

In the 21st century, with the exhaustion of priority attention by criminal policy for perpetrators, legislators as well as practitioners and organisations that are dedicated to the prevention and prosecution of crime are turning their focus toward the direct subject of criminal acts, acknowledging numerous rights and strengthening the position of victims.

The development of the science of victimology into a genuine discipline, the fading of hopes related to the attempts of improving the behaviour change of perpetrators, the need for the acceleration and simplification of the criminal proceedings, the appearance of the managerial approach in science and legal practice clearly led to the "rediscovery" of the role of the victim. This was coupled with tendencies that placed the process of and reasons for becoming a victim, as well as other related subject matters such as latency, secondary and tertiary victimisation, the sense of security after becoming a victim and compensation, at the centre of research. The issue of fair treatment and compensation of victims has received greater emphasis in international documents and, as a result, in the various national justice systems.[1]

The aims of this paper are to outline the situation of victims of crime and their treatment in Hungary, to explain the Hungarian legislation on victim-protection, victims' rights and state compensation, as well as the opportunities for, and regulation of, restorative justice. In the introduction, the study concentrates on the main results of

---

1 Directive 2012/29/EU of the European Parliament and of the Council of 25 October 2012 Establishing Minimum Standards on the Rights, Support and Protection of Victims of Crime, and Replacing Council Framework Decision 2001/220/JHA, Directive No. 2012/29/EU, 14.11.2012, Official Journal of the European Union 315/57; https://eur-lex.europa.eu/legal-content/EN/TXT/PDF/?uri=CELEX:32012L0029&from=en [09.09.2019].

the victims surveys carried out by the National Institute of Criminology (hereinafter OKRI), led by the author of this chapter. It also gives an overview of the different circumstances and reasons for why criminal acts stay in latency, which phenomena, according to the research studies, are similar to international trends: victimisation is of a much greater extent than is indicated in the official statistics in Hungary.

Related to the question of victims' rights and compensation, the second part of the study presents the most important regulatory steps towards the implementation of restorative justice methods and the current situation in Hungary. It also introduces two important pilot projects which aim to improve the position of victims in reaching reconciliation and the extension of restorative justice tools related to the reconciliation between criminal victims and offenders in Hungary: the MEREPS (Mediation and Restorative Justice in Prison Settings) and the Peacemaking Circle project.

2. The Situation of Victimisation and Victim Protection in Hungary

2.1 Current Stage of Victim Protection Instruments

In Hungary, intensive efforts started as early as the 1990s to reform the role of the victim in the criminal procedure. The reform was initiated under pressure of substantial changes in criminality which was partly the consequence of the regime change. There were several novelties, such as a rapid increase in criminal activity and a change in its structure, increasing recidivism and undetected crime; while international requirements and conventions on victims' rights also called for change.

In the late 1990s, a system of national institutions was established to provide information and support for victims. The Victim Support Services were created as part of the Office of Justice within the Ministry of Justice, and later, in 2007, a mediation department was also integrated into the Office. After many changes, from the 1st of January 2017, the central management of victim support belongs to the Ministry of Justice, and the Victim Support Services work within the framework of the government agencies. With regards to victim protection, in accordance with international documents, the emphasis was shifted towards information (i.e., providing information on the offender's release and on compensation, healthcare and social issues) and on the state compensation.[2] The applicable Act[3] has been in effect since 2005 and it states that the work of the Victim Support Services should provide sup-

---

2 Government Resolution No. 1074/1999 on the legislative tasks and other measures to be taken in the interest of the protection of victims of crimes and their relatives and on the compensation and relief of damage, Resolution No. 1074/1999, 01.01.1999, Official Gazette 1074/1999.

3 Act CXXXV of 2005 on Crime Victim Support and State Compensation, Law No. CXXXV, 04.09.2009, Official Gazette CXXXV/2005.

port in the following areas: promotion of interests, immediate financial assistance, proof of victim status, support of witnesses, provision of protected shelter and state compensation (partial) for the victims of serious violent crimes. According to the regulation, the followings options are available in the field of the means of promotion of interest: information, legal advice, emotional support and other assistance. Pursuant to the 1999 Government Resolution, a national network of rapporteurs for victim-protection was established within the police. The rapporteurs are responsible for cooperating with the police units carrying out investigations, inquiries and other activities and also for referring victims to the Victim Support Services.[4] NGOs, established before the system of government institutions, are active in the field of psychological and other non-financial assistance but cover a much smaller area and typically focus on specialized victim support groups, for example, the White Ring Public Benefit Association or the ESZTER Foundation[5], which provides support for victims of sexual crimes, or NANE Association[6], which supports the victims of domestic violence.[7]

The recognition of the necessity for victim-protection and efforts to reinforce victims' rights have intensified the need to enable victims to play a more active role in the procedure and decide about their own needs. One of the most important means of doing so was to enable restorative methods by introducing mediation in 2006.

2.2 Overview of Victimisation – Victim Surveys in Hungary

In order to find out more about victimisation, we must start from the official statistics. These are constantly updated and contain all official data relating to victimisation. In Hungary, the most comprehensive official statistical data in respect of the victims of crimes are included in the annual police statistics, providing information on the known victims of the most significant reported crimes. These statistics are useful but reflect reality in a limited way. The reason for that is that the data on the victims of crime are recorded at the end of the investigation, so the registers do not contain any later changes in the course of the criminal proceedings. It will not be shown in the statistics if, for example, the court proceedings later establish that no criminal act occurred, which means that there can be no victim in the case in the legal sense; or if the court qualifies the act as something other than as specified in the charge. Despite all these deficiencies, the victims' statistics are necessary and useful. The victims'

---

4 See Resolution No. 1074/1999.

5 Eszter Foundation for the Rehabilitation of Sexual Violence.

6 NANE – Association Women for Women Together Against Violence.

7 Fehér Gyűrű 2019; NANE Segélyvonal 2019.

data are collected by a separate publication, and as a result, it has become possible to map the trends and circumstances of victimisation.[8]

The authorities, however, do not have knowledge of all victims but only of those who are involved in the criminal justice process. This is not sufficient for the development of a successful model for prevention, as more information is needed for that, not only regarding the declared victims during a legal procedure but also regarding those who are endangered and victims unknown to the authorities. As the UN pointed out in the Vienna Declaration of 2000,[9] when formulating a valid crime prevention model, reliance on police records is not sufficient, but the actual number and characteristics of victims should also be known.

The criminal cases registered in the statistics – for the reasons described above – do not cover all the acts actually committed and suffered at a given place and time, therefore not including the number of victims either. The phenomenon of latency is scientifically accepted in criminology: it is well-known that a certain part of criminal acts are never discovered and they never become known by the authorities.[10] According to some estimates, these "dark numbers" are at least twice or even four or five times (and according to other sources, ten times) more than the registered crimes.[11] In the absence of data, we can only learn more about the cases that are not available in the statistics through empirical examination.

Besides administrative problems, the fact that cases remain hidden is mainly related to the public's willingness to report crimes, as criminal acts are mostly discovered on the basis of the reports made by the people. This means that latency basically lies in the fact that citizens for some reason fail to report the crimes to the authorities.[12] Several circumstances may play a role in this; e.g., the person concerned may have had a previous bad experience in respect of the proceedings of the authority, either first-hand or through his/her immediate environment. Therefore the victim comes to the conclusion that it is not worth reporting the crime, either because s/he was treated unfairly or because the perpetrator will not be arrested anyhow (loss of trust). The cause may simply be fear (of the authority or of the perpetrator), physical (violence) or psychological (shame, blackmail) barriers, the relatively small value of the

8 *Barabás* 2004.

9 Vienna Declaration on Crime and Justice: Meeting the Challenges of the Twenty-first Century, Declaration No. A/conf.187/4/Rev.3, 15.04.2000; https://www.un.org/ruleoflaw/blog/document/vienna-declaration-on-crime-and-justice-meeting-the-challenges-of-the-twenty-first-century/ [08.10.2019] [in English only].

10 *Korinek* 1988, pp. 12–18.

11 *Penney* 2014.

12 *Korinek* 1988, p. 24.

damage suffered, or the fact that the perpetrator is a relative or an acquaintance.[13] Consequently, personal decision is the most important factor with respect to latency. Besides this, the authorities' so-called "selective" practice, i.e., the authorities' refusal to record the report of the crime, may also be an explanation why cases remain hidden. This may be a result of the pressure to be successful in statistical terms as the main indicator of the effectiveness of the police's work is the proportion of solved cases; therefore the police tries to select the cases as early as they can, even the phase of reporting.[14] As the role of victims came to the fore, ground was gained by efforts which – in addition to understanding the causes and process of victimisation – intended to explore issues that had been neglected until then, such as latency, secondary or tertiary victimisation,[15] the possibility of compensation and the sense of security/the fear of crime.

2.2.1 The Early Years

The wide international perspective and the foreign recognition of Hungarian scholars in criminology is proved by the fact that there was a substantial amount of victimisation research as early as the eighties, though Hungary's participation was not untroubled in international life at that time because of the political regime. Perhaps partly as a result of it, neither the political leadership nor the justice system were able to make use of the correlations and conclusions revealed by the victimisation research.[16] Following the change of the political system, the number of empirical studies continued to increase, and these researches mostly focused on a certain segment of victimisation (e.g., domestic violence, housebreaking, rape, etc.).

In Hungary, the first survey concerning victimisation was carried out by *László Korinek* in Baranya county in 1982.[17] In this study, in addition to examining the proportion of latent offences, he investigated the population's sense of security and their opinion about the criminal investigation authorities and judicial agencies. This survey, which can be regarded as a trail-blazer in terms of methodology, was the first in Hungary to give an account of criminal acts that remained hidden.

---

13 *Barabás* 2004; *Korinek* 1988. The International Crime Victims Survey (ICVS) has found very similar results, see *van Dijk, Kesteren & Smit* 2007, pp. 112–113.

14 If the case seems to be impossible to unravel at the very beginning, then the authorities may advise the complainant to abstain from reporting the crime. Of course, we cannot talk of a deliberate strategy in this instance; on the contrary, it happens as an autonomous mechanism of the organisation and the realisation of self-defensive considerations, see *Korinek* 1996.

15 *Fattah* 1991.

16 *Lévay* 2006, p. 175.

17 *Korinek* 1988.

In the period between autumn 1999 and summer 2000, the Central Statistical Office (Központi Statisztikai Hivatal; hereinafter KSH) collected data relating to the life-style of the population and a block of questions related to victimisation was included within the framework of the so-called "Lifestyle time-balance" (Életmód-időmérleg) survey. The researchers at National Institute of Criminology (Országos Kriminológiai Intézet; hereinafter OKRI) provided professional assistance for the evaluation of the obtained survey-responses. The large-sample survey dealt with the fundamental issues of victimisation in an investigatory manner, considering the preceding five years, and covering the personal circumstances and physical location of victims, the elements of their sense of security and, in connection with the reporting of crimes, with latency too. Based on the research, it was proved again that a significant number of violations of the law remain latent. Although no exact results could be established, it seemed certain that at least a third of all the acts mentioned did not become known to the authorities.[18]

Under *Korinek*'s leadership, Hungary participated in the first round of The International Crime Victims Survey (ICVS) conducted simultaneously in the Federal Republic of Germany and the USA in 1989.[19] In addition to this, the UN conducted ICVSs that included Budapest twice in the same decade; these surveys were overseen by *Imre Kertész* on the Hungarian side. The examinations were organised by the United Nations Interregional Crime and Justice Institute (hereinafter UNICRI) and dealt with the issues of victimisation among the population considering the preceding five years. While during the first survey in 1995, 25% of the questioned indicated that they had become victims of a crime, 32% did so in the second one in 1999. The percentage of reporting was 47% on the average, which means that, according to the respondents, more than half of the cases were not reported to the police.[20]

These examinations confirmed the assumption that the number of registered criminal acts/victims and the acts suffered do not correspond to each other in reality. This means that the proportion of latent cases is significant in a certain sphere of crimes (e.g., damaging motor vehicles, sexual crimes, theft of personal property), whereas in other types of acts (e.g., motor vehicle thefts) there was no significant difference between the Uniform Statistical Database of the Police and Prosecution (ERÜBS)[21] and the survey data. Besides exploring the rate and causes of latency, the research studies dealt with several other issues related to victimisation – for example, the fear of crime, general opinion on the work carried out by the authorities, compensation, attitudes to punishment and prevention.

---

18 *Barabás* 2009a.

19 *Arnold & Korinek* 1989.

20 *Kertész* 2001; *Zvekic & Kerész* 2000.

21 Prosecutor's Office of Hungary 2019.

After the turn of the millennium, there were several large-scale surveys conducted by the OKRI dealing with victimisation and related issues: latency, fear of crime, sense of insecurity, communal and situational crime prevention and restorative justice. Each survey was supported by funds from grants (e.g., EU subsidies). Until now, no comprehensive victim survey has been conducted with state financing.

2.2.2 Victims and Opinions – The First "Victim Survey" in Hungary[22]

In 2002 and the first half of 2003, the first survey that can be regarded as a"victim survey" carried out in Hungary was led by the OKRI.[23] It examined the characteristics of victimisation in Hungary through interviewing 10,000 people. This victimological survey offers a unique chance for researchers to gather information according to the type the characteristics of victims, the frequency of victimisation, the emotions and fears of the victims and what happened in their lives after the crime. Since then, there have been no examinations of similar scope in Hungary that explored this problem in such depth, from so many aspects and on such a massive sample.

One of the goals was to determine how many people are victimised annually in Hungary and how many cases are not reported to the police and for what reasons. Based on the results of international and Hungarian researches, we had reasons to suppose that this figure is much higher than the ones in the official statistics. The researchers asked detailed questions exploring the more recent cases, i.e., those closest to the time of the interview (the past twelve months). The methodological reason for this was partly that they took into account the peculiarity of human memory, which may impair the accurate recollection of distant events, thereby also corrupting the results of the survey.

During the examination of latency, the first thing that became clear was that the number of criminal acts not coming to light was in fact extremely large in Hungary. In respect of the last year (2002), only 739 crimes were reported out of 2,276 according to the statements (approximately 32%).[24]

Researchers examined if there is a correlation between the willingness to report and the type of the crime, the gender of the victims and their ages. No such connection was found either among people who were victimised only once or among those who were victimised more times. Thus, there were no significant differences between those who report and those who do not the incidents concerning their ages. It is worth noting that the willingness to report crimes appears to be higher in the

---

22 Supported by the Hungarian Széchenyi Project.

23 For more information about the results, see *Irk* 2004.

24 *Barabás* 2004.

age group of 45 to 60 and lower in the age group 26 to 35. There was no difference between men and women.[25]

The presumption that people mainly fail to report petty cases also proved to be true. The statement was right for those cases where the extent of the disadvantage stemming from the crime-reporting significantly exceeds the advantages of the police procedure. On the other hand, in those cases where reporting the crime should lead to a certain event (for example, to the payment of the insurance company in case of car theft), the rate of reporting is rather high. It was also asked why the victims failed to report the given act. The most frequent answer was the distrust of and discontent with the police (43%) followed by the answers mentioning “little damage” or “no damage” (28%).[26]

The victims’ sense of security seemed worse than that of those who did not become victims, just as in previous results. This was apparent from answers given to the questions concerning opinions on the safety of the interviewed persons’ residences as well as from opinion on the extent of crime. It was interesting that, as regards leaving their homes after dark, those who did not become victims were more inclined to choose staying at home than those who have already become victims previously. The explanation for this can be that the victims are more used to accepting the thought of crime but it can also be explained by the fact that they happen to belong to the younger generation and would go out in the evenings more often anyway. Examining anxieties, most of those who did not become victims were not particularly influenced by crime, while this proportion was also worse among victims. On the other hand, it is also clear that, in case of, for example, ‘thinking about the possibility of violence in the street’, those who have already been assaulted are more prone to imagine another assault (35% of victims think it is possible in general, compared with 50% of those who have been assaulted). However, respondents consider the situation even worse in the sphere of housebreakings, when even those who did not become victims previously truly fear suffering such a crime, presumably on the basis of what they have experienced in their environment.[27]

2.2.3 “Insecurities in European Cities” – Sense of Insecurity in the Cities of Europe

The international research titled “Insecurities in European Cities”(hereinafter InSec) took place under the aegis of OKRI during the period 2001 and 2004. The survey examined the opinion of people concerning crime, victimisation, the fear of crime, the defence strategy and punishment in two districts of five European cities (Amster-

25 *Barabás* 2009a.

26 *Barabás* 2004.

27 *Barabás* 2004.

dam, Hamburg, Vienna, Cracow and Budapest).[28] The international team then had the opportunity to compare the results of the five cities.[29]

In Hungary, two districts of the capital with different local conditions were chosen and altogether 1,000 adult residents were interviewed in these two locations. The sample of five hundred persons in each district was selected and the sample was representative according to the age and sex of the adult population living there. The characteristics of the examined areas differed significantly from each other in respect of their physical parameters and their location within the city, as well as their criminal data and the local efforts of crime prevention. According to these aspects, we distinguished a more prosperous and a relatively poorer district (the latter being more infected with crime). Just as was shown in the criminal statistics, there is a significant difference between the experiences of the residents of the two districts concerning victimisation. During the survey conducted by means of questionnaires, 50% more of those living in the "worse" district claimed to have suffered a criminal act than those from the better district. According to the results of the survey, the injured usually fall victim in the immediate surroundings of their homes (61%). Evidently, the victims suffered the burglaries in their own flats, but motor vehicle thefts and such typical street crimes as pickpocketing or robbery also happened close to the victims' homes, most often in the street where they lived.[30]

It turned out during the survey that the extent of crime and that of the fear of crime did not overlap at all.[31] This is clearly shown by the results of the survey, namely the volume of fear of crime was lower in the worse positioned district, in which permanently and strongly infected in terms of crime than in the so-called better higher positioned district, which was only recently integrated into the capital, and the level of crime was significantly lower than the other location. However, it must be admitted that the crime numbers were changing fast here as well. The response of those living in the more dangerous district to the question: "How often do you leave your home after dark?" indicated a greater frequency than that of those from the safer district. Since the indicators of criminal acts were clearly worse in the less well-to-do district, its residents are either braver than those from the better situated one, or they are aware of the fact that the majority of criminal acts are typically not committed at night.[32]

Related to the willingness to punish, the respondents were asked within the sphere of violent acts. The incidence of these acts is relatively low (7–8%) within the

---

28 European Commission 2004.

29 *Barabás, Irk & Kovács* 2005.

30 European Commission 2004.

31 *Wynne* 2008.

32 European Commission 2004.

totality of crimes in contrast with the incidence of crimes against property (about 70% at the time of questioning). However, similarly to international trends, the number of violent cases suddenly started to increase in Hungary around 2004, 2005. This is especially conspicuous when compared to the generally falling crime trends. The specific question examined the respondents' opinions on whether there was a need for more severe punishments in order to prevent violent crimes.[33]

The proportion of the answers given to this question show that Hungarian respondents do distinguish themselves by being either too strict or too liberal, although they seemed rather less rigorous. 47% of respondents did not think that the use of more severe punishment as a means of prevention was appropriate, while the types of answers "I think it is by and large or perfectly appropriate" represented a proportion of 39%. Comparing the proportions of those who wanted stricter punishments for violent crimes in the five countries, we get an interesting outcome: the more severe punishments were the least approved of by Hungarians (the percentage of those fully approving of them was 22%). In comparison, the strongest willingness to punish could be seen among the respondents from Cracow, 76% of whom fully agreed with using more severe punishments, whereas the proportion of the respondents from Amsterdam was 49%, that of the Viennese was 50% and that of the respondents from Hamburg was 57%.[34]

2.2.4 "Crime Prevention Carousel"

The purpose of the AGIS[35] project Crime Prevention Carousel (2005–2007; coordinated by the Max Planck Institute for Foreign and International Criminal Law) was to examine the issues of the built environment, victimisation and fear of crime and in respect of these issues, of situational crime prevention too. The members of the international team (British, Dutch, German, Polish and Hungarian experts) paid particular attention to the investigation of the crime and victimisation prevention effects of town rehabilitation projects, aiming at the renewal of the built environment.[36]

Altogether 1,500 residents were visited in the given areas in Hungary. Of these, 342 answered affirmatively to the question concerning possible victimisation during the preceding three years. 12% of the respondents marked that they had been victims once, while the others claimed that they had become victims twice or more. The

---

33 European Commission 2004.

34 *Sessar, Herrmann, Keller, Martin & Breckner* 2007, pp. 44–105.

35 AGIS was a EU funding programme for scientific research.

36 *Lukas* 2007; for the Hungarian national project report, see Országos Kriminológiai Intézet 2006.

residents were mainly afraid in deserted and dark places (e.g., subways, pubs and the area around the market) in the housing estate.[37]

Just as in the previous survey, it turned out that women were represented in a larger proportion among victims than in the official statistics. The survey entitled "Victims and Opinions" showed similar results in respect of the proportion of the sex. Typically, more women mentioned damage against the property of great value such as car theft or burglary, whilst men were more prone to call back memories on bicycle theft and car break-ins.[38]

Reports to the police were made by approximately 50% of the interviewed men and 71% of the women who were asked. This may be related to the fact that they talked about greater damage, probably covered by an insurance company. There were no differences with regards to trust, bad experience and other causes between the sexes and the different age groups, and the respondents also mentioned experiencing damage in a similar proportion. The answers showed that women's sense of security decreases much more after the crime, as more than 50% of women felt they were in danger following the crime, only 30% of men felt the same.[39]

One of the most important results of the survey was the fact that 42% of victims had not reported the case to the police, although this was not surprising on the basis of the earlier observations. According to the responses, the most frequent reason for this (in more than half of the cases) was that "they did not believe that the perpetrator would be captured". In addition to this, many respondents mentioned the bad experience they or their family members had had in the course of previous procedures; that they had had no time to deal with the case; or that there had been only little or no damage. Four percent of those who failed to report the case had settled it among themselves, which means, they applied some kind of "domestic" conflict resolution. Only 10% of those reporting (197) knew that the perpetrator was later arrested, and only 12 persons declared that they had knowledge of the further course of the procedure (5 mentioned that the perpetrator had been found guilty). This experience obviously does not increase the victims' willingness to report crime.[40]

2.2.5 Victim's Reconciliation – Perpetrator's Accountability

Within the framework of the research entitled: The opinion of the residents of Budapest on crime and restorative justice,[41] in 2011, OKRI researchers carried out a

---

37 *Barabás & Windt* 2007.

38 *Barabás* 2009a.

39 *Barabás* 2004.

40 *Barabás* 2004.

41 The residential survey entitled: The Opinion of the Residents of Budapest on Crime and Restorative Justice was conducted within the framework of the international research

survey of a sample of 500 adults from Budapest, which consisted of questions concerning crime, punishment, victimisation and restorative justice. The survey – which could be regarded as representative in respect of sex and age – helped confirm the majority of the earlier research results, although the study relied on a relatively small sample.

As regards victimisation, the results of the previous surveys were confirmed. Contrary to the 2% victimisation rate shown in the official statistics, approx. one fifth (20%) of the respondents said that they had suffered a criminal act during the year preceding the questioning, with altogether 50 respondents mentioning more than one crime. The 152 respondents who became victims suffered a total of 259 criminal acts in the year before the questioning; 99 persons suffered only one act. This rate shows a ten times bigger victimisation rate than the official rate. Looking back on their lives, only 37% of those interviewed reported that they had never been a victim before.[42]

Regarding the criminal acts suffered in the previous year, reports were made in just a bit more than half of the cases (52%). The respondents preferred not to report the cases such as theft, robbery, damage to property, bodily harm, vandalism or domestic violence, whereas they did go to the police to report the crime in the case of harassment, a car break-in, car theft, burglary or abuse of data (mainly because of the insurance). This result confirmed the observations that latency differs according to the type of criminal act. Thus, in cases of minor importance, when reporting would only mean an additional burden for the victim, or in cases when the victim is defenceless or afraid of the perpetrator, ashamed or blames himself/herself (e.g., the cases of domestic violence or sexual assault), latency is significant. On the other hand, the low willingness to report crimes did not show any relation with the sex and age of the respondent.[43]

According to the results, those who have become victims at a certain point of their lives, regard their living area as much less safe. This is obviously related to their bad frame of mind arising from victimisation. However, it should also be remembered that the most frequent answers were burglaries, car thefts and thefts from cars and these acts are often connected to peoples' places of residence, therefore making this connection a rational one.[44]

Mediation and Restorative Practice in Prison Settings, with the financial support of the European Codmmission's Criminal Justice Programme (JLS/2008/JPEN015-30-CE-0245615/00-52), see *Barabás* 2009b.

42 *Barabás* 2012.

43 *Barabás* 2015.

44 *Barabás & Windt* 2009, pp. 12–15.

In addition to this, 246 of the 500 respondents – that is, nearly half of the respondents – thought that they could be assaulted in the street near their flats (136 women and 110 men). This fear – which can be regarded as irrational, since it proved to be independent of the place of respondents' residence – can be attributed to the result of the media propaganda suggesting an increase in violence rather than to another rational cause (other rational factors are for example the following: sex, age, previous victimisation, and crime that could not be resolved).[45]

We discovered that the population (within this the residents of the capital) do not see crime in its true colours and that they misjudge its trends for various reasons. There are several circumstances that can play a role in this; sex, age or previous victimisation may have a significant influence. Only 3% of those questioned guessed roughly the number of registered criminal acts in the previous year, 55% greatly underestimated it, and a third more or less overestimated it.[46]

2.2.6 Tackle Insecurity in Marginalized Areas

MARGIN,[47] which stands for "Tackle Insecurity in Marginalized Areas", has received funding from the European Union Horizon 2020 Programme. The project, which started in 2015 and ended in 2017, provided policymakers with evidence-based tools for developing and assessing strategies targeted at the reduction of insecurity among different demographic and socioeconomic groups. It aimed to create sustainable modes of cooperation between stakeholders dealing with security issues, and in order to reach this general objective it sets up an international environment for knowledge exchange involving some of the leading EU institutions in Crime Victimisation Surveys (CVSs). To achieve this general objective, the project had been designed to establish an international environment for knowledge exchange that enables the identification and analysis of factors influencing public and personal perceptions of (in)security.

One of the main questions of the project was to seek the relationship between lifestyle, routine activities and feeling unsafe, which has received great attention in criminal victimisation studies. Scholars generally agreed that an individual's lifestyle is a critical factor associated with the perception of risk. Criminologists have identified three elements that in convergence increase the likelihood of being vic-

---

45 *Barabás* 2015.

46 *Barabás* 2015.

47 The project searched for the root causes of insecurity in Europe in cooperation with the 6 partners: Universitat de Barcelona (UB) – National Institute of Criminology (OKRI) – Institut national des hautes études de la sécurité et de la justice (INHESJ) – Università degli Studi di Milano Bicocca (UNIMIB) – University College London (UCL) – EuroCrime Research Training and Consultancy srl (ECR) – Departament d'Interior, Generalitat de Catalunya (INT), see MARGIN: Tackle Insecurity in Marginalized Areas 2019.

timised: the presence of a motivated offender, an attractive target/victim, and the absence of capable guardianship.[48]

Identifying behaviours that may generate an increased unsafe feeling among citizens was one of the issues that in the expectations would have marked a difference between the MARGIN project and previous research. Accordingly, one of the fundamental objectives of the fieldwork was to explore the relationship between people's lifestyle and their perception of insecurity bearing in mind that this relationship is always bidirectional: engaging in risky behaviours may expose people to unsafe situations and, in turn, experiencing victimisation and/or episodes that make people feel unsafe may push them to avoid some types of behaviours in the future. With these premises, the analysis of the relationship between lifestyle and insecurity suddenly appeared as strongly related to people's perception of social disorder and their understanding of which behaviours are acceptable in public spaces or which ones are not.[49]

The project focused on the four dimensions of insecurity: the objective dimension (victimisation); the subjective dimension (fear of crime); the socio-economic dimension (social vulnerability); and the socio-geographic dimension (neighbourhood effect). In two selected neighbourhoods of each city (Barcelona, London, Milan, Paris and Budapest) we implemented quantitative (data analysis and survey) and qualitative (in-depth interview, participant observation, focus group) research methods. Based on an in-depth review of five CVS at the EU level,[50] a panel of 12 international experts on the topic of insecurity assessment had been involved in an iterative design process in order to define a number of indicators enabling the assessment of insecurity among different social groups.[51]

---

48 *Valente* 2017; On the other hand, if the link between lifestyle and victimisation has received great attention in the criminological literature the relationship between daily activities and people's perception of insecurity (including, but not limited to, fear of being victimised) has been less explored. As a matter of fact, people may feel unsafe even without experiencing any form of victimisation, which is actually quite uncommon in the area analysed during our field work.

49 Additional information available online at http://marginproject.eu.

50 The following surveys were considered: Cadre de vie et sécurité (France), Crime Survey for England and Wales (UK), Encuesta de Seguridad Pública de Cataluña (Spain), Sicurezza dei cittadini (Italy) and Victims and Opinion Research (Hungary), see MARGIN: Tackle Insecurity in Marginalized Areas 2019.

51 The main outcome of the Delphi method was the design of the MARGIN Questionnaire on Perception of Insecurity, which is available online in six languages (English, Spanish, Catalan, French, Hungarian and Italian) including a set of items enabling the assessment of how demographic, socio-economic and socio-geographic variables might influence public and personal perceptions of insecurity. Further modules included standardised questions on victimisation and perceptions of insecurity derived from existing CVS, see *Barabás* 1996, pp. 142–157.

The MARGIN Questionnaire on Perception of Insecurity was used to carry out four small-scale surveys in the cities of Barcelona, Budapest, Paris and London with a total sample of 402 respondents. Furthermore, a large-scale survey was also implemented in Italy (15,428 respondents). Italy was chosen for this trial because the use of victimisation surveys had been less common there in the past than in the other five countries involved in the project.[52]

Consistent with previous research, female respondents and the elderly report higher levels of feelings of unsafety compared to their male counterparts. At the same time, respondents displaying high levels of perceived disorder within the neighbourhood tended to show higher levels of subjective insecurity as well. Our analysis revealed the incidence of future-oriented anxieties and self-perceived stigmatisation on people's perception of insecurity. In particular, the findings emerging from the analysis of the survey in Italy support the idea that people's concerns about the deterioration of their health and/or economic situation coupled with the perception of being looked down upon by others due to religious beliefs, sexual orientation or ethnic background may, in turn, increase their feeling of insecurity.[53]

The small-scale survey was carried out in Hungary by using the MARGIN questionnaire on a sample of 115 respondents living in a marginalised area of the capital. The survey in Budapest was carried out from July to September 2016. As regards the question of victimisation, the proportion of hidden cases was lower than in the previous surveys, but the extent of sense of insecurity from other aspects, i.e., the fear of being victimised, showed similar tendencies as earlier. According to the results of the mixed surveys (Delphi) method, socio-economic and socio-geographic factors have a significant impact on the perception of insecurity, as along with the phenomenon of social exclusion and social cohesion or the deprived, marginalised position of the neighbourhoods.[54]

3. The Possibilities of Using Restorative Methods in Hungary

Besides the unfair treatment of the victims, one of the key problems of criminal proceedings is the circuitousness of the justice system in Hungary. The process can drag on from as early as the investigation phase. This is not necessarily justified by the gravity of the cases; sometimes proceedings involve less serious crimes with several perpetrators and/or multiple events (e.g., a series of crimes have been committed), which require a longer time or the prosecution asks for an expert opinion for deciding a certain issue, which can take years to obtain. Final closure of a certain case can also drag on due to the multiple-level proceeding. Hence, the perpetrator can easily

---

52 *Barabás* 2018.

53 *Valente* 2017.

54 *Barabás* 2018.

be on trial for several years after committing the crime and may not even remember exactly what the case was as he may have committed other crimes in the period in between. In addition, the victim's rights, which stand on weak grounds anyway, are clearly violated and she or he may feel victimised again when they have to testify and relive events years after suffering the offence. Endeavours to simplify and hasten proceedings are therefore no coincidence. One such tool today is mediation.

In Hungary, the use of mediation in criminal matters had been debated for over a decade. However, the opinions were divided even among professionals arguing for mediation on whether it should function as part of or outside the criminal procedure. One argument by those opposing mediation was that it was alien to the function and purpose of criminal law and legal practice, to the mindset of the Hungarian population and legal practitioners, or even to the solutions applied by Hungarian legal institutions. If the purpose of punishment is to impose retribution in proportion to the acts committed, then the "exemption" from other sanctions, offered by reconciliation, could by no means be incorporated into penal practice. The idea of a restorative approach prompted doubts on whether the victim or the state had the right to dispense with the procedure in the event of reparation.[55]

Those debates were brought to an end by Act LI of 2006 on the Amendment to the Criminal Procedure Code, adopted in February 2006, virtually at the last minute, as Hungary, following its accession to the EU, was under an obligation to introduce mediation in criminal proceedings pursuant to Article 10 of the Council Framework Decision of 15 March 2001. The Framework Decision set a deadline for compliance with this requirement by 22 March 2006.[56]

3.1 Legal Framework

The changes related to mediation were specified in Act LI of 2006, which amended a number of provisions of both the Criminal Procedure Code and the Criminal Code.[57] Following this, from January 2007 onwards, it was possible for offenders and their victims to reach an agreement within the framework of criminal proceedings.

According to these developments, as a general rule, mediation is available before the court phase and up until the formal accusation if the offender pleads guilty. The mediation procedure may be initiated by the public prosecutor, the parties and their representatives. If the statutory conditions are met, or if the victim and the suspect

---

55 *Barabás* 2015.

56 Amendment to the Criminal Procedure Code, Law. No. LI/2006, 01.07.2006, Official Gazette LI/2006.

57 Act C of 2012 on the Criminal Code, Law No. C/2012, 13.07.2012, Official Gazette C/2012; Act XIX of 1998 on Criminal Proceedings, Law No. XIX/1998, 23.03.1998, Official Gazette XIX/1998.

agree, the prosecutor may suspend the procedure for a maximum of six months to allow the parties to reach and implement their agreement. Mediation remains available if for some reason the possibility of using the mediation procedure only arises during the court phase.[58]

However, statutory restrictions apply to the mediation procedure, which means that it cannot be applied in all cases. This is because active repentance, which is a ground for exemption of culpability (as regulated in Section 29 of the Criminal Code) and the foundation for the application of mediation, can only be applied with regard to misdemeanours against life, physical integrity, health, personal freedom, dignity and certain fundamental rights, and furthermore in cases of traffic misdemeanours, misdemeanours against property or intellectual property and/or of felonies punishable by a maximum of three years of imprisonment. It is a major deficiency of the regulation that mediation cannot be applied in all cases. That is especially unjustified e.g., in the case of violent crime against property (Chapter XXXV of the Criminal Code), or crimes against sexual freedom and sexual offences (Chapter XIX).[59]

Additionally, mediation is excluded in a number of cases, for instance, if the offender is a habitual offender committing a similar crime for the second time or committing a crime more than twice, if the offender commits the crime as a member of a criminal organisation or if the crime results in death.[60]

The new Criminal Code entered into force in 2013, and it extended the scope of application of mediation Now it is possible to take into account subsequently, within the framework of the mediation procedure, any reparations provided by the offender and accepted by the victim before the mediation procedure. It should be noted that reparations are not limited to the reparations of a financial nature. They may include any other activity, including an apology, if the activity is accepted by the victim.[61]

The other key legislation in connection with mediation is Act CXXIII of 2006 on Mediation in Criminal Cases, which regulates the activity of mediators, their duties and other related practical matters. Furthermore, since 1 January 2014, it has been possible to use mediation in cases of petty/administrative offences.[62] However, this may not be consistent with the actual purpose of the legal institution because, with these minor offences that do not even constitute crimes, the victims usually do not suffer severe psychological damage and the offender typically will not be impris-

---

58 See Law No. C/2012; Law No. XIX/1998.

59 See Law No. C/2012; Law No. XIX/1998.

60 See Law No. C/2012.

61 See Law No. C/2012.

62 Act CCXL of 2013 on the Execution of Punishments, Actions, Court-ordered Supervision and Postcharge Non-criminal Detention, Law No. CCXL/2013, 01.01.2013, Official Gazette CCXL/2013.

oned. As a result, the parties find mediation to be a burden in these cases. Finally, according to the new prison law, since 2015 it has also been possible to use mediation in prison settings, but only for conflicts between prisoners in petty (disciplinary) conflicts.[63]

3.2 Research on Restorative Justice

Even before mediation was introduced in practice, a number of research projects were carried out asking sentenced persons and victims about whether mediation could be applied in Hungary.[64] Therefore, these were mainly attitude surveys.

After mediation was introduced, research continued in three directions. First, researchers partly examined the recently launched scheme's efficacy, problems with it and the possibility of correcting any errors. In the OKRI during 2008 and 2009, a focus group project was carried out to examine the lessons of the mediation procedure from the side of the prosecutors' practice.[65] It was during this project that the difficulties contributing to the differences between the counties' practices were identified. It also became evident that any barrier to the application of mediation practically violates the victims' right to be reached restorative justice equally in all regions of the country.

Various Hungarian research projects looked at the population's attitude toward mediation. These showed that, although people do not reject the idea of a settlement, many of them were very uncertain in the first years of practice.[66] According to a study on attitudes towards restorative methods, victims do not refuse to refer to such means. Those who have been victims are willing to confront the offender for various reasons. However, their willingness slowly decreases as time passes from the time of the crime.[67]

Another group of studies, as a second direction, focused on the attitude and satisfaction of the parties involved in mediation. According to a 2007 study, led by the Partners Hungary Foundation, those participants who completed a satisfaction survey were very satisfied because

1) they could participate in the mediation procedure voluntarily;
2) they felt like active participants in the process and were able to influence it;
3) victims had access to reparations acceptable to them more quickly and easily;

---

63 See Law No. CCXL/2013.

64 *Barabás* 1996, pp. 142–157; 2004, pp. 161–201.

65 *Barabás & Windt* 2009.

66 *Barabás* 2007.

67 *Barabás & Windt* 2009.

4) perpetrators had to face the consequences of their actions, had the opportunity to apologise and to provide the reparations they had agreed to;
5) the opportunity to meet the offender allowed victims to process the psychological trauma caused by the crime, and their fear was reduced or disappeared;
6) victims had the opportunity to learn why the crime had been committed, which allowed them to avoid re-victimisation;
7) perpetrators could avoid the continuation of the procedure (and avoided a criminal record) or their sentence might be reduced without any limitation; and
8) on average, the mediation procedure took three months and the criminal procedure could be completed within three months after the mediation.[68]

This means that the engagement of the victim, the ability to make a decision in their own case, the opportunity to answer the victim's questions (e.g., "Why me?", "What could I have done to prevent this?") and the speed of the procedure were all considered as positive results of mediation.

The third direction of research focused on the extension of the mediation practice. As part of these research projects, pilot methods were used to extend the practical application of mediation. These projects included the MEREPS (Mediation and Restorative Justice in Prison Settings) project, implemented as part of the cooperation between OKRI and the Foresee Research Group, and the Peacemaking Circles project, which tested a new model of restorative justice.[69]

The EU-funded Peacemaking Circles pilot project took place between September 2011 and August 2013, through the partnership of three countries (Belgium, Germany and Hungary). In Hungary, four counties were involved.[70] As opposed to mediation, reconciliation circles involve a larger group in the discussion of the conflict. Beyond victims and offenders, circles engage the community affected by the conflict (family, friends, colleagues, schoolmates, the residential environment, the neighbourhood, and, in the case of a crime against community property, the community itself). However, reconciliation circles also attempt to involve the officials in the criminal procedure, i.e., judges, prosecutors, police officers and the representatives of other supporting professions. Although neither of these pilots resulted in the extension of the statutory regulations, their novel approach and successes have contributed to the recognition of the usefulness of restorative methods.

---

68 Partners Hungary Foundation 2008.

69 *Barabás* 2015.

70 Foresee Research Group 2012.

3.2.1 The MEREPS Project

The EU funded the MEREPS project, implemented between 2009 and 2012, through the partnership of four countries (Belgium, Germany, Hungary and the UK). The project focused on how mediation and other restorative practices could be applied in prison settings, with special regard to offenders who committed serious crimes and the victims of such crimes. In addition, it was studied whether these procedures contribute to supporting the prison staff and inmates in the peaceful resolution of their internal conflicts and to the reintegrating of offenders into society after release. The methods of restorative justice were tested in practice in a prison environment in the form of a pilot project. In this way, it was possible to study the effectiveness of these approaches.[71]

This research was based on the duality of the examination of prisoners from both the sociological and the psychological aspect. During the examination in Hungary, three different research methods were employed to investigate the chances of applying restorative techniques, namely in-depth interviews (100), questionnaires (200) and focus group interviews (8). None of these means were able to reveal the innermost thoughts of the respondents or the "truth" itself, but we hoped that, by combining these methods, we could get nearer to the truth, noting, however, that research carried out in prisons was capable of finding out the truth to only a limited degree. Respondents do not always say the truth. This may be caused by their fear of the consequences, by their desire to live up to the questioner's expectations or to impress them. The interviews were significant because, through them, individual opinions could be revealed and a more personal relationship was established between the researcher and the respondent, while the analysis of questionnaires facilitated the in-depth and thorough evaluation of the data. The focus group examination demonstrated the system of collective expectations and the ways and limits of an individual's submission, through interaction between the group members. The premise of the research was that the willingness to repent and to participate in mediation is influenced by the intention to integrate or reintegrate into society: the stronger this urge, the stronger is the readiness to cooperate.[72]

According to the examination, the first and maybe most important condition for the meeting of the prisoner and the victim is the empathic ability of the offender. It is probable that a person with strong empathic abilities will not commit any offences, as he would forecast what the victim would undergo, which would hold him back. In prison, such a level of empathic abilities can be expected of those offenders who are, at least subsequently, able to acknowledge that they caused pain to the victims.

---

[71] *Barabás, Fellegi & Windt* 2012.

[72] *Barabás et al.* 2012.

This acknowledgement helps the offender to experience the victim's pain, the ideal consequence of which is sincere repentance.[73]

The majority of inmates are unable to overcome egocentricity, i.e., they only consider their own interests when thinking and acting. This is illustrated by the fact that many prisoners alleged that they regretted what they had done but they were not sorry for the victim but only for the fact that, as a consequence of their offence, they were sent to prison (next time I'll be "smarter"). Although empathic ability develops in early childhood, it can also be improved later. Compared to the adults, we can mention a much lower level of empathy among juvenile offenders; the victim's feelings did not even come up during the research or if they did indeed, the juveniles did not understand them. Therefore, in their case, we can hardly speak about sincere repentance. Because of this fact, it would be worthwhile to hold training for the prisoners to improve their empathy, as successful participation can prevent the prisoner from committing a crime in the future. It is not by chance that *van Ness* mentions the programmes for improving empathy among restorative training.[74]

Besides empathy, other important factors are the extent to which the individual relates to the community that surrounds him and the values represented by this community (differences may occur in the degree to which a person makes his self-esteem dependent on external valuation). If the community condemns the act in unison and the individual is responsive to the negative opinion of the community members, it is natural that he will feel ashamed of himself. This feeling may be constructive, in which case we call it a "reintegrative shame".[75] The prisoner who is surrounded by a close community, whose external relationships remain active even during his imprisonment, and who is also responsive to the opinion of the community, tends to feel reintegrative shame, which supports the endeavour to resolve the conflict with the victim.

The survey ran into several difficulties with regard to juvenile offenders, where the application of restorative means would be especially important. While they usually spend much less time in prison, this is exactly the period when they become real criminals. As many of them mentioned, a short prison term is enough for them to learn new criminal techniques and become even more aggressive or injured. A new subcultural order, in which violence lends power and independence, develops among juvenile offenders. On the other hand, perpetual uncertainty also appears as deprivation, since the obtained status is not permanent: anyone can be attacked at any time. In such situations, immature personalities who have suffered multiple injuries are virtually unsuited for meeting their previous victim or for understanding the latter's situation without any prior mental support and emotional development.

---

73 *Barabás et al.* 2012.

74 *Van Ness* 2006, pp. 312–323.

75 *Braitwaite* 1989.

The basic idea behind concepts of reconciliation and restoration is that the affected persons are directly entitled to decide how the caused problems can be solved. The majority of imprisoned juvenile offenders is not suitable for this. Due to this very reason, the use of restorative means requires special preparation in their cases. In addition to their psychological and mental development, a change in prison culture, as well as the reinforcement of family ties, is also crucial.[76]

3.2.2 The Potential of Peacemaking Circles – Dealing With Cases Traditionally or by Using the Circle Method

The EU-funded Peacemaking Circles pilot project took place between September 2011 and August 2013, through the partnership of three countries (Belgium, Germany and Hungary). In Hungary, four counties were involved.[77]

The uniqueness of the peacemaking circle as a new restorative method lies in facilitating reconciliation between the parties, ensuring compensation for the victim, as well as promoting the reintegration of the offender. It is particularly distinctive in that it allows the involvement of "victims", interpreted in a broader sense, in the process of justice, thus fostering reconciliation on the community level, the reinforcement of community, as well as the (re)integration of the offender. The main research questions of the project were whether the so-called peacemaking circles method can be implemented into the European continental legal systems, giving the victims, the offenders and the communities a better chance for reconciliation, and to develop good practices in Europe. In the course of the research in Hungary, the advantages/disadvantages of using the peacemaking circle method were examined in four pilot cases. The perpetrators were young adults, minors and children, which highlights how important using the method and involving the community may be with respect to offenders of this age group. The cases included deterioration, theft at a dormitory and battery and depriving a person of personal freedom during a school fight. This project and its results have highlighted the manifold and versatile application of the peacemaking circle, as well as the wide scope of cases where its use may be important for resolving the raw injuries of victims and the local problems of the community beyond interpersonal conflicts.[78]

The question of whether the method could be suitable in the case of more severe crimes and whether "traditional" actors of the justice system (prosecutor, judge, policeman probation officer) could also be involved was raised during the project. However, the role of the actors will change and the role of the mediator/facilitator is becoming more accentuated and active in the circle method than in the traditional

---

76 *Barabás* 2012.

77 Foresee Research Group 2012.

78 Foresee Research Group 2012.

criminal procedure. It seems that the involvement of the representatives of the justice system would be justified if the peacemaking circle method were possible with severe crimes as well. In such cases, the penal procedure could go hand in hand with a community-led process and a joint decision could be made about the appropriate punishment, with the involvement of representatives of the justice system (prosecutor/judge). This is a highly progressive approach, which remains a distant possibility in continental legislations that work on the basis of legality.[79]

The results of the survey also showed a wide range of cases where it might be important to use this method to solve problems, beyond the interpersonal conflicts of the local community. Hungarian legislation prescribes that the only people who can take part in the mediation process are the parties directly involved, two supporters each, and their legal representatives. Therefore, reconciliation is not possible for a wider circle of victims (including family members, relatives, neighbours and community members). It remains unclear if the offenders were able to see any of the pain that they had inflicted, and if those more broadly affected by the act (for instance, youth with a syndrome or the school community) found relief during mediation.[80]

In respect of engaging additional participants, the involvement of judicial representatives in the peacemaking circles is useful but it might seem problematic at the same time, exactly because of the nature and basic principle of the circles (ensuring the principle of equality). The judicial representative who orders such a procedure to take place, who "returns" to his initial role in the penal procedure in case of an unsuccessful process, cannot participate as an equal party. Furthermore, it might be problematic for the judicial representative to discover information in the peacemaking circle about further crimes, in connection with which he is obligated to take action ex officio. Additionally, this type of participation is questionable because involving the judicial representative as an "equal party" strips the representative of the given body of its very function and this might undermine trust in the appropriate functioning of the justice system. For instance, if the perpetrator and the policeman acting in the case get closer to each other during the peacemaking circle, the perpetrator might be unwilling to relinquish this closeness during the next police action, therefore possibly requiring a stronger measure or proving the measures unsuccessful, causing further conflict.[81]

In the course of the pilots' implementation, the peacemaking method, involving the broader community, proved it could be particularly suitable for supporting victims, reintegrating offenders, supporting families, strengthening/renewing the community, handling discrimination, violence and interpersonal conflicts, as well as supporting injured families and communities – tasks that traditional tools/methods are

79 Foresee Research Group 2012.

80 Foresee Research Group 2012.

81 Foresee Research Group 2012.

completely unsuitable for.[82] This is why it would be important to expand the use of the restorative approach and its various methods as widely as possible.

4. Conclusions

Although in Hungary there is no victim survey of the type used in the English-speaking countries, other kinds of victim examinations have long been established. The results of such research studies emphasise that the issues of latency and the sense of fear, security and insecurity must be addressed specifically both among the residents and purposefully among those who are already victims. Similarly to international tendencies, victimisation rates are much higher than indicated in the official statistics in Hungary, because many cases do not reach the authorities.

There are many factors that play a part in the victims' failure to report the acts to the police. One of the most important of these is the distrust in the authorities and scepticism – arising from previous experiences – concerning the success of the procedure or the possibility that the damage suffered will increase exponentially in the official procedure but may not be recovered at the end of the same. It was also established that Hungarians (at least those living in the surveyed areas) are more prone to punishing crimes than the citizens of other European countries. On the contrary, they seem to be more tolerant, and they do not wish to pursue the fight against violent crime through more severe punishments. The fear-paradox is also true for the Hungarian case: Hungarian citizens are mostly not afraid of those acts that have the greatest probability of occurrence, not even those to whom these could actually happen – at least according to the statistics.

At the same time, we have to face the fact that people are also aware of the causes leading to latency, as probably there is no family in Hungary nowadays without at least one close or distant relative or acquaintance who has suffered a criminal act which remained hidden. This is why it is particularly important for the authorities and the agencies responsible for supporting victims to take care of the victims in accordance with the international standards.

Though the conclusions of the surveys relating to the extent of hidden crime cannot be regarded as equivalent to the results of the data collection concerning the known phenomena, they can be a great help in the proper interpretation of the latter and in revealing new correlations. As such, the conclusions drawn from victim surveys may support the future work of the acting authorities, the police, the public prosecutor's office and even the court making the decision in the case. They can point out weak spots and call attention to the need for change. Besides, in order

---

[82] *Pranis* 2005.

to evaluate the criminal statistics, to judge the tendencies objectively and to carry out an international comparison, we should have reliable data about the extent, the composition and especially the dynamics of not only the crimes that are known to the authorities but also those that remain hidden. Without this, we can only obtain a distorted view of the actual criminal conditions of a country.

This discernment could serve as a basis for the development of preventive measures. Social crime prevention using a strategic approach – which also involves interventions, the purpose of which, in addition to reducing the effects of the factors giving rise to crime, is the reinforcement of society's ability to defend itself and the reduction of the detrimental financial and moral effects of crime – can only be effective with regard to the victims of criminal acts if we assess the circumstances of victimisation and the different target groups correctly and determine the concrete things to be done on the basis of this. To this end, however, we need more wide-ranging information about victimisation in addition to the statistics.

Over and above all this, according to the new Directive, the EU member states have obligations to carry out victim surveys.[83] Thus, the introduction of regular wide-spectrum surveys will be inevitable in the future: these will not only ensure the measurement of the trends in actual victimisation but, with the appropriate measures, could improve citizens' sense of security and help the administration of justice in becoming more effective and more humane in the long run.

Related to broadening the potential of restorative justice tools, the results clearly reflect the view that the direct adoption of the new methods of restorative tools is quite distant from the Hungarian legal system, which is based on the principle of legality, but it is not impossible. However, these new methods (mediation in prison or peacemaking circle) exceed the level of energy and flexibility used in the routine mediation cases.

In the course of the pilots' implementation, the restorative justice methods, involving the wider community, proved they could be particularly suitable for supporting victims, reintegrating offenders, supporting families, strengthening/renewing the community, handling discrimination, violence and interpersonal conflicts, as well as supporting injured families and communities – tasks that traditional tools/methods are completely unsuitable for.[84]This is why it would be important to expand the use of the restorative approach and its various methods as widely as possible.

The development is likely to help with bridging the gap between the unconditional demand for the implementation of the state's penal authority and the assertion of victims' rights. The use of civil law conflict resolution methods in criminal pro-

---

83 See Directive No. 2012/29/EU.

84 *Pranis* 2005.

ceedings could lead to a drop in traditional punishments, while it could do more to repair the harm caused by offences, and provide feedback to social and educational policy-makers on the pressures towards crime that need to be addressed.[85]

5. Summary in Hungarian

A tanulmány első részében a bűncselekmények áldozataink magyarországi helyzetét, és az ezzel kapcsolatos főbb kérdéseket mutatja be. Ennek során a jogi szabályozás mellett ismerteti azokat a kutatási eredményeket, amelyek az Országos Kriminológiai intézet vezetésével illetve részvételével zajlottak az elmúlt 15 évben. Fontos ugyanis, hogy a hivatalos dokumentumok valamint statisztikai adatok mellett a jelenségeket a „tények mögé nézve", empirikus módon is vizsgáljuk. Ezáltal válik lehetővé egy adott országban, egy adott jelenség – jelen esetben az áldozattá válás – tényleges megismerése. A kutatások rámutatnak arra, hogy miközben a szabályozás és az áldozatok támogatására kiépített intézményrendszer teljes mértékben megfelel az európai normáknak, a valóságban a bűncselekmények sértettjei továbbra is ki vannak téve a hatóságok által előidézett másodlagos viktimizáció veszélyének, számtalan korábbi rossz tapasztalatuk miatt nagyfokú a látencia, vagyis a bűncselekmények rejtve maradása, melynek oka elsősorban az, hogy az érintettek nem tesznek feljelentést. Mindezek miatt ugyanakkor jóval nagyobb mértékű az áldozattá válástól való félelem a lakosság körében, mint ahogy azt a tényleges bűnözési helyzet indokolná. Ez egybecseng azokkal a külföldi eredményekkel, amelyek az OKRI által együttműködésben folytatott, valamint más nemzetközi kutatásaiból (például ICVS), kiderülnek. Az áldozatok kompenzációjának kérdése sem megoldott, az egyébként teljes mértékben EU konform törvényi szabályozás ellenére sem. Ez az oka annak, hogy a tanulmány második részében a resztoratív igazságszolgáltatás szabályozásával, lehetőségeivel, és az azzal kapcsolatos hazai és nemzetközi kutatásokkal is foglalkozik, amelyek rámutatnak a resztoratív eszközök bővítésének lehetőségeire is.

Literature

Arnold, H.R. & Korinek, L. (1989): Victimisation, attitude towards crime and related issues: Comparative research results from Hungary, in: G. Kaiser, H. Kury, & H.J. Albrecht (eds.), Victims and criminal justice. Vol. I. Freiburg, pp. 99–121.

Barabás, A.T. (2018): The dimensions of insecurity in urban areas. Research on the Roots of unsafety and fear of crime in European cities. Budapest.

Barabás, A.T. (2015): Restorative justice in Hungary: A rapidly growing field of practice. Restorative Justice 3, pp. 387–395.

---

[85] *Cornwell, Blad & Wright* 2014.

Barabás, A.T. (2012): Prisons, where are we heading?, in: T. Barabás, B. Fellegi, & S. Windt (eds.), Responsibility-taking, relationship-building and restoration in prisons. Budapest, pp. 263–278.

Barabás, A.T. (2009a): Áldozattá válás Magyarországon: a statisztika és az empirikus vizsgálatok valóságképe [Victimisation in Hungary: Statistical and empirical survey], in: A. Borbíró (ed.), A kriminálpolitika és a társadalmi bűnmegelőzés kézikönyve II. [Handbook on criminal policy and social crime prevention II.]. Budapest, pp. 39–55.

Barabás, A.T. (2009b): Mediation and restorative justice post-sentence: The Hungarian experience; http://mereps.foresee.hu/uploads/media/00105-Pages_from_Barabas_Tunde_paper.pdf [08.10.2019] [in English only].

Barabás, A.T. (2007): Vélemények a büntetésről és a kiegyezés lehetőségéről [Opinions on crime and the possibility of reconciliation]. Belügyi Szemle [Internal Affairs Review] 55, pp. 74–89.

Barabás, A.T. (2004): General victimology, latency, in: F. Irk (ed.), Victims and opinions I. Budapest, pp. 161–201.

Barabás, A.T. (1996): A mediáció esélyei Magyarországon egy empirikus vizsgálat tükrében [The chances of mediation in Hungary according to an empirical survey], in: F. Irk (ed.), Kriminológiai és Kriminalisztikai Tanulmányok No. 33 [Criminology and forensics studies No. 33]. Budapest, pp. 142–157.

Barabás, A.T. & Windt, S. (2009): Az ügyész szerepe a mediációban: Az első év tapasztalatai [The role of the prosecutor in mediation: the experience of the first year], in: G. Virág (ed.), Kriminológiai Tanulmányok [Criminology papers]. Budapest, pp. 132–168.

Barabás, A.T. & Windt, S. (2007): Levels of victimisation, in: T. Lukas (ed.), Crime prevention in high-rise housing. Berlin, pp. 63–85.

Barabás, A.T., Fellegi, B. & Windt, S. (2012): Responsibility-Taking, relationship-building and restoration in prisons. Budapest.

Barabás, A.T., Irk, F. & Kovács, R. (eds.) (2005): Félelem, bűnözés és bűnmegelőzés Európa öt nagyvárosában [Fear, crime and crime prevention in five cities of Europe]. Budapest.

Braithwaite, J. (1989): Crime, shame and reintegration. New York.

Cornwell, D., Blad, J. & Wright, M. (eds.) (2014): Civilising criminal justice: An international restorative agenda for penal reform. New York.

Fattah, E.A. (1991): Understanding criminal victimization. Scarborough.

Irk, F. (ed.) (2004): Victims and opinions. Vol. I–II. Budapest.

Kertész, I. (2001): Áldozattá válási felmérés [Victimisation Survey], in: E. Róth (ed.), Kriminálpolitikaiválaszok a bűnözés kihívásaira, különös tekintettel a szervezett bűnözésre és abüntetőjogi szankciórendszerre [Criminal policy answers to the challenges of crime, with special regard to organised crime and the sanctions system of criminal law]. Budapest, pp. 34–51.

Korinek, L. (1996): A bűnözés visszatükröződése [The Reflection of Crime], in: K.K. Gönczöl, L. Korinek & M. Lévai (eds.), Kriminológiai ismeretek [Criminology studies]. Budapest, pp. 75–92.

Korinek, L. (1988): Rejtett bűnözés [Hidden crime]. Budapest.

Lévay, M. (2006): A magyar kriminológiai gondolkodás fejlődése [The development of criminological thought in Hungary], in: K. Gönczöl, K. Kerezsi, L. Korinek, & M. Lévay (eds.), Kriminológia – Szakkriminológia [Criminology – Special criminology]. Budapest, pp. 153–200.

Lukas, T. (ed.) (2007): Crime prevention in High-Rise Housing. Lessons from the Crime Prevention Carousel; https://www.mpicc.de/de/publikationen/crime-prevention-in-high-rise-housing/ [08.10.2019] [in English only].

Penney, L.T. (2014): Dark figure of crime (Problems of estimation); https://onlinelibrary.wiley.com/ [08.10.2019] [in English only].

Pranis, K. (2005): The little book of circle process: The new/old approach to peacemaking. Brattleboro.

Sessar, K., Herrmann, H., Keller, W., Martin, W. & Breckner, I. (2007): Insecurities in European cities. Crime-related fears within the context of new anxieties and community-based crime prevention; http://cordis.europa.eu/docs/publications/1001/100124091-6_en.pdf [08.10.2019] [in English only].

Valente, R. (2017): MARGIN Final report; https://inhesj.fr/sites/default/files/ondrp_files/Margin/Final%20report%20-%20Evidence%20from%20the%20MARGIN%20project.pdf [08.10.2019] [in English only].

Van Dijk, J., van Kesteren, J. & Smit, P. (2007): Criminal victimisation in international perspective; Key findings from the 2004–2005 ICVS and EU ICS 2007, O&B 257; http://www.unicri.it/services/library_documentation/publications/icvs/publications/n61.htm [08.10.2019] [in English only].

Van Ness, D.W. (2006): Prisons and Restorative Justice, in: G. Johnstone, & D.W. van Ness (eds.), Handbook of restorative justice. London, pp. 312–324.

Wynne, T. (2008): An investigation into the fear of crime: Is there a link between the fear of crime and the likelihood of victimisation? Internet Journal of Criminology; https://www.scribd.com/document/87580950/Wynne-Fear-of-Crime [08.10.2019] [in English only].

Zvekic, U., & Kertész, I. (2000): Bűncselekmények áldozatai a rendszerváltás országaiban [The victims of crime in the transition countries]. Budapest.

Documents

European Commission (2004): EU research on social sciences and humanities. Insecurities in European Cities. Crime-related fears within the context of new anxieties and community-based crime prevention; https://publications.europa.eu/en/publication-detail/-/publication/b70a1112-94bb-4d47-9cbf-76ddc3e8a48d/language-en [08.10.2019] [in Hungarian and English].

Fehér Gyűrű [White Ring] (2019): Kezdőoldal [Home]; http://fehergyuru.eu/ [08.10.2019] [in Hungarian and English].

Foresee Research Group (2012): Introduction of the peacemaking circles; http://www.foresee.hu/en/segedoldalak/news/592/bf41d09c06/5/ [08.10.2019] [in English only].

MARGIN: Tackle Insecurity in Marginalized Areas (2019): Home; http://marginproject.eu/ [08.10.2019] [in English only].

NANE – Association Women for Women Together Against Violence (2019): Kezdőoldal [Home]; http://nane.hu/ [08.10.2019] [in Hungarian only].

Országos Kriminológiai Intézet [National Institute of Criminology] (2006): Crime Prevention Carousel. Hungarian National Report. Budapest; https://intranet.mpicc.de/files/pdf1/national_report_hungary.pdf [08.10.2019] [in English only].

Partners Hungary Foundation (2008): A büntetőügyekben alkalmazható közvetítő tevékenység bevezetésének tapasztalatai [Experiences of mediation in penal matters in Hungary]; http://bunmegelozes.easyhosting.hu/dok/b_ugyek_mediacio.pdf [08.10.2019] [in Hungarian only].

Prosecutor's Office of Hungary (2019): A rendőrség és az ügyészség egységes statisztikai adatbázisa [Uniform statistical database of the police and prosecution]; http://ugyeszseg.hu/kozerdeku-adatok/statisztikai-adatok/ [08.10.2019] [in Hungarian and English].

Hungary

Victimology in Hungary

Ákos Kara, Anna Kiss, Eszter Sárik &
Viktória Szentmihályi-Soós

1. Introduction

The aim of this chapter is to provide the reader with a general overview of the state of the art of victimology in Hungary. The article intends to reflect on the basic theoretical and scientific (theory of science) dilemmas of victimology, on some aspects of victim's morphology, and – first and foremost – on the position of the victim in the legal context (the procedural rights of victims), mostly with regard to the Hungarian Criminal Procedure Law.

Victimology as a discipline has been in search of itself for a long time. This uncertainty is partly the consequence of the circumstances of its "birth", as the "two spiritual fathers" of the science represented different approaches both in the definition and interpretation of victimology. Even the date of its 'genesis' was (and is still) surrounded by contradictions. While most of the Eastern European authors refer to *Benjamin Mendelsohn* as the person to have described the first steps of victimology, the Western European authors tend to quote *Hans von Hentig* as the creator of the independent branch of science called victimology. These scientific debates are by far not theoretical because the contradictions between *Mendelsohn*'s and *von Hentig*'s approaches determine both the definition and position of victimology in the context of social sciences.[1]

Mendelsohn formulated a broad concept of victimology in which the new field of science would become (or could have become) independent from criminology, as he considered "all kind of harms" as victimological situations regardless of the source of this pain. Such harm could mean suffering from natural disasters, being exposed

---

1 *Korinek* 2010.

to abuse by employers, as well as being hurt in a traffic accident.[2] Therefore, according to *Mendelsohn*: "Criminology has a different nature from victimology. The first mostly concentrates on one factor among the many which might cause pain and suffering, whilst the latter should concern all factors which conclude in suffering and pain."[3] Contrary to *Mendelsohn*'s point of view,[4] *von Hentig* considered victimology as part of criminology and formulated that "victimology is a branch of criminology which focuses on the victims of criminal acts, and all topics related to it."[5] *Von Hentig* named this discipline criminal victimology.[6]

Hungarian scholars usually rely on *von Hentig*'s approach and interpret victimology within the context of criminology, regardless of the fact that they would name *Mendelsohn* as the founding father of the science. In Hungary, research into victimology and victimisation began in 1962. On the one hand, the development of this branch of science started with an empirical criminological examination of certain types of crime and, on the other hand, theoretical announcements have been made based on the Hungarian adaptation of foreign and international knowledge since 1969. Within the framework of the Hungarian Criminology Society, the Victimological Section was established in 1989, and the White Ring (Fehér Gyűrű) public benefit association was established to support victims of crime and prevent crime.[7] Still, no independent university department has ever been dedicated to the branch of victimology; in Hungary the discipline is (and has always been) taught within the theoretical framework of criminology.

Over the past decades, Hungary has seen a large amount of victimology publications (see the most important publications in the bibliography). A significant number of theoretical articles and experimental materials were published, where the name of *Ilona Görgényi, Anna Kiss, Lenke Fehér* and *Tünde Barabás* should definitely be mentioned as the Hungarian pioneers of this discipline. It is noteworthy that in

---

2 *Görgényi* 2001a; 2011b.

3 *Rácsok* 2013.

4 *Mendelsohn*'s interest was diverted from crime and crime prevention to the prevention and mitigation of victimity, in the broadest sense. *Mendelsohn* believed that the subjects of research should be not only the victims of crime and power abuse but also the victims of accidents, natural disasters and other "acts of God". He advocated the development of general victimology, as a discipline which would be independent from criminology and criminal law and which would help countries to minimize human suffering and plight, see *Kostic* 2010.

5 *Görgényi* 2001a; 2011b.

6 Besides victimology as a broad concept and "criminal victimology", it is notable that the classification of these so-called "modern victimology" also exists, which is strongly related to the postmodern concept of crimes and criminality, treating power as a central issue.

7 *Tóth* 2003.

1999, the bibliography of victim protection was published as a special issue of the Interior Review (Belügyi Szemle), which was organised by the Pest County Police Headquarters. In addition, the official publication of the National Institute of Criminology, the so-called Studies on Criminology (Kriminológiai Tanulmányok), was dedicated to the topic of victimology in 2005. Criminological publications contained several suggestions that were used in the legislative process (see the publications and research on victimology detailed in *Section 3*). In the following sections, this legal development will be discussed.

2. The Position of the Victim: Procedural Questions Regarding the Victim

Recently, the position of the victim has been the subject of an increasing number of surveys. In the course of the development of criminal law, the victim lost their former leading role in the procedure and was pushed to the periphery of justice. Legal experts have come to realise that this tendency is drastically unfair to the victim.[8] To quote the well-known song by the Doors, "they are riders on the storm, swept away by sand".

It is not easy to understand this, especially when news about crimes influence us day by day. People fall victim to crimes every day, and this experience often has grievous psychological, social, and financial consequences. In many cases, the administration of justice fails to restore the damage caused by the offence. They are severely disregarded during criminal proceedings, and the possibilities for the enforcement of any compensation are highly limited. Consequently, the government must provide victims with other types of assistance.[9]

Recently, similarly to the beginning of the 20th century, more and more people have been calling for a restoration of the victim's proper place and role in the drama that we call criminal procedure (see the publications and research on victimology detailed in *Section 3* and *4*). This is only possible by extending the rights of the victim. An increasing number of people demand the restoration of the former role of the victim. To address this situation, a rising number of specialists have turned the spotlight on the victims of crime. Consequently, the question arises: Should we recommence the former leading role of the victim in the pursuit of crime? By no means. This is not the solution! A solution is only possible if the victim's rights increase, and if guarantees to make the restriction of victims' rights impossible are built into criminal procedure. European documents on the

---

8 *Albrecht & Kilchling* 2005; *Barabás* 2015; *Kiss & Farkas* 2018; *Lupária* 2015; *Róth* 2004; 2011.

9 Possible opportunities are suggested in the chapter "Victimisation and victim-related questions of restorative justice in Hungary", see *Barabás* in this book.

legal position of the victim increasingly call attention to the need for changes in legislation.[10] However, we still have problems concerning the improvement of the victim's situation.

There are several reasons for these ambiguous questions. In the early 1990s, the aim was to develop jurisdiction with respect to the disciplines of fair procedure, and the state was too busy to deal with victim's rights. Later, this aim was replaced by a practical way of thinking. The new goal was to provide effective justice through faster and simpler criminal proceedings. The situation of the courts of justice, which have almost surpassed the limit of their functioning abilities, may actually be made easier by making the procedures less complicated, but the simplification and acceleration of the procedure alone are not enough to create effective justice. Legislatures should also consider human rights issues because simplified procedures lacking guarantees do not work out in the long run. Human rights apply not only to the defendant but also to the victim, and most victims are dissatisfied with the performance of law enforcement authorities (police, prosecution, and courts).

The status of victims of criminal offences has been a major political issue in the European Union, and as such, it has been given particular attention in recent years. In this regard, the 2001 Council Framework Decision[11] on the standing of victims in criminal proceedings deserves to be emphasised. This was the first legal act that specifically dealt with the status of victims on a European level and provided general and legally binding rights for victims. However, the transposition of the Framework Decision into national law was not successful in many respects, since a number of Member States did not fully implement it. In 2011, during the Hungarian Presidency, the Council adopted a resolution, the so-called "Budapest Roadmap".[12] In the resolution, the Member States agreed that action

---

10 Council Framework Decision of 15 March 2001 on the Standing of Victims in Criminal Proceedings, Decision No. 2001/220/JHA, 15.03.2001, Official Journal of the European Communities 82/1; https://eur-lex.europa.eu/legal-content/EN/TXT/PDF/?uri=CELEX:32001F0220&from=EN [09.09.2019]; Directive 2012/29/EU of the European Parliament and of the Council of 25 October 2012 Establishing Minimum Standards on the Rights, Support and Protection of Victims of Crime, and Replacing Council Framework Decision 2001/220/JHA, Directive No. 2012/29/EU, 14.11.2012, Official Journal of the European Union 315/57; https://eur-lex.europa.eu/legal-content/EN/TXT/PDF/?uri=CELEX:32012L0029&from=en [09.09.2019]; Regulation (EU) No 606/2013 of the European Parliament and of the Council of 12 June 2013 on Mutual Recognition of Protection Measures in Civil Matters, Regulation No. 606/2013, 29.06.2013, Official Journal of the European Union 181/4; https://eur-lex.europa.eu/legal-content/EN/TXT/PDF/?uri=CELEX:32013R0606&from=EN [09.09.2019].

11 See Decision No. 2001/220/JHA.

12 Resolution of the Council of 10 June 2011 on a Roadmap for Strengthening the Rights and Protection of Victims, in Particular in Criminal Proceedings, Resolution No. 2011/C

should be taken at the level of the European Union in order to strengthen the rights of victims and to increase their support and protection. Accordingly, Member States revised and supplemented the Framework Decision. As a result, Directive 2012/29/EU of the European Parliament and of the Council establishing minimum standards on the rights, support, and protection of victims of crime, and replacing Council Framework Decision 2001/220/JHA, was adopted.[13] The Directive reinforces the rights granted by the Framework Decision in many respects and introduces new ones. In addition to state aid and assistance, the Directive aims to promote the victim's awareness and lays importance on the role of the victim in criminal proceedings. There are three major groups of victims' rights in the Directive: provision of information and support, participation in criminal proceedings, and protection of victims and recognition of victims with specific protection needs.

The Directive prescribed 16 November 2015 as a transposition deadline. The transposition was realised in Act CLI of 2015[14] in Hungary. The Act entered into force on 1 November 2015. As a result of the legislation, Hungary could finally notify the European Commission of full compliance with the provisions of the Directive. It is worth mentioning, however, that also on the basis of the 2014 survey on the criminal procedural law of the Member States prepared by the European Union Agency for Fundamental Rights, it could be established that Hungary had a leading role among the Member States in assuring victims' rights in criminal proceedings even before transposing the Directive into Hungarian national law. Consequently, the Hungarian procedural rules mostly met the objectives of the Directive even before the implementation, so the legislature amended the provisions of the effective Criminal Procedure Code only to such an extent that was strictly necessary to comply with the regulation of the Directive as a whole.[15]

2.1 Hungarian Criminal Procedure

The Hungarian criminal procedure has three phases: investigation, indictment, and the court proceeding/trial. The criminal procedure in Hungary begins with the investigation of the crime, usually carried out by the police under the supervision of the public prosecutor. When the investigation is over, the public prosecutor decides whether charges should be brought and whether the case should go to court for trial

---

187/01, 28.06.2011, Official Journal of the European Union 187/1; https://eur-lex.europa.eu/legal-content/EN/TXT/PDF/?uri=CELEX:32011G0628(01)&from=EN [09.09.2019].

13 See Directive No. 2012/29/EU.

14 Act CLI of 2015: Amending Certain Laws Necessary to Transpose Directive 2012/29/EU of the European Parliament and of the Council of 25 October 2012 Laying down Minimum Standards on the Rights, Support and Protection of Victims of Crime.

15 See Directive No. 2012/29/EU.

or – if there is not enough evidence or if it is established that the offender should not be punished – should be closed at this stage. When the case is brought to court for trial, the court examines the evidence presented and decides whether the defendant is guilty or not.[16]

In 2016, the government of Hungary adopted the proposal of the Minister of Justice on the new concept of criminal procedure. The new law was passed in June 2017. The Code came into effect in July 2018 and confirmed the victim's procedural position. We would like to point out that the concept of the new Criminal Procedure Code discussed and adopted by the government at its session on 11 February 2015 defined the strengthening and emphasising of the procedural position of victims as a clear objective. The concept set out the following aims:

> The new Act must support the protection of victims and the interests thereof with all possible means […]. It is necessary to broaden the scope of guarantees ensuring that vulnerable persons regarding the limited ability to enforce their interests due to their age, status or circumstances, are able to exercise their rights in the same way as those who do not have such disadvantages, irrespective of their procedural position.[17]

It has to be highlighted that in 2014 and 2015, in the implementation period of the Directive, the drafting of the new Criminal Procedure Code was already on the agenda. The transposition of the Directive thus provided a great opportunity to review the structure of the provisions concerning victims of the effective Criminal Procedure Code. It could be stated that in the effective Act, fragmented rules related to certain procedural roles and procedural phases are typical. Thus, in the new Criminal Procedure Code, a consistent, thoughtful, and coherent regulation for victims has been established in line with the requirements set out in the Directive.[18]

2.2 The Victim's Roles in Hungarian Criminal Proceedings

2.2.1 About the Victim

According to the EU Directive, "victim" means: a natural person who has suffered harm, including physical, mental or emotional harm or economic loss which was directly caused by a criminal offence; family members of a person whose death was directly caused by a criminal offence and who have suffered harm as a result of that person's death.[19]

---

16 Criminal Procedure Code, Law No. 9917, 17.11.2017, Official Gazette 99/2017.

17 See Law No. 9917.

18 See Directive No. 2012/29/EU.

19 See Directive No. 2012/29/EU.

The definition being used in the Hungarian laws – until 30 June 2018 – was: "a victim is the party whose rights or lawful interests have been violated or jeopardised by the criminal offence." Therefore, according to the Hungarian criminal procedure, it is not only a natural person but also a legal entity (for example, a company) that can be titled as victim. However, Hungarian law does not consider indirect victims (e.g., family members) as victims, though in the case of the death of the victim, the relative directly in line (the brother or sister, the spouse or common-law partner of the victim) and the legal representative of the victim may exercise the rights of the victim. The essence of the change in the definition of a victim is a clear reference to *direct injury* that was inserted in the text of the new Criminal Procedure Code.[20] According to the new wording, the victim is a person whose right or legitimate interest was *directly* violated or threatened by the criminal offence. The unambiguous appearance of *directness* means a clarification as compared to the effective text. The purpose of the legislature with this change was to make it clear that the admission of *indirectly injured persons* into criminal proceedings as victims is not justified.[21] Practitioners interpret the issue this way, but it was necessary to insert *directness* into the normative text as well. It must be underlined that the Directive itself also calls directly injured persons victims. It should be pointed out that Hungarian national law fulfils the regulation of the Directive by considering not only natural persons who have suffered harm as a direct consequence of a criminal offence, but also legal persons who have suffered such harm as victims. This is a definite step forward as compared to the regulation of the Directive.[22]

2.2.2 Victim's Position: The Many-Faceted Victim

The victim has been able to fill various positions in the justice process for years. According to their legal position, they can be a 'simple' victim, a "denunciator" who reports the crime, a private complainant, a witness, a private party, a private prosecutor, or a *substitute* private prosecutor. *Erika Róth* states that the victim is either on the side of the state helping to enforce its criminal claim, or substitutes for it in the criminal relation in every position.[23] Although criminological literature most often uses the term victim, the legal language – primarily the Criminal Procedure Law – prefers the term "injured party" and as such, it has the right to receive information and protection. This position can be equalised with the so-called *simple victim*.

---

20 See Law No. 9917.

21 *Kiss* 2018a; 2018b.

22 *Kiss* 2018a; 2018b.

23 *Róth* 2004.

The *"denunciator" and private complainant* is the person who reports the crime. In criminal proceedings, investigation is based on information about how the offence was committed. The data may be obtained by the investigating authority such as the police official, or from the crime report and the private indictment. In many cases, the victim stands as a witness as well, they are the so-called *victim-witnesses* who may have knowledge of the facts waiting to be proven and may be heard as a witness.[24]

The *private party* is the victim enforcing a civil claim in criminal proceedings. The private party may enforce the civil claim against the defendant, arising out of the offence forming the subject of the indictment. According to the law in force, the victim can be a *private prosecutor*. Unless provided otherwise by the relevant Act, in the case of an assault, invasion of privacy, violation of secrecy of correspondence, libel, defamation, and irreverence, the prosecution shall be represented by the victim as a private prosecutor, provided that the offender may be prosecuted upon private motion.[25]

In criminal proceedings, when by the law the charge shall be represented by the public prosecutor, in case of passivity on the part of the prosecutor, the victim may represent the charge as a *substitute private prosecutor*. The victim can act as a substitute private prosecutor in three instances: if the prosecutor drops the charges; if the prosecutor or investigation officials reject the denunciation; or if the prosecutor or investigation officials terminate the investigation. The victim can be a substitute private prosecutor, or in the case of the victim's death, immediate relatives, such as the spouse, the companion, or a legal representative can continue with the proceedings.[26]

2.2.3 Victims' Rights

The victim has several rights in respect of the criminal procedure which are as follows: the right to ask for *information*, the right to *protection*, the right to *participation*, the right to *interpretation and translation*, the right to *criminal charges* (reimbursable victim expenses), and the right to apply for *mediation* too. In some cases, due to their special properties and vulnerability (i.e., age, sexual orientation, etc.) victims can be assigned additional rights. In the following paragraph we will attempt to interpret these rights in order to specify the victims' position in the criminal procedure.[27]

---

24 *Kiss* 2018b.

25 *Kiss* 2018b.

26 *Kiss* 2004b.

27 *Kiss* 2018b.

The victim has the right to ask for *information* about the justice system, about services available to them, and about the progress of their case and the status of the person who harmed them. The wish of victims as to whether or not they want to receive information shall bind the competent authority, unless that information must be provided due to the right of the victim to actively participate in the criminal proceedings.[28]

The victim has the right to protection, which means that victims have the right to have their security and privacy considered, and to receive reasonable and necessary protection from intimidation and retaliation. The right to protection includes not just the right to the confidential treatment of data but it refers also to the special protection of specified witnesses. Victims can ask that their identity not be publicly disclosed. According to the law, in order to protect the life, physical integrity, or personal freedom of the witness, as well as to ensure that the witness fulfils the obligation of giving testimony and to ensure that the testimony is given free from any intimidation, the witness should be afforded protection. Concerning the *confidential treatment of the personal data* of a witness: the court, the prosecutor, and the investigating authority proceeding in the case shall ensure that the data of the witness are treated confidentially and may not become known via some other data of the procedure. The court, the prosecutor and the investigating authority establish the identity of the witness by way of examining documents suitable for identification. And last but not least, the confidential treatment of the personal data of the witness may only be terminated with the consent of the witness. From the time of ordering the confidential treatment of the personal data of the witness, the copies of documents containing such personal data may only be given to participants in the criminal proceedings without the personal data of the witness.[29]

A witness may be declared *specially protected* in four cases: if their testimony relates to the substantial circumstances of a particularly serious case; if the evidence expected by their testimony cannot be substituted; if the identity, the place of residence, and the fact that they are intended to be heard by the prosecutor or the investigating authority is not known by the accused and the defence counsel; or if the exposure of the witness's identity would seriously jeopardise the life, the health, or the personal freedom of either the witness or the relatives thereof. In exceptionally justified cases, the chairperson of the court's panel proceeding, the prosecutor, or the investigating authority may initiate that the defendant, the counsel for the defendant, the victim, other interested parties, the representative of the victim, and other interested parties be protected. The documents pertaining to personal protection shall be kept together with the documents of the criminal case. With the exception of the decision on the request and initiation, the documents shall be handled confidentially. The participa-

28 See Directive No. 2012/29/EU.

29 See Law No. 9917; *Belovics & Tóth* 2017.

tion of the defendant, victim, and witness in the *witness protection programme*[30] are specified in a separate law.[31]

The victim has the right to *participation*, which necessarily includes more than their simple presence. Victims have the right to present victim impact statements and have them considered. Victims' views about decisions that affect their rights must also be considered.[32]

In financial terms, victims are conferred with rights too. Victims have the right to have the court consider making a *restitution* order for their financial losses and to have any unpaid amount enforced through a civil court. Altogether, the law refers to them as *criminal charges*. Additionally, they are entitled to reimburse the following expenses: travel and accommodation expenses; costs of the expert invited by the victim with the consent of the prosecution/court; expenses of full or partial video or audio recordings of the proceedings/stenography; expenses for one copy of the case files; communication expenses (phone, fax, post) and the representative's fee.[33]

Criminal proceedings are conducted in Hungarian, but the victims can use their mother tongue, their regional or minority language, or any other language that they choose both verbally and in writing. If the use of their mother tongue would lead to undue difficulties, the use of another language known to them will be decided upon. They are entitled to an *interpreter* free of charge.[34]

The victim may propose at any stage of the proceedings to refer the case to penal *mediation* if the conditions for such a procedure are fulfilled. Mediation is applied only once in the course of proceedings; for certain crimes against the person, crimes against property or traffic offences, if the crime is punishable with a maximum of five years' imprisonment; with victim's consent and that of the offender. The meeting of the perpetrator with the victim can play a significant role in the perpetrator's

---

30 Such a programme shall not affect their respective rights and obligations related to the criminal proceedings; and in respect of the participants of the programme, the provisions of this Act shall apply with the following derogation: persons participating in the programme shall be summoned or notified by the body responsible for their protection, further, official documents to be served on such persons may only be delivered by the body responsible for their protection; and they shall state their original personal identification data during criminal proceedings, but give the address of the body responsible for their protection as their place of residence or stay. No one – including the authorities – may be provided with a copy of documents containing the personal data of persons participating in the programme and any information regarding such persons, unless they hold the permission of the body responsible for the protection of such persons, see Law No. 9917.

31 See Law No. 9917.

32 See Law No. 9917.

33 See Law No. 9917.

34 See Law No. 9917.

ability to evaluate the consequence and damage that they had caused in reality, while it assists the victim in processing the events and in finding peace.[35]

According to the requirements of the Directive, in 2015, criminal procedure law changed in Hungary, due to which not just the wording but the approach to the victim was changed. These changes largely widened the rights of the victim and also strengthened their protection. Their right to participation and to communication was strengthened (the victim is entitled to be represented by legal aid counsel in all criminal proceedings; and to clear communication both verbally and in writing in all criminal proceedings). Emphasis was put on avoiding time-consuming situations (the victim is entitled to not have to repeat the procedural actions related to them if it is possible), as well as humiliating and dangerous ones. It means the victim is entitled to know if the defendant is at large or has been released. The victim is entitled not to meet the defendant if it is possible.[36]

The legislature, having taken into consideration the recommendation of the European Commission on victim protection, created new legal institutions: *the victim statement* and *the waiver restitution.* According to this, the victim is entitled at any time during the criminal proceedings to declare what kind of physical, psychological harm, financial disadvantage they have suffered as a result of the criminal offence, whether they wish the establishment of the guiltiness of the defendant and the punishment thereof. A victim statement is a forward-looking opportunity for the victims that their interests are taken into account by the authorities, that the acting bodies consider them not only additional actors in the criminal proceedings but persons suffering harm. In the light of the Directive, the new Code determines that if the victim no longer wishes to exercise their rights in criminal proceedings, they may make a declaration at any time about it. Naturally, the statement does not prevent the victim from being questioned as a witness, if it is deemed necessary (so the victim must fulfil their obligation to testify) and does not exempt from the obligation to appear in person at certain procedural actions. The victim may revoke the statement at any stage of the criminal proceedings. The text, however, clearly states that if the statement is withdrawn, the victim cannot exercise their rights retroactively. This could lead to a delay in the proceedings.[37]

2.2.4 Rights of Vulnerable Persons

In the last few decades, the possibility of individualisation and the consideration of individual needs of a person involved in criminal proceedings have been given more and more emphasis. The essence of the new system is that first of all, the bodies

35 See Law No. 9917.

36 See Directive No. 2012/29/EU.

37 See Law No. 9917.

acting in criminal proceedings must make a decision in all cases when the need for individualisation arises and the decision should be based on a unified set of criteria. Thus, if the court, the prosecutor's office, or the investigative authority observes that specific needs emerge concerning the person involved in criminal proceedings, it must be decided whether the person can be considered a person requiring special treatment. Once the decision is made, the system of the measures that are capable to handle the individual needs of the person concerned in the most appropriate way can be applied. With the legal institution of special treatment, the legislature would like to express that special attention, protection, caution, and active behaviour by the court, the prosecutor's office, and the investigative authority is required in criminal proceedings.[38]

The new Act on the Criminal Procedure[39] defines those persons that may primarily be concerned with special treatment as victims and witnesses. However, in specific cases, the law extends the applicability of certain measures covered by special treatment to the defendant as well. The basis of the system of special treatment is that the participation of the person concerned in criminal proceedings is somehow impeded. The purpose of the system is to compensate for such an obstacle to the greatest possible extent. The law lists those circumstances related either to the individual or the criminal offence which may justify the application of special treatment. The list is formulated in a non-exhaustive manner and includes in particular the age, mental, physical and health status of the person concerned, as well as the flagrantly violent nature of the criminal act. The decision on the establishment of special treatment may be made officially or on the motion of the person concerned, or their supporter.[40]

The law concretely enumerates those cases where it is compulsory for the acting bodies to establish special treatment: if the person concerned has not yet reached the age of 18, if they are a disabled person, or they are a victim of a criminal offence against sexual freedom and sexual morality.[41]

What measures are covered by the institution of special treatment? In this respect, the legislator's main objective was to create a gradual set of tools, which can be classified in two groups. The first group contains those measures with the aim to protect the rights of the person concerned, as well as to ensure their gentle treatment (soft measures). These soft measures have a less meaningful effect on the course of

---

38 *Kiss* 2018a; 2018b.

39 See Law No. 9917.

40 *Kiss* 2018a; 2018b.

41 However, the establishment of special treatment does not entail the mandatory application of all the elements of the system. The acting body sorts out the suitable measure on the basis of the specificity of the person requiring special treatment in accordance with the principle of necessity and proportionality. However, from the latter rule, the law sets out exceptions, see Law No. 9917.

criminal proceedings; basically the law expects the bodies to act with extraordinary caution.[42]

Among others, the following soft measures belong to the first group: increased caution when communicating with the person concerned; increased caution in order to protect the privacy of the person concerned; the execution of certain procedural acts without delay; the requirement to avoid unjustified repetition of the procedural act; the carrying out of the procedural act in a room designed for that purpose or in any other suitable place, etc.[43]

The second group covers protection measures that may, in a particular case, limit the rights of other participants in criminal proceedings (hard measures). These legal tools are less flexible and can only be applied if, in connection with one's participation in criminal proceedings, the life, the physical integrity, or the personal freedom of the person requiring special treatment is endangered or in order that the person concerned can exercise their rights and fulfil their obligations without intimidation or influence. Obviously, soft measures and hard measures can be applied concurrently.

It is important to come to the point of the legal tools ensuring the protection of the person concerned.[44] Such hard measures, for example, may include:

- Omitting the confrontation of the witness requiring special treatment;
- Initiating the personal protection of the person concerned;
- Placing the witness under special protection or the initiation thereof, etc.

The law determines special provisions in three separate cases related to the obligatory establishment of special treatment: for persons not having reached the age of 18, for persons under the age of 14 (in which case obviously the rules applicable to persons under 18 are also compulsory to apply), and for victims of criminal offences against sexual freedom and sexual morality. In this context, the law establishes further binding rules in case the victim has not reached the age of 18 or 14. In cases

---

42 These legal tools can be applied more freely and the system is not completely closed. Besides the listed measures, it is possible to apply other solutions in view of the needs of the person concerned.

43 See Law No. 9917.

44 The principle of gradualism appears in connection with the persons affected by the legal tools. While for the victim and the witness requiring special treatment the entire system of measures is available, a limited scope of the tools may be applied for defendants. In case of a defendant, primarily soft measures may be ordered. If, however, the defendant is under 18 years of age, the authorities must strive to make audio and video recordings of a procedural act requiring the participation of the defendant. If the defendant has not reached 14 years of age, the making of audio and video recordings is obligatory, see Law No. 9917.

where victims and witnesses requiring special treatment are under the age of 14, the investigative authority may ensure, in the course of the investigation, that the procedural act is carried out by the same person on every occasion, if this does not endanger the effectiveness of the procedural act. However, as regards the victim of a criminal offence against sexual freedom and sexual morality, the law again renders more stringent rules when it determines that, as a main rule, such victims shall be heard by a person of the same sex during the investigation and, in the course of other procedural acts involving the victim, a person of the same sex from the authorities has to be present, and the investigative authority must also ensure that the procedural act requiring the participation of the victim is conducted by the same person on every occasion. For the victims of sexual offences, the law makes an exception from the above-mentioned rules on the motion or the consent of the person concerned, or if this is inevitable for the success of the criminal proceedings. If the victim of a sexual offence has not reached the age of 18, the law requires the compulsory application of certain legal tools. For example, it is a clear obligation to make audio and video recordings of the procedural act and the defendant and the defence lawyer cannot be personally present at the procedural act involving the victim. In the latter case, the participation of the affected persons should be ensured in other ways, for instance with the use of a telecommunications system. The law does not allow any exception to this rule for the sake of the protection of victims, not even with the consent of the person concerned.[45]

2.3 Groups of Victims' Rights in Hungarian Law

There are three groups of victims' rights in Hungarian criminal proceedings: Provision of information and support; Participation in criminal proceedings; Protection of victims and recognition of victims with specific protection needs.[46]

Provision of information and support

- right to understand and to be understood;
- right to receive information from the first contact with a competent authority;
- right of victims when making a complaint;
- right to receive information about their case; and
- right to interpretation and translation.[47]

---

45 See Law No. 9917.

46 *Kiss* 2018b.

47 See Law No. 9917.

Participation in criminal proceedings

- rights to be heard;
- rights in the event of a decision not to prosecute;
- right to safeguards in the context of restorative justice services;
- right to legal aid;
- right to reimbursement of expenses;
- right to the return of property; and
- right to decision on compensation from the offender in the course of criminal proceedings.[48]

Protection of victims and recognition of victims with specific protection needs

- rights to protection;
- right to avoid contact between victim and offender;
- right to protection of privacy;
- individual assessment of victims to identify specific protection needs;
- right to protection of victims with specific protection needs during criminal proceedings; and
- right to protection of child victims during criminal proceedings.[49]

The new rules intend to give more attention to the victim's interests, and to promote their enforcement. Although these amendments and improvements can be assessed as positive, the question remains: how will the rights provided by law be applied during the enforcement of the law? It will be possible to evaluate this over the next few years. During the creation of the new Criminal Procedure Code, particular attention was paid to the enforcement of the rights of victims and, in general, persons belonging to vulnerable groups. There was a change in the legislature's approach in this regard. The new provisions appear in a simplified and more practical form.[50]

3. Criminal Statistics

In the previous paragraphs, the legal position of the victim was discussed, which is crucially important if an objective picture is to be drawn on the position of the victim and victimology in general. In the following section, reality will be explored from the perspective of statistics and also the victims' position and morphology will be also clarified from the research point of view.

---

48 See Law No. 9917.

49 See Law No. 9917.

50 *Kiss* 2018b.

In Hungary, data on victims are registered by two institutes (constituting two databases), which can be reduced to one if one goes beyond the surface. Victim data are collected by the police and the prosecution authorities but the Central Statistical Office (hereinafter KSH) also publishes information on victims, though the latter also relies on the Aggregated Statistics of Police and Prosecutors' Office. KSH only interprets these pieces of information and puts them in a broader social context, leaving the world of jurisdiction behind.

Hungarian sources only provide researchers with a limited amount of data, as they do not examine the details regarding the victim's habits (except their alcohol and drug consumption patterns), or the amount of material and financial damage that society had to suffer due to criminal acts. The pieces of information are restricted to criminal victimisation, so the interpretation is necessarily restricted to the scope of the Criminal Code. It must also be considered that the partial gaps in data also stem from the fact that, in criminal procedure (due to its nature), much more attention is paid to the offender than to the victim.

When interpreting the Hungarian statistics, it is inevitable to take into consideration the fact that in 2011 a new Criminal Code came into force. Due to the new law, there were important amendments which influenced the criminal statistical system too. Some crime categories were reduced from several to one, and in other cases, the value limit of crimes was lifted (for example Crimes against property), due to which many crimes fell out of the scope of crime statistics: these offences were registered as misdemeanours from this time on. The data examined and interpreted below come from the Aggregated Statistics of the Police and Prosecutors' Office (hereinafter ASoPPO).

The official data gathering on the position of victims was started by the Chief Prosecutor's Office in 1993, but a comprehensive registry of victims was last published for the period between 2004 and 2008. These materials contained those crimes in which natural persons were concerned as victims and the crimes were of great significance, such as homicide, battery, and robbery. The official 'prosecution-brochures' detailed the basic demographic features of the victims such as age and sex, and also, the relationship between the injured person and the offender. Hereby, we will give an overview on the statistical aspects of victimology, relying on the source of ASoPPO but we will only follow up the data of the period 2009–2016 (in some cases, detailed data are only available for the period 2012–2016). It is also important to see when analysing these data that the police and prosecution data are based on so-called statistical papers, which are filled out by the practitioners after the cases have been closed with legally binding and final decisions.

Parallel to the decreasing tendencies of criminality between 2009 and 2016, the number of offenders decreased radically during these years. Moreover, the number of victims diminished even more radically than the number of registered offenders. The latter decrease from 2009 to 2016 was only 13.6% contrary to the 27.3% decline-rate of victimisation in the same period (*Tables 1, 2,* and *3*).

Table 1 Offenders and Victims

Year	Offenders	Victims
2009	112,830	213,661
2010	122,529	247,778
2011	112,895	260,279
2012	100,239	275,175
2013	103,572	245,601
2014	105,588	214,715
2015	98,987	183,125
2016	98,136	155,292

Source: StatOffice 2010–2017.

Table 2 The Number of Victims 2009–2016 According to the "Old" CC (Act IV of 1978)

Crime categories	2009	2010	2011	2012	2013	2014	2015	2016
Crime against the person	21,970	25,778	25,510	25,750	21,920	4,343	769	344
Traffic crime	4,176	3,722	3,388	3,200	2,705	643	98	20
Crime against marriage, family, and sex morals	5,761	5,311	6,058	5,625	9,534	1,023	280	77
Crime against state and public integrity	2,121	2,436	2,264	2,074	1,645	640	144	95
Crime against public order	9,370	12,102	10,486	10,269	8,769	1,769	302	92
Economic crime	495	8,114	12,074	16,731	5,368	406	84	27
Crime against property	169,738	190,255	200,426	211,488	133,449	15,925	4,806	2,159
Military crime	30	60	73	38	37	43	10	0
Total	213,661	247,778	260,279	275,175	183,427	24,792	6,493	2,814

Source: StatOffice 2010–2017.

Table 3 The Number of Victims 2013–2016 According to the "New CC"

Crime groups	2013	2014	2015	2016
Criminal offences against humanity	0	0	0	0
War criminal offences	0	0	0	0
Criminal offences against life, limb, and health	1,652	12,108	13,181	12,484
Medical procedures and criminal offences against order of research	0	0	0	0
Criminal offences against health	5	0	0	0
Criminal offences against personal freedom	43	487	629	544

Table 3 cont. *The Number of Victims 2012–2016 According to the "New CC"*

Crime groups	**2013**	**2014**	**2015**	**2016**
Sexual freedom and sexual criminal offences	152	984	1,354	1,453
Criminal offences against children and against family law	505	3,350	3,929	3,863
Criminal offences against human dignity and fundamental rights	909	9,476	10,236	9,722
Criminal offences against traffic regulations	422	2,304	2,890	3,258
Criminal offences against environment and nature	71	0	0	0
Criminal offences against state	0	0	0	0
Criminal offences in connection with classified information and against public records and registers recognised as national assets	0	0	0	0
Criminal offences against judicial system	27	109	110	91
Criminal offences of corruption	7	0	0	0
Malfeasance in office	2	39	39	80
Criminal offences against public officials	106	838	900	906
Criminal offences against public security	19	3	0	1
Criminal offences against economic sanctions imposed under international commitment for reasons of public security	0	0	0	0
Criminal offences against public peace	1,678	8,628	9,327	8,575
Criminal offences against public confidence	842	0	0	0
Criminal offences related to administrative procedures	30	0	12	40
Criminal offences against property	1,091	4,202	3,984	3,530
Criminal offences against property	54,294	146,724	129,505	106,331
Criminal offences against intellectual property rights	0	2	2	1
Criminal offences relating to counterfeiting currencies and philatelic forgeries	272	597	464	328
Criminal offences against public finances	1	0	0	0
Money laundering	0	0	0	0
Economic and business criminal offences	1	13	11	1,204
Criminal offences against consumer rights and violation of competition laws	0	0	0	0
Illicit access to data and criminal offences against information systems	37	25	17	19
Criminal offences against military obligations	0	0	0	0
Military criminal offences	8	34	42	48
Total	62,174	189,923	176,632	152,478

Source: StatOffice 2014–2017.

This decline is more impressive if we consider the fact that this tendency has no statistical peaks, so the downward tendency was permanent during this time period.

Table 4 The Aggregated Number of Crimes against Property in the Old and the New Criminal Code, 2009–2016

2009	2010	2011	2012	2013	2014	2015	2016
169,738	190,255	200,426	211,488	187,743	162,649	134,311	108,490

Source: StatOffice 2010–2017.

Table 5 The Aggregated Number of Crimes against Persons in the Old and the New Criminal Code, 2009–2016

2009	2010	2011	2012	2013	2014	2015	2016
21,970	25,778	25,510	25,750	21,920	25,927	24,188	22,550

Source: StatOffice 2010–2017.

This tendency may arise from the aforementioned legal changes but also from the low rates of reporting. Behind the spectacular diminishing tendencies of criminality, the Hungarian government's severe approach to criminality may also appear.

In the related, interim years when the new Criminal Code came into force, both of the laws were used by the courts, depending on which regulation was more favourable for the accused person. These transitional periods make statistical analysis and data gathering more complicated and hinder, or at least make more difficult, a valid comparison between the years under review. The problem is made more complicated by the fact that the crime categories of the Criminal Code were also changed. Despite all these challenges, some major conclusions on the diversity and the distribution of the crimes can be boldly drawn.

It seems quite obvious that the most often committed and suffered crimes belong to the category of crimes against property: the number of victims was always between 100,000 and 200,000 in the period under review, peaking in 2012 with 211,488 injured parties. The decline is rather remarkable even if we consider the change in the law and add the figures of the old and the new Criminal Codes: in 2016 there were only 108,490 victims of property crimes. That means that the number of crimes against property have nearly halved compared to 2009 and the years before *(Table 4)*.

The number of crimes committed against the person did not radically change from 2009 to 2016. Though we can detect a minimum value at the beginning and at the end of the period, the average figure was rather stable, somewhere between some 21,000 and some 25,900 *(Table 5)*.

The same conclusion can be drawn regarding the victims of traffic crimes. The number of victims never reached 4,500 but was never under 2,500 either: it hovered around 3,000 *(Table 6)*.

Table 6 The Aggregated Number of Traffic Crimes in the Old and the New Criminal Code

2009	2010	2011	2012	2013	2014	2015	2016
4,176	3,722	3,388	3,200	3,127	2,947	2,988	3,278

Source: StatOffice 2010–2017.

It is beyond doubt that the distribution of the victims (and the offenders) is more or less determined by the amount of crimes committed against property.[51] The question that automatically arises is why the amount of these crimes was halved within such a short period. Some aspects of the radical decline can be interpreted by the legal alterations, as the original classification was modified in this context too. Namely: the original title under which these crimes were regulated was split into three: Violent Crimes against Property, Offences against Property, and Crimes against Intellectual Property Rights. Still, if we add the two newly formed crime types to the traditional offences against property, the numbers remain below the original level of 150,000 to 200,000 crimes per year. The answer is rather unclear, though of course the press[52] (and via the press, the public) warmly welcomes the steep fall in the figures indicated in the crime statistics. The official summary of the criminal data highlighted the decline in the number of thefts, which fell from 141,469 (2014) to 92,149 (2016). The report also stated that the proportion of crimes against property only represented 52% in the totality of crimes in 2016, which is a new phenomenon as the rate of property crimes used to be 60% to 70% for several decades.[53]

If we consider the gender factor among the victims, there is no significant difference between males and females: the radical and permanent decrease can be detected in both genders among the registered victims. If the 2016 data are compared with the numbers from 2009, it is obvious that the current numbers represent only the 80% of the victims in respect of women and 68% of males as compared to the base year, which means that the victimisation tendencies seem to be more stable with regard to women.

---

51 The validity of the comparison can be underpinned by the fact that the expert of statistical analysis at the National Institute of Criminology, *József Kó*, also referred to the same data groups – Crimes against Property, Crimes against the Person and Traffic Crimes – when he conducted examinations about the problems and dilemmas of crime statistics in Hungary, see *Kó* 2019.

52 *Szilágyi* 2017.

53 It is also important to acknowledge that if we compare violent and vandalism-related crimes, a growing tendency can be detected in both types, whose increase is faster in terms of violent crimes. In 2002, the number of violent crimes was 19,349, which grew by nearly 4,000 (23,446) by 2012, meaning that the data from 2012 reached 121.2% of the same crime category as compared to the data of 10 years before. Examining the same data in the same period for vandalism-related crimes, the proportion was only 116.9%. This is especially important if we consider the fact that these rates remained stable when we compared them to the total number of crimes.

Table 7 Victims by Gender

Gender	Year							
	2009	**2010**	**2011**	**2012**	**2013**	**2014**	**2015**	**2016**
Male	130,909	148,832	154,461	161,286	142,282	124,073	106,446	89,339
Female	82,752	98,946	105,818	113,889	103,319	90,642	76,679	65,953
Total	**213,611**	**247,778**	**260,279**	**275,175**	**245,601**	**214,715**	**183,125**	**155,292**

Source: StatOffice 2010–2017.

However, this decrease proves to be rather significant for this victim group, especially because males are always more exposed to victimisation than females *(Table 7)*.

As for the age distribution, we can provide data from the period 2012–2016, which is more or less stable too. Adults and young adults (over the age of 18) had to suffer more criminal situations than previously, whilst children (under the age of 14) and the elderly were less affected *(Table 8)*.

Table 8 Victims by Age (numbers and percentages)

Age distribution	Year				
	2012	**2013**	**2014**	**2015**	**2016**
Children	7,569	10,2 91	5,285	4,003	3,562
Juveniles	8,967	8,337	7,438	6,886	5,924
Adults	219,916	193,795	172,676	147,472	125,319
Elderly	38,694	33,502	29,806	24,760	20,475
Total	**275,173**	**245,925**	**215,205**	**183,121**	**155,280**
Children	2.8%	4.2%	2.5%	2.2%	2.3%
Juveniles	3.3%	3.4%	3.5%	3.8%	3.8%
Adults	79.9%	78.8%	80.2%	80.5%	80.7%
Elderly	14.1%	13.6%	13.9%	13.5%	13.2%
Total	**100%**	**100%**	**100%**	**100%**	**100%**

Source: StatOffice 2013–2017.

It is important to acknowledge that the proportion of adults still represents 80% of all victims. The share of the elderly is relatively high (on average, between 13% and 14%), which is in line with the information that we obtained from research projects.[54] It should not be forgotten that crimes against property might distort the validity of conclusions, as these crimes are usually reported by the male, adult member of

54 *Bolyky* 2018; *Tamási, Bolyky & Sárik* 2014.

Figure 1 The Relationship between the Victims and the Offenders

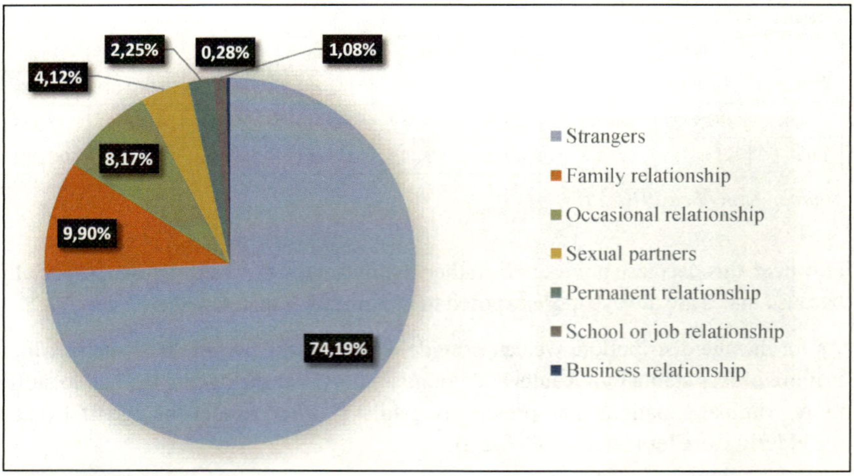

Source: StatOffice 2016.

the household, whilst the property on which the crime was committed is commonly owned by the family.

The relationship between the offender and the victim *(Figure 1)* should also be analysed, as this can bring one closer to the issue of the interdependence of the victim. Though the proportion of the missing data is rather huge (53.26%) in this context, the official statistics suggest that nearly three quarters of the crimes are committed by and against strangers. In case the perpetrator and victim had any relationship with each other, 9.9% of the crimes were committed within the family, 8.17% happened in casual relationships, and 4.12% of the crimes affected sexual partners. In this respect, colleagues or business relations were not typical.

In terms of violent crimes and street vandalism, the data differ a lot. The proportion of crimes committed against strangers was smaller than a half of the sample (44.75%); in 17.3% of the cases the victims were family members, 20.7% were casual partners and in 10.13% of the cases sexual partners were affected by the offence. However, if we dissect the most violent crimes (and especially homicides), it can be revealed that most of them are perpetrated within the family, or against sexual partners.[55] In this crime category, felonies hardly ever target strangers.[56]

---

55 *Bolyky* 2018; *Tamási* 2005.

56 Although it would be of crucial importance to gain knowledge about the victims' personal features and behaviour during (or even before) the criminal act in order to be able draw a more or less reliable picture on the victim in morphological terms, statistics provide us only with poor information. The only background-related information in this respect is the question of the victims' alcohol and drug use during victimisation. It is clear that most

These statistics are suitable for outlining long-time tendencies and trends which can serve as important tools for drafting crime-prevention strategies.[57] However, these data should be considered and interpreted only with limitations because they only represent the tip of the iceberg. According to criminological studies and experts' opinions, the number of crimes and victims is likely twice (or even 3 or 4 times) as many as the number of registered crimes.[58] Besides administrative problems, this is partly the consequence of the low reporting will of Hungarian citizens, which is also due to the negative experience of the victim or of their acquaintances.

The best example of this is the topic of hate crimes. Without going into details regarding this topic, we can boldly state that the interpretation of hate crimes (and hate-motivated acts) can be best understood by using diverse sources that will definitely lead to different conclusions. If hate motivated acts were interpreted purely by the official statistics, we would say that Hungary has hardly any tasks to tackle *(Table 9)*.

It is obvious that neither the number of victims nor the number of offences are crucially high, especially if we consider the nearly 10 million inhabitants of Hungary.

There was no radical increase in the reported cases of hate crimes in the past five years, not even in the course of the migration flow; this is valid for the violent crimes too. There were 6 homicide cases upon bias or hate motivation in between 2010 and 2015 and in the same period altogether 43 assaults were committed with the same motivation.[59] However, if the phenomenon was studied more deeply or the reports of NGOs were taken into account, the picture would be modified a lot. According to the data of the Fundamental Rights Agency (FRA), 5% of the Jewish community, 21% of LGBTQ people (Lesbian, Gay, Bisexual, and Transgender), and 12% of the Roma people being interviewed suffered violence or were threatened with violence in the past five years.[60] These data sharply contradict the official statistics.

---

of the victims (50.86%) were not influenced by alcohol or drugs (or any other mind-altering substances). Whilst the proportion of victims consuming alcohol before the felony was 2.45%, the proportion of those who used drugs did not even reach the proportion of 1% (0.07 for drug users and 0.03 for using other mind-altering substances). In respect of vandalism-related and violent crimes, the proportion of missing data was only 9.84% and according to ASoPPO, 71.97% of the passive subjects were sober and 17.82% of the victims were drunk. These data suggest that those who were involved in violent acts were much likely to be influenced by mind-altering substances than those involved in other types of crimes, see *Bolyky* 2018; *Tamási* 2015.

57 *Görgényi* 2001a; 2001b; *Tóth* 2003.

58 *Görgényi* 2001a; 2011b; 2006.

59 StatOffice 2011–2016.

60 *Dombos* 2018.

*Table 9 Crimes Traditionally Interpreted as Hate Crimes**

Hate crime	2012		2013		2014		2015		2016	
	victim	offence	victim	offence	victim	offence	victim	offence	victim	offence
"Violence against member of community"	36	21	43	39	48	37	32	30	33	24
"Incitement against community"	5	2	3	0	4	5	4	0	5	2
"Use of symbols of totalitarianism"	58	11	46	10	44	6	23	7	23	4
"Open denial of Nazi crimes and communist crimes"	6	2	5	2	19	7	13	6	10	4
"Blasphemy of national symbols"	0	0	0	0	0	0	0	0	0	0

Source: StatOffice 2013–2017.

* The table contains data both from the so-called 'old' Criminal Code (Act IV of 1978) and the crimes regulated by the new Criminal Code (Act C of 2012). The data collection is a summary of the so-called classical bias-motivated crimes.

Research conducted on this subject is mostly restricted to file analyses[61] and case studies[62] as other sources besides criminal files are just restrictedly available for criminologists. However, these sources only enable researchers to focus on content-problems and use qualitative methods. So the studies performed by the experts of the National Institute of Criminology[63] and in sporadic cases, by the Working Group against Hate Crimes (GYEM)[64] were first and foremost[65] dedi-

---

61 *Amberg* 2013; *Jovánovics* 2013.

62 *Átol, Dombos, Jovánovics, Tóth, Pap & Udvari* 2013; *Ivány* 2012; *Kirs & Pap,* 2017; *Pap* 2017, *Uszkiewicz* 2013.

63 *Bárd & Tóth* 2016a; 2016b; *Póczik* 2011; *Utasi* 2011.

64 *Balogh, Dinók & Pap* 2012; *Jovánovics* 2013.

65 The Hungarian papers and examinations are mostly addressed to legislative and judicial problems and also to practical issues of investigation, see *Balogh et al.* 2012; *Udvari* 2013; *Uszkiewicz* 2013. On the one hand they concentrate on whether Hungarian hate crime legislation complies with the international treaties and norms (see *Átol et al.* 2013), and on the other hand the papers and presentations examine definition-related questions which might appear theoretical but which influence practice a lot, see *Demeter* 2017; *Dombos* 2015; 2017; *Dombos & Pap* 2015; *Iványi & Udvari* 2014; *Jovánovics* 2013; *Kirs* 2017; *Pap* 2016). The best example of the latter is the crime called "Violence against a member of a community", which is dissected from different approaches, but in most of the examinations the victim's approach is highlighted, see *Dinók* 2013; *Iványi* 2012; *Jovánovics* 2013; *Jovánovics & Pap* 2013). The text of the regulation alone does not give

cated to the question: how the hate aspect of a crime could best be detected and proved by the authorities and what can and should be done in order to reduce under-reporting of crimes as well as to minimize the number of disguised crimes. The significance of the hate crime was also discussed from the police point of view, and scientific papers and presentations were prepared to aid police in its recognition.[66]

4. The Dilemmas of Researching Domestic Violence Victimisation

While empirical research on victimology began in the late 1960s, it was not until the 1990s that the discipline unfolded completely. *Ilona Görgényi* (who is often referred to as the "theoretical mother of victimology" in Hungary)[67] has made significant efforts to transplant international legal institutions into the Hungarian criminal legislation and has published chapters on victimology in handbooks on criminology[68]. She also conducted empirical research on victims[69] and was involved in international surveys[70] too. *Görgényi* published an entire book on victimology in 2001 and a book on restoration and criminal mediation in 2006. *Anna Kiss* was the first researcher who concentrated on the importance of the victims' position during criminal procedures and made tremendous efforts to strengthen this position in her publications.[71] Besides her work, a rather wide range of studies were conducted on the legal position of the victim, the legal protection of the injured party[72] *Tünde Barabás* examined restorative justice in Hungary and was successful in promoting mediation.[73]

Though the legal aspects of the issue can be boldly titled the "hardware" of victimology, victimological research cannot and should not be restricted to this theme. In Hungary, various themes were the subject of empirical and theoretical research. Some of the victim-related research projects were about discovering general questions, such as the phenomenon of the dark figures of criminality (unreported crime),[74] the causes of the low reporting data, and another (and not less) important group of

---

a definite idea on whether any sensitive groups or identity itself is protected by the law, or whether the protection refers to being a member of a minority group in society.

66 *Uszkiewicz* 2013.

67 *Görgényi* 1991; 1993a; 1993b; 1994; 1995; 2004a; 2004b; 2005.

68 *Görgényi* 1999; 2006.

69 *Görgényi* 2000.

70 *Görgényi* 2001a; 2001b.

71 *Kiss* 1997; 2004a; 2004b; 2005; 2006a; 2006b; 2018a; 2018b; *Kiss & Farkas* 2018.

72 *Bárd* 2015a; 2015b; *Király* 2008; *Tóth* 2003.

73 *Barabás* 2005; 2014; 2015.

74 *Korinek* 1988; 2017; *Kó* 2005.

studies searches for special answers on certain questions related to specified crimes (i.e., crimes against property,[75] violent crimes,[76] crimes against official persons,[77] etc.).

Though studies or at least research questions within nearly all criminal domains (such as homicide and violent crimes)[78] exist regarding the victim, there are some topics that should mainly be approached from the victims' point of view. What does that mean? There are themes that would show a dramatically different interpretation in view of criminal statistics and from the victims' aspect. In the field of sexual crimes, crimes happening in the family or online crimes, the sensitivity of privacy would modify the willingness to report which would automatically lead to dramatic uncertainty in the number of registered victims. People feel ashamed of being used as sexual objects, people feel ashamed of being abused by family members, and people would like to keep up the appearance of a good and loving family, despite all the cruelty and pain they suffer.[79]

These sensitive issues are usually covered and discovered by two main sources,[80] namely scientific research (usually relying on file examinations and interviews in addition to official criminal data) and the work done by the NGOs. These sources differ a lot in terms of their scope, their content and, last but not least, in their objectives. Scientific research describes a phenomenon on its own, based on purely scientific methods. The aim of such studies is to disseminate knowledge on a certain issue; whilst the guidelines developed for and by NGOs (usually relying on their own questionnaires and interviews) primarily aim to raise awareness.

We will discuss research efforts which concentrated on the topic of domestic violence. The subject was chosen for two main purposes: first, to enable the readers to follow up the development of the research in this crucially important issue and, second, to call attention to the contradictions which may lie in the approach of researchers and the (sometimes biased) rights' defenders.

On the topic of domestic violence, the book entitled "Family dreads",[81] which was edited by *György Virág*, provided the readers with a general overview of the phe-

---

75 *Kránitz* 2005.

76 *Görgényi* 1990; *Nagy* 2005.

77 *Nagy* 2012.

78 *Bolyky* 2018; *Nagy* 2005.

79 This statement is also valid in respect of hate crimes. The sensitivity of the victimisation, as well as the sensitivity and inconvenience of reporting are quite similar here too. People who were to suffer crimes due to their ethnicity, their religion or nationality can be in a similarly grievous, trying and humiliating situation as those who were violated in their sexual integrity or were to suffer crimes within their families, committed by family members.

80 As stated above, official statistics do not operate as reliable sources in this context.

81 *Virág* 2005.

nomenon of domestic violence based on the examination of 1500 criminal files. The authors – *Lenke Fehér, Szilvia Gyurkó, Mária Herczog, Erzsébet Tamási, Gábor Szöllősi, György Virág*, and *Szandra Windt* – dealt with the difficulty of the fact that the presence of violence within the family was mostly secret and denied, or at least uninteresting. The volume was extremely valuable, as it did not miss analysing the victimisation of men and the elderly (parents and grandparents) besides the 'classical' forms of domestic violence: female and child victimisation. From 1,453 examined cases, 302 were minors, 130 adult men (husband or men living in a partnership), 157 parents, 598 women (wives and extramarital partners), 154 other male relatives, 73 other female relatives, and 39 assaults were committed against the adult sons or daughters of the perpetrator. The vast majority of the victims were women (mostly wives and partners) in respect of the classical forms of abuse, such as assault. However, it has become obvious that violence is more or less 'men-business', a statement which is true both in terms of perpetrators and victims (at least in the most serious cases). Namely, in respect of homicides or violence against minors. Sixty-one per cent of the victims of domestic homicide are men and two-thirds of the victims of acts committed against minors were boys.[82]

The phenomenon was also explained by a special approach in the book "Sinful victims"[83] written by *Erzsébet Tamási*. The author assessed the position of men victimised by relatives and in family circumstances. Domestic violence generally means public accusation of male aggression against women and children as, according to the choreography of conflicts between partners, women are victims and men are perpetrators. Women are seen as having been ill-treated even as victims but when men are hurt by the hands of women, they are collectively forgotten by society. The book of *Tamási* drew attention to this social taboo, and summed up the results of international and domestic research not only regarding abusive parties but also the victim's role. The empirical part of the study was based on the above mentioned sample, namely the research sample of the National Institute of Criminology.

Among others, it is important to mention that a paper was drafted on the topic of dating-violence, edited and written by *Mária Herczog* and *Szilvia Gyurkó.*[84] The research conducted within the institutional framework of the National Institute of Criminology involved interviews with 206 university and college students about the abuse they suffered in their romantic relationships (from physical and psychological aspects alike) but also the violence and neglect that they endured during their childhood too. These young people, despite belonging to the upper classes of society,

---

82 The volume discussed the conceptual questions of domestic violence, the main problems of its definition and handling, and its research history. It also reviewed international documents and models and presented the details of domestic legislation, see *Virág* 2005.

83 *Tamási* 2005.

84 *Herczog & Gyurkó* 2006.

experienced bad parental treatment in a high percentage during their childhood: 24% of them were physically abused, 20% sexually abused, and more than one third of them suffered psychological maltreatment. In terms of partner violence, it has transpired that despite the fact that 71% of the students had relationships, 90% of them had not suffered physical violence from their partner, which rate proved to be the same in respect of psychological violence.

Many comprehensive writings and books have also been published on the topic of child abuse in Hungary. One of the most well-known experts who should definitely be mentioned is *Mária Herczog*. Besides launching and editing a professional journal in the field of child protection ("Család, Gyermek, Ifjúság", Family, Child and Youth), she was the author of more than one hundred articles and several books. The book "Child Abuse" was published in 2007 for the 10th anniversary of the Act on Child Protection (Act XXXI of 1997 on Child Protection). The volume attempted to analyse theoretical and practical problems, investigate various forms of abuse and neglect, and formulate possible new phrases and concepts.[85]

In the field of the mistreatment of children, it was not only the classical forms of abuse and neglect that were researched and explained by Hungarian authors but also the postmodern phenomenon of internet misuse too. *Katalin Parti* (also a researcher of the National Institute of Criminology) published a book on the phenomenon of child pornography in the 21st century "Child pornography on the Internet".[86] *Parti*'s work revealed both the legal problems of internet-violence and the dilemmas which may occur in the course of criminal procedure, for instance with regards to the rule of the forensics. The author also highlighted the importance of the perpetrators' personality and their potential mental problems. According to the survey, two-thirds of the offenders were punished for intended sexual demeanour, but among them not a single offender was declared sexually aberrant by the psychological examination.

A profound work titled "Partner abuse against older women" was published by the Hungarian Academy of Sciences, Sociology Research Institute, which was written by *Olga Tóth* and *Katalin Róbert* on the topic of the abuse affecting elderly women.[87] The research project consisted of three parts. In the first round, 450 questionnaires were given to institutions and professionals who could find examples of the abuse of elderly women by their partners during their work. In the second round, the professionals who had come across such cases, or who had suggestions and ideas to solve the problem, were interviewed. In the third round, deep interviews were conducted with victims. The sample included 33 institutions which met all criteria of the research, which represented 41.8% of the institutions that have completed the questionnaire. It proved to be a real problem that a significant number of the

85 Child Protection Act, Law No. 311997, 31.12.1997, Official Gazette 31/1997.

86 *Parti* 2009.

87 *Tóth & Róbert* 2010.

institutions of the social care system, especially the institutions providing special care for the elderly, had not met with cases at all. One-third of general social service institutions, and 14% of services for elderly institutions, have case experience. For the 56% of the institutions that had reported cases, the number of victims was 1–3 in the period under review. There were 3–10 cases in the period under review at 19% of the institutions that had cases and only law enforcement organisations met with a higher number of cases. The research originated from the hypothesis that experts can assist in finding victims who are willing to give interviews. However, a section of the experts willing to give interviews had no case knowledge at all. All in all, nine interviews could be taken with elderly victims who suffered abuse. Despite the thorough examination, the most important lesson that could be learnt from the study was that the abuse of the elderly women is not widespread in Hungary and that the institutions had very little information on the issue.

Although a large range of topics was examined by researchers in the field of domestic violence, there is no doubt that 'the ever hot issue' would be the crimes committed against women. The first book published on this subject was *Krisztina Morvai*'s volume "Terror in the family – Wife abuse and law".[88] The book became very popular, not just among scientists but also among rights' defenders. As the prologue says: "The criminal lawyer has been investigating the phenomenon of wife abuse for two years, in the course of which she conducted more than fifty in-depth interviews with abused women, their children, abusive men and their practitioners, and analysed hundreds of police and court files in an intelligible way. Separate chapters cover the tasks of various public bodies (police, public prosecutor's office, court, child protection and social authorities), various professions concerned (such as lawyers, doctors) and civil society groups to reduce the phenomenon of domestic violence, prevent tragedies, to support victims".[89] Although the volume relied on valid data and judicial decisions and the methodological standards were diligently complied with, the author's conclusions left the sphere of objectivity, which fuelled much debate afterwards. Still, the advantages of the volume must be recognized, as this pioneering work was very instructive and forward-looking.

The book of *Krisztina Morvai* provided a basis for many initiatives to deal with the topic of domestic violence. NGOs – such as Nők a Nőkért Együtt az Erőszak Ellen Egyesület, NANE (Women for Women Together Against Violence), Keret Koalíció (Frame Coalition – Coalition Against Violence for Survivors), PATENT Jogvédő Egyesület, Patriarchátust Ellenzők Társasága (PATENT Rights Defender Association– Society against Patriarchy), ESZTER Alapítvány az Erőszakos Szexuális Támadást Elszenvedettek Rehabilitációjára (ESZTER Foundation for the Re-

---

88 *Morvai* 1998.

89 *Morvai* 1998, p. 1.

habilitation of Women Who Suffered Sexual Attacks) – were established to provide assistance and help for (mainly) female victims of (domestic) violence.

These foundations, associations, and societies are not just important for their practical work but because they also develop manuals, guidelines, and brochures on the relevant topics.[90] These works partly rely on profound studies and well-based research findings but it is also important to acknowledge that the messages they intend to convey and spread intentionally use exaggerations to make the phenomenon more visible in society, which can be well demonstrated by the volume "Stuck in the system",[91] which was to address the jurisdictional implications of domestic violence. "The volume demonstrated through case studies, surveys and research findings that sexist, offender-friendly attitudes rule in the various institutions of the Hungarian judicial system, which makes it extremely difficult for the victims to protect themselves and their children from further abuse."[92] These words, quoted from the preface, clearly suggest that despite the positive goals and aims, the NGOs (sometimes) tend to exaggerate and emphasise just one side of the coin. It is beyond doubt that the problems indicated by them should (and must) be accepted, but it would be irresponsible to say that all authorities perform their duties in a sexist and offender-friendly manner. These sweeping statements may cause more harm than good. In order to call attention to a problem, declarations should be formulated profoundly and carefully, and first and foremost, they should avoid fuelling aggressive debates and conflicts between those groups who are sensitively affected by these issues.

5. Conclusions

Both criminology and victimology are interdisciplinary branches of science, which contain the elements of criminal law, psychology, and sociology, as well as some

---

90 The so-called FRAME Coalition (Coalition Against Sexual Violence for Survivors) summarised their recommendations regarding methodological issues on the topic of sexual violence. *Judit Spronz, Judit Wirth* and *Gábor Kuszing* – representatives of the NANE (Women for Women Together Against Violence) and Patent Associations – have published a Methodological Guide which contains common recommendations from the experts of women's rights NGOs involved in helping victims, governmental and non-governmental organisations, as well as civil service providers for dealing with the victims and offenders of partner violence based on international good practices and recommendations. There were projects developed in order to help children who had witnessed domestic and partner violence (The B-Side Project – Stopping The Domino Effect – Support Programmes For Children – Good Practices And Directives, and a manual was formulated for helping victims of sexual violence, developed by the FRAME Coalition), see Project B-SIDE (2019): The B-SIDE project: A barrier to stop the in-door effect; http://www.cwdv-barriertostopindoordominoeffect.eu/en/index.php/the-b-side-project-a-barrier-to-stop-the-in-door-domino-effect [01.10.2019] [in English only].

91 *Wirth* 2009.

92 *Wirth* 2009, p. 10.

aspects of history. Due to their comprehensive character and the cause of their birth, criminological and victimological research serves certain practical goals too. On the one hand, criminology (and victimology), as nearly all social sciences nowadays, have been put to the postmodern test and forced to become practical and useful in terms of 'reality', which means, in this context, the promotion and development of effective criminal policy.[93] On the other hand (seemingly forming a contradiction with the statements above), criminology (and victimology too) is not just pressed by practice and policy-makers but it necessarily has to rely on moral values which are as optional (creating the illusion as if they could be chosen from a menu in a café)[94] as all other things and thoughts in the 21st century.[95] It can be concluded that criminology and, as a part of it, victimology, represents a special field of science which partly reflects reality but – and as a consequence of its relations to criminal law and criminal politics – also intensively shapes it.[96]

Due to the interdisciplinary and multidisciplinary position of victimology and the comprehensive knowledge of this field of science, victimology can be best understood by the topics covered by the discipline. According to the classification of *Tóth*), the topics of victimology can be discussed in eight main research fields:

1) consider the position of the victim within the criminal procedure and to examine his/her legal protection provided by criminal law (victim's position);
2) reveal the victims' features with regard to the typology of crimes as well as their social, psychological, and biological characteristics (victimological morphology);

---

93 *Sárik* 2018.

94 *Rácsok* 2013.

95 According to *Haines* and *Sutton*, the discussion on the goals and the function of criminology has been taken so far that even the fact of criminology being a science has, on occasion, been doubted. They stated: "We will be provocative and argue that to understand core values and the sanctions both positive and negative, that criminologists apply to one another, it may be useful to treat criminology as a form of religion" (*Haines & Sutton* 2000, p. 147). It is beyond doubt that in some (not necessarily marginal) aspects, criminology is not a pure science: it necessarily contains the elements of morality, based on philosophy (and taking this idea further, sometimes even on religion). In this, we can face the elements of risks too, because if sciences in the postmodern era hold up their tasks of formulating opinions on any social questions, their statements can automatically be interpreted and transformed into the vocabulary of political ideologies too, see *Haines & Sutton* 2000.

96 This statement is absolutely in line with the related sentences of *Miomira Kostić*, who acknowledged the (partly) political aspects of the discipline of victimology: "Victimology is considered to be a sub-discipline of criminology which includes three different groups of people and their respective interests. This area has been the subject matter of frequent debates and analyses which have brought together the intellectuals, the activists of many non-governmental organisations, as well as the law-making authorities, yielding a lot of tension in this "boiling pot" of diverse interests" (*Kostic* 2010, p. 66).

3) examine the extent and quality of unreported cases, the typical behaviour of victims and also the causes behind why they are not motivated to report crimes to the police (victimological latency);

4) interpret the relationship between the offender and the victim in order to understand the background of interpersonal relations and conflicts (victimological interdependence);

5) research situations and circumstances in which victims found themselves before, during, and after the criminal act and, also, to highlight the nature of the behaviour conducted by them during the process of the crime (victimological habit);

6) examine the behaviour of the injured party within the context of law enforcement in respect of reporting and sharing relevant information with authorities (victimological information);

7) estimate the amount of damage the victim suffered by the criminal act, in terms of health, bodily (physical) integrity, and property, based on which the efficiency of the judicial system can be evaluated (victimological compensation); and

8) to calculate the potential risks of being victimised based upon the social and living conditions of people (also with the aid of information on victimisation gained from law enforcement agencies). Based upon these findings, to formulate programmes and suggestions for crime prevention in order to avoid attacks (victimological prophylaxis).[97]

In our chapter, we intended to reflect on victim's morphology and victims' habits with the help of victimological data and research findings but, first and foremost, we aimed to clarify the position of the victim. It is well known that the data of criminal statistics only represent the tip of the iceberg: criminality and the injuries suffered due to criminal acts represent a much higher proportion in society than suggested by the data appearing in statistics. In this chapter we also tried to call attention to the contradictions which may lie in the interpretation of criminal data. In terms of victimology, it means that the state can be interested in representing lower numbers, whilst the rights' defenders might tend to exaggerate a certain problem with the aim of raising awareness and making people alert to it. It is important to bear in mind that in order to understand reality as clearly as possible, researchers should keep the largest possible distance from the given sources (either official ones, or those provided by NGOs); even their fields of research should be double checked, using the compulsory rule of self-reflection, which was formulated and is stressed by postmodern science. In addition, the chapter also sought to emphasise the importance of legislation, namely the fact that the actual situation and signif-

---

97 *Tóth* 2003.

icance of each procedural actor is based on its position in criminal proceedings. This statement is especially true when we speak of the victim who has been abandoned for many centuries. In our opinion, criminal legislation may operate as the most objective source of interpretation because the legal framework reflects reality the best, in terms of how the victim is treated in the drama of criminal procedure. Still, it should not be forgotten that without scientific research and the tremendous work of researchers in the field of victimology, codification alone would not have placed the victim in its current position.

6. Summary in Hungarian

A tanulmány általános áttekintést nyújt az olvasó számára az áldozat helyzetéről Magyarországon. A cikk célja az áldozattan elméleti és tudományos (tudományelméleti) dilemmáinak, az áldozat-morfológia néhány aspektusának, és elsősorban az áldozat jogi környezetben betöltött szerepének (az áldozatok eljárási jogainak) bemutatása, különös tekintettel az új büntetőeljárási törvényre. A dolgozat célja, hogy leírja, hogyan kezelik az áldozatot, de egy pillantást vetünk arra is, hogy kit értünk konkrétan áldozat alatt. Milyenek az áldozatok statisztikai szempontból? Alkothatunk-e valós képet az áldozatokról a statisztikák tükrében? Milyen kutatást végeznek Magyarországon az áldozattal kapcsolatban?

Literature

Albrecht, H.J., & Kilchling, M. (2005): Victims of terrorism – Policies and Legislation in Europe. Council of Europe Expertise PC-S AV 04. Strasbourg.

Amberg, E. (2013): Gondolatok a gyűlölet-bűncselekmények rendészetéről, [Thoughts about hate crimes in law-enforcement]. Tanulmányok „A változórendészet aktuális kihívásai" című tudományos konferenciáról [Papers reflecting the conference, entitled:" The actual challenges of the changing law enforcement"] XIV, pp. 439–446.

Átol, D., Dombos, T., Jovánovics, E.M., Tóth, B., Pap, A.L. & Udvari, M. (2013): Közösség tagja elleni erőszak [Violence against the member of a community]. Alternatív kommentár [Alternative commentary] 4, pp. 71–79.

Balogh, L., Dinók, É., & Pap, A.L. (2012): A jog által láthatatlan? A gyűlölet-bűncselekmények szabályozási kérdései és gyakorlati problémái [Not visible by law? The regulation dilemmas and practical problems of hate crimes]. Fundamentum [Fundamentum], 4, pp. 91–98.

Barabás, A.T. (2015): Restorative justice in Hungary: A rapidly growing field of practice. Restorative Justice 3, pp. 387–395.

Barabás, A.T. (2014): Áldozatok és igazságszolgáltatás [Victims and jurisdiction]. Budapest.

Barabás, A.T. (2005): Az áldozattá válás sajátosságai Magyarország egyes régióiban [The features of victimisation in the different regions of Hungary], in: F. Irk (ed.), Kriminológiai Tanulmányok [Studies on Criminology]. Budapest, pp. 41–68.

Bárd, K. (2015a): Az áldozatok jogállása a nemzeti és a nemzetközi büntetőeljárásban [The position of the victim in the Hungarian and in the international criminal procedure], in:

P. Hack, M.E. Király, L. Korinek & A. Patyi (eds.), Gályapadból laboratóriumot: Tanulmányok Finszter Géza professzor tiszteletére. [From the desk of galley to the laboratory. Complimentary Copy in honor of Prof. Géza Finszter]. Budapest, pp. 205–216.

Bárd, K. (2015b): Victim's rights and due process, in: R. Uitz (ed.), Freedom and its enemies. The Hague, pp. 189–205.

Bárd, P., & Tóth, Z. (2016a): Gyűlölet-bűncselekmények Magyarországon I. [Hate crimes in Hungary I.]. Ügyészségi Szemle [Journal for Prosecution] 2, pp. 30–46.

Bárd, P., & Tóth, Z. (2016b): Gyűlölet-bűncselekmények Magyarországon III. [Hate Crimes in Hungary III.] Ügyészségi Szemle [Journal for Prosecution] 4, pp. 52–80.

Belovics, E. & Tóth, M. (2017): Büntetőeljárásjog. Harmadik, aktualizált kiadás [Criminal procedure law. Third edition]. Budapest.

Bolyky, O. (2018): Az emberölések jogi és kriminológiai jellemzői, különös tekintettel a mentális tényezők büntetőjogi értékelésére. Doktori értekezés. [The criminological and legal features of homicides, with special regard to the criminal law evaluation of the mental factors. Doctoral dissertation]. Budapest.

Demeter, Á. (2017): UN UPR recommendations and the development of the expert-front. Budapest.

Dinók, H. (2013): A gyűlölet-bűncselekmények – dogmatika és joggyakorlat [Hate crimes – Dogmatics and jurisprudence]. Belügyi Szemle [Journal of Police Studies] 61, pp. 52–67.

Dombos, T. (2018): Hate crimes in Hungary. Budapest.

Dombos, T. (2017): Data-protection issues in the context of hate crimes, by witness-hearings. Budapest.

Dombos, T. (2015): Jogalkalmazási problémák a gyűlölet-bűncselekményekkel kapcsolatos eljárásokban [Problems in the legal practice of procedures of hate-crimes]. Budapest.

Dombos, T., & Pap A.L. (2015): Using research results in training and education. Budapest.

Görgényi, I. (2006): A viktimológia [Victimology], in: K. Gönczöl, K. Kerezsi, L. Korinek & M. Lévay (eds.), Kriminológia – Szakkriminológia [Criminology – Specialized Criminology]. Budapest, pp. 273–296.

Görgényi, I. (2005): Az áldozat fogalma és megítélése [The concept of the victim and its assessment], in: Z. Rózsahegyi (ed.), Áldozatsegítés Európában [Victim-protection in Europe]. Budapest, pp. 7–32.

Görgényi, I. (2004a): A bűncselekményáldozata a büntetőeljárás során az Európai Unióban [The victims of crime in the criminal procedure in the European Union], in: M. Lévay (ed.), Az Európai Unióhoz való csatlakozás kihívásai a bűnözés és más devianciák elleni fellépés területén. [Challenges of joining the European Union in the fight against crime and other deviations]. Miskolc, pp. 267–301.

Görgényi, I. (2004b): Ötletek a készülő áldozatvédelmi törvényhez – az áldozat büntető eljárásjogi helyzete de lege ferenda [Ideas for the new law on victim protection – The position of the victim in the criminal procedure, de lege ferenda], in: E. Sárik & K. Marosi (eds.), Kriminológiai Közlemények [Papers on Criminology]. Budapest, pp. 105–131.

Görgényi, I. (2001a): A viktimológia alapkérdései [The fundamental questions of victimology]. Budapest.

Görgényi, I. (2001b): Kutatási eredmények Miskolcról egy nemzetközi viktimizációs felmérés keretében [Research findings in Miskolc as part of an international victim survey], in: I. Görgényi (ed.): Facultas nascitur – 20 éves a jogászképzés Miskolcon [Facultas nascitur – The 20th anniversary of the legal education in Miskolc]. Miskolc, pp. 181–202.

Görgényi, I. (2000): Nemzetközi és hazai viktimizációs felmérések [International and Hungarian surveys on the victims of crime], in: I. Tauber (ed.), Tanulmányok Vigh József 70. születésnapjára [Complimentary copy in honour of the 70th birthday of Vigh József]. Budapest, pp. 86–108.

Görgényi, I. (1999): A viktimológia [Victimology], in: K. Gönczöl, L. Korinek & M. Lévay (eds.), Kriminológiai ismeretek, bűnözés, bűnözéskontroll [Criminological knowledge, crime, crime control]. Budapest, pp. 93–107.

Görgényi, I. (1995): Az állam általi kártalanítás rendszere Nagy-Británniában, [The state compensation-system in Great Britain]. Kriminológiai Közlemények [Papers on Criminology] 51, pp. 106–118.

Görgényi, I. (1994): A bűncselekmények áldozatait segítőszervezetek Európában és szerepük a bűnmegelőzésben [The victim protector organisations in Europe and their role in crime prevention], in: I. Gönczöl (ed.), Büntetőpolitika, bűnmegelőzés [Criminal policy, crime prevention]. Budapest, pp. 74–104.

Görgényi, I. (1993a): A bűncselekmények áldozatainak okozott kárjóvátétele [The restitution of damage suffered by the victims of crime] Jogtudományi Közlöny [Official Gazette of Legal Sciences] 6, pp. 231–241.

Görgényi, I. (1993b): Hungarian aspect of victimology, in: S.P Singh & P.C. Friday (eds.), Global perspectives in victimology. London, pp. 212–218.

Görgényi, I. (1991): Női áldozatokról az ENSZ, Európa Tanács dokumentumai és a szakirodalom tükrében [The position of female victims in view of the document of the UN and the European Council]. Magyar Jog [Hungarian Law] 11, pp. 688–693.

Görgényi, I. (1990): Az 1980-as évek erőszakos bőnözésének viktimológiai jellemzői Magyarországon [The features of violent criminality in the 1980s in respect of victimology in Hungary]. Magyar Jog [Hungarian Law] 12, pp. 1021–1032.

Haines, F., & Sutton, A. (2000): Criminology as Religion? British Journal of Criminology 40, pp. 146–162.

Herczog, M., & Gyurkó, S. (2006): Randevú-erőszak – partnerbántalmazás a családi együttélést megelőzően [Rendezvous violence – Partner abuse before living together] in: F. Irk (ed.), Kriminológiai és Kriminalisztikai Tanulmányok [Papers on Criminology and Criminalistics.] Budapest, pp. 136–155.

Ivány, B. (2012): Minősíthetetlen szigorúság [Unqualifiable seriousness]. Budapest.

Ivány, B., & Udvari M. (2014): Küzdelem a gyűlölet-bűncselekmények visszaszorításáért [Fight against hate-crimes]. Budapest.

Jovánovics, E. (2013): Gyűlölet vagy előítélet? Szavak vagy tettek? Definíciókérdések, elhatárolások [Hatred or prejudice? Words or acts? Definitions, questions and differentiations]. Belügyi Szemle [Journal of Police studies] 12, pp. 68–76.

Jovánovics E., & Pap A.L. (2013): Kollektív bűnösség a 21. század Magyarországán: magyarellenesség vádja cigányokkal szemben két emblematikus perben [Collective guilt in 21st-century Hungary: The charge of an anti-Hungarian attitude in two emblematic criminal cases]. Fundamentum, pp. 153–157.

Király, T. (2008): A büntetőeljárási jog [The criminal procedure law]. Budapest.

Kirs, E. (2017): A gyűlölet-bűncselekmények nyomozásának jellemzői hibái a strasbourgi sztenderdek alapján [The typical mistakes in investigations of hate-crime cases according to Strasbourg-standards]. Budapest.

Kirs, E., & Pap, A.L. (2017): Az Emberi Jogok Európai Bíróságának ítélete a gyűlölet-bűncselekmények esetén folytatott nyomozásról [The legal summary of the sentences of the European Court of Human Rights on the investigation of hate crimes]. Állam- és Jogtudomány [State and Legal Science] 4, pp. 141–151.

Kiss, A. (2018a): A különleges bánásmódot igénylő személyek jogai az új büntetőeljárási törvényben [Rights of vulnerable persons in the new Act on Criminal Procedure]. Kriminológiai Tanulmányok [Studies on Criminology] 55, pp. 103–119.

Kiss, A. (2018b): A sértett szerepe a büntetőeljárásban [The role of the victim in the Criminal Procedure]. Budapest.

Kiss, A. (2006a): A közvetítői eljárásról [About the mediation process], in: F. Irk (ed.), Kriminológiai Tanulmányok [Studies on Criminology]. Budapest, pp. 241–264.

Kiss, A. (2006b): A sértett fogalma a büntetőeljárásban [The role and concept of the victim in the criminal procedure], in: C. Fenyvesi, C. Herke, B. Mészáros & S. Alamoreanu (eds.), Bizonyítékok. Tiszteletkötet Tremmel Flórián egyetemi tanár 65. születésnapjára [Evidences. Honorary volume for the 65th birthday of Prof. Flórián Tremmel]. Pécs, pp. 287–293.

Kiss, A. (2005): Az adhéziós eljárás szerepe a büntetőeljárásban [About the adversarial process in the criminal procedure], in: F. Irk (ed.), Kriminológiai Tanulmányok [Studies on Criminology]. Budapest, pp. 367–380.

Kiss, A. (2004a): A sértett szerepe a büntetőeljárásban [The position of the victim in the criminal procedure], in: K. Marosi & E. Sárik (eds.), Kriminológiai Közlemények [Papers on Criminology]. Budapest, pp. 132–138.

Kiss, A. (2004b): Additional private prosecution, in: K. Gönczöl & M. Lévay (eds.), New tendencies in crime and criminal policy in Central and Eastern Europe. Special Edition of the Proceedings of Criminology. Miskolc, pp. 392–396.

Kiss, A. (1997): A sértett szerepe a büntetőeljárásban [The role of the victim in the criminal procedure], in: F. Irk (ed.), Kriminológiai és Kriminalisztikai Tanulmányok [Studies on Criminology and Criminalistics]. Budapest, pp. 232–254.

Kiss, A., & Farkas, K. (2018): The position of victims in Hungary with special regard to the efficiency of criminal proceedings, in: J. Andraško, J. Hamuľák & M. Kahounová (eds.): Constitutional, Statutory and Criminological Attributes for Crime Victims. Bratislava Legal Forum. Collection of Papers from the International Academic Conference 22nd – 23rd of February 2018 = Ústavnoprávne, stavnoprávne, zákonné a kriminologické atribúty o obetiach trestných činov. Bratislavské právnické fórum 2018. Zborník príspevkov z medzinárodnej vedeckej konferencie 22.–23. februára 2018. Comenius University in Bratislava, Faculty of Law, Bratislava, 2018, pp. 86–97; https://www.flaw.uniba.sk/file admin/praf/Veda/Konferencie_a_podujatia/bpf_2018_new/Zbornik_BPF2018_sekcia_1.pdf [02.10.2019] [in Slovakian only].

Kó, J. (2019): A bűnügyi statisztika aktuális kérdései [Current issues of criminal statistics]. Budapest.

Kó, J. (2005): Félelem keletről nyugatra: A bűnözéstől való félelem területi sajátosságai Magyarországon, [Fear from the East to the West: The dimensions of fear in Hungary in a geographical dimension], in F. Irk (ed.), Kriminológiai Tanulmányok [Studies on Criminology]. Budapest, pp. 41–67.

Korinek, L. (2017): Félelem a bűnözéstől, rejtett bűnözés [Fear of crime, latent criminality], in: A. Borbíró, K. Gönczöl, K. Kerezsi & M. Lévay (eds.), Kriminológia Tankönyv [Handbook of criminology]. Budapest, pp. 371–391.

Korinek, L. (2010): Kriminológia I–II. [Criminology I–II.]. Budapest.

*Korinek, L. (*1988): Rejtett bűnözés [Latent criminality]. Budapest.

Kostić, M. (2010): A contemporary theoretical approach to crime and its victim. Facta Universitatis Series: Law and Politics 8, pp. 65–78.

Kránitz, M. (2005): A vagyon elleni bűncselekmények áldozatainak területi jellemzői [The geographical features of victims of property crimes], in: F. Irk (ed.), Kriminológiai Tanulmányok [Studies on criminology]. Budapest, pp. 112–139.

Lupária, L. (ed.) (2015): Victims and criminal Justice. European standards and national good practices. Milan.

Morvai, K. (1998): Terror a családban – Feleségbántalmazás és a jog [Terror in the family – wife abuse and law]. Budapest.

Nagy, L.T. (2012): A közfeladatot ellátó személyek elleni erőszakról – egy empirikus kutatás tükrében [Perceptions of the assault on a person entrusted with public functions – conclusions of empirical study, in: Collegium Doctorum. Miskolci Egyetem Deák Ferenc Doktori Iskola [Collegium Doctorum. Miskolc University of Law, Deák Ferenc Doctoral School]. Miskolc.

Nagy, L.T. (2005): Az erőszakos bűncselekmények áldozatainak területi jellemzői [The geographical features of victims of violent crimes], in: F. Irk (ed.), Kriminológiai Tanulmányok [Studies on criminology]. Budapest, pp. 92–112.

Pap A.L. (2017): Jogalkalmazási fejlemények (és adalékok) a zaklatás tárgykörében [The development of legal practice on the topic of harassment]. Budapest.

Pap, A.L. (2016): Gyűlölet-bűncselekmények a magyar jogrendszerben [Hate crime in the Hungarian national legal order]. Budapest.

Parti, K. (2009): Gyermekpornográfia az interneten [Child pornography on the internet]. Miskolc.

Póczik, S. (2011): A gyűlöletbeszéd és a holokauszt tagadás szankcionálása a németnyelvű országokban [Hate speech and the punishment of the denial of the Holocaust in German-tongue countries], in: G. Virág (ed.), Kriminológiai Tanulmányok [Studies on criminology]. Budapest, pp. 127–143.

Rácsok, G. (2013): A film mint missziói eszköz korunk változó vallásosságának kontextusában, Hittudományi doktori értekezés a missziológia tárgykörében [Film as a means of religious missiology in the context of our era of fluid religiosity. Doctoral dissertation in Theological Studies]. Sárospatak.

Róth, E. (2011): Position of victims in the criminal procedure in the context with requirements of the European Union. European Integration Studies 9, pp. 109–120.

Róth, E. (2004): What is the real interest of the victim?, in: K. Gönczöl & M. Lévay (eds.), New Tendencies in crime and criminal policy in Central and Eastern Europe. Miskolc, pp. 396–404.

Sárik, E. (2018): Vallásosság, értékrend, ifjúság a kriminológia kontextusában. [Religion, values, youth in the context of criminology]. Pécs.

Tamási, E. (2005): Bűnös áldozatok, [Sinful victims]. Budapest.

Tamási, E. (ed.) (2015): Különös kegyetlenséggel – Fiatalkorú és fiatal felnőtt emberölést elkövetők kriminológiai vizsgálata [With particular cruelty – The criminological study of juvenile and young adult killers]. Budapest.

Tamási, E., Bolyky, O. & Sárik, E. (2014): Az emberöléshez vezető út rizikófaktorai fiatalkorúak és fiatal felnőttek körében. [The risk factors of homicides among juveniles and young adults], in: G. Vókó (ed.), Kriminológiai Tanulmányok [Studies on criminology]. Budapest, pp. 130–164.

Tóth, O., & Róbert, K. (2010): Idősnők partner általi bántalmazása [Partner abuse of older women]. Budapest.

Tóth, T. (2003): A viktimológia ismeretelmélete. A viktimológia története és vizsgálódásának tárgya [The theory of victimology. The history of victimology and the scope of its examination]. Budapest.

Udvari, M. (2013): Hova tűnnek a gyűlölet-bűncselekmények? Jogalkalmazási anomáliák, rendőrségi és ügyészségi ügykezelés [Where do hate crimes vanish? Irregularities in the administration of Police and Prosecution]. Belügyi Szemle [Journal of Police Studies] 12, pp.77–83.

Uszkiewicz, E. (2013): (Mit (nem) mutatnak a számok? [What do the numbers fail to show?]. Belügyi Szemle [Journal of Police Studies] 12, pp. 84–91.

Utasi, J. (2011): A gyűlölet-bűncselekmények háttere [The background of hate crimes], in: G. Virág (ed.), Kriminológiai Tanulmányok [Studies on criminology]. Budapest, pp. 115–126.

Virág, G. (ed.) (2005): Családi iszonyok. A családi erőszak kriminológiai vizsgálata [Family Dreads. The criminological research of domestic violence]. Budapest.

Documents

Prosecution Statistics Brief (ASoPPO) (2017): Büntetőjogi szakterület 2016 [Criminal law 2016]; http://ugyeszseg.hu/pdf/statisztika/Buntetojogi_szakterulet_2016.pdf [02.10.2019] [in Hungarian only]; cited as: StatOffice 2017.

Prosecution Statistics Brief (ASoPPO) (2016): Büntetőjogi szakterület 2015 [Criminal law 2015]; http://ugyeszseg.hu/pdf/statisztika/Buntetojogi_szakterulet_2015.pdf [02.10.2019] [in Hungarian only]; cited as: StatOffice 2016.

Prosecution Statistics Brief (ASoPPO) (2015): Büntetőjogi szakterület 2014 [Criminal law 2014]; http://ugyeszseg.hu/pdf/statisztika/Buntetojogi_szakterulet_2014.pdf [02.10.2019] [in Hungarian only]; cited as: StatOffice 2015.

Prosecution Statistics Brief (ASoPPO) (2014): Büntetőjogi szakterület 2013 [Criminal law 2013]; http://ugyeszseg.hu/pdf/statisztika/Buntetojogi_szakterulet_2013.pdf [02.10.2019] [in Hungarian only]; cited as: StatOffice 2014.

Prosecution Statistics Brief (ASoPPO) (2013): Büntetőjogi szakterület 2012 [Criminal law 2012]; http://ugyeszseg.hu/pdf/statisztika/Buntetojogi_szakterulet_2012.pdf [02.10.2019] [in Hungarian only]; cited as: StatOffice 2013.

Prosecution Statistics Brief (ASoPPO) (2012): Büntetőjogi szakterület 2011 [Criminal law 2011]; http://ugyeszseg.hu/pdf/statisztika/Buntetojogi_szakterulet_2011.pdf [02.10.2019] [in Hungarian only]; cited as: StatOffice 2012.

Prosecution Statistics Brief (ASoPPO) (2011): Büntetőjogi szakterület 2010 [Criminal law 2010]; http://ugyeszseg.hu/pdf/statisztika/Buntetojogi_szakterulet_2010.pdf [02.10.2019] [in Hungarian only]; cited as: StatOffice 2011.

Prosecution Statistics Brief (ASoPPO) (2010): Büntetőjogi szakterület 2009 [Criminal law 2009]; http://ugyeszseg.hu/pdf/statisztika/Buntetojogi_szakterulet_2009.pdf [02.10.2019] [in Hungarian only]; cited as: StatOffice 2010.

StatOffice: see Prosecution Statistics Brief.

Montenegro

Victimology and Victim Protection

Velimir Rakočević & Aleksandra Jovanović

1. Introduction

According to the Montenegrin constitution adopted in 2007, Montenegro is a civil, democratic, and ecological state. It is also a country founded on social justice and the rule of law.[1] Montenegro is a member of the United Nations, the Organization for European Security and Cooperation (OSCE), and the European Council. Since 2010, it has also been a candidate for EU membership. The country is also a member of NATO (since June 2017). Montenegro is situated in Southeast Europe on the Balkan Peninsula. Montenegrin territory covers 13,812 square kilometres. It borders Croatia, Bosnia and Herzegovina, Serbia, and Albania and it is separated from Italy by the Adriatic Sea. The length of the cost is 293.5 square kilometres. According to the country's Statistical Office (MONSTAT) data from 2017, there are 620,029 inhabitants: 313,793 females and 306,236 males.[2] The ethnic composition of the population is as follows: Montenegrins (44.69%), Serbians (26.73%), Bosnians (8.65%), Albanians (4.91%), Muslims[3] (3.31%), Roma people (1.01%), Croatians (0.97%), and other (7.44%). Montenegrin is the official language. But also Serbian, Albanian, Bosnian, and Croatian are used officially.[4] According to the constitution of Montenegro, all religious organisations have the same rights and function separately from the state. The majority of the population is Orthodox Christian (72.07%), followed by Muslim (19.11%), and Catholic (3.44%).[5] Out of all inhabitants older than 15,52% have finished high school, however, 27,285 out of that number are university stu-

---

1 Constitution of Montenegro, Law. No. 01-514/22, 22.10.2007, Official Gazette 1/2007.

2 StatOffice 2018.

3 Based on the national and ethnic affiliation 3.31% of the population declared itself as Muslims; see StatOffice 2011.

4 Based on the Constitution of Montenegro, the official language is Montenegrin; however, languages in official use are also Serbian, Albanian, Bosnian and Croatian; see Article 13 (language and writing) of the Law No. 01-514/22.

5 StatOffice 2018.

dents. In Montenegro, 17% of inhabitants have higher (BA, BSc), whether by using "the old" or "the new" Bologna system of education. The average age of people who completed secondary school (but were not educated further) is 44 years, and the average age of people who only completed primary school, is 56. There are 964 doctors of sciences, whose average age is 54 years, and a population that counts 3,713 masters of sciences is noticeably younger, with an average age of 41 years.[6] According to the MONSTAT data, 6,464 people died in 2017, out of which 3,385 were males and 3,079 were females. The birth rate in 2016 was positive and it counted a plus of 1,105 people. In 2017, the national rate of population increase was positive (159 people), while the rate of migration was higher in Montenegro from the north to the central region and the south region of the country because of economic reasons.[7] In 2017, 68% of the population lived in urban areas.[8] According to Montenegrin economic indicators, the country falls into the category of a developing state. National gross income in 2016 was 4,007,000,000 EUR and it was nominally higher than in 2015 (by 6.9%). The primary income balance with foreign countries was positive for 2016 (52,600,000 EUR). National gross income per inhabitant counted 6,439 EUR in 2016. The unemployment rate in Montenegro was 20% in 2016.[9]

The criminal justice system of Montenegro consists of criminal courts, the state prosecution service, the police force, and the prison administration. The police force falls under the Ministry of Interior. The police director is appointed and dismissed by the government, based on the suggestions of the Ministry of Interior. The police director keeps the responsible minister and the government informed and must not be politically active or be a member of a political party. The police director submits to the competent working body of the Assembly a special report on the results in the fight against organized crime and corruption twice a year, and at the latest on 1 June and 1 December. If the competent working body of the Assembly does not accept the report, it shall inform the Minister that may initiate the dismissal procedure of the Director of the Police before the deadline for appointment.[10]

The police have a wide variety of tasks to conduct. These include (but are not limited to): protecting citizens, maintaining security and public order, preventing and solving crimes, protecting property, securing public gatherings, safeguarding certain individuals, supervising traffic, supervising state borders, controlling the movement of foreigners, ensuring international police cooperation, etc. Security centres are carrying out police affairs on the territory of local units, the capital and the capital city, which relate to: the protection of life, personal and property security; prevention

---

6 StatOffice 2018.

7 StatOffice 2018.

8 StatOffice 2018.

9 StatOffice 2018.

10 Law of Internal Affairs, Law No. 044/12, 09.08.2012, Official gazette 44/2012.

and detection of criminal offences and the detection and deprivation of their liberty, 47 actors; maintenance of public order and traffic safety; control of movement and residence of foreigners; certain criminal-technical tasks and conduct other activities within the scope of the Centre. Security Centre operations are carried out within narrow organizational units, as follows: Departments of Security, Police Stations and Police Units.[11]

The legal system (legislation and courts)[12] is responsible for the organisation and regulation of courts, the election of judges, and all matters necessary for the orderly and timely functioning of courts. The country's courts exercise judicial power. Judges are independent. The following courts exist in Montenegro:

1) base Courts,
2) High court,
3) Economic court,
4) Appellate court,
5) Administrative court, and
6) Supreme court.[13]

The law on state prosecution[14] regulates the founding, organisation, and supervision of the state prosecution service, including its internal workings, mandate, composition, and mode of functioning. The State Prosecutor's Office carries out its function based on the constitution, laws, and certified international guidelines. Within the State Prosecutor's Office, five departments have been established: the Supreme State Prosecution Office, the Chief Prosecution Office, the Special State Prosecution Office, the High State Prosecution Offices, and the Basic State Prosecution Offices were founded within the area of Montenegro, with the residence in Podgorica.

Criminal sanctions are carried out by the Institute for Execution of Criminal Sanctions, which consists of Podgorica Penitentiary, Podgorica Prison, and Bijelo Polje Prison. The Law on the Execution of Prison Sentences, Fines, and Security Measures[15] regulates imprisonment (up to forty-years-imprisonment), monetary fines, security measures, rights and obligations of prisoners, etc. The Office for the Enforcement of Criminal Sanctions, pursuant to the Regulation of the Government of Montenegro, is an administrative body in the Ministry of Justice. The Office for the Execution of Criminal Sanctions shall perform tasks related to the following:

---

11 Law of Internal Affairs, Law No. 001/15, 05.01.2015, Official gazette 01/2015.

12 Law on Courts, Law No. 01-283/2, 01.02.2002 Official Gazette 5/2002.

13 See Article 1 (subject of the law) of the Law No. 01-283/2.

14 Law on State Prosecution, Law No. 01-242/2, 04.03.2015, Official Gazette 11/2015.

15 Law on the Execution of Prison Sentences, Fines, and Security Measures, Law No. 01-626/2, 10.07.2015, Official gazette 36/2015.

execution of criminal sanctions, as follows: sentences of imprisonment and juvenile imprisonment, security measures carried out in accordance with the law in the Institute for the Execution of Criminal Sanctions; sentences of imprisonment pronounced in the misdemeanour procedure[16] and measures for securing the presence of the defendant in the criminal procedure – detention; as well as other tasks assigned to him in jurisdiction.[17]

Montenegro has had several state and legal arrangements, from the time of the Socialist Federal Republic of Yugoslavia, through to the Federal Republic of Yugoslavia, then the State Union of Serbia and Montenegro, and finally the restoration of independence in 2006. It is important to underline that there were no armed conflicts during the 1990s on its territory, and multinational and multi-religious balance was kept with only a few minor conflicts. There were several mass demonstrations, out of which the biggest took place in the 1980s, which resulted in the government being overthrown. There were violent mass demonstrations in 1997 and 2006, but in both cases, the police intervened and dispersed the demonstrations.[18] All the mass protests took place in the capital, Podgorica.

There has been an increase in the number of migrants in Montenegro during the last years. In 2016 and 2017, the number of migrants increased by 80%, compared to the previous year.[19] In the Asylum Seekers Centre in Spuz, there are currently 128 persons, most of whom are from Algeria but also from other countries such as Pakistan, Syria, Palestine, and Cuba too. In 2017, 746 asylum seekers were accepted.[20] Asylum seekers can stay in Montenegro until the end of the first instance procedure, conducted by the Ministry of Internal Affairs. In case of appeal, they can stay until the end of the second instance procedure. If the asylum seeker receives refugee status, the state is obliged to take care of them for another six months.

1.2 The Development of Victimology in Montenegro

Little has been written about the development of victimology in Montenegro. *Vukašin Pešić*, the first Professor of Criminology at the University of Veljko Vlahović in Titograd (from 1972 to 1978) has noted in his book on criminology: "Be-

---

16 The misdemeanour is the action that constitutes a violation of public order, determined by law or other regulation and for which is prescribed sanction; see Article 2 (the term misdemeanour) of the Law on Misdemeanours, Law No. 039/11, 11.01.2011, Official gazette 39/2011.

17 See Article 3 (execution of foreign courts' decisions) of the Law on enforcement of criminal sanctions, Law No. 32/2011-3, 01.07.2011, Official Gazette 40/2011.

18 *Rakočević* 2010.

19 Ministry of Internal Affairs 2018.

20 Ministry of Internal Affairs 2018.

cause of different methodological approaches and other reasons, the victimological problematics neither was thoroughly explored, nor separated from other sciences".[21] A further Montenegrin book on criminology, written by Professor *Krsto Perović* and, did not contain a chapter on victimology.[22] Professor *Velimir Rakočević* did, however, write a chapter on victimology in his book "Criminology". In this chapter, the following topics were addressed: the origin and development of victimology, the concept and subject of victimology, the most important features of modern victimology, the goals and tasks of victimology, the concept and typology of victims, the concept and types of victim predispositions, the victimisation of women and children, victims of massive violations of human rights, the victim's contribution to the discovery of a crime, and victim compensation.[23]

Victimology has been taught as an independent scientific discipline since 2006 at the Faculty of Law, University of Montenegro. It is an elective unit at an undergraduate level and a compulsory unit for Master and Doctoral Studies. At the Department of Security and Criminalistics victimology is taught as a part of criminology.

In Montenegro, organisations standing up for women's rights were the first to point out the phenomenon of domestic violence, and their work began with the launch of SOS contact numbers for female and child victims of domestic violence in 1996. After three years of work, it became apparent that a large number of women in Montenegro were forced to leave home due to domestic violence. This realisation led to the establishment of a shelter for victims of domestic violence. The first shelter, entitled Women's Safe House (WSH), was established in mid-1999. The shelter for women and children who are victims of violence certainly the most important program is the Safe Women's House, in which more than 3,000 people were accommodated, and over 6,000 people asked for some sort of help, which is an extremely large number for Montenegro, since the founding of the shelter until 2013.

In addition to shelter services, the Safe Women's House has provided support services to women who were victims of violence from the very beginning, including providing basic information, establishing contacts with institutions relevant for a particular problem, and psychological counselling. Up until December 2013, over 449 people contacted WSH for some kind of help.[24]

In addition, WSH has also developed programs to raise awareness about domestic violence as well as educational programs. As a part of its work, the WSH has published: "Handbook for sexual and reproductive health", "Sexual violence – A handbook for children and youths", "Handbook for elderly people to fight domestic

---

21 *Pešić* 1980.

22 *Perović* 1998.

23 *Rakočević* 2007.

24 Women's Safe House 2013.

violence", "What do we know about economic abuse of women".[25] The WSH organised seminars for training officers of state institutions (police, judiciary, centres for social work) on the topic of domestic violence, organized a seminar for overcoming discrimination among mothers who come from different socio-cultural backgrounds, implemented the project "Empowering Young Women for Monitoring Governmental Policies in the Area of Gender Equality", 2011/2013, and participated in a number of awareness-raising activities.

The work of the organisation is based on international standards set by non-governmental organisations. The WSH cooperates with numerous international organisations. Moreover, it is a member of the Balkan Human Rights Network, the Regional Anti-Human Trafficking Network ACTA and Penelope, the RECOM coalition. The RECOM is an organisation that promotes the establishment of a Regional Commission and creates an accurate, official and objective record of war crimes and other grave human rights violations, the recognition of victims and their suffering, and the prevention of reoffending to gather facts about war crimes and other serious violations of human rights in the territory of the former Yugoslavia in the period from 1991 to 2001.[26]

After establishing the shelter, the WSH received support for trainings and strengthening human resources, as well as material and financial assistance in most cases from international and humanitarian organisations, embassies, foundations, and charities. At the beginning of 2004, the government of Montenegro, in cooperation with the International Organization for Migration and the OSCE, opened a shelter for victims of human trafficking.

2. Montenegrin Legislation Provides a Normative Basis for the Protection of Victims of Criminal Offences

The Law on the Compensation to Victims of Crimes of Violence[27] regulates the conditions, methods, and procedures, for exercising the right to compensation for victims of violent criminal offences. Under this law, a violent crime is defined as a criminal offence committed with intent. This can include: a criminal offence committed with the use of physical force, a criminal offence against sexual freedom, a criminal offence that endangers a person's life, body, or property by means of a highly dangerous act, or a dangerous criminal offence that results in the death, serious bodily injury, or serious violation of the physical and mental health of one

---

25 *Perović-Ivanović* 2008; 2009a; 2009b; 2009c.

26 Center for peace, non-violence and human rights 2019.

27 Law on the Compensation to Victims of Crimes of Violence, Law No. 01-624/2, 07.07.2015, Official gazette 35/2015.

or more persons (and it is prescribed under the Criminal Code of Montenegro[28] as a serious form of the basic criminal acts, committed with intent).

Article 3 of the Criminal Code of Montenegro states that a victim of a violent crime is a person whose death, serious bodily injury, or serious violation of physical and mental health has occurred due to the commission of a crime of violence.[29] The victim is also a person who has suffered death, serious bodily injury, or severe mental and physical health damage due to the crime of violence, referred to in Article 2, paragraph 1, indent 1 of this law,[30] even when the perpetration of this criminal offence was not directed at that person.

The victim is also a person who has suffered death, serious bodily injury, or severe mental and physical health damages in the following situations: attempt to prevent the commission of the crime of violence, when assisting the police in capturing the perpetrator of the crime of violence and while helping the victim. A victim has the right to compensation, such as compensation for lost salary, compensation for health care costs (costs of treatment and stay in the hospital), and compensation for the costs of a funeral. When the death of the victim occurs, the victims' dependents are entitled to compensation for damages and the right to compensation for loss of future support prescribed by law.

The Criminal Code of Montenegro stipulates in Article 1: "The protection of people and other basic social values constitutes the basis for determining criminal offences and the prescription of criminal sanctions necessary for the suppression of these acts".[31]

The Code of Criminal Procedure of Montenegro in Article 1 establishes procedures and rules to ensure fair trials.[32] Article 59 stipulates the rights of the injured party as a prosecutor or subsidiary prosecutor.[33] When a state prosecutor concludes that there is no basis for prosecution for a criminal offence for which a party is prosecuted *ex officio* or has no basis to prosecute against any of the reported accomplices, the prosecution shall, within eight days, notify the injured party and give instructions so that they may continue prosecution themselves if so desired. The injured party has the right to undertake or continue prosecution within 30 days of receiving this notice. If the state prosecutor withdrew the indictment, the

---

28 Criminal Code of Montenegro, Law No. 070/03, 25.12.2003, Official gazette 70/2003.

29 See Article 3 (no punishment without guilt) of the Law No. 070/03.

30 See Article 2 (lawfulness in the determination of criminal offences and the prescribing of criminal sanctions) of the Law No. 070/03.

31 See Article 1 (the basis and limits of criminal complaint) of the Law No. 070/03.

32 See Article 1 (subject and purpose of the law) of the Criminal Procedure Code of Montenegro, Law No. 057/09, 26.08.2009, Official gazette 57/2009.

33 See Article 59 (injured as a prosecutor) of the Law no. 057/09.

injured party may, by taking over the prosecution, keep the issued indictment or bring a new one. Rules are also in place should the prosecution fail to notify the injured party in the stipulated manner. If the injured party dies within the time limit for prosecution or during the proceedings, his/her spouse, partner, children, parents, adopted children, adopted parents, siblings may, within three months of his/her death, undertake prosecution, or give a statement that they will continue the proceedings.

The Law on Protection of Witnesses regulates the conditions and the procedure for providing protection and assistance to a witness if there exists a well-founded fear the witnesses is exposed to real and serious danger.[34] Protection and assistance may also be provided to a close person at the witness's request. The protection of witnesses (or their close relatives) is provided through the application of the witness protection program. The protection program offers a set of measures, stipulated by law, to ensure the protection of the protected individual's life, health, physical integrity, and freedom. Those to be protected must consent to the measures (in the case of a minor, the parents or legal guardians must consent). In Montenegrin criminal legislation, the criminal and legal protection of children and especially vulnerable persons is strengthened. This means that if some of the numerous criminal offences were committed against a particularly vulnerable category of persons, the perpetrator will be punished more severely.

2.1 Review of Other Acts that Protect Victims of Criminal Offences

In Montenegro, the following legislative acts deal with the protection of victims of criminal offences:

1) Law on Treatment of Juveniles in Criminal Proceedings,[35]
2) Law on Internal Affairs,[36]
3) Law on Mediation,[37]
4) Law on Misdemeanours,[38]
5) Law on Gender Equality,[39]

---

34 Law on Protection of Witnesses, Law No. 01-1372/2, 25.10.2004, Official gazette 65/2004.

35 Law on Treatment of Juveniles in Criminal Proceedings, Law no. 01-1507/2, 29.12.2011, Official gazette 64/2011.

36 See Law No. 044/12.

37 Law on Mediation, Law No. 026/12, 06.06.2012, Official gazette 29/2012.

38 See Law No. 039/11.

39 Law on Gender Equality, Law No. 035/15, 07.07.2015, Official gazette 35/15.

6) Law on the Prohibition of Discrimination,[40] and
7) Law on Protection against Domestic Violence.[41]

2.2 Position of the Witness-Victim in Montenegrin Criminal Procedure

The Montenegrin Code on Criminal Procedure regulates the position of witness during criminal proceedings.[42] Persons who are likely to be able to provide information about the criminal offence, about the perpetrator, or about other important circumstances, are invited as witnesses. The injured party may also be heard as witnesses. Every person invited as a witness is obliged to respond to a call, and unless otherwise provided by this law, they are obliged to testify.[43] The following persons cannot be heard as witnesses:

1) a person who could violate the duty of keeping confidential information or the regulations that cover secrecy of the information (unless the authorised body relieves them of duty);
2) counsel for the defence;
3) a person who could violate their duty of keeping a professional secret (a religious confessor, a lawyer, a health worker, a journalist, etc.); and
4) a minor who, given their age and mental development, is unable to understand the significance of the right or obligation to testify.[44]

The following persons are released of their duty to testify:

1) a perpetrator's spouse or *de facto* partner or
2) direct blood relatives of the perpetrator.

The court that conducts the procedure is obliged to warn the persons that they are not obliged to testify. The warning and the answer are entered into the court record. If there are reasonable grounds that a person is relieved from proving testimony against one of the perpetrators, the same person is released of testimony for other perpetrators, if due to the nature of their testimony it cannot be restricted

---

40 Law on Prohibition of Discrimination, Law No. 042/17, 30.06.2017, Official gazette 42/2017.

41 Law on Protection against Domestic Violence, Law No. 046/10, 27.07.2010, Official gazette 46/2010.

42 See Law No. 057/09.

43 See Article 107 (persons who can be heard as witnesses) of the Law No. 057/09.

44 See Article 108 (persons who cannot be heard as witnesses) of the Law No. 057/09.

only to the other perpetrators.[45] The court's decision cannot be based on a testimony when a person who should not have been examined as a witness was examined as a witness, or a person that was not obliged to testify, and they were not warned about this or they did not explicitly waive their right. The same applies if the warning or the waiver were not entered into the record, or if the testimony was obtained by using torture.[46] The witness has the right not to answer certain questions if there is a possibility that would expose him/her to embarrassment or prosecution, and the court is obliged to provide information accordingly.[47] Summons of the witness is carried out by sending a written summons stating the name, surname, and occupation of the invited person, the time and place of arrival, the criminal case in question, and a designation that they are invited as a witness (along with a warning about the consequences of an unjustified absence). The summons of a juvenile witness under 16 years old is carried out via their parents unless this is, due to exceptional circumstances, not possible.

Witnesses who cannot attend the hearing due to a valid reason (not in the country, poor health, disability, etc.) can be heard elsewhere (generally at their home). In exceptional cases, witnesses can provide testimony using technical devices. In such cases, the summons of witnesses may be done via a phone or other means of electronic communication, if they accept to answer such a call.[48] Witnesses are questioned separately and without the presence of other witnesses. The witness is obliged to provide oral answers. The witness will be warned beforehand about their obligation to speak the truth and that concealing evidence or providing false testimony is a criminal offence. The witness will be acquainted with these rights and this will be record. When examining juveniles, especially if they are affected by the crime, witness examination should be conducted in a cautious manner to avoid damaging the psychological status of the juvenile. If necessary, the questioning should be conducted with the assistance of a psychologist or other competent person. If the injured party is a victim of a criminal offence against sexual freedom or a trial, then they have the right to be questioned in a separate room by the judge and recording clerk, while the prosecutor, the defendant, and the defence attorney may watch it on a screen from another room, with an option to ask questions. The court is obliged to inform them about their rights, which shall also enter the record. Court can decide to apply this provision to the testimony of the damaged party, who is the victim of discrimination.[49] When examining a witness, deception is not allowed to obtain answers. The injured party who is interrogated

45 See Article 109 (persons exempt from the duty of testimony) of the Law No. 057/09.

46 See Article 110 (testimonies, on which a court decision cannot be based) of the Law No. 057/09.

47 See Article 111 (denial of answering some questions) of the Law No. 057/09.

48 See Article 112 (calling witnesses) of the Law No. 057/09.

49 See Article 113 (method of hearing witnesses and court warnings) of the Law No. 057/09.

will be asked if they want to obtain the proprietary claim.[50] The defendant who is questioned as a witness will be asked if he wants to have a proprietary claim in the criminal proceedings. If the injured party does not want the property legal claim to be obtained in criminal proceedings, he can accomplish it in a civil procedure through a civil action. An interpreter is to be provided by the court if necessary.[51]

The protection of witnesses against intimidation is also regulated by this law. If there is a grounded fear that the witness, by providing evidence, could expose themselves, their family, or any other person closely connected to them, to serious danger for life, health, physical integrity, freedom, or property, the witness may refuse to testify until protection is provided.

Witness protection may also be provided outside criminal proceedings, in accordance with the law governing the protection of witnesses.[52] Witnesses can provide testimony under a pseudonym or use other means to remain anonymous (e.g., voice or image encryption). If the special way of hearing witness testimony relates only to concealment of data, the hearing will be conducted using a pseudonym for the witness and, for the rest of the hearing, the hearing will be conducted according to the general provisions of the law on witness testimony. If the special way of hearing witness testimony in the proceedings relates to concealment of information and to the concealment of a witness's face, the hearing will be conducted via technical devices for the transmission of image and sound. The face and the voice of a witness will be altered during the hearing. During the hearing, a witness will be in a room that is separate from the courtroom. The investigating judge will forbid any question that may lead to the identity of the witness being revealed. When the hearing is over, the witness will sign the record using a pseudonym (in the presence of investigating judge and recording clerk). Persons who, by any means, find out information about the identity of the witness are obliged to keep it as a secret.[53] These provisions are to be applied throughout the entire trial.

The Code of Criminal Procedure provides special protection for cooperating witness or in other words crown witness. During the hearing of the cooperating witnesses, the public is excluded, unless the council, upon the proposal of the state prosecutor (and with the consent of the cooperating witness), makes a different decision. Before making a decision, the president of the panel, in the presence of the defence counsel, will inform cooperating witnesses about the proposal of the state prosecutor and inform them about the right to be heard without the public being present. When a co-

---

50 See Article 114 (examination and confrontation of witnesses) of the Law No. 057/09.

51 See Article 116 (examining witnesses through an interpreter) of the Law No. 057/09.

52 See Article 120 (protection of witnesses from intimidation) of the Law No. 057/09.

53 See Article 120 (protection of witnesses from intimidation) of the Law No. 057/09.

operating witness makes a statement that he/she agrees to be heard in the presence of the public, the statement will be entered on record. The state prosecutor may suggest the provision of special protection for cooperating witness, their relatives, or other persons close to them.[54]

2.3 How to Improve the Position of Victims in Montenegrin Criminal Procedure

If the victim is a witness in criminal proceedings, it is very important that they should be informed properly, have legal assistance, have the right to privacy, and the right to compensation. It is particularly important to provide physical security as well as psychological and emotional support to the victim. The process of victimisation and the provision of testimony in front of Montenegrin courts is often a traumatic experience. The reasons for such a state are the feeling of fear because of the presence of the aggressor, that is, the accused in the court, the suffered victimisation, and the lack of support during the examination and investigation. Because of this, and especially because of the risk of intimidation of the witness, the victim frequently refuses to testify against the accused and, due to a lack of evidence, the prosecution is forced to abandon prosecution due to a lack of evidence. Psychological support for victims is thus not only of particular importance in terms of overcoming early traumatisation, but also of vital importance to help ensure that conditions for the provision of safe testimony exist.

Montenegro needs to establish an integral system of victim support to the victims of all kinds of crimes. Such an integral system must serve the needs of victims, witnesses, and other aggrieved parties and, importantly, should create special procedures to prevent repeated victimisation.

3. Challenges in the Field of Criminality in Montenegro

While crimes come in all manifestations, this next section will focus on those crimes that are considered to represent the greatest danger to the state's vital structures.

3.1 Organised Crime

Organised crime poses a serious threat to the rule of law and the development of a modern Montenegro. Increased organised criminal activity began shortly after the Yugoslav republics separated. Organised crime groups in the region commit various types of crimes, including the trafficking of drugs and people, the smuggling of

---

54 See Article 131 (protection of witnesses – co-operators) of the Law No. 057/09.

goods, arms, and explosives, as well as the international smuggling of vehicles. As noted, these groups (and their leaders) mainly emerged from the countries formed after the dissolution of the former Yugoslavia.[55]

The connection between criminal groups from Montenegro and those across the Balkans and Europe (Belgium, the Netherlands, Spain, Italy, Germany, France and Denmark, among others) is evident in almost all processed acts of organised crime.[56] The phenomenology of registered acts of organised crime is dominated by drug abuse, violent crime, illegal migration, the smuggling of motor vehicles and other goods, as well as organised financial crime.[57]

Bearing in mind that organised crime encompasses a broad range of crimes, a very large number of victims from disparate categories exist. In criminal proceedings, these victims are not always sufficiently informed of their rights and help and support is often lacking. Moreover, during trials, victims of organised crime are often exposed to inconvenience and further victimisation due to prolonged court proceedings.

3.2 Narcotic Abuse and Illegal Migration

Crimes in the domain of the abuse of narcotic substances represent one of the largest challenges in Montenegro. In 2013, the police intercepted and seized 1,345,781 kilograms of drugs, most of which were marijuana, cocaine, heroin, and synthetic drugs. Searches of shipping containers in the port of Bar by Montenegrin customs officials uncovered 227,600 kilograms of cocaine, *en route* from Ecuador to Albania.[58] According to the same sources, illegal immigration has increased every year, particularly in 2015.

The situation in the field of narcotic abuse is characterised by very good organisation, joint activities, and a very high participation by Montenegrin citizens in international organised criminal groups. Registered drug trafficking is growing significantly due to:

1) Montenegro's geostrategic position;
2) the enormous increase in vehicle smuggling and people trafficking across borders, coupled with more liberal controls; and

---

55 Supreme State Prosecutor's Office of Montenegro 2015; 2016; 2017; 2018b.

56 Supreme State Prosecutor's Office of Montenegro 2015; 2016; 2017; 2018b.

57 Supreme State Prosecutor's Office of Montenegro 2015; 2016; 2017; 2018b.

58 Ministry of Internal Affairs 2014; 2015; 2016; 2017.

3) a state border that facilitates illegal trafficking and drug transport, combined with a lack of professional staff, funding, and equipment for the work of police officers in these extremely complex operational tasks.[59]

The profitability of criminal behaviour related to drug abuse, regardless of the detection and interception of trafficking channels and the neutralising of some international criminal groups, is encouraging criminals to participate in the abovementioned illegal activities. Official data indicate that organised crime groups in the country are setting up direct connections with traffickers and drug dealers in other countries, allowing them to organise the trafficking and sale of drugs, thereby achieving very high profits. Drug abuse is connected to other criminal activities, such as arms smuggling, people trafficking, usury and, increasingly, money laundering, whereby the money gained by drug smuggling is invested in legitimate businesses. The smuggling of cannabis products from Albania causes the most serious security problem for Montenegro. Some of the smuggled drugs remain in Montenegro, while most of them are smuggled into the countries of the region and of the European Union, such as Croatia, Italy, Germany, and the Netherlands. For a number of Montenegrin citizens, the earnings gained by the smuggling and selling drugs provides a motive for participation in these activities (particularly the cannabis trade). Despite significant police involvement, including cross-border police cooperation, the situation has not significantly improved.[60]

The main heroin trafficking corridors from the Near East and Middle East to Western Europe do not pass through Montenegrin territory. However, part of the heroin that remains in the region is trafficked into Montenegro for local consumption or transits into other countries in the region. Montenegro has a small market, and subsequently, according to the assessment of the Centre for Combating Drugs and Smuggling, in the years 2013 and 2014, around 2–5% of the drugs that arrive in Montenegro stay in Montenegro, while the rest is distributed for selling elsewhere.[61] Prosecuted cases, international investigations, operational findings, and information gained from cooperation with international police confirm the involvement of Montenegrins in the organisation of cocaine trafficking from South America to illegal markets in the countries of the European Union.[62] The very high profits made from trafficking and selling cocaine are controlled by well-organised criminal groups that invest the illegally obtained money in legitimate businesses, such as real estate. Montenegrin cit-

---

59 Ministry of Internal Affairs 2014; 2015.

60 Ministry of Internal Affairs 2014; 2015.

61 Ministry of Internal Affairs 2014; 2015.

62 Strategy of Montenegro for the Prevention of Drug Abuse 2013–2020 and the Action Plan 2013–2016, 01.02.2013; https://docplayer.net/6317438-Strategy-of-montenegro-for-the-prevention-of-drug-abuse-2013-2020.html [19.04.2019].

izens, in particular sailors, are also involved in the previously mentioned trafficking as couriers or dealers (in Montenegrin waters and elsewhere).

Drugs and drug addiction are changing the traditional understanding of crime, given that a large number of crimes are perpetrated under the influence of drugs, or committed in order to obtain money to buy them. Drug-related crimes are characterised by their sheer volume, organised nature, and professionalism. Moreover, the accessibility of drugs in Montenegro can lead to possible victimisation. This is especially a risk concerning young people growing up in difficult/unfavourable circumstances, and it is unsurprising that a significant number of young people have been victimised. That said, regarding the social status of victims of drug abuse, there is no difference between rich and poor, that is, young drug addicts are equally represented amongst all social classes.

Although the exact number of the users of narcotic drugs and psychoactive substances is unknown, it seems that their number is not decreasing. Some experts are prone to claim that the use of narcotics has taken on epidemic proportions, due to the large presence of dealers in the streets and the low cost of narcotics. Montenegrin society is not excluded from this monstrosity, and the victims are young people who often resort to drugs out of curiosity, sometimes to rebel against their parents and a society that does not understand them, and sometimes out of ignorance.

A 2013 Europol report on Montenegro states that Adriatic ports are used to bring in drugs, such as cocaine, usually concealed in cargoes of citrus fruits, as well as in shipments of wine or coffee. Montenegro is also a destination of interest to traffickers due to its weaker controls and corruption among customs officials.[63]

The problem of illegal migration into Montenegro has to do with the country's border to Greece, through which illegal immigrants, mostly undocumented, pass and enter the territories of Albania, Macedonia, Serbia, and Kosovo, using Montenegro as a transit country. Croatia's entry into the EU further complicates Montenegro's position. Bearing in mind that illegal migrants are looking for the shortest way into the EU, it is expected that illegal migration through Montenegro will continue to increase. It is important to point out that illegal migration in Montenegro, for the time being, is still characterised by transiting of people through the territory of Montenegro to the EU, and mostly they are economic migrants. Analysing issues through contacts with neighbouring countries, there is a very high level of concern about the growth of illegal migration from the Middle East, Asia, and North Africa. The major routes of migrant trafficking are Turkey – Greece – Albania – Montenegro – EU and Turkey – Greece – Albania – Kosovo – Montenegro – EU. The following routes are used on a smaller scale: Turkey – Greece – Macedonia – Serbia – Montenegro – EU

---

63 Ministry of Internal Affairs 2015.

and Turkey – Greece – Macedonia – Kosovo – Montenegro – EU.[64] To enter Montenegro, migrants commonly use forest areas near the border crossings of 'Sukobin', 'Božaj', and 'Kula', or low-visibility regions that are not covered by technical monitoring devices or a sufficient number of new technology-enhanced patrol cars.

The major organisers of illegal migration are criminal organisations from the Western Balkans or Western Europe. They mainly appear as part of a widespread international criminal network, which, according to the assessments of the Police Authority of Montenegro, is made up of criminal groups from Turkey, Greece, Albania, Kosovo, and Montenegro.[65] Local and uncategorised roads and waterways are used to circumvent official border crossings for the purpose of illegal migration. Recognising the significance of the establishment of an efficient and comprehensive mechanism to combat illegal migration and human trafficking, the Montenegrin legal system is striving to improve the legal framework and achieve a professional level of sophistication to counter these phenomena.

The police claim that although there has been an increase in the number of migrants going through Montenegro recently, this number is not worrying at the moment. According to police data, during 2018, about 1,500 migrants went through the territory of Montenegro. On average, there were about twenty to thirty migrants a day; a year ago, the number was around five per day. The police admit that criminal groups are involved in the illegal migration of migrants. According to their experience, in the majority of cases, criminals and their organisations are citizens of those countries from which the migrants themselves are either from of crossing through. When it comes to migrants, there are no prosecuted cases of trafficking. Only two cases of people smuggling were processed. The Office for Combating Trafficking of Human Beings explains that they could not prove coercion, which is the basis for the existence of the crime of trafficking. The police and the Office claim that the migrants are especially monitored, since in other countries they have even been forced to "donate" organs to cross the border. Given that, due to crises, war horrors, and poverty, they were forced to leave their homes, these people are already victims. Media coverage and announcements of the new migrant wave have raised additional awareness about this topic.[66]

3.3 Smuggling of Motor Vehicles

Between 2010 and 2015, the number of vehicles found in Montenegro, which were the subject of a crime abroad, amounted to 1,070, while the number of vehicles

---

64 Ministry of Internal Affairs 2015.

65 Ministry of Internal Affairs 2015.

66 Ministry of Internal Affairs 2018.

found abroad that had been stolen in Montenegro came to 119. During the same period, the number of vehicles entered into Interpol's database by Montenegrin authorities was 390.[67]

The international smuggling of motor vehicles is connected to criminal groups from several countries and exhibits a clear division of tasks and roles. Through its organisational network structure and firm connections, criminal groups have maintained continuity in the smuggling of motor vehicles and fraud related to vehicle insurance and the forgery of documentation.

The Balkan car criminal organisation within which the members of this organisation operate in Montenegro is one of the better-organised groups in Europe. Europe's open borders facilitate this and the lack of a unified database of vehicles makes car theft relatively simple.

Police data show that in the past few years, in the other republics of the former Yugoslavia, as well as in Montenegro, there has been a chain that accepted vehicles with *cancelled car insurance coverage* and for that purpose, companies of professional mechanics were also organised to alter or remove motor vehicle identification numbers.[68] In addition, parts from vehicles that were not sold in Montenegro were altered and then put into circulation. Most vehicles are smuggled across Lake Skadar into Albania, and then to other neighbouring countries. The smuggling of motor vehicles today is less frequent than it was in the 1990s. The smuggling channels have been effectively cut off due to enhanced cooperation with Interpol and Europol. It is considered that Montenegro is not large enough for the sale of a large number of stolen cars. Additionally, the opening of a large number of marketplaces for used vehicles and car dealerships that include loans and leasing options for new vehicles seems to have closed the door on car smugglers. However, there are still trafficking channels that go through Montenegro to the Middle East.[69]

3.4 Money Laundering

The crime of money laundering is categorised under the group of crimes against the transfer of payments and business operations. Crimes in this area make up about 15% of registered crimes. In 2014, 841 cases of business crime were discovered, which is an increase of 11.8% compared to 2013. In many cases, the processes involving money laundering were perpetrated by members of criminal groups over a long period.[70]

---

67 Results of Interpol NCB for the period 2010–2014; see Ministry of Internal Affairs 2015.

68 Ministry of Internal Affairs 2002; 2003; 2004; 2005.

69 Ministry of Internal Affairs 2002; 2003; 2004; 2005.

70 Ministry of Internal Affairs 2015.

Cases of organised crime are directed towards the acquisition of property with later attempts to incorporate this by appropriate ways into legal channels. Money laundering is a synthesis of organised crime and the so-called legal activities pursued by organised crime groups. They attempt to transfer the money, gained through the above-mentioned crimes, into the legal economy. In Montenegro, particularly risky areas include gambling, privatisation, building construction (including the purchase of real estate), and luxury and other goods as appropriate means to conceal the origin of money.

A Europol report from 2013 warns that Montenegro has a problem with the laundering of money from illegally obtained gains into the legal economy and legal businesses. It is alleged that illegally obtained money, mainly from Russia, often ends up in Montenegro via investments in land, hotels, and villas on the Montenegrin coast. The report points out that some of the 3,600 criminal groups registered in Europe include Montenegro as a part of their territory. Thus, the involvement of the criminal underworld in various forms of economic crime and fraud in Montenegro is a known feature.[71]

Montenegrin offshore companies are used to disguise the criminal origin of funds, so it is possible to return local, illegally obtained money to the country through privatisation or through the selling of companies to foreign investors. Wherever offshore companies appear, there are serious grounds to suppose that money laundering was conducted through them. The mechanism is simple. The domestic "classical" company sells the goods of the offshore firm of the same owner at the lowest possible price, even below the market, which is the basis for taxation, in this case in Montenegro, minimal. After that, the offshore firm sells the same goods to the right buyer at market price, with real profits, but since the profit has not been formally realized in the domestic system, but in Cyprus, the Virgin Islands, Gambia or some other taxes paradise where no tax is paid, the money that was supposed to get into the Montenegrin budget went to a private account. Everything is by law, and state cash and citizens are denied.

Despite many problems, recent legislative progress has been made in this field, in particular concerning the issuance of a more precise definition of the elements of the crime of money laundering. Secondary legislation has also been adopted in order to implement the Law on the Prevention of Money Laundering and the Financing of Terrorism.[72]

---

71 Ministry of Internal Affairs 2015.

72 *Rakočević* 2010, p. 117.

3.5 Professional Murders

For the purpose of this paper, recent analysis of all murders in the past 25-year period has been conducted. The results found that between 1990 and 2015, there were at least 522 aggravated murders, and 105 (20.11%) of them were professional murders (murders committed by professional murderers).[73] Of these, 36 (34.28%) murders were solved, while 69 (65.71%) remain unsolved.

It has been proven that the low percentage of resolved murders is caused by a lack of traces of identification as well as a high level of organisation and professionalism in the commission of the crimes (as evidenced by the destruction of the devices used, etc.). The factors that *contributed* to the unsuccessful identification of the perpetrators are the numerous shortcomings in the operations of the responsible organs, which would not be the case if modern methods and techniques of detecting and solving professional murders were applied. The conclusion is that the successful and effective detection and prevention of professional murders can be achieved, as long as a scientific and practical basis for the research and prevention of these crimes is appropriately created and developed. In respect of the age of victims of professionally executed murders, most were persons aged 31–40 years – 38 (55.07%), followed by the age of 41–50 (20.28%), followed by victims aged 21–30 years – 12 (17.39%) and 51–60 years old – 5 (7.24%). All victims of professionally executed murders were male. The victims of these murders were members of the criminal groups in 49 (71.07%) cases, entrepreneurs – 8 (11.59%), random victims – 7 (10.14%), police officers – 2 (2.89%), and journalists – 1 (1.44 %).[74]

4. Victimisation by Type of Crime in Montenegro

In this part of the study, we will summarise the state of victimisation by crime type for the years 2017, 2016, and 2015. In 2017, 1,631 victims of criminal offences were registered. Out of that number, 1,006 (61.67%) were men, while 625 were women (38.32%). The number of victims of property crimes was 445 (27.28%). The number of victims of criminal offences against the safety of public transport was 332 (20.35%). (In Criminal Code of Montenegro, 27 head of law, there is regulated the special group of criminal offences against the safety of public transport such as threatening of public traffic -article 339, piracy-article 345, etc.) Victims of criminal offences against marriage and family amounted to 255 (15.63%). Victims of crimes against life and body amounted to 225 (13.79%).[75]

---

73 Supreme State Prosecutor's Office of Montenegro 2018a.

74 *Rakočević* 2016.

75 StatOffice 2016; 2017; 2018.

Based on the inspection of the MONSTAT report for 2016, it is stated that 1,491 victims of various crimes were registered in total. This is not a realistic statistic as unreported crimes are not included. Most victims experienced a property crime (theft, aggravated theft, extortion, robbery, the criminal offence of usury (it means contracting disproportionate property gains). For this group, there were 456 registered victims. In second place were the victims of criminal offences against the safety of public transport, which registered 256 victims. In third place were victims of crimes against marriage and family (234 registered victims). 230 victims of crimes against life and body were recorded. There were significantly fewer registered victims of others criminal offences. Men made up more than half of the victims (940 victims (63.04%)) and 38 (2.54%) juveniles were registered as victims of the above offences.

In 2015, a total of 1,393 persons were registered as victims of criminal offences. Out of that number, there were 948 men (68.05%) and 445 women (31.99%). Most victims were for offences relating to property (444), then safety of public transport (253), life and body (222), and marriage and family (197).

As can be seen, property crimes accounted for roughly 25–30% of all crimes. For the purposes of this study, it is important to point out that criminal groups in this area are well organised and victims are often ill prepared. For example, in a number of cases, the victims left doors to their houses unlocked, windows open, or keys under doormats. Money and other valuables were also left in visible locations. However, we think that the biggest problem in this area is the fact that neighbours did not react (in most cases). Moreover, state authorities have shown no efficacy in the detection and prosecution of perpetrators, and there is no compensation for victims. Victims came from all walks of life and there was no difference found between native citizens and foreigners. Repeat victimisation was also recorded.

Victims of traffic crime were the second most common victim group. Such a large number of victims are affected by subjective and objective factors. Subjective factors relate to aggressive behaviour in traffic and objective factors include poor road networks. Young drivers and pedestrians made up a large proportion of the victims in this group.

In third place were criminal offences against marriage and family. Montenegro only criminalised domestic violence in 2002. Until then, it was considered to be a private relationship and state authorities could not intervene. In this area, unreported cases were likely high (possibly five to ten times more than the reported cases). Victims usually do not charge violators out of fear that of revenge or, very often, because of their economic dependence on the perpetrator. Husbands were the most common perpetrators and the most common victims were women, children, and the elderly (male or female).

In the last five years, according to the data of the state authorities, about 60 cases of under-age marriage were registered in Montenegro. In the last two years, only 49 cases were reported to the police. Contracted marriages are one of the biggest problems facing the Roma population in Montenegro. In addition to poverty and discrimination problems, girls of Roma ethnicity are exposed to another type of violence, and these are contracted marriages, where practically parents sell their underage daughters.[76]

The fourth most common group of victims were those who suffered from crimes against life and body (battery, murder, etc.). Young males were the most common victims here.

5. Discussion

We still cannot talk about victimology as a science in the Montenegrin context, since there is no victimological association in the country, scientific conferences and research in this field are not organised, and there is no specialised journal in the field of victimology. The scientific development of victimology remains lacking, due in part to the lack of victimology research projects (for instance, there are only a few – incomplete – surveys on victimisation). That said, normative planning has improved, so that nowadays Montenegrin legislation is compatible with international victim protection standards. However, problems occur when laws are to be implemented in practice. Victims of criminal offences should receive support and assistance (as too should members of their families). However, in practice, the accused often received more protection than victims do. The obligation of society is to establish a balance between the rights of the accused and the injured party. It has been noticed that police and prosecutors lack specialised knowledge on communication skills with injured persons. It is necessary to work on recognising the psychological characteristics of the victims of violence in order to enable authorised persons to better deal with situations where victims are in fear, when they cry, or when they are silent. Victims should be supported by professionals who can identify their needs and understand their problems. Victims often need help during the investigation phase, in order to avoid psychological trauma, that is, to avoid secondary victimisation that involves going through the situation in which they were victimised, again. It is necessary to establish support services for victims of crime, educate personnel, and adequately equip victim support rooms. Montenegro is in the process of joining the European Union, which is why it has a special obligation to fulfil obligations under the United Nations Declaration concerning rights of victims of criminal offences and recommendations of the European Parliament Directive. In the process of joining the EU, Montenegro has special obligations under the Action Plan for Chapter 23 (Justice

---

76 Ministry of Internal Affairs 2018.

and fundamental rights) and Chapter 24 (Justice, freedom, and security). A national strategy for assisting victims and is planned. The establishment of a civil service to assist victims of criminal offences that would bring together all the authorities and institutions dealing with this issue is also planned.

6. Summary in Montenegrin

Rad se fokusira na početak razvoja viktimologije u Crnoj Gori kroz predstavljanje pravnog okvira za zaštitu žrtava krivičnih djela i pregled žrtava kriminala. Postoje brojni zakoni koji regulišu prava i položaj žrtava krivičnih djela u Crnoj Gori, od kojih navodimo:

1) Zakon o naknadi štete žrtvama krivičnih djela,
2) Krivični zakonik,
3) Zakonik o krivičnom postupku,
4) Zakon o zaštiti svjedoka,
5) Zakon o postupanju prema maloljetnicima u krivičnom postupku.

U radu je prikazan broj povrijeđenih – žrtava krivičnih djela koja su počinili punoljetne osobe i maloljetnici za period od 2015–2018 godine. Prikazane su vrste krivičnih djela kojima su žrtve pogođene, od kojih se po učestalosti ističu krivična djela protiv imovine, sigurnost javnog saobraćaja, braka i porodice i života i tijela kao i oštećeni po polu i starosti. Nedostaju statistički podaci o žrtvama novih oblika kriminaliteta. Očigledno je da nedostaje naučni pristup u istraživanju problema viktimizacije i da nema razvijenih mehanizama za sprječavanje viktimizacije.

Literature

Perović, K. (1998): Kriminologija [Criminology]. Niksic.

Perović-Ivanović, A. (ed.) (2009a): Priručnik za starije osobe za borbu protiv nasilja u porodici [Handbook for older people for fight against domestic violence]. Podgorica.

Perović-Ivanović, A. (ed.) (2009b): Seksualno nasilje: priručnik za mlade [Sexual violence: A handbook for children and youths]. Podgorica.

Perović-Ivanović, A. (ed.) (2009c): Šta znamo o ekonomskom zlostavljanju zena [What we know about economical abuse of woman]. Podgorica.

Perović-Ivanović, A. (ed.) (2008): Priručnik za seksualni I reproduktivno zdravlje [Handbook for sexual and reproductive health]. Podgorica.

Pešić V. (1980): Kriminologija [Criminology]. Titograd.

Rakočević, V. (2016): Research on issues of detection, solving and evidence collecting in cases of professionally executed murders. Revija za kriminalistiko in kriminologijo [Journal of Criminal Investigation and Criminology] 67, pp. 348–357.

Rakočević, V. (2010): Krivična djela sa elementima organizovanog kriminaliteta [Crimes with elements of organised criminality]. Podgorica.

Rakočević, V. (2007): Kriminologija [Criminology]. Podgorica.

Documents

Center for peace, non-violence and human rights [Centar za mir, nenasilje i ljudska prava] (2019): Aktivnosti – REKOM – Inicijativa za REKOM [Activities – REKOM – Initiative for REKOM]; http://www.centar-za-mir.hr/aktivnosti-rekom-inicijativa-za-rekom/ [27.04.2019] [in Croatian and English].

Ministry of Internal Affairs (2018): Izvještaj Ministarstva unutrašnjih poslova o radu I stanju u upravnim oblastima, za 2017. godinu [Report of the Ministry of internal affairs on work and state in administrative areas for 2017]; http://www.mup.gov.me/biblioteka/izvjestaji [19.04.2019] [in Montenegrin only].

Ministry of Internal Affairs (2017): Izvještaj Ministarstva unutrašnjih poslova o radu I stanju u upravnim oblastima, za 2016. godinu [Report of the Ministry of internal affairs on work and state in administrative areas for 2016]; http://www.mup.gov.me/biblioteka/izvjestaji [19.04.2019] [in Montenegrin only].

Ministry of Internal Affairs (2016): Izvještaj Ministarstva unutrašnjih poslova o radu I stanju u upravnim oblastima, za 2015. godinu [Report of the Ministry of internal affairs on work and state in administrative areas for 2015]; http://www.mup.gov.me/biblioteka/izvjestaji [19.04.2019] [in Montenegrin only].

Ministry of Internal Affairs (2015): Izvještaj Ministarstva unutrašnjih poslova o radu I stanju u upravnim oblastima, za 2014. godinu [Report of the Ministry of internal affairs on work and state in administrative areas for 2014]; http://www.mup.gov.me/biblioteka/izvjestaji [19.04.2019] [in Montenegrin only].

Ministry of Internal Affairs (2014): Izvještaj Ministarstva unutrašnjih poslova o radu I stanju u upravnim oblastima, za 2013. godinu [Report of the Ministry of internal affairs on work and state in administrative areas for 2014]; http://www.mup.gov.me/biblioteka/izvjestaji [19.04.2019] [in Montenegrin only].

Ministry of Internal Affairs (2005): Izvještaj Ministarstva unutrašnjih poslova o radu i stanju u upravnim oblastima, za 2004. godinu [Report of the Ministry of internal affairs on work and state in administrative areas for 2004]; http://www.mup.gov.me/biblioteka/izvjestaji [19.04.2019] [in Montenegrin only].

Ministry of Internal Affairs (2004): Izvještaj Ministarstva unutrašnjih poslova o radu i stanju u upravnim oblastima, za 2003. godinu [Report of the Ministry of internal affairs on work and state in administrative areas for 2003]; http://www.mup.gov.me/biblioteka/izvjestaji [19.04.2019] [in Montenegrin only].

Ministry of Internal Affairs (2003): Izvještaj Ministarstva unutrašnjih poslova o radu i stanju u upravnim oblastima, za 2002. godinu [Report of the Ministry of internal affairs on work and state in administrative areas for 2002]; http://www.mup.gov.me/biblioteka/izvjestaji [19.04.2019] [in Montenegrin only].

Ministry of Internal Affairs (2002): Izvještaj Ministarstva unutrašnjih poslova o radu i stanju u upravnim oblastima, za 2001. godinu [Report of the Ministry of internal affairs on work and state in administrative areas for 2001]; http://www.mup.gov.me/biblioteka/izvjestaji [19.04.2019] [in Montenegrin only].

Statistical Office of Montenegro (StatOffice) (2018): Statistički godišnjak 2018 [Statistical yearbook 2018]; http://monstat.org/eng/publikacije_page.php?id=1518 [19.04.2019] [in Montenegrin and English]; cited as: StatOffice 2018.

Statistical Office of Montenegro (StatOffice) (2017): Statistički godišnjak 2017 [Statistical yearbook 2017]; http://monstat.org/eng/publikacije_page.php?id=1426 [19.04.2019] [in Montenegrin and English]; cited as: StatOffice 2017.

Statistical Office of Montenegro (StatOffice) (2016): Statistički godišnjak 2016 [Statistical yearbook 2016]; http://monstat.org/eng/publikacije_page.php?id=1402 [19.04.2019] [in Montenegrin and English]; cited as: StatOffice 2016.

Statistical Office of Montenegro (StatOffice) (2011): Popis stanovništva, domaćinstva i stanova u Crnoj Gori 2011. Godine [Population and housing census in Montenegro in 2011]; https://www.monstat.org/userfiles/file/popis2011/saopstenje/saopstenje(1).pdf [27.04.2019] [in Montenegrin only]; cited as: StatOffice 2011.

StatOffice: see Statistical Office of Montenegro.

Supreme State Prosecutor's Office of Montenegro (2018a): Izvještaj o radu Vrhovnog državnog tužilaštva Crne Gore za period od 1990-2015. godine [Report on the work of the Supreme State Prosecutor of Montenegro for the period 1990–2015], http://www.tuzilastvocg.me [19.04.2019] [in Montenegrin only].

Supreme State Prosecutor's Office of Montenegro (2018b): Izvještaj za 2017. godinu [Report of 2017]; http://www.tuzilastvocg.me/media/files/IZVJESTAJ%202017%20%20.pdf [19.04.2019] [in Montenegrin only].

Supreme State Prosecutor's Office of Montenegro (2017): Izvještaj za 2016. godinu [Report of 2016]; http://www.tuzilastvocg.me/media/files/Izvje%C5%A1taj%20o%20radu%20Tu%C5%BEila%C4%8Dkog%20savjeta%20i%20Dr%C5%BEavnog%20tu%C5%BEila%C5%A1tva%20za%202016.godinu.pdf [19.04.2019] [in Montenegrin only].

Supreme State Prosecutor's Office of Montenegro (2016): Izvještaj za 2015. godinu [Report of 2015]; http://www.tuzilastvocg.me/media/files/izvjestaj%20o%20radu%20vdt%20za%202015-compressed.pdf [19.04.2019] [in Montenegrin only].

Supreme State Prosecutor's Office of Montenegro (2015): Izvještaj za 2014. godinu [Report of 2014]; http://www.tuzilastvocg.me/media/files/Izvjestaj%20o%20radu%20Drzavnog%20tuzilastva%20za%202014.pdf [19.04.2019] [in Montenegrin only].

Women's Safe House (2013): Podaci o broju prijavljenih slučajeva nasilja za 2013. godinu [Report on the number of reported cases of violence in 2013]; http://szk.org.me/izvjestaji/podaci-o-broju-prijavljenih-slucajeva-nasilja-za-2013-godine/ [19.04.2019] [in Montenegrin only].

North Macedonia

Victimology and Victim Protection

Gordana Lažetić & Aleksandra Gruevska Drakulevski

1. Introduction

This paper deals with the situation in the Republic of North Macedonia and offers a short overview of the concepts regarding the victims of crime, advantages of restorative justice, as well as procedural rights of the victims, rights and protection of minor victims and vulnerable categories of victims. Successful procedural rights and protection of vulnerable victims can be provided only if there are skilled staff and approved treatment methods within relevant and competent bodies and authorities. The features of criminal justice systems – be they more offender-oriented or more victim-oriented – are significant when analysing victimology. Victimology, rights of victims and their protection seems to have a significant influence on the development of modern criminal law, victim's rights are not at the margins of the criminal law anymore and victim's consent has been prescribed as a legislative precondition for different types of proceedings and final penal outcomes. The dark figures of committed crimes shall be linked with the position of the victim in the criminal justice system to help assess the victim's motivation to report a crime. The legislature is obliged to provide compensation for victims of violent crimes and compensation for minor victims, which is in accordance with the European standards. The paper offers a short overview of the statistical data regarding specific groups of victims, taking into consideration the data from the State Statistical Office. When analysing the relationship between the media and their portrayal of crime, delinquency and the fear of crime, the probability of reporting on a crime in the news is greater if the victim is a minor.

2. General Country Background

2.1 Basic Facts on Country and Population

With a surface area of 25,713 km^2, according to the official data from the State Statistical Office, on 31.12.2016 in the Republic of North Macedonia, there were a total number of 2,073,702 inhabitants which is 13,908 persons or 0.7% more compared to 2011, and 31,761 persons or 1.6% more compared to 2006.[1] The Macedonian population is increasingly ageing. In the period 2006–2016, the proportion of young population (age group 0–14) in the total population dropped from 18.9% to 16.6%, whereas the share of older population (age group 65 and over) grew from 11.2% to 13.3%.[2] The country is subdivided into 84 administrative municipalities. The population density is 80.6 inhabitants per km^2. The last census was conducted in 2002. However, the official data regarding the distribution of the population by the ethnicity are as follows: Macedonians (64.18%); Albanians (25.17%); Turks (3.85%); Roma (2.66%); Serbs (1.78%); Bosnians (0.84%); Vlachs (0.48%); others (1.04%). The most common religion is Orthodox Christianity, practiced by most of the ethnic Macedonians. Islam is the second-largest religious group (consisting of mainly Macedonian citizens from Albanian, Turkish and Bosnian ethnicity). In the period 2006–2016, there has been a continuous increase in the number of immigrated foreigners in the Republic of North Macedonia.[3]

In 2015, 8,887 persons changed their place of residence within the Republic of North Macedonia, and net migration was 2,144 persons. The country was inevitably involved in the refugee crisis in Europe as part of the so-called Western Balkans Route.[4] Starting in October 2014, throughout 2015, and until the first quarter of 2016, the North Macedonia was a transit country, especially for refugees fleeing from the war in Syria and Iraq, who chose countries in the European Union as their point of destination.[5]

2.2 Economic Indicators

The political situation in the country in the past ten years almost devastated the country's economy, so it is not surprising that the North Macedonia is a country with one of the lowest GDP per capita in Europe. GDP annual growth rate in North Macedonia was on average 2.72% from 2001 until 2017, with a peak of 10.70% in the second quarter of 2005 and a record low of –12.70% in the third quarter of 2001. The economy of the country expanded 0.2% year-on-year in the third quarter of 2017, recovering from a 1.3% decline in the previous quarter. Household consumption went up to 2.9%, following a 4.4% rise in the previous quarter. Also, imports slowed to 2.1% (5.6% in the second quarter), while exports advanced at a faster 5.5% (11.0%). In addition,

1 StatOffice 2017.

2 The changes in the age structure are reflected in the number of deaths in the country. The constant increase in the number of deaths caused an increase in the mortality rate of 9.9% in 2016, compared to 2006 when it was 9.1% (deaths per 1,000 inhabitants); see StatOffice 2017.

3 StatOffice 2017.

4 Amnesty International 2015; Human Rights Watch 2017.

5 *Chudoska Blazhevska & Juberías* 2016.

gross capital formation fell less (–9.4% from –18.6%). In contrast, government spending contracted 3.6%, compared to 0.4% increase in the preceding quarter. The structure of GDP in 2014 and in 2015 was dominated by the section Services with 53.8% and 54.2%, respectively. Data about economically active population, employment and unemployment should be taken as basic and indispensable for monitoring the changes on the labour market. Namely, in the third quarter of 2017, the labour force numbered 954,814 persons, of which 743,451 were employed, while 211,363 were unemployed. The activity rate in this period was 56.8%, the employment rate was 44.2%, while the unemployment rate was 22.1%. The at-risk-of-poverty rate calculated according to the recommendations of Eurostat was 22.1% in 2014, 21.5% in 2015, while 21.9% of people lived below the poverty threshold in 2016.[6] The indicator for the inequality of income distribution, the "Ginicoefficient",[7] decreased by 0.1 compared to 2015, while the S80/S20 indicator (which shows the ratio between the sum of the highest and the lowest 20% of equivalent income of persons in the household), remained at the same level as in 2015.[8] According to the data presented within the Corruption Perceptions Index for 2016 (measured by Transparency International), in orange and red countries, citizens face the tangible impact of corruption on a daily basis. The North Macedonia falls into the red zone. The country is at the 90th place together with Indonesia, Liberia and Morocco.[9]

3. Current State of Victimology

Regarding victimology as a scientific discipline in the Republic of North Macedonia, we need to emphasise that at the universities, victimology is typically studied as a part of other subjects. This is a theoretical limitation since victimology and research in victimology has a great significance.

At the University of "Ss. Cyril and Methodius", Law Faculty "Iustinianus Primus" in Skopje, Institute of Criminal Law, Department of Criminology and Penology, which is rated as the best University and Law Faculty in the country,[10] until June 2018, Victimology was not a specific subject. Some aspects related to victims of crime, such as the victim of the criminal act, the risk of victimisation, type of victims, the victim's contribution to the commitment of certain types of crime, as well as the measures of protection of certain categories of victims are studied within

6 StatOffice 2018a.

7 The Gini coefficient is a measure of statistical dispersion intended to represent the income or wealth distribution of a nation's residents, and is the most commonly used measurement of inequality.

8 StatOffice 2018a.

9 Transparency International 2017.

10 Academic Ranking of World Universities 2016.

criminology, criminal law, criminal procedure, and justice for children. The authors of this study have made an effort to include Victimology as a subject in the curriculum of the Master's studies in criminal law at the Faculty starting in the academic year (2018–2019). Several professors from the Faculty were involved in conducting a research project "Students Views on the Police in the Republic of Macedonia". The purpose of the study is to understand the students' experience with the criminal justice system and possible victimisation. This is a reliable research project in the field of victimology.[11] The work of *Lažetić* in the field of restorative justice, juvenile justice and victimology is significant.[12]

The other law faculties in the country do not have victimology as a separate subject. Only, at the University of "St. Kliment Ohridski" in Bitola, the Faculty of Security has a specific subject Victimology in the third year of undergraduate studies. Furthermore, they offer study course in Victimology with Restorative Justice in their Master's studies. *Oliver Bačanović* is recognisable in the country for his work in the field of victimology.[13] Another professor that has published papers in the field of victimology is *Vesna Stefanovska.*[14]

Victimological papers can be found in several journals in the country, such as the Macedonian Journal for Criminal law and Criminology, Iustinianus Primus Law Review, Yearbook of the Law Faculty "Iustinianus Primus" in Skopje, Police Academy Yearbook, as well as Yearbook of the Law faculty, University of "Goce Delčev", Štip.

Data on victims of certain types of crime, such as domestic violence, traffic accidents, human trafficking, are available at the websites of the Ministry of Internal Affairs, the Sector for Border Affairs and Migration, National Commission for Combating Human Trafficking and Illegal Migration, Institute for Social Activities. Also, data on certain types of victims can be obtained from the Centres for Social Affairs. Another governmental actor is the Ministry of Labour and Social Policy. The State Statistical Office of the Republic of North Macedonia publishes an annual Statistical Review on Population and Social Statistics and Perpetrators of Criminal Offences,

---

11 *Bužarovska-Lažetić & Misoski* 2011; *Bužarovska, Bachanović, Kalajdziev, Gruevska Drakulevski, Misoski, Gogov, Ilic & Jovanova* 2014.

12 *Bužarovska, Nanev & Koshevaliska* 2016; *Dimitrojska, Burarovska & Saltirovska* 2017; *Lažetić & Bužarovska* 2006, 2015.

13 More information is available online at http://www.fb.uklo.edu.mk/EN/CVEN/CV.Oli ver.pdf [14.06.2019]. We should mention his work along with his younger college on "Victimization in penal institutions", "Victimization of prison employees and difficulties in their work", "Victimization and substance abuse among young people: Results of the ISRD-3 survey (International Survey of Self-Announcement of Juvenile Delinquency)", "Migrant and refugee crisis – Victimological aspects", all of which presented at the conferences of the Victimology Society of Serbia; see Viktimološko društvo Srbije 2019.

14 More information is available online at http://www.fb.uklo.edu.mk/EN/CVEN/ CV.VesnaS.pdf [14.06.2019].

but these reviews neither collect nor present statistical data on victims of crime. Regarding victims of crime, the "News Release: Violent Deaths in the Republic of Macedonia, published annually" it is of great importance as it offers data on violent deaths in the Republic of North Macedonia in terms of "accidents", "suicides" and "homicides", by sex and age. Another relevant institution regarding victimology issues is the Ombudsman of the Republic of North Macedonia's Department for Protection of Children Rights, which aims to more actively and widely get involved into the protection of all the children`s rights.

Several governmental agencies and non-governmental organizations (NGO) are involved in victim protection in the country: The Helsinki Committee for Human Rights of the Republic of Macedonia (MHC), the International Organisation for Migration Mission in Skopje (IOM), the Macedonian Red Cross, Open Gate La Strada, for action against violence and Human Trafficking, The Association for Emancipation, Solidarity and Equality of Women – ESE, National Network to End Violence against Women and Domestic Violence "Voice against Violence", as well as The First Children's Embassy in the World "Megjashi" (FCEWM) – Republic of North Macedonia which is helping to bring down the wall of silence concerning children's rights, especially related to physical, sexual and economic abuse of children. UNICEF focuses on the protection of the rights of the children. Similarly, the work and influence of UNDP in the country is noticeable. Another organisation devoted to protection of victim's rights in the Republic of North Macedonia is the OSCE Mission to Skopje. Country assessments in the field of the protection of the rights of the victims has been prepared by: Amnesty International, Human Rights Watch, Freedom House, as well as The United States Department of Justice, Executive Office for Immigration Review, Macedonia.

In *Table 1* (see *next page*), the authors summarises the main focus area of different Governmental/State-Related Institutions and NGOs that are active in different aspects related to victim protection, as well as the web pages where more detailed information can be found.

4. Relevant Legal Framework in Terms of Criminal Policy

Restorative justice

The concept of restorative justice has been introduced in the Macedonian theory more than three decades ago.[15] However, the first legislative steps toward introducing restorative proceedings and restorative outcomes into Macedonian criminal legislation have been made during the last decade and a half.

---

15 *Arnaudovski, Bužarovska-Lažetić, Celevski & Nanev* 2004; *Bačanović* 2009, 2010; *Bužarovska-Lažetić & Misoski* 2009, 2011; *Kambovski* 1984; *Kanevčev* 2006; *Lažetić & Bužarovska* 2015; *Lažetić-Bužarovska* 2003, 2006; *Marjanović* 1995, 1996.

Table 1 *Key Governmental/State-Related Institutions and NGOs Involved in Victim Protection*

Ministry/ Institution/NGO		**Main Focus**	**Internet Site**
Ministry of Internal Affairs		Crime statistics and analysis	http://www.mvr.gov.mk/analiza/kriminal/31
	Sector for Border Affairs and Migration	Migrant and refugee crisis	http://www.mvr.gov.mk/profilepage/sektor-za-granichni-raboti-i-migracii
National Commission for Combating Human Trafficking and Illegal Migration		Human trafficking and illegal migration	http://nacionalnakomisija.gov.mk/en/
Institute for Social Activities		Domestic violence	http://zsd.gov.mk
Ministry of Labour and Social Policy			http://www.mtsp.gov.mk
	Sector for Child Protection and Sector for Inspectional Supervision of the Application of Legal and Other Regulations in the Field of Social Protection and Child Protection	Child protection	
	National Mechanism for Referral to Victims of Human Trafficking	Human trafficking	
State Statistical Office of the Republic of North Macedonia		Statistical data	http://www.stat.gov.mk
Ombudsman of the Republic of North Macedonia		Domestic violence Trafficking in humans Migrants and refugees Discrimination Torture Children victims of physical, psychological and sexual harassment	http://ombudsman.mk/EN

Ombudsman of the Republic of North Macedonia	"Department for Protection of Children Rights"	Children's rights	http://ombudsman.mk/EN/protection_of_children_rights/department_for_protection_of_children_rights.aspx
	National Preventive Mechanism (NPM)	Protection of persons deprived of their liberty in places of detention, against torture and other cruel, inhuman or degrading treatment or punishment	http://ombudsman.mk/EN/national_preventive_mechanism/npm_in_rm.aspx
Helsinki Committee for Human Rights of the Republic of Macedonia (MHC)		Human rights	http://mhc.org.mk
International Organisation for Migration Mission in Skopje (IOM)		Migration and human trafficking	http://iomskopje.org
Macedonian Red Cross		Protecting and supporting victims	http://ckrm.org.mk
Association for Action Against Violence and Human Trafficking Open Gate		Violence and human trafficking	http://www.lastrada.org.mk
Association for Emancipation, Solidarity and Equality of Women – ESE		Violence Domestic violence Human trafficking	http://www.esem.org.mk
National Network to End Violence against Women and Domestic Violence "Voice against Violence"		Domestic violence	http://www.glasprotivnasilstvo.org.mk/en/about-us/
First Children's Embassy in the World "Megjashi" (FCEWM)		Children's rights	http://www.childrensembassy.org.mk/home.nspx
UNICEF		Children's rights	https://www.unicef.org/tfyrmacedonia/
UN Development Agency (UNDP)			http://www.mk.undp.org/content/the_former_yugoslav_republic_of_macedonia/en/home.html

Table 1 cont. Key Governmental/State-Related Institutions and NGOs Involved in Victim Protection

Ministry/ Institution/NGO	**Main Focus**	**Internet Site**
OSCE Mission to Skopje	Human trafficking Terrorism Violence Human rights	http://www.osce.org/mission-to-skopje
Amnesty International	Country assessment in the field of the protection of the rights of victims	https://www.justice.gov/sites/default/files/pages/attachments/2016/02/25/amnesty-international_2015_full-report.pdf#macedonia
Human Rights Watch	Country assessment in the field of the protection of the rights of victims	https://www.justice.gov/sites/default/files/pages/attachments/2016/02/01/hrw_2005_macedonia.pdf
Freedom House	Country assessment in the field of the protection of the rights of victims	https://freedomhouse.org/report/freedom-world/2017/macedonia
The United States Department of Justice, Executive Office for Immigration Review, Macedonia	Human rights Human trafficking Terrorism	https://www.justice.gov/eoir/country/macedonia-topical

Definition of "victim of crime"

A definition of a "victim of a crime" was introduced in the Macedonian legislation in 2008.[16] The necessity emerged from the amendments in the criminal offences regarding human trafficking and, in that time, the newly introduced criminal offence for trafficking of minors, where the term "victim" was included. The definition of "victim of crime" in the Penal Code contains the same elements as included in the definition prescribed in the UN Declaration of Basic Principles of Justice for Victims of Crime and Abuse of Power, as well as the first EU Directive toward the position of the victim in the criminal proceeding. The definition of "victim of crime" in the Code of Criminal Procedure is almost identical as in the Penal Code.[17]

Procedural rights of the victims

The Code of Criminal Procedure prescribes the procedural rights of the victims.[18] According to Article 56 of the Law No. 150, the victim should be provided with information about the proceeding. The procedural rights of the victim during the criminal proceeding encompasses the right of the victim to take part during the procedure as damaged party for the purpose to accomplish the property-legal claim.[19] According to Article 53 para. 1 of the Law No. 150, the victim of a crime shall be provided with special care and attention, as well as, getting an effective psychological and other professional assistance and support by bodies, institutions and organisations that provide help for victims of crime.[20]

Special protection for victims of serious crimes

An advisor is provided for at the expense of the State budget (before giving a statement or filing of property-legal claim) if there is a victim that suffers serious psychophysical damages or in case of other serious consequences of the crime, and compensation for material and non-pecuniary damage from the State budget is provided for too. [21]

Protection of victims as witnesses

The protection of victims as witnesses is provided by two laws: Code of Criminal Procedure and Law on Witness Protection. The provisions are harmonised with the

---

16 Article 122 (meaning of legal terms) of the Penal Code, Law No., 83004, 10.09.2008, Official Gazette 139/2008.

17 Article 21 (meaning of terms) of the Code of Criminal Procedure, Law No. 150, 18.11.2010, Official Gazette 150/2010.

18 See Article 53 (victim's rights) of the Law No. 150.

19 See Article 56 (victim not informed of the right to participate in the procedure as a damaged party) of the Law No. 150.

20 See Article 53 (victim's rights) of the Law No. 150.

21 See Article 53 (victim's rights) of the Law No. 150.

European instruments regarding witness protection. Procedural protection is stipulated in the Code of Criminal Procedure.[22]

Consent of the victim as legislative precondition

In accordance with the alternative measure, conditional termination of the criminal procedure, the procedure will be conditionally terminated after conducting a hearing and receiving consent from the victim, as necessary preconditions.[23] In line with the role of the public prosecutor for discretionary decisions, there is a possibility for conditional postponement of the criminal prosecution by the public prosecutor where there is a necessity of provided consent from the victim prior the public prosecutor's decision.[24]

Special rights of vulnerable categories of victims[25]

There are three categories of vulnerable victims regarding different criteria: the age, serious threat for their life, health or physical integrity and harmful consequences for their psychological or physical health. The statements of victimised minors can be the subject of video and audio recording and these recordings can be used as an evidence. For preventing secondary victimisation, in exceptional cases due to newly established circumstances in the case, the court may order another additional interview of the minor victim. There are some special rights of victims of crimes against sexual freedom and sexual morality, humanity and international law, as well.[26]

Examination of particularly vulnerable victims and witnesses

The Code of Criminal Procedure prescribes a special manner for the examination of victims and witnesses that are considered as particularly vulnerable.[27] Particular vulnerability relates to age, health, the nature and the consequences of the criminal offence or to the children as victims of human trafficking, violence or sexual abuse.

Minor victim

A "minor victim" shall refer to a minor under the age of 18. The definition of minor victim in the Law on justice of children is in line with the definition in the latest EU Directive regarding the minimum standards on the rights, support and protection of

---

22 Law No. 150.

23 See Article 58-a (terms of termination) of the Law No. 83004; *Kambovski* 2015.

24 See Articles 43 (conditional postponement of the criminal prosecution) and 44 (waiving of criminal prosecution) of the Law No. 150.

25 See Article 54 (special rights of victims of vulnerable categories of victims) of the Law No. 150.

26 See Article 55 (special rights of victims of crimes against sexual freedom and sexual morality, humanity and international law) of the Law No. 150.

27 See Article 232 (examination of particularly vulnerable victims and witnesses) of the Law No. 150.

victims of crime. The Law on justice of children has been promoting a child-sensitive approach by providing protection of minor victims in the very extensive definition of "child in risk". Since 2008, there is a criminal offence "Trafficking of a Minor" in the Penal Code where the consent given by the minor is completely irrelevant for the level of criminal responsibility of the defendant accused of trafficking.[28]

Protection of a child as damaged party or witness in the criminal procedure

The Law on justice for children stipulates several basic rights of the minor victim, as well as for child witnesses.[29] The minors should be treated with protection of their dignity, without any discrimination, there should be possibilities for special protection from secondary victimisation or re-victimisation, as well as providing psychological and other professional assistance and support from bodies, institutions and organisations for assistance to minors.

Special rights for procedural protection of the child

Minor victims and child witness should be provided with special measures for procedural protection and special care and protection when they are victims of human trafficking, violence or sexual abuse, crimes against humanity and international law or other serious acts committed against children punishable with imprisonment for more than four years.

Compensation for victims of crime

According to the European standards there should exist the possibility for providing compensation for victims of violent crimes. There is no such a law in the Macedonian legislation, although all relevant conventions have been ratified and there is an obligation for the country to establish a State fund for compensation for victims of violent crimes. Within the criminal procedure, there is a possibility for the damaged party to file a (property legal) claim that may refer to a compensation of a damage, returning objects or nullification of a certain legal matter.[30] In accordance with the provision of the Penal Code, there is a possibility for the protection of the damaged party in two cases:

a) the damaged party who, after a criminal proceeding, has been referred to a civil litigation; and
b) when the damaged party has learned about the criminal judgement after the completion of the proceedings and was not able to file a property legal claim.[31]

---

28 See Article 418-g (trafficking of a minor) of the Law No. 83004.

29 Article 145 (protection of children as damaged party or witness in the criminal procedure) of the Law on Justice for Children, Law No. 148/2013, 31.12.2013, Official Gazette 148/2013.

30 Law No. 150.

31 See Article 99 (protection of the damaged party) of the Law No. 83004.

Compensation for children

In accordance with the Law on justice for children, compensation for a minor victim as a damaged party from a violent criminal offence shall be provided by funds within the budget of the Ministry of Justice when necessary conditions are fulfilled.[32]

Mediation procedure

Victim offender mediation toward minors was introduced in the Macedonian legislation in 2007.[33] Regarding the adults, mediation procedure was introduced with the Code of Criminal Procedure in 2010. Principles of mediation procedure, conditions for mediators, costs of the mediation process and other issues are prescribed by the Law on mediation.[34]

Prevention, Suppression and Protection from Domestic Violence

The Law on prevention, suppression and protection from domestic violence, regulates the responsible and obligatory actions of the institutions and associations, their mutual coordination and cooperation, in order to prevent and suppress domestic violence and to provide protection of the victims.[35] There is a broad definition of domestic violence in the law,[36] but it does not define it as gender-based violence and does not recognise girls and women as an especially vulnerable group.[37] In order to eliminate immediate and serious danger to life and physical integrity of the victim and the members of her family, the law provides temporary protection measure.[38] The Law anticipates that the government will need to enact a new National Strategy on the prevention and protection from domestic violence in the period of 2015–2020, which will determine specific steps to improve the protection system and will create a budget plan for its implementation.[39] The protection of victims of domestic violence, and victims of human trafficking in social protection institutions (including protecting their health) is provided by the Law on social protection.

---

32 Law No. 148/2013.

33 Law No. 148/2013.

34 Law on Mediation, Law No. 188/2013, 31.12.2013, Official Gazette 188/2013.

35 Article 1 (subject of the law) of the Law on Prevention, Suppression and Protection from Domestic Violence, Law. No. 138/2014, 31.12.2014, Official Gazette 138/2014.

36 See Article 3 (definition of domestic violence) of the Law No. 138/2014.

37 *Saltirovska & Dimitrijoska* 2017.

38 Law No. 138/2014.

39 *Saltirovska & Dimitrijoska* 2017.

5. A Picture of the Victimisation Reality, Based on Data and Research Findings

Regarding the facts and figures about victimisation in the country, as stressed in *Chapter 2,* all of the conducted research was partial, dealing with specific groups of victims, such as, victims of domestic violence, victims of human trafficking and migrants, children victims of physical, psychological and sexual harassment, victims of traffic accidents, etc. Up until now, no major national or international victimisation surveys or victimological research projects have been conducted apart from the research mentioned above. Also, we cannot present an estimated number of victims per year (prevalence and incidence rates), but we present the victim data on the most important categories of crime. For some of the types of crime we give the rate of perpetrators (since data on victims are missing) per 100,000 inhabitants. For some of the types of victims of specific types of crime, the authors also present characteristics (sex, age, nationality, education) of victims in the country. In the following, the authors analyse data on specific groups of victims, namely, victims of violent crimes, victims of domestic violence, children victims of physical, psychological and sexual harassment, victims of sexual assault, victims of human trafficking and smuggling of migrants.

5.1 Victims of Violent Crime

According to the State Statistical Office data, there were 421 violent deaths in the Republic of North Macedonia in 2017, which is a decrease of 15.3% compared to the previous year. Violent deaths accounted for 2.1% of the total number of deaths. The data on violent deaths in the Republic of North Macedonia for the period 1994–2017 are presented in *Table 2*.

The gender structure for violent deaths in 2017, as in previous years, shows higher male participation with 75.1%. In the total number of violent deaths, "accidents" ranked first with 66.0%, followed by "suicides" with 26.4% and "homicides" with 7.6%. In the category "accidents", the group "other external causes of accidental injury" was predominant with 26.1%. In the category "suicides", deaths caused by "hanging, strangulation and suffocation" were most frequent with 15.7%. The dominant cause of death in the category "homicides" was "assault by other and unspecified firearm discharge", making up 2.4% of the total number of violent deaths.

The data on violent deaths by external causes of death, sex and age are summarised in *Table 3*.

Regarding the victims of violent crime, we also present the data from the Ministry of Internal Affairs that refers to the registered perpetrators of homicides and bodily injuries for the period 2010–2016. As can be seen from the figures, the territo-

Table 2 Violent Deaths in the Republic of North Macedonia, 1994–2017

Years	Violent deaths in the country				Structure (%)			
	Total	Accidents*	Suicides	Homicides	Total	Accidents	Suicides	Homicides
1994	632	471	128	33	100.0	74.5	20.3	5.2
1995	538	380	130	28	100.0	70.6	24.2	5.2
1996	590	402	143	45	100.0	68.1	24.2	7.6
1997	636	438	155	43	100.0	68.9	24.4	6.8
1998	693	497	151	45	100.0	71.7	21.8	6.5
1999	761	542	169	50	100.0	71.2	22.2	6.6
2000	720	512	148	60	100.0	71.1	20.6	8.3
2001	737	455	151	131	100.0	61.7	20.5	17.8
2002	743	525	149	69	100.0	70.7	20.1	9.3
2003	630	428	136	66	100.0	67.9	21.6	10.5
2004	708	473	179	56	100.0	66.8	25.3	7.9
2005	587	392	143	52	100.0	66.8	24.4	8.9
2006	653	435	165	53	100.0	66.6	25.3	8.1
2007	743	536	159	48	100.0	72.1	21.4	6.5
2008	598	397	161	40	100.0	66.4	26.9	6.7
2009	613	417	167	29	100.0	68.0	27.2	4.7
2010	588	422	122	44	100.0	71.8	20.7	7.5
2011	527	370	128	29	100.0	70.2	24.3	5.5
2012	584	378	172	34	100.0	64.7	29.5	5.8
2013	552	364	170	18	100.0	65.9	30.8	3.3
2014	493	311	147	35	100.0	63.1	29.8	7.1
2015	513	361	114	38	100.0	70.4	22.2	7.4
2016	497	354	125	18	100.0	71.2	25.2	3.6
2017	421	278	111	32	100.0	66.0	26.4	7.6

Source: StatOffice 2018b.

* Accidents include: Transport accidents; Pedestrian injured in transport accident; Pedal cyclist or motorcycle rider injured in transport accident; Car, pick-up truck or van occupant injured in transport accident; Occupant of heavy transport vehicle injured in transport accident; Bus occupant injured in transport accident; Other land transport accidents; Other transport accidents; Accidental poisoning by and exposure to noxious substances; Complications of medical and surgical care; Falls; Exposure to smoke, fire and flames; Exposure to forces of nature; Accidental drowning and submersion; Other external causes of accidental injury).

rial distribution of homicides is as follows: most of the homicides are committed on the territory of Administrative region Skopje and SVR Kumanovo, and the

Table 3 Violent Deaths by External Causes of Death, Sex and Age, 2017

Codes of causes of death*			Sex	Total	0–4	5–14	15–24	25–34	35–44	45–54	55–64	65+ and unknown
VIOLENT DEATHS (V01–Y89)			Male	378	9	8	29	38	56	53	73	112
			Female	119	1	3	4	8	12	8	14	69
ACCIDENTS (V01–X59; Y10–Y89)			Male	267	9	7	21	28	42	34	49	77
			Female	87	1	2	4	7	9	4	5	55
V01–V99	Transport accidents		Male	90	3	2	8	15	17	10	21	14
			Female	17	1	–	–	3	4	–	1	8
	V01–V09	Pedestrian injured	Male	3	1	–	–	–	–	–	2	–
			Female	–	–	–	–	–	–	–	–	–
	V10–V29	Pedal cyclist or motorcycle rider injured	Male	5	–	1	1	2	–	–	–	1
			Female	–	–	–	–	–	–	–	–	–
	V40–V59	Car, pick-up truck or van occupant injured	Male	48	2	1	6	7	8	8	8	8
			Female	11	–	–	–	3	3	–	1	4
	V60–V69	Occupant of heavy transport vehicle injured	Male	–	–	–	–	–	–	–	–	–
			Female	–	–	–	–	–	–	–	–	–
	V70–V79	Bus occupant injured	Male	–	–	–	–	–	–	–	–	–
			Female	–	–	–	–	–	–	–	–	–
	V80–V89	Other land transport accidents	Male	28	–	–	1	5	8	1	8	5
			Female	5	1	–	–	–	–	–	–	4
	V30–V39; V90–V99	Other transport accidents	Male	6	–	–	–	1	1	1	3	–
			Female	1	–	–	–	–	1	–	–	–

Table 3 cont. Violent Deaths by External Causes of Death, Sex and Age, 2017

X40–X49	Accidental poisoning by and exposure to noxious substances	Male	18	–	–	4	3	5	3	–	3
		Female	4	–	–	–	1	–	1	1	1
Y40–Y84	Complications of medical and surgical care	Male	–	–	–	–	–	–	–	–	–
		Female	–	–	–	–	–	–	–	–	–
W00–W19	Falls	Male	28	–	–	–	–	1	5	3	19
		Female	23	–	–	–	–	–	–	–	23
X00–X09	Exposure to smoke, fire and flames	Male	4	–	–	–	–	–	1	–	3
		Female	6	–	–	–	–	1	–	–	5
X30–X39	Exposure to forces of nature	Male	1	–	–	–	–	–	–	1	–
		Female	–	–	–	–	–	–	–	–	–
W65–W74	Accidental drowning and submersion	Male	21	2	2	2	2	3	–	1	9
		Female	13	–	–	–	1	4	1	1	6
W20–W64; W75–W84; W85–W99; X10–X20; X58–X59; Y10–Y34	Other external causes of accidental injury	Male	105	4	3	7	8	16	15	23	29
		Female	24	–	2	4	2	–	2	2	12
SUICIDES (X60–X84)		Male	98	–	1	7	7	11	18	24	30
		Female	27	–	1	–	1	3	3	8	11
X60–X65; X68–X69	Poisoning by solid and liquid substances	Male	11	–	–	1	2	–	2	2	4
		Female	3	–	–	–	–	–	–	2	1
X66–X67	Poisoning by gases and vapours	Male	–	–	–	–	–	–	–	–	–
		Female	–	–	–	–	–	–	–	–	–

X70	Hanging, strangulation and suffocation	Male	52	–	1	4	2	5	10	11	19
		Female	15	–	–	–	–	2	3	3	7
X71	Drowning and submersion	Male	2	–	–	–	–	–	–	1	1
		Female	3	–	1	–	–	1	–	1	–
X72–X74	Exposure to firearm discharge	Male	13	–	–	1	–	4	1	4	3
		Female	–	–	–	–	–	–	–	–	–
X75	Exposure to explosive material	Male	–	–	–	–	–	–	–	–	–
		Female	–	–	–	–	–	–	–	–	–
X76–X77	Exposure to smoke, fire, flames, steam, hot vapours and hot objects	Male	–	–	–	–	–	–	–	–	–
		Female	–	–	–	–	–	–	–	–	–
X78–X79	Stabbing with sharp or blunt object	Male	–	–	–	–	–	–	–	–	–
		Female	1	–	–	–	–	–	–	1	–
X80	Jumping from a high place	Male	4	–	–	–	1	–	1	1	1
		Female	3	–	–	–	–	–	–	1	2
X81	Jumping or lying before moving object	Male	–	–	–	–	–	–	–	–	–
		Female	–	–	–	–	–	–	–	–	–
X82	Crashing of motor vehicle	Male	–	–	–	–	–	–	–	–	–
		Female	–	–	–	–	–	–	–	–	–
X83–X84	Mixture of specified and unspecified means	Male	16	–	–	1	2	2	4	5	2
		Female	2	–	–	–	1	–	–	–	1
MURDERS (X85–Y09)		Male	13	–	–	1	3	3	1	–	5
		Female	5	–	–	–	–	–	1	1	3
X91	Assault by hanging, strangulation and suffocation	Male	1	–	–	–	–	–	–	–	1
		Female	1	–	–	–	–	–	–	–	1

Table 3 cont. Violent Deaths by External Causes of Death, Sex and Age, 2017

X92	Assault by drowning and submersion	Male	1	–	–	–	–	–	–	–	1
		Female	–	–	–	–	–	–	–	–	–
X93	Assault by handgun	Male	1	–	–	–	–	1	–	–	–
		Female	–	–	–	–	–	–	–	–	–
X94	Assault by rifle, shotgun and larger firearm	Male	–	–	–	–	–	–	–	–	–
		Female	–	–	–	–	–	–	–	–	–
X95	Assault by other and unspecified firearm	Male	1	–	–	–	–	1	–	–	–
		Female	2	–	–	–	–	–	–	1	1
X99	Assault by sharp object	Male	2	–	–	1	–	1	–	–	–
		Female	1	–	–	–	–	–	1	–	–
Y00	Assault by blunt object	Male	4	–	–	–	2	–	–	–	2
		Female	1	–	–	–	–	–	–	–	1
Y01	Assault by pushing from high place	Male	–	–	–	–	–	–	–	–	–
		Female	–	–	–	–	–	–	–	–	–
Y04	Assault by bodily force	Male	–	–	–	–	–	–	–	–	–
		Female	–	–	–	–	–	–	–	–	–
	Other (not covered by groups X85–Y09)	Male	3	–	–	–	1	–	1	–	1
		Female	–	–	–	–	–	–	–	–	–

* International Statistical Classification of Diseases and Related Health Problems.

Source: StatOffice 2018b.

bodily injuries on the territory of SVR Skopje, SVR Strumica, SVR Shtip, SVR Bitola, SVR Tetovo, SVR Ohrid, etc. The data are presented in *Tables 4* and *5*.

Table 4 Homicides and Bodily Injuries, 2010–2016

	2010	2011	2012	2013	2014	2015	2016
Homicides	40	29	28	20	25	21	17
Registered perpetrators	46	34	28	18	24	23	20
Rate per 100,000 inhabitants	1.82	1.32	1.28	0.91	1.21	1.01	0.96
Bodily injuries	248	239	211	216	213	154	173
Registered perpetrators	333	293	251	242	243	191	209
Rate per 100,000 inhabitants	11.28	10.88	9.65	9.83	10.31	7.41	9.77

Source: Ministry of Internal Affairs 2017.

Table 5 Homicides and Bodily Injuries by Administrative District, 2010–2016

	2010		2011		2012		2013		2014		2015		2016	
	H	BI	H	BI	H	BI	H	BI	H	BI	H	BI	H	BI
SVR Skopje	13	53	13	56	8	61	8	75	8	68	6	56	4	45
SVR Bitola	3	33	–	39	3	33	1	35	1	28	–	21	3	22
SVR Veles	–	36	2	25	4	10	2	15	6	13	1	9	1	8
SVR Kumanovo	7	20	4	28	2	21	3	23	1	12	3	5	4	10
SVR Ohrid	5	27	3	27	3	15	–	20	2	22	4	16	1	17
SVR Strumica	4	20	3	22	2	19	1	16	–	16	1	15	2	25
SVR Tetovo	4	27	4	20	4	21	3	15	3	24	7	16	2	21
SVR Shtip	4	32	–	22	2	31	2	17	4	30	–	16	–	25

Source: Ministry of Internal Affairs 2017.

H = homicide; BI = bodily injury; SVR = Administrative region

We conclude that the number of homicides in the country are relatively low compared to the homicide rates per 100,000 inhabitants in other countries in the world. For instance, in 2016 it was at 0.96 per 100,000 inhabitants and the level of bodily injuries was at 10.9 per 100,000 inhabitants.

5.2 Victims of Domestic Violence

Surveys on domestic violence in the country confirm the existence of almost all forms of domestic violence, however, it is necessary to regularly monitor, collect statistical data and conduct surveys in order to determine the trends of all forms of domestic violence. This is especially important for our country because we are facing a problem of non-existence of official data on domestic violence.[40] In the Republic of North Macedonia, the problem of domestic violence, and especially violence against women, for a long time did not attract the attention of the social, scientific and expert community. In 2004, domestic violence was for the first time incriminated in the Penal Code of the Republic of North Macedonia.[41] To date, the phenomenon of domestic violence is the subject of scientific research dedicated to determining the prevalence, dynamics, characteristics of domestic violence and determining the scope, manifestations and risks of domestic violence against women, children and the elderly. In the Republic of North Macedonia women are the most frequent victims of domestic violence.[42] Although domestic violence against men has not been sufficiently explored, however, it has been found that men can also be victims of domestic violence.[43]

According to the relevant data of the Ministry of Internal Affairs in 2017, there were a total of 973 victims of domestic violence, 78% were females and 22% were males. Most of them were victims of bodily injury and verbal/physical threats. The analysis also refers to the relative links between the perpetrator and the victim. The data are presented in *Table 6.*

5.3 Children as Victims of Physical, Psychological and Sexual Harassment

Misuse or neglect of a child, or child abuse, are general terms covering a large number of acts of perpetration or omission ranging from death to serious injuries, emotional pain, malnutrition or illness.[44]

There are six types of abuse or child negligence: physical abuse, sexual abuse, emotional abuse, physical neglect, educational neglect and emotional neglect.[45] In the Republic of North Macedonia, the research "Neglected and Stigmatised" analysed the dynamics and the occurrence of sexual abuse of children in the country.[46] Regarding domestic violence against children, 20.7% of women victims in the Republic of North Macedonia reported that the violence was directed towards their children. "When it comes to the child's age, most of the victims are preschool children, which is understandable since they have physical and psychological

---

40 *Gruevska Drakulevski* 2013.

41 *Čačeva & Mirčeva* 2009; *Popovska, Rikalovski & Viljagomez* 2012.

42 *Gruevska Drakulevski* 2013.

43 *Gruevska Drakulevski* 2013.

44 *Gelles* 1998, p. 181.

45 *Gelles* 1998, p. 181.

46 *Čačeva & Mirčeva* 2009, pp. 8–9.

Table 6 Review of Victimisation in Relation to Domestic Violence, 2017

Criminal act (according to the Penal Code)	Perpetrators	Victims												
		Sex		Relationship with perpetrator										
		Male	Female	Marital partner		Non-marital partner		Former marital partner		Child		Parent		Other
				Husband	Wife	Male	Female	Ex-Husband	Ex-Wife	Son	Daughter	Father	Mother	
Murder (art.123 par. 2)	2		2	–	1	–	–	–	–	–	–	–	–	1
Murder (art. 123 par. 2 in relation to art. 19)	4	1	3	–	1	–	–	–	–	1	–	–	2	–
Bodily injury (art.130 par. 2)	538	128	449	14	235	1	54	2	25	42	21	44	48	91
Severe bodily injury (art. 131 par. 2)	16	5	11	1	6	–	2	–	–	–	–	–	1	6
Coercion (art.139 par. 2)	6	1	5	–	–	–	1	–	–	–	1	1	1	2
Threatening the safety (art. 144 par. 2)	333	81	283	7	147	–	23	3	37	18	7	40	47	35
Unlawful deprivation of liberty (art. 140 par. 2)	4	1	3	–	1	–	1	–	–	–	–	–	–	2
Total	903	217	756	22	391	1	81	5	62	61	29	85	99	137

Source: Ministry of Internal Affairs 2017.

inferiority in relation to older children".[47] It is also highlighted that domestic violence against children in most cases is the longest, since older family members who are exposed to domestic violence have the option and opportunity to report the violence that is being committed against them, but this possibility is rare for children, because they are very small, on the one hand, and in most of the cases they are not informed how they can protect their rights and their integrity, and, on the other hand, after a certain period they experience domestic violence as quite normal, as is the need for food and drinking water. All this leads to a huge dark number of children – victims of domestic violence.[48]

The Ombudsman of the Republic of North Macedonia in the framework of the project "Prevention of child exploitation in the South East Europe, Sexual Exploitation of children in Macedonia", with financial support of the regional office of "Save the Children" Sarajevo, Bosnia and Herzegovina, conducted a research project entitled "Children-victims on sexual exploitation and paedophilia for the period of 01.01 2008 to 30.06 2011".

The aim of the research was to collect data from all bodies and institutions in order to assess the situation about sexual abuse and exploitation of children in the Republic of North Macedonia. In cases of sexual exploitation of children, socio-pathological occurrences exist, including alcoholism in the family, psychical illness, drugs addiction and prostitution of the female parent. The research upon sexually violated children indicates that they do not always have physical injuries, but often we realise that there are psychological disturbance and disorders, which means, aggressive behaviour of a child, problems in communication, problem with concentration, insomnia, depression and other problems that may have a permanent influence on the psychical development of the child. All child victims came from dysfunctional families, without parental care. The general conclusions are that the most frequent sexual abuse of children is "sexual abuse of minor", followed by "rape" and "illegitimate marriage with a minor". The most frequent penalty is imprisonment. Regarding the gender of the victims, the data point at higher presence of female victims, mostly between 14 and 16 years old. Roma children present most of the victims. The data also show that the children have either their elementary school level or have not finished it yet.

5.4 Victims of Sexual Assault

According to the data of the Ministry of Internal Affairs, in 2016 there was a total of 33 perpetrators of rape and 36 committed criminal acts. For the same year, there were 28 perpetrators of sexual assault upon a child under 14 years old. Data from the Ministry of Internal Affairs on these two *delicta carnis* are presented in *Tables 7* and *8*.

---

47 *Bačanović* 1999.

48 *Gruevska Drakulevski* 2013.

Table 7 Delicta Carnis, 2010–2016

	2010	2011	2012	2013	2014	2015	2016
Rapes	28	41	43	38	45	42	36
Perpetrators	31	39	36	36	48	33	33
Rate per 100,000 inhabitants	1.28	1.87	1.96	1.73	2.17	2.02	1.73
Sexual assaults upon a child	61	35	34	47	43	38	30
Perpetrators	71	37	35	51	54	38	28
Rate per 100,000 inhabitants	2.79	1.60	1.55	2.14	2.07	1.83	1.44

Source: Ministry of Internal Affairs 2017.

Table 8 Delicta Carnis According to Administrative District, 2010–2016

	2010		2011		2012		2013		2014		2015		2016	
	R	SA	R	SA	R	SA	R	SA	R	SA	R	SA	R	SA
SVR Skopje	1	7	2	7	8	10	5	8	5	10	10	6	6	5
SVR Bitola	3	8	8	8	3	3	4	9	5	3	8	16	4	8
SVR Veles	2	7	4	2	3	1	6	3	11	6	3	–	4	2
SVR Kumanovo	7	1	5	2	5	4	3	7	5	3	6	1	3	2
SVR Ohrid	–	6	–	3	1	3	3	1	10	1	4	3	4	1
SVR Strumica	4	11	9	6	6	8	7	7	2	3	3	5	6	5
SVR Tetovo	4	2	2	–	2	1	2	3	–	8	3	4	3	2
SVR Shtip	7	19	11	7	15	4	8	9	7	9	5	3	6	5

Source: Ministry of Internal Affairs 2017.

R = Rape; SA = Sexual attack upon a child; SVR = Administrative district.

According to the data, the rate of rape has fluctuated with the most rapes in 2014 (45) and the least in 2010 (28). In some cases, the rape was conducted by several perpetrators. The Republic of North Macedonia has a medium rape rate (5.0) of 100,000 inhabitants compared to the other countries in the world. In 2010, there were 61 cases of sexual assault upon a child who has not turned 14 years of age, followed by a decrease in the following years with slight fluctuations. Most of the crimes were committed on the territory of SVR Skopje, Shtip, Bitola, Strumica, and Veles. The rate of *delicta carnis* per 100,000 inhabitants is relatively low – 1.73. *Tables 7* and *8* summarise the data.

5.5 Victims of Human Trafficking and Smuggling Migrants

The National Commission for Combating Human Trafficking and Illegal Migration has drafted documents to form the National Strategy and National Action Plan for Combating Human Trafficking and Illegal Migration for the period 2017–2020. According to the US Department of State, The Republic of North Macedonia is a source, transit and destination country for men, women and children subjected to sex trafficking and forced labour. According to the data of the Ministry of Internal Affairs, the number of smuggled migrants has seen an upward trend with a peak in 2015 (142 criminal acts of smuggling migrants) (see *Table 9*).

Table 9 Smuggling Migrants, 2010–2016

	2010	2011	2012	2013	2014	2015	2016
Smuggling migrants	27	27	39	52	94	142	80
Perpetrators	58	44	70	98	166	212	123
Rate per 100,000 inhabitants	1.23	1.23	1.78	2.37	4.53	6.83	3.84

Source: *Ministry of Internal Affairs 2017.*

Next, the number of illegal migrants increased from 2015 to 2016 (127,358 > 1,49). This was heavily influenced by the refugee and migrant crisis (2015–2017) that took place in our country, as well. Most of the illegal migrants in 2016 were Albanian citizens, which is an increase of 7.8% in correlation to the previous year. Regarding the illegal migration of Afghan and Syria citizens, they note a drastic reduction of –63% and –77% respectively (see *Tables 10 a* and *10 b*).

Table 10 a Illegal Migrants, 2010–2013

Illegal migrants	**2010**	**2011**	**Increase/ reduction**	**2011**	**2012**	**Increase/ reduction**	**2012**	**2013**	**Increase/ reduction**
Total	1,103	469	–57.5%	469	682	45.4%	682	1,132	66%
Albanian citizens	892	216	–75.7%	216	328	51.8%	328	400	21.9%
Afghan citizens	16	57	256.25%	57	65	14%	65	134	106.15%
Syrian citizens	–	–	–	–	–	–	–	116	–

Source: *Ministry of Internal Affairs 2017.*

Table 10 b Illegal Migrants, 2013–2016

Illegal migrants	2013	2014	Increase/ reduction	2014	2015	Increase/ reduction	2015	2016	Increase/ reduction
Total	1,132	1,750	54.6%	1,750	1,949	11.4%	1,949	127,358	6,434.53%
Albanian citizens	400	624	56%	624	347	–44.4%	347	374	7.8%
Afghan citizens	134	291	117.16%	291	95,782	32,814.78%	95,782	35,079	–63%
Syrian citizens	116	570	391.38%	570	216,393	37,863.68%	216,393	49,633	–77%

Source: Ministry of Internal Affairs 2017.

Regarding the victimological aspects of the problem, indicators for the identification of victims of trafficking are: direct indicators designed to identify victims (e.g., height, gender, location of origin, transit and destination, documentation, transport, escort, physical appearance); specific indicators according to the type of trade, but they differ for adults and child victims of trafficking; indirect indicators for identifying potential victims. Most of the victims are children, aged 10–18 years old. Next, most of them are female and, as to their country of origin, they are from the Republic of North Macedonia. For more details see *Tables 11, 12* and *13.*

Table 11 Victims of Trafficking in Persons by Age, 2010–2014

Age	2010	2011	2012	2013	2014
Total	12	11	8	15	8
10–14	5	3	3	7	4
15–18	7	7	2	2	2
19–24	–	1	3	5	2
25–29	–	–	–	1	–
30 and over	–	–	–	–	–

Source: Ministry of Labour and Social Policy 2015.

Table 12 Victims of Trafficking in Persons by Sex, 2010–2014

Sex	2010	2011	2012	2013	2014
Total	12	11	8	15	8
Male	–	–	2	–	1
Female	12	11	6	15	7

Source: Ministry of Labour and Social Policy 2015.

Table 13 Victims of Trafficking in Persons by Country of Origin, 2010–2014

Country	2010	2011	2012	2013	2014
Total	12	11	8	15	8
North Macedonia	11	10	4	9	7
Albania	–	–	3	2	–
Bulgaria	–	1	–	–	–
Serbia	–	–	–	3	–
Kosovo	–	–	–	1	–
Bosnia and Herzegovina	–	–	1	–	–
Romania	1	–	–	–	1

Source: Ministry of Labour and Social Policy 2015.

Education of the victims

In studying the education of victims of human trafficking, the low level of education attracts particular attention. The highest number of victims are with uncompleted primary education, followed by victims who were not involved in the educational process (illiterate), or with completed primary education, next, are victims with an incomplete secondary, completed secondary and (with the lowest number of victims) incomplete or complete university education.

Occupation of the victims

Since the victims – minors or adults – had mostly no complete primary education, most of their occupations are those for which there is no need for vocational or higher education (waitresses, strippers, prostitutes, companions, entertainers). However, there were also victims who had completed secondary or higher education and worked as officer employees, teachers, etc.

Marital status of the victims

The victims were generally unmarried (given the greater prevalence of minors); a much lower number of victims were either divorced or widowed.

In order to protect victims of human trafficking, the Ministry of Labour and Social Politics opened a state shelter in February 2011 (Centre for Victims of Human Trafficking) where victims of trafficking are sheltered. Also, the Ministry of Labour and Social Politics continues the cooperation with the Association for Action against Violence and Human Trafficking "Open Gate" and for psychological support with the Association for Assistance and Support for Children and Families at Risk "For a Happy Childhood".

In 2016, the Republic of North Macedonia continued to be used as a transit country by migrants from the countries of the Middle East and Africa. In 2016, the number of identified victims increased. Six victims of human trafficking were identified and were given direct help and support. A total of 125 potential victims (78 adults and 47 children) were identified when illegally crossing the state border and were also given direct help and support. A total of 35,177 migrants were found at the entrance to the Republic of North Macedonia, while smuggling of 1,961 migrants was prevented. The six female victims that were identified included three children, half of them came from the Skopje region, one from Kicevo, one from Gostivar and one from the Republic of Serbia. Regarding the place of exploitation, the most common was the internal trade where the exploitation was performed mostly in the area of Gostivar, in three cases, two cases in Ohrid and one in Skopje. All victims were sexually exploited, one of the victims was exploited in a forced marriage.

Victims were provided with assistance and help at the Centre for Victims of Human Trafficking. In 2016, mobile teams in the two transit centres conducted 3,295 migrant referrals to services offered by various organisations (international and non-governmental) and state institutions, in the transit centres themselves. In 2016, mobile teams provided direct assistance to 8,627 migrants with specific needs.

6. Public and/or Media Discourses About Victims, Victim Rights, Protection and Victimisation

The relationship between the media, on the one hand, and crime and delinquency, on the other hand, can be considered from several aspects, including the influence of the media on criminal and delinquent behaviour; the distorted picture of crime and delinquency; the fear of crime; the creation of a false picture of the perpetrators and victims of crime and delinquency; as well as a distorted picture of the (un)successful authorities; the media and its failure to respect the principle of the presumption of innocence.

According to the Law on Audio and Audio-visual Media Services, providers of audio-visual media services must not broadcast programs that can seriously harm the physical, psychological or moral development of minors, especially programs that contain pornography or unnecessary violence.[49]

The media create a false picture of the perpetrators and victims of crime and delinquency, as well as a distorted picture of (un)successful authorities in combating and preventing crime and delinquency. An important prerequisite for publishing the news is the characteristics of the victim. The probability of reporting in the news is greater if the victim is a child. There is also a template in the media presentation of the perpetrators, who, according to media reporting, are mostly older persons who enjoy a higher social status that does not correspond with the profile of the perpetrators of crimes according to official statistics and surveys. The media, burdened with the need of sensationalism, often forget the interests of the juvenile perpetrator against whom criminal procedure is conducted. It is not uncommon for reporting by journalists to be contrary to and/or violate the ban on interviewing children under the age of 16 without the consent of their parent or guardian, even in cases where such reporting is directly contrary to the rights of children.[50]

In the area of protecting children's rights, it is necessary to protect the identity of anyone who, by pure chance, was or has become a victim of sexual exploitation and sexual abuse. So, their privacy should be protected and information should not be published about the victim to avoid any further victimisation of the child. Journalistic ethics also include the principle of "limiting the damage". This involves not reporting the names of victims, names of minors or information that is not materially linked to the news, which could, for example, harm someone's reputation.[51] According to the Law on justice for children, the court should protect the privacy of children and their families. Thus, in each juvenile court, proceedings the public should be excluded.[52]

Next, the exaggeration and reporting of sensational violent crime creates fear among the population, and such fear further influences criminal policy. For example, the Penal Code was amended regarding "paedophilia" (Sexual assault upon a child who has not turned 14 years of age) in terms of significant more severe criminal policy for these crimes, introducing a new security measure (medical and pharmacological treatment of perpetrators of such crimes) and a separate register of perpetrators.[53]

---

49 Article 50 (protection of minors) of the Law on Audio and Audio-visual Media Services, Law No. 184, 26.12.2013, Official Gazette 148/2013.

50 Article 9 of the Code of Ethics of Journalist, 14.11.2001; https://www.printfriendly.com/p/g/PqELMZ [19.06.2019].

51 Article 7 of the Code of Ethics of Journalist, 14.11.2001; https://www.printfriendly.com/p/g/PqELMZ [19.06.2019].

52 See Law No. 148/2013.

53 See Article 188 (sexual attack on a child who has not reached the age of 14) of the Law No. 83004.

But, according to statistics, these crimes account for less than 1% of crimes in the Republic of North Macedonia. So far, no research has been conducted in the Republic of North Macedonia on the correlation between sensationalist reporting and the creation of fear among the population and, further, the impact of that fear on criminal policy.

According to the Law on audio and audio-visual media services, broadcasters should protect the identity of victims of violence.[54] Journalists shall also respect the privacy of every person, except in cases when this is contrary to the public interest. Journalists are also obliged to respect personal pain and grief.[55] Moreover, they shall not consciously create or process information that jeopardises human rights and freedoms, shall not use hate speech and shall not encourage discrimination of any sort (nationality, religion, sex, social class, language, sexual orientation, political orientation, etc.).[56]

We can conclude that the media will not stop reporting on crime and delinquency, but nevertheless the findings about the negative influence of the media on criminal behaviour should at least be conceived by the media before they make reports. They should not report according to the maxim 'If it bleeds, it leads'. The Code of Journalists should be upheld to ensure professionalism.

7. Expert Assessment and Constructive Criticism With Suggestions for Improvement

Since 2007, an ongoing process of legislative reform has occurred in the Republic of North Macedonia. Within this process, research has been undertaken by different NGOs on victims of domestic violence and human trafficking, child victimisation and physical, psychological and sexual harassment, etc. However, thus far a major national victimisation survey has not been conducted. Whilst obstacles for such a survey exist, the necessity for such a survey exists so that a better picture of crime and victimisation can be garnered. We suggest that the official body for gathering and analysing the data should be the State Statistical Office of the Republic of North Macedonia. It is a specialised and independent organisation whose basic functions are collecting, processing and disseminating statistical data about the demographic, social and economic situation of Macedonian society.

Regarding victimology as a scientific discipline in the Republic of North Macedonia, we emphasise that at the universities, mostly, victimology is studied as a part

---

54 See Article 61 (principles) of the Law No. 148/2013.

55 Article 7 of the Code of Ethics of Journalist, 14.11.2001; https://www.printfriendly.com/p/g/PqELMZ [19.06.2019].

56 Article 10 of the Code of Ethics of Journalist, 14.11.2001; https://www.printfriendly.com/p/g/PqELMZ [19.06.2019].

of criminology, criminal law and criminal procedure. This is a theoretical limitation since victimology and research in victimology has a great significance. It is almost impossible to explain the aetiology of crime and delinquency without understanding the victim of the crime.

There are several governmental actors and NGOs involved in victim protection, as mentioned previously. Their activities have influenced many legislative changes. Many laws have been enacted: some laws have resulted in more sever punishments and others in better victim protection. Attention has also been drawn to the plight of victims, shifting away from the previous offender-centric focus of the criminal law.

In legislative terms, the situation of victims, their rights and their protection has improved since 2004. New possibilities are enshrined by law to better help, support and protect victims. Due to frequent cases of paedophilia and domestic violence, the general prevention was re-actualised, so the criminal policy regarding these criminal offences has been made more severe to create a stronger deterrent. However, the awareness about victims' rights is not at a satisfactory level due to the fact that legislative enactments, which are quite comprehensive and almost completely harmonised with EU standard, are not well implemented. Indeed, NGOs are seen as being far more effective than state bodies and authorities. For the latter, continuous training programs, campaigns and better funding are required. NGOs should also receive institutional and financial support.

Finally, each country, including ours, has the obligation to create a comprehensive framework, policies and measures for the protection and assistance of all victims of crime, to provide support and assistance to organisations and law enforcement agencies for effective co-operation in order to adopt an integrated approach to support and help victims.

8. Conclusions

Although the legislation exists to improve the position of victims in the criminal justice system, the impression exists that the law has not been satisfactorily implemented thus far. The criminal justice system remains more offender-oriented than victim-oriented. Although the legislative framework of the North Macedonia is in line with international and European standards, the most serious problems are linked to the level of implementation. Criminal policy regarding paedophilia, human trafficking and domestic violence has become harsher in the last decade, but the number of these crimes (at least paedophilia and domestic violence) has increased, so the deterrent effect of the criminal legislation has not been achieved so far.

In regard to property legal claims within criminal procedure, the practice shows that there are many cases where the victim (as a damaged party) has been referred to a civil litigation. Mediation is also very rare in practice due to a lack of experience and knowledge about its long-term advantages.

For successful implementation of the provision on procedural rights and the protection of vulnerable victims, services should be provided by different bodies with skilled staff and approved treatment methods. NGOs should also be used to establish and run different types of shelters and to provide therapy and counselling. The state should encourage and support empirical research regarding different issues connected with the position of victims in general and during criminal proceedings; issues concerning child victims must be researched as well.

As a result of the analysis of the paper, the authors make several suggestions:

- There is a need for the complete adoption and implementation of EU standards regarding information, support and protection of victims so that they will be able to participate in criminal proceedings.
- In accordance with Directive 2012/29/EU of the European Parliament and of the Council of 25 October 2012 establishing minimum standards on the rights, support and protection of victims of crime, and replacing Council Framework Decision 2001/220/JHA, the definition of "victim of crime" should be extended to encompass the family members: the spouse, the person who is living with the victim in a committed intimate relationship, in a joint household and on a stable and continuous basis, the relatives in direct line, the siblings and the dependants' of the victim as well as a family members of a person whose death was directly caused by a criminal offence and who have suffered harm as a result of that person's death.
- There is a need to provide compensation to victims of violence. This does not exist at the moment, although North Macedonia has ratified all the relevant international instruments and has already accepted the obligation to implement this compensation domestically.
- In the forthcoming amendments of the Law on justice of children, there is a necessity to reintroduce the legislative grounds for the establishment of a fund to compensate child victims of violent crime.
- Due to the tendency to strengthening the position of victims during criminal procedure, there is a need for the procedural possibility to exist that victimised minors be accompanied by representatives from specialised NGOs (be they specialised in providing help and support for victims in general or for victims of particular offences (trafficking, domestic violence, paedophilia, etc.).

9. Summary in Macedonian

Trudot dava opšta slika za sostojbata na viktimologijata, politikata vo odnos na žrtvite, legislativata povrzana so žrtvite i momentalnata sostojba na poddrška na žrtvite i zaštita na žrtvite vo Republika Severna Makedonija. Avtorite na trudot se osvrnuvaat na podatocite za žrtvite od oficijalnite statistiki za viktimizacija, kako i podatocite od anketite za žrtvite i analiza na relevantnite zakonski propisi povrzani so pravata na žrtvite, nivnata poddrška i nivnata zaštita povrzana so viktimizacija i zaštita na žrtvite vo i nadvor od krivičnata postapka. Avtorite gi analiziraat podatocite od Državniot zavod za statistika, centrite za socijalni raboti, policijata, obvinitelstvoto i sudovite, kako i relevantnite graǵanski združenija čija primarna aktivnost e poddrška i zaštita na žrtvite i nivnite prava i mediumskoto informiranje za žrtvite. Isto taka, avtorite davaat kratok pregled na zakonskata legislativa vo vrska so pravata na žrtvite, nivnata poddrška i zaštita, potoa, zakonskata regulativa za restorativnata pravda i karakteristikite na graǵanskite dejstvija vo krivičnata postapka i formite na nadomestok. Trudot se odnesuva na nekolku prašanja, kako što se opšti podatoci za državata; sostojbata na disciplinata viktimologija; pravnata ramka vo odnos na kriminalnata politika; kus pregčed na podatocite od istražuvanjata; javnite i/ ili mediumskite diskursi; ekspertska procenka i kritika so predlozi za podobruvanje; zaklučoci i rezime. Avtorite na trudot zaključuvaat deka sostojbata so viktimologijata ne e na zadovolitelno nivo so ogled na faktot što viktimologijata e relativno zanemarena oblast na kriminologija vo zemjata. Postoi potreba od sproveduvanje seopfatni istražuvanja za žrtvite, nivnite prava, poddrška i zaštita na žrtvite.

Literature

Arnaudovski, L., Bužarovska-Lažetić, G., Celevski, D. & Nanev, L. (2004): Strategija za implementacija na alternativnite merki [Strategy for the implementation of alternative measures]. Skopje.

Bačanović, O. (2010): Restorativna pravda u makedonskom kaznenom zakonodavstvu i poteškoće u njenoj implementaciji [Restorative justice in Macedonian criminal legislation and difficulties in its implementation]. Temida 13, pp. 5–24.

Bačanović, O. (2009): Restorativna Pravda I Zakon o maloletničkoj pravdi sa posebnim osvrtom na medijaciju [Restorative Justice and Law on Juvenile Justice with a special focus on mediation]. Crnogorska Revija za krivično pravo I kriminologijo [Montenegrin Journal of Criminal Law and Criminology] 2, pp. 405–422.

Bačanović, O. (1999): Decata – zrtvi na semejnoto nasilstvo [Children – Victims of domestic violence]. Bezbednost – Revija za kriminilistika, krimonologija I krivicno pravo [Security – Journal of Criminalistics, Crimology and Criminal Law] 1–2, p. 45.

Bužarovska-Lažetić, G. (2009): Spogoduvanje I medijacija [Collaboration and mediation]. Macedonian Review of Criminal Law and Criminology 2, pp. 215–260.

Bužarovska-Lažetić, G., & Misoski, B. (2011): Restorative aspects of Juvenile Justice in Macedonia. Teme [Themes] 2, pp. 365–383; http://teme2.junis.ni.ac.rs/public/journals/1/previousissues/teme2-2011/teme%202-2011-02.pdf [14.06.2019] [in English only].

Buzarovska, G., Bachanovic, O., Kalajdziev, G., Gruevska Drakulevski, A., Misoski, B., Gogov, B., Ilic, D., & Jovanova, N. (2014): Students' views on the police in the Republic of Macedonia. Varstvoslovje [Journal of Criminal Justice and Security] 16, pp. 435–452.

Bužarovska, G.L., Nanev, L., & Koshevaliska, O. (2016): [Restorative justice towards children]. Macedonian Review of Criminal Law and Criminology 1; http://journal.maclc.mk/2016/16.pdf [14.06.2019] [in Macedonian only].

Chudoska Blazhevska, I., & Juberías, C.F. (2016): La posición de Macedonia en la crisis de los refugiados de 2015 [The position of Macedonia in the refugee crisis of 2015]. Balkania [Balkans] 7, pp. 223–251; https://www.balkania.es/index.php?journal=Balkania&page=article&op=view&path%5B%5D=133&path%5B%5D=126 [14.06.2019] [in Spanish only].

Čačeva, V, & Mirčeva, S. (2009): "Zapostaveni i žigosani", Analiza na sostojbata: seksualna zloupotreba na deca ["Neglected and stamped", Analysis of the situation: Sexual abuse of children]. Skopje.

Dimitrojska, S., Buzarovska, G., & Saltirovska, Z. (2017): Risk factors for recidivism in juvenile criminal offenders. European Journal of Social Sciences, Education and Research 4, pp. 167–173.

Gelles, J.R. (1998): Family violence, in: M. Tonry (ed.), The handbook of crime and punishment. Oxford, pp. 178–206.

Gruevska Drakulevski, A. (2013): Domestic violence in the Republic of Macedonia. Macedonian Review of Criminal Law and Criminology 20, pp. 109–162.

Kambovski, V. (2015): Naučen i praktičen Komentar na Krivičniot zakonik na Republika Makedonija [Scientific and practical commentary on the Criminal Code of the Republic of Macedonia]. Skopje.

Kambovski, V. (1984): Alternativi za kaznata zatvor [Alternative to punishment of prison]. Godišnik na Institutot za socioloski i političko pravni istražuvanja [Yearbook of the Institute of sociological and political legal research] 1, pp. 291–309.

Kanevčev, M. (2006): Uslovno prekinuvanje na krivičnata postapka [Conditional termination of the criminal procedure]. Macedonian Review of Criminal Law and Criminology 13, pp. 87–96.

Lažetić, G., & Bužarovska, G. (2015): Macedonia, in: F. Dünkel, J.G. Holten, & P. Horsfield (eds.), Restorative justice and mediation in penal matters, vol. 1. Mönchengladbach, pp. 501–528.

Lažetić, G., & Bužarovska, G. (2006): Maloletnička pravda – od retributivnost kon restorativnost [Juvenile justice – From retribution towards restorative justice]. Macedonian Review of Criminal Law and Criminology 3, pp. 113–137.

Lažetić-Bužarovska, G. (2006): Restorativna Pravda od aspect na megjunarodnite dokumenti [Restorative justice in the aspect of international documents], in: Godišnik na Pravniot fakultet "Justinijan Prvi" – Skopje vo čest na prof. dr. Ljupčo Arnaudovski [Yearbook of the Law Faculty "Justinian the First" – Skopje in honour of prof. dr. Ljupčo Arnaudovski]. Skopje, pp. 630–645.

Lažetić-Bužarovska, G. (2003): Alternativi za zatvorot [Alternatives to imprisonment]. Skopje.

Marjanović, G. (1996): Alternativi za zatvorot I zatvoranjeto [Alternative to prison and imprisonment]. Godišnik na Pravniot fakultet vo Skopje [Yearbook of the Law Faculty in Skopje] 37, pp. 249–263.

Marjanović, G. (1995): Vo potraga po alternatuvu za zatvorot [In search of an alternative to prison], in: Godišnik na Pravniot fakultet "Justinijan Prvi" – Skopje vo čest na prof. dr. Ljupčo Arnaudovski [Yearbook of the Law Faculty "Justinian the First" – Skopje in honour of prof. dr. Ljupčo Arnaudovski]. Skopje, pp. 187–201.

Popovska, L., Rikalovski, V., & Viljagomez, E. (2012): „Izveštaj od studijata za nacionalnata anketa za semejno nasilstvo", publikacija izrabotena vo ramkite na Programata na Obedinetite Nacii za „Zajaknuvanje na nacionalnite kapaciteti za prevencija na semejno nasilstvo" ["Study Report on National Survey on Family Violence", a publication prepared within the United Nations program for "Stimulating National capacities for the prevention of domestic violence"]. Skopje; http://mtsp.gov.mk/WBStorage/Files/semejno_nasilstvo_anketa.pdf [14.06.2019] [in Macedonian only].

Saltirovska, Z., & Dimitrijoska, S. (2017): Legal and institutional functionality in the protection of women – Victims of domestic violence in the Republic of Macedonia – Present situation and future perspectives. European Journal of Social Sciences Education and Research 10, pp. 131–139; http://journals.euser.org/files/articles/ejser_may_august_17_nr_2/Zorica.pdf [14.06.2019] [in English only].

Documents

Academic Ranking of World Universities (2016): Macedonian HEIs ranking 2015–2016; http://www.shanghairanking.com/Macedonian_HEIs_Ranking/Macedonian-HEIs-Ranking-2015-2016.html [14.06.2019] [in English only].

Amnesty International (2015): Europe's borderlands: Violations against refugees and migrants in Macedonia, Serbia and Hungary; https://www.amnesty.org/download/Documents/EUR7015792015ENGLISH.PDF [14.06.2019] [in English only].

Human Rights Watch (2017): World report 2017, events of 2016; https://www.hrw.org/sites/default/files/world_report_download/wr2017-web.pdf [14.06.2019] [in English only].

Ministry of Internal Affairs (2017): Homicides and bodily injuries [Ubistva I telesni povredi]; https://mvr.gov.mk/statistiki/kriminal [14.06.2019] [in Macedonian only].

Ministry of Labour and Social Policy (2015): Programa za pomoš I poddrška pri reintegracija na deca reintegracija na deca žrtvi na trgovija žrtvi na trgovija [Program for assistance and support at reintegration of children reintegration of children victims of trade viction of trade with people]; http://www.mtsp.gov.mk/content/pdf/programa_reintegracija_deca.pdf [14.06.2019] [in Macedonian only].

State Statistical Office (StatOffice) (2018a): Istražuvanje za prihodite i uslovite za život, 2017 [Survey on income and living conditions, 2017]; http://www.stat.gov.mk/PrikaziPoslednaPublikacija_en.aspx?id=%2068 [14.06.2019] [in Macedonian and English]; cited as StatOffice 2018a.

State Statistical Office (StatOffice) (2018b): Nasilni smrtni slučaj vo Republika Severna Makedonija [Violent deaths in the Republic of North Macedonia]; http://www.stat.gov.mk/GSearch_en.aspx?cx=005984792435174779271%3Av7t0sn-wu1a&cof=FORID%3A10&ie=UTF-8&q=violent+deaths&sa=Search; [14.06.2019] [in Macedonian and English]; cited as StatOffice 2018b.

State Statistical Office (StatOffice) (2017): Makedonija vo figuri [Macedonia in figures, 2017]; http://www.stat.gov.mk/PrikaziPublikacija_1_en.aspx?rbr=676 [14.06.2019] [in Macedonian and English]; cited as StatOffice 2017.

StatOffice: see State Statistical Office.

Transparency International (2017): Corruption perceptions index 2016; https://www.transparency.org/whatwedo/publication/corruption_perceptions_index_2016 [14.06.2019] [in English only].

Viktimološko društvo Srbije [Victimology Society of Serbia] (2019): O nama [About us]; http://www.vds.rs/index.html [14.06.2019] [in Serbian and English].

Romania

Andra-Roxana Trandafir & Flaviu Ciopec

1. Introduction

As shown very often with respect to Romania, since the middle of the 19th century, the country has experienced so many reforms in the field of justice in general and of criminal legislation in particular as never before. While the focus is always on the offender, as is the case in other states, this does not mean that there is no interest in victims or victim protection, especially since as a member of the EU, Romania has implemented many of the measures required at European level, mainly in the Criminal Procedure Code (hereinafter CPC). Several entities, either public institutions or NGOs, are fighting for the rights and the protection of different categories of victims. This can also be seen in media coverage and the general social attitude, which are extremely important in some areas and can direct the professionals' approach towards the victims.

In order to analyse the particularities of victim protection and victimology in Romania, we shall present a short general background of the country, the current state of victimology, the status of the legislation related to victims and their protection including the status of implementation of EU regulations, the most important data with respect to victims as well as public and media discourse in this field. The main problems and possible solutions will be presented separately in order to draw some general conclusions.

2. General Country Background

Romania is located in Central and South-Eastern Europe and is the 12th largest country in the continent, comprising an area of 238,391 km^2. The Republic of Moldavia (formerly part of Romania) is in the East. The shore of the Black Sea lies in the South-East. The last demographic census organized in 2011 shows a population of 20.121.641; public data (Romanian National Institute of Statistics) speak about 19,760,314 inhabitants in Romania in 2016, out of which approx. 51% are women. The urbanized population stands at 54%. Romanians make up about 89.9% of the population, the rest mainly comprises Hungarians (6.5% of the population) and

Gypsies (3.3% of the population). Other minorities include Ukrainians, Germans, Turks, Lipovans and Tatars. The main religion is the Orthodox one (86.5% of the population), followed by the Roman-Catholic (4.6%), the Protestants (3.2%) and the Pentecostals (1.9%).[1] In terms of economy, Romania is an upper-middle income country. One of the worst setbacks is the lack of infrastructure (both motorways and railways) and the fluctuating fiscal legislation, which tend to discourage foreign investments. The Romanian GDP reached the official level of 186.7 billion dollars in 2016 (approximately 168 billion EUR). Regarding the employment rate, official data show that 66.3% of the population, aged 20–64, were working in 2016;[2] the unemployment rate slightly decreased to 5.9% (from 6.8% in 2015).

The country is governed on the basis of multi-party democratic system and of the segregation of the legislative, executive and judicial powers, all provided by the Constitution. Romania is divided into 5 macro regions which comprise a total number of 41 counties and the municipality of Bucharest, the capital of the country.

3. Current State of Victimology

The interest for victims and victimology in the academic milieu is rather narrow. The most prominent approaches are made by the University of Bucharest, where the curriculum contains a course on Victims' Sociology, as well as a course on Victims' Social Assistance and Victimology in the third year of studies (before graduation) at the Faculty of Sociology and Social Assistance. The same faculty organizes several Master of Arts (MA) programmes that are related to this area of interest. Thus, within the Social Deviance and Criminality MA programme, there is a course on Victimology within the Probation Services MA programme, and there is a course on the Assistance of Victims, while within the MA programme of Prevention and Fight against Illicit Drug Trafficking there is a course on Victims' Sociology. Lastly, within the MA programme on Risk Groups and Local Aid Services there is a course held on Victims of Human Trafficking: Specialized Services and Interventions.[3]

Another academic institution that holds specialized MA programmes is the Faculty of Philosophy and Social-Political Sciences within the Alexandru Ioan Cuza University in Iasi. Thus, within the MA programme on Probation services, mediation and social assistance of crime victims, there is a course of Victimology dedicated to the second year of studies, and within the MA programme of Community Security and Violence Control there is a course on Criminology and Victimology, destined for the first year of study.[4]

---

1 StatOffice 2013.

2 StatOffice 2016.

3 University of Bucharest 2019b.

4 University of "Alexander Ioan Cuza" in Iaşi 2019.

There have not yet been specific approaches dedicated to the topic within the Babeş-Bolyai University in Cluj-Napoca, the Craiova University, the Lucian Blaga University in Sibiu or the West University of Timişoara, which is a powerful indicator of the small concern paid to this topic in the academic world. A notable exception is the MA programme on Judicial Psychology and Victimology held at the Faculty of Psychology and Education Sciences at the Spiru Haret University in Bucharest, where a course on Victims and Aggressors in the Family Milieu is destined for the second year of the study.[5] Essentially, academic courses in the discussed domain are thus affiliated to Faculties of Sociology and Social assistance. At the Law Faculties within the Hexagon,[6] there are organized lectures on Criminology[7], which also approach the elements of victimology, however, there are no courses especially dedicated to this academic subject.

Although one of the founding fathers of victimology is a researcher of Romanian origins – in 1947, *Mendelsohn* submitted his study on victims to the Romanian Society of Psychiatry. The works in this domain are either very scarce or unsubstantial. In 2003, *Tănăsescu* published the volume "Criminology, aggressology, victimology, detentology",[8] in 2004, *Butoi* authored a monograph on "Victimology",[9] and in 2006,[10] *Hotca* wrote "Protection of victims: Elements of victimology".[11]

In Romania there is no society or institute specialised in victimology or dedicated to the study of victims. The Romanian Society of Criminology and Criminalistics (hereinafter RSCC),[12] established in 1990, publishes the Penology, Criminalistics and Criminology Review, with four issues per year. All contributions to this journal have been republished in two volumes,[13] which also comprise a few studies on victims. Nonetheless the RSCC is not an important player in the field.

---

5 University Spiru Haret 2019.

6 An informal academic network grouping the most representative Romanian Law faculties from the main university centres of state higher education: Bucharest, Cluj-Napoca, Iasi, Craiova, Sibiu and Timisoara. Annually, within the Hexagon, a competition for criminal law, civil law, constitutional law and sports contest is organized by rotation, see University of Bucharest 2019a.

7 For the state of art of criminology within law schools in Romania, see *Trandafir* 2014.

8 *Tănăsescu* 2003.

9 *Butoi* 2004.

10 Law on Certain Measures to Ensure the Protection of Victims of Crime, Law No. 211, 27.05.2004, Official Gazette 211/2004.

11 *Hotca* 2006.

12 Romanian Society of Criminology and Criminalistics 2019.

13 Romanian Society of Criminology and Criminalistics 2019.

A National Institute of Criminology was to be established as early as 2001[14] with the aim of scientific diagnosis and prediction of criminality. It was founded the following year[15] and was affiliated to the Ministry of Justice. Later, on the 31st January 2007 it was dissolved,[16] only to be re-established in 2017,[17] but it does not function yet due to lack of staff. Its fragmented existence did not provide the opportunity for serious literature in the domain. The only exceptions consist of a study on domestic violence,[18] published in 2004 and a study on the analysis of the violence phenomenon in Romania (1990–2002),[19] published in 2003.

However, in the matter of victim protection, there are several active NGOs. The informal network We break silence over sexual violence was created in May 2014, within a project financed by the NGO Fund Romania and comprises 15 NGO members.[20] The network ensures legal aid service for the victims of sexual violence,[21] where victims can have a confidential discussion on their trauma with specialists, as well as legal aid from the Pro Bono attorneys in the Pro Bono Network for Human Rights.[22]

---

14 Governmental Decision No. 455 of 2001 on the Approval of the Governing Programme Action Plan for the period 2001–2004, Decision No. 455, 23.05.2001, Official Gazette 267/2001.

15 Governmental Decision No. 722 of 2002 on the Amendments to the G.D. No. 212 of 2001 on the Organization and Functioning of the Ministry of Justice, Decision No. 722m 06.08.2002, Official Gazette 580/2002.

16 Governmental Decision No. 1918 of 2006 on the Amendments to the G.D. No. 83 of 2005 on the Organization and Functioning of the Ministry of Justice, Decision No. 1918, 09.01.2007, Official Gazette 13/2007.

17 Governmental Decision No. 14 of 2017 on the Establishment, Organization and Functioning of the National Institute of Criminology, Decision No. 14, 16.01.2017, Official Gazette 44/2017.

18 *Liiceanu, Saucan & Micle* 2004.

19 *Liiceanu, Saucan, Micle, Istrate, Rujoiu & Bărbulescu* 2003.

20 Association for Freedom and Gender Equality (Asociația pentru Libertate şi Egalitate de Gen), Equality and Human Rights Action Center (Centrul de Acțiune pentru Egalitate şi Drepturile Omului), Association Center for Curricular Development and Gender Studies (Centrul Filia), Front Association (Asociația Front), Eastern European Reproductive Health Institute (Institutul Est European pentru Sănătatea Reproducerii), Partnership Center for Equality (Centrul Parteneriat pentru Egalitate), Association for Promoting Gipsy Women's Rights (Asociația pentru Promovarea Drepturilor Femeilor Rrome), Women's Association Against Violence (Asociația AFIV Artemis), Feminist Analysis Society (Societatea de Analize Feministe Ana), Transcena Association (Asociația Transcena), Quantic Group (Grupul Quantic), Alternative Step Association (Asociația Pas Alternativ), Psychosphere Association (Asociația Psihosfera), Center for Mediation and Community Security (Centrul de Mediere şi Securitate Comunitară), Association Victory Against Violence, Abuse and Discrimination (Asociația VIVAD), see Partnership Center for Equality 2019.

21 Association for Liberty and Equality of Gender 2013.

22 The Pro Bono Network for Human Rights 2019.

Within the aforementioned network, several studies have been elaborated: The Joint-Opinion on legislative amendments need to be adopted after the ratification of Istanbul Convention on preventing and combating violence against women and domestic violence;[23] Guide for the Victims of Sexual Violence[24] or Sexual Violence as a Form of Violence against Women.[25]

Another informal structure is the Network on Prevention and Fight of Violence against Women, reuniting those organisations which are active in promoting women rights, protecting gender violence victims and fighting gender discrimination.[26] Such network was shaped out between 2011–2014 especially through lobbying, advocacy, advertising campaigns in the support of amending Law No. 2003–217 on the prevention and combating of domestic violence, especially as to the enactment of the restricting order.[27]

Several studies were published by the aforementioned network, namely: the Practical guide for victims of domestic violence;[28] the National Report on implementation of the restricting orders, edition 2013, 2014 and 2015; the Exploratory Study on the Implementation of the Protection Order and the Domestic Violence Provisions of the Criminal Code of Romania in 2012–2016;[29] the Exploratory Study on Social Services for Domestic Violence Victims 2013; How much is a victim of domestic violence? Analysis of public financing services 2014.

Another renowned NGO is the Social Alternatives of Iași, which coordinated the publication of several works, namely: the Guide to Children Hearing in Judicial

---

23 Equality and Human Rights Action Centre 2016.

24 We break the silence about sexual violence 2016.

25 Association for Freedom and Gender Equality 2013.

26 Asociația pentru Libertate și Egalitate de Gen (Association for Liberty and Gender Equality), Centrul de Acțiune pentru Egalitate și Drepturile Omului (Equality and Human Rights Action Center), Centrul Filia (Association Center for Curricular Development and Gender Studies), Asociația Front (Association Front), Institutul Est European pentru Sănătatea Reproducerii (Eastern European Reproductive Health Institute), Centrul Parteneriat pentru Egalitate (Center Partnership for Equality), Asociația pentru Promovarea Drepturilor Femeilor Rrome (Association for Promoting Gipsy Women's Rights), Asociația AFIV Artemis (Women's Association Against Violence - Artemis), Societatea de Analize Feministe Ana (Feminist Analysis Society - Ana), Asociația Transcena (Association Transcena), Grupul QUANTIC (Quantic Group), Asociația Pas Alternativ (Association Alternative Step), Asociația Psihosfera (Association Psychosphere), Centrul de Mediere și Securitate Comunitară (Center for Mediation and Community Security), Asociația VIVAD (Association Victory Against Violence, Abuse and Discrimination).

27 Law on the Prevention and Combating Domestic Violence, Law No. 2003–217, 18.07.2018, Official Gazette 205/2014.

28 Anais Association 2017.

29 Network for Preventing and Combating Violence against Women 2017.

Proceedings (2009),[30] coordinated by *Pivniceru* and *Luca*; the Victims' Protection (2009);[31] Information Guide to Human Trafficking. Prevention, Fight and Victims' Assistance (2006); Institutional Practices Guide to Conducting Cases involving Underage (Victims), 2005; Human Trafficking, Offender, Victim, Offense (2005).

Within another NGO – the Association Pro Refugiu – a specialised programme work is in progress. Pro Victims Justice[32] through an Enhanced Rights Protection and Stakeholders Cooperation is coordinated by the Association Pro Refugiu in partnership with Centre for the Study of Democracy Bulgaria, Crime Prevention Council of Lower Saxony Germany, Scandinavian Human Rights Lawyers Sweden, and National Association of the Romanian Bars. The project is implemented with the financial support of the European Union, Justice Programme, for a period of 24 months, starting from 1 September 2017 until 31 August 2019.

The NGO's objectives are to design and promote methods and instruments in order to ensure proper assistance for victims of crime. It is also supposed to promote the recognition of their rights and to help the victims within the procedures when they access the justice system: from an early contact with the investigators until the end of the trial; and also to strengthen the victims' position within the justice framework through the exchange of best practices/transfer of expertise/cross-border networking among several countries.

The research performed hereby was shaped to concrete form in the following works: the Survey Report on Victims of Crimes Rights Competent Stakeholders in Romania, Bulgaria, Germany, Sweden (2018);[33] Manual for Lawyers, Prosecutors and Judges. Strengthening Legal Knowledge for a Better Protection of Victims of Human Trafficking Rights in the Judicial Proceedings (2017);[34] and the Handbook for Legal, Social, Health Professionals Involved in the Protection of the Rights and the Assistance of Victims of Human Trafficking (2017).[35] Moreover, it must be noticed the contribution of APADOR-CH (first and most visible national NGO in the field of human rights protection) with a special project named Improving Access to Justice in Romania for Victims of Trafficking in Human Beings (2017).[36]

It is easily to perceive that private legal entities are more active in the field of research and protection of the victims than public authorities. As an outstanding ex-

30 *Pivniceru & Luca* 2009.

31 Social Alternative 2019.

32 Pro Victims Justice 2019.

33 *Berbec, Ilcheva, Nordström, Heinonen, Feito & Freudenberg* 2018.

34 *Mosneagu et al.* 2017.

35 *Berbec et al.* 2017.

36 *Rotundă* 2017.

ception, it is worth noting that the National Agency against Trafficking in Persons[37] develops several programmes for victims of these specific offences. As a follow-up of the Agreement concluded between the Government of Romania and the Swiss Federal Council on the implementation of the Swiss-Romanian Cooperation Programme to Reduce Economic and Social Disparities within the Enlarged European Union, the National Agency Against Trafficking in Persons has implemented the project Supporting Romanian NGOs for Direct Assistance of Victims of Human Trafficking for a period of 38 months, starting in February 2015. Within other projects (RO21-MAI-ANITP-PDP-3 and RO20-MJ-ANITP-PDP 1), both financed by Norway Grants, the study on Compensation for Victims of Human Trafficking in Romania[38] and the Analysis of Assistance Services for Victims of Trafficking in Human Beings have been elaborated.

4. Relevant Legal Framework in Terms of Criminal Policy

In 2012, the European Council and the European Parliament adopted a historic piece of EU legislation strengthening to a great extent the rights of victims of crime (Directive 2012/29/EU; hereinafter Directive) and replacing the Framework Decision 2001/220/JHA of 15 March 2001 on the standing of victims in criminal proceedings.[39] This way, all European countries (except Denmark) committed themselves to improvement of the rights, support and protection of all victims of crime by the 16th November of 2015.

There are a few Member States that have either not yet fully transposed the Directive (Slovenia) or despite having transposed the Directive, may not be fully legally compliant (Malta, Lithuania, Poland, Romania).[40] Western European countries were the first to incorporate and recognise victims' rights in their national legislation in the 1970s and 1980s, while Central and Eastern European countries (Bulgaria, Croatia, Hungary, Latvia, Malta, Lithuania, Romania and Slovakia) started embedding these in the 2000s.[41]

37 National Agency against Trafficking in Persons 2019.

38 *Dragotă* 2017.

39 Directive 2012/29/EU of the European Parliament and of the Council of 25 October 2012 Establishing Minimum Standards on the Rights, Support and Protection of Victims of Crime, and Replacing Council Framework Decision 2001/220/JHA, Directive No. 2012/29/EU, 14.11.2012, Official Journal of the European Union 315/57; https://eur-lex.europa.eu/legal-content/EN/TXT/PDF/?uri=CELEX:32012L0029&from=en [09.09.2019].

40 European Parliamentary Research Service 2017.

41 European Union Agency for Fundamental Rights 2014.

On 27th May 2004, Romania adopted the Law No. 2004–2011[42] on certain measures to ensure the protection of victims of crime (hereinafter Victims' Act). The legislative act intended to regulate certain measures for informing the victims of crime with regard to their rights, as well as for providing the victims of crime with psychological counselling, free legal assistance and financial compensation from the State. The Explanatory Memorandum of the Act explicitly stated that the Framework Decision 2001/220/JHA has been considered as a standard for the adoption of the said Act. Subsequently, the Act was amended in 2007, following the accession of Romania to the European Union. One of the amendments was to expressively declare the transposition of the Directive 2004/80/EC of 29 April 2004 into national law on the compensation of crime victims.[43]

On 1st February 2014, the new CPC (Law 2010-135)[44] entered into force in Romania. The CPC provides several provisions on the rights and the protection of the victims of crime. The Explanatory Memorandum of the CPC refers only to the Framework Decision 2001/220/JHA and contains no reference to the Directive 2012/29/EU, although the new code was enacted by a law adopted in 2013[45] that is after the Directive.

For long time, the Directive 2012/29/EU was neither fully transposed into domestic legal order, nor on time. The single Act which expressly refers to the transposition of the said Directive was adopted on the 18th May 2016 by the Government by issuing the Emergency Ordinance No. 2016-18.[46] This act stipulated that only certain provisions of the Directive are transposed.[47] The Government Ordinance was subjected to approval by the Parliament, but the legislative procedure is still pending. On this matter, an infringement case was opened against Romania by the European Commission in January 2016, as well as against other countries.[48] The last call of the Commission for complying with the Directive was set on January 8, 2019. As a last resort, Romania adopted the Emergency Ordinance No. 2019-24, expressly referred to the transposition of certain provisions of the Directive.[49] The area of

42 See Law No. 2004-2011.

43 Council Directive 2004/80/EC of 29 April 2004 Relating to Compensation to Crime Victims, Directive No. 2004/80/EC, 06.08.2004, Official Journal of the European Union 261/15.

44 Criminal Procedure Code, Law No. 2010-135, 15.07.2010, Official Gazette 486/2010.

45 Law No. 2013-255 on the Enactment of the Criminal Procedure Code, Law No. 2013-255, 14.08.2013, Official Gazette 515/2013.

46 Government Emergency Ordinance No. 2016-18, Ordinance No. 2016-18, 23.05.2016, Official Gazette 389/2016.

47 See Directive No. 2012/29/EU.

48 Victim Support Europe 2016.

49 Government Emergency Ordinance no 2019-24, Ordinance No. 2019-24, 01.04.2019, Official Gazette 24/2019.

victims' protection has begun to be explored in Romania at sectoral level through attempts to provide solutions for certain categories of victims. Thus, through Law No. 2001-678 on preventing and combating trafficking in human beings (hereinafter Human Trafficking Act),[50] a form of protection was designed for the victims of this type of crime. Law No. 2002-682 on the protection of witnesses (hereinafter Witness Protection Act)[51] aims to ensure the protection of victims who can act as witnesses in criminal proceedings and are called upon to testify before judicial bodies. Through Law No. 2003-217 on the prevention and combating of domestic violence (hereinafter Domestic Violence Act),[52] another form of protection has been envisaged for persons being subjected to domestic violence. Finally, Law No. 2004-272 on the protection and promotion of children's rights (hereinafter Child's Rights Act)[53] provided protection for minor victims. The Victims' Act[54] was adopted as a consequence of these sectoral policies and was the first legislative instrument to propose an extended strategy on the protection of victims without being a successful model. Symptomatic for the level of interest in this field is the fact that after four consecutive years of annual regulations, since 2004, no strong initiative has taken place from this point of view in Romania, at legislative level. However, the entry into the EU imposed another paradigm. Romania is compelled to strive to comply with European requirements and to incorporate European law into national legislation. As shown before, the Act 2019-24 was adopted by the Government in an extraordinary procedure in order to avoid European penalties.

4.1 Definition of the Victim

The Romanian CPC contains a legal definition of a victim.[55] The specific term used by the CPC is that of the injured person *(persoana vătămată)*. As concerns equivalence of legal meaning of injured person with victim, it is to be noted that CPC uses both expressions. The difference is that injured person is the victim who participates in a criminal proceeding as a main subject.[56] The victim who does not

---

50 Law No. 2001-678 on Preventing and Combating Trafficking in Human Beings, Law No. 2001-678, 11.12.2001, Official Gazette 783/2001.

51 Law No. 2002-682 on the Protection of Witnesses, Law No. 2002-682, 18.04.2014, Official Gazette 288/2014.

52 Law No. 2003-217 on the Prevention and Combating of Domestic Violence, Law No. 2003-217, 24.03.2014, Official Gazette 205/2014.

53 Law No. 2004-272 on the Protection and Promotion of Children's Rights, Law No. 2004-272, 05.03.2014, Official Gazette 159/2014.

54 See Law No. 2004-2011.

55 See Article 79 (Injured party) of the Law No. 2010-135.

56 This was also the view of the previous criminal procedure code, which provided that the person who suffered a physical, moral or material injury, if involved in the criminal proceedings, is called injured party.

want to participate in criminal proceedings has to inform the judicial body, who could call such person as a witness if it deems it necessary.[57] It is clear, therefore, that the CPC recognises a legal status for the victim, depending on whether that person participates in criminal proceedings or not. This is not the European concept of the term, where such conditions does not exist. It is to be noted that the definition of the victim in Human Trafficking Act is closer to the Directive requirements,[58] excluding participation in the criminal proceedings as a condition for being a victim.

Expressing the victim's desire to participate in the criminal trial seems irrevocable. Once the will on not participating as an injured person and being heard as a witness exists, the victim no longer retains the option to come back on the decision. In this respect, CPC states that the quality of witness takes precedence over the status of the expert, the lawyer, the mediator or the representative of one of the parties or of a main subject, as with respect to the facts and the circumstances that the person knew before acquiring this quality.[59]

The Directive includes also family members of a person whose death was directly caused by a criminal offence and who have suffered harm as a result of that person's death in the notion of victim. Family members means the spouse, the person who is living with the victim in a committed intimate relationship, in a joint household and on a stable and continuous basis, the relatives in direct line, the siblings and the dependents of the victim.[60] Family members of a victim are not included in the category of victims under the CPC, and, accordingly, they do not enjoy the exercise of all the rights recognised by the Directive. However, family members of a victim enjoy similar protection measures to threatened witness.[61] However, a family member claiming a patrimonial right (compensation for the economic loss/emotional harm incurred by the death of a relative) could be accepted as a victim.[62]

As amended, Victims' Act provides a definition for victim and family members of the victim, by simply transposing[63] the definition contained in the Directive. At this moment, the Victims' Act enlarged the notion of the victim and surpassed indirectly the RCPP norms, being the reference standard in the field. Accordingly, the defini-

---

57 See Article 81 (Rights of the injured party) of the Law No. 2010-135.

58 See Article 2 of the Law No. 2001-678.

59 See Article 114 (Persons heard as witnesses) of the Law No. 2010-135.

60 See Directive No. 2012/29/EU.

61 See Article 113 (Protection of injured person and civil party) of the Law No. 2010-135.

62 Articles 1390 (Person entitled to compensation in case of death) and 1391 (Remedy of the non-pecuniary damage) of the Civil Code, Law No. 2009-287, 20.03.2017, Official Gazette 20/2017.

63 See Law No. 2004-2011.

tion of family members in the Penal Code[64] or in the Domestic Violence Act[65] (art. 5) are to be considered as subsidiary.

The new definition of victim incorporated in the Romanian legislation also clarified the debate about the legal protection of civil partnerships between persons of the opposite or same sex. This is to remember that such partnership concluded or contracted abroad either by Romanian citizens or by foreign citizens are still not recognised under the Romanian Civil Code.[66] Since the equivalence of forms of cohabitation with marriage is basically prohibited in Romania, this could mean that the civil law refuses the status of a victim to persons living in such a partnership. No such interpretation is still available based on the new legal approach.

The Romanian Constitutional Court (hereinafter Court) has ancipated this issue, by ruling as unconstitutional the legal condition of cohabiting. The Court stated[67] that the cohabitation as a legal condition provided by the criticized law for asking the judge to issue a protection order violates the right to life and the right to physical and mental integrity of the person whose life, physical or mental integrity or freedom is endangered by an act of violence committed by a member of the family. In a different decision,[68] the Court found the legislative solution regulated by CPC unconstitutional, based on the fact that it excludes the persons, who have established similar relations to those existing between spouses, from the right to refuse to be heard as a witness as it violates the provisions on the equality of citizens before the law referred to in Constitution. The decision seems to permit a broader interpretation of the legal notion of family, including persons who just cohabit with each other and in an extensive view, civil partnership.

Some specific provisions exist in the Witness Protection Act related to the protected witness, i.e., the witness themselves (including the victim who does not want to participle in criminal proceedings), the members of their family and the persons close to them. Family members of the protected witness are the spouse, parents and children, while the close person of the protected witness is the person with whom the witness is linked by strong emotional ties.[69]

---

64 Article 177 (Family member) of the Penal Code, Law No. 286/2009, 17.07.2009, Official Gazette 286/2009.

65 See Article 5 of the Law No. 2003-217.

66 See Article 277 (Prohibition or equivalence with marriage of certain forms of cohabitation) of the Law No. 2009-287.

67 Constitutional Court of Romania, Decision No. 264, 27.04.2017.

68 Constitutional Court of Romania, Decision No. 562, 19.09.2017.

69 See Article 2 of the Law No. 2002-682.

4.2 Status and Rights of Victims in Criminal Proceedings

As we have already shown, the victim wishing to participate in the criminal trial acquires the position of an injured person. As such, the victim may participate in the criminal proceedings both on the criminal and on the civil side. On the criminal side, the victim is recognized as a main subject, without being part of the trial. The distinction is formal, since the main subjects have the same rights and obligations as the parties.[70] The victims does not become a party in the proceedings because they do not fall under the scope of the party's definition, namely the person who is or is being sued. Thus, the victim does not take part in the criminal action, which belongs entirely to the Public Ministry. Under the previous CPC by 2006, the victim had the role of private accusation for a limited category of offences: assault, bodily harm, threat, libel, slander, theft among relatives, breach of trust, trespassing and criminal mischief.[71] In this capacity, the victim initiated the criminal action, without the prosecutor's intervention, directly before a criminal judge, being a genuine holder of the criminal action for the offences indicated above. In this situation, the quality of party within the criminal trial of the victim could not be denied. After 2006, the Public Ministry gained monopoly power over criminal proceedings and excluded the victim from setting the criminal action in motion. As a consequence, the victim has become only a main subject of the proceedings. On the civil side, the victim may choose to take civil action against the defendant in the criminal proceedings. In this situation, the victim becomes a civil party and may cumulate the quality of the main subject in the same case.[72] We shall refer to civil action below (see *Section 4.3*).

In a criminal trial, the victim has several rights,[73] which are the same for both injured and civil party .[74] A victim who considers him- or herself affected in their legitimate rights and interests may complain against measures and acts of criminal prosecution. The complaint is addressed to the prosecutor who supervises the activity of the criminal investigation body and is filed either directly with them or with the criminal investigation body.[75] Against the solutions of not to proceed with or to end the investigation or not to prosecute the offender, the victim has the possibility to file a complaint which falls in the competence of a preliminary chamber judge.[76] In exercising this control, the Preliminary Chamber Judge will be able to:

---

70 See Article 33 (Main participant of trial) of the Law No. 2010-135.

71 Article 279 (Authorities where the complaint is filed) of the Criminal Procedure Code, Law No. 1968-29, 11.01.2006, Official Gazette 78/1997.

72 See Articles 84 (Civil party) and 85 (Rights of the civil party) of the Law No. 2010-135.

73 See Article 81 (Rights of the injured party) of the Law No. 2010-135.

74 See Article 85 (Rights of the civil party) of the Law No. 2010-135.

75 See Article 336 (Rights to file a complaint) of the Law No. 2010-135.

76 See Article 340 (Complaint against decisions not to prosecute and not to refer to court) of the Law No. 2010-135.

1) if the prosecution has not been initiated, allow the complaint, vacate the challenged solution and refer the case file back to the prosecutor to start or complete the prosecution, or, as the case may be, to initiate the criminal proceedings and complete the prosecution; and
2) if the prosecution was initiated by the prosecutor, to allow the complaint, vacate the challenged solution and order the beginning of the trial on the facts and persons indicated in the order of the criminal action, when the legally supplied evidence is sufficient.

Against the decision of the first court, the victim has the right to file an appeal, but only on the criminal side of the case.[77] The civil party has the right to appeal on the civil side, and on the criminal side only if the solution on this side has influenced the solution on the civil side. The victim cannot file an appeal for review,[78] but instead may file an appeal on the time frame of the criminal trial.[79]

4.3 Compensation System for Victims

National law allows victims to become civil parties in criminal proceedings in order to claim damages caused by the commission of an offence. A victim becomes a civil party upon their request, which is decided before the judicial examination of the case in court. Otherwise a victim could file an action with a civil court only. The court may order disjoinder of a civil action when its settlement leads to exceeding the reasonable term for the ruling on the criminal action.[80] Nevertheless, the settlement of the civil action, under these conditions, shall remain under the competence of the criminal court.

The civil action may be filed in criminal proceedings up to the moment when evidence is submitted before the court.[81] Judicial bodies are under the obligation to inform victims on the existence of such right.[82] A civil action initiated in criminal proceedings aims at establishing civil liability in tort of the persons liable under the civil law for damages caused by having committed an act that is the subject matter of the criminal act.[83] A civil action is used by a victim or by their successors, who become civil parties against the defendant and, as applicable, against the party with civil liability.

---

77 See Article 408 (Decision subject to appeal) of the Law No. 2010-135.

78 See Law No. 2010-135.

79 See Article 488 (Submission of the challenge) of the Law No. 2010-135.

80 See Article 19 (Object and exercise of civil action) of the Law No. 2010-135.

81 See Article 20 (Claim damage as a civil party) of the Law No. 2010-135.

82 See Article 111 (Hearing of injured person) of the Law No. 2010-135.

83 See Article 19 (Object and exercise of civil action) of the Law No. 2010-135.

If victims or their successors do not become civil parties in criminal proceedings, they may file an application for damages caused by a criminal offence to a civil court. A victim or their successors who became civil parties in criminal proceedings may file an application for damages to a civil court if: the criminal court issued no ruling on the civil action, by a final decision or if the criminal trial was suspended.[84] A victim or their successors who initiated an application for damages before a civil court may leave this court and address the criminal investigation body, the judge or the court, if the criminal action was initiated subsequently or if criminal proceedings were resumed following suspension; also, if more damages were discovered after they became a civil party to the criminal proceedings.

Taking in consideration the Directive's provisions (i.e., Member States shall promote measures to encourage offenders to provide adequate compensation to victims) national law states that compensation to victim provides for the offender the opportunity to secure latitudes of penalty reduced by one-third. For instance, there shall be legal mitigating circumstances the covering of all the material damage caused by an offence, during the criminal investigation or the trial, until the first hearing, if the offender has not benefited from this circumstance within five years prior to committing the crime.[85]

Finally, Romania has established a compensation system with state financing through the Victims' Act for the following categories of victims:

a) persons who have been the subjects of an attempted murder and murder, crime of bodily injury, rape, sexual intercourse with a minor and sexual assault, crime of trafficking in human beings and trafficking in minors; terrorist offences, and any other intentional offence committed with violence;
b) the needy spouse, children and persons dependent on the deceased, as a result of the offences referred to above.[86]

Financial compensation is granted if the offence has been committed on the territory of Romania and the victim is:

a) Romanian citizen;
b) foreign citizen or stateless person legally residing in Romania;
c) a citizen of a Member State of the European Union, legally present on the territory of Romania at the time the offence was committed;

---

84 See Article 27 (Ruling on the civil action before the civil court) of the Law No. 2010-135.

85 See Article 75 (Mitigating circumstances) of the Law No. 286/2009.

86 See Law No. 2004-2011.

d) a foreign citizen or a stateless person residing in the territory of a Member State of the European Union, legally present on the territory of Romania at the time the offence was committed; or
e) for victims who do not fall into these categories, the financial compensation is granted on the basis of the international conventions which Romania is party to.[87]

Financial compensation is not granted if:

a) it is established that the deed does not exist or is not provided by the criminal law or that the deed was committed in legitimate defence against the victim's attack;
b) the victim receives a final sentence for participating in an organized criminal group;
c) the victim receives a final sentence for one of the offences indicated above;
d) the court decides in favour of the perpetrator extenuating circumstances for overstepping the boundaries of legitimate defence against the victim's attack or the extenuating circumstance of the provocation;
e) the victim did not notify the criminal prosecution bodies within 60 days from the date of the offence. Victims who have not reached the age of 18 and those under judicial interdiction are not required to notify the criminal prosecution bodies of the offence;
f) the victim did not file the financial compensation request within one year, depending on the situation, from the date of the final decision of the criminal court or the date when the prosecutor ordered the filing. If the perpetrator is unknown, the victim may file the application for financial compensation within 3 years from the date when the offence was committed;
g) the victim was a civil party in the criminal trial;
h) the perpetrator is insolvent or missing; or
i) the victim obtained full compensation for the damage suffered by an insurance company.[88]

If the victim is a minor and their legal representative has not filed the application for financial compensation within 1 year or 3 years, these terms start to run from the date the victim reaches the age of 18. Financial compensation is granted to the victim for the following categories of damage incurred through the crime:

---

87 See Article 23 of the Law No. 2004-2011.

88 See Law No. 2004-2011.

1) hospitalisation expenses and other categories of medical expenses incurred by the victim;
2) material damage resulting from the destruction, degradation or inappropriate use of the victim's property or from dispossession due to the offence;
3) the gains which the victim is deprived of due to the offence;
4) funeral expenses; or
5) maintenance of which the victim is deprived due to the offence.[89]

Financial compensation for this material damage is granted up to an amount equivalent to ten gross minimum country salaries[90] set for the year in which the victim filed the financial compensation claim. Amounts of money paid by the perpetrator for civil damages and the compensation obtained by the victim from an insurance company for the damages caused by the offence are deducted from the amount of the financial compensation granted by the state to the victim.

The application for financial compensation is filed with the court in whose area of jurisdiction the victim resides and is settled by two judges of the special commission for providing financial compensation to the victims. The necessary funds for granting the financial compensation or the down payment for the victims of the crimes are provided by the state budget, through the budget of the Ministry of Justice. The State, through the Ministry of Justice, subrogates the victim's rights to financial compensation or an advance payment to recover the sums paid to the victim. The request for financial compensation and the application for a down payment may be made by non-governmental organisations that carry out their activity in the field of victim protection, if the victim signs them.

4.4 Forms of Settlement Between Victim and Offender

The CPC provides three forms of settlements between victim and offender:

a) withdrawal of the victim's prior complaint in the case of offences for which such withdrawal vacates criminal liability;
b) reconciliation between the victim and the offender; or
c) conclusion of a mediation agreement under the law.[91]

---

89 See Article 27 of the Law No. 2004-2011.

90 As for 2019, 1 gross minimum country salary amounts 2080 lei = approx. 440 euros, see Governmental Decision No. 937 of 2018 on the Determination of Gross Minimum Country Salary, Decision No. 937, Official Gazette 1045/2018.

91 See Article 16 (Cases where the public action is obstructed) of the Law No. 2010-135.

Withdrawal of the preliminary complaint cancels criminal liability in the case of criminal offences for which the criminal action is initiated upon a preliminary complaint, if the manifestation of unilateral will occurs expressly, unambiguously and unconditionally until a final decision is taken. Withdrawal takes effect *in personam*, only in regard to the offender against whom the complaint has been withdrawn. In the case of offences for which a criminal complaint is required to initiate the criminal proceedings and was initiated ex officio (the victim is a person with restrained or no legal capacity, or a legal person whose legal representative is the offender), withdrawal of the complaint shall take effect only if it has been recognized by the prosecutor. The measure seeks to protect victims in a vulnerable position from potential pressure to withdraw the complaint.[92]

Reconciliation is a ground which vacates criminal liability only in the case of offences prosecuted *ex officio* and only if the law expressly provides this (theft and grand theft, theft for the purpose of use, acquiring the property found, fraud, insurance fraud), as a consequence it does not apply to offences where a preliminary complaint is needed. The reconciliation agreement must be explicit, unambiguous, complete and unconditional and intervene until the court hearing. Reconciliation takes effect *in personam,* only with respect to the persons between which it takes place. Therefore, reconciliation between the legal person who committed the offence and the victim shall have no effect on the individuals who participated in the same act (RPC art. 159 para. 5). In order to have the effect of exonerating from criminal liability, the prosecutor's consent to the reconciliation between the injured legal person and their representative, the perpetrator of the offence, is also necessary.[93]

Romania introduced restorative justice services in 2006 by adopting a law on mediation, applicable even in certain criminal cases. The mediation agreement is a *sui-generis* ground for cancelling criminal liability, provided for in a special law, distinct from reconciliation, which may intervene throughout the criminal proceedings until the final[94] decision on the criminal case has been made. The mediation agreement is applied in accordance with the Law 2006-192 on Mediation and the Mediators' Profession (hereinafter Mediation Act),[95] both on the criminal side and on the civil side, but it can also cover only one side, unlike reconciliation that must have a total character. Initiation of the mediation agreement can be made both before (pre-trial mediation) and after the commencement of the criminal trial (trial mediation). In the

---

92 See Article 158 (Withdrawal of prior complaint) of the Law No. 286/2009.

93 See Article 159 (Reconciliation) of the Law No. 286/2009.

94 High Court of Justice, Decision No. 9, 17.04.2015. The decision of the Supreme Court was invalidated by the Constitutional Court, which provides that the conclusion of a mediation agreement on the offences for which reconciliation is allowed by law can take place only the court hearing, see Constitutional Court, Decision No. 397, 15.06.2016.

95 Law 2006-192 on Mediation and the Mediators' Profession, Law No. 2006-192, 22.05.2006, Official Gazette 441/2006.

latter case, the criminal trial may be suspended during the mediation procedure, but not more than 3 months.[96]

Mediation is a way of resolving conflicts amicably, with the help of a specialized third party as a mediator, under conditions of neutrality, impartiality, confidentiality and with the free consent of the parties. Mediation relies on the trust which the parties invest in the mediator, as a person able to facilitate negotiations between them and to provide them with support for the settlement of the conflict, by reaching a mutually convenient, efficient and durable solution. The mediator has the duty to make all arrangements so that the parties reach a mutually convenient agreement within a reasonable time.[97] The parties and subjects of the proceedings cannot be compelled to accept the mediation procedure, participation in such a procedure is undoubtedly voluntary and based on the free consent of the parties.[98] The victim has the right to terminate the mediation at any time, by informing in writing the other party and the mediator.[99] No other conditions are required.

In a previous version, the law on mediation provided that the parties shall be bound by the obligation to attend the session where they are informed on the advantages of mediation, including, if necessary, after the onset of a trial before the competent courts, in order to settle accordingly the conflicts on civil, family, criminal matters, as well as on other matters. The court had the power to dismiss a request as inadmissible in case the applicant did not meet their obligation to attend the information session on the advantages of mediation, prior to filing the request in court.[100]

The Court declared the texts contrary to the fundamental law on the ground that the obligation imposed on the parties to participate in the meeting where they were informed on the advantages of mediation under the sanction of inadmissibility of the petition is an unconstitutional measure, contrary to the principle of free access to justice.[101] At present, no provisions related to advantages, process or outcome of the mediation are in force anymore. Nevertheless, judicial and arbitration bodies, as well as other authorities with jurisdictional powers, shall inform the parties on the possibility and on the advantages of using the mediation procedure and shall advise them to resort to it in order to settle conflicts between them.[102]

---

96 See Articles 70 and 71 of the Law No. 2006-192; Article 367 (Stay of court proceedings) of the Law No. 2010-135.

97 See Articles 1 and 30 of the Law No. 2006-192.

98 See Article 67 of the Law No. 2006-192.

99 See Article 60 of the Law No. 2006-192.

100 See Article 2 of the Law No. 2006-192.

101 Constitutional Court of Romania, Decision No. 266, 07.05.2014.

102 See Article 6 of the Law No. 2006-192.

Before the last amendment of the Mediation Act (due to Emergency Governmental Ordinance No. 2019-24) mediation aims at reaching a mutually convenient solution for all the parties involved in the procedure.[103] Therefore, the interest of the victim did not expressly prevail. Taking into consideration that, under the national law, the mediation in criminal proceedings apply only to criminal offences for which the withdrawal of the prior complaint or the reconciliation of the parties excludes criminal liability, mediation appeared to be more in favour of the offender. At his moment, as amended, the Mediation Act expressly provides for the condition of confession of the perpetration of the deed by the offender in order to engage in mediation. Accordingly, the mediation begins only when the victim is acknowledged as such by the offender, i.e., interest of the victim is highly supported.[104]

4.5 Prevention of Secondary Victimisation

One the of major concerns in victimology refers to the risk of secondary and repeated victimisation, to intimidation and to retaliation of the victim by the offender. Romania has done little to provide effective protection of victims against this kind of risk.

Once the status of threatened or vulnerable witness has been granted (to a victim), the judicial body shall order application of one or more of specific measures.[105] According to the Directive, Member States shall establish the necessary conditions to enable avoidance of contact between victims and their family members, where necessary, and the offender within premises where criminal proceedings are conducted, unless the criminal proceedings require such contact.[106] Member States shall ensure that new court premises have separate waiting areas for victims. At this moment, such provisions exist *de lege lata* in national law.[107]

In the case of victims for whom special protection has been established under the law, the judicial body may order one or more of the following measures wherever possible and when it considers that the proper conduct of the process or rights and interests of the parties are not affected: interviews of the victim by the judicial body with which a complaint has been filed, on the commission of an offence shall be immediately carried out and, if this is not possible, shall be made after the filing of the complaint without undue delay; repeated interviews of the injured person is only

---

103 See Ordinance No. 2019-24.

104 See Law No. 2006-192.

105 See Articles 126 (Protection measures ordered during the criminal investigation) and 127 (Protection measures ordered during the trial) of the Law No. 2010-135.

106 See Article 19 (Right to avoid contact between victim and offender) of the Directive No. 2012/29/EU.

107 See Article 35 of the Law No. 2004-2011.

made if this is strictly necessary for the criminal proceedings; at the hearing, the victim may be accompanied, upon their request, by their legal representative and by another person designated by the victim, unless the judicial body decides otherwise; interview them on certain premises designed or adapted for that purpose; interview them through or in the presence of a psychologist or other specialist in counselling victims; their interview and possible re-examination shall be carried out by the same person if this is possible and the judicial authority considers that it does not prejudice the appropriate course of the trial or the rights and interests of the parties. The interview by the criminal investigating bodies of persons who have been victims of the offence of domestic violence, rape, sexual assault, sexual intercourse with a minor and sexual abuse of minors, of the offence of ill-treatment applied to the minor, harassment and sexual harassment, as well as in other cases in which, owing to the circumstances of the offence, this is deemed necessary, it is carried out only by a person of the same sex with the victim, at their request, except when the judicial body considers that this prejudices the proper conduct of the process or the rights and interests of the parties.[108] Victims of human trafficking may be temporarily accommodated, upon request, in centres for the assistance and protection of victims of trafficking in human beings or in shelters protected for victims of trafficking.[109]

4.6 Victim Support Services

Victim support services are typically set up as public or non-governmental organisations. Access to support services is not dependent on a prior formal complaint. Until recently, the probation services played an important role because, according to Law No. 2013-252 on the Organising of the Probation System (hereinafter Probation Act)[110] they had to carry out the duties of protecting and assisting the victims of offences provided for in special laws, until such duties are taken over by another institution. At this moment, the role was undertaken by the General Directorates for Social Assistance and Child Protection, as public entities dependent of the County Councils (one for every county of Romania and 6 more for every Bucharest's districts). In order to provide support and protection services for victims of crime, in the organizational structure of each general directorate, a compartment is established to support the victims of crime, the structure in which at least three specialists will function, respectively: social worker, psychologist, legal adviser. The main function of these services is to perform the assessment of each person identified as a victim of a crime in order to ensure the access of the victims as quickly as possible to the

108 See Articles 111 (Hearing of injured person) and 113 (Protection of injured person and civil party) of the Law No. 2010-135.

109 See Article 32 of the Law No. 2001-678.

110 Article 123 of the Law No. 2013-252 on the Organisation of the Probation System, Law No. 2013-252, 14.08.2012, Official Gazette 512/2012.

psychological, medical and social assistance or legal counselling according to their individual needs. The victim support services shall draw a report for each individual assessment and send the report to the judicial body in charge with criminal investigation, when the victims take part of the proceedings as witness, injured party or civil party. Moreover, the above-mentioned services shall organize a National Registration Book of Victims for every person identified as such and subjected to an assessment. All the data contained in the registration book must be deleted after 1 year. The assessment of each victim is based on the following criteria:

1) the type of the offence and the circumstances of its commission, insofar as they are available or can be offered by the authorized bodies;
2) the physical and mental impact that the crime had on the victim;
3) the personal characteristics of the victim;
4) the data regarding the perpetrator of the crime, as far as they are available;
5) the type of relationship or the state of dependence on the offender;
6) the possible communication difficulties of the victim;
7) the criminal history and, as the case may be, information regarding the victim's belonging to criminal groups; and
8) any other relevant aspects.

Public authorities acting in co-operation with non-governmental organizations, shall: organize campaigns of public appraisal in this field of protecting the victims of crime to ensure, free of charge, the operation of a telephone line available permanently for the information of victims of crime; develop and disseminate documentary material on the prevention, causes and consequences of domestic violence; develop educational programmes for parents and children in order to prevent domestic violence.[111]

In order to prevent trafficking in human beings, The National Agency against Trafficking in Human Beings (hereinafter Agency), in cooperation with interested institutions, as well as with non-governmental organisations, international organisations and civil society representatives, engaged in preventing trafficking in human beings, protecting and assisting their victims, shall organise awareness campaigns on the phenomenon of trafficking in human beings and the risks to which victims may be subject, shall produce and disseminates documentary material on the risks to which persons, potential victims of trafficking in human beings may be exposed; develop educational programmes to prevent trafficking in human beings,[112] shall monitor as-

---

[111] See Laws No. 2004-2011 and 2003-217.

[112] Educational activities in the field of formal and non-formal education for pre-university students and students in university education, information and counseling activities for parents and pupils on the consequences of trafficking in human beings, seminars for informing teachers in the field of children's rights and trafficking in human beings.

sistance to the victim of trafficking in human beings and facilitate their participation in the criminal proceedings.[113]

5. Victimisation in Romania: Data and Research Findings

Von Hentig pointed out:

> Why in history has everyone always focused on the guy with the big stick, the hero, the activist, to the neglect of the poor slob who is at the end of the stick, the victim, the passivist – or maybe, the poor slob (in bandages) isn't all that much of a passivist victim – maybe he asked for it?[114]

These words are not still valid only in terms of literature (see, for instance, the current state of victimology in Romania), but also when it comes to data and research findings. We shall thus analyze the situation of the official criminal statistics to see whether there are important data on victims in order to underline the focus of some data on special groups of victims. As we will see, there is little importance given to the characteristics of victims.

5.1 Official Criminal Statistics

The attention generally paid to the offender also means that statistics focus on gathering data on the offender and less on the victim. For example, if we look at the official data published yearly by the National Institute for Statistics,[115] we can see that all data relate to criminality in general or to the number and socio-demographic characteristics of the offenders.

We can of course deduct some general information about the victims – for example, if we look at *Table 1*, showing the types of crimes perpetrated in 2016 (final convictions), we can see that roughly one third of the crimes for which a final conviction decision has been issued relate to road traffic offences. While such crimes do not include negligent homicide or injuries caused following a traffic accident (but mostly driving without license or under the influence of alcohol), they already show a great risk for all the population (either drivers or pedestrians). This is actually confirmed by the great number of victims of road traffic accidents from other sources. We can also see the homicide rate (4.55) or the total number of crimes against persons (5,744; rate 2.75), but it does not mean that the rate of victims is the same, as some of the crimes have multiple victims.

---

113 See Law No. 2001-678.

114 *Von Hentig* 1948.

115 StatOffice 2017.

Table 1 Types of Crime Perpetrated in 2016 (Final Convictions)

Type of crime	Number	Per 100.000 inhabitants
Crimes against persons – total	5,744	2.75
Homicide	900	4.55
Bodily harm causing death	59	0.3
Bodily harm	469	2.37
Negligent homicide	479	2.42
Rape	330	1.67
Crime against property	7661	38.76
Threatening or injuring a public official	283	1.43
Road traffic crimes	10,839	54.85
Total	32,720	166

Source: StatOffice 2017.

The situation is quite similar in Eurostat statistics[116] (see, for instance, statistics related to assault, robbery, kidnapping, theft, burglary, offences of sexual violence, rape, sexual assault or data related to suspects and offenders by sex - number and rate for the relevant sex group, by age, by citizenship, etc.). However, data on intentional homicide do show the number of victims as collected by health statistics on cause of death, showing a decrease especially since 2012 *(Table 2)*. More data on victims are not, however, available for Romania (i.e., intentional homicide victims by victim-offender relationship and sex – number and rate for the relevant sex group, intentional homicide victims by age and sex - number and rate for the relevant sex and age groups, intentional homicide victims in largest cities by sex), as they may be for other European States. Nonetheless, as we shall see, some of the data are available upon request at a national level.

Table 2 Number of Victims as Collected by Health Statistics on Cause of Death (2008–2015)

2008	2009	2010	2011	2012	2013	2014	2015
470	397	404	335	378	336	298	291

Source: World Health Organisation 2016.

Annual reports of some public institutions or authorities pay moderate attention to victims and mainly focus on specific crimes or group of victims. There is no official estimation on the dark figure of victims, but EU agencies, media or NGOs present such estimations, although they are not always supported by any survey or study in

116 Eurostat 2019.

this respect. It should also be stated that data from the International Crime Victimization Survey (ICVS) regarding Romania date back to 1996 and 2000 and concern only the capital (Bucharest). Therefore it would be difficult do draw a conclusion or compare data because statistics on victims were inexistent or compiled differently at that time.

5.2 Special Groups of Victims

As mentioned above, while public official statistics focus little on victims, there is an increase in attention offered to special groups of victims, either in the annual reports of some public institutions or at the level of the Superior Council of the Judiciary. Such data are not classified, but they are available only upon request (justifying a scientific purpose, for example or – at least some of them – based on the Law No. 544/2001 offering access to information of public interest) or made public by some of the representatives of the said authorities.[117] An analysis of these data reveals five special groups of victim: domestic violence victims, minors, victims of rape, victims of human trafficking and of road traffic accidents, which are to be detailed below.

5.2.1 Domestic Violence

Data on domestic violence, from the victims' perspective, are presented in the most recent Annual Report of the Public Ministry – General Prosecutor's office,[118] made public in March 2018. It should be noted that such data have been collected by the authorities only since 2014. The above-mentioned Report shows that prosecutors have issued an indictment for 1,491 offenders in 2017, meaning 2.5% of the total number of offenders for whom an indictment has been given. The Report underlines a great number of serious crimes perpetrated between family members (homicide, rape, bodily harm or assault). We may also note the great number of offenders which are accused of family abandonment, meaning the commission by an individual having a legal obligation of support with regard to an individual entitled to receive such support of: abandoning, sending away or leaving them helpless and thus subjecting them to physical or moral suffering, failure, in bad faith, to fulfil their obligation of support provided by the law or failure, in bad faith, to pay for two months the support allowance established by the court.

The geographical distribution of criminal offences related to domestic violence, presented in the Annual Report of the Public Ministry, shows an unequal distri-

---

117 Law on Offering Access to Information of Public Interest, Law No. 544/2001, 23.10.2001, Official Gazette 663/2001.

118 Public Ministry 2018.

Table 3 Number of Victims Regard to the Offender–Victim Relationship in Domestic Violence Cases (2017)

Type of Offence and Share of Minor Victims (in numbers)	**Victim is … of the offender**			
	Spouse	**Parent**	**Child**	**Sibling**
Total	302	136	223	132
*Minors**			162	18
Homicide	43	27	39	29
Minors			17	
Homicide (completed)	22	19	23	14
Minors			11	
Assault and battery	213	72	55	68
Minors			30	
Bodily harm or negligent bodily harm	3	7	2	3
Minors			1	
Bodily harm causing death	4	5		1
Minors				
Ill treatment of underage persons			18	
Rape			44	14
Minors			37	12
Family abandonment			622	
Minors			557	
Failure to comply with measures taken for a juvenile's custody			9	

Source: Public Ministry 2018.

* Number of minor victims of crimes (out of the total number). Data are presented in the same manner for the whole table.

bution, with greater numbers in the North-Western departments and some of the Northern-Eastern departments and smaller ones in the South and South-Western part of the country. We believe that such data are not fully reliable, given that they refer to numbers of victims (and not to rates of victims per 100,000 inhabitants, for example). Also, the Southern part of Romania generally has higher criminality rates (especially compared to the North-Eastern part), supported by all the statistics showing criminal convictions.

The relationship between the offenders and the victims is presented in *Table 3.* As it may be seen, there is a special count regarding offences against minors for some of the offences, underlined as well by the Report of the Public Ministry. Similar data can be read in the previous report (for 2016).

Worrying data on domestic violence are also shown by some NGOs working for the protection of women's rights.[119] Such data were obtained upon request from the Romanian Police for the first month of 2016[120] and show that 8,926 complaints for battery against family members were reported within that period. According to these data, 79% of the victims are women and 92.3% of the offenders are men. Out of the 81% cases of rape which were reported, the victim was the partner of the offender in 21% of cases and son or daughter in 44.4% situations. All perpetrators of rape were men. The NGOs underline that such data refer only to reported cases, but that the European Union Agency for Fundamental Rights published a study in 2014, which shows that 1 of 4 women in Romania was physically or sexually abused by her partner.[121]

5.2.2 Minors

As it may be seen from the data on domestic violence, specific attention is already offered to minors who are victims of criminal offences. The seriousness of crimes perpetrated against minors, as well as the increased number of offences determined the Public Ministry to elaborate a study on The role of the prosecutor within justice for minors. Protection of minors. Victim of domestic violence and exploited minors.[122]

Some very interesting data on minors have been published by a (former) member of the Superior Council of the Judiciary in 2016.[123] The data show both the situation of the offenders who were minors at the time of the criminal offence was perpetrated and the one of the minors who were victims of crimes, focusing on the period 2011–2015 *(Figure 1)*.

When looking at the specific criminal offences, the data show that every day a person is being indicted for killing a child (either intentionally or negligently), another one for sexually abusing a minor (rape or sexual intercourse with a minor) and another one who committed a theft or burglary against a minor. The author of the comments on these statistics shows that minors are more and more used for producing pornographic materials and that more than 250 minors are being trafficked every year (according to court files). The data thus refer to files finalized with final convictions and not only to reported cases; they can be read in *Table 4.* We may see that most data correlate to the ones shown in the Report of the Public Ministry,[124] meaning that the largest number of minors were vic-

---

119 Network for Preventing and Combating Violence against Women 2017.

120 Network for Preventing and Combating Violence against Women 2016.

121 European Union Agency for Fundamental Rights 2012.

122 This study has not been made public by the Public Ministry.

123 *Danilet* 2016.

124 Public Ministry 2018.

Figure 1 *Minors – Victims of Criminal Offenses (Data from Final Convictions) (2011–2015)*

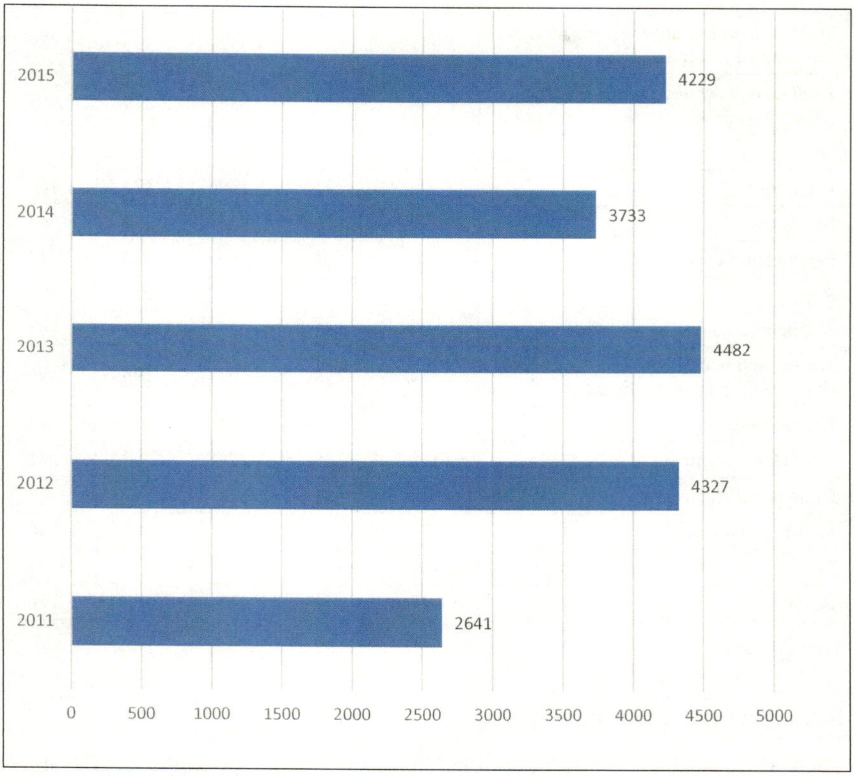

Source: Danilet 2016.

tims of family abandoning and then negligent homicide, trafficking of minors, rape, battery and bodily harm, sexual intercourse with a minor, and burglary. This is consistent with the conclusion of the Public Ministry in the sense that the number of serious crimes perpetrated against minors is worrying and should lead to effective measures for their protection. The statistics are very much detailed for county court files *(judecatorii)* and tribunals,[125] showing the criminal offences for which most files are created (i.e., trafficking of minors tried by tribunals stand for 39.8% cases, homicide for 12.9%, while at the level of county courts, 27.2% of files refer to family abandoning, 9.05% to rape and each 7.6% to battery, negligent bodily harm and sexual intercourse with a minor).

125 *Danilet* 2016.

Table 4 Number of Underage Victims (Final Convictions) (2011–2015)

	2011	2012	2013	2014	2015
Total number of minor victims in files finalized with convictions	2,641	4,327	4,482	3,733	4,229
Total number of files finalized with convictions in which minors are victims	1,756	2,803	2,835	2,379	2,405
Out of which:					
Homicide	96	141	130	123	100
Negligent homicide	209	312	324	234	205
Bodily harm causing death	15	21	19	13	14
Rape	148	242	319	236	193
Sexual intercourse with a minor	97	186	217	112	157
Battery and bodily harm (both intentional or negligent)	184	278	299	196	196
Kidnapping	13	21	24	22	21
Trafficking of minors	178	325	286	359	261
Child pornography	12	14	24	47	76
Family abandoning	376	516	553	495	556
Theft	134	161	154	118	124
Burglary	147	258	226	155	156

Source: Danilet 2016.

5.2.3 Victims of Rape

There are few specific statistics or discussions concerning rape and most of them are related, as we have already seen, to domestic violence. Through the same channel as in case of minors,[126] some data were published for the last three years before the new Criminal Code entered into force (2014). While they also focus on the offenders, some information refers to victims (i.e., 25% of the victims are minors under 15 years of age, 5 of the crimes have led to victim's death). The data also refer to sexual intercourse with a minor, showing that half of the victims were less than 15 years old. As it may be seen, most numbers actually refer to minors as well.

5.2.4 Human Trafficking

With respect to human trafficking, the first data available are to be found in the 2017 Report of the Public Ministry. The Report shows that out of 1,766 files on human trafficking (out of which 738 were reported in 2017), 532 were solved in 2017. Indictments and plea-bargaining agreements have been issued in 132 files, counting

[126] *Danilet* 2015.

451 offenders (more than half being arrested). According to the Report, the total number of victims in 2017 was 609, out of which 225 were minors.[127]

The last available Report of the National Agency against Human Trafficking[128] concerns the year 2015 and contains important data about the characteristics and regional distribution of victims. The Agency counted 1465 offenders, out of which one legal person, most of them being accused of sexual exploitation (80.75%) and labour exploitation (12.5%). Most legal qualifications were forced labour, procuring, child pornography.

5.2.5 Road Traffic Accidents

As mentioned above, some of the most numerous criminal offences in Romania are related to road traffic accidents. Whether we speak about crimes against persons (negligent homicide, negligent bodily harm) following a traffic accident or offences like driving without license or under the influence of alcohol, statistics show a big issue in this respect. One of the explanations is related of course to the poor infrastructure in Romania, with only 748 km of operable highways. Irrespective of this, the situation of the victims of such offences is worrying.

Statistics from the Romanian Police[129] show that 8,624 accidents occurred in 2017 (a number similar with the one in 2016), which resulted in 1,951 deaths and 8,172 seriously injured persons. *Table 5* shows the dynamics of road traffic accidents in 2016–2017. It results that there is no actual improvement (the situation has been slightly the same since 2001, according to the same statistics).

Table 5 Dynamics of Road Traffic Accidents (2016-2017)

	2016	**2017**	**(+/–)**	**%**
Serious accidents				
Total	8,688	8,642	–46	–0.53
Deaths	1,931	1,951	+38	+1.95
Serious injuries	8,287	8,172	–115	–1.41
Minor injuries	3,622	3,602	–20	–0.55
Minor accidents				
Total	22,064	22,462	+398	+1.77
Minor injuries	27,654	28,430	+776	+2,73

Source: Romanian Police 2019b.

127 Public Ministry 2018.

128 National Agency against Trafficking in Persons 2019.

129 Romanian Police 2019b.

5.3 Characteristics of Victims

As mentioned above, there is little focus on the characteristics of victims (gender, age, nationality, education, social status, etc.) in Romania. No particular attention is given to the regional/local distribution of the victims in the official statistics. However, some data exist in connection to these aspects, although many are available only upon request. For instance, following a request for public information for the Balkan Homicide Study, the General Prosecutor's Office communicated also some data on victims. The statistics concern files of the prosecutors for the years 2011–2016 and are divided for each prosecutor's office (affiliated to a tribunal, to a court of appeal or to the High Court of Cassation and Justice).

The first important information relates to the gender of the victims of homicides. In 2016, for instance, 627 were male (out of which 26 minors) and 154 women (11 minors). The relationship victim-offender is also mentioned; however, in most cases (589 out of 781) it is mentioned that the victim and the offender have 'other relationship' (other than being a parent, child, sister/brother, son/daughter, grandparent, cousins, or aunts/uncle) or "no relationship". Most probably, such data are actually missing. There are no other details such as age of the victim, nationality, education, social status – as it is the case for the offender. As the data are divided for each prosecutor's office, we may get an idea about the place (city/village) where homicides are perpetrated, taking into consideration that, according to the Criminal Procedure Code, the first criterion for determining competence is the place where the crime was committed. Except for the capital, which ranks first for the period 2011–2016, leading departments are in the North-Eastern part of Romania and in the South-Western one, which is consistent with the two regions seen as poorer. What is interesting is that the last two counties, in terms of numbers of homicides for the relevant period, are Harghita and Covasna, meaning the area inhabited mostly by Hungarians (in the central part of Romania), and generally seen as a region of conflict with Romanians. However, these data do not show if the victim actually comes from the same place where the crime was committed; therefore, we cannot speak about a local or regional distribution of victims of homicide.[130]

A broader analysis about characteristics of victims in 2017 is made by the National Agency against Human Trafficking,[131] which actually looks at data from a victimological perspective. The study shows that females represent 76.4% of the trafficked victims and that 88% of the total number of victims have completed little studies (less than 8 classes), while 8% have no education. There is no actual correlation between trafficking and victim's domicile (rural or urban); however, only 1.8% of the victims live within the capital of the country. Six departments in Romania report

---

[130] StatOffice 2017.

[131] National Agency against Trafficking in Persons 2017.

45.2% of the victims (Dolj, Iasi, Sibiu, Galati, Prahova and Neamt), but no particular correlation can be made in terms of quality of life in these departments and trafficking.[132] The study underlines that 45% of the recruitments are made by a friend or an acquaintance, which also correlates with the victims' low level of education. Consequently, we may conclude that, while some efforts have been made, there is still little attention paid to victims, especially when it comes to officially gathering data on their characteristics.

6. Public and/or Media Discourses About Victims, Victims' Rights and Protection

As showed above, most NGOs active in the field of victims' protection, as well as statistics, focus on specific group of victims. Consequently, public and media discourses take into consideration mainly the same groups. We shall thus analyse the public attention given to victims of domestic violence, including minors, rape, also including minors and road traffic accidents. It should be stated, however, that sometimes the discourse of public authorities concerns victims in general. For example, the most recent Annual Report of the Public Ministry shows that

> In the context of high level of work at the level of prosecutors' offices and changing legal framework, it is necessary that prosecutors show necessary attention to human rights, in order to ensure a balance between offender's right to defence and the legal protection of the victim.[133]

6.1 Domestic Violence

The increased attention given by public authorities to domestic violence in the past years and the publication of several statistics in this field have also lead to an increased focus of the media in this field. This was also "helped" by some recent tragic cases which were broadly presented by the media (e.g., a husband killing his wife in the kindergarten where she was working, breaching the protection order, another husband killing his wife and some of her colleagues in a beauty salon, a father killing his wife and children because some voices told him they will be happier this way, etc.).[134]

---

132 For instance, Dolj and Iasi are poorer areas, but it is not the case for Sibiu.

133 Public Ministry 2018.

134 Romanian media is generally seen as showing much attention to tragic events (i.e., there is even an expression which now constitutes Romanian folklore – "5 o'clock news", meaning the TV news broadcasting the most recent crimes, rapes, violence, etc.).

For example, the most recent Report of the Public Ministry is discussed in TV shows and newspapers.[135] In this respect, the media highlight the problem of children left home by their parents, who now live in Spain or Italy where they work,[136] subject to family abandoning or to physical or sexual abuse perpetrated by other family members. The media wonder why, despite such data, politicians still wait to vote a law project on domestic violence referred to the Parliament by the Romanian Government. This shows another general tendency of Romanian media and even population always to "blame" politicians.

The discourse of the NGOs involved in this field focuses also on legislative and institutional changes which could be made in order to reduce the phenomenon. For example, when addressing the problem of rape against a family member, the Network for Preventing and Fighting Violence against Women[137] shows that the low number of cases reported to the police proves the lack of confidence in the public authorities as well as the fact that the legal provisions and public services do not provide for immediate safety. This is why the network considers that a solution could be the emergency protection order, issued in maximum 24 hours as of the moment when the offence was perpetrated. NGOs and media also believe that, in order to develop public policies able to prevent and fight such crimes, it is highly necessary that Romanian authorities collect detailed data in order to understand who the offenders are, who the victims are, what the relationship between them is and where the offences are perpetrated.[138]

Lawyers or other legal professionals are sometimes requested by media to discuss statistics. For example, when analysing the 2016 Report of the Public Ministry, a legal website invited a lawyer to draw some conclusions. One of the ideas she issued was that, with respect to domestic violence, we should add a zero to the numbers.[139]

---

135 Digi24 of 07.03.2018; Statistici îngrijorătoare: Sute de copii uciși de propriii părinți. Lazăr: „E o cifră nepermis de mare" [Worrying statistics: Hundreds of children killed by their parents. Lazar: "It's a figure not allowed high"]; https://www.digi24.ro/stiri/actualitate/justitie/statistici-ingrijoratoare-sute-de-copii-ucisi-de-propriii-parinti-sau-frati-lazar-e-o-cifra-nepermis-de-mare-890979 [14.10.2019] [in Romanian only].

136 According to Government Decision No. 405/2017 for the approval of the National Strategy for all Romanians for 2017–2020, approximately 3,5–4 million Romanians were living abroad in 2016, more than half living in Spain and Italy, see Government Decision No. 405/2017 for the Approval of the National Strategy for All Romanians for 2017–2020, Decision No. 405/2017, 27.06.2017, Official Gazette 485/2017.

137 Network for Preventing and Combating Violence against Women 2017.

138 Digi24 of 07.03.2018.

139 CluJust 2019 of 09.03.2017; Av. Iona Trană despre statistica pe violenta în familie: "Cifrele reale ar trebui să poarte cel putin o cifră în plus" [Av. Iona Trana on statistics on domestic violence: "Real figures should carry at least one more figure"]; https://www.clujust.ro/av-ioana-trana-despre-statistica-pe-violenta-in-familie-cifrele-reale-ar-trebui-sa-poarte-cel-putin-o-cifra-in-plus/ [14.10.2019] [in Romanian only].

This is consistent to the general perception of the population and to the idea presented above – that victims often lack confidence in the public authorities and prefer not to report such offences. Very often, the media and the NGOs see the increase of reported cases as an increase of confidence in the public authorities and in their solutions.[140]

It must be stressed that not only the media's allegations are important in this field, but also the public discourse of some authorities. For instance, in the 2017 Annual Report of the Public Ministry, it is stated that for 2018 and following years, more attention should be paid to the protection of minors, to the victims of domestic violence and discrimination, to victims of human trafficking and exploitation, to vulnerable victims (handicapped persons), fighting hate or prejudice crimes (especially online criminal offences) and to the creation of an institutional relationship with the organizations activating in the field of human rights protection. Unfortunately, these directions are not accompanied by specific legislative proposals.[141]

The Romanian Police has a specialized section on their website for domestic violence[142] and also set in motion a campaign aiming to prevent such crimes, named Broken Wings, together with Association Necuvinte. A TV spot, a documentary movie and safety guidelines were created for the purpose of this campaign, which were widely diffused in the country, including schools.

Also, the National Institute for Public Health[143] has analysed the situation of domestic violence in the past years, also showing the effects of the protection orders issued by courts after the entry into force of the Law No. 2012-25 on amending the Act of preventing and fighting with domestic violence.[144] The results of public barometers show that, one year after the entry into force of this law, only 47% of women knew of its existence and 74% were not aware of any specialised entity which could provide support for victims.

6.2 Rape

When it comes to rape, the media tend to show things from a very tragic perspective. Titles such as Two minors are being raped every day in Romania,[145] Every 4

---

140 Network for Preventing and Combating Violence against Women 2017.

141 Public Ministry 2018.

142 Romanian Police 2019a.

143 National Institute for Public Health 2016.

144 Amendment to the Act of preventing and fighting with domestic violence, Law No. 2012-25, 13.03.2012, Official Gazette 165/2012.

145 Incomod of 18.01.2018; Statistic, două minore sunt violate zilnic în România! Cifrele sunt în creştere! FOTO-DOCUMENTE [Statistically, two minors are raped daily in Romania! The figures are rising! PHOTO-DOCUMENTS]; https://www.ziarulincomod.ro/

hours a person is being raped in Romania[146]or Five rapes occur daily in Romania[147] can often be seen in the newspapers. The media underline that, in any event, data provided by public authorities are not real considering that many victims choose not to report rapes,[148] although they note that the number of reported cases increases yearly, especially in case of minors. Also, the media focus on public perception on rape, showing, for instance that 55% of Romanians believe that rape can be justified or 1 out of 5 think that rape should not be illegal,[149] following data from the Special Eurobarometer on Gender-Based Violence.[150]

The media are indeed often being overly critical of the role of the authorities. For example, it underlines that, when it comes to domestic violence and more particularly to violence against women, the authorities limit themselves to stupid advice,[151] offering the example of the Romanian Police, who states: decent clothes and modest behaviour does not invite to solicitation, or that of the local police in Vaslui Department, according to which the great number of rapes in the area has several causes: lack of education, excessive use of alcohol and a possible genetic component.

It should be stated that Vaslui Department, apart from being one of the poorest in Romania, is also known for the case of a young girl raped by seven men in 2015. This case received a lot of attention in the media and from NGOs,[152] which showed that

---

statistic-doua-minore-sunt-violate-zilnic-in-romania-cifrele-sunt-in-crestere-foto-documente/ [14.10.2019] [in Romanian only].

146 Ziare.com of 25.02.2018; In Romania, are loc un viol la fiecare 4 ore. Un proiect de lege prevede pedepse pana la inchisoare pe viata pentru violatori [In Romania, there is a rape every 4 hours. A draft law provides for life sentences for rapists]; http://www.ziare.com/stiri/crima/in-romania-are-loc-un-viol-la-fiecare-4-ore-un-proiect-de-lege-prevede-pedepse-pana-la-inchisoare-pe-viata-pentru-violatori-1503294 [14.10.2019] [in Romanian only].

147 Ziarul Românesc.net of 26.11 2016; În România, în fiecare zi au loc cinci violuri. Multe dintre ele sunt justificate, cred majoritatea românilor [In Romania, there are five rapes every day. Many of them are justified, most Romanians believe]; https://ziarulromanesc.net/focus/romania/in-romania-in-fiecare-zi-au-loc-cinci-violuri-multe-dintre-ele-sunt-justificate-cred-romanii/ [14.10.2019] [in Romanian only].

148 *Foarfă* 2017.

149 Stirile Pro TV of 28.11.2016; Studiu UE: 55% dintre romani cred ca violul poate fi justificat. Unu din cinci nu ar vrea nici macar sa fie illegal [EU study: 55% of Romanians believe that rape can be justified. One in five wouldn't even want to be illegal]; https://stirileprotv.ro/stiri/stirileprotv-special/studiu-ue-55-dintre-romani-cred-ca-violul-poate-fi-justificat-unu-din-cinci-nu-ar-vrea-nici-macar-sa-fie-ilegal.html [14.10..2019] [in Romanian only].

150 European Commission 2016.

151 *Alexandrescu* 2015.

152 ACTEDO of 30.07.2015; Violul de la vaslui – Simptom al proastei aplicări a legislației europene în România [ape from Vaslui – Symptom of the bad application of the European legislation in Romania]; http://actedo.org/VIOLUL-DE-LA-VASLUI-SIMPTOM-AL-

the offenders had actually a lot of supporters, but also that the solutions envisaged by the politicians were mainly related to chemical castration. NGOs emphasized that, traditionally, victims were only seen as accessories in Romanian or EU criminal procedures and that attention is always given to the offender and that the Directive 2012/29/UE was not properly transposed in the Romanian legislation. The correct implementation of this Directive would have led, according to these opinions, to a better protection of the victim, mainly through the prevention of disclosure of sensitive information and, thus, of blaming the victim; consequently, the rape in Vaslui is seen just as a symptom of the real problem: a society which, although permanently subject to victimisation, is not capable of hearing and supporting victims, in a State which does not provide for the necessary legal framework for victims. The main problem would be the lack of efficient services that could offer support to victims of rape.[153]

It should also be stated that, following an increased attention in the media for rape and rape offenders, a politician drafted a law project aiming to change penalties for such crime in order to align them to penalties applicable for aggravated homicide (life imprisonment or imprisonment from 15–25 years). This supports the idea that the only way to fight rape is to increase penalties.

6.3 Road Traffic Accidents

When it comes to road traffic accidents, the media also depart from statistics, using headlines such as "Worrying statistics. Romania ranks 2 in Europe when it comes to deaths following road traffic accidents"[154]. 27,000 accidents took place in Romania in 2016.[155] Newspapers show that most accidents occur during the day, in summer and that a main cause is the use of alcohol,[156] although Romania has zero tolerance

PROASTEI-APLICARI-A-LEGISLATIEI-EUROPENE-IN-ROMANIA/ [14.10.2019] [in Romanian only].

153 ACTEDO of 30.07.2015.

154 *Matei* 2017.

155 AutoBild Romania of 20.01.2017; Statistică neagră – 27.000 de accidente rutiere s-au petrecut în România în 2016 [Black statistics – 27,000 road accidents happened in Romania in 2016]; https://www.auto-bild.ro/headline/statistica-neagra-27-000-de-accidente-rutiere-s-au-petrecut-romania-2016-114817.html [14.10.2019] [in Romanian only].

156 HotNews.ro of 30.05.2016; Cate accidente rutiere au loc anual in Romania si cate victime mor? O statistica ce ne poate da de gandit [How many road accidents occur annually in Romania and how many victims die? A statistic that can give us some thought]; https://economie.hotnews.ro/stiri-finante_banci-21038603-cate-accidente-rutiere-loc-anual-romania-cate-victime-suferit-statistica-judete.htm [14.10.2019] [in Romanian only].

for such practice[157]. Retrospectives of road traffic accidents are often presented[158] and, generally, 5 o'clock news always show at least one serious accident which occurred during the day.

The Romanian media, especially the legal websites, saluted the first conviction of a person for attempted aggravated homicide and aggravated homicide and not for negligent homicide, because the offender caused an "accident" driving a car in high speed in the city of Iasi, not observing the red lights and driving on the opposite side of the road. The final penalty was imprisonment for 19 years and 8 months.[159]

It should be added that the Romanian police has a dedicated subsection on their website for serious accidents.[160] An association of road traffic victims[161] was created, trying to perform activities such as fighting for victim's right to obtain damages for their losses, road traffic education, proposals of legislative changes in this area, commemoration of victims of road traffic accidents, etc.

7. Expert Assessment and Constructive Criticism with Suggestions for the Improvement in the Field of Victim Protection

What can be firstly argued against the Victims' Act is that, until recently, it did not tackle rigorously and thoroughly the protection of victims of crime. The legislative act had no general strategy for all victims. Secondly, there were no national provisions concerning 'a respectful, sensitive, tailored and professional approach to victims' as the Directive suggests. Additionally, there were no specific domestic provisions concerning child victims. Obviously, all these aspects result from the fact that the provisions of the Directive had not been fully transposed. The situation was remarkably changed after the adoption of the Emergengy Governmental Ordinance

---

157 Depending of the level of intoxication, such offence can be a misdemeanour or a criminal offence; if a person is injured, irrespective on how serious the injuries are, it is always a criminal offence. In the absence of alcohol or drug intoxication, only injuries having specific consequences (i.e., loss of pregnancy, disability, more than 90 days of medical care) represents a criminal offence.

158 Ţimonea 2018.

159 CluJust of 15.03.2018; Condamnat pentru omor calificat în urma unui accident rutier grav. Pedeapsa finală: 19 ani si 8 luni, plus daune morale de 1 milion de lei [Convicted of qualified murder after a serious road accident. Final penalty: 19 years and 8 months, plus moral damages of 1 million lei]; https://www.clujust.ro/condamnat-pentru-omor-calificat-in-urma-unui-accident-rutier-grav-pedeapsa-finala-19-ani-si-8-luni-plus-daune-morale-de-1-milion-de-lei/ [14.10.2019] [in Romanian only].

160 Romanian Police 2019b.

161 Traffic Accident Victims Association of Romanian 2019.

2019-24. Accordingly, all these issues were *prima facie* addressed. It is important to monitor the very application of the new act in order to assert a real shift.[162]

The need to create a common law in the area of victims' protection seemed to be fulfilled. Special legislation (domestic violence, trafficking in human beings, terrorism, etc.) will continue to exist alongside with this common law. The European Commission has prepared an analysis of the conformity and completeness of the transposition in national member states (including Romania) of the Directive. One of the authors of this study was involved in that assessment.

To sum up, lack of transposition of the Directive is due to the fact that, traditionally, the victim had a minor role in the criminal proceedings. Apparently, the national approach, which allows the victim to become a civil party in a criminal trial should grant the victim a high level of protection. In reality, this situation has impregnated the protection of victims by an individualist philosophy that has transformed itself into the opposite of what it aimed to protect. Hence it appears that the victim has the task of defending themselves, of promoting their interests and, in general, of achieving their own protection. However, this approach seems to be in contradiction with the Directive, which has imposed positive obligations on Member States, starting from the victim's anthropological and procedural weak position.

It can also be argued that the importance of victim protection is part of the new criminal paradigm, which tends to move away from the policy exclusively centred on the offender. In this respect the appearance of the 'nothing works' doctrine is no accident. In the context of combating a new generation of offences (organised crime, terrorism, money laundering, etc.), emphasis has been placed on marginal aspects such as detecting, tracking, freezing and confiscating money, and less on punishing offenders. We believe that the strengthening of the victims' protection is based on the same philosophy, aimed at removing or mitigating the consequences of crime, previously of lower importance.

With respect to statistics, as it results from the data shown above, a first assessment relates to the poor data collected for victims, especially for the case of socio-characteristics and relationship victim-offender. As some of the NGOs in the field and even the National Agency against Trafficking in Person point out, a first step for fighting crime would be to have reliable data on victims, showing their gender, age, domicile, level of education, relationship with the offender and with other victims; also, it would be important to have information on whether they received legal and psychological support before/after reporting the case. There should also be data on the number of complaints withdrawn by the victims.

The main problem underlined by the analysis and studies which focus on victims of domestic violence, for instance, relates to the protection order. For instance, in an

---

162 See Law No. 2004-2011; Ordinance No. 2019-24.

exploratory study on the protection order for 2012–2016, GRADO Association[163] noticed that 88% of the persons who requested a protection order were women and only 43% of such requests were granted by the courts. The most important issues in connection to the protection order are the duration of the procedure for obtaining such order (which does not cover the first 10–14 days, when the risk of recidivism is at its highest risk), the lack of statistics concerning breached order of protection and criminal files created for such offenders and lack of harmonization of existing data on domestic violence coming from several institutions. Of course, some solutions can be envisaged, such as the possibility to obtain an emergency protection order (i.e., within 24 hours) and an effective control on the observance of such order. Another issue, which was pointed out by the Director of the National Institute of the Judiciary in an interview given to one of the authors of this paper for another study in February 2018, refers to the training of judges and prosecutors. She underlined that, very often, magistrates are being trained only in terms of legislation, but do not actually look at the social and criminological side of the criminal phenomenon. From this perspective, focus on cross-sectorial training of magistrates and police agents should be made (e.g., meetings with victims of trafficking in person, trainings provided by social workers, etc.). Moreover, due to the fact that, as it may be seen in case of rape, a great part of the population believe that serious crimes can be justified, the public stakeholders should also pay attention to education in this field, especially in rural area, where domestic violence of any kind is seen as traditional, with popular sayings such as "Violence comes from Heaven" or "If he doesn't beat you, he doesn't love you". Such education should be performed in schools, through television, newspapers, posters and other efficient forms of disseminating information on these victimisations rural areas.

8. Conclusion

As has already been stated in the national doctrine,[164] criminal law is confronted with an evolution of the status of the victim – from the position of a forgotten actor to the "new star" of the criminal law scene. Following the effervescence of regulations in the early 2000s, attention to victims has dramatically decreased from a legislative point of view. The adoption of the Law No. 2004-2011 was perceived as a high achievement peak of our criminal policy, which, combined with the new configuration of the Code of Criminal Procedure, entered into force in 2014 and created the illusion of a sufficient regulation. This non-transparency still persists, despite the launch of the infringement procedure against Romania in January 2016. It explains why attempts to amend the legislation are only partial. However, it is clear that the European Directive on the protection of victims has not been fully transposed. The disregard of the topic

---

163 GRADO 2019.

164 *Pașca* 2001, p. 35.

is also seen in the absence of a structured research framework: there is no dedicated research institute, there are no studies and no books are published. The Criminology Society and the National Institute of Criminology are anything but less research angels. In addition, victimology is a subject of study but still marginal and only within the faculties of sociology (the master degree programme). The only important voices seem to be the NGOs that have had consistent initiatives, both by consolidating impact networks (15–20 members) and by supporting projects and publishing studies. Their activity is also responsible for some legislative success: implementation and optimization of the protection order for victims of domestic violence.

As shown above, there is no actual concern for gathering specific data on victims, which leads to lack of knowledge about their characteristics, that might prevent criminal offences especially in some cases (e.g., human trafficking, domestic violence).

As a general conclusion, it could be stated that victims' problems reflect in fact the country's problems, which means that solutions could be searched not only in terms of criminal legislation or activities performed by the public authorities or institutions involved in this sector, but also from an economic, social and sometimes even religious perspective.

9. Summary in Romanian

În România există un paradox privind victimologia: deşi ţara l-a dat lumii pe „părintele" noţiunii, *Benjamin Mendelsohn,* acesta şi cercetările lui sunt puţin cunoscute, iar victimologia nu este studiată ca atare în universităţi. Aceasta nu înseamnă totuşi că nu există interes pentru victime sau protecţia acestora. Statisticile conţin anumite date despre victime şi statutul lor, mai ales cele de la nivelul Parchetului General. De asemenea, mai multe entităţi militează pentru apărarea drepturilor şi protecţia unor categorii specifice de victime (i.e. persoanele condamnate pe motive politice, victime ale evenimentelor din 1989 etc.). Asociaţii mai recente vorbesc despre problemele actuale (i.e. victime ale accidentelor de circulaţie, întrucât România conduce statisticile privind numărul victimelor acestor infracţiuni; victime ale infracţiunilor legate de violenţa în familie – o problemă socială posibil specifică Balcanilor; victimele unui incendiu devastator într-un club de noapte din Bucureşti; victime ale abuzurilor comise în cadrul procedurilor judiciare; bullying-ul în şcoli etc.). Nu trebuie uitat că victimizarea este întotdeauna influenţată de istoria unei ţări, ceea ce înseamnă că o persoană nu întotdeauna se percepe victimă a unei infracţiuni (i.e. femeile în cazul violenţei în familie) sau nu se găseşte o victimă (i.e. oferirea de bani unui medic pentru a-i mulţumi pentru serviciile prestate). Articolul acoperă principalele aspecte în aceste domenii şi subliniază particularităţile victimologiei, ale protecţiei victimelor şi ale victimizării în România, arătând cele mai importante probleme, atât la nivel legislativ, cât şi la nivelul punerii în aplicare a reglementărilor aplicabile.

Literature

Alexandrescu, V. (2015): EXCLUSIV: Statisticile oficiale 1990–2014, obținute de PUTEREA. Violul la români. Vasluienii au trimis şi în Parlament un violator [EXCLUSIVE: Official statistics 1990–2014, obtained by POWER. Rape to Romanians. Vaslui also sent a rapist to Parliament], in Puterea, 23.07.2015; https://www.puterea.ro/dezvaluiri/exclusiv-statisticile-oficiale-1990-2014-obtinute-de-puterea-violul-la-romani-vasluienii-au-trimis-si-in-parlament-un-violator-117893.html [14.10.2019] [in Romanian only].

Berbec, S., et al. (2017): Handbook for legal, social, health professionals involved in the protection of the rights and the assistance of victims of human trafficking; http://ec.justice-project.prorefugiu.org/wp-content/uploads/2017/11/Handbook-Final-Version-EN.pdf [09.10.2019] [in English only].

Berbec, S., Ilcheva, M., Nordström, R., Heinonen, H., Feito, P. & Freudenberg, D. (2018): Survey report: Victims of crimes rights competent stakeholders in Romania, Bulgaria, Germany, Sweden; https://provictimsjustice.prorefugiu.org/wp-content/uploads/2018/02/Survey-Report.pdf [09.10.2019] [in English only].

Butoi, T. (2004): Victimologie. Curs universitar. Perspectiva psihologiei victimale asupra cuplului penal victimă-agresor [Victimology. University course. The perspective of the victim psychology on the victim-aggressor criminal couple]. Bucharest.

Danilet, C. (2016): Statistici 2011-2015 (ep.1 si 2): Delincventa juvenila si minorii victim [2011–2015 statistics (ep. 1 and 2): Juvenile delinquency and minor victims], in Contributors.ro, 28.03.2016; http://www.contributors.ro/administratie/justitieordine-publica/statistici-2011-2015-ep-1-delincventa-juvenila/ [09.10.2019] [in Romanian only].

Danilet, C. (2015): Infracțiuni privind viața sexuală. Statistici 2011–2015 [Sex offences. 2011–2015 statistics], in Juridice.ro, 24.07.2015; https://www.juridice.ro/388297/infractiuni-privind-viata-sexuala-statistici-2011-2015.html [09.10.2019] [in Romanian only].

Dragotă, C. (2017): Compensation for victims of human trafficking in Romania; http://anitp.mai.gov.ro/ro/docs/Proiecte/RO21/Documente%20elaborate/Studiul%20privind%20drepturile%20EN%20mic.pdf [09.10.2019] [in English only].

Foarfă, C. (2017): Cât de greu este să treci peste un viol, în România, mai ales când agresorul ți-e prieten [How hard it is to get over a rape in Romania, especially when the aggressor is your friend], in Vice News, 24.08.2017; https://www.vice.com/ro/article/8xxvvb/cat-de-greu-este-sa-treci-peste-un-viol-in-romania [14.10.2019] [in Romanian only].

Hotca, M.A. (2006): Protecția victimelor. Elemente de victimologie [Protection of victims. Elements of victimology]. Bucharest.

Liiceanu, A., Saucan, D.S. & Micle, I. (2004): Violenta domestic si criminalitatea feminine [Domestic violence and female crime]. Bucharest; http://criminologie.org.ro/wp-content/uploads/2015/08/Violenta-domestica-Studiu.pdf [14.10.2019] [in Romanian only].

Liiceanu, A., Saucan, D.S., Micle, I., Istrate, M., Rujoiu, O. & Bărbulescu, A. (2003): Analiza fenomenului violenţei în societatea Românească (1990–2002). Etiologie şi dinamică [Analysis of the phenomena of violence in Romanian society (1990–2002). Etiology and dynamics]; http://criminologie.org.ro/wp-content/uploads/2015/08/Analiza-Fenomenului-Violentei-in-Societatea-Romaneasca.pdf [14.10.2019] [in Romanian only].

Matei, T. (2017): Statistici înfiorătoare: România este pe locul 2 în Europa la numărul de morți în accidente rutiere [Frightening statistics: Romania ranks second in Europe in the number of road accident deaths], in ActiveNews, 29.03.2017; https://www.activenews.ro/stiri-social/Statistici-infioratoare-Romania-este-pe-locul-2-in-Europa-la-numarul-de-morti-in-accidente-rutiere-142302 [14.10.2019] [in Romanian only].

Mosneagu, A.P., et al. (2017): Manual for lawyers, prosecutors and judges; http://project-ecjusticeprogramme.prorefugiu.org/wp-content/uploads/2017/05/Legal-Practitioners-Manual-EN-Version.pdf [09.10.2019] [in English only].

Paşca, V. (2001): The victim – A great actor in a minor role. Revista de drept penal [Criminal Law Magazine] 2, p. 35.

Pivniceru, M.M. & Luca, C. (2009): Ghid de audiere a copilului în procedure judiciare [Guide for hearing the child in court proceedings]. Bucharest.

Rotundă, M. (2017): Îmbunătăţirea accesului la justiţie în România pentru victimele traficului de personae [Improving access to justice in Romania for victims of human trafficking]. Bucharest.

Tănăsescu, I. (2003): Criminologie. Agresologie.Victimologie. Detentologie [Criminology. Agressology. Victimology. Detentology]. Bucharest.

Ţimonea, D. (2018): Cele mai grave accidente rutiere din 2017. Tragediile care s-au soldat cu aproape 2.000 de morţi şi multe mii de răniţi [The worst road accidents of 2017. The tragedies that resulted in nearly 2,000 dead and many thousands injured], in Alba Iulia, 02.01.2018; https://adevarul.ro/locale/alba-iulia/cele-mai-grave-accidente-rutiere-2017-tragediile-s-au-soldat-aproape-2000-morti-multe-mii-raniti-1_5a491b3bd7af743f8dea73f6/index.html [14.10.2019] [in Romanian only].

Trandafir, A.R. (2014): Crime and criminology in Romania. Focus on the New Criminal Code, in: A.M. Getoš Kalac, H.J. Albrecht & M. Kilchling (eds.), Mapping the criminological landscape of the Balkans: State of Art in criminology and crime with an expedition into the criminal landscape of the Balkans. Berlin, pp. 315–328.

Von Hentig, H. (1948): The criminal and his victim. New Haven.

Documents

Anais Association (2017): Ghidul practic pentru victimele violenţei în familie [Guidelines for victims of domestic violence]; http://violentaimpotrivafemeilor.ro/wp-content/uploads/2017/08/Ghid-practic-A5-ANAIS-INT-12.pdf [09.10.2019] [in Romanian only].

Association for Liberty and Equality of Gender (2013): Consiliere on-line [A.L.E.G.'s online counselling]; https://aleg-romania.eu/2013/09/16/consiliere-on-line/ [09.10.2019] [in Romanian and English].

Equality and Human Rights Action Centre (2016): Joint opinion on the ratification of the Istanbul convention; http://actedo.org/joint-opinion-ratification-council-europe-istanbul-convention/ [09.10.2019] [in English only].

European Commission (2016): Public opinion; https://ec.europa.eu/COMMFrontOffice/publicopinion/index.cfm/Survey/getSurveyDetail/instruments/SPECIAL/surveyKy/2115 [09.10.2019] [in English only].

European Parliamentary Research Service (2017): Victims' Rights Directive 2012/29/EU – European Implementation Assessment. Brussels; http://www.europarl.europa.eu/RegData/etudes/STUD/2017/611022/ EPRS_STU(2017)611022_EN.pdf [09.10.2019] [in English only].

European Union Agency for Fundamental Rights (2014): Victims of crime in the EU: The extent and nature of support for victims. Luxembourg; http://fra.europa.eu/en/publication/2014/victims-crime-eu-extent-and-nature-support-victims [09.10.2019] [in English only].

European Union Agency for Fundamental Rights (2012): Survey on violence against women in EU (2012); https://fra.europa.eu/en/publications-and-resources/data-and-maps/survey-data-explorer-violence-against-women-survey [09.10.2019] [in English only].

Eurostat (2019): Crime and criminal justice – Overview; https://ec.europa.eu/eurostat/web/crime/overview [09.10.2019] [in English only].

GRADO (2019): Acasă [Home]; https://grado.org.ro/ [09.10.2019] [in Romanian and English].

National Agency against Trafficking in Persons (2019): Acasa [Home]; http://anitp.mai.gov.ro/ [09.10.2019] [in Romanian only].

National Agency against Trafficking in Persons (2017): Analiză succintă asupra traficului de persoane în 2017. Perspectivă victimologică [Short analysis on human trafficking in 2017. Victimological Perspective]; http://www.anitp.mai.gov.ro/ro/docs/Cercetare/Analize/analiza%20succinta%20victime%20identificate%20in%202017%20mod.pdf [24.10.2019] [in Romanian only].

National Institute for Public Health (2016): Analiză de situatie [Analysis of the situation]; http://insp.gov.ro/sites/cnepss/wp-content/uploads/2016/01/Analiza-de-situatie-2015-7.pdf [09.10.2019] [in Romanian only].

Network for Preventing and Combating Violence against Women (2017): Exploratory study on the implementation of the Protection order and the Domestic violence provisions of the Criminal Code of Romania in 2012–2016; http://violentaimpotrivafemeilor.ro/wp-content/uploads/2017/07/Study-Network-VAW-RO-2017.pdf [09.10.2019] [in English only].

Network for Preventing and Combating Violence against Women (2016): Statistici privind violența în familie: aproape nouă mii de cazuri de lovire şi alte violențe şi 80 de violuri în familie, în primele 6 luni ale anului [Statistics on domestic violence: almost nine thousand cases of rape and other violence and 80 rapes in the family, in the first 6 months of the year]; https://violentaimpotrivafemeilor.ro/statistici-privind-violenta-in-familie-aproape-noua-mii-de-cazuri-de-lovire-si-alte-violente-si-80-de-violuri-in-familie-in-primele-6-luni-ale-anului/ [09.10.2019] [in Romanian only].

Partnership Center for Equality (2019): Acasa [Home]; http://www.cpe.ro/ [09.10.2019] [in Romanian only].

Pro Victims Justice (2019): Home; https://provictimsjustice.prorefugiu.org/ [09.10.2019] [in English only].

Public Ministry (2018): Raport de activitate pe anul 2018 [Annual activity report 2018]; http://www.mpublic.ro/sites/default/files/PDF/raport_activitate_2018.pdf [09.10.2019] [in Romanian only].

Romanian National Institute of Statistics (2017): Statistics for 2017; http://statistici.insse.ro:8077/tempo-online/ [24.10.2019] [in Romanian only]; cited as StatOffice 2017.

Romanian National Institute of Statistics (2016): În anul 2016, rata de ocupare a populaţiei în vârstă de muncă (15–64 ani) a fost de 61,6%, în creştere faţă de anul anterior cu 0,2 puncte procentuale [In 2016, the employment rate of the working age population (15–64 years) was 61.6%, up from the previous year by 0.2 percentage points.]; http://www.insse.ro/cms/sites/default/files/com_presa/com_pdf/somaj_2016r.pdf [09.10.2019] [in Romanian only]; cited as StatOffice 2016.

Romanian National Institute of Statistics (2013): Ce ne spune recensământul din 2011 despre religie? [What does the 2011 census reveal about religion?]; http://www.insse.ro/cms/files/publicatii/pliante%20statistice/08-Recensamintele%20despre%20religie_n.pdf [09.10.2019] [in Romanian only]; cited as StatOffice 2013.

StatOffice: see Romanian National Institute of Statistics.

Romanian Police (2019a): Campanii/Proiecte [Campaigns/Projects]; https://www.politiaromana.ro/en/prevention/campaigns-projects// [09.10.2019] [in Romanian and English].

Romanian Police (2019b): Infotraffic; https://www.politiaromana.ro/ro/info-trafic/situatia-accidentelor-rutiere-grave-inregistrate-in-ultimele-24-de-ore-la-nivel-national [09.10.2019] [in Romanian and English].

Romanian Society of Criminology and Criminalistics (2019): Prima pagină [First page]; http://criminologie.org.ro/ [09.10.2019] [in Romanian only].

Social Alternative (2019): Justitie [Justice]; http://www.alternativesociale.ro/en_GB/justitie/ [09.10.2019] [in Romanian and English].

The Pro Bono Network for Human Rights (2019): Pro bono legal aid; http://proboNo.actedo.org/en/category/pro-bono-legal-aid/ [09.10.2019] [in Romanian and English].

Traffic Accident Victims Association of Romania (2019): Acasa [Home]; http://avacromania.ro/ [09.10.2019] [in Romanian only].

Transcend Association (2019): Membri [Members]; https://violentaimpotrivafemeilor.ro/membri-actuali/ [09.10.2019] [in Romanian only].

University of "Alexander Ioan Cuza" in Iaşi (2019): Faculty of philosophy; https://www.fssp.uaic.ro/en/about-faculty [09.10.2019] [in Romanian and English].

University of Bucharest (2019a): Hexagonul Facultăților de Drept [Heyagon of law faculties]; https://drept.unibuc.ro/Hexagonul-Facultatilor-de-Drept-Bucuresti-editia-2019-s816-ro.htm [09.10.2019] [in Romanian only].

University of Bucharest (2019b): School of sociology and social work; https://sas.unibuc.ro/en [09.10.2019] [in Romanian and English].

University Spiru Haret (2019): Facultatea de psihologie si stiintele educatiei [Faculty of psychology and educational sciences]; https://pse-b.spiruharet.ro/images/secretariat/Orare/orar_master_PJV_anul_II.pdf [09.10.2019] [in Romanian only].

Equality and Human Rights Action Centre - ACTEDO (2016): We break the silence about sexual violence, Ghid pentru victimele violenței sexuale [Guide for victims of sexual violence]; http://actedo.org/wp-content/uploads/2016/06/Ghid-pentru-victime_Rupem-tacerea-despre-violenta-sexuala.pdf [09.10.2019] [in Romanian only].

World Health Organisation (2016): Statistics on causes of death; https://www.who.int/healthinfo/mortality_data/en/ [24.10.2019] [in English only].

Victim Support Europe (2016): The EU victims' directive on EU day for victims of crime 2016: Infringement cases opened against 16 Member states; https://victimsupport.eu/news/the-eu-victims-directive-on-eu-day-for-victims-of-crime-2016-infringement-cases-opened-against-16-member-states/ [09.10.2019] [in English only].

Serbia

Victimology and Victim Protection

Vesna Nikolić-Ristanović & Sanja Ćopić

1. Introduction

The Republic of Serbia (hereinafter Serbia) is situated in the centre of the Balkan Peninsula in Southeast Europe. Serbia is a former republic of the Socialist Federal Republic of Yugoslavia (SFRY). After the break-up of the SFRY, Serbia and Montenegro established a federation called the Federal Republic of Yugoslavia; this was later reconstituted into the State Union of Serbia and Montenegro in 2003. In 2006, both Serbia and Montenegro proclaimed their independence. Serbia is a parliamentary republic.

Serbia covers an area of 88,499 square kilometres.[1] According to the latest population census, which was conducted in 2011 by the Statistical Office of the Republic of Serbia (SORS), Serbia had 7,186,862 inhabitants.[2] The estimated number of population in 2016 was 7,058,322: 3,437,630 males and 3,620,692 females. Thus, females constitute 51.3% of the population in Serbia.[3] Data from 2016 also suggest that the natural population growth rate in Serbia is, in fact, negative (–5.11 per 1,000 inhabitants).[4] According to the 2011 population census, the average age in Serbia was 42.3 (43.5 for females and 40.8 for males),[5] while in 2016, the average age was 42.9 (41.5 for males and 44.2 for females).[6] Almost 60% of the population lived in

---

1 StatOffice 2017a.

2 The 2011 census was not conducted on the territory of Kosovo and Metohija. In the municipalities of Preševo and Bujanovac, decreased census coverage was recorded due to a boycott by the majority of the Albanian national community. All further demographic data relate to Serbia without Kosovo and Metohija; see StatOffice 2017a.

3 StatOffice 2014, p. 27; 2017a.

4 StatOffice 2017a.

5 StatOffice 2017b, p. 10.

6 StatOffice 2017a.

urban areas.[7] Serbs constituted the majority of the population of Serbia (83.3%). The most numerous ethnic minorities were recorded as being Hungarians (3.5%), Roma (2.1%), Bosnians (2.0%), and Croats (0.8%).[8] Concerning religion, more than two-thirds of the population (84.6%) declared themselves Orthodox Christian.[9]

According to the 2011 population census, one half of the population aged over 14 had a secondary education; this is followed by those with primary (20.8%) and tertiary education i.e., higher – and university – level educational attainment (16.2%); 2.7% had no formal education and the share of persons with an incomplete primary education was 11%.[10] The 2016 Labour Force Survey suggested that 53.3% of the population over 15 was active in the labour market: the employment rate was 45.2% and the rate of unemployment was 15.3%.[11] The rate of employment among the younger working-age population (15–24) was 18.7% and the rate of unemployment 34.9%. The employment rate for females was 38.1%: 14.7 percentage points less than the employment rate for males (52.8%).[12] According to the SORS's data, in Serbia, the GDP per capita for 2016 was 4,904 EUR. The Gender Equality Index for Serbia was 52.4% in 2014.[13] In the period 2014–2016, the index value increased by 3.4 points and in 2016 it was 55.8%.[14] Compared to the average results from the Gender Equality Index in the 28 European Union Member States, the value in Serbia is still lower. However, the gap between the EU-28 average and Serbia decreased in 2016 compared to 2014, when it was 12.6 points.[15] The most severe gender gaps in Serbia in 2014 were in the fields of work and money, while in 2016 the difference compared to the EU-28 was more pronounced in the domains of power, time, and money, and lesser in the domains of health, knowledge, and work.[16]

In 2015, Serbia faced a refugee crisis. According to the data of the Serbian Commissariat for Refugees and Migration, in 2015, 579,518 persons expressed their inten-

---

7 StatOffice 2014, p. 13.

8 Albanians are also among the most numerous ethnic minorities, but the figures from the 2011 census are very low and unreliable due to the aforementioned boycott by the majority of Albanian national community; see StatOffice 2014.

9 StatOffice 2014, p. 63.

10 StatOffice 2014, p. 39.

11 StatOffice 2017c, p. 17.

12 StatOffice 2017c, p. 21.

13 *Babović* 2016. The Gender Equality Index for the European Union was 52.9% in 2012, and 66.2% in 2015; see *Babović* 2016. The data are available online at: http://eige.europa.eu/gender-equality-index.

14 *Babović* 2018.

15 *Babović* 2016; 2018.

16 *Babović* 2016, p. 29; 2018, p. 22.

tion to seek asylum in the Republic of Serbia – 313,335 men and 92,188 women.[17] The majority of asylum seekers came from Syria (52.1%) and Afghanistan (27.8%), followed by Iraq (13.3%), Iran (2%), and Pakistan (1.6%). This was 35 times more than the number of asylum seekers in 2014 (16,490).[18] However, out of the total number of those that expressed an intention to seek asylum, only 586 persons (0.1%) filed an application for asylum.[19] The number of those who expressed an intention to seek asylum in Serbia significantly decreased in 2016 (12,811), due to the closure of the Western Balkan migration route.[20] In 2016, based on the decision of the Government of the Republic of Serbia, citizens coming from countries in which their lives were endangered were issued with a "proof of entry" into the territory of Serbia. In total, 96,236 such "proofs" were issued, which legalised the stay of undocumented migrants in the territory of Serbia for 72 hours, protecting them from punishment due to illegal entry and enabling them to use accommodation and medical services.[21]

The Serbian criminal justice system consists of:

1) the police;
2) the public prosecution;
3) the judiciary; and
4) the prison administration.

The police force in Serbia is under the jurisdiction of the General Police Directorate of the Ministry of Interior.[22] The police force is the central organisational unit of the Ministry of Interior, and operates at the national, regional, and local level. The police force is headed by the Director of the Police who reports to the Minister of the Interior. The police force's organisation, work, competences and powers are regulated by the Law on Police.[23] The public prosecution is an autonomous state body, which prosecutes perpetrators of criminal and other punishable offences and undertakes measures for the protection of constitutionality and legality; its organisation and jurisdiction are governed by the Law on Public Prosecution.[24] The Public Prosecution of the Republic of Serbia consists of the Republican Public Prosecution, the appellate public prosecutions, the higher public prosecutions, the basic pub-

---

17 Commissariat for Refugees and Migration 2015, p. 56.

18 United Nations High Commissioner for Refugees 2015.

19 Commissariat for Refugees and Migration 2015, p. 58.

20 Commissariat for Refugees and Migration 2016, p. 58.

21 Commissariat for Refugees and Migration 2016, p. 59.

22 *Kešetović* 2013, p. 221.

23 Law on Police, Law No. 6/2016-3, 28.01.2016, Official gazette 6/2016.

24 Law on Public Prosecution, Law. No. 116/2008-27, 22.12.2008, Official gazette 116/2008.

lic prosecutions, and the public prosecutions with special jurisdiction, including the Public Prosecution for Organised Crime and the Public Prosecution for War Crimes. The Republican Public Prosecution, the Public Prosecution for Organised Crime, and the Public Prosecution for War Crimes are established for the territory of the Republic of Serbia. According to the Law on the Organisation of Courts,[25] judicial power in Serbia is vested in courts of general and special jurisdiction. Courts of general jurisdiction are basic courts (66), higher courts (25), appellate courts (4), and the Supreme Court of Cassation. Courts of special jurisdiction are commercial courts, the Commercial Appellate Court, minor offences courts, the Higher Minor Offences Court, and the Administrative Court. The Prison Administration, i.e., the Administration for the Enforcement of Penal Sanctions is a body within the Ministry of Justice whose organisation and work are governed by the Law on the Execution of Criminal Sanction.[26]

The aim of this chapter is to present an overview of victim-related developments in Serbia, including the development of victimology and the movement for victims' rights, and the development of legislation relevant to the protection of victims.

2. An Overview of Victim-Related Developments in Serbia[27]

Similarly to other countries in the region, the development of initiatives for the improvement of the position of crime victims in Serbia started about twenty years later compared to those found in other Western countries. In Serbia, public interest in the victims of crime began in 1980s, primarily via feminist advocacy groups that pushed for the rights of women and children.[28] During 1990s, other factors also influenced victim-related developments. These included the following: initiatives of human rights organisations, the development of victimology as an academic discipline, an increase of crime in Serbia, the sufferings of civilians related to ethnic conflicts on the territory of the former Yugoslavia, war related humanitarian initiatives, as well as international activities relevant for the rights of victims that started with the UN Declaration on Basic Principles of Justice for Victims of Crime and Abuse

---

25 Law on Organisation of Courts, Law. No. 104/2009-3, 16.12.2009, Official gazette 104/2009.

26 Law on the Execution of Criminal Sanction, Law No. 55/2014-10, 23.05.2014, Official gazette 55/2014.

27 The text that follows is based on parts of the book *Crime Victims: International and Serbian perspective* that describe developments of victimology and the victims' rights movement in Serbia, which were written by *Vesna Nikolić-Ristanović*; see *Lindgren & Nikolić-Ristanović* 2011.

28 For more details, see *Lindgren & Nikolić-Ristanović* 2011.

of Power,[29] and were further intensified during the 1990s and 2000s. Activism for victims' rights has grown since 2012, i.e., after the ratification of the Council of Europe Convention on Preventing and Combating Violence against Women and Domestic Violence[30] (Istanbul Convention) and acceptance of the candidacy of Serbia for membership in the European Union (EU). Civil society advocacy turned toward harmonisation of Serbian legislation and legal practice with the Istanbul Convention and the Directive of the European Parliament and of the Council of 25 October 2012 on establishing minimum standards on the rights, support and protection of victims of crime (EU Victims' Rights Directive). [31]

The most intensive victim-related developments that brought positive changes in Serbia occurred after political changes, from the year 2000 onwards. Since then, the development of the movements for women and human rights have become more intense, leading to broader, more systematic, and successful victim awareness campaigns and the development of victim support services.[32] Consequently, during the 2000s, the state finally started to deal with victims' issues as a result of the influence of civil society advocacy and in order to fulfil its international obligations (although it should be noted that the state often acted in a sporadic and non-comprehensive way). Finally, the development of victim-related initiatives benefited from Serbia's membership in the Council of Europe and the EU accession process. Thus, victim-related developments in Serbia have gone through four distinct phases, each characterised by different social, political, and economic conditions:

1) the period until 1991;
2) the period during the wars on the territory of the former Yugoslavia (1991–2000);
3) the period between political changes in Serbia in 2000 and acceptance of its EU candidacy (2012); and
4) the period since 2012.[33]

---

29 Declaration of Basic Principles of Justice for Victims of Crime and Abuse of Power, No. A/RES/40/34, 29.11.1985; https://www.un.org/documents/ga/res/40/a40r034.htm [17.04.2019].

30 Council of Europe Convention on Preventing and Combating Violence against Women and Domestic Violence, No. 210, 11.5.2011; https://rm.coe.int/168008482e [07.03.2018].

31 Directive of the European Parliament and of the Council of 25 October 2012 on establishing minimum standards on the rights, support and protection of victims of crime, Directive No. 2012/29/EU, 14.11.2012, Official Journal of the European Union, 315/2012; https://eur-lex.europa.eu/legal-content/EN/TXT/PDF/?uri=CELEX:32012L0029&from=en [07.03.2018].

32 *Nikolić-Ristanović* 2007.

33 It is important to note that this categorisation has been made based on the predominant characteristics of developments in different periods and that it is not possible to make

The first public discussions about violence against women were organised during the 1980s in Belgrade by the feminist group "Women and Society". The members of this group were also engaged in other awareness raising activities, such as media interviews, round tables, speeches in various institutions, etc.[34] Representatives of other women's groups, together with researchers, presented federal state authorities with proposals to change laws on domestic violence and marital rape. This advocacy was designed to raise public awareness and better protect female victims of violence and it continued to exist during the ethnic conflicts that erupted across the former Yugoslavia as well. During the 1990s, women's groups and feminist researchers helped make issues such as domestic violence, sexual violence, and human trafficking visible, including particularly those who were victimised on the territories directly affected by ethnic conflicts. Moreover, the first proposal to criminalise domestic violence and marital rape was prepared and submitted by the "Group for Women's Rights of the European Movement in Serbia"[35] in the mid-1990s.[36]

During the 1990s, women's groups activists also established SOS hotlines, shelters, and counselling services for women and children. The first SOS hotlines were established in 1990 while the first Serbian shelter for battered women (and children) was established in 1994. Apart from battered women, the shelter also accommodated female victims of war (rape victims, refugees, etc.), who accounted for 22.3% of the occupants who spent time in the shelter between 1994 and 1999.[37] Later on, shelters for battered women were established in other parts of Serbia. After 2000, shelters for victims of human trafficking were also opened.

The development of victim services run by non-state organisations intensified after social changes in 2000. In general, the development of victim services in the 1990s and 2000s was under the strong influence of the women's movement. However, broader societal elements and human rights organisations also played a pivotal role. As in other countries, human rights organisations were mostly interested in victim's rights related to the criminal procedure and punishment of offenders; contrary to this, victim support organisations mostly took a more flexible and empowering approach to support victims, trying to meet victims' needs irrespective of their involvement in the criminal justice system. Thus, the first victim services in Serbia were specialised services for women and children who had been victims of violence.

a clear timeline between them. Each new period practically started during the previous one.

34 *Blagojević* 1998.

35 The Group was the predecessor of the Victimology Society of Serbia.

36 Although not successful, this advocacy was very important in terms of raising awareness among state officials and the general public. Namely, the provision about the punishment for marital rape was included in the draft Criminal Code as an alternative to the traditional rape definition, and was, for the first time ever, discussed in the Parliament.

37 *Ćetković* 1998.

Later on, other specialised services were developed, such as services for torture and war victims. However, until the late 1990s, victim advocacy and support in Serbia was mostly limited to women and child victims of violence. Since the establishment of the Victimology Society of Serbia (VDS) in 1997, and largely thanks to its advocacy, many positive changes have now been initiated to benefit all victims of crime.

The VDS was established as a not-for-profit and non-governmental organisation committed to work towards the development of victims' rights and victimology as an academic discipline.[38] Soon after its establishment, the VDS initiated numerous new programs in Serbia. The following initiatives should be particularly stressed:

1) launch of the first Serbian academic journal on victimisation, human rights, and gender – "Temida";
2) development of victimological research;
3) legislation and policy/practice reform proposals;
4) introducing data on victims in the official judiciary statistics governed by the SORS;
5) public awareness campaigns on victims' issues;
6) introduction of victimology at the universities and into regular education of professionals in various fields.

Almost all initiatives of the VDS had a "pioneer character" and led to important societal changes. The VDS has also organised numerous national and international conferences on topics of victimisation, including war victimisation, domestic violence, truth and reconciliation, and alternative sanctions. In order to foster victimological research and practice, the VDS established three awards in 2009 and has granted them regularly ever since:

1) the award for the contribution to the promotion of victims' rights;
2) the award "Third way" that is awarded to individuals or organisations who have contributed to the development of a non-conflict and comprehensive approach to dealing with the consequences of war and the promotion of peace in Serbia; and
3) the award for a talented young researcher in the field of victimology.

Largely based on the VDS's initiatives, drafts, and joint-advocacy with other non-governmental organisations (NGOs), new laws have been passed with provisions that are of importance for victims. Finally, the first and so far the only generic victim support service, which offers support to victims of all crimes and of both

38 More information about the VDS is available online at www.vds.org.rs.

sexes, was established in 2003 as a special unit of the VDS, named "VDS info and victim support".

Post 2000, victim services were established by state institutions as well, mostly within social welfare institutions. Legal changes that related to domestic violence and human trafficking led to an increase in available funds for financing partnerships between NGOs and state institutions and this was particularly beneficial for this development. State services mostly followed the predominant trend set by NGOs, focusing on services for women and child victims of violence (domestic violence and human trafficking). Since 2010, new trends suggest the suspension of some NGO victim services (SOS hotlines and shelters) which had been developed with a lot of enthusiasm and which generated precious experience for activists. These activities were partly taken over by state institutions which often have less appropriate knowledge and experience for meeting the needs of victims. In terms of victim/witness support, in 2006 the first witness service was established in the War Crime Chamber of the District Court in Belgrade (today the Higher Court in Belgrade) – the service for assistance and support to victims and witnesses of war crimes. Since 2015, witness services have been established in all higher public prosecutor's offices and courts in Serbia to inform and provide support to victims (injured parties) and witnesses.

In sum, the development of both non-state and state victim services and programs in Serbia was neither linear nor systematic. Although very important, these developments mostly came about as a result of the efforts of enthusiastic groups and individuals, partially supported by fragmented state efforts. Although a certain level of cooperation between different services exists, a national network of local victim services (as seen in other countries) has not yet been established in Serbia.

3. Development of Victimology in Serbia

Many important works were published between 1960 and 1981 in the former Yugoslavia that helped to establish and develop victimology throughout the region (including in Serbia). Authors who published during this period included: *Marina* (Macedonia), *Makra, Šeparović, Carić, Pospišl-Završki*, and *Puškarić* (Croatia), *Vodopivec, Pečar, Šeparović, Šelih*, and *Kobe* (Slovenia), as well as *Aćimović, Simić, Krstić, Kapamadžija*, and *Pihler* (Serbia).[39] These authors opened the door for the development of victimology by introducing the victim's perspective into dealing with different forms of crime. Moreover, they presented global victimology research and debates to a domestic academic and research audience. They established a systematic understanding of victimological knowledge and research during the 1980s, which was then put to great use

---

39 *Kramarić* 1982; *Šeparović* 1985.

thereafter (in the case of Serbia, especially during the 2000s when the research on crime victims intensified).

Development of victimology as a science in Serbia, as in other countries of the former Yugoslavia, was delayed for several decades in comparison with developments in other countries. Additionally, the break-up of the SFRY influenced the specific dynamics of its development in Serbia and resulted in a slightly different approach to addressing the problems of victims. In the sections that follow, an overview is provided about victimology research and development of victimology as an academic discipline during the four aforementioned periods of victim-related development in Serbia.

3.1 The First Period in the Development of Victimology in Serbia (1980–1992)

The first period in the development of victimology in Serbia is characterised by the emergence of systematic works dealing with victimology and the problems of victims, as well as the first empirical research and initiatives to improve the position of victims. In addition, this period, in contrast to those thereafter, took place within the wider, Yugoslav, social and academic context. Thus, a characteristic of the period was mutual cooperation among a large number of researchers and practitioners from both the former Yugoslavia and other countries.

Several victimological events were of pivotal importance during this period. Firstly, in 1984 the first international conference on victims' rights and the first post-graduate course in victimology and victim assistance were organised in Dubrovnik. The fifth symposium of the World Society of Victimology was held in Zagreb in 1985, which was followed by the establishment of the Yugoslav Victimology Society in 1988 by professor *Zvonimir Šeparović*, the president of the World Society of Victimology at the time. The Society had its headquarters in Zagreb (Croatia) but its members were drawn from all other parts of Yugoslavia, including very active members from Serbia, some of whom were also members of the Society's presidency and organising committees during the fifth symposium of the World Society of Victimology.[40] Establishment of the Yugoslav Victimology Society contributed to a closer relationship between researchers and practitioners from various parts of the former Yugoslavia. It was also a period that saw the consolidation of victimology as a science, and a period that witnessed the first concrete initiatives to improve the position of victims in Serbia.

---

40 The disintegration of Yugoslavia and the ethnic conflicts that followed led to the end of the Yugoslav Victimology Society. It was later transformed into the Croatian Victimology Society.

During the 1980s and the beginning of the 1990s, authors from Serbia published and presented their victimological works at victimological conferences. The research on victims was conducted by the Institute of Criminological and Sociological Research in Belgrade, as well as by researchers from other institutions. The works were primarily based on the results of empirical research and were dedicated to various topics, such as:

1) mentally ill people as victims and victim's testimony in criminal procedure;[41]
2) political prisoners as victims;[42]
3) victims of terrorism;[43]
4) UN activities and victims;[44]
5) victims of traffic accidents;[45]
6) the first contact of a victim with the police;[46]
7) the legal position of victims of sexual violence;[47]
8) young people and children as victims;[48]
9) the legal position of crime victims;[49]
10) fear of crime;[50] and
11) spousal abuse.[51]

Additionally, the topic of the 14th annual conference of the Association for Criminal Law and Criminology, which was held in 1982 in Aranđelovac, was "The Injured Party in the Criminal Law".

The first comprehensive book on victimology and victims of crime was published in 1984: "The influence of the victim on the phenomenon of crime", written by *Vesna Nikolić-Ristanović*.[52] It was based on her master thesis, which was defended at the

---

41 *Aćimović* 1979; 1981.

42 *Janković* 1989.

43 *Aćimović* 1980; *Šeparović* 1998.

44 *Šeparović* 1998.

45 *Nikolić-Ristanović* 1987.

46 *Nikolić-Ristanović & Mrvić* 1988.

47 *Nikolić-Ristanović* 1989a.

48 *Nikolić-Ristanović* 1988; *Radovanović* 1988; 1989.

49 *Bejatović* 1993; *Nikolić-Ristanović* 1989b.

50 *Nikolić-Ristanović* 1995; *Nikolić-Ristanović & Mrvić* 1990.

51 *Nikolić-Ristanović* 1993;1996.

52 *Nikolić-Ristanović* 1984.

University of Belgrade's Law Faculty under the supervision of two internationally recognised professors of criminology, *Milan Milutinović* and *Mihajlo Aćimović*. The establishment and development of victimology, its aims and tasks, different notions of its subject, and the concept of the victim, basic victimological terms, and the importance of assistance and support to victims were presented for the first time in this book. The book was based on both theoretical and empirical research on the following topics:

1) crime victims;
2) characteristics that make them vulnerable;
3) the victim-offender relationship;
4) victim's behaviour that can contribute or prevent victimisation;
5) consequences of victimisation and recovery processes; and
6) the legal position of victims.

Several years later, in 1989, the second comprehensive research-based book on victim's issues was published by *Nikolić-Ristanović*.[53] The book, entitled "Women as crime victims", was the first PhD thesis done and published in Serbia dealing with issues such as domestic violence, marital rape, inadequate victim legislation, the position of rape victims (before the police, the prosecutor, and the court), and shelters and hotlines for battered women. Apart from dealing with the victimisation of women by gender-based violence, this book also dealt with women as victims of other forms of crime, such as bodily injuries, theft, robbery, insult, and fraud. Along with the basic empirical research, based on data from court files, the first victimisation survey in Serbia was also conducted. This was a pilot study on the sample of 206 female pupils and students in Belgrade. Similarly to other foreign surveys, the participants were asked if they had been victimised by certain forms of crime in the period from 1980 to 1985. The book served as an important platform to advocate legal change.[54] Both books ("The influence of the victim on the phenomenon of crime" and "Women as crime victims") presented an excellent basis for further victimological research developments in Serbia.

3.2 The Second Period in the Development of Victimology in Serbia (1992–2000)

War and economic sanctions shaped the entirety of social life in Serbia during this period, and consequently the development of victimology as well. War sufferings, first indirectly and then directly, as well as mass violations of human rights by the

---

53 *Nikolić-Ristanović* 1989b.

54 In 1990, the book "Women as victims of crime" was publicly launched at one of the public panels organised by the group Women and Society; see *Blagojević* 1998.

regime of *Slobodan Milošević*, were part of everyday life in Serbia during the 1990s. At the same time, in the early 1990s, political pluralism and freedom of association, as part of the political transition to a democratic society, created conditions for the development of a civil society, which was evident in the establishment of various NGOs. War victimisation, a large influx of refugees, marital and domestic violence by war participants who returned from the battlefield, as well as political violence and other violations of human rights by the state authorities, captured the attention of activists, humanitarian organisations, and academic researchers. In this period, NGOs played an important role in the collection and dissemination of data on people's suffering; they also provided assistance and support to victims, which the state was unable or unwilling to provide (for example, when it came to victims of human rights violations committed by the state agencies themselves, or against members of ethnic groups who were considered enemies).

Due to economic sanctions, funding for research carried out by state institutions was dramatically cut. However, some civil society initiatives were launched and international funds became available to Serbia, which consequently influenced both research and practices on victims. Most victimology research during this period were carried out by NGOs and individual researchers, often on the topic of victims of war and state violence.

In this period, empirical research was conducted on the victimisation of women in war, including rape and forced pregnancies,[55] and police violence against citizens.[56] This research aimed to not only collect data and information but to also empower victims and provide them with assistance and support. Such action research included the collection of qualitative data about women's experiences of violence and the provision of support to help them recover from the consequences of their victimisation.[57] During this period, empirical (mostly qualitative) research on the relationship between domestic violence and female crime[58] and the impact of war and transition on violence against women and society's response to it[59] were conducted as well.

Additional issues that were researched included:

---

55 *Nikolić-Ristanović* 2000a; 2000b; *Nikolić-Ristanović, Konstantinović-Vilić, Mrvić-Petrović, Stevanović & Knežić* 1996; *Nikolić-Ristanović, Mrvić-Petrović, Konstantinović-Vilić & Stevanović* 1995.

56 *Nikolić-Ristanović, Stevanović & Knežić* 1997.

57 *Nikolić-Ristanović* 2000a; *Nikolić-Ristanović et al.* 1995; 1996.

58 *Nikolić-Ristanović* 2000c.

59 *Nikolić-Ristanović* 1994; 1996; 1999a; 2002a; 2008; *Nikolić-Ristanović & Milivojević* 2000.

1) psychological consequences of war;[60]
2) war victimisation;[61]
3) victim compensation;[62] and
4) the impact of war and economic sanctions on the living conditions in women's prisons.[63]

The first comprehensive studies on child abuse[64] and incest[65] were published. Important works relevant for the protection of children from abuse were published in this period as well.[66] In addition, in 1996, the Institute of Criminological and Sociological Research participated in the International Crime Victim Survey (ICVS). The first (and so far the only) Serbian crime victimisation survey was conducted in Belgrade on a sample of 1,094 respondents.[67]

In this period, the establishment of the Victimology Society of Serbia-VDS in 1997 was important for the development of victimology too. After its establishment, the VDS intensified victimological research in Serbia. In 1998, the VDS started to publish an academic journal on victimisation, human rights, and gender entitled "Temida",[68] which has been regularly published ever since. It is the first and still the only journal dealing with issues of victimisation, human rights, and gender in Serbia, but it has also been recognised in the broader region and beyond. Every issue is dedicated to a specific victim-related topic. "Temida" is recognised as an academic journal by the Serbian Ministry of Education, Science, and Technological Development and has become a valuable source for students, professionals, and anyone else interested in victim research and issues. It publishes articles in both Serbian and English.

3.3 The Third Period in the Development of Victimology in Serbia (2000–2012)

As already mentioned, the establishment of the VDS created favourable conditions that, along with political changes in 2000 and a larger influx of foreign donations,

---

60 *Bojanin & Išpanović-Radojković* 1994; *Kaličanin, Bukelić, Išpanović-Radojković & Lečić-Toševski* 1993.

61 *Milivojević* 1999; *Nikolić-Ristanović* 1999b; 2000a.

62 *Mrvić-Petrović* 2001.

63 *Nikolić-Ristanović* 1997.

64 *Banjanin-Đuričić* 1998.

65 *Mršević* 1997.

66 *Obretković* 1997; 1998.

67 *Nikolić-Ristanović* 1998a; 1998b; *Zvekić* 2001.

68 More information on the academic journal "Temida" is available online at http://www.vds.rs/TemidaMenuEng.htm.

enabled numerous victimology efforts to be launched across the country. This lead to the preconditions needed to consolidate victimology as a science and a practice in Serbia. During this period, significant victimological research was conducted, primarily by researchers gathered around the VDS and the Autonomous Women's Centre.

The VDS carried out numerous victimological studies, including:

1) victimisation surveys on partner and domestic violence[69];
2) research on victim support services;[70]
3) trafficking in women, children, and men and the system of assistance to victims of human trafficking;[71]
4) victims and restorative justice;[72]
5) victims and reconciliation in post-conflict society;[73]
6) legal position of victims;[74]
7) non-governmental organisations and assistance to victims in Serbia;[75]
8) discrimination of women in the labour market;[76] and
9) living conditions and the level of respect of human rights of imprisoned women.[77]

In 2001, the VDS carried out the first national survey on domestic violence, while in 2009 another survey of this type was conducted in the province of Vojvodina. Both studies were based on a combination of the victimisation survey and feminist methodology, and included face-to-face interviews with respondents. Both studies were action-oriented: they aimed to empower female victims of domestic violence, raise awareness about domestic violence, and provide information about existing (both state and non-state) victim support services, and to contribute to change of social response to this form of crime. In 2003, the VDS conducted the first comprehensive

---

69 *Nikolić-Ristanović* 2002b; 2010.

70 *Ćopić* 2007; *Milivojević & Mihić* 2003; *Nikolić* 2007; *Nikolić, Nikolić-Ristanović & Petrović* 2010; *Nikolić-Ristanović* 2007.

71 *Bjerkan* 2005; *Ćopić & Nikolić-Ristanović* 2006; *Nikolić-Ristanović* 2009; *Nikolić-Ristanović & Ćopić* 2010; 2011a; *Nikolić-Ristanović, Ćopić, Simeunović-Patić, Milivojević & Mihić* 2004.

72 *Ćopić* 2010.

73 *Nikolić-Ristanović & Hanak* 2004; *Nikolić-Ristanović & Srna* 2008.

74 *Nikolić-Ristanović & Ćopić* 2011b.

75 *Nikolić-Ristanović* 2011a.

76 *Nikolić-Ristanović, Ćopić, Nikolić & Šaćiri* 2012.

77 *Ćopić & Šaćiri* 2012; *Ćopić, Stevković & Šaćiri* 2012.

ethnographic survey on trafficking in persons in Serbia. In addition, the first survey on discrimination and victimisation of women in the labour market (a victimisation survey), which included the collection of data on sexual harassment and work related violence, was also conducted by the VDS.[78]

Since 2010, the VDS has regularly organised annual conferences, which present a great opportunity for constructive discussion, comprehensive exchange, and professional meetings for researchers and practitioners from Serbia and abroad.

Apart from the VDS, other NGOs (domestic and international), institutions, and individual researchers conducted relevant victimological researches as well.[79] They conducted surveys on domestic violence, trafficking in women and children, child abuse, the elderly as victims, fear of crime, homophobic violence, sexual harassment, work related abuse, war victimisation, victim services, compensation for victims, etc. For example, the NGO "Autonomous Women's Centre – Centre for Promotion of Women's Health" from Belgrade conducted a survey on domestic violence on a sample of 1,456 women from Belgrade in 2002, as a part of the World Health Organization's multicountry study on violence against women and women's health.[80] The Autonomous Women's Centre also conducted several studies on court practice regarding domestic violence.[81] In 2010, the NGO "Secons" conducted a prevalence survey on domestic violence in Serbia, excluding the Autonomous province of Vojvodina.[82] During 2004 and 2009–2010, studies on the abuse of the elderly were conducted as well.[83] It is particularly important to mention a major survey on child abuse and neglect that was conducted during 2010 and 2011 by the Faculty of Special Education and Rehabilitation, as part of a broader FP7-funded project called Balkan epidemiological study on child abuse and neglect (BECAN).[84]

The first book in Serbia that had a term victimology in its title was published in 2009: "The frameworks of victimology", which was written by *Ivana Simović-Hiber*.[85] During 1998, victimology started to be taught, for the first time in Serbia, as a part of the criminology course at the Law Faculty, University of Niš. Professor *Slobodanka Konstantinović-Vilić* lectured the course, on the basis of the criminology textbook written by herself and professor *Vesna Nikolić-Ristanović*. Professors

78 *Nikolić-Ristanović et al.* 2012.

79 It is worth mentioning that a large part of this research was conducted by VDS members, who conducted research either for their master or PhD theses or while working with other NGOs and institutions.

80 *Garcia-Moreno, Jansen, Ellsberg, Heise & Wats* 2006; *Otašević* 2005.

81 *Konstantinović-Vilić & Petrušić* 2004; 2007.

82 *Babović, Ginić & Vuković* 2010.

83 *Kostić* 2010; *Stevković & Dimitrijević* 2011.

84 *Hanak, Tenjović, Išpanović-Radojković, Vlajković & Beara* 2013.

85 *Simović-Hiber* 2009.

Konstantinović-Vilić and *Nikolić-Ristanović*, for the first time ever in Serbia, introduced a special chapter in a university textbook on victimology as well as topics such as crime victims, victimology, child abuse, domestic violence, marital rape, the battered women's movement, feminist methodology, and feminist theory.[86] This textbook was later up-dated and amended to include many other victimological topics, such as trafficking in persons, work-related abuse, stalking, abuse of the elderly, etc.[87]

Since 2007, victimology has been taught as a separate course at the Law Faculty (University of Niš), Faculty of Special Education and Rehabilitation and Faculty of Security (University of Belgrade), as well as at the Academy of Criminalistics and Police Studies in Belgrade. In the period between 2004 and 2008, at the Faculty of Special Education and Rehabilitation of the University of Belgrade, professor *Vesna Nikolić-Ristanović* put much more emphasis on spreading knowledge about victim-related issues through her criminology course. For this purpose, extensive literature on victimology has been introduced as course reading material for the students. Moreover, in 2007, victimology became a separate elective course at the Faculty of Special Education and Rehabilitation (University of Belgrade). Apart from that, the course on child abuse in the family became an elective course at the same faculty too.

The development of victimology in this period, the results of the efforts of NGOs, as well as the demands of the international community, have led to a whole range of activities and important changes in practice:

1) enhancement of legislation on victims, in particular legislation related to domestic violence, sexual violence, and human trafficking;
2) intensification of campaigns to raise public awareness about victims' rights and advocacy for changes of practice;
3) establishment of the first general victim support service within the VDS;
4) intensified establishment of victim support services by civil society organisations and the establishment of state services;
5) conducting a series of victimological research, primarily regarding victims of gender-based violence and child victims;
6) the inclusion of data on victims in the official judiciary statistics;[88]

---

86 *Konstantinović-Vilić & Nikolić-Ristanović* 1998.

87 *Konstantinović-Vilić & Nikolić-Ristanović* 2003; 2004.

88 Since 2007, data on crime victims (their gender and age) have been recorded. The data are collected from the country's courts by the SORS. As such, the data only contain information on victims that had their cases heard before a court. However, even in these court cases, victim data are often missing. Therefore, the official statistics cannot be used to assess the true level of victimisation in Serbia.

7) introduction of victimology as a separate subject into the curriculum at faculties in Serbia, development and licensing of practical trainings for professionals of different background, and production of readers and manuals;
8) initiation of regular annual (international) conferences of the VDS about victims' rights, etc. In addition, advocacy by the VDS (and other NGOs) contributed to improvements concerning the legal position of imprisoned women and better treatment of battered women who had killed their abusers.

3.4 The Fourth Period in the Development of Victimology in Serbia (2012–2018)

For the development of victimology in Serbia post-2012, the following events have been of pivotal importance:

1) acceptance of Serbia's candidacy for EU accession (2012) and related legislative harmonisation activities (including the EU Victims' Rights Directive);
2) ratification of the Istanbul Convention and related legislative harmonisation activities; and
3) local, regional, and global social contexts, particularly the so-called "refugee crisis" and terrorism (and related security issues).

As before, the focus has remained on improving conditions for women and child victims of violence, particularly in the context of legislative harmonisation in accordance with the Istanbul Convention (this will be discussed below). Serious social efforts that have aimed to establish improved conditions for all victims of crime have also been spurred-on by the EU accession talks. As part of these negotiations, Serbia has prioritised the implementation of the EU Victims' Rights Directive.[89] In the context of Serbia's accession negotiations with the EU, and as a part of the preparatory process for the development of a national victim support system in Serbia, during 2016 and 2017, within the project entitled "Victim support service in Serbia", Victim Support Europe and the World Bank conducted several important research activities. This included measuring the compliance of Serbian legislation with the EU Victims' Rights Directive, research into victim support services in other countries as possible models for Serbia, research into organisations and institutions in Serbia and selected Balkan countries that provide assistance and support to victims, campaigns for raising awareness about crime victims, the development and updating of the victim services database, and the establishment and coordination of a network of victim support services.[90]

89 Multi-Donor Trust Fund for Justice Sector Support in Serbia & World Bank 2017c.

90 Multi-Donor Trust Fund for Justice Sector Support in Serbia & World Bank 2017a; 2017b; 2017c; *Nikolić-Ristanović, Ćopić, Nikolić & Šaćiri* 2018.

These activities were conducted in cooperation with relevant ministries and state institutions, as well as with civil society organisations, particularly with the VDS, which was actively involved in all these activities, and was generally in charge of conducting the research on victim support services in Serbia and the development and maintenance of a database concerning these services.

Victimological research and academic papers published in this period largely reflect the aforementioned processes of legislative harmonisation and local and international social contexts. In addition, research has focused on victims' rights, needs, and support, court practices regarding domestic violence, systems of assistance and protection for victims of domestic violence, etc.[91] Additionally, since a large number of migrants and refugees have recently passed through Serbia or temporarily remained there, special attention has been given to providing assistance and support to refugees and asylum seekers; this has been reflected in a number of academic papers.[92] In particular, security and victimisation in contemporary wars as well as issues on migration and terrorism (including assistance to victims) were important topics covered in scientific meetings and academic journals during this period.

A major subject of analysis has been the practical implementation of the Istanbul Convention.[93] Research and advocacy of civil society focused on femicide in this period as well.[94] In addition, attention has also focused on exploring the following topics: media's relationship to victims, sexual harassment, work related violence, fear of crime, cyber victimisation, restorative justice, victimisation of people with mental disabilities, victims of hate crimes, the elderly as victims, victims of peer violence, ecological crime, discrimination, etc.

Within the third round of the International Self-Report Delinquency Study (ISRD3), the Faculty of Special Education and Rehabilitation, University of Belgrade, in cooperation with the Victimology Society of Serbia, conducted a self-reported delinquency study in Serbia. The study was conducted in 2013 and 2014 on a representative sample of primary and secondary school students. A victimisation survey was implemented as a part of this study.[95] In 2013, a victimisation survey was also carried out by the VDS in country's multi-ethnic border communities: this occurred in the FP7 research project ALTERNATIVE.[96]

---

91 *Jovanović, Simeunović-Patić & Macanović* 2012; *Nikolić-Ristanović* 2013a; 2015; *Nikolić-Ristanović & Simić* 2014.

92 *Ćopić & Ćopić* 2017; 2018; *Krstić* 2012.

93 *Branković* 2013; *Petrušić, Konstantinović-Vilić & Žunić* 2015; *Soković* 2014.

94 *Batrićević* 2016; *Konstantinović-Vilić* 2013; *Pavićević, Glomazić & Ilijić* 2016; *Rakić* 2017; *Simeunović-Patić & Jovanović* 2013; *Spasić, Kolarević & Luković* 2017.

95 *Nikolić-Ristanović* 2016.

96 *Nikolić-Ristanović, Ćopić, Petrović & Šaćiri* 2017.

An important novelty in the development of victimology in Serbia has been the interest of researchers in topics related to positive victimology, such as posttraumatic growth, the place of yoga in victim support and victimisation prevention, mindfulness and happiness as factors that can contribute to recovery process and decrease of risk from victimisation and fear of crime, etc.[97] At most conferences of the VDS, papers on positive victimology were presented. Moreover, positive criminology was a key theme for an issue of the academic journal "Temida" in 2015. Also during this period, the first systematised bibliography of victimological literature published in Serbia in the period 1980–2012 was published. This represents an important source for exploring the development of victimology in Serbia.[98]

The number of faculties in Serbia in which victimology is studied as a separate subject also increased: from three in the previous period to eight. According to data collected by the VDS in 2017, victimology was studied most often as an elective subject at an undergraduate or postgraduate level (six faculties).[99] As a compulsory subject, victimology is studied at two faculties: at the Faculty of Special Education and Rehabilitation, University of Belgrade (undergraduate),[100] and at the Faculty of Applied Security, Educons University in Sremska Kamenica (postgraduate [masters]).[101]

---

97 *Nikolić-Ristanović* 2010; 2014a; 2014b; 2015; *Vasiljević-Prodanović* 2015.

98 *Madžarac & Vukotić* 2012.

99 Law Faculty, University of Niš; Faculty of Security and Law Faculty at the University of Belgrade; Academy of Criminalistics and Police Studies; Faculty of Applied Security at the Educons University in Sremska Kamenica; Law Faculty, University of Priština and the Department for Legal Sciences at the International University in Novi Pazar; see *Nikolić-Ristanović & Ćopić* 2017.

100 In 2015, the Faculty of Special Education and Rehabilitation, University of Belgrade, became the only faculty in Serbia to teach victimology as an obligatory course at undergraduate level.

101 Victimological issues have also been explored during this period within other courses (see *Nikolić-Ristanović & Ćopić* 2017), such as:

1) Violence against children;
2) Women and prison;
3) Juvenile delinquency;
4) Qualitative methods in criminology and victimology;
5) Research in criminology, victimology and social response to delinquency (Faculty of Special Education and Rehabilitation, University of Belgrade);
6) Legal gender studies;
7) Gender equality and gender based violence (Law Faculty, University of Niš); and
8) Gender law (Law Faculty, University of Belgrade).

4. Development of a Legal Framework to Protect Victims

A number of measures have been taken by Serbian authorities to improve the position of crime victims in recent years. New laws have been passed and existing laws have been re-examined and modified. In addition, various policy documents, such as strategies, national action plans, and protocols have been adopted; various state bodies have also been established to effectively implement these new laws into practice; Serbian NGOs (and international donors) have also been vital in the implementation of these changes (in particular the draft laws designed by the VDS).[102] As also noted above, the EU accession process and the harmonisation of Serbian legislation with the EU acquis, as well as the ratification of numerous international treaties, has also pushed this process onwards.

The first legal changes, which marked the beginning of major improvements to the legal position and protection of victims in Serbia, occurred soon after social and political changes in 2000.[103] In general, legal reforms have proceeded in three main directions. Firstly, reforms to the substantive criminal law, particularly those that occurred during 2002 and 2003. These reforms were primarily related to criminalising domestic violence, marital rape, and human trafficking, which in turn established a favourable legal basis for the protection of these particular victim categories.[104] This trend continued with further reforms to the Serbian Criminal Code, through criminalising, for instance, sexual harassment, stalking, and female genital mutilation. Improved measures were also put in place to stop re-victimisation after trial. Secondly, from 2001 numerous criminal procedure reforms took place. This resulted in the establishment of a basis for, at least to some extent, the active role of victims in criminal procedures and the creation of further measures to hinder secondary victimisation. The third direction of reforms can be seen in the adoption of special laws to better protect certain categories of victims, inducing children, victims of organised crime, victims of war crimes, victims of domestic violence, victims of work-related abuse, discrimination, etc.[105] In recent years, hints of restorative justice have also begun to enter the criminal and juvenile justice system.

In the text that follows, the analysis will turn towards the

1) position of victims in criminal proceedings;
2) introduction of elements of restorative justice;

---

102 *Lindgren & Nikolić-Ristanović* 2011.

103 *Ćopić* 2011; *Lindgren & Nikolić-Ristanović* 2011; *Nikolić-Ristanović* 2006.

104 *Ćopić* 2011; *Dokmanović* 2011; *Konstantinović-Vilić & Petrušić* 2011; *Nikolić-Ristanović* 2006.

105 *Jovanović* 2011; *Nikolić-Ristanović* 2011b; *Petrušić & Stevanović* 2011.

3) legal protection for vulnerable victims; and
4) protection from re-victimisation and secondary victimisation.

4.1 Victim (Injured Party) in Criminal Proceedings

The term 'victim' does not exist in Serbian criminal legislation. Instead, the term 'injured party' is used. It is defined in the Criminal Procedure Code (CPC) as a person whose personal or property rights have been violated or endangered by a crime.[106] The injured party can have several procedural roles (which can also be combined). Although an injured party is generally a direct victim of a crime, he/she is not necessarily a party to the proceedings. In most cases, a victim, i.e., an injured party, will appear in the criminal procedure in the capacity of a witness, as most crimes are prosecuted *ex officio*, i.e., the public prosecutor is the only legitimate prosecutor who can initiate a criminal procedure. However, an injured party is always a potential (subsidiary) prosecutor in cases of crimes prosecuted *ex officio*.[107] For certain criminal offences, defined by the Criminal Code, an injured party can initiate a criminal procedure by submitting a private charge (criminal offences prosecuted *ex parte*); thus, in these cases, he/she will have a position of a private prosecutor in the criminal procedure. For a certain category of criminal offences prosecuted *ex officio*, the public prosecutor can initiate a procedure only upon previous proposal given by the victim, i.e., the injured party. Finally, the injured party can also appear in a criminal procedure as a person who claims damage restitution.

Prior to the reforms that began in 2000, the injured party still had most of the rights relevant to his/her active role in the criminal procedure, such as: the right to propose evidence and view the case files; to be informed on the dismissal of criminal charges or withdrawal of criminal prosecution; to file a complaint against the decision of the public prosecutor not to take or refrain from criminal prosecution; to be informed about the possibilities to take over the criminal prosecution and present charges; to ask questions and make objections or give explanations about statements of other actors, and to present closing arguments; to appear as a subsidiary or private prosecutor (including access to free legal representative if a subsidiary prosecutor without appropriate financial recourses), etc.

After 2000, reforms introduced a number of novelties: return of the injured party's proposition as a condition for criminal prosecution of certain criminal offences prescribed by law, extension of the right of an injured party to a complaint, removal of some limitations on the rights of a private prosecutor, and some possibilities to

---

106 Article 2 of the Criminal Procedure Code, Law No. 72/2011-3, 28.09.2011, Official gazette 72/2011.

107 *Škulić* 2000, p. 7.

access restorative justice.[108] Depending on the stage of the criminal procedure, the public prosecutor and the court will now inform the injured party of his/her rights. An injured party can exercise his/her rights on his/her own or via a legal representative. However, victims do not have an access to free legal aid and they have to bear expenses of legal representation by themselves, unless the perpetrator is convicted and obliged to pay for the costs of the procedure, including costs of the victim's legal representative. Although an injured party has the right to assert a claim for damages, the court is not obliged to decide on this during the criminal proceedings and victims are mainly referred to civil procedures to resolve a damages claim.[109]

Recent procedural law reforms have resulted in a reversal of some previous steps. It now seems that an objection is the only legal remedy given to an injured party in certain number of cases, but this is not an effective legal remedy. Possibilities for an injured party to gain the status of a subsidiary prosecutor have decreased in comparison to the CPC from 2001, since this possibility does not exist prior to an indictment being confirmed. As will be seen below, instead of enhancing the victim's role, when some forms of diversion measures (i.e., prosecutorial discretion) are applied, the legislature has taken a backward step and made the victim completely passive in these cases. In 2014, the CPC introduced plea barging to all criminal courts (it has been used in Serbia's special courts for war crimes and organised crime since 2009), but it completely excludes an injured party from participating in this process, which impairs the victim's position.[110]

4.2 Introducing Restorative Justice into the Criminal and Juvenile Justice System

Peaceful settlement of disputes in Serbia and other parts of the former Yugoslavia have a long history.[111] Until the 19th century, there were different organisational forms of social response to disputes among people: the court of good people, special commissions, the court of the elderly, etc., which applied customary law to solve conflicts and disputes among community members. One may also find elements of restorative justice in response to crimes in the period after World War II, in the form of peace councils and other self-governing courts.[112] However, it was only after reforms post-2005 that a basis was created for the broader inclusion of restorative justice into the Serbian criminal and juvenile justice system. Elements of restorative justice are contained in the provisions of the Criminal Procedure Code, the Criminal

---

108 *Ćopić* 2011; 2015; *Grubač & Beljanski* 2002; *Nikolić-Ristanović & Ćopić* 2006.

109 *Janković Jovanović & Vasić* 2017.

110 Criminal Procedure Code, Law No. 55/2014-41, 23.05.2014, Official gazette 55/2014.

111 *Sahati* 1985.

112 *Sahati* 1985, pp. 180–181.

Code,[113] and the Law on Juvenile Offenders and Criminal Protection of Juveniles,[114] as well as in various by-laws. In 2005, the first Law on Mediation was adopted; it was later amended and, in 2014, replaced by a new law.[115] The new law regulates mediation, which can be applied in criminal matters, but only with regard to claims for restitution and compensation.

In 2001, the CPC introduced prosecutorial discretion. The public prosecutor may postpone a criminal prosecution for a criminal offence punishable with a fine or imprisonment for up to five years, if the suspect agrees to fulfil one or more obligations,[116] some of which may lead to the material satisfaction of a victim (although it is not necessary for the parties to meet). However, when applying this provision, the public prosecutor does not have to ask for the consent of the injured party nor is the prosecutor obliged to inform the injured party in advance about a decision to postpone prosecution. This can therefore result in secondary victimisation of a victim. In respect to this provision, the legislature made a backwards step in comparison to the rules found in the CPC from 2001. Previously, at least for the implementation of certain obligations, the public prosecutor needed the victim's consent prior to their application (e.g., for paying certain amount of money to the benefit of a humanitarian organisation, fund or public institution, and for performing certain community service or humanitarian work). In the 2006 and 2009 reforms to the CPC, the list of possible obligations was broadened and it was possible to now implement them not only in the pre-trial stage, but also once a trial had begun.[117] Thus, instead of further enhancement of this particular institute, basing it more on restorative jus-

---

113 Criminal Code, Law No. 85/2005-30, 06.10.2005, Official gazette 85/2005; Law No. 55/2014-41.

114 Law on Juvenile Offenders and Criminal Protection of Juveniles, Law No. 85/2005-99, 06.10.2005, Official gazette 85/2005.

115 Law on Mediation in Dispute Resolution, Law No. 55/2014-48, 25.05.2014, Official gazette 55/2014.

116 These are:

1) to rectify the detrimental consequence caused by the criminal offence or indemnify the damage caused;
2) to pay a certain amount of money to the benefit of a humanitarian organisation, fund or public institution;
3) to perform certain community service or humanitarian work;
4) to fulfil maintenance obligations which have fallen due;
5) to attend alcohol or drug treatment programme;
6) to submit to psycho-social treatment for the purpose of eliminating the causes of violent conduct; and
7) to fulfil an obligation determined by a final court decision, or observe a restriction determined by a final court decision.

117 *Bejatović, Đurđić, Škulić, Ilić, Kiurski, Matić, Lazić, Nenadić & Trninić* 2012, p. 14.

tice principles that could have given victims more active role, the legislator made a step backward and entirely excluded participation of the victim. Another institute with restorative justice potential foreseen in the CPC is settlement between a private prosecutor and the suspect. In cases of criminal offences prosecuted *ex parte*, a judge can call the private prosecutor and the suspect to introduce them to the process of mediation. If the parties consent, the judge can refer them to mediation. If mediation results in an agreement, the judge will dismiss the case.

Elements of restorative justice are visible in two provisions of the Criminal Code. Firstly, in the settlement between an offender and an injured party. The court may decide not to punish a perpetrator (of a criminal offence punishable by imprisonment of up to three years or a fine) if the offender has fulfilled all obligations from an agreement previously reached with the victim. Additionally, the court may also decide not to punish a perpetrator of a criminal offence (punishable by imprisonment of up to five years) if, following the commission of the offence and before learning that he has been uncovered, the offender eliminates the consequences of the offence or compensates damages caused by the crime. Although it is not necessary for the parties to meet and enter into a dialogue, this provision may result in the material satisfaction of a victim. Secondly, elements of restorative justice are visible in provisions on suspended sentence with protective supervision. The court may order protective supervision of an offender serving a suspended sentence during probation, which includes assistance, care, and protection measures provided by the law. Protective supervision may consist of one or more obligations, including eliminating or mitigating the damage caused by the offence, particularly reconciliation with the victim.

Elements of restorative justice are also introduced into the Law on Juvenile Offenders and Criminal Protection of Juveniles. Firstly, diversion orders can be made at different stages of the procedure against a juvenile. One of them is the settlement with the injured party (via compensation, apology, work, or otherwise) to alleviate the detrimental consequences suffered (in part or in full).[118] Secondly, the court may order one or more alternative sanctioning measures if relevant demands or bans are necessary to influence the juvenile and his/her behaviour. These are, *inter alia*, the following alternative sanctions:

1) to apologise to the injured party;
2) to compensate for the damage caused, within his/her personal capacity; and
3) to participate, without remuneration, in the work of a humanitarian organisation or perform community work of a social, local, or environmental character.

---

118 *Ćopić & Maletić* 2016.

4.3 Legal Protection of Certain Categories of Victims

When speaking about legal protection of certain categories of victims, we mainly refer to those victims considered most vulnerable (i.e., victims of domestic violence, sexual violence, human trafficking) as well as some other groups of victims, such as victims of work-related violence. Legal changes relating to domestic and sexual violence, as well as human trafficking, were initiated at the behest of, and largely based on drafts written by the VDS's experts. The basis for these changes was a legislative draft submitted to the authorities in 1998, with the idea to be included in the draft of the Criminal Code of the Federal Republic of Yugoslavia.[119] The draft consisted of the "New Model of Legal Protection from Domestic Violence",[120] a draft concerning the chapter on sexual violence based on a new conception of sexual violence offences, and a draft concerning the criminal offence of human trafficking. Later on, in 2002, a more systematic and comprehensive draft, called the "New Model of Laws on Trafficking in People" was prepared. In general, advocacy for legal reforms was primarily oriented towards the harmonisation of reforms affecting the Criminal Code, the Criminal Procedure Code, the Family Code, the Law on Civil Procedure, the Law on Weapons and Munitions, the Law on Misdemeanours, and the Law on the Movement and Residence of Foreign Nationals.

Advocacy for legal reforms resulted in domestic violence being criminalised in the Criminal Code of Serbia in 2002. Domestic violence is a separate criminal offence, prosecuted *ex officio*; it includes not only physical violence but also psychological violence against a family member. Family member is broadly defined and can include partners, former partners, children, and other relatives (including in-laws), as well as foster and adoptive parents. Reforms also introduced protection (restraining) orders into the Family Code[121] in 2005. A range of protection orders can now be issued by way of a civil procedure,[122] while their violation is punishable as the most lenient form of a criminal offence of domestic violence. This is a good example of

---

119 Although this law was never passed, the VDS's draft was used as a basis for the new Criminal Code of Serbia in the 2000s.

120 The "New Model of Legal Protection from Domestic Violence" followed two years of monitoring the trials of battered women who killed their abusers and awareness-raising campaigns organised by women's NGOs. The first draft (later modified to reflect existing legislative trends) was based on the research findings and reports on trial monitoring, as well as on the research of international and domestic law, while the Minnesota Domestic Abuse Act and the Duluth Model were used as guidelines for its drafting.

121 Family Code, Law No. 18/2005-26, 18.02.2005, Official gazette 18/2005.

122 The Family Code contains the following protection orders: injunction for an abuser to move out of a flat or house disregarding his/her property or rental rights on the real estate; injunction for moving a victim into a flat or house disregarding property or rental rights on the real estate; prohibition of approaching a family member at a certain distance; prohibition of access to the area around the workplace and home of a family member; prohibition of further harassment of a family member (non-molestation order).

the interaction between criminal and civil norms; the Criminal Code supports the protective measures provided by the Family Code. In 2013, Serbia ratified the Istanbul Convention. This was followed by the adoption of the Law on the Prevention of Domestic Violence[123] in 2016, which came into effect in June 2017. The purpose of the Law is to secure effective prevention of domestic violence and to provide urgent, adequate, and efficient protection and support to victims of domestic violence. Thus, it rests upon the 3P approach: prevention, protection, and prosecution. Domestic violence is broadly defined to include physical, sexual, psychological, or economic violence (a definition that is broader when compared to the definition of the criminal offence of domestic violence in the Criminal Code). It is stipulated that victims of domestic violence have the right to information, the right to free legal aid, and the right to an individual plan of protection and support. The Law foresees two emergency measures: temporary removal of the perpetrator from the property (house or flat) and a temporary restraining order, i.e., a ban on contact with the victim.

Advocacy for legal reforms on sexual violence has resulted in numerous legislative changes. Marital rape became punishable in 2002. Reforms of the Criminal Code in 2005 brought additional improvements:

1) providing for more severe punishments for all sexual offences, particularly for sexual violence against children and disabled persons, as well as in cases when a sexual crime results in victim's pregnancy; and
2) providing for a new concept of rape which assures the same protection to victims regardless of gender and sexual orientation, which means that the provision of rape includes both heterosexual and homosexual rape as well as coercion to vaginal as well as oral, anal, and similar sexual acts. A step forward in providing protection to victims, particularly to victims of gender-based violence, was made by introducing stalking, sexual harassment, and female genital mutilation into the Criminal Code in 2016,[124] while the protection of victims of all these forms of violence falls under the Law on the Prevention of Domestic Violence.

Finally, advocacy for legal reforms concerning human trafficking has resulted in its criminalisation as a separate criminal offence, which is in line with the trafficking definition given in the UN Protocol to Prevent, Suppress and Punish Trafficking in Persons, Especially Women and Children,[125] and providing for the delay of depor-

---

123 Law on the Prevention of Domestic Violence, Law No. 94/2016-3, 24.11.2016, Official gazette 94/2016.

124 Criminal Code, Law No. 94/2016-7, 24.11.2016, Official gazette 94/2016.

125 Trafficking in persons is defined in Article 3a of the Protocol to Prevent, Suppress and Punish Trafficking in Persons; see Protocol to Prevent, Suppress and Punish Trafficking in Persons, No. 55/25, 15.11.2000; https://www.ohchr.org/en/ProfessionalInterest/Pages/ProtocolTraffickingInPersons.aspx [18.04.2019]. It encompasses three main elements:

tation of victims of trafficking and issuing them with a temporary residence permit. Additionally, the 2005 Criminal Code criminalised the trafficking of children for the purpose of adoption as a separate criminal offence.[126]

It is worth mentioning that the 2011 Law on Social Protection[127] brought certain novelties relevant to the protection of victims. Both victims of domestic violence and human trafficking are recognised as users of social welfare services. The Law recognises the prevention of and protection from abuse, neglect, and exploitation as goals of social protection. Additionally, counselling and support to victims of violence, as well as SOS hotlines, are now recognised as social protection services.

By passing the Law on Prevention of the Abuse at the Workplace[128] in 2010, as well as a set of anti-discrimination laws (the Law on the Prohibition of Discrimination,[129] the Law on Gender Equality,[130] and the Law on Prevention of Discrimination against Persons with Disabilities[131]) a legal basis for protecting victims of work-related violence and different forms of discrimination was established. For example, the Law on the Prevention of the Abuse in the Workplace prohibited workplace abuse (including sexual harassment) and established several countermeasures (i.e., of a restorative, preventive, protective, and repressive nature). Employers are also now responsible for the well-being and protection of their employees. Finally, the law puts the burden of proof at the perpetrator.[132]

4.4 Protection from Re-Victimisation and Secondary Victimisation

Legal changes to protect victims from re-victimisation and secondary victimisation were largely initiated by the VDS. Relevant provisions are contained in several laws:

---

the action (recruitment, transportation, transfer, harbouring or receipt of persons), *the means* (threat or use of force or other forms of coercion, of abduction, of fraud, of deception, of the abuse of power or of a position of vulnerability or of the giving or receiving of payments or benefits to achieve the consent of a person having control over another person), and *the purpose* (exploitation, including exploitation for prostitution or other forms of sexual exploitation, forced labour or services, slavery or practices similar to slavery, servitude or the removal of organs).

126 Law No. 85/2005-30.

127 Law on Social Protection, Law No. 24/2011-15, 04.04.2011, Official gazette 24/2011.

128 Law on Prevention of the Abuse at the Workplace, Law No. 36/2010-3, 28.05.2010, Official 36/2010.

129 Law on the Prohibition of Discrimination, Law No. 22/2009-3, 30.03.2009, Official gazette 22/2009.

130 Law on Gender Equality, Law No. 104/2009-61, 16.12.2009, Official gazette 104/2009.

131 Law on Prevention of Discrimination against Persons with Disabilities, Law No. 33/2006-3, 17.04.2006, Official gazette 33/2006.

132 Law No. 36/2010-3.

Criminal Code, Criminal Procedure Code, Law on the Program of Protection of the Participants in the Criminal Procedure,[133] Law on Juvenile Offenders and Criminal Protection of Juveniles, Law on Misdemeanours, etc.

4.4.1 Protection from Re-Victimisation

The Serbian CPC has important provisions for the protection of victims from physical abuse and threats in the courtroom. The authority conducting proceedings is required to protect an injured party or a witness from an insult, threat, or any other attack that endangers his/her safety (basic protection). In certain cases, special police protection measures can also be applied.

The Serbian Law on Misdemeanours[134] also contains a provision on a protection order: the prohibition of access to the victim (the injured party), property, or a place where the misdemeanour was committed. It aims to prevent contact between the offender and the victim when the victim feels that he/she is endangered. However, unlike protection orders in the Family Code, which can be issued only to the perpetrator of domestic violence, this protection order is applicable to all misdemeanours.

In 2009, the Criminal Code introduced a security measure called the prohibition of approaching and communicating with the victim, which aims to avoid re-victimisation after the trial. It includes:

1) prohibition of approaching the victim within a certain distance;
2) prohibition of access to the area around the workplace or home of the victim; and
3) prohibition of further harassment of the victim or communication with her/him.[135]

Protection from intimidation and re-victimisation is also provided by provisions of the Law on the Program of Protection of the Participants in the Criminal Procedure.[136] This Law established a basis for protecting the physical integrity of a broad circle of persons, including a victim and persons close to the victim. Protection is not limited to the trial (protection in the courtroom), but is also possible before and after the effective conclusion of criminal proceedings. A protection program encompasses the following measures: physical protection of persons and property, change of a place of residence, concealing of identity and ownership information, and change of identity, which may be followed by changing physical characteristics of a protected

133 Law on the Program of Protection of the Participants in the Criminal Procedure, Law No. 85/2005-150, 06.10.2005, Official gazette 85/2005.

134 Law on Misdemeanours, Law No. 65/2013-6, 25.06.2013, Official gazette 65/2013.

135 Criminal Code, Law No. 72/2009-53, 03.09.2009, Official gazette 72/2009.

136 Law No. 85/2005-150.

person. However, the Law is limited in two ways: by the form of the criminal offence and the relevance of the testimony of a person that should be granted protection. Protection is limited to only three groups of criminal offences: criminal offences against the constitutional order and security, criminal offences against humanity and other values protected by international law, and criminal offences of organised crime. Moreover, protection can only be granted if there is a real danger to life, health, physical integrity, freedom, or property due to testifying or providing information in criminal proceedings, and without that testimony or information, it would be considerably more difficult or impossible to prove the commission of a crime. This leads to the conclusion that victims (injured parties) which "are not important witnesses" will not be able to be included in this program of protection.[137]

4.4.2 Protection from Secondary Victimisation

By introducing best practice in questioning vulnerable victims as witnesses, the Serbian CPC establishes a legal framework for the protection of victims from secondary victimisation, which is of paramount importance, particularly if keeping in mind that witnesses, including victims are still the irreplaceable source of evidence.[138] Protection can be granted for vulnerable witnesses and protected witnesses. Additionally, protection from secondary victimisation can be achieved by using other evidence in criminal proceedings (which may eliminate or at least limit the extent of a victim's examination), as well as through the training and specialisation of the authorities responsible for collecting testimony and evidence in certain criminal cases.

According to the CPC, a 'particularly vulnerable witness' is a witness who is particularly vulnerable due to his/her age, experience, lifestyle, gender, state of health, nature, the manner or the consequences of the criminal offence committed, or other circumstances.[139] The Code foresees several measures of questioning in order to avoid secondary victimisation, including:

1) indirect questioning, which means that a particularly vulnerable witness may be examined only through the authority conducting the proceedings, who will treat the witness with particular care, endeavouring to avoid possible detrimental consequences of the criminal proceedings on the personality and/ or physical and mental state of the witness;
2) examination with the assistance of a psychologist, social worker, or other professional;
3) examination via video-link; and

137 *Paunović* 2006, p. 452.

138 *Brkić* 2014.

139 For more information about this particular institute, see *Brkić* 2014.

4) examination outside of the court premises. Additionally, as a principle, a particularly vulnerable witness may not be confronted with the defendant.

If, by giving testimony or answering certain questions, a witness would expose him/herself or persons close to him/herself to a substantial danger to life, health, freedom, or property, he/she can be granted the status of a protected witness. This status may be granted *ex officio* by the court, or at the request of the public prosecutor or the witness. The court may impose one or more measures of special protection, which include questioning the protected witness under conditions and in a manner ensuring that his/her identity is not revealed to the general public, and in exceptional circumstances, also not to the defendant and his/her defence counsel. Such measures can include the exclusion of the public from the trial and the prohibition of publication of data about the identity of the witness. The CPC foresees several ways in which protection could be achieved: alteration or erasure of data on the identity of the witness from the record, concealment of the witness's appearance, examination from a separate room with distortion of the witness's voice, and examination using video-link.

It is worth mentioning here that the reforms of the CPC in 2006 were the most prosperous. Apart from introducing above-mentioned institutes, 2006 CPC brought another important novelty: it was possible to prohibit asking the victim (injured party) or a witness certain questions. These prohibitions related to sexual lifestyle and habits, political or ideological opinions, racial, national, or ethnical status, moral views, familial circumstances. Such questions were prohibited if they were not directly linked to solving the particular criminal case. The essence of these provisions was to eliminate stigmatisation, secondary victimisation, and re-traumatisation of a victim. Unfortunately, later reforms to the CPC excluded this provision and it no longer exists in the Serbian criminal justice system.

The Law on Juvenile Offenders and the Criminal Protection of Juveniles foresees special rules for questioning minor victims to prevent secondary victimisation, including the following: limiting the number of questioning (in principle, the questioning may be conducted at most twice), questioning with the assistance of a psychologist, counsellor, or other qualified person, questioning via video-link, etc. In principle, confrontation between the juvenile victim and the defendant is prohibited. Finally, a juvenile victim must have a legal representative from the first hearing of the defendant.[140]

Applying some other provisions, such as those on hearing cooperating convicted person, may also be relevant for protecting victims from secondary victimisation, in terms that it may prevent putting a burden of testifying on a victim and mostly basing the court decisions on his/her testimony.

---

[140] Law No. 85/2005-99.

Lastly, increasing awareness among state actors and authorities about the damaging effects of secondary victimisation in certain cases is also of vital importance. This has led to the specialisation of evidence-gathering. For example, in cases of organised crime or war crimes, all procedures are conducted in courts of special jurisdiction situated in Belgrade (establishing substance matter instead of territorial jurisdiction). This can prevent victims being exposed to threats, intimidation, or revenge in their local communities. Moreover, prosecutors and judges are now better educated and sensitised, being aware that relevant preconditions are necessary to prevent secondary victimisation.

5. Discussion and Conclusions

Similar to other countries, research in the field of victimology in Serbia initially focused on crime victims. However, over time the field was extended to include victims of war and human rights violations. Thus, we may argue that the study of victims of conventional crime has been marginalised in some way in comparison with the study of victims of domestic violence, human trafficking, war, discrimination, and work-related violence, as well as other forms of human rights violations.

If, however, the explicit declaration of domestic authors on the subject of victimology is considered, it should be noted that only in the earliest period of development of victimology, during the 1980s, did the narrowest notion prevail. At that time, it was advocated by *Milutinović* and *Nikolić-Ristanović*.[141] Today, advocacy for a wider understanding of the subject of victimology prevails, though it still remains within the framework of dealing with crime victims. *Nikolić-Ristanović*, who had advocated in her earlier works that victimology should deal only with victims of crime, later adopted a broader definition.[142] Namely, in the textbook "Criminology", together with *Konstantinović-Vilić*[143] and *Kostić*,[144] in accordance with the wider understanding of the notion of crime, she broadened the definition of the subject of victimology in accordance with the manner determined by representatives of critical and radical victimology.[145] According to these authors, the subject of victimology involves dealing with issues related to victims of all forms of crime, including both those prescribed as punishable acts and violations of human rights that are not foreseen as criminal offences by national laws, although international documents require their punishment. Thus, as argued by these authors, apart from victims of conventional crime, victims of all other crimes, as defined above, present the subject of victimolo-

---

141 *Milutinović* 1979; *Nikolić-Ristanović* 1984.

142 *Nikolić-Ristanović* 1984.

143 *Konstantinović-Vilić & Nikolić-Ristanović* 1998; 2003; 2004.

144 *Konstantinović-Vilić, Nikolić-Ristanović & Kostić* 2010; 2012.

145 *Mawby & Walklate* 1994; *Ronel* 2015; *Ronel & Toren* 2012.

gy, including victims of white-collar crime, structural crime, war, and state violence. In addition, in accordance with the main assumptions of critical victimology, these authors consider that linking science and activism is of pivotal importance for victimology, i.e., studying both the social context in which victimological knowledge is gained and its potential impact on the real improvement of the victim's position.

Similarly, *Ignjatović* and *Simeunović-Patić* define the subject of victimology in the following way: it encompasses dealing with victims of wrongful acts, whether they are prescribed as criminal offences by national laws or constitute "serious violations of fundamental human rights determined in the international treaties that protect human rights".[146] *Simović-Hiber,* however, uses the definition of victimology, whereby the subjects are victims of crime (which is understood in legal terms, i.e., as criminal offences prescribed by national laws) and the abuse of state power. This understanding falls between the narrowest and broadest concepts of victimology.[147]

Finally, *Nikolić-Ristanović* argues for the broadest notion of the subject of victimology, arguing for a science that deals with all victims of suffering, regardless of whether they are considered victims of crime in any sense or not.[148] *Nikolić-Ristanović* considers that current victimology developments, both in Serbia and worldwide, form a good basis for further expansion towards inclusion of all victims in the subject category. As *Mendelsohn* wrote at the very beginning of the development of victimology, "victimology should deal with all victims in the same way as medicine deals with all patients and all diseases or as criminology deals with all perpetrators and all types of crime".[149]

When it comes to the subject of victimology in Serbia, it is necessary to emphasise the importance given to special forms of victimology, such as feminist, narrative, positive, transnational, and cultural victimology, and more recently, environmental victimology. Nevertheless, it is evident that, as in other countries, despite a broadening of the subjects that fall under the term of victimology, it primarily remains a science that relates to crime victims (albeit though now understood in a broader sense).

In Serbia, as in other countries, a single movement for the rights of victims has not been created. Instead, separate or non-coordinated initiatives and movements are often involved. Various approaches to solving problems of victims are visible, being quite often underlined by different ideologies. Moreover, as expected, trends in Serbia are more similar to those in Europe than, for example, in the United States of America. It can be argued that, from the very beginning, a combination of a retributive and a social approach to the problems of victims prevailed in Serbia. A retrib-

---

146 *Ignjatović & Simeunović-Patić* 2011, p. 17.

147 *Simović-Hiber* 2009.

148 *Nikolić-Ristanović* 2013b.

149 *Mendelsohn* 1976, p. 21.

utive-instrumental approach is present as well. This approach reduces the care for victims primarily to advocacy for their adequate treatment by state authorities in order to provide evidence and, consequently, harsher penalties for the perpetrators. Thus, care for victims is seen as a means to achieve repression, although this goal is not necessarily requisite for the victim. This approach is particularly visible in relation to victims of human rights violations and war crimes. It can be very dangerous, since it encourages victims to be vengeful and unrealistic about punishment, but it does not help them cope with trauma. There is also another form of instrumental approach, which makes support and assistance to victims conditional on the victim's cooperation with the criminal justice system or on not sending a victim back to the abuser or the trafficker, or on previous checks by certain state agencies to see whether the person is recognised as a victim, etc. In these cases, it is obvious that the interest of the state to combat certain forms of crime and other political interests, and related stereotypes about genuine and wrong, that is, good and bad victims, are put ahead of the needs and interests of the victims. In recent years, the rhetoric of "the war on crime" and "the war against the mafia" has had a particularly strong impact in Serbia, primarily related to drug trafficking, human trafficking, and the smuggling of migrants.

Finally, restorative justice measures, particularly the possibility of victim-offender reconciliation, have created conditions for abolitionist approach, i.e., for improving the position of victims by offering the possibility of informal conflict resolution. However, these measures are designed in a way that benefits the perpetrator more than the victim.[150] Consequently, in the context of the newly introduced measures of restorative justice in Serbia, one can still speak of an instrumental/rehabilitation approach that is guided by the interests of the perpetrator, rather than about an abolitionist or informal approach, which would take equal care of both the victim and the offender.

In conclusion, we can state that the situation of crime victims in Serbia has received increasing attention during recent decades, both by researchers and by society at large. A number of reforms and improvements have been carried out to improve the availability of assistance programs and support for victims. Examples of these reforms are legal changes, increased awareness about certain categories of victims, and development of non-state and state victim services.

One factor behind the increase in victim awareness is the work of the women's movement to expose male violence against women and, in parallel, against children. In recent years, other particularly vulnerable groups of victims have also been focused on, such as victims of homophobic crimes, human trafficking, and war crimes. However, in Serbia, many victims of crime, such as victims of robbery, burglary,

---

150 *Ćopić* 2011; 2015; *Nikolić-Ristanović & Ćopić* 2006.

traffic accidents, or the relatives of murdered people, are still largely invisible and are not recognised as victims in need of assistance and protection.

There is, however, a risk that even awareness about certain victims will only result in rhetoric and not action. The British victimologists *Mawby* and *Walklate* state that "crime victims" have received a large symbolic value in the justice system and in the debate on penal policy.[151] This does not, however, necessarily lead to an improvement in their situation. It can actually lead to frustration on the part of crime victims if their actual situation does not reflect the ambitions expressed by the society. This can erode their faith and trust in society, since they do not receive the aid and support that they have heard so much about.

Thus, unlike developments in many other countries, a holistic approach to victims is still unrecognisable in Serbia. Therefore, it is of utmost importance that during past years, primarily under the influence of international law, institutions and organisations (primarily the European Union and the Council of Europe) more favourable climate for wider social acceptance of the holistic approach to the rights of victims have been created. This holistic approach, which has been further developed by the VDS since its establishment in 1997, should help create systemic and best-practice solutions for the problems of victims in Serbia.

Analysis of Serbian policies and legislation on victims has proven that, in spite of progress, there are numerous shortages, gaps, and inconsistencies, which inhibit adequate implementation of laws in practice.[152] Many victims are still left unrecognised. There are no legal obligations on specific authorities to provide support to victims as required under the EU law.[153] The number of victims that can obtain assistance and support from victim support services is generally very low. There is no systematic and comprehensive state effort to support victims and prevent victimisation. There is no national network of victim support services, nor is there a national referral mechanism. Support is primarily linked to criminal proceedings, excluding access to victims outside the justice system. Appropriate education is lacking among police officers, judges, prosecutors, and lawyers on the proper treatment of victims, as well as the prevention of secondary victimisation.

To conclude, strengthening the rule of law and fundamental rights, including victims' rights, is a serious challenge for Serbia during the EU accession process. In this respect, transposition and implementation of the EU Victims' Rights Directive into national legislation and practice has been recognised as a key objective, as defined in the Accession Action Plan for Chapter 23 (Judiciary and fundamental rights). The

---

151 *Mawby & Walklate* 1994, p. 169.

152 *Ćopić* 2011; *Lindgren & Nikolić-Ristanović* 2011; *Nikolić-Ristanović* 2011a.

153 Analysis of victims' rights and services in Serbia and their alignment with EU Directive 2012/29/EU; see Multi-Donor Trust Fund for Justice Sector Support in Serbia, World Bank & Victim Support Europe 2017b; 2017c.

Accession Action Plan states that the normative framework will be aligned with the EU Victims' Rights Directive, establish victim support services, and create the capacities for the full implementation of minimum standards on the rights, support, and protection of victims of crime. Therefore, the accession process is an important opportunity to develop an effective and efficient legal and institutional framework for victims' rights, protection, and support.

6. Summary in Serbian

Interesovanje istraživača i javnosti za žrtve kriminaliteta u Srbiji primetno je tokom proteklih nekoliko decenija. Tokom 1980-ih javljaju se prvi sistematizovani naučni radovi i empirijska istraživanja u oblasti viktimologije, kao i prve inicijative za poboljšanje položaja žrtava, posebno zahvaljujući zalaganjima feministkinja. Na dalji razvoj vezan za žrtve, tokom 1990-ih, poseban uticaj imali su i sledeći faktori: inicijative organizacija za ljudska prava, razvoj viktimologije kao akademske discipline, porast kriminaliteta u Srbiji, etnički sukobi na prostoru bivše Jugoslavije, humanitarne intervencije povezane sa ratom. Zalaganja organizacija civilnog društva su u velikoj meri doprinela promeni odnosa države prema pitanjima žrtava. Najintenzivniji razvoj, koji je doveo do brojnih pozitivnih promena, usledio je tek nakon političkih promena 2000. godine. Od 2012. godine, u kontekstu pristupnih pregovora Srbije i harmonizacije zakonodavstva sa pravom EU i drugim međunarodnim ugovorima, stvoreni su povoljni uslovi za šire društveno prihvatanje holističkog pristupa pravima svih žrtava i pružanju pomoći i podrške. Brojne reforme su doprinele unapređenju pravne zaštite žrtava i dostupnosti pomoći i podrške žrtvama. Pa ipak, još uvek postoje brojni nedostaci i nekonzistentnost propisa i politika, što otežava adekvatnu primenu zakona u praksi i jednak pristup uslugama podrške i zaštite za sve žrtve. Polazeći od toga, u ovom poglavlju dat je pregled razvoja vezanog za žrtve u Srbiji, uključujući razvoj viktimologije i pokreta za prava žrtava, kao i razvoj zakonodavnog okvira relevantnog za zaštitu žrtava.

Literature

Aćimović, M. (1981): Žrtvin iskaz u krivičnom postupku [Victim's statement in the criminal proceedings]. Jugoslovenska revija za kriminologiju i krivično pravo [Yugoslav Journal of Criminology and Criminal Law] 2, pp. 215–222.

Aćimović, M. (1980): Diskusija na savetovanju o savremenim oblicima terorizma [Discussion at the seminar about contemporary forms of terrorism]. Arhiv za pravne i društvene nauke [Archive of Law and Social Studies], pp. 1–2.

Aćimović, M. (1979): Duševno obolela lica kao žrtve krivičnih dela [Mentally ill people as crime victims]. Zbornik Pravnog fakulteta u Nišu [Proceedings of the Law Faculty in Niš] 18, pp. 103–110.

Babović, M. (2018): Gender equality index for the Republic of Serbia. Measuring gender equality in the Republic of Serbia 2016. Belgrade.

Babović, M. (2016): Gender equality index for Serbia. Measuring gender equality 2014. Belgrade.

Babović, M., Ginić, K. & Vuković, O. (2010): Mapiranje porodičnog nasilja prema ženama u Centralnoj Srbiji [Mapping domestic violence against women in Central Serbia]. Belgrade.

Banjanin-Đuričin, N. (1998): Udarac po duši: sociološka studija zlostavljanja dece u porodici [A blow to the soul: Sociological study on child abuse in the family]. Belgrade.

Batrićević, A. (2016): Krivičnopravna reakcija na femicide [The reaction to femicide in criminal law]. Temida 3-4, pp. 431–452.

Bejatović, S. (1993): Oštećeni u krivičnom postupku [An injured party in the criminal procedure]. Belgrade.

Bejatović, S., Đurđić, V., Škulić, M., Ilić, G., Kiurski, J., Matić, M., Lazić, R., Nenadić, S. & Trninić, V. (2012): Primena načela oportuniteta u praksi: izazovi i preporuke [The application of the principle of opportunity in practice: Challenges and recommendations]. Belgrade.

Bjerkan, L. (ed.) (2005): The life on one's own: The rehabilitation of victims of trafficking for sexual exploitation. Oslo.

Blagojević, M. (1998): Ka vidljivoj ženskoj istoriji: ženski pokret u Beogradu 90-tih [Towards visible women's history: Women's movement in Belgrade in the 1990s]. Belgrade.

Bojanin, S. & Išpanović-Radojković, V. (1994): Adolescenti i stresovi rata [Adolescents and war stress]. Belgrade.

Branković, B. (2013): Vesti iz budućnosti: Istanbulska konvencija i odgovornost države za borbu protiv nasilja nad ženama. Funkcionisanje opštih servisa – operacionalizacija dužne priježnosti [The news from the future: Istanbul convention and the responsibility of the state for combating violence against women. Functioning of the generic services – Operationalisation of the due diligence]. Belgrade.

Brkić, S. (2014): Posebno osetljivi svedoci [Particularly vulnerable witnesses]. Zbornik radova Pravnog fakulteta u Novom Sadu [Proceeding of the Faculty of Law in Novi Sad] 2, pp. 211–227.

Ćetković, N. (1998): U traganju za sigurnim zenskim mestom [In the search of safe women's place]. Belgrade.

Ćopić, S. (2015): Restorativna pravda i krivičnopravni sistem: teorija, zakonodavstvo i praksa [Restorative justice and criminal justice system: Theory, legislation and practice]. Belgrade.

Ćopić, S. (2011): Položaj i zaštita žrtve u krivičnom postupku [Position and protection of victims in the criminal procedure], in: V. Nikolić-Ristanović & S. Ćopić (eds.), Prava žrtava i EU: izazovi pružanja pomoći [Victims' rights and the EU: Challenges of victim support]. Belgrade, pp. 135–160.

Ćopić, S. (2010): Restorativna pravda i krivičnopravni sistem [Restorative justice and criminal justice system]. Niš.

Ćopić, S. (2007): Službe za žrtve u Srbiji: rezultati istraživanja [Victim support services in Serbia: survey results]. Temida 2, pp. 13–28.

Ćopić, S. & Ćopić, S. (2018): Zaštita prava migranata u Srbiji: Od humanitarnog zbrinjavanja ka integraciji i socijalnoj inkluziji [Protection of migrants' rights in Serbia: From humanitarian protection to integration and social inclusion]. Zbornik Instituta za kriminološka i sociološka istraživanja [Proceedings of the Institute for Criminologcal and Sociological Research], 2, 7–27.

Ćopić, S. & Ćopić, S. (2017): Migranti, azilanti, izbeglice: Određenje i razgraničenje osnovnih pojmova i implikacije na pravni status lica i nivo njihove zaštite [Migrants, asylum seekers, refugees: Defining main terms and making distinctions between them. Implications on legal status and the level of protection]. Teme [Themes] 1, pp. 1–22.

Ćopić, S. & Maletić, N. (2016): Implementation of diversion order settlement with the injured party: The practice of the Centre for social work in Belgrade, in: I. Stevanović & A. Batrićević (eds.), Krivične i prekršajne sankcije i mere: izricanje, izvršenje i uslovni otpust [Criminal and misdemeanor sanctions and measures: Imposing, enforcement and conditional release]. Belgrade, pp. 295–306.

Ćopić, S. & Nikolić-Ristanović, V. (2006): Mehanizam praćenja trgovine ljudima u Srbiji [Mechanism of monitoring trafficking in human beings in Serbia], in: J. Škrnjug (ed.), Praćenje fenomena trgovine ljudima – BiH, Hrvatska, Srbija [Mechanisms for the monitoring trafficking in human beings phenomenon – Bosnia and Herzegovina, Croatia, Serbia]. Belgrade, pp. 67–96.

Ćopić, S. & Šaćiri, B. (2012): Žene u zatvoru u Srbiji: uslovi za život osuđenica u Kazneno-popravnom zavodu za žene u Požarevcu [Women in prison in Serbia: Living conditions for female prisoners in the Correctional Institution for Women in Požarevac]. Temida 4, pp. 23–44.

Ćopić, S., Stevković, L. & Šaćiri, B. (2012): Tretman i ostvarivanje prava osuđenica u Kazneno-popravnom zavodu za žene u Požarevcu [The treatment and the realization of the female prisoners' rights in the Correctional Institution for Women in Požarevac]. Temida 4, pp. 45–71.

Dokmanović, M. (2011): Međunarodni i evropski standardi o žrtvama rodno baziranog nasilja i usklađenost zakonodavstva Srbije sa njima [International and European standards on victims of gender based violence and the level of harmonization of Serbian legislation with them], in: V. Nikolić-Ristanović & S. Ćopić (eds.), Prava žrtava i EU: izazovi pružanja pomoći [Victims' rights and the EU: Challenges of victim support]. Belgrade, 17–36.

Garcia-Moreno, C., Jansen, H.A.F.M., Ellsberg, M., Heise, L. & Wats, C. (2006): Prevalence of intimate partner violence: findings from the WHO multi-country study on women's health and domestic violence. The Lancet 368, pp. 1260–1269.

Grubač, M. & Beljanski, S. (2002): Nove ustanove i nova rešenja u Zakoniku o krivičnom postupku SR Jugoslavije [New institutes and solutions in the Criminal Procedure Code of the FR Yugoslavia]. Belgrade.

Hanak, N., Tenjović, L., Išpanović-Radojković, V., Vlajković, A. & Beara, M. (2013): Epidemiološko istraživanje nasilja nad decom u Srbiji [Epidemiological research of violence against children in families in Serbia]. Temida 2, pp. 75–102.

Ignjatović, Đ. & Simeunović-Patić, B. (2011): Viktimologija [Victimology]. Belgrade.

Janković, I. (1989): Political prisoners as victims, in: Z. Šeparović (ed.), Victimology: International action and study of victims, Vol. II. Zagreb, pp. 69–75.

Janković Jovanović, A. & Vasić, M. (2017): Victims within Criminal Law in Serbia. Belgrade.

Jovanović, S. (2011): Zlostavljanje na radnom mestu: pravna zaštita žrtava u međunarodnoj i nacionalnoj perspektivi [Work related abuse: Legal protection of victims in the international and national perspective], in: V. Nikolić-Ristanović & S. Ćopić (eds.), Prava žrtava i EU: izazovi pružanja pomoći [Victims' rights and the EU: Challenges of victim support]. Belgrade, pp. 119–134.

Jovanović, S., Simeunović-Patić, B. & Macanović, V. (2012): Krivičnopravni odgovor na nasilje u porodici [Criminal legal responses to domestic violence]. Novi Sad.

Kaličanin, P., Bukelić, J., Išpanović-Radojković, V. & Lečić-Toševski, D. (1993): Stresovi rata [War stresses]. Belgrade.

Kešetović, Ž. (2013): Serbian police: Troubled transition from police force to police service, in: G. Meško, C.B. Fields, B. Lobnikar & A. Sotlar (eds.), Handbook on policing in Central and Eastern Europe. New York, pp. 217–238.

Konstantinović-Vilić, S. (2013): Femicid kao oblik rodno zasnovanog nasilja [Femicide as a form of gender based violence]. Zbornik radova Pravnog fakulteta u Nišu [Proceedings of the Faculty of Law in Niš] 64, pp. 33–52.

Konstantinović-Vilić, S. & Nikolić-Ristanović, V. (2004): Kriminologija [Criminology]. Niš.

Konstantinović-Vilić, S. & Nikolić-Ristanović, V. (2003): Kriminologija [Criminology]. Niš.

Konstantinović-Vilić, S. & Nikolić-Ristanović, V. (1998): Kriminologija [Criminology]. Niš.

Konstantinović-Vilić, S. & Petrušić, N. (2007): Krivično delo nasilje u porodici – aktuelna pravosudna praksa u Nišu i Beogradu [Criminal offence of domestic violence – Current legal practice in Nis and Belgrade]. Belgrade.

Konstantinović-Vilić, S. & Petrušić, N. (2011): Instrumenti pravne zaštite od nasilja u porodici u Srbiji: funkcionisanje, efikasnost i nedostaci [Instruments of legal protection from domestic violence in Serbia: Functioning, effectiveness and shortcomings], in: V. Nikolić-Ristanović & S. Ćopić (eds.), Prava žrtava i EU: izazovi pružanja pomoći [Victims' rights and the EU: Challenges of victim support]. Belgrade, pp. 69–85.

Konstantinović-Vilić, S. & Petrušić, N. (2004): Krivično delo nasilja u porodici – pravna praksa u Republici Srbiji [Criminal offence of domestic violence – Legal practice in the Republic of Serbia]. Niš.

Konstantinović-Vilić, S., Nikolić-Ristanović, V. & Kostić, M. (2012): Kriminologija [Criminology]. Niš.

Konstantinović-Vilić, S., Nikolić-Ristanović, V. & Kostić, M. (2010): Kriminologija [Criminology]. Niš.

Kostić, M. (2010): Viktimitet starih ljudi [Victimisation of the elderly]. Niš.

Kramarić, I. (1982): Jugoslovenska bibliografija iz oblasti viktimologije (1961–1981) [Yugoslav bibliography in the field of victimology (1961–1981)]. Jugosloveska revija za kriminologiju i krivično pravo [Yugoslav Journal of Criminology and Criminal Law] 3, pp. 365–368.

Krstić, I. (2012): Zaštita prava migranata u Republici Srbiji [Protection of migrants' rights in the Republic of Serbia]. Belgrade.

Lindgren, M. & Nikolić-Ristanović, V. (2011): Crime victims: International and Serbian perspective. Belgrade.

Madžarac, V. & Vukotić, J. (2012): Bibliografija viktimološke literature u Srbiji 1980–2012 [Bibliography of the victimological literature in Serbia 1980–2012]: Belgrade.

Mawby, R. & Walklate, S. (1994): Critical victimology. London.

Mendelsohn, B. (1976): Victimology and contemporary society' trends. Victimology 1, pp. 8–28.

Milivojević, S. (1999): Nasilje u porodici za vreme agresije NATO alijanse na SR Jugoslaviju [Domestic violence during NATO aggression on the FR Yugoslavia]. Temida 2, pp. 45–47.

Milivojević, S. & Mihić, B. (2003): Organizacije koje pružaju pomoć žrtvama kriminaliteta u Beogradu (rezultati istraživanja) [Non-governmental organizations assisting victims of crime in Belgrade – Survey results]. Temida 1, pp. 37–43.

Milutinović, M. (1979): Kriminologija [Criminology]. Belgrade.

Mršević, Z. (1997): Incest između mita i stvarnosti [Incest in between the myth and reality]. Belgrade.

Mrvić-Petrović, N. (2001): Naknada štete žrtvi krivičnog dela [Compensation to crime victims]. Belgrade.

Nikolić, J. (2007): Službe za decu i specijalizovane organizacije za osobe sa invaliditetom i Rome u Beogradu [Services for children and specialized organization for disabled persons in Roma and Belgrade]. Temida 2, 29–40.

Nikolić, J., Nikolić-Ristanović, V. & Petrović, N.M. (2010): Stanje raspoloživih usluga i kapaciteta za pomoć žrtvama nasilja u porodici u Vojvodini i upoznatost i zadovoljstvo žena sa njima [Available services, capacity to help victims of domestic violence in Vojvodina and the awareness and satisfaction of women with these services]. Temida 2, 61–79.

Nikolić-Ristanović, V. (ed.) (2016): Delinkvencija i viktimizacija maloletnih lica u Srbiji: Rezultati Međunarodne ankete samoprijavljivanjem delinkvencije [Delinquency and victimisation of minors in Serbia: The results of the International Self-Report Delinquency Study]. Belgrade.

Nikolić-Ristanović, V. (2015): Osobe sa dijagnozom kancera kao žrtve/preživeli: obrasci viktimizacije, osnažujuća podrška i posttraumatski rast [Persons with cancer diagnosis as victims/survivors: Patterns of victimization, empowering support and posttraumatic growth]. Temida 3-4, pp. 31–52.

Nikolić-Ristanović, V. (2014a): Joga i žrtve [Yoga and victims]. Temida 1, pp. 47–64.

Nikolić-Ristanović, V. (2014b): Making people happy is the best crime prevention: Towards happy-making criminology. European Journal of Criminology 4, 401–409.

Nikolić-Ristanović, V. (2013a): Praćenje primene zakonskih rešenja o nasilju u porodici u Srbiji: nalazi pilot istrazivanja [Monitoring the application of domestic violence legislation in Serbia: pilot survey findings]. Belgrade.

Nikolić-Ristanović, V. (2013b): Different understandings of the notion of victim and their consequences on social attitude towards victimisation, in: M. Ambrož, K. Filipčić & A. Završnik (eds.), Zbornik za Alenko Šelih [Commemorative for Alenka Šelih]. Ljubljana, pp. 383–399.

Nikolić-Ristanović, V. (2011a): Izazovi pružanja pomoći žrtvama u Srbiji [Challenges of victim support in Serbia], in: V. Nikolić-Ristanović & S. Ćopić (eds.), Prava žrtava i EU: izazovi pružanja pomoći [Victims' rights and the EU: Challenges of victim support]. Belgrade, pp. 163–178.

Nikolić-Ristanović, V. (2011b): Pravna zaštita žrtava ratnih zločina u Srbiji [Legal protection of victims of war in Serbia], in: V. Nikolić-Ristanović & S. Ćopić (eds.), Prava žrtava i EU: izazovi pružanja pomoći [Victims' rights and the EU: Challenges of victim support]. Belgrade, 103–118.

Nikolić-Ristanović, V. (2010): Moguća primena joge u viktimologiji [Possible use of yoga in victimology], in: P. Nikić (ed.), Joga – svetlost mikrouniverzuma [Yoga – The light of the microuniversum]. Belgrade, pp. 161–166.

Nikolić-Ristanović, V. (ed.) (2010): Nasilje u porodici u Vojvodini [Domestic violence in Vojvodina]. Novi Sad.

Nikolić-Ristanović, V. (ed.) (2009): Male victim of trafficking in Serbia. Belgrade.

Nikolić-Ristanović, V. (2008): Preživeti tranziciju: svakodnevni život i nasilje nad ženama u postkomunističkom i posleratnom društvu [Surviving transition: Everyday life and violence against women in post-communist and post-war countries]. Belgrade.

Nikolić-Ristanović, V. (2007): Razvoj službi za pomoć i podršku žrtvama kriminaliteta u Srbiji [Development of services for victims in Serbia]. Temida 2, pp. 5–11.

Nikolić-Ristanović, V. (2006): Zaštita žrtava i svedoka u kontekstu pravnih i društvenih reformi u Srbiji [Protection of victims and witnesses in the context of legal and social reforms in Serbia]. Pravni život [Legal Life] 9, pp. 1079–1089.

Nikolić-Ristanović, V. (2002a): Social change, gender and violence: Post-communist and war-affected societies. Dordrecht.

Nikolić-Ristanović, V. (ed.) (2002b): Porodično nasilje u Srbiji [Domestic violence in Serbia]. Belgrade.

Nikolić-Ristanović, V. (2000a): Women, violence and war. Budapest.

Nikolić-Ristanović, V. (2000b): Žrtve ratova u bivšoj Jugoslaviji: obim, struktura i obrasci viktimizacije [War victims in the former Yugoslavia: Scope, structure and characteristics of victimisation]. Temida 2, pp. 11–21.

Nikolić-Ristanović, V. (2000c): Od žrtve do zatvorenice: nasilje u porodici i kriminalitet žena [From a victim to a prisoner: Domestic violence and women's crime]. Belgrade.

Nikolić-Ristanović, V. (1999a): Viktimizacija kriminalitetom u Beogradu: uticaj rata i društvenih promena [Crime victimisation in Belgrade: The influence of war and social changes]. Temida 1, pp. 31–43.

Nikolić-Ristanović, V. (1999b): Žrtve agresije NATO-a na SRJ: struktura viktimizacije [Victims of NATO aggression on the FRY: the structure of victimisation]. Temida 2, pp. 22–29.

Nikolić-Ristanović, V. (1998a): The international crime victim survey in Belgrade (FRY), in: The international crime victim survey in countries in transition – National reports. Rome, pp. 547–565.

Nikolić-Ristanović, V. (1998b): Victims and police in Belgrade. International review of victimology 1, pp. 49–63.

Nikolić-Ristanović, V. (1997): Prison for women in Serbia. Temida 1, pp. 5–10.

Nikolić-Ristanović, V. (1996): Domestic violence against women in the conditions of war and economic crisis, in: C. Sumner, M. Israel, M. O'Connell R. & Sarre (eds.), International victimology. Canberra, pp. 75–79.

Nikolić-Ristanović, V. (1995): Fear of Crime in Belgrade. International Review of Victimology 6, pp. 15–33.

Nikolić-Ristanović, V. (1994): Feminist research as process of empowering: an example of research on violence against women in war, in: What can we do for ourselves. Belgrade, pp. 111–115.

Nikolić-Ristanović, V. (1993): Bračno nasilje: teoretski okvir i rezultati dosadašnjih istraživanja [Spouse abuse: Theoretical framework and up-to-date research findings]. Sociološki pregled [Sociological Review] 1/4, pp. 275–293.

Nikolić-Ristanović, V. (1989a): The state of woman as victim of sex offenses in the criminal procedure of Yugoslavia, in: Z. Šeparović (ed.), Victimology: International action and study of victims, Vol. II. Zagreb, pp. 191–194.

Nikolić-Ristanović, V. (1989b): Žene kao žrtve kriminaliteta [Women as crime victims]. Belgrade.

Nikolić-Ristanović, V. (1988): Krivičnopravna zaštita dece od nasilja u porodici (situacija u Jugoslaviji) [Criminal protection of children from domestic violence (Situation in Yugoslavia)], in: Z. Šeparović (ed.), Nasilje u obitelji [Domestic violence]. Dubrovnik, pp. 75–79.

Nikolić-Ristanović, V. (1987): Viktimizacija pešaka u saobraćaju i mere za njeno suzbijanje [Victimisation of pedestrians and the measures of its suppression]. Jugoslovenska revija za kriminologiju i krivično pravo [Yugoslav Journal of Criminology and Criminal Law] 2, pp. 113–130.

Nikolić-Ristanović, V. (1984): Uticaj žrtve na pojavu kriminaliteta [The influence of the victim on the phenomenon of crime]. Belgrade.

Nikolić-Ristanović, V. & Ćopić, S. (eds.) (2017): Viktimološko društvo Srbije: 20 godina zalaganja za prava svih žrtava [Victimology Society of Serbia: 20 years of standing up for the rights of all victims]. Belgrade.

Nikolić-Ristanović, V. & Ćopić, S. (2011a): Combating trafficking in human beings for labour exploitation in Serbia, in: C. Rijken (ed.), Combating trafficking in human beings for labour exploitation. Nijmegen, pp. 223–282.

Nikolić-Ristanović, V. & Ćopić, S. (eds.) (2011b): Prava žrtava i EU: izazovi pružanja pomoći [Victims' rights and the EU: Challenges of victim support]. Belgrade.

Nikolić-Ristanović, V. & Ćopić, S. (2010): Pomoć i podrška ženama žrtvama trgovine ljudima u Srbiji [Assistance and support to women victims of trafficking in persons in Serbia]. Belgrade.

Nikolić-Ristanović, V. & Ćopić, S. (2006): Položaj žrtve u Srbiji: klasični krivični postupak i mogućnosti restorativne pravde [The position of victims in Serbia: Criminal procedure and possibilities of restorative justice]. Temida 1, pp. 67–75.

Nikolić-Ristanović, V. & Hanak, N. (2004): Od sećanja na prošlost ka pozitivnoj budućnosti – kakav model istine i poverenja/pomirenja je potreban Srbiji [From remembering the past towards positive future – what kind of model and trust/reconciliation is needed in Serbia]. Belgrade.

Nikolić-Ristanović, V. & Milivojević, S. (2000): Viktimizacija žena nasiljem u porodici: uticaj socijalnih faktora vezanih za društvene promene i životnu dob [Victimisation of women by domestic violence: The impact of social factors related to social change and the age]. Temida 1, pp. 20–28.

Nikolić-Ristanović, V. & Mrvić, N. (1990): Strah od kriminaliteta u Beogradu [Fear of crime in Belgrade]. Zbornik Instituta za kriminološka i sociološka istraživanja [Proceedings of the Institute for Criminological and Sociological Research] 1, pp. 343–361.

Nikolić-Ristanović, V. & Mrvić, N. (1988): Prvi kontakt žrtve sa policijom – pomoć i podrška, ili ponovna viktimizacija [Victim's first contact with the police – Assistance and support, or re-victimisation]. Revija za kriminologiju i krivično pravo [Journal of Criminology and Criminal Law] 4, pp. 81–92.

Nikolić-Ristanović, V. & Simić, V. (eds.) (2014): Međusektorska saradnja u procesu zaštite žrtava nasilja u porodici u Kragujevcu [Inter-sector cooperation in the process of protection of women victims of domestic violence in Kragujevac]. Kragujevac.

Nikolić-Ristanović, V. & Srna, J. (eds.) (2008): Mogući put do pomirenja u Srbiji: zajednička akcija za istinu i pomirenje [Possible path to reconciliation in Serbia: Join action for truth and reconciliation]. Belgrade.

Nikolić-Ristanović, V., Ćopić, S., Nikolić, J. & Šaćiri, B. (2018): Podrška žrtvama u izabranim državama Balkana: Komparativna perspektiva [Victim support in the selected Balkan countries: Comparative perspective]. Belgrade.

Nikolić-Ristanović, V., Ćopić, S., Nikolić, J. & Šaćiri, B. (2012): Diskriminacija žena na tržištu rada [Discrimination of women at the labour market in Serbia]. Belgrade.

Nikolić-Ristanović, V., Ćopić, S., Petrović, N. & Šaćiri, B. (2017): Conflicts, victimisation and restorative justice in intercultural settings: an example of action research in Serbia, in: I. Vanfraechem & I. Aertsen (eds.), Action research in criminal justice – Restorative justice approaches in intercultural settings. New York, pp. 99–116.

Nikolić-Ristanović, V., Ćopić, S., Simeunović-Patić, B., Milivojević, S. & Mihić, B. (2004): Trafficking in people in Serbia. Belgrade: OSCE.

Nikolić-Ristanović, V., Konstantinović-Vilić, S., Mrvić-Petrović, N., Stevanović, I. & Knežić, B. (1996): Žene Krajine: rat, egzodus i izbeglištvo [Women from Krajina: War, exodus and refugee]. Belgrade.

Nikolić-Ristanović, V., Mrvić-Petrović, N., Konstantinović-Vilić, S. & Stevanović, I. (1995): Žene, nasilje i rat [Women, violence and war]. Belgrade.

Nikolić-Ristanović, V., Stevanović, I. & Knežić, B. (1997): The use of physical force and other coercive measures during the civil and student protest against the annulment of the municipal elections results in Serbia. Temida 1, pp. 24–33.

Obretković, M. (1998): Nasilje u porodici i prava deteta na zaštitu [Domestic violence and child's right to protection]. Temida 1, pp. 3–8.

Obretković, M. (1997): Multidisciplinarni model zaštite dece – žrtava nasilja [Multidisciplinary model of protection of children –Victims of violence]. Temida 3-4, pp. 3–10.

Otašević, S. (ed.) (2005): Nasilje u partnerskim odnosima i zdravlje [Violence in partner relationships and health]. Belgrade.

Paunović, S. (2006): Program zaštite učesnika u krivičnom postupku [The program of protection of participants in the criminal procedure], in: D. Radovanović (ed.), Novo krivično zakonodavstvo: dileme i problemi u teoriji i praksi [New criminal legislation: Dilemmas and problems in theory and practice]. Belgrade, pp. 449–463.

Petrušić, N. & Stevanović, I. (2011): Pravna zaštita dece u Srbiji i međunarodni standardi [Legal protection of children in Serbia and international standards], in: V. Nikolić-Ristanović & S. Ćopić (eds.), Prava žrtava i EU: izazovi pružanja pomoći [Victims' rights and the EU: Challenges of victim support]. Belgrade, pp. 87–102.

Pavićević, O., Glomazić, H. & Ilijić, L. (2016): Femicid kao deo strukture nasilja [The femicide as a part of the culture of violence]. Temida 3-4, pp. 453–476.

Petrušić, N., Konstantinović-Vilić, S. & Žunić, N. (2015): Institucionalni seksizam: prepreka efikasnoj zaštiti od nasilja u porodici [Institutional sexism: An obstacle to an effective protection against domestic violence]. Temida 1, pp. 31–54.

Radovanović, J. (1989): Loneliness among the young as victimisation, in: Z. Šeparović (ed.), Victimology: International action and study of victims, Vol. II. Zagreb, pp. 87–190.

Radovanović, J. (1988): Zlostavljanje i zapostavljanje dece: subjektivno iskustvo deteta [Abuse and neglect of children: Subjective experience of a child], in: Z. Šeparović (ed.), Nasilje u obitelji [Domestic violence]. Dubrovnik, pp. 99–101.

Rakić, J. (2017): Genitalno sakaćenje žena – od tradicije do femicide [Female genital mutilation – From tradition to femicide]. Temida 2, pp. 241–267.

Ronel, N. (2015): Why victimology should stay positive – The ongoing need for positive victimology. Temida 3-4, pp. 5–16.

Ronel, N. & Toren, T. (2012): Positive victimology: An innovation or "more of the same"? Temida 2, pp. 171–180.

Sahati, E. (1985): Uloga mirovnog veća u krivičnom postupku [The role of the peace council in the criminal procedure]. Jugoslovenska revija za krivično pravo i kriminologiju [Yugoslav Journal of Criminal Law and Criminology] 2–3, pp. 177–183.

Simeunović-Patić, B. & Jovanović, S. (2013): Žene žrtve ubistva u partnerskom odnosu [Women victims of homicide in partner relationship]. Belgrade.

Simović-Hiber, I. (2009): Okviri viktimologije [The frameworks of victimology]. Belgrade.

Soković, S. (2014): Žrtve i savremene tendencije u kontroli kriminaliteta [Victims and contemporary tendencies in crime control]. Temida 1, pp. 5–27.

Spasić, D., Kolarević, D. & Luković, Z. (2017): Femicid u partnerskim odnosima [Femicide in partnership relations]. Temida 3, pp. 411–434.

Stevković, L. & Dimitrijević, J. (2011). Viktimizacija starih u porodičnom i institucionalnom okruženju [Victimisation of the elderly in the family and in the institutions], in: V. Nikolić-Ristanović & S. Ćopić, S. (eds.), Prava žrtava i EU: Izazovi pružanja pomoći žrtvama [Victims' rights and the EU: Challenges of victim support]. Belgrade, pp. 335–354.

Šeparović, Z. (1998): Viktimologija - studije o žrtvama [Victimology – A study on victims]. Zagreb.

Šeparović, Z. (1985): Viktimologija - studije o žrtvama [Victimology – A study of victims]. Zagreb.

Škulić, M. (2000): Oštećeni u krivičnom postupku – kako poboljšati njegov položaj [Injured party in the criminal procedure – How to improve his position]. Temida 3-4, pp. 5–19.

Vasiljević-Prodanović, D. (2015): Pozitivna psihologija i njen doprinos pozitivnoj viktimologiji [Positive psychology and its contribution to the development of positive victimology]. Temida 3-4, pp. 17–30.

Zvekić, U. (2001): Žrtve kriminala u zemljama u tranziciji [Crime victims in countries in transition]. Belgrade.

Documents

Commissariat for Refugees and Migration (2016): Migracijski profil Republike Srbije za 2015. godinu [Migration Profile of the Republic of Serbia for 2016]. Belgrade; http://www.kirs.gov.rs/docs/migracije/migracioni%20profil%202016.pdf [25.3.2018] [in Serbian and English].

Commissariat for Refugees and Migration (2015): Migracijski profil Republike Srbije za 2015. godinu [Migration profile of the Republic of Serbia for 2015]. Belgrade; http://www.kirs.gov.rs/docs/migracije/migracioni%20profil%202015.pdf [25.3.2018] [in Serbian and English].

Multi-Donor Trust Fund for Justice Sector Support in Serbia & World Bank (2017a): Analysis of the harmonisation of the regulation on police of the Republic of Serbia compared to the provisions contained in the EU Directive 2012-29 on establishment minimum standards on the rights, support and protection of victims of crime. Belgrade; https://victimsupport.eu/activeapp/wp-content/files_mf/1506075535Legalanalysis_FINAL_%D0%95ngl.pdf [16.01.2018] [in English only].

Multi-Donor Trust Fund for Justice Sector Support in Serbia, World Bank & Victim Support Europe (2017b): Operating networks for victim support services. Belgrade; https://victimsupport.eu/activeapp/wp-content/files_mf/1506075235WB_networkoperationsreport_final.pdf [16.01.2018] [in English only].

Multi-Donor Trust Fund for Justice Sector Support in Serbia, World Bank & Victim Support Europe (2017c): Overview of existing victim support services in Serbia. Belgrade; http://www.mdtfjss.org.rs/en/mdtf_activities/2017/victims-access-to-support-services-in-serbia#.XLggldJMSUl [16.01.2018] [in English only].

Statistical Office of the Republic of Serbia (StatOffice) (2017a): [Demografska statistika 2016] Demographic yearbook 2016. Belgrade [in Serbian and English]; cited as: StatOffice 2017a.

Statistical Office of the Republic of Serbia (StatOffice) (2017b): [Žene I muškarci u Republici Srbiji] Women and men in the Republic of Serbia. Belgrade [in Serbian and English]; cited as StatOffice 2017b.

Statistical Office of the Republic of Serbia (StatOffice) (2017c): [Anketa o radnoj snazi u Republici Srbiji] Labour force survey in the Republic of Serbia, 2016. Belgrade [in Serbian and English]; cited as StatOffice 2017c.

Statistical Office of the Republic of Serbia (StatOffice) (2014): [2011 Census atlas] 2011 Census atlas. Belgrade [in Serbian and English]; cited as: StatOffice 2014.

StatOffice: see Statistical Office of the Republic of Serbia.

United Nations High Commissioner for Refugees (2015): Tražioci azila u 2015. godini [Asylum seekers in 2015]. Belgrade; http://www.unhcr.rs/dokumenti/statisktike/azil.html [30.1.2018] [in Serbian and English].

Slovenia

Victimology and Victimological Research – Past, Present, and Future Challenges[1]

Gorazd Meško, Katja Eman, Rok Hacin & Urška Pirnat

1. Introduction

Slovenia, which gained independence from the former republic of the Socialist Federal Republic of Yugoslavia in 1991, is a parliamentary republic.[2] Slovenia covers an area of 20,273 square kilometres. According to the latest census conducted by the Statistical Office of the Republic of Slovenia, on 1 April 2017, Slovenia had 2,064,836 inhabitants; the average age was 43 years-old. The number of females (1,039,823) exceeded the number of males (1,025,013) in 2017, while the number of foreign nationals currently living in Slovenia amounts to 115,841 (5.6% of the population).[3] Slovenia has three official languages:

1) Slovene,
2) Hungarian (second official language in the territory of eastern Slovenia inhabited by the Hungarian national minority), and
3) Italian (second official language in the territory of south-western Slovenia inhabited by the Italian minority).[4]

In 2016, 443,608 people had no formal education or had not completed elementary school, 925,832 people had finished secondary school, and 388,358 people had completed some form of higher education. In 2016, population growth in Slovenia was positive (656 people); the same also applied to migration (1,051 new residents), as

---

1 This chapter is based on part of a national research project entitled Safety and Security in Local Communities, which was financed by the Slovenian Research Agency (2015–2018; grant number: P5-0397).

2 *Konte* 1996.

3 StatOffice 2017b.

4 Government of the Republic of Slovenia 2017.

16,623 foreign nationals migrated to Slovenia and 15,572 Slovenes left the country.[5] In 2016, 984,334 people were living in urban areas; Slovenia has 104 urban areas out of which 67 have a status of a town; however, the population only exceeds 50,000 in two of them (Ljubljana – 288,919 and Maribor – 111,079).[6] According to key economic indicators, Slovenia belongs to the group of developed countries, with a GDP of 18,693 EUR per capita (2017). Slovenia suffered during the 2008 economic crisis, the effects of which can still be observed today, and approximately 79,000 people were still unemployed in 2017 (an unemployment rate of 7.8%).[7]

The Slovene criminal justice system consists of:

1) the police,
2) state prosecution service,
3) the judiciary, and
4) the prison administration.

The Slovene Police Force is a centralised organisation operating at national, regional, and local levels. The Slovene Police Force is headed by the Director General who reports to the Minister of the Interior. Police powers are regulated by the Police Tasks and Powers Act and the Police Organisation and Work Act.[8] The State Prosecutor's Office is an independent entity within the Ministry of Justice and is regulated by the State Prosecution Service Act.[9] The Slovene judiciary is organised as a three-level system (55 local and district courts, 4 high courts, and the Supreme Court), which is regulated by the Courts Act.[10] The Prison Administration of the Republic of Slovenia is an independent body within the Ministry of Justice. It is responsible for the execution of prison sentences in Slovenia. It is headed by the Director General who is responsible to the Minister of Justice. The implementation of penal sanctions is regulated by the Criminal Sanctions Act.[11]

Since 1991, when Slovenia gained its independence after the Ten-Day War, the country has not been involved in armed conflicts. In the past 25 years, no terrorist attacks were recorded. In 2010, student demonstrations in Ljubljana resulted in the

---

5 StatOffice 2017b.

6 Ministry of the Environment and Spatial Planning 2017; StatOffice 2017b.

7 StatOffice 2017a.

8 Police Organisation and Work Act, Law No. 003-02-2/2013-10, 15.02.2013, Official Gazette 15/2013; Police Tasks and Powers Act, Law. No. 003-02-1/2013-2, 07.02.2013, Official Gazette 15/2013.

9 State Prosecution Service Act, Law No. 110-139/2011, 22.07.2011, Official Gazette 58/2011.

10 Courts Act, Law No. 700-04/93-16/30, 27.09.2007, Official Gazette 94/2007.

11 Criminal Sanctions Act, Law No. 713-03/92-5/69, 29.09.2006, Official Gazette 110/2006.

damaging of the Parliament building and in 2012, massive protests against the government and politicians took place in larger Slovene towns, starting in Maribor and reaching their climax in Ljubljana: the protests resulted in police interventions.[12] In 2015, Slovenia was exposed to a severe migration crisis with the number of daily illegal border crossings peaking at 11,000 migrants.[13] In 2015, the intake of refugees was restricted to 2,500 arrivals per day. Moreover, the Slovene army was sent to the border with Croatia, where they assisted police in conducting border patrols.[14] After the passing of legislation, which enabled the Slovene Police Force to use additional technical means at the state border, a wire fence was erected along a 135 kilometre section of the external Schengen border. At the beginning of 2016, the number of migrants decreased due to poor weather conditions. Overall, more than 400,000 migrants crossed the Slovene border during the migration/refugee crisis.[15]

The aim of this paper is to present Slovene victimological research since its inception in 1967.[16] The first part of the paper presents certain theoretical concepts of victimology, as defined by Slovene authors, and provides an overview of the development of victimology in Slovenia and related legal frameworks. The second part of the paper presents victimological research prior to 1991, when Slovenia was part of Yugoslavia and, after 1991, when Slovenia gained its independence. An overview of more than 70 studies conducted in the last 50 years is provided. Furthermore, official statistical data on crime victims and data gained from victimisation surveys conducted in Slovenia are also presented. The final part discusses the implications of previous studies on the development of victimology in Slovenia and the Slovene criminal justice system, with a view to foster the future development of victimology both in Slovenia and in Europe.

2. Theoretical Concepts and the Development of Victimology in Slovenia

Victimological research is essential for understanding situations in which individuals become victims of crime and/or understanding persons who have experienced victimisation. Victimology is defined as a science that deals with the study of victims, the causes and different types of victimisation, the processes and consequences of victimisation, as well as the study of social reactions to victimisation.[17] Victimology is also described as a science that examines the causes of victimisation and

---

12 *Merljak, Belovič, Božič & Potič* 2012.

13 Uniformed Police Directorate 2016.

14 United Nations High Commissioner for Refugees 2016.

15 Uniformed Police Directorate 2016.

16 *Šelih* 1967.

17 *Davies, Francis & Jupp* 2004; *Peršak* 2015.

the characteristics of victims during primary, secondary, and tertiary victimisation. Primary victimisation studies focus on victimisation risks related to lifestyle, as well as the socialisation with criminal peers and friends.[18] In the field of secondary[19] and tertiary victimisation,[20] efforts are directed towards the professionalization (especially sensitisation) of police officers, prosecutors, and judges dealing with crime victims, as well general attitudes towards the victims of crime.[21]

In Slovenia, victimology and victims first became the subject of scientific research via examinations conducted in the 1960s, 1970s, and 1980s at the Institute of Criminology, and later, from the 1990s onwards, at the Faculty of Criminal Justice and Security of the University of Maribor (FCJS UM). The participation of the FCJS UM had a clear advantage from the very beginning of its operation: this advantage stemmed from its close cooperation with the police and other criminal justice agencies. This turned out to be very useful in the process of raising awareness about victims as well as their rights and needs for protection. The FCJS UM did not only take part in the process of educating and training police officers, and subsequently also prosecutors and judges, about how to improve their work when dealing with victims, but also developed close cooperative efforts with non-governmental organizations (NGOs) in this field. In Slovenia, NGOs working with victims are highly developed and well organised. They have also established an active and enduring cooperation with the police. The most successful NGOs working with victims in Slovenia include:

1) Association SOS Help-line for Women and Children Victims of Violence,
2) Association for Nonviolent Communication,
3) White Ring of Slovenia – Association for Victims of Crime,
4) Association Key – Centre for Combating Trafficking in Human Beings,
5) Institution Emma – Victim Assistance Centre, and
6) smaller regional and local associations that often cooperate closely with larger NGOs, which are usually situated in the capital and have regional offices.

---

18 Primary victimisation refers to personal victimisation, where an actual person becomes a first-hand victim of a crime; see *Meadows* 2014.

19 Secondary victimisation (also known as post-crime victimisation) relates to further victimisation following the original victimisation. For example, when a victim of crime meets with law enforcement authorities in the process of criminal proceedings after experiencing a criminal offence.

20 Tertiary victimisation means that a person is victimised by their family, neighbours, or other people in society because of the experienced crime. For example, a man leaves a raped wife because he cannot accept the fact that she was touched by another man (a similar response may also come from the woman's children or relatives). Alternatively, *Meadows* defines tertiary victimisation as an event in which society as a whole becomes a victim; see *Meadows* 2014.

21 *Kanduč* 2002b; *Meško* 2016; *Petrovec* 2005.

Furthermore, the entire territory of Slovenia is well covered with safe houses, crisis centres, and youth centres operating around the clock: each of these offer constant assistance and support to victims.

In Slovenia, zero tolerance of any form of violence has been the norm for many years. At the end of 2008, the Domestic Violence Prevention Act was adopted, which introduced special protection and investigative measures for victims, especially children, and paved the way for the provision of assistance to victims by governmental and non-governmental organisations.[22] In 2016, the Domestic Violence Prevention Act was amended in order to remedy the shortcomings that had become evident in practice and further to protect the victims (e.g., banning corporal punishment of children in the family).[23] Nevertheless, the need to understand that the underlying causes of victimisation (and its consequences) have an impact on the development of crime prevention techniques, as well as the necessity to raise the awareness of potential crime victims, remains important. Moreover, findings from victimological studies offer an insight into crime itself, i.e., the context in which crimes occurs.[24] This means that studying victims, violence, and related phenomena have – and continue to be – the central focus of criminologists and victimologists in Slovenia.

The growing number of victims of criminal offences, the lack of awareness concerning the consequences of victimisation, limited preventive efforts, and growing concerns about human rights were the main factors that influenced the beginnings of victimological research in Slovenia. The first victimological study, conducted in 1967, exposed the importance of victimology in the fight against crime.[25] From its very beginning, victimological research focused on the applicability of foreign research models in the Slovene context. Results of empirical studies, which confirmed the applicability of models from abroad, motivated researchers to devise a theoretical framework of victimology in Slovenia.[26] This also contributed to legislative changes and the development of new crime prevention techniques, including the introduction of self-protective measures against property crime and awareness-raising activities concerning violence against children (as children are a particularly vulnerable victim group).[27] In Slovene law, the role of victims in criminal proceedings is defined in the following acts:

---

22 Domestic Violence Prevention Act, Law No. 003-02-2/2008-9, 11.02.2008, Official Gazette 16/2008.

23 Act Amending the Domestic Violence Act, Law No. 003-02-8/2016-10, 02.11.2016, Official Gazette 68/2016.

24 *Meško* 1998.

25 *Šelih* 1967.

26 *Šelih* 1994.

27 *Šelih* 2012.

1) the Crime Victim Compensation Act[28] regulates the rights to compensation for victims of violent crimes (Article 1 defines victims' rights to compensation in cases of intentional violent crime;[29] Article 8 defines damages on the basis of which victims have the right to compensation;[30] Article 25 defines the obligations of the police to provide victims with information about their rights[31]);
2) the Criminal Code[32] provides protective measures for victims after a crime has been committed (Article 65 defines protective measures [restraining orders against perpetrators]; Article 143 regulates the protection of victims' personal data); and
3) the Criminal Procedure Act[33] prescribes the assistance afforded to victims in the scope of criminal procedures (Article 162 defines that victims of minor criminal offences have the power to consent to the suspension of prosecution of a criminal offence if the offender is willing to remove the harmful consequences of the criminal offence; Article 331 regulates the protection of victims of crime under the age of 15 [it restricts the possibilities for direct questioning during the main hearing]).

The following section presents an overview of victimological research in Slovenia over the past 50 years with a specific focus on:

---

28 Crime Victim Compensation Act, Law No. 001-22-114/05, 07.11.2005, Official Gazette 101/2005.

29 The Crime Victim Compensation Act regulates the right to compensation for victims of intentional violent crime (as well as their dependants). It also outlines the claim proceedings and the relevant decision-making authorities. The Act regulates the competent authorities and the proceedings to be applied in the case of cross-border situations; see Article 1 (Contents of the Act) of the Law No. 001-22-114/05.

30 Article 8(1) stipulates that the eligible person is obliged, except in cases referred to in the preceding Article, to claim indemnification in accordance with the Act governing the criminal procedure, or to bring an action for compensation. Moreover, if the victim acts in accordance with paragraph 1, he or she is eligible to compensation pursuant to the Act, if he or she, in accordance with the Act, can prove that the implementation was not successful; see Article 8 (Types of recognized damage) of the Law No. 001-22-114/05.

31 Article 25(1) states that the Slovene Police Force shall provide information on the possibilities, terms, and conditions concerning enforcement of the rights to the persons intending to enforce them. Moreover, at the request of the person referred to in paragraph 1, the Slovene Police Force shall issue an acknowledgement that the act was detected, reported, and dealt with as a criminal offence. The contents of the certificate shall be determined by the Minister of Justice, in agreement with the Minister of the Interior; see Article 25 (Duties of police) of the Law No. 001-22-114/05.

32 Criminal Code, Law No. 713-01/12-8/2, 14.06.2012, Official Gazette 50/2012.

33 Criminal Procedure Act, Law No. 713-01/11-24/2, 19.04.2012, Official Gazette 32/2012.

1) victimisation surveys,
2) different types of victimisation,
3) provision of assistance to victims,
4) satisfaction of crime victims with the police,
5) fear of crime, and
6) implementation of restorative justice.

3. Victimological Research in Slovenia Before 1991

Prior to Slovenia's independence in 1991, victimological research followed worldwide trends. During this period, 11 victimological studies were conducted in Slovenia, with the first studies focusing on the victimisation of individual groups. In following years, the focus shifted to research on the provision of assistance to victims and structural victimisation.[34]

The first victimological study in Slovenia focused on the role of victimology in combating crime. The study successfully sparked a theoretical discussion regarding the criminological aspects of crime victims.[35] A new perspective on victims, the typology of victims, and victimisation processes were also highlighted. Moreover, researchers exposed the need for further victimological research to benefit criminal policy development and crime prevention. The first empirical study of victims of assault and murder was conducted in the municipality of Šmarje pri Jelšah.[36] The study explored assaults, the nature and circumstances of such offences, as well as the characteristics of the offenders and victims. The findings showed that the backward economic and social trends in the area were the most significant contributors to victimisation and, in terms of prevention, adequate criminal policy should be implemented to improve economic and social conditions among the local population. *Pečar* studied the contribution of victims to their own victimisation in cases of homicide.[37] His findings revealed that in 50% of all cases, the victims somehow provoked the offence and had a problem with alcohol abuse. Moreover, the analysis showed no major differences between victims and offenders regarding their social class, as both groups were members of the lower socioeconomic class. In the same year, the effect of a third person on the offender-victim relationship was studied.[38] The findings paved the way for the introduction of an operational definition of "involved bystanders" and their impact on offenders and victims. This research, conducted in

---

34 *Šelih* 1994.

35 *Šelih* 1967.

36 *Podjaveršek* 1970.

37 *Pečar* 1971a.

38 *Pečar* 1971b.

1972, focused on a somewhat neglected aspect of criminology and victimology.[39]As with most other social sciences, modern victimology, which is an interdisciplinary scientific discipline, makes use of numerous findings of psychology, psychiatry, sociology, criminology, biology, and law. Furthermore, the contribution of victims to their victimisation differs a great deal, thus making their role vary from instigating, attracting, participating, and so forth. *Uderman* conducted a study of homicides in Slovenia and confirmed previous findings regarding offenders' characteristics, as most of them were of low socioeconomic status with poor levels of education.[40] The study of the potential forms of victimisation in supermarkets revealed factors that created opportunities for victimisation, including the social atmosphere in stores, insufficient controls, anonymity of the customers, and impersonal relationships.[41] *Kobe* addressed the position of victims in judicial proceedings.[42] He proposed the introduction of restitution for victims in criminal proceedings and suggested practical solutions for the implementation of restitution within the existing legal framework. *Vodopivec* studied the extent of restitution in cases of assault and property crime.[43] By analysing court files, she learnt that a third of victims were satisfied with the restitution of damage before the court trial. *Pečar* researched the (in)visibility of crime in society and the detection of potential victimisation.[44] He found that awareness of victimisation by victims is dependent on their social status, their attitudes towards crime, the damage suffered, and their confidence in the criminal justice system. He concluded that these factors, together with victims' preparedness to report crime to the authorities, require further attention of researchers. The first victimological survey in Slovenia revealed that approximately 60% of criminal offences against property and 70% of various types of violent crime remained unreported.[45] The main reasons for non-reporting included:

1) insignificance of the incident or damage,
2) perception of victimisation,
3) acquaintance with the offender, and
4) social status of the victim.

Pečar focused on victimogenic relationships in families. The results revealed that family victimisation usually arises from mutual conflicts or from the victimological

---

39 *Pečar* 1972.

40 *Pečar* 1971a; *Uderman* 1972.

41 *Pečar* 1978.

42 *Kobe* 1977.

43 *Vodopivec* 1977.

44 *Pečar* 1979.

45 *Pečar* 1982.

cycle; negative emotions were identified as the primary cause of crime within a family. Moreover, a large amount of unreported crime in domestic violence was observed.[46] *Pečar* conducted a study on the involvement and contribution of third persons in criminogenic situations.[47] He stated that third persons influenced primary, secondary, and tertiary victimisation. His reflection on 'involvement' included: motivation for the involvement, types of involvement, and relationships with the criminal couple (an offender and his/her victim, as well as the victim and his/her offender). During this period, new areas were investigated by Slovene criminologists and victimologists. Victimological research went beyond the limits of criminal legislation and took a broader look at victimological perspectives. Thereby, new topics were studied in Slovenia, such as the abolition of the death penalty,[48] shops as criminogenic and victimogenic entities,[49] human rights and the rights of the child,[50] children and domestic violence,[51] and persecution.[52]

4. Victimological Research in Slovenia After 1991

Victimological research conducted in Slovenia since 1991 (post-independence) has consisted of more than 70 victimological studies, focusing on:

1) victimisation surveys,
2) different types of victimisation,
3) assistance to victims of crime,
4) satisfaction of victims of crime with their treatment by competent authorities,
5) fear of crime, and
6) implementation of restorative justice.

4.1 Victimisation Surveys

Ten years after *Pečar* conducted the first victimisation study in Slovenia,[53] *Pavlović* took part in the International Crime Victim Survey (ICVS) collecting victimisation data in Ljubljana, the capital of Slovenia.[54] The results of the study showed

---

46 *Pečar* 1984a.

47 *Pečar* 1984b.

48 *Bavcon* 1979; *Zlobec* 1981.

49 *Pečar, Maver & Zobec* 1981.

50 *Kobe* 1988.

51 *Dobnikar* 1989; *Pavlović* 1990.

52 *Bavcon* 1990.

53 *Pečar* 1982.

54 *Pavlović* 1993.

that more than 64% of respondents or other household members were victims of at least one criminal offence during the last five years. Moreover, only 38% of crimes were reported to the police. Theft of a vehicle, theft from a vehicle, and burglary were the most common types of reported victimisation, while sexual offences, attempted burglary, and robbery were the most underreported crimes. The most common reasons for not reporting crime to the police included: perceptions that the crime committed was not too serious and feelings that the police could not help solve the crime anyway. In 50% of all cases of reported crimes, victims were satisfied with the work of the police. The next round of this study in 1997, which was expanded from the Ljubljana area to the entire country, showed that there were no significant differences in victimisation between the inhabitants of Ljubljana and the inhabitants of other parts of Slovenia.[55] Consumer fraud, vehicle vandalism, and theft from vehicles represented the most common types of reported victimisation, while theft of a vehicle, robbery, attempted burglary, and corruption were the least common. In 2001, the findings of the third round of the survey in Slovenia showed that crime remained at approximately the same level compared to the results of previous studies. Such a relatively stable crime rate was also confirmed by police statistics. The major increases in the number of crimes were detected with respect to the thefts of bicycles and robberies, while the number of thefts from a vehicle, vehicle vandalism, sexual offences, and assaults dropped significantly. Respondents were inclined to report property crime and physical attacks to the police, while sexual offences remained mostly unreported. In comparison with the results of the study carried out in 1997, the percentage of reported robberies and thefts increased, while the number of reported sexual offences decreased. Respondents' satisfaction with the police remained at approximately the same level as in the previous studies. Moreover, victims of burglaries and sexual offences were satisfied with the police, while victims of robberies and physical assaults were least satisfied with the police.[56]

A comparison between official police statistics and findings of victimisation studies pointed to a gap between official data and research results regarding crime trends in Slovenia. Police statistics showed that in the period from 1992 to 1997, crime was declining; in contrast, victimisation studies suggested an increase in crime, with the highest growth detected in the areas of violent and non-contact property crime. In 2001, a comparison between data from police statistics and victimisation surveys showed no significant differences in crime trends.[57]

---

55 *Pavlović* 1998; 1999a; 1999b; 1999c.

56 *Pavlović* 1998; 1999a; 1999b; 1999c; *Umek* 2004.

57 *Pavlović* 1998; 1999a; 1999b; 1999c.

4.2 Types of Victimisation Studies

The following section presents studies focusing on different aspects of victimisation:

1) violent crime,
2) crimes against the elderly,
3) mobbing – violence at the work place,
4) victimisation related to migration, refugees and hate speech,
5) victimisation of consumers,
6) environmental crime, and
7) cybercrime.

4.2.1 Violent Crime

Dekleva studied the phenomenon of bullying in primary and secondary schools, and introduced the definition of peer violence and looked at different types of violence in schools (and its consequences).[58] Additionally, his research exposed the positive role of mediation in cases of juvenile bullying. More than 20 years later, *Kaučič-Gačnik* offered a detailed definition of bullying, its victims, and consequences.[59] She defined bullying as physical, psychological, or verbal violence lasting for a longer period and affecting the victim's mental development. The findings of her study highlighted the need to establish prevention programmes in schools, which would be based on a partnership between parents and the school. *Cvek* and *Pšunder* carried out a research study on peer violence and victimisation in primary schools.[60] Their findings showed that one-quarter of all pupils were victims of bullying and peer violence. Moreover, they found that the majority of victims of bullying reported such incidents to their parents, and that the types of victimisation depended on the child's gender (boys experienced physical violence more often, while girls were more frequently exposed to psychological violence). *Razpotnik* and *Dekleva* defined a theoretical framework for understanding peer violence and bullying in contextual and socio-pedagogical aspects.[61] They found that violence among youths often occurs through the discrimination of specific social groups, particularly immigrants from former Yugoslav republics. Children, whose parents immigrated to Slovenia, were more frequently victims of bullying; the findings also revealed that nationalist feelings represented the main cause for bullying immigrant peers. Recent research has focused on peer violence in cyberspace. *Pšunder* conducted a theoretical study

---

58 *Dekleva* 1995.

59 *Kaučič-Gačnik* 2007.

60 *Cvek & Pšunder* 2013.

61 *Razpotnik & Dekleva* 2015.

on cyberbullying, in which she defined this phenomenon and presented different forms of violence in cyberspace.[62] Moreover, she suggested some prevention measures based on the awareness of cyberbullying (forms and consequences) by school teachers. The most recent research on bullying examined the link between offenders and domestic violence incidents; it used a sample of elementary school pupils and found correlations between pupils that were exposed to domestic violence and their deviant behaviour exhibited in various forms of bullying. In contrast, pupils with a stable family situation expressed less aggressive behaviour.[63]

The topic of domestic violence in Slovenia has been relatively well research, with numerous studies focusing on different types and forms of domestic violence. *Kanduč* carried out a study on victims (children and women) of violence and their contribution to victimisation.[64] His findings showed that violence against children was a consequence of inappropriate reactions by their parents in stressful situations caused by a child. In addition, the author emphasised particularly those circumstances due to which female victims of violence decide not to leave the perpetrator. These include:

1) the psychological state of the victims, in which they are unable to make decisions,
2) emotional attachment to the perpetrator, also known as traumatic bonding,
3) the fact that victims are caught in a social trap,
4) victims' sacrifice for the family,
5) victims' identification with the perpetrator,
6) the fact that victims blame themselves for their victimisation, and
7) the victims' lack of economic resources which prevents them to live on their own.

On the basis of a literature review, *Černič, Šprah, Šoštarič, Rožman* and *Kneževič* conducted an analysis of data obtained from governmental and non-governmental organisations to determine the scope of violence against women.[65] The most common forms of victimisation included offences against human rights and liberties (52%), offences against life and limb (28%), offences against public law and order (13%), and offences against sexual inviolability (8%). In 2002, approximately 6% of all Slovene women were victims of some form of intimate violence by their partners. *Leskošek, Urek* and *Zaviršek* studied violence against women with the aim of

62 *Pšunder* 2012.

63 *Filipčič, Bertok, Karajić, Klemenčič & Muršič* 2017.

64 *Kanduč* 2002.

65 *Černič, Šprah, Šoštarič, Rožman & Kneževič* 2003.

determining the victimisation of women due to different forms of violence (physical, sexual, psychological, and economic violence and the violation of rights).[66] Psychological violence was identified as the most common form of violence against women (49%), while 23% of women experienced domestic violence, 14% were subjected to economic violence, and 6.5% of women experienced sexual violence. Women between the age of 30 and 39 were identified as the most vulnerable group. *Frangež* and *Dvoršek* conducted a study on the characteristics of detecting sexual abuse in children.[67] Based on a review of police cases involving sexual assaults on children and interviews with prosecutors and criminal investigators, their findings emphasised the role of educational and care institutions in detecting sexual violence against children. *Pavšič Mrevlje* conducted a study in which she analysed police statistics and data to identify the characteristics of victims and circumstances of domestic violence.[68] She found that the areas of violence against children, the elderly, homosexual partners, and parents were studied inadequately and thus did not allow for the implementation of effective prevention programmes. *Smolej* studied violence against children and the impact of the newly adopted Criminal Code on the detection and investigation of domestic violence. The findings revealed that the new classification of domestic violence and the use of restraining orders improved the protection of victims but also caused some unintended consequences (e.g., individuals involved in family quarrels abused established mechanisms for their personal revenge against other family members – false acquisitions, restraining orders, etc.).[69]

Following the most recent review of criminological research on violence in Slovenia, the topic of violent crime is quite well researched and studies focus on offenders, victims, causes, consequences, and the prevention of violent crime. However, some forms of violence have changed in the past few years. Bullying has become more frequent in cyberspace, domestic violence has decreased due to a newly adopted zero-tolerance strategy, and the influence of mainstream media has changed the understanding of violence (particularly sexual violence). An analysis of statistical data showed that in the period from 2000 to 2016, all forms of reported violent crime decreased, while the clearance rates of investigated crimes were rather high (91%).[70]

4.2.2 Crimes Against the Elderly

Klančnik and *Pavšič Mrevlje* analysed police statistics regarding criminal offences committed against elderly citizens and found that crime against the elderly is in-

---

66 *Leskošek, Urek & Zaviršek* 2010.

67 *Frangež & Dvoršek* 2013.

68 *Pavšič Mrevlje* 2014a.

69 *Smolej* 2011.

70 *Eman & Hacin* 2017.

creasing.[71] Results showed that the majority of crimes against the elderly involved property crimes (80%), crimes against human rights and freedoms (5%), economic crimes (5%), and crimes against life and limb (3%). Moreover, results revealed that men were more frequently victims of crimes against life and limb, and crimes against human rights, while women were more frequently victims of sexual offences and property crime. In 2014, *Pavšič Mrevlje* conducted an empirical study on the victimisation of the elderly in the Municipality of Ljubljana by measuring the scope of victimisation, the consequences for victims, their response to victimisation and their satisfaction with the police when reporting victimisation.[72] The results revealed that 19.6% of all respondents were victimised at least once in the previous year. Theft and vandalism (60%), fraud (16%), threats and harassment (12%) represented the most frequent types of crime against the elderly. More than 50% of all respondents reported the crime to the police and more than 80% were satisfied with the police response. *Pavšič Mrevlje* and *Nivala* compared the victimisation of the elderly in Slovenia and Sweden.[73] Results revealed that property crime was the prevailing form of victimisation in both countries. Furthermore, the elderly in Slovenia were more frequently victims of harassment, threats, theft, and fraud than their peers in Sweden. Strangers represented the most frequent offenders in both countries, while children comprised the second group of most violent offenders victimising the elderly in Slovenia.

4.2.3 Mobbing – Violence at the Workplace

A significant amount of research on mobbing and other forms of victimisation at the workplace has been conducted in Slovenia in the past 10 years. *Dolinar, Jere* and *Meško* conducted a case study to examine mobbing and violence in the working environment and concluded that this type of victimisation could often have been prevented by adopting adequate legislation, implementing good prevention practices, increasing public awareness, and giving a more prominent role to organisations dealing with the prevention of mobbing.[74] *Dolinar, Jere, Meško, Podbregar* and *Eman* measured the perceptions and forms of mobbing, as well as responses to it, and found that more than 40% of respondents experienced the avoidance, offensive gestures, ignorance, gossiping, criticism, receiving unclear comments, and inappropriate assessment of their work.[75] *Česen, Damej, Kečanovič, Modrej, Pečnik, Posel* and *Lazar* found that in the past five years, 19% of the Slovene population experienced mobbing, whereby the most common forms of mobbing included gossiping, the delegation of tasks for which the victims were over-qualified, criticism, ridicule, and unfair assessments of

---

71 *Klančnik & Pavšič Mrevlje* 2013.

72 *Pavšič Mrevlje* 2014b.

73 *Pavšič Mrevlje & Nivala* 2017.

74 *Dolinar, Jere & Meško* 2009.

75 *Dolinar, Jere, Meško, Podbregar & Eman* 2010.

work.[76] Results showed that victims of mobbing were commonly not alone, as in 65% of all cases they were victimised together with other employees, and in 27% of all cases the victimisation was experienced by entire working groups. *Selič* and *Jakopin* conducted a study on mobbing among trainee doctors in Slovenia and found that 71% of trainee doctors experienced mobbing at the workplace.[77] The most common forms of mobbing included withholding significant information, verbal aggression, spreading rumours, receiving working assignments for which they were over-qualified, and working assignments above their capacity. Victims of mobbing reported symptoms of illness (anxiety and irritability). *Vene* studied unethical and hateful communication as a factor leading to mobbing.[78] Results of interviews revealed that all participants experienced some form of unethical or hateful communication (shouting, cursing, insults, verbal threats, etc.); however, not all of them experienced mobbing. The most common consequences of mobbing included psychological trauma, reduced productivity, frequent sick leave, and the termination of the victim's employment contract.

4.2.4 Victimisation Related to Migration, Refugees, and Hate Speech

In light of recent migration events in Europe, victimisation of migrants was examined at the theoretical level, while studies focusing on different forms of migrant victimisation were conducted in Slovenia. *Bučar-Ručman* emphasised the importance of structural violence at a global and local level as a cause of subsequent victimisation of migrants in Western European countries.[79] He introduces a system in which migrants are considered as objects of immigration control and immigration policy, which differentiates between desired and undesired migrants based on an economic perspective. Migrants easily become victims on the basis of stereotypes and prejudice towards "other people". As stated by *Kanduč* and *Bučar-Ručman*, migrant workers moving to Slovenia were a direct result of high unemployment rates in the countries of former Yugoslavia. Victimisation of migrant workers is characterised by structural violence and socioeconomic hardship, which are additionally affected by the state's legislation and the passive nature of control mechanisms.[80] The results of a study on human trafficking in Slovenia showed that the rates of human trafficking (for the purpose of forced begging) and trafficking in children were low, whereas no evidence of trafficking in human organs, tissue, or blood was detected. The causes of such victimisation stem from the vulnerability of migrant workers and deteriorating social conditions in their countries of origin.[81] In the light of the recent refugee crisis

---

76 *Česen, Damej, Kečanovič, Modrej, Pečnik, Posel & Lazar* 2009.

77 *Selič & Jakopin* 2010.

78 *Vene* 2012.

79 *Bučar-Ručman* 2016.

80 *Kanduč & Bučar-Ručman* 2017.

81 *Frangež & Bučar-Ručman* 2017.

in 2015 and the role of Slovenia in the migration route, institutions responsible for dealing with migrants and migration management in Europe were studied. In Slovenia, an increase in the number of refugees led to the adoption of restrictive measures by the government, changes in the legislation, securitisation and militarisation.[82] However, research studies on migration and policing in Slovenia emphasised pluralisation, Europeanisation, demilitarisation, and academisation as the general trends in the area of migration policing.[83] In order to raise awareness and increase tolerance towards migrants and refugees in accordance with the United Nations Sustainable Development Goal 4.7,[84] a part of a national project on safety and security in local communities (2015–2018) also covered issues related to the incorporation of topics about migrants and refugees in education and training programmes at universities.[85]

Pečar began conducting research into hate crime as a form of violent crime. The scope of his research addressed the issue of heterogeneous societies and the hatred towards different social groups. He emphasised that hate crimes are generally directed towards different cultural and/or religious groups.[86] From the victimological perspective, the issue of hate speech was first addressed by *Salecl* in her essay on violence against national, racial, and gender differences.[87] The author discussed the regulation of hate speech and emphasised the importance of legislative aspects, as they empower victims of hate speech. Victims decide if their identity was threatened or damaged because of their gender, race, or nationality. *Varga* studied hate speech in the legislative context, highlighted the characteristics of victims and identified homosexuals, disabled persons, migrants, refugees, and minorities as the most vulnerable social groups exposed to hate speech.[88] *Završnik* examined the legal elements of stereotypes and discussed how to draw a line between a criminal offence and a stereotype and define them accordingly.[89] Moreover, he discussed the motives of hate speech offenders, which often cannot be proven due to the following reasons:

1) offenders hide their true motive because sanctions for hate speech are higher,
2) offenders do not know their reasons for hate speech, and
3) psychoanalytical reasons – offenders repress or suppress their true reasons for expressing violence.

---

82 *Bučar-Ručman* 2018.

83 *Modic* 2016.

84 UNESCO 2017.

85 *Bučar-Ručman* 2014; *Meško, Hacin, Pirnat & Eman* 2018, *Modic* 2016.

86 *Pečar* 1993.

87 *Salecl* 2002.

88 *Varga* 2007.

89 *Završnik* 2006.

With respect to the victims of hate speech, *Završnik* stressed the importance of the victim status that has to be gained by the victims themselves; such a status cannot be awarded only to the most typical groups of hate speech victims but also to the hidden victims of hate speech. In 2007, some progress was achieved when hate speech was criminalised and the elements constituting hate speech were defined as a criminal offence. The main issue of the article on hate speech in the Criminal Code revolved around the fact that acts of hate crime referred to vulnerable groups of victims from a historical perspective and could not focus on all types of victims. The response of the criminal justice system to hate speech was based on repressive law without alternatives.[90] The findings of an analysis of anonymously reported hate speech on the internet in Slovenia suggested that only 3% of all reported hate speech cases met the criteria of a criminal offence and were further reported to the police. A survey on the perception of hate speech in Slovenia showed that among respondents who expressed concern regarding the issue of hate speech, the highest rate of concern was expressed by women and the elderly.[91] Lately, researchers have been focusing on examining hate speech from a legislative perspective, since the Criminal Code does not explicitly define hate speech as an independent criminal offence, but recognises it in the scope of the criminal offence of spreading hate in public.[92] Due to the recent refugee crisis in 2015, a rise in hate speech towards refugees, particularly Muslims, has been observed. Hate speech towards refugees, which is frequently expressed on the internet and in social media, derives from the fear of terrorism, population mixing, Islamophobia, and social conflicts.[93]

4.2.5 Victimisation of Consumers

Mičović studied the exposure of preschool children to food additives and focused on measuring children's food intake in kindergartens to determine the level of daily intake of additivities, which was then compared to the acceptable daily intake.[94] The findings revealed that the daily intake of food additives by children in kindergartens did not exceed the acceptable daily levels. However, children and their parents were not aware of the level of additives in consumed food and did not have a choice to select food with fewer additives. The victimisation of consumers was included in the study on food safety carried out by *Mičović*, in which she analysed invisible threats in the context of Routine Activity Theory.[95] By conducting two public surveys, the author confirmed the violation of consumers' rights to be informed about the content

---

90 *Završnik* 2007.

91 *Vehovar, Motl, Mihelič, Berčič & Petrovčič* 2012.

92 *Ferlinc* 2018; *Kogovšek* 2017; *Završnik & Zrimšek* 2018.

93 *Bajt* 2018; *Bajt & Frelih* 2018.

94 *Mičović* 2010.

95 *Mičović* 2011.

of products and their right of choice, as adequate information on the quality of food was not provided to consumers, which meant that consumers' rights regarding food safety were violated. The need for a systematic supervision of food and the essential role of the Consumer Protection Office in raising consumers' awareness were the main concerns identified in the study.

4.2.6 Environmental Crime

In recent years, Slovene victimological research focused on environmental crime and victims of environmental crime. Environmental crime was studied from criminological and criminal justice perspectives, while victims of environmental crime were defined in a broader context – apart from human beings, victims of environmental crime may also be found in all seven elements of the natural environment.[96] By analysing statistical data regarding crime against the environment in Slovenia, the torture of animals, game poaching, as well as the burdening and destruction of the environment, were identified as the most frequent criminal offences against the environment.[97] Social conditions (environmental resources as a source of survival) and economic factors (environmental resources as a source of profit) were considered the main causes of environmental crime.[98] *Eman* also exposed problems regarding the victims of environmental crime, as they are frequently not aware of their victimisation and of the consequences of such crime for the environment, natural habitats, and human beings.[99] *Meško, Bančič, Eman* and *Fields* made a step forward and presented the situational crime prevention measures to environmental threats in order to protect the environment.[100] Slovene researchers also expanded their national research endeavours to the regional problems of environmental protection, as environmental crime is not solely a national problem.[101] Recently, new topics have been arising in the field of environmental crime, such as victimisation issues relating to water crimes,[102] (electronic) waste trafficking,[103] and corruption.[104]

---

96 *Eman* 2011; 2012; *Eman & Meško* 2009; 2014.

97 *Eman* 2008a; 2011; 2013; *Eman, Meško & Fields* 2009; *Eman, Meško, Dobovšek & Sotlar* 2013.

98 *Barišič Jaman, Franca & Eman* 2015; *Eman & Franca* 2013; *Meško & Eman* 2012.

99 *Eman* 2008b; 2011; 2012.

100 *Meško, Bančič, Eman & Fields* 2011.

101 *Eman & Meško* 2013; *Eman et al.* 2013; *Eman, Meško & Fields* 2013; *Meško, Sotlar & Eman 2012; South, Eman & Meško 2014.*

102 *Eman* 2016; *Eman & Humar* 2017; *Eman, Kuhar & Meško* 2016; 2017; 2018.

103 *Eman & Franca* 2016; *Meško & Eman* 2012.

104 *Eman* 2014.

4.2.7 Cybercrime

Meško and *Bernik* conducted an online survey on a sample of internet users regarding their perception of cybercrime, experience with victimisation in cyber-space, and preventive measures.[105] Results showed that:

1) cybercrimes were related to the use of social networks,
2) the fear of cybercrime was related to users' awareness about the possible victimisation by cybercrime, and
3) users reported that they were relatively well-informed about the various types of cybercrime.

Moreover, they identified three factors affecting the fear of crime experienced by the users of cyberspace:

1) inappropriate activities in cyberspace (identity theft, phishing, spreading rumours, dissemination of personal data in social networks, child pornography, cyberterrorism, hate speech and slander),
2) harassment in cyberspace (e-mail harassment, harassment on social networks, extortion and dissemination of indecent material on the internet), and
3) threats in cyberspace (computer viruses, unauthorised computer access and control, computer hacking, software cracking and computer vandalism).[106]

Dimc and *Dobovšek* conducted a web survey on cybercrime as a contemporary security threat and found that approximately 40% of internet users believed that cyberspace was safe and more than three-quarters of respondents were aware of the consequences of their activities in the virtual world.[107] Approximately 50% of all respondents believed that they had sufficient knowledge for the safe use of the internet and would report crime in cyberspace to the police. *Završnik* identified the importance of the following aspects for the prevention of child pornography on the internet:

1) raising children's awareness and ability to use self-protective measures,
2) protecting children and encouraging them to report suspicious behaviour, and
3) the criminal prosecution of offenders.[108]

He also highlighted the significance of cyberbullying prevention in educational measures and the need to raise the awareness of children, their parents and teachers.

---

105 *Meško & Bernik* 2011.

106 *Bernik & Meško* 2011.

107 *Dimc & Dobovšek* 2013.

108 *Završnik* 2015.

Denžič studied the perception of risks in the virtual world and highlighted the fact that young people did not believe they could become victims of cybercrime.[109] Her results implied that cyberspace users did not perceive threats in the cyber world as more dangerous than those in the 'real world'. Findings from the recent research study on citizens' cybersecurity showed that increased rates of cybercrime contributed to a greater awareness of potential threats and harm in cyberspace.[110] The importance of research was further emphasised with respect to children and minors in cyberspace where authors examined various threats that emerged when this vulnerable group of users was given easy access to the internet. Pornography, receiving sexual messages, offline meetings with online contacts, bullying, harassment, misuse of personal data, and internet addiction were recognised as the key online risks for children and minors in cyberspace.[111] Lately, the focus has been set on online banking users and their self-protective behaviour in cyberspace. The results of a study conducted on a sample of online banking users showed that users were well informed about the threats associated with online banking, however, their use of self-protective measures was insufficient (unchanged passwords, use of unsafe webpages, failure to check the validity of a digital certificate).[112] A new national project on the safety and security of cyberspace users and their criminological, victimological, and preventive aspects started in 2018. The project focuses on the development of a new model of impact factors leading to higher threats and the victimisation of users – potential victims (e.g., trust, fear, previous victimisation, behavioural patterns, and the use of cyber-security solutions). Efforts are also in planning to map the threats associated with cyber-security to reduce cybervictimisation.[113]

4.3 Provision of Assistance to Crime Victims

Meško addressed the need for the development of appropriate assistance for victims of violent crime.[114] Assisting such victims is essential as they can experience serious physical injuries and psychological trauma. Moreover, various consequences of victimisation depend on the type of victimisation; therefore, victim assistance must be based on each victim's individual needs in criminal proceedings. In this respect, the provision of support to reduce subsequent victimisation is of great importance. *Koprol* emphasised the need for proper training and education

---

109 *Denžič* 2016.

110 *Bernik* 2016.

111 *Tomažič & Bessa* 2017.

112 *Prislan & Lobnikar* 2018.

113 *Meško* 2018.

114 *Meško* 1998.

of police officers dealing with victims of crime.[115] Results showed that police officers should establish a high-quality professional relationship with the victim in order to provide them with assistance. Major changes in the police organisation have taken place to guarantee a higher degree of quality in contacts between police officers and crime victims in police procedures. Šelih stressed the important role of non-governmental organisations and their contributions in helping victims of crime, particularly in combatting violence.[116] Assistance to victims of violent crime has improved significantly in the last decade due to campaigns carried out by a non-governmental organisation, close cooperation between the police and other institutions, and the development of providing legal assistance to victims. Assistance to children, as well as the elderly, has received a great deal of attention, as they constitute the most vulnerable groups of victims.[117]

4.4 Satisfaction of Victims of Crime With the Police

The satisfaction of victims of crime with the police has been assessed by numerous studies. *Umek* and *Meško* examined the effects of crime on victims and police officers' attitudes towards crime victims in two Slovene towns.[118] Results indicated that victims experienced strong emotional reactions after a crime had been committed and approximately 80% of victims stated they were satisfied with the police officers' attitudes during the crime reporting process. Moreover, victims were satisfied with police officers' concerns regarding the investigation into the case, the gathering of information, and the provision of advice to victims. *Gorenak* studied the satisfaction of victims of property crimes in police procedures and found that more than 70% of victims were satisfied with the work of the police at all stages (reporting a crime, crime scene investigation, and crime investigation).[119] However, victims expressed their dissatisfaction with the lack of additional contacts or visits by the police after they had reported a crime. Results of a study on the satisfaction of victims of property crimes with the police revealed that the professional work conducted by the police in their contacts with crime victims and the quality of communication between police officers and victims were the main factors that influenced the victims' satisfaction with the police.[120] Moreover, the type of criminal offence had no influence on the general satisfaction with police work.

---

115 *Koprol* 2007.

116 *Šelih* 2012; *Veselič* 2007.

117 *Eman & Hacin* 2017.

118 *Umek & Meško* 1999.

119 *Gorenak* 2003.

120 *Dvoršek, Maver & Meško* 2006.

4.5 Fear of Crime

The concepts of fear of crime and fear of potential victimisation were first mentioned by *Meško* and *Pavlović* when they introduced the basic characteristics of fear of crime and the significance of feelings of vulnerability.[121] In 1999, *Meško* and *Umek* presented a socio-psychological and demographic model for studying the fear of crime and focused on examining correlations between living environments and the fear of crime, as their research was conducted in an urban environment.[122] Findings suggested that fear of crime correlated with certain perceptions regarding dangerous people and areas, while gender, age, the socioeconomic situation of an individual, their social network, and previous experiences of victimisation were identified as the main factors that contributed to fear of crime.[123] *Meško, Fallshore* and *Jevšek* analysed the role of the police in reducing fear of crime and emphasised the importance of paying attention to the most vulnerable and fearful groups of people by implementing community-based policing to bring about increased reassurance.[124] *Meško, Šifrer* and *Vošnjak* compared fear of crime in urban and rural areas and found that the level of urbanisation of an area represented an important factor when explaining fear of crime and other processes in local communities. Overall, fear of crime and concerns about potential future victimisation tend to be greater in urban areas.[125] They found a negative correlation between victimisation and fear of crime (previous victimisation did not affect threat-perceptions among people but had an impact on the perception of potential risks of future victimisation). In general, the results also showed that fear of crime or feelings of being threatened did not affect attitudes toward punitiveness. Moreover, the importance of planning a safe urban environment, social crime prevention, and implementing community policing for reducing the fear of crime (i.e., reassurance) was exposed.[126] A study on fear of crime, which was based on the application of crime mapping tools, was conducted in the Municipality of Trbovlje.[127] The level of fear in ten local communities was mapped and areas in the municipality characterised by high and low levels of fear were identified. The outskirts of the municipality were identified as areas where fear of crime was lower; the study also identified a positive correlation between the official crime rates and levels of fear of crime.

---

121 *Meško & Pavlović* 1998.

122 *Meško & Umek* 1999.

123 *Meško & Areh* 2003; *Meško & Šifrer* 2008.

124 *Meško, Fallshore & Jevšek* 2007.

125 *Meško, Šifrer & Vošnjak* 2012.

126 *Vošnjak* 2011.

127 *Hacin & Eman* 2014.

4.6 Implementation of the Restorative Justice Concept

Kanduč attempted to identify the actual and normative positions of victims of crime.[128] By analysing the concept of restorative justice and victim restitution, he established a theoretical framework for implementing the concept of restitution. A few years later, *Bošnjak* studied restorative justice and introduced a criminal law and criminal policy concept of restorative justice that could be implemented in the Slovene criminal justice system.[129] *Filipčič* studied the role of mediation in criminal proceedings, conducted a theoretical analysis of the institute of mediation, and analysed data obtained from surveys involving state prosecutors and mediators, as well as court files regarding victim-offender mediation.[130] Their results showed that almost 50% of all state prosecutors believed they should not be dealing with minor criminal offences. They supported the idea of increasing private lawsuits, where the victim would assume the role of a prosecutor. State prosecutors showed positive attitudes towards the concept of mediation, yet they rarely relied on it. Insufficient information about the offenders and victims in criminal reports represented the main reasons for failing to use mediation. *Završnik* studied conceptual issues regarding the implementation of restorative justice in the criminal law system.[131] He explored the principle of restorative justice and the modern criminal law system in terms of its incompatibility with the implementation of restorative justice due to differences in the conceptual framework, as restorative justice represents a relatively new perspective on crime itself. The author argued that when considered as a substitute for dealing with certain types of crime, restorative justice cannot be part of the modern criminal law system. The following section presents some statistical data on crime victims.

5. Victims of Crime in Slovenia in Figures

In Slovenia, there are two major sources of statistical data on crime victims. The first comprises the official crime statistics of the Ministry of the Interior, which contain information on victims of crime included in the Annual Police Reports.[132] The characteristics of victims of crime with respect to their gender, age, nationality, and the type of crime they experienced obtained in the period between 2010 and 2017 are presented in *Table 1*. The number of victims decreased from 44,334 in 2010 to 34,449 in 2017 (in 2017, the victim rate amounted to 1,667 victims per 100,000 inhabitants). During this period, the number of male victims was higher

---

128 *Kanduč* 1997.

129 *Bošnjak* 1999; 2000.

130 *Filipčič* 2008.

131 *Završnik* 2008.

132 Ministry of the Interior, Police 2011; 2012; 2013; 2014; 2015; 2016; 2017; 2018.

Table 1 Victims of Crime in Slovenia 2010–2017

		2010	2011	2012	2013	2014	2015	2016	2017
Gender	Male	25,503	25,768	27,761	28,569	25,418	20,904	21,667	19,556
	Female	18,831	18,866	19,388	19,442	17,611	14,656	14,002	14,893
Age (in years)	< 17	2,859	2,725	2,885	2,504	2,383	2,056	2,171	2,133
	18–20	1,964	1,864	1,842	1,605	1,533	1,311	1,271	1,167
	21–30	8,693	8,318	8,585	1,894	7,175	6,005	5,428	5,081
	31–40	9,243	9,688	10,103	10,268	9,216	7,471	7,546	7,137
	41–50	8,540	8,579	9,302	9,500	8,671	7,063	7,192	6,908
	51 <	13,017	13,441	14,415	15,695	14,036	11,654	12,061	12,023
Nationality (country of origin)*	Slovenia	41,798	41,313	43,278	43,221	39,435	32,378	32,246	31,109
	EU countries	797	1,120	1,417	2,122	1,281	1,309	1,179	1,397
	Other	1,739	2,201	2,454	2,668	2,313	1,873	2,244	1,943
Type of crime*	Conventional crime**	42,836	42,289	44,182	43,358	38,149	31,762	31,931	30,453
	Economic crime	1,498	2,345	2,967	4,653	4,880	3,798	3,738	3,996
	Organised crime	37	51	22	33	27	52	32	67
	Juvenile crime	1,107	967	885	874	793	614	626	656
Total		44,334	44,634	47,149	48,011	43,029	35,560	35,669	34,449

Source: Data taken from Ministry of the Interior, Police 2011; 2012; 2013; 2014; 2015; 2016; 2017; 2018.

* In several cases, individuals were victims of more than one type of crime.

** Conventional crime refers to property crime and violent crime, including sexual crime.

than the number of female victims. The majority of victims were older than 51, followed by victims between 31 and 40 years of age and victims aged between 41 and 50, most of whom were Slovene citizens. In the observed period, the number of foreign nationals who were victimised in Slovenia increased. Individuals victimised by conventional crimes accounted for more than 90% of all victims, while the number of victims of conventional crime, organised crime, and juvenile crime decreased. At the same time, the number of victims of economic crime increased by almost 200%.

Table 2 presents the consequences of criminal offences that resulted in death, grievous bodily injury, minor bodily injury, and financial damage from 2010 to 2017. The number of victims who experienced bodily injury decreased in this period, while the amount of loss incurred by victims decreased from EUR 577,313 to EUR 510,041 (the greatest financial damage in the 2010–2017 period was inflicted upon victims in 2014). Moreover, the number of victims who died as a result of a crime decreased by 20%; this figure peaked in 2015 with 56 fatalities.[133]

Table 2 Consequences of Criminal Offences in Slovenia 2010–2017

	2010	**2011**	**2012**	**2013**	**2014**	**2015**	**2016**	**2017**
Death	33	48	43	40	30	56	43	26
Grievous bodily injury	297	262	278	245	240	224	192	159
Minor bodily injury	2,846	2,620	2,489	2,330	2,099	1,921	1,748	1,307
Financial damage (in EUR)	577,313	271,788	537,397	376,453	755,326	454,885	590,936	510,041

Source: Data taken from Ministry of the Interior, Police 2011; 2012; 2013; 2014; 2015; 2016; 2017; 2018.

Victimisation surveys comprise the second source of data on crime victims in Slovenia. The first ICVS was conducted in 1992 and was later replicated in 1997 and 2001.[134] The share of victims from 1992, 1997, and 2001[135] (according to the type of victimisation observed) is presented in *Table 3.*[136] Vandalism to cars,

---

133 Ministry of the Interior, Police 2011; 2012; 2013; 2014; 2015; 2016; 2017; 2018.

134 *Pavlović* 1993; 1998; 1999a; 1999b; 1999c; Umek, 2004.

135 In 1992, 1,000 individuals from Ljubljana participated in the study. In 1997 and 2001, the study was conducted at the national level. In 1997 and in 2001, 2,053 and 3,886 individuals respectively participated in the study.

136 Questions about victimisation referred to the experience of victimisation in the past five years.

theft from cars, and bicycle theft were the most frequent forms of victimisation reported by respondents. The number of victims of all offences declined from 1997 to 2001, when the study was conducted at the national level. The largest share of respondents experienced vandalism to cars, theft from cars, and fraud. Moreover, only a handful of respondents reported that they had experienced a sexual offence, assault, or robbery in the past five years, while the percentage of respondents who were victimised by these types of offences decreased between 1997 and 2001. A comparison of results from Ljubljana with the national sample reveals that the share of victims of various criminal offences in Ljubljana is proportionate to the share at the national level.

*Table 3 Proportion of Victims of Crime According to the Type of Offence**

Type of offence	1992	1997	2001**
Theft of cars	1.2%	1.3%	1.3%
Theft from cars	19.3%	18.1%	11.5%
Vandalism of cars	27.1%	23.2%	18.6%
Motorcycle theft	2.7%	1.0%	1.3%
Bicycle theft	14.4%	9.6%	9.5%
Burglary	7.2%	8.6%	6.2%
Attempted burglary	8.5%	5.8%	4.2%
Personal theft	13.6%	12.1%	8.0%
Robbery	1.6%	3.3%	3.1%
Sexual offence	9.8%	5.1%	2.3%
Assault	8.5%	13.3%	7.8%
Fraud	–	14.0%	11.1%
Corruption	–	1.4%	2.1%

Source: Data taken from ICVS 2017.

* The SPSS data file of all rounds of the victimisation survey is available online at: http://wp.unil.ch/icvs/codebooks/.

** In Slovenia, the last ICVS was conducted in 2001.

Table 4 presents the share of crime reported to the police in 1992, 1997 and 2001. More than 90% of respondents reported the theft of cars. The number of respondents who were victimised by theft from cars, vandalism of cars, burglary, attempted burglary, robbery, personal theft, assault, and fraud, and were prepared to report these offences to the police increased from 1997 to 2001. However, the willingness to report car theft, motorcycle theft, bicycle theft, sexual offences, and corruption decreased. A decrease in the willingness to report sexual offences to the police is particularly worrisome. A comparison of results from Ljubljana and the national sample reveals that the share of victims who reported various

Table 4 Proportion of Crime Reported to the Police

Type of offence	1992	1997	2001*
Theft of cars	91.7%	92.6%	91.8%
Theft from cars	58.3%	52.2%	72.8%
Vandalism to cars	20.4%	29.4%	31.7%
Motorcycle theft	96.3%	85.7%	73.5%
Bicycle theft	56.7%	48.5%	47.6%
Burglary	63.1%	61.4%	69.0%
Attempted burglary	20.0%	22.5%	32.7%
Robbery	18.8%	35.3%	50.4%
Personal theft	36.3%	33.7%	44.2%
Sexual offence	7.3%	10.5%	9.0%
Assault	29.4%	35.1%	35.8%
Fraud	–	3.8%	4.2%
Corruption	–	3.6%	2.4%

Source: Data taken from ICVS 2017.

* In Slovenia, the last ICVS was conducted in 2001.

criminal offences to the police in Ljubljana is proportionate to the one observed at the national level.

The provision of help to victims by specialised agencies and victim satisfaction with the treatment they received are presented in *Table 5*. Results show that only a handful of victims received help from specialised agencies (the highest share was recorded with respect to the victims of assault). Moreover, the share of victims of burglary who received help from specialised agencies decreased from 1997 to 2001, while the share of victims of robbery and assault increased, and

Table 5 Provision of Help to Victims by Specialised Agencies and Satisfaction with Treatment

	1997		2001*	
	Help from specialised agencies	Victim satisfaction	Help from specialised agencies	Victim satisfaction
Burglary	6.4%	73.5%	3.3%	68.2%
Robbery	2.5%	71.8%	2.6%	77.6%
Sexual offence	2.4%	85.0%	2.4%	82.9%
Assault	6.5%	76.2%	6.6%	75.0%

Source: Data taken from ICVS 2017.

* In Slovenia, the last ICVS was conducted in 2001.

the share of victims of sexual assault who received help from specialised agencies remained the same. Approximately three-quarters of victims of burglary, robbery, sexual offences, and assault were satisfied with their treatment (victims of sexual offences reported the highest level of satisfaction). In the 1997–2001 period, victims' satisfaction with their treatment decreased (except for victims of robbery).

6. Discussion

The importance of the development of victimology is observed in the growing body of research in this area. In the beginning, victimological research in Slovenia focused on different types of victims and their contribution to crime. Later on, researchers paid greater attention to the provision of assistance to the victims of crime.[137] Studies also assessed changes in applicable legislation.[138] The results of several studies had practical implications for police work, particularly in terms of a proper approach to, and treatment of, victims during and after they reported a crime to prevent secondary victimisation and increase the efficiency of criminal investigations.[139] With respect to police work, studies on fear of crime have focused on fear-reduction strategies, mainly through police reassurance.[140] Studies on different forms of victimisation have focused on broader aspects of crime victims, ranging from conventional crime victimisation (especially property and violent crimes) to unconventional and hidden forms of victimisation. Research topics covered hate speech victimisation, consumer victimisation, environmental victimisation, crimes against the elderly, and cybercrime victimisation. The substantial contribution of victimological research is also observable in the victimological literature used at the relevant faculties.[141]

Official statistical data show that the number of victims of crime and the number of bodily injuries have decreased in recent years, while the financial consequences of crime have increased. Victims of property crime represent the most common type of victims, while in terms of demographic factors, men and the elderly tend to be victims of crime more frequently. These findings suggest the importance of pursuing further studies on the satisfaction of police work among victims of property crime and elderly victims. The findings of victimisation studies show that most property crimes were related to vehicles, while assault was the most common type of crime against a person. Car theft was the most frequently reported property crime, while

---

137 *Šelih* 2012.

138 *Filipčič* 2008; *Smolej* 2011; *Završnik* 2008.

139 *Dvoršek et al.* 2006; *Gorenak* 2003; *Koprol* 2007.

140 *Meško et al.* 2007; *Meško, Vošnjak, Muratbegović, Budimilić, Bren & Kury* 2012; *Vošnjak* 2011.

141 *Kanduč* 2002b; *Meško* 2007.

robbery and personal theft were the most frequently reported crimes against a person. Moreover, fraud and corruption recorded a very low rate of reporting. The rate of help provided to victims by specialised agencies was low, despite the fact that victim satisfaction with these agencies was high with respect to all types of crime.

We can conclude that victimology has gained importance among research endeavours in Slovenia and that significant progress has been recorded. At the very beginning, i.e., in the 1960s, the first studies focused on the victimisation of individuals and groups contributing to their victimisation (offender-victim relationship). The role of victimology in responding to crime and theoretical discussions regarding criminological aspects of crime victims represented the initial perspectives on victims, the typology of victims, and victimisation processes. Currently, new types of crime, such as mobbing, environmental crime, cybercrime, and crimes against the elderly, as well as new social circumstances relating to migration, migrants, and refugees, are opening new avenues for future victimological studies.

The public discourse on victims, victimisation, and victims' position has been developing in an increasingly positive and protective direction throughout the previous decades. The greatest progress can be observed in the field of domestic violence, where victimised women were initially not considered victims by the police, criminal justice agencies, nor the public. Since the 1980s and 1990s, however, when the need for the development of appropriate assistance to victims of violent crimes was addressed and the role of the victim in criminal proceedings, as well as the prevention of secondary victimisation, became more prominent, Slovene society has been developing a zero tolerance towards violence.[142] This is particularly true for domestic violence, where significant progress has been made. As a result, victims of violence suffering behind closed doors, including male victims, now receive every possible assistance and are treated respectfully. The role of non-governmental organisations in helping victims and contributing to the effective fight against violence was also addressed.[143] Moreover, Slovenia achieved notable progress and is one of very few countries in the world to offer obligatory (i.e., as part of the offender's sentence) therapeutic help to perpetrators, which is provided by the Association for Nonviolent Communication.

The media discourse about victimisation and victim protection varies according to the type of media, however, the majority of mainstream media still report on crime and victimisation realistically and respectfully, also considering victim protection (especially when reporting on crimes involving children). In Slovenia, only one newspaper (Slovenske Novice) reports about crime cases by employing deliberate exaggeration in order to increase its circulation.[144] On the other hand, daily news-

142 *Meško* 1998.

143 *Šelih* 2012; *Veselič* 2007.

144 *Petrovec* 2005.

papers, as well as specialised magazines (e.g., Naša žena, Jana, Lisa, etc.), focus on more specific victimisation-related topics, such as vulnerable groups, forms of victimisation, victim protection, and crime prevention. Furthermore, victim-related media campaigns, supported by NGOs, are very often observed on an almost daily basis. Thus, it is not possible to talk about any differentiation prevailing in the general public between "good" and "bad" victims or similar representations that could be linked to the "ideal victim" stereotype.

As mentioned above, secondary and tertiary victimisation of some victims by the police and the courts was present in the 1980s and 1990s. However, the need to focus on the education and training of criminal justice agencies was promoted at a very early stage and has led to the development of professional, respectful, and supportive attitudes toward victims (especially for victims of sexual offences and domestic violence). In Slovenia, the police have made significant progress, as major changes in the police organisation took place with a view to provide more quality contacts between police officers and crime victims.[145] Nowadays, police officers tend to establish a quality relationship with the victim in order to provide them with necessary assistance. Furthermore, the police work closely with NGOs to offer victims the help they require. This professional police attitude towards crime victims is also evident from various surveys on victim satisfaction. Three previous studies showed that more than 70% of victims were satisfied with police attitudes during the reporting of a crime and the subsequent investigations.[146] Victims only expressed dissatisfaction about the lack of additional contacts or visits by the police after having reported a crime. Furthermore, victimological studies proved to be very useful for developing positive approaches that could be applied by officers working in the field. For example, *Meško* identified a very negative attitude of police officers towards crime victims (some police officers reported far more negative feelings towards victims than towards perpetrators), thus identifying a very clear need for police training.[147] Apart from the immediately introduced communication training for police officers dealing with victims, the Slovene Police Force published a booklet entitled *When I become a crime victim* in 2004.[148]

We can conclude by stating that in Slovenia, numerous (both empirical and theoretical) studies have been conducted in the field of victimology and that the gathering of information from crime victims in police statistics confirms the importance of victimology studies in Slovenia, which is significant particularly in terms of responding to traditional and new forms of victimisation. Victimological research is mainly conducted as part of criminological and criminal justice research. Publications on victims

---

145 *Koprol* 2007.

146 *Dvoršek et al.* 2006; *Gorenak* 2003; *Umek & Meško* 1999.

147 *Meško* 2000.

148 *Štirn* 2004.

and victimological perspectives contribute to the development of an independent science. As a subject, victimology has been included in higher education curricula at the Faculty of Law, University of Ljubljana, and the FCJS UM, for many years.

Victimology and victimologists (mainly criminologists) have had an impact on criminal policy and public perceptions. This impact has varied over time, depending on the orientation of the governing political party, the importance of the topic, or public awareness. In the future, victimology in Slovenia should pay a greater deal of attention to new types of crime, such as cybercrime and environmental crime, the factors causing new forms of victimisation, such as dark web crime, or crimes against animal and plant species, as well as to victimisation related to migration and refugees. In the last decade, victimology followed general concerns and prevailing public awareness, thus focusing more on various violations of human rights, particularly with respect to vulnerable groups of victims, such as children, women, and the elderly.

With respect to financial resources and the legal basis necessary for improving the situation of victims and developing a positive, more tolerant attitude towards victims, Slovenia has responded adequately and adopted the most up-to-date legislation for combatting violence (zero tolerance), including within the parent-child relationship. Nevertheless, there are still problems related to the government's priorities in the field of victimological research. This is especially true in relation to the ICVS, which used to be conducted by the Institute of Criminology. The study was then taken over by the Statistical Office of the Republic of Slovenia and has not been conducted since 2001.

As elsewhere in Europe, victimology has become globalised, international, and focused on the violations of human rights (particularly those of individual social groups). In the future, this field could be expanded in an effort to motivate victimologists to focus more on the offender-victim-environment relationships and develop methods for the prevention of (re)victimisation.

Attention must also be given to "normalised" violence (individual, structural, or cultural) as well as traditional social practices that lead to the victimisation of specific groups and individuals. An interesting and eye-opening essay on "Violence under the Mask", consisting of stories illustrating how, even in the present, some forms of ritualised violence are maintained and reinforced, is a case in point.[149] This publication calls for a more qualitative, anthropological study of victims and abusive social practices that are often ignored in the mainstream victimology literature (e.g., violence of various medical institutions towards different social groups, victimisation of people without a legal status, violence in Slovene traditions and customs, football hooliganism, and false reports of the sexual abuse of children).

---

149 *Petrovec* 2015.

7. Summary in Slovene

V poglavju se osredotočamo na viktimologijo, katero opredeljujemo kot vedo, ki se ukvarja s preučevanjem žrtev, vzrokov in različnih oblik viktimizacije, postopkov in posledic viktimizacije, kot tudi s preučevanjem družbenih odzivov na viktimizacijo. V Sloveniji, vlogo žrtve v kazenskih postopkih opredeljujejo:

1) Zakon o odškodnini žrtvam kaznivih dejanj,
2) Kazenski zakonik in
3) Zakon o kazenskem postopku.

Pregled literature je razkril, da je bilo v zadnjih 50 letih opravljenih več kot 70 študij o žrtvah, ki so se osredotočile na:

1) viktimizacijske študije,
2) različne oblike viktimizacij,
3) nudenje pomoči žrtvam,
4) zadovoljstvo žrtev kriminalitete z delom policije,
5) strah pred kriminaliteto in
6) izvajanje restorativne pravičnosti.

Uradna statistika kriminalitete Ministrstva za notranje zadeve in podatki o žrtvah kriminalitete pridobljeni iz viktimizacijskih študij predstavljata glavna vira statističnih podatkov o žrtvah kriminalitete v Sloveniji. Analiza statističnih podatkov je pokazala, da je število žrtev v zadnjih 15 letih v upadanju. Viktimološko raziskovanje v Sloveniji bi se v prihodnosti moralo osredotočiti na preučevanje novih oblik kriminalitete (npr. kibernetska kriminalitete, okoljska kriminalitete, itd.), ki povzročajo nove oblike viktimizacij.

Literature

Bajt, V. (2018): Online hate speech and the 'refugee crisis' in Slovenia, in: Ž. Žagar, N. Kogovšek Šalamon & M. Lukšič Hacin (eds.), The disaster of European refugee policy: perspective from the 'Balkan route'. Newcastle upon Tyne, pp. 133–155.

Bajt, V. & Frelih, M. (2018): Crimmigration and nationalism in Slovenia. Understanding causes and consequences of criminalization of migration: International conference. Ljubljana, p. 24.

Barišić Jaman, S., Franca, B. & Eman, K. (2015): Preiskovanje nezakonite sečnje dreves v Republiki Sloveniji [Investigation of illegal logging in the Republic of Slovenia]. Revija za kriminalistiko in kriminologijo [Journal of Criminal Investigation and Criminology] 66, pp. 44–55.

Bavcon, L. (1990): Strašna moč "velikih idej" in oblasti: v opomin: žrtve ne smejo biti zaman [The awesome power of "great ideas" and authority: In reminder: victims must not be in vain]. Naši razgledi: štirinajstdnevnik za politična, gospodarska in kulturna vprašanja [Ouw views: Biweekly for political, economic and cultural issues] 39, pp. 382–384.

Bavcon, L. (1979): Prispevek k razpravam o smrtni kazni [Contribution to the debate on death penalty]. Pravnik: revija za pravno teorijo in prakso [Jurist: Journal of Legal Theory and Practice] 34, pp. 155–162.

Bernik. I. (2016): Cybersecurity of Slovenia and its citizens, in: G. Meško, K. Eman & U. Pirnat (eds.), 2nd National conference on local safety and security: Safety and security in local communities; http://press.um.si/index.php/ump/catalog/view/144/124/201-1 [20.08.2018].

Bernik. I. & Meško. G. (2011): Internetna študija poznavanja kibernetskih groženj in strahu pred kibernetsko kriminaliteto [Internet study of familiarity with cyber threats and fear of crime]. Revija za kriminalistiko in kriminologijo [Journal of Criminal Investigation and Criminology] 62, pp. 242–252.

Bošnjak, M. (2000): Teoretična, ideološka in kriminalitetnopolitična izhodišča obnavljalne pravičnosti [Theoretical, ideological and criminalpolitical foundations of restorative justice]; Proceedings of scientific debate 1. Ljubljana, pp. 17–50.

Bošnjak, M. (1999): Pomembnejše značilnosti restorativne pravičnosti [Some of the most important characteristics of restorative justice]. Revija za kriminalistiko in kriminologijo [Journal of Criminal Investigation and Criminology] 50, pp. 299–306.

Bučar-Ručman, A. (2018): Securitization and militarization of migration management in Europe: The case of refugee migration through Slovenia in 2015/2016, in: D. Siegel & V. Nagy (eds.), The migration crisis?: Criminalization, security and survival. The Hague, pp. 293–319.

Bučar-Ručman, A. (2016): Structural violence and migration: Explaining global and local total institutions. Inter Faculty 7, pp. 37–55.

Bučar-Ručman, A. (2014): Migracije in kriminaliteta: pogled čez meje stereotipov in predsodkov [Migrations and crime: View over the boundaries of stereotypes and prejudices]. Ljubljana.

Cvek, M. & Pšunder, M. (2013): Učenci, žrtve medvrstniškega nasilja [Students, victims of peer violence]. Revija za elementarno izobraževanje [The Journal of Elementary Education] 6, pp. 105–116.

Černič, M.I., Šprah, L., Šoštarič, M., Rožman, I. & Kneževič, D. (2003): Nasilje nad ženskami ali kako doseči ničelno tolerance [Violence against women – How to achieve zero tolerance]. Ljubljana.

Česen, T., Damej, M., Kečanovič, B., Modrej, A., Pečnik, P.S., Posel, E. & Lazar, E. (2009): Mobing, trpinčenje, šikaniranje: nekaj usmeritev za pogum pri ohranjanju dostojanstva [Mobbing, harassment, scandal: Some guidelines for courage in maintaining dignity]. Ljubljana.

Davies, P., Francis, P. & Jupp, W. (eds.) (2004): Victimology: Theory, research and policy. New York.

Dekleva, B. (1995): Pogledi na nasilje in ustrahovanje med vrstniki [Views on violence and intimidation among peers], in: Children-peers-violence. Ljubljana, pp. 24–43.

Denžič, J. (2016): Zaznava ogroženosti v realnem in virtualnem svetu [Perceived risk in the real and the virtual world]. Ljubljana.

Dimc, M. & Dobovšek, B. (2013): Percepcija kibernetske kriminalitete pri nekaterih uporabnikih interneta v Sloveniji in ZDA [Perception of cybercrime by selected internet users in Slovenia and USA]. Varstvoslovje [Journal of Criminal Justice and Security] 15, pp. 338–356.

Dobnikar, M. (1989): O nasilju [On violence]. Socialno delo [Social Work] 28, pp. 317–323.

Dolinar, P., Jere, M. & Meško, G. (2009): Skrito nasilje na delovnem mestu – med zanikanjem in trpljenjem – študija primera [Hidden violence at workplace – between denial and suffering], in: Varstvoslovje med teorijo in prakso. 10. Slovenski dnevi Varstvoslovja [Criminal justice between the theory and practice – 10th annual days of criminal justice]; https://www.fvv.um.si/dv2009/Zbornik/clanki/dolinar_jere_mesko.pdf [19.08.2018].

Dolinar, P., Jere, M., Meško, G., Podbregar, I. & Eman, K. (2010): Trpinčenje na delovnem mestu – zaznavanje. pojavne oblike in odzivi [Mobbing – Perception, forms and responses]. Revija za kriminalistiko in kriminologijo [Journal of Criminal Investigation and Criminology] 61, pp. 272–285.

Dvoršek, A., Maver, D. & Meško, G. (2006): Policijsko delo z oškodovanci premoženjske kriminalitete – med prijaznostjo in učinkovitostjo [Police work with victims of property crime – Between kindness and efficiency]. Revija za kriminalistiko in kriminologijo [Journal of Criminal Investigation and Criminology] 57, pp. 57–68.

Eman, K. (2016): Water crimes – a contemporary (security) issue. Crimen: časopis za krivične nauke [Crimen: Journal of criminal justice] 7, pp. 44–57.

Eman, K. (2014): Ekološka kriminaliteta kot priložnost za koruptivna ravnanja [Environmental crime as an opportunity for corruption], in: D. Smolej & B. Dobovšek (eds.), Korupcija kot pereča oblika okoljske problematike v Republiki Sloveniji [Corruption as the form of environmental problem in the Republic of Slovenia]. Ljubljana, pp. 37–55.

Eman, K. (2013): Environmental crime trends in Slovenia in the past decade. Varstvoslovje [Journal of Criminal Justice and Security] 15, pp. 240–260.

Eman, K. (2012): Crimes against the environment – Comparative criminology and criminal justice perspectives. Ljubljana.

Eman, K. (2011): Ekološka kriminaliteta v kriminologiji: razvoj nove veje kriminologije v Sloveniji [Environmental crime in criminology: The development of a new branch of criminology in Slovenia]. Revija za kriminalistiko in kriminologijo [Journal of Criminal Investigation and Criminology] 62, pp. 312–324.

Eman, K. (2008a): Ekološka kriminaliteta kot oblika lastne viktimizacije [Environmental crime as the form of victimisation], in: J. Šifrer (ed.), Javna in zasebna varnost: zbornik prispevkov, 9. Slovenski dnevi Varstvoslovja [Public and private security: Conference proceedings, 9th annual days of criminal justice. Ljubljana, p. 16.

Eman, K. (2008b): Uvod v fenomenološko analizo ekološke kriminalitete [Introduction to the fenomological analysis of environmental crime]. Varstvoslovje [Journal of Criminal Justice and Security] 10, pp. 220–239.

Eman, K. & Franca, B. (2016): Trgovanje z električno in elektronsko opremo - problem moderne družbe [Trading of electrical and electronic equipment – A contemporary problem of modern society]. Revija za kriminalistiko in kriminologijo [Journal of Criminal Investigation and Criminology] 67, pp. 248–261.

Eman, K. & Franca, B. (2013): Vpliv ekonomske krize na gibanje ekološke kriminalitete v Sloveniji [Impact oft he economic crisis on environmental crime trends in Slovenia]. Revija za kriminalistiko in kriminologijo [Journal of Criminal Investigation and Criminology] 64, pp. 358–370.

Eman, K. & Hacin, R. (2017): Pregled kriminološkega raziskovanja nasilja v Sloveniji po letu 1991 [An overview of criminological research on violenece in Slovenia since 1991]. Revija za kriminalistiko in kriminologijo [Journal of Criminal Investigation and Criminology] 68, pp. 209–217.

Eman, K. & Humar, S. (2017): (Vsiljena) privatizacija vodnih virov - nova oblika kriminalitete zoper vodo (in ljudi) z vidika kritične ekološke kriminologije [(Forced) water resource privatization – A new form of crime against water (and people) in terms of critical green criminology]. Revija za kriminalistiko in kriminologijo [Journal of Criminal Investigation and Criminology] 68, pp. 116–134.

Eman K. & Meško, G. (2014): Environmental crime and criminology: Crime phenomena and development of a green criminology in Slovenia. Saarbrücken.

Eman K. & Meško, G. (2013): Green issues in South-Eastern Europe, in: N. South & A. Brisman (eds.), Routledge international handbook of green criminology. Routledge, pp. 230–240.

Eman, K. & Meško, G. (2009): Ekološka kriminologija – poskus opredelitve in razprava [Environmental crime – Attempt of defining it and discussion]. Varstvoslovje [Journal of Criminal Justice and Security] 11, pp. 357–381.

Eman, K., Kuhar, S. & Meško, G. (2018): Kriminaliteta zoper vodo v Sloveniji [Water crimes in Slovenia]. Revija za kriminalistiko in kriminologijo [Journal of Criminal Investigation and Criminology] 69, pp. 44–53.

Eman, K., Kuhar, S. & Meško, G. (2017): Water crimes and policing. Varstvoslovje [Journal of Criminal Justice and Security] 19, pp. 105–119.

Eman, K., Kuhar, S. & Meško, G. (2016): Providing water supply in local communities - case study of Slovenia, in: G. Meško & B. Lobnikar (eds.), Criminal justice and security in Central and Eastern Europe: Safety, security, and social control in local communities: conference proceedings. Ljubljana, pp. 368–374.

Eman, K., Meško, G., & Fields, C.B. (2013): Environmental crime: A new security challenge, in: A. Maas (ed.), Global environmental change: New drivers for resistance, crime and terrorism. Baden-Baden, pp. 15–35.

Eman, K., Meško, G. & Fields, C.B. (2009): Crimes against the environment: Green criminology and research challenges in Slovenia. Varstvoslovje [Journal of Criminal Justice and Security] 11, pp. 574–592.

Eman, K., Meško, G., Dobovšek, B. & Sotlar, A. (2013): Environmental crime and green criminology in South Eastern Europe - Practice and research. Crime, Law and Social Change: An International Journal 59, pp. 341–358.

Ferlinc, A. (2018): Sovražni govor z vidika splošnega pojma kaznivega dejanja [Hate speech from the view point of general concept of criminal offense]. Pravna praksa [Legal Practice] 37, pp. 25–27.

Filipčič, K. (ed.) (2008): Poravnavanje v kazenskem postopku [Mediation in criminal procedure]. Ljubljana.

Filipčič, K., Bertok, E., Karajić, E., Klemenčič, I. & Muršič, M. (2017): Nasilje v družini kot dejavnik medvrstniškega nasilja [Domestic violence as a risk factor of bullying]. Revija za kriminalistiko in kriminologijo [Journal of Criminal Investigation and Criminology] 68, pp. 218–234.

Frangež, D. & Dvoršek, A. (2013): Nekateri kriminalistični vidiki odkrivanja spolnih zlorab otrok v Sloveniji [Some criminal investigation aspects of child sexual abuse detection in

Slovenia]. Revija za kriminalistiko in kriminologijo [Journal of Criminal Investigation and Criminology] 64, pp. 63–73.

Frangež, D. & Bučar-Ručman, A. (2017): Specific forms of human trafficking in Slovenia: Overview and preventive measures. Police Practice and Research: An International Journal 18, pp. 230–244.

Gorenak, V. (2003): Stališča oškodovancev kaznivih dejanj do policijskih postopkov kot merilo uspešnosti policijskih organizacij [Attitudes of victims of crime towards police proceedings as a criterion for the evaluation of the efficiency of police organisations]. Revija za kriminalistiko in kriminologijo [Journal of Criminal Investigation and Criminology] 54, pp. 41–51.

Hacin, R. & Eman, K. (2014): Study of the fear of crime in the Municipality of Trbovlje using crime mapping tools. Revija za kriminalistiko in kriminologijo [Journal of Criminal Investigation and Criminology] 65, pp. 299–315.

Kanduč, Z. (2002a): Vprašanje (so)odgovornosti pri intimnih viktimizacijah in "zločinih brez žrtev" " [A question of (co)responsibility in intimate victimisation and victimless crimes]. Revija za kriminalistiko in kriminologijo [Journal of Criminal Investigation and Criminology] 53, pp. 337–351.

Kanduč, Z. (ed.) (2002b): Žrtve. viktimizacije in viktimološke perspektive [Victims, victimizations and victimological perspectives]. Ljubljana.

Kanduč, Z. (1997): Izboljševanje normativnega in dejanskega položaja žrtve kaznivega dejanja [Enhancing the normative and actual situation of a victim of crime]. Revija za kriminalistiko in kriminologijo [Journal of Criminal Investigation and Criminology] 48, pp. 255–265.

Kanduč, Z. & Bučar-Ručman, A. (2016): Razredna vojna, delo in migracije: primer delavcev migrantov v Sloveniji [Class war, labour and migration: The case of migrant workers in Slovenia]. Dve domovin [Two Homelands], 43, pp. 77–89.

Kaučič-Gačnik, I. (2007): Viktimizacije v šolskem okolju [Victimisation in the school environment], in: G. Meško (ed.), Izbrana poglavja iz viktimologije I: mala čitanka viktimologije za varstvoslovce [Selected chapters from victimology I: A small book on victimology for criminal justice students]. Ljubljana, pp. 95–111.

Klančnik, A.T. & Pavšič Mrevlje, T. (2013): Kriminaliteta nad starejšimi in izhodišča za varno staranje v Sloveniji [Crime against the elderly and guidelines for a safer aging in Slovenia]. Varstvoslovje [Journal of Criminal Justice and Security] 15, pp. 385–397.

Kobe, P. (1977): Položaj žrtve v sodnem postopku s posebnim ozirom na adhezijski postopek [The victim's position in the criminal procedure with special regard to the "adhesion procedure"]. Revija za kriminalistiko in kriminologijo [Journal of Criminal Investigation and Criminology] 28, pp. 3–11.

Kobe, P. (1988): Kazenskopravna ureditev človekovih pravic in svoboščin [Criminal law provision on human rights and freedoms], in: P. Jambrek, A. Perenič & M. Uršič (eds.), Varstvo človekovih pravic: razprave, eseji in dokumenti. [Protection of human rights: debates, essays and documents]. Ljubljana, pp. 98–124.

Kogovšek, Š.N. (2017): Prispevek k razumevanju izziva pregona kaznivega dejanja 'javnega spodbujanja sovraštva, nasilja ali nestrpnosti' [A contribution to understanding the challenge of prosecuting 'a public incitement to hatred, violence or intolerance']. Časopis za kritiko znanosti [Journal of Criticism of Science] 45, pp. 74–87.

Konte, B. (ed.) (1996): Kronika človeštva [Chronicle of mankind]. Ljubljana.

Koprol, T.P. (2007): Tipologija žrtev kaznivih dejanj [Typology of victims of crime], in: G. Meško (ed.), Izbrana poglavja iz viktimologije I: mala čitanka viktimologije za varstvoslovce [Selected chapters from victimology I: A small book on victimology for criminal justice students]. Ljubljana, pp. 35–46.

Leskošek, V., Urek, M. & Zaviršek, D. (2010): Nacionalna raziskava o nasilju v zasebni sferi in v partnerskih odnosih. Končno poročilo 1. faze raziskovalnega projekta [National research on violence in domestic sphere and in partnership: Final report of the 1st phase of the research project]. Ljubljana.

Meadows, R.J. (2014): Understanding violence and victimization (6th ed.). Upper Saddle River.

Merljak, S., Belovič, M., Božič, A. & Potič, A. (2012): Protesti proti oblasti: Ljubljana v živo [Protests against the governement: Ljubljana live], in: Delo, 30.11.2012; http://www.delo.si/novice/slovenija/protesti-proti-oblasti-ljubljana-v-zivo.html [18.08.2018].

Meško, G. (2018): On some aspects of cybercrime and cybervictimization: editorial. European journal of crime, criminal law and criminal justice 26, pp. 189–199.

Meško, G. (2016): Kriminologija [Criminology]. Ljubljana.

Meško, G. (2000): Storilci kaznivih dejanj, storilci prekrškov in žrtve kriminalitete v očeh slovenskih policistov [Views of Slovenian police officers on the perpetrators of criminal offences, misdemeanours and victims of crime]. Varstvoslovje [Journal of Criminal Justice and Security] 2/3, pp. 264–273.

Meško, G. (1998): Nekatere razsežnosti nasilne viktimizacije [Some aspect of violent victimization]. Teorija in praksa [Journal of Theory and Practice], 35, pp. 1076–1088.

Meško, G. (ed.): (2007): Izbrana poglavja iz viktimologije I: mala čitanka viktimiologije za varstvoslovce [Selected chapters from victimology I: A small book on victimology for criminal justice students]. Ljubljana.

Meško, G. & Areh, I. (2003): Strah pred kriminaliteto v urbanih okoljih [Fear of crime in urban environment]. Revija za kriminalistiko in kriminologijo [Journal of Criminal Investigation and Criminology] 54, pp. 144–152.

Meško, G. & Bernik, I. (2011): Cybercrime: Awareness and fear; https://www.academia.edu/1470364/Cybercrime_Awareness_and_Fear_Slovenian_Perspectives [21.08.2018].

Meško, G. & Eman, K. (2012): Organised crime involvement in waste trafficking - case of the Republic of Slovenia. Kriminalističke teme [Criminalistics themes] 12, pp. 79–96.

Meško, G. & Pavlović, Z. (1998): Strah pred kriminaliteto – izzivi za raziskovanje [Fear of crime – a challenge to research]. Revija za kriminalistiko in kriminologijo [Journal of Criminal Investigation and Criminology] 49, pp. 346–353.

Meško, G. & Šifrer, J. (2008): Strah pred kriminaliteto v mestnem okolju – raziskava [Fear of crime in urban environment - Research]. Varstvoslovje [Journal of Criminal Justice and Security] 10, pp. 539–560.

Meško, G. & Umek, P. (1999): Značilnosti socialnopsihološkega in demografskega modela strahu pred kriminaliteto [Characteristics of sociopsychological and demographic model of fear of crime]. Revija za kriminalistiko in kriminologijo [Journal of Criminal Investigation and Criminology] 50, pp. 131–137.

Meško, G., Bančič, K., Eman, K. & Fields, C.B. (2011): Situational crime-prevention measures to environmental threats, in: G. Meško, D. Dimitrijević & Fields C.B. (eds.), Understanding and managing threats to the environment in South Eastern Europe: [proceedings of the NATO Advanced Research Workshop on Managing Global Environmental Threats to Air, Water and Soil, Ljubljana, Slovenia, 28-30 June 2010]. Dordrecht, pp. 41–67.

Meško, G., Fallshore, M. & Jevšek, A. (2007): Policija in strah pred kriminaliteto [Police and fear of crime]. Revija za kriminalistiko in kriminologijo [Journal of Criminal Investigation and Criminology] 58, pp. 340–351.

Meško, G., Hacin, R., Pirnat, U. & Eman, K. (2018): Migration issues in Slovenia: Beyond the rhetoric of university-level criminology and crime prevention education for sustainable development, in: H. Kury & S. Redo (eds.), Refugees and migrants in law and policy: Challenges and opportunities for global civic education. Cham, pp. 492–527.

Meško, G., Sotlar, A. & Eman, K. (eds.) (2012): Ekološka kriminaliteta in varovanje okolja - multidisciplinarne perspective [Environmental crime and protection of the environment – Multidisciplinary perspectives]. Ljubljana.

Meško, G., Šifrer, J., & Vošnjak, L. (2012): Strah pred kriminaliteto v mestnih in vaških okoljih v Sloveniji [Fear of crime in urban and rural environments in Slovenia]. Varstvoslovje [Journal of Criminal Justice and Security] 14, pp. 259–276.

Meško, G., Vošnjak, L., Muratbegović, E., Budimilić, M., Bren, M. & Kury, H. (2012): Fear of crime in urban neighbourhoods: A comparative analysis of six capitals. Varstvoslovje [Journal of Criminal Justice and Security] 14, pp. 397–421.

Mičović, E. (2011): Varstvo potrošnikov in varna hrana - tveganja in nevidne viktimizacije [Consumer protection and food safety – Risks and invisible victimisations]. Revija za kriminalistiko in kriminologijo [Journal of Criminal Investigation and Criminology] 62, pp. 3–11.

Mičović, E. (2010): Prepoznavanje nevidnih viktimizacij z vidika zagotavljanja varne hrane in varstva potrošnikov [Recognizing invisible victimization regarding food safety and consumer protection]. Ljubljana.

Modic, M. (2016): The convergence between migration and policing: The Slovenian perspective. Dve domovini [Two Homelands], 43, pp. 47–59.

Pavlović, Z. (1999a): Mednarodni anketi o kriminaliteti oz. viktimizaciji Slovenija (Ljubljana) 1992-1997 (2. del) [International crime (victimisation) surveys – Slovenia (Ljubljana) 1992-1997 (2nd part)]. Revija za kriminalistiko in kriminologijo [Journal of Criminal Investigation and Criminology] 50, pp. 30–37.

Pavlović, Z. (1999b): Mednarodni anketi o kriminaliteti oz. viktimizaciji Slovenija (Ljubljana) 1992-1997 (3. del) [International crime (victimisation) surveys – Slovenia (Ljubljana) 1992–1997 (3rd part)]. Revija za kriminalistiko in kriminologijo [Journal of Criminal Investigation and Criminology] 50, pp. 122–130.

Pavlović, Z. (1999c): Mednarodni anketi o kriminaliteti oz. viktimizaciji Slovenija (Ljubljana) 1992–1997 (4. sklepni del) [International crime (victimisation) surveys – Slovenia (Ljubljana) 1992–1997 (4th concluding part)]. Revija za kriminalistiko in kriminologijo [Journal of Criminal Investigation and Criminology] 50, pp. 234–239.

Pavlović, Z. (1998): Mednarodni anketi o kriminaliteti oz. viktimizaciji Slovenija (Ljubljana) 1992–1997 (1. del) [International crime (victimisation) surveys – Slovenia (Ljubljana) 1992–1997 (1st part)]. Revija za kriminalistiko in kriminologijo [Journal of Criminal Investigation and Criminology] 49, pp. 257–265.

Pavlović, Z. (1993): Mednarodna anketa o viktimizaciji: Ljubljana 1992 [International crime survey – Ljubljana 1992]. Revija za kriminalistiko in kriminologijo [Journal of Criminal Investigation and Criminology] 44, pp. 129–138.

Pavlović, Z. (1990): "Nasilje nad ženskami, zlasti v družini": sklepi seminarja seminarja ["Violence against women, especially within the family": Conclusion of the seminar]. Revija za kriminalistiko in kriminologijo [Journal of Criminal Investigation and Criminology] 41, pp. 126–129.

Pavšič Mrevlje, T. & Nivala, J. (2017): Victimisation of the elderly in the municipalities of Ljubljana and Uppsala. International Review of Victimology 23, pp. 33–46.

Pavšič Mrevlje, T. (2014a): Kaj nam povedo slovenske raziskave in podatki policije o nasilju v družini? [What does Slovenian research and police data tell us about domestic violence], in: B. Flander, I. Areh & M. Modic (eds.), Conference proceeding of the 15th Slovenian days of Criminal Justice; https://www.fvv.um.si/dv2014/zbornik/Pavsic-Mrevlje.pdf [20.08.2018].

Pavšič Mrevlje, T. (2014b): Viktimizacija starejših v Mestni občini Ljubljana [Victimization of the elderly in the Municipality of Ljubljana]. Revija za kriminalistiko in kriminologjjo [Journal of Criminal Investigation and Criminology] 65, pp. 96–107.

Pečar, J. (1993): Nasilje in prisila [Violence and coercion]. Revija za kriminalistiko in kriminologijo [Journal of Criminal Investigation and Criminology] 44, pp. 34–48.

Pečar, J. (1984a): Viktimologija družine [Victimology of family]. Revija za kriminalistiko in kriminologijo [Journal of Criminal Investigation and Criminology] 35, pp. 135–150.

Pečar, J. (1984b): "Induktologija" – znanje o vplivanju na kazensko dvojico ["Inductology" – The knowledge of influences exercised on the criminal couple]. Revija za kriminalistiko in kriminologijo [Journal of Criminal Investigation and Criminology] 35, pp. 299–311.

Pečar, J. (1982): Neprijavljena konvencionalna kriminaliteta zoper posameznika [Unreported conventional crime against individual]. Revija za kriminalistiko in kriminologijo [Journal of Criminal Investigation and Criminology] 33, pp. 118–129.

Pečar, J. (1979): Družbena "vidnost" kriminalitete in družbeno nadzorstvo [Social "visibility" of crime and social control]. Revija za kriminalistiko in kriminologijo [Journal of Criminal Investigation and Criminology] 30, pp. 35–46.

Pečar, J. (1978): Viktimološke sestavine samopostrežne trgovine [Victimological components of self-services stores]. Revija za kriminalistiko in kriminologijo [Journal of Criminal Investigation and Criminology] 29, pp. 264–274.

Pečar, J. (1972): Involved bystanders: examination of a neglected aspect of criminology and victimology. International Journal of Contemporary Sociology 2, pp. 81–87.

Pečar, J. (1971a): Vloga žrtev pri ubojih na Slovenskem [The role of the victim in criminal homicide in Slovenia]. Revija za kriminalistiko in kriminologijo [Journal of Criminal Investigation and Criminology] 22, pp. 258–265.

Pečar, J. (1971b): Vpleteni "opazovalci" – viktimološka razčlemba [Involved bystanders – Victimological aspect]. Revija za kriminalistiko in kriminologijo [Journal of Criminal Investigation and Criminology] 22, pp. 172–184.

Pečar, J., Maver, D. & Zobec, Ž. (1981): Tatvine v samopostrežnih prodajalnah Thefts in self-service shops]. Ljubljana.

Peršak, N. (2015): Viktimologija [Victimology], in: A. Šelih, & K. Filipčič (eds.), Kriminologija [Criminology]. Ljubljana, pp. 126–182.

Petrovec. D. (2005): Kult žrtve [Cult of victim]. Ljubljana.

Petrovec, D. (2015): Nasilje pod masko [Violence under mask]. Ljubljana.

Podjaveršek, A. (1970): Kazniva dejanja telesnih poškodb v občini Šmarje pri Jelšah Jelšah [Offences of assault in the commune Šmarje pri Jelšah]. Revija za kriminalistiko in kriminologijo [Journal of Criminal Investigation and Criminology] 21, pp. 97–104.

Prislan, K. & Lobnikar, B. (2018): Analiza vedenja uporabnikov spletnega bančništva [Analysis of online banking users behaviour]. Varstvoslovje [Journal of Criminal Investigation and Criminology] 20, pp. 25–44.

Pšunder, M. (2012): Medvrstniško nasilje preko interneta in primerjava s tradicionalnim nasiljem [Peers violence over the Internet and comparison with traditional violence], in: M. Senekovič, O. Dečman Dobrnjič & J. Ferk (eds.), Modeli vzgoje v globalni družbi [Education models in the global society]. Ljubljana, pp. 43–48.

Razpotnik, Š. & Dekleva, B. (2015): Medvrstniško nasilje v šoli – socialnopedagoški pogledi [Peer violence in school – socialpedagogic views]. Socialna pedagogika [Journal Social Pedagogy] 19, pp. 217–230.

Salecl, R. (2002): Besede in nasilje [Words and violence], in: Z. Kanduč (ed.), Žrtve. viktimizacije in viktimološke perspective [Victims, victimisations and victimological perspectives]. Ljubljana, pp. 14–27.

Selič, P. & Jakopin, A. (2010): Trpinčenje na delovnem mestu – razširjenost in posledice pri specializantih medicine v Sloveniji v letu 2009 [Mobbing of trainee doctors in Slovenia: Prevalence and impact on their health in 2009]. Revija za kriminalistiko in kriminologijo [Journal of Criminal Investigation and Criminology] 61, pp. 286–294.

Smolej, D. (2011): Zloraba in zanemarjanje otrok – storilci starši [Abuse and mistreatment of children – Parents perpetrators], in: T.P. Mrevlje (ed.), Zbornik prispevkov. 12. Slovenski dnevi Varstvoslovja [12th Slovenian days of Criminal Justice and Security]. Ljubljana.

South, N., Eman, K. & Meško, G. (2014): History of green criminology, in: G. Bruinsma & D. Weisburd (eds.), Encyclopedia of criminology and criminal justice. New York.

Šelih, A. (2012): Victimological research in Slovenia. Temida [Temida] 15, pp. 121–134.

Šelih, A. (1994): Viktimološko raziskovanje v Sloveniji [Victimological research in Slovenia]. Revija za kriminalistiko in kriminologijo [Journal of Criminal Investigation and Criminology] 45, pp. 356–360.

Šelih, A. (1967): Viktimologija in njena vloga v boju zoper kriminaliteto [Victimology and its role in the war on crime]. Revija za kriminalistiko in kriminologijo [Journal of Criminal Investigation and Criminology] 18, pp. 37–42.

Štirn, M. (2004): Ko postanem žrtev kaznivega dejanja [When I become a victim of crime]. Ljubljana.

Tomažič, T. & Bessa, N.V. (2017): Ongoing criminal activities in cyberspace: From the protection of minors to the Deep Web. Revija za kriminalistiko in kriminologijo [Journal of Criminal Investigation and Criminology] 68, pp. 412–423.

Uderman, B. (1972): Uboji na Slovenskem (1954-1967) [Homicide in Slovenia (1954-1967)]. Revija za kriminalistiko in kriminologijo [Journal of Criminal Investigation and Criminology 23, pp. 13–20.

Umek, P. (2004): Viktimizacijska študija 2001 [Victimisation study 2001], in: G. Meško (ed.), Preprečevanje kriminalitete – teorija. praksa in dileme [Prevention of crime – theory, practice and dilemmas]. Ljubljana, pp. 149–162.

Umek, P. & Meško, G. (1999): Žrtve premoženjskih deliktov o delu policistov in kriminalistov [Victims of property offences and their assessment of police officers' and crime investigators' work]. Revija za kriminalistiko in kriminologijo [Journal of Criminal Investigation and Criminology] 50, pp. 339–344.

Varga, A. (2007): Žrtve besednega nasilja – sovražni govor [Victims of verbal violence – Hate speech], in: G. Meško (ed.), Izbrana poglavja iz viktimologije I: mala čitanka viktimologije za varstvoslovce [Selected chapters from victimology I: A small book on victimology for criminal justice students]. Ljubljana, pp. 275–288.

Vehovar, V., Motl, A., Mihelič, L., Berčič, B. & Petrovčič, A. (2012): Zaznava sovražnega govora na slovenskem spletu [Perception of hate speech in Slovene web]. Teorija in praksa [Theory and Practice] 49, pp. 171–189.

Vene, T. (2012): Mobing, grožnja zaposlenim [Mobbing, threat to employees]. Revija za univerzalno odličnost [Journal of universal excellence] 1, pp. 11–19.

Veselič, Š. (ed.) (2007): Nasilje!: kaj lahko storim? [Violence!: What can I do?]. Ljubljana.

Vodopivec, K. (1977): Povrnitev škode žrtvam kaznivih dejanj [Restitution to victims of criminal offences]. Revija za kriminalistiko in kriminologijo [Journal of Criminal Investigation and Criminology 28, pp. 241–257.

Vošnjak, L. (2011): Strukturalna analiza socio-demografskega. socialnopsihološkega in celostnega modela zaskrbljenosti ljudi glede kriminalitete in sodobnih oblik negotovosti [A structural analysis of socio-demographic, social psychological, and holistic model of people's anxiety regarding crime and contemporary forms of insecurity]. Ljubljana.

Završnik, A. (2015): Kibernetska kriminaliteta [Cybercrime]. Ljubljana.

Završnik, A. (2008): Konceptualne zagate restorativne pravičnosti – nova paradigma modernega odzivanja na kriminaliteto? [Conceptual problems of restorative justice – a new paradigm of a contemporary response to crime?]. Revija za kriminalistiko in kriminologijo [Journal of Criminal Investigation and Criminology] 59, pp. 125–140.

Završnik, A. (2007): Sovražni govor po predlogu KZ-1 [Hate speech under the proposition of Criminal Code-1]. Pravna praksa [Law practice] 4; https://www.pravnapraksa.si/Lite/Kazalo.aspx?Src=zNblVXQY1zSI0YqaH4aXViOQxjuE1q+kWaTdh3BaQQe6Nez-J60ydGc1dJilCCiCsVLFCzkuztv4U2nYRM/oyVA== [20.08.2018].

Završnik, A. (2006): Regulacija sovražnega govora: kriminološki in kazenskopravni vidik [Regulation of hate speech: Criminological and criminal justice perspectives]. Dialogi [Dialogues] 45, pp. 51–73.

Završnik, A. & Zrimšek, V. (2017): Sovražni govor po slovenski kaznovalni zakonodaji in sodni praksi [Hate speech in the view of Slovene criminal legislation and legal practice]. Časopis za kritiko znanosti [Journal of Criticism of Science] 45, pp. 59–73.

Zlobec, J. (ed.) (1989): Smrtna kazen: zbornik [Death penalty: Proceedings]. Ljubljana.

Documents

Government of the Republic of Slovenia (2017): O Sloveniji [About Slovenia]; http://www.vlada.si/o_sloveniji/ [19.08.2018] [in Slovene and English].

International Crime Victimisation Survey (ICVS) (2017): Data analysis – SPSS syntax [Data File]; http://wp.unil.ch/icvs/codebooks/ [18.08.2018] [in English only]; cited as: ICVS 2017.

Ministry of the Environment and Spatial Planning (2017): Mesta in urbana središča [Towns and urban centres]; http://www.mop.gov.si/si/delovna_podrocja/urbani_razvoj/mesta_in_urbana_obmocja/ [15.08.2018] [in Slovene and English].

Ministry of the Interior, Police (2018): Poročilo o delu policije za 2017 [Annual report on the work of the police 2017]; http://www.policija.si/images/stories/Statistika/LetnaPorocila/PDF/LetnoPorocilo2017.pdf [19.08.2018] [in Slovene only].

Ministry of the Interior, Police (2017): Poročilo o delu policije za 2016 [Annual report on the work of the police 2016]; http://www.policija.si/images/stories/Statistika/LetnaPorocila/PDF/LetnoPorocilo2016.pdf [19.08.2018] [in Slovene only].

Ministry of the Interior, Police (2016): Poročilo o delu policije za 2015 [Annual report on the work of the police 2015]; http://www.policija.si/images/stories/Statistika/LetnaPorocila/PDF/LetnoPorocilo2015.pdf [19.08.2018] [in Slovene only].

Ministry of the Interior, Police (2015): Poročilo o delu policije za 2014 [Annual report on the work of the police 2014]; http://www.policija.si/images/stories/Statistika/LetnaPorocila/PDF/LetnoPorocilo2014.pdf [19.08.2018] [in Slovene only].

Ministry of the Interior, Police (2014): Poročilo o delu policije za 2013 [Annual report on the work of the police 2013]; http://www.policija.si/images/stories/Statistika/LetnaPorocila/PDF/LetnoPorocilo2013.pdf [19.08.2018] [in Slovene only].

Ministry of the Interior, Police (2013): Poročilo o delu policije za 2012 [Annual report on the work of the police 2012]; http://www.policija.si/images/stories/Statistika/LetnaPorocila/PDF/LetnoPorocilo2012.pdf [19.08.2018] [in Slovene only].

Ministry of the Interior, Police (2012): Poročilo o delu policije za 2011 [Annual report on the work of the police 2011]; http://www.policija.si/images/stories/Statistika/LetnaPorocila/PDF/LetnoPorocilo2011.pdf [19.08.2018] [in Slovene only].

Ministry of the Interior, Police (2011): Poročilo o delu policije za 2010 [Annual report on the work of the police 2010]; http://www.policija.si/images/stories/Statistika/LetnaPorocila/PDF/LetnoPorocilo2010.pdf [19.08.2018] [in Slovene only].

Statistical Office of the Republic of Slovenia (StatOffice) (2017a): Delo in brezposelnost [Jobs and unemployment] [Data File]; http://www.stat.si/StatWeb/Field/Index/17 [15.08.2018] [in Slovene only]; cited as: StatOffice 2017a.

Statistical Office of the Republic of Slovenia (StatOffice) (2017b): Prebivalstvo [Residents] [Data File]; http://www.stat.si/StatWeb/Field/Index/17 [15.08.2018] [in Slovene only]; cited as: StatOffice 2017b.

StatOffice: see Statistical Office of the Republic of Slovenia.

UNESCO (2017): Historical efforts to implement the UNESCO 1974 recommendation on education in ligh of 3 SGDs targets; http://unesdoc.unesco.org/images/0024/002472/247275E.pdf [20.08.2018] [in English only].

Uniformed Police Directorate (2016): Ilegalne migracije na območju Republike Slovenije [Illegal migrations on the area of the Republic of Slovenia]; http://www.policija.si/images/stories/Statistika/MejnaProblematika/IlegalneMigracije/2015/December2015.pdf [21.08.2018] [in Slovene only].

United Nations High Commissioner for Refugees (2016). The Balkan migrant Crisis: An introduction; https://data2.unhcr.org/ar/documents/download/46801.

Turkey

Victimology and Victim Protection

Tuba Topçuoğlu & Selman Dursun

1. General Country Background

After the fall of the Ottoman State, the Republic of Turkey was founded on 29 October 1923, in Ankara, the country's new capital. Turkey, at the crossroads of Europe and Asia, is located at the northeast end of the Mediterranean Sea in southeast Europe and southwest Asia, and is bordered by the Black Sea to the north, the Mediterranean Sea to the south and the Aegean Sea to the west. Turkey is primarily a Western Asian country, with a small portion of Eastern Thrace located in Southeast Europe. The surface area of Turkey is 814,578 square kilometres, of which 97% are in Asia and 3% in Europe (referred to as Thrace). The Bosporus, the Sea of Marmara and the Dardanelles separate the European and the Asian parts of the country. Turkey has traditionally been a country of emigration; however, of those who did immigrate to Turkey, until the late 1980s, the majority of arrivals were from the Balkans. After the collapse of the USSR, a new wave of migrants came from former Soviet republics.[1] The Syrian civil war, which started in 2011, has further affected Turkey: Turkey is currently hosting the largest number of refugees in the world, with nearly 3,586,679 Syrian refugees under temporary protection (almost half are children).[2] In addition to this refugee crisis, Turkey suffers from a decades-long struggle with terrorism. There have been 4,106 terrorist attacks in Turkey between 1970 and 2016.[3] Turkey also recently witnessed several political events, such as a series of suicide bombings and an attempted coup-d'état on 15 July 2016 (the latter resulted in 248 deaths and 2,193 serious injuries). After the initial declaration in July 2016, Turkey extended a state of emergency several times and, finally, ended it in July 2018.[4]

---

1 Human Resource Development Foundation 2007, p. 227.

2 Ministry of the Interior, General Directorate of Migration Management 2018a.

3 START 2016.

4 Hurriyet of 01.02.2020; Türkiye'de Ohal Sona Erdi; http://www.hurriyet.com.tr/gundem/ohal-uygulamasi-sona- erdi-40901478 [19.01.2019].

Turkey is a secular state and the political system is based on the principle of separation of powers between legislative, executive and judicial branches. After a constitutional referendum on 16 April 2017, the Turkish Constitution changed from a parliamentary to a presidential system. Accordingly, the Prime Ministership has been abolished and the President of Turkey is the head of the executive branch of government as well as the head of state. The President is elected directly by popular vote. While legislative power is vested in the Grand National Assembly of Turkey, judicial power is exercised by independent courts.

Although public administration in Turkey is divided between central and local authorities, Turkey maintains a highly centralised administrative system. The country is divided into provinces, districts and sub-districts. The central administration is organised at the provincial, district and sub-district levels and includes various governmental ministries and agencies (as well as their provincial and district branches). In Turkey, there are 81 provincial, 919 district and a number of sub-district administrations. Local administration in Turkey is comprised of special provincial administrations, municipalities (including metropolitan municipalities) and villages. At present, there are 81 special provincial administrations, 30 metropolitan municipalities, 1,398 municipalities and 18,336 village administrations in Turkey.[5]

After Russia and Germany, Turkey has the third largest population in Europe. As of 31 December 2017, and based on the address-based population registration system, Turkey had 80,810,525 inhabitants (50% male) with an annual growth rate of 1.2%.[6] The population in Turkey was around 67,804,000 in 2000 and has thus increased by 19% during the last seventeen years. About 92% of the population live in urban areas, while the remainder lives in towns and villages. Amongst the 81 provinces, Istanbul is the largest city in terms of population (15,029,231), followed by the capital Ankara (5,445,026), Izmir (4,279,677) and Bursa (2,936,803). The country's population density was 105 people per square kilometre in 2017, ranging from 11 to 2,892 among all the provinces. With 2,892 inhabitants per square kilometre, Istanbul had (and still has) the highest population density, followed by Kocaeli (521), Izmir (356), Yalova (297), Gaziantep (294), Bursa (282), Hatay (270) and Ankara (222). Tunceli has the lowest population density with 11 inhabitants per square kilometre, followed by Ardahan (20), Erzincan (20), Sivas (22), Bayburt (22) and Artvin (23).

The population in Turkey is relatively young, with 24% of the country's population falling within the 0–14 age bracket. The 15–64 age bracket corresponds to 67.5% of the population while the 65 and above age bracket makes up 8.5% of the total pop-

5 Ministry of the Interior 2018.

6 The last population census was carried out in 2000 in Turkey. In 2006, the address-based population registration system was established, and the first results based on the new system were announced in 2008 for the previous year; this and all the subsequent statistical information on Turkey in this paragraph was taken from TurkStat 2018a.

ulation. According to the address-based population system, there were 40,535,135 men and 40,275,390 women in 2017. The median age was 31 for men and 32 for women. Within the population aged 15 years and over, 27.4% were single, 63.4% married, 5.5% widowed and 3.7% divorced. The birth rate for 2017 was 16.1 births while the death rate was 5.3 deaths per thousand people. The estimated fertility rate in 2017 was 2.07 children per woman. The infant mortality rate for 2016 was 10 deaths per thousand live births, and life expectancy was 75.3 years for males and 80.7 years for females in 2014.

The foreign-born component of Turkey's population accounts for about 2% of the country's population. According to the address-based population system records in 2017, 19% were born in Bulgaria, followed by Germany with 14.4%, Iraq with 10.4%, Syria with 5.7%, Afghanistan with 4.1% and Azerbaijan with 3.7%. There are no official statistics on the ethnic or religious composition of the country's population.

Turkey is an upper-middle income country with a gross domestic product of 12,112 US dollars (in current prices) per capita (in 2014). Based on the Income and Living Conditions Survey conducted in 2016, the Gini coefficient by household disposable income was 0,404. Among the population aged 15 years and over in 2017, the labour force participation rate was 52.8% while the unemployment rate was 10.9%. Of those in the labour force, 19.4% were employed in agriculture, 26.5% in industry and 54.1% in services. Turkey is a founding member of the UN, OECD, OSCE, a member of NATO, the Council of Europe and an associate member of the EU.[7]

2. Current State of Victimology

Victimology is currently not an institutionalised scientific discipline in Turkey. It is generally taught as a graduate selective course at some of the country's law faculties. There are only two textbooks on victimology[8] and all victimology courses use these books as the course material. Currently, there is no national victimological society and not a single Turkish academic journal focuses on victimology. Information on victims is scarce as police statistics on crime and victims are not available to the public[9] and, in addition, Turkey does not conduct regular victimisation surveys at the national level. Therefore, no national set of data exists about the number and the characteristics of victims (reported or unreported). There are, however, a number of national surveys that focus on specific types of victimisation, such as violence against women.[10] Given the significance of the topic and the push for

7 Ministry of Foreign Affairs 2018a.

8 *Sokullu-Akıncı & Dursun* 2016; *Polat* 2014.

9 *Sözüer & Topçuoğlu* 2014.

10 *Altınay & Arat* 2007; 2009; Ministry of Family and Social Policies, General Directorate on the Status of Women 2015; Prime Ministry, Institution of Family Research 1995; 1998.

women's rights since the 1980s, the first comprehensive study on domestic violence against women was carried out in 1993/4 on behalf of the Family Research Institution of the Turkish Prime Ministry.[11] This was followed by another national study on the prevalence and correlates of violence against women in 2008 (with a follow-up study in 2014).[12] While numerous victimisation surveys have occurred at the local level, methodological drawbacks of most empirical research (e.g., lack of representative samples, inadequacy of research design, etc.) make it difficult to obtain an accurate picture of either the actual prevalence rates or the risk factors of victimisation.

Despite these drawbacks, victimological research is developing in Turkey. An examination of empirical victimological studies conducted in Turkey suggests that researchers generally focus on issues such as intimate partner violence, sexual abuse, victimisation at school (e.g., peer-bullying), cyber-bullying and victimisation at work (e.g., mobbing, violence against healthcare workers). In recent years, Turkey has taken part in some international studies on victimisation. For example, Turkey participated in the International Crime Victims Survey (ICVS) in 2005 with a city-based sample in Istanbul.[13] Turkey also participated in the Balkan Epidemiological Study on Child Abuse and Neglect (BECAN)[14] and the International Self-Report Delinquency 3 (ISRD 3) study, an international comparative survey on delinquency and victimisation of school children (the latter was carried out in 2017 with a city-based sample in Istanbul). Nevertheless, there are still a number of areas that have not yet attracted adequate scholarly attention in Turkey, such as secondary victimisation, repeat victimisation, elderly victimisation, victims of trafficking, victims of white-collar crime, environmental victimisation, tourism and victimisation, victimisation within prisons and victimisation of minorities.

Several governmental and state-related institutions, in cooperation with various non-governmental organisations (NGOs), provide victim support and victim protection. Such institutions and organisations play a key role in the study of victimology in Turkey. Key governmental and state-related institutions that actively provide protection and assistance for victims of various types of crime, such as women victims of violence, child victims of crime and victims of human trafficking, are listed in *Table 1.*

---

11 Prime Ministry, Institution of Family Research 1995.

12 Ministry of Family and Social Policies, General Directorate on the Status of Women 2015; Ministry of Family and Social Policies and Hacettepe University Institute of Population Studies 2015.

13 *Jahic & Akdaş* 2007; *Jahic & Akdaş Mitrani* 2010.

14 *Akço, Dağlı, İnanıcı, Kaynak, Oral, Şahin, Sofuoğlu & Ulukol* 2013.

Table 1 Key Governmental/State-Related Institutions Involved in Victim Protection

Ministry	Institution	Main focus	Internet site
Ministry of Family and Social Policies	General Directorate of Status of Women	Women	http://kadininstatusu.aile.gov.tr
	Violence Prevention and Monitoring Centres		https://kadininstatusu.aile.gov.tr/uygulamalar/siddet-onleme-ve-izleme-merkezi
Ministry of Family and Social Policies	General Directorate of Child Services	Children	http://cocukhizmetleri.aile.gov.tr
	Child Support Centres		http://cocukhizmetleri.aile.gov.tr/uygulamalar/cocuk-destek-merkezleri
Ministry of Health	Child Monitoring Centres	Child victims of sexual abuse	https://www.saglik.gov.tr
Ministry of Interior	General Directorate of Migration Management	Victims of human trafficking	http://www.goc.gov.tr/En_3
	Department for the Protection of Victims of Human Trafficking		
–	Ankara Metropolitan Municipality, Women's shelter	Victims of human trafficking, women	https://www.ankara.bel.tr
–	Kırıkkale Shelter Home	Victims of human trafficking, women	–
Ministry of Justice	General Directorate of Prisons and Detention Houses, Department of Probation	Victims of crime	http://www.cte.adalet.gov.tr/index.html http://www.cte-ds.adalet.gov.tr/en/index_en.html
	General Directorate for Penal Affairs, Department of Victim Rights		http://www.magdur.adalet.gov.tr

The Ministry of Family and Social Policies[15] was founded in 2011. It encompasses eight service units, including the General Directorate of Family and Community Services, the General Directorate of Social Assistance, the General Directorate on the Status of Women, the General Directorate of Child Services, the General Directorate of Persons with Disabilities and Elderly Services and the Department of Fall-

15 After the submission of this chapter, with the Decree Law No.703 dated 9 July 2018, the Ministry of Family and Social Policies merged with the Ministry of Labour and Social Security under the Ministry of Labour, Social Services and Family, which was renamed as the Ministry of Family, Labour and Social Services with the Presidential Decree on the Organisation of the Presidency published on 10 July 2018.

en Soldiers' Relatives and Veterans' Affairs.[16] The General Directorate on the Status of Women was assigned as the coordinating body on issues of violence against women and honour killings pursuant to the Prime Ministry Circular in 2006.[17] The General Directorate is responsible for the coordination and provision of various protective, preventive, educational, counselling and rehabilitative social services to women.[18] Accordingly, in 2012, numerous Violence Prevention and Monitoring Centres (V PMCs) were established.[19] These centres provide services to victims of violence, including accommodation, temporary financial assistance, counselling and guidance, legal and medical assistance and employment support.[20] Currently, there are 49 VPMCs in Turkey.[21] Furthermore, in addition to the services provided through the VPMCs and other women's shelters directly linked to the Ministry of Family and Social Policies, various help and support services are available to female victims of violence through health institutions, local administrations, bar associations and NGOs. Amongst all NGOs, those initiated by women's groups are the strongest in Turkey (given the long history – going back to the Ottoman period – and the accomplishments of the women's movement in Turkey).[22] Currently, there are 143 women's shelters in Turkey, with a total capacity of 3,444 beds.[23] Of these, 109 are affiliated with the Ministry of Family and Social Policies and 32 are under the administration of municipalities. While one women's shelter is affiliated with the Ministry of Interior General Directorate of Migration Management, another is owned by an NGO.[24] These shelters provide various services to women who are victims of abuse or violence of any form, including counselling, psychological support, legal support, medical care support, temporary financial

---

16 Ministry of Family and Social Policies 2017; Article 6 of the Decree Law on the Establishment and Functions of the Ministry of Family and Social Policies, Law No. 633, 03.06.2012, Official Gazette 08.06.2011/27958.

17 Ministry of Family and Social Policies 2018; Prime Ministry, Circular on Measures to be taken for the prevention of Violence against Children and Women and Honour Killings, No. 2006/17, Official Gazette 04.07.2006/26218.

18 Article 9 of the Decree Law on the Establishment and Functions of the Ministry of Family and Social Policies.

19 Article 14 of the Law on Protection of Family and Prevention of Violence against Women, Law No. 6284, 08.03.2012, Official Gazette 20.03.2012/28239.

20 Article 15 of the Law on Protection of Family and Prevention of Violence against Women.

21 Ministry of Family and Social Policies, General Directorate on the Status of Women 2017, p. 4.

22 The women's movement is quite strong and autonomous in Turkey, especially since the 1980s. Accordingly, the movement has been very influential on government responsiveness to violence against women; see *Sözüer, Baytaz & Kelep* 2012; *Tekeli* 2010; *Yeşilyurt Gündüz* 2004.

23 Ministry of Family and Social Policies 2018.

24 Ministry of Family and Social Policies 2018.

aid, allowances, kindergarten services, vocational training courses, group work and scholarships for children.

The General Directorate of Child Services (previously named Agency of Social Services and Child Protection before 2011) also functions under the Ministry of Family and Social Policies and is responsible for the coordination and provision of various protective, preventive, educational, counselling and rehabilitative services for children.[25] The General Directorate is responsible for carrying out protective and supportive measures for juvenile victims of crime as well as security measures for juveniles who have drifted into crime, as determined by the Child Protection Law.[26] Within the Turkish child protection system, Child Support Centres are especially important, since they provide services to three specific groups of children: children who are victims of crime, children who have drifted into crime and children living on the streets.[27] These are specialized residential rehabilitation centres based on the age, gender and special needs of the children; they provide psycho-social services to children who are in need of protection (i.e., children whose physical, mental, social or emotional development and personal safety is in danger, children who are neglected or abused or children who are victims of crime). Assistance is also provided to delinquent children.[28] As of December 2017, there are 65 Child Support Centres in Turkey, accommodating around 1,640 children.[29]

The Ministry of Health is the governmental agency responsible for the diagnosis of sexual abuse cases as well as for extending treatment and rehabilitation services.[30] Child Monitoring Centres under the Ministry of Health are especially important in this context. After the ratification of the Council of Europe's Convention on the Protection of Children against Sexual Exploitation and Sexual Abuse (Lanzarote Convention) in 2011, Turkey has taken important steps and necessary legislative measures to ensure that interviews with children take place in premises specifically designed for this purpose, are carried out by trained professionals and, wherever

---

25 Article 8 of the Decree Law on the Establishment and Functions of the Ministry of Family and Social Policies.

26 The Law on Child Protection, Law No. 5395, 03.07.2005, Official Gazette 15.07.2005/25876.

27 Ministry of Family and Social Policies, General Directorate of Child Services 2018; Article 14 of Law No. 6518, 06.02.2014, Official Gazette 19.02.2014/28918.

28 Ministry of Family and Social Policies, General Directorate of Child Services 2018; Article 4 of the Regulation on Child Support Centres, Official Gazette 29.03.2015/29310; Article 3 of the Law on Social Services Law No. 2828, 24.05.1983, Official Gazette 27.05.1983/18059; the Law on Child Protection.

29 Ministry of Family and Social Policies, General Directorate of Child Services 2018.

30 International Children's Center, University of Hacettepe, Institute of Public Health & Society of Public Health Specialists 2015, p. 23.

possible, are conducted by the same persons to avoid secondary victimisation.[31] In 2012, Child Monitoring Centres were established to conduct interviews and provide medico-legal examinations of child victims of sexual abuse.[32] As of April 2016, there were 27 Child Monitoring Centres in Turkey.[33] In addition, various help and support services are available to children through universities and NGOs (see *Table 2*). Within this context, university-based child protection implementation and research centres, which provide diagnostic and therapeutic services for abused children and carry out preventive studies, are especially important.[34]

Table 2 Selected NGOs Dealing With Certain Types of Victims

NGOs	Main focus	Internet site
Mor Çatı Women's Shelter Foundation	Violence against women Sexual abuse of children	https://www.morcati.org.tr/en
The Foundation for Women's Solidarity	Violence against women, human trafficking	https://www.kadindayanismavakfi.org.tr/english
Child Protection Centres Support Society	Children	http://cokmed.org
Society for Prevention of Child Abuse and Neglect	Children	–
Human Resource Development Foundation	Human trafficking	http://www.ikgv.org/eng_ikgv_gecici/ing_index.html
Family Counsellors Association	Human trafficking	http://ailedanismanlari.org

Furthermore, it is also important to mention one of the new legal and institutional changes that took place in Turkey in relation to combating human trafficking. After the collapse of the Soviet Union, human trafficking has emerged as a major phenomenon in Turkey. In response, Turkey has taken important steps to fight human

31 Article 35 of the Council of Europe Convention on the Protection of Children against Sexual Exploitation and Sexual Abuse; Council of Europe Convention 2007.

32 The Prime Minister's Circular on Child Monitoring Centres, No. 2012/20, Official Gazette 04.10.2012/28431; Bar Association of Trabzon, Committee on Children's Rights 2015, p. 6.

33 Milliyet of 17.04.2016, Adli Sürecin Travmasını Mimimuma İndiriyoruz; http://www.milliyet.com.tr/-adli-surecin-travmasini-minimuma/pazar/haberdetay/17.04.2016/2228400/default.htm [14.05.2018].

34 For more information about the establishment and the activities of the university-based child protection implementation and research centres in Turkey, see *Akço et al.* 2013, pp. 305–307.

trafficking and help trafficked persons. All measures are conducted in cooperation with relevant stakeholders.[35] With the adoption of the new Law on Foreigners and International Protection in 2013, a new specialized institution, called the General Directorate of Migration Management, was established within the Ministry of Interior.[36] The General Directorate has a special Department for the Protection of Victims of Human Trafficking. This Department is responsible for the coordination of counter-trafficking actions and all measures to assist trafficked persons. Turkish authorities are currently working in co-operation with two state-related institutions (Ankara Metropolitan Municipality and Kırıkkale shelter homes) and one NGO (Human Resource Development Foundation) to provide shelters and assist victims of human trafficking (see *Tables 1 & 2*).[37]

Finally, the General Directorate of Prisons and Detention Houses and the General Directorate of Penal Affairs, both under the Ministry of Justice, have special departments that deal with the needs and rights of victims. In the provinces, there are Victim Support Services Bureaus and Protection Board Bureaus under the Probation Department. These bureaus work in co-ordination with all state and non-governmental institutions that deal with victim protection and support, and provide both counselling services and psycho-social programmes.[38] In addition, the Department of Victim Rights, established in 2013 under the General Directorate of Penal Affairs, is responsible for providing various counselling and support services to victims, including psycho-social services and social and economic help; it is also responsible for the development of alternative compensation and intervention programmes based on the needs of the victims of crime.[39]

3. Relevant Legal Framework in Terms of Criminal Policy

3.1 Introduction

General interest in victims and victims' rights in Turkey is relatively new. Especially since the 1990's, the main focus of the law has been on the rights of suspects and the accused. The victim—the other side of crime's coin—has long been neglected. However, with the 2004–2005 reform of Turkish penal law, important regulations on victims came into force. The term "victim" can be defined differently from criminological

---

35 *Dündar & Özer* 2012, p. 19.

36 Article 103 of the Law on Foreigners and International Protection, Law No. 6458, 04.04.2013, Official Gazette 11.04.2013/28615.

37 Ministry of the Interior, General Directorate of Migration Management 2018b.

38 Articles 19 and 20 of the Regulation on Probation Services, Official Gazette 05.03.2013/28578.

39 Ministry of Justice, General Directorate of Penal Affairs, Department of Victim Rights 2018a.

and normative perspectives. From a criminological perspective, the victim refers to a person who has suffered harm, pain or death as a result of the actions of another person.[40] From a normative perspective, however, there is no clear definition of the victim or the injured party within the basic penal laws of Turkey.[41] Therefore, in the penal law literature, it is possible to find various definitions (either narrow or broad).[42] Victims of domestic violence (especially women), sexual crime (especially children) and mass economic crime (e.g., fraud) have featured prominently in the Turkish media and public discourse. Media coverage of crimes and victims is very influential on political and public discourse; moreover, it can lead to new progressive regulations on related crimes and their victims. Examples of such progressive reforms are the establishment of the Child Monitoring Centres in 2012 for child victims of sexual abuse, the establishment of the aforementioned VPMCs for victims of domestic violence and the 2017 establishment of judicial interview rooms in the courthouses for the questioning of children and other vulnerable individuals (as victims, witnesses or perpetrators).[43]

---

40 *Sokullu-Akıncı & Dursun* 2016, pp. 1–3. According to the UN Declaration of Basic Principles of Justice for Victims of Crime and Abuse of Power of 1985, victims refer to people who, individually or collectively, have suffered harm, including physical or mental injury, emotional suffering, economic loss or substantial impairment of their fundamental rights, through acts or omissions that are in violation of criminal laws operative within the Member States, including those laws proscribing criminal abuse of power. This term also includes, where appropriate, the immediate family or dependents of the direct victim and persons who have suffered harm in intervening to assist victims in distress or to prevent victimisation (Annex, Articles 1–2 of the Declaration). Thus, not only direct (primary) victims but also indirect (secondary) victims, such as the family/dependents of victims, witnesses of crime, and even the whole society are included (*Sokullu-Akıncı & Dursun* 2016, loc. cit.).

41 In the Regulation on Probation Services (Official Gazette 05.03.2013/28578), a victim is defined as a person who needs support due to physical, emotional or financial consequences of the crime committed against him/her or one of his/her family members (Article 4/1-p).

42 In the doctrine of substantive penal law, a victim is defined as the owner of the object of the crime. For example, the owner of a stolen object is the victim of a crime of theft crime; see *Özgenç* 2017, p. 206; *Koca & Üzülmez* 2017, pp. 114–115. However, in penal procedural law, the term "injured party" is used rather than the term "victim"; it describes a person whose protected legal value (e.g., right to life, property right, etc.) or legal interest has been violated. The concept is further categorized as direct/narrow and indirect/wide. Pursuant to this understanding, a person who is killed is the direct victim of murder, but her/his relatives are considered the indirect injured party; see *Öztürk, Tezcan, Erdem, Sırma Gezer, Saygılar Kırıt, Özaydın, Alan Akcan & Tütüncü* 2016, pp. 231–233.

43 For more detailed information on Child Monitoring Centres and VPMCs, see *Sokullu-Akıncı & Dursun* 2016, pp. 78–80, 316–320. For more information on judicial interview rooms, see Ministry of Justice, General Directorate of Penal Affairs, Department of Victim Rights 2018b; Delegation of the European Union to Turkey 2019. The Child Monitoring Centres and judicial interview rooms are organised by administrative regulations, whereas the VPMCs are established by law.

3.2 General Overview of National Legal Provisions Related to Victims

Currently, there is no special act on victims in Turkish law. Provisions are, however, included in the Turkish Penal Code and the Penal Procedure Code. In addition, victim-related provisions can be found in the Child Protection Law, the Law on the Protection of the Family and the Prevention of Violence against Women, the Law on Probation Services and the Law on Combating Terrorism. While the concept of victim is not defined in these laws, they each contain various provisions about victim rights and/or protections.

In this context, various provisions of the Turkish Penal Code[44] provide an opportunity for victim restitution. For example, the compensation for damage is regulated as an alternative sanction for short-term imprisonment,[45] as a condition for the suspension of a prison sentence[46] or as effective remorse.[47] In the Penal Procedure Code,[48] victims' rights during the penal process are regulated under a separate section. The victim's role in various transactions, their role as public claimants and the use of victim-offender mediation are also foreseen.[49] The Child Protection Law[50] also contains several protective and supportive measures for children,[51] not only for those who have drifted into crime but also for those who are neglected, abused or victimised.[52]. The Law on the Protection of the Family and the Prevention of Violence against Women[53] regulates protective and preventive measures for female victims of violence.[54] In this Law, the concept of violence has a very

---

44 Law No. 5237, 26.09.2004, Official Gazette 12.10.2004/25611.

45 See Article 50/1-b of the Law No. 5237. This means one year or less imprisonment (see Article 49/2 of the Law No. 5237).

46 See Article 51/2 of the Law No. 5237.

47 For example, see Article 168 of the Law No. 5237.

48 Law No. 5271, 04.12.2004, Official Gazette 17.12.2004/25673.

49 These regulations will be discussed in detail below.

50 Law No. 5395, 03.07.2005, Official Gazette 15.07.2005/25876.

51 "Child" refers to a person who has not reached the age of 18 (see Article 3/1-a of the Law No. 5395).

52 In this context, the Child Protection Law includes two different terms: "child in need of protection" and "child that has drifted into crime" (see Article 3).

53 Law No. 6284, 08.03.2012, Official Gazette 20.03.2012/28239. This Law is based on the Council of Europe/Istanbul Convention on Preventing and Combating Violence against Women and Domestic Violence. This Convention is clearly mentioned in the Law as a reference for the basic principles related to this subject (see Article 1/2-a).

54 See Articles 3–13 (protective and preventive measures) and Articles 14–15 (on VPMCs) of the Law No. 6284.

broad definition.[55] In the Law on Probation Services,[56] it is also stated that Probation Centres must provide counselling and assistance to victims to help resolve psycho-social and economic problems.[57] Finally, in the Law on Combating Terrorism[58], the payment of compensation is regulated for those who suffer material damage either due to terrorism or counter terrorism activities.[59]

With regards to the historical development of victim regulations in Turkey, it is necessary to stress the penal law reform of 2004–2005, in particular the victim-related regulations in the Penal Procedure Code, Child Protection Law and the Law on Probation Services. It is also important to mention a draft law on victims' rights.[60] In the draft law, a victim is defined as a person who has directly suffered physical, mental, psychological or economic harm as a result of the commission of a crime.[61] The draft law sets forth the basic principles, rights and services for victim protection and regulates the specific services for victims with certain characteristics (named as vulnerable groups). Furthermore, state compensation for remedying the plight of victims is regulated for the first time. Moreover, the regulations on the central and provincial organisation of the Victims' Rights Department[62] (under the Ministry of Justice) are also important in terms of the establishment of the institutional infrastructure to protect and develop victims' rights.

3.3 The Provisions of the Penal Procedure Code Which Regulate the Status and Rights of the Victim in the Penal Procedure

The fourth book of the Penal Procedure Code[63] is devoted to victims' rights and the participation of victims in criminal proceedings. Victims' rights during the in-

---

55 See Article 2/1-d of the Law No. 6284.

56 Law No. 5402, 03.07.2005, Official Gazette 20.07.2005/25881.

57 See Articles 12/1-c and 13/1-c of the Law No. 5402. In the Regulation on Probation Services, the establishment of a Victim Support Services Bureau is foreseen to coordinate and execute work intended for victim support (Article 19 of the Regulation).

58 Law No. 3713, 12.04.1991, Official Gazette 12.04.1991/20843.

59 See Articles 21–22 of Law No. 3713. The Law on the Compensation of Damages arising from Terrorism and Combating Terrorism (Law No. 5233, 17.07.2004, Official Gazette 27.07.2004/25535), and Law on Cash Compensation and Determination of Monthly Salary (Law No. 2330, 03.11.1980, Official Gazette 06.11.1980/17152) include specific regulations on this topic.

60 Draft Law on Victims' Rights; http://www.magdur.adalet.gov.tr/tasari-01177 [23.05.2018].

61 See Article 2/1-g of the Draft Law on Victims' Rights.

62 For the website of the Victims' Rights Department, see http://www.magdur.adalet.gov.tr [23.05.2018].

63 See Turkey in the Annex for Articles 233–243 of the Law No. 5271.

vestigation and the prosecution phases[64] are regulated separately. These rights are provided by the prosecutor and the judicial police (who assist the prosecutor) during the investigation phase and by the competent court during the prosecution phase.[65] In each phase, there are four common rights:

1) The right to demand the gathering of evidence during the investigation phase and to demand the invitation of witnesses during the prosecution phase

2) The right to review and copy the casefile. During the investigation phase, this right may be restricted, if it would endanger the secrecy and the aim of the investigation.

3) The right to demand the appointment of a lawyer on her/his behalf by the Bar Association in cases of sexual assault and those crimes which lead to imprisonment of more than five years, if s/he has no lawyer. In cases where the victim has not attained the age of 18, is deaf or dumb, or is unable otherwise express their wishes, a lawyer shall be appointed on their behalf if they do not already have one.

4) The right to resort to legal remedies against the decision of the public prosecutor not to prosecute during the investigation phase and against the final decisions of courts at the prosecution phase, provided that s/he has been an intervening party in the lawsuit.

In addition to these rights, victims also have the right to be notified about the main trial and to participate in the criminal case during the prosecution phase.[66] Through participation, the victim is allowed to be present in various procedural transactions, to personally participate in cross-examination (with the help of the judge or through a lawyer)[67] and may apply for legal remedies independent of the public prosecutor.[68]

In both phases (i.e., investigation and prosecution), the victim is heard like a witness, and provisions related to the testimony shall apply, excluding the oath. To prevent secondary victimisation, there are specific rules for the hearing of some victims. For example, as a rule, a child or a victim who has suffered psychological damage due to the committed crime shall be heard only once in relation to the investigation or prosecution of the committed crime and, during the hearing, there shall be an expert

---

64 The term "prosecution" refers to the phase beginning with the decision on the admissibility of the indictment and ending with the final judgment (Article 2/1-f of the Law No. 5271).

65 See Article 234/3 of the Law No. 5271.

66 See Article 234/1-b of the Law No. 5271.

67 See Article 201 of the Law No. 5271.

68 See Article 242 of the Law No. 5271.

present who has expertise in the fields of psychology, psychiatry, medicine and/or education.[69]

3.4 The Compensation System and Legal Services for Victims

Under Turkish law, there is still no general (state) compensation system specifically designed for victims. However, as pointed out above, there is a draft law on this subject. In the draft law, state compensation is to be regulated for the victims of crimes, such as intentional killing, aggravated injury and torture, sexual assault and abuse.[70] Under current legislation, reference can be made to the provisions on temporary financial assistance, alimony and health insurance for victims of violence in accordance with the Law on the Protection of the Family and the Prevention of Violence against Women,[71] and the compensation of victims of terrorism.

As a legal service that can help the victims, the establishment of Victim Support Services Bureaus has been considered under the Law on Probation Services.[72] However, these bureaus are still not completely active. Within this framework, the Department of Victims' Rights was established under the Ministry of Justice in 2013[73] and the draft law on victims' rights aims to organize this department nationwide. Currently, as a legal service, the VPMCs established by the Ministry of Family and Social Policy are active for the victims of violence. In addition, NGOs offer support for victimised women.[74]

3.5 Civil Actions Within the Penal Procedure

In the current penal procedure system, victims can participate in criminal proceedings but they are not entitled to claim damages within the criminal proceeding. The

---

69 See Article 236 of the Law No. 5271.

70 See Article 19 of the Draft Law on Victims' Rights.

71 See Articles 17–19 of the Law No. 6284.

72 According to the Article 19/3–4 of the Regulation on Probation Services, the duties of a Victim Support Services Bureau are as follows:

a) to receive and evaluate victims' requests,

b) to inform victims about persons and entities where they can get help/receive aid,

c) upon the victim's request

  1) to inform them about the trial process and

  2) to implement psycho-social support programmes. In addition, each bureau operates in full coordination with all relevant institutions, organizations and persons carrying out related activities for the victims.

73 Ministry of Justice, General Directorate of Penal Affairs, Department of Victim Rights 2018c.

74 See *Section 2*: Current State of Victimology.

victim must file a claim at the civil court for compensation. The penal court, however, is obliged to clearly indicate in its final judgement whether the victim has a right to ask for compensation.[75]

Prior to the Turkish penal law reform in 2004–2005, the victim was able to claim her/his personal rights through participation in the criminal case, and the penal court could rule on compensation provided that it would not dramatically lengthen the proceeding.[76]

3.6 Regulations Related to Restorative Justice

In the context of restorative justice, various penal, procedural and enforcement regulations include provisions that consider the victim, promote the victim's interests and compensate the victim for damages. For example, as an effective remorse regulation in crimes against property, if compensation is paid, a significant penalty reduction is foreseen.[77]

As mentioned above, compensation of the victim's loss may substitute a short-term prison sentence of one year or less.[78] Moreover, the compensation of the victim's loss is a pre-condition for various other court orders, such as the suspension of a prison term,[79] postponement of the filing of a public claim[80] or postponement of the pronouncement of a sentence[81] (while these rules are designed with perpetrators in mind, they also protect the interests of victims).

The most important regulation on restorative justice is mediation. This institution was regulated for the first time with the 2004–2005 Turkish penal law reform. Previously, only crimes which could be investigated and prosecuted on complaint were indicated as crimes eligible for mediation, and the confession of guilt and compensation for damage were stipulated as pre-conditions.[82] In the Penal Procedure Code, only the procedure for mediation by the prosecutor, the court or the mediator was regulated.[83]

---

75 See Article 232/6 of the Law No. 5271.

76 Former Penal Procedure Code, Law No. 1412, 04.04.1929, Official Gazette 20.04.1929/1172.

77 See Article 168 of the Law No. 5237.

78 See Article 50/1-b of the Law No. 5237.

79 See Article 51/2 of the Law No. 5237.

80 See Article 171/3-d of the Law No. 5271.

81 See Article 231/6-c of the Law No. 5271.

82 See Article 73, repealed paragraph 8 of the Law No. 5237.

83 See Articles 253–254 of the Law No. 5271.

Through legal reforms,[84] the provisions on mediation within the Turkish Penal Code were moved into the Penal Procedure Code and the scope of mediation was extended. In addition to crimes investigated and prosecuted on complaint, some minor crimes (regardless of dependency on a complaint) were included as well. Sexual crimes and those crimes where the provisions of effective remorse apply, have been excluded even if they depended on complaint. The pre-conditions, such as the confession of crime and compensation of the damage were repealed, and the will of the parties has become important.

Finally, with further reform amendments in 2016,[85] some other crimes (such as threat, theft and fraud) and all juvenile crimes punishable by less than three years imprisonment have also been included within the scope of mediation.[86] In addition, those crimes for which the provisions of effective remorse apply can also be handled through mediation. The 2016 amendments also created an autonomous structure for mediation via the establishment of a mediation office within the prosecutor's office,[87] in accordance with the provisions of the Recommendation of the Council of Europe concerning mediation in penal matters, No. R (99)19.[88] Lastly, mediation fees are now considered court expenses and are compensated by the state treasury.[89]

4. Picture of the Situation of Victimisation in Turkey Based on Data and Research Findings

Official data sources with regards to crime victims in Turkey are extremely scarce. Official statistics on victims comprise both police and judicial data sources. Police statistics on suspects and victims are collected by the General Directorate of Public Security in urban areas, whereas the Turkish Gendarmerie is responsible for recording crimes committed in sub-districts and villages. As previously mentioned,[90]official statistics on crime victims compiled by the police and the gendarmerie are not accessible to the public. There is, however, one exception. Since 1997, data on juveniles received into security units of the police and the gendarmerie are compiled and published annually by the Turkish Statistical Institute. This study initially covered

---

84 Law No. 5560, 19.12.2006, Official Gazette 19.12.2006/26381.

85 Law No. 6763, 24.11.2016, Official Gazette 02.12.2016/29906.

86 See Article 253/1 of the Law No. 5271.

87 See Article 253/24 of the Law No. 5271.

88 See Articles 5 and 20 of the Council of Europe Recommendation (Council of Europe 1999). In this context, the Department of Alternative Dispute Resolutions was established under the Ministry of Justice. For the website of the Department, see http://www.alternatifcozumler.adalet.gov.tr [25.05.2018].

89 See Article 253/22 of the Law No. 5271.

90 *Sözüer & Topçuoğlu* 2014.

27 provinces in Turkey; but since 2007 the coverage was extended to all 81 provinces. These statistics cover data on juveniles who are brought into security units for a variety of reasons. Therefore, they include data on juvenile crime victims as well as juvenile suspects.

Figure 1 presents data on the number of juvenile suspects and juvenile victims received into security units between the years 2008–2016. Within this publication, juvenile victim is defined as a child who has suffered material/tangible or intangible harm as a result of the commission of a criminal offense, and hence it includes physical and emotional harm, property damage or economic loss. An examination of the number of juvenile victims brought into security units reveals an increasing trend over the last eight years. It can also be seen in *Figure 1* that while the number of juvenile suspects was larger than that of juvenile victims between the years 2008–2010, since 2011 the number of juvenile victims increasingly exceeds that of juvenile suspects. In 2016, while 158,343 children were brought to security units due to crime victimisation, the number of juvenile suspects was 108,675. Overall, 55% (86,519) of the juvenile victims were male while 45% (71,824) were female.[91] The age distribution of juvenile victims for both genders in 2016 is displayed in *Figure 2*. The figure indicates that overall, within both genders, children aged 15–17 years are the most likely to be victimised (43% for males, 48% for females). This is followed by children aged below 11 years (35% for males, 29% for females) and then those aged between 12–14 years (22% for males and 23% for females). Although more detailed information on juvenile suspects is available (e.g., type of crime, education level, drug use, etc.), official police and gendarmerie data on juve-

Figure 1 Juvenile Suspects and Juvenile Victims Received Into Security Units, 2008–2016

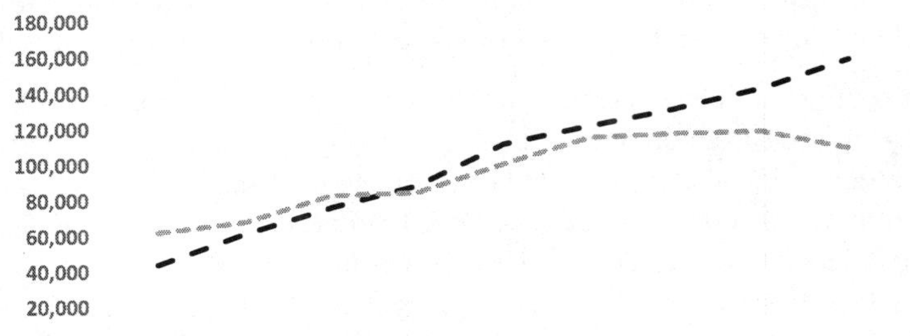

	2008	2009	2010	2011	2012	2013	2014	2015	2016
Juvenile victims	44,153	61,645	76,428	88,582	111,857	121,717	131,172	142,179	158,343
Juvenile suspects	62,430	68,344	83,393	84,916	100,831	115,439	117,486	118,245	108,675

Source: Data taken from TurkStat 2018b.

91 TurkStat 2018b.

Figure 2 Juvenile Victims by Age and Gender, 2016

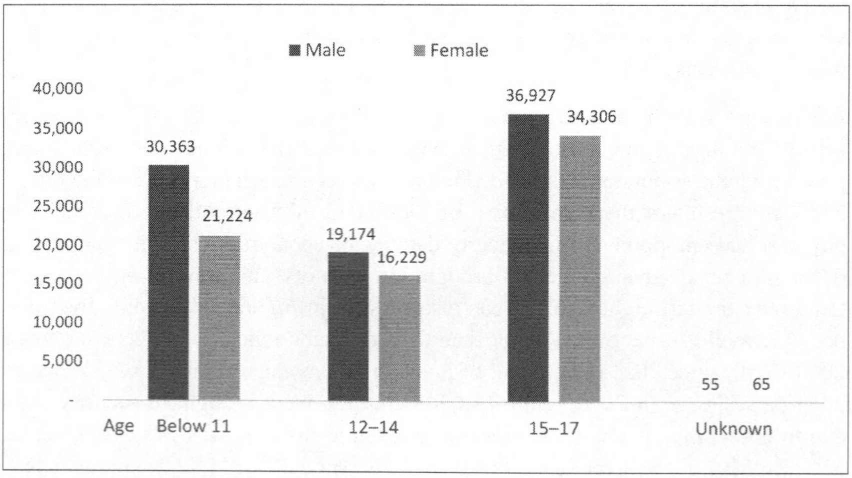

Source: Data taken from TurkStat 2018b.

nile crime victims are limited. However, since 2014, official data on juvenile crime victims are further categorised by type of crime victimisation. In 2016, although there were 158,343 juvenile victims in total, 95 (0.06%) were victims of misdemeanour, 19,070 (12%) were victims of crimes that are prosecuted on complaint and the remainder (139,178; 87.9%) were victims of other crimes.[92] A further examination of the latter category indicates that a majority of the juveniles were victims of violent offences. According to the most recent statistics available, while 83,607 (60%) juveniles were victims of assault in 2016, 16,877 (12%) were victims of sexual crimes.[93] Unfortunately, official statistics on juvenile victims do not include more detailed information such as the type of the relationship between the victim and the offender.

In contrast to police and gendarmerie data, judicial statistics in Turkey are annually published; unfortunately, they include highly limited data on crime victims. Further, it should also be noted that a number of changes, such as the criminal law reform which took place in 2004–2005, limit the comparability of judicial statistics for different time periods in Turkey. Besides the criminal law reform, another significant change relates to the data compiling method and the counting rules employed by the General Directorate of Criminal Records and Statistics.[94] Prior to 2009, all judicial data were compiled by mail; but since 2009 these data are electronically obtained from the National Judiciary Network Information System which includes

92 TurkStat 2018b.

93 TurkStat 2018b.

94 *Sözüer & Topçuoğlu* 2014, pp.384–385.

data based on a different counting rule.[95] Furthermore, previously between the years 2006–2009, official statistics on the number of victims were relatively more detailed and included information on the type of crime victimisation as well.[96] Since 2009, these statistics include only the total number of victims (and complainants) within the cases brought (which include cases from the preceding year, new cases and those brought through reversal by the Supreme Court) and those judged at the criminal courts each year. These figures are only divided by gender and nationality; no further detailed information is available about victims.

Figure 3 displays the total number of victims and complainants within the new cases brought at the criminal courts category during the years 2009–2017. Overall, males are more likely than females to be victims, though the disparity seems to have decreased over the last eight years. The number of male victims peaked at 736,137 in 2010 and then decreased to a minimum of 546,144 in 2017, indicating a 26% decrease. The number of female victims continuously increased from 2009 (except for the slight decrease in 2014) and reached a maximum of 373,743 in 2015, indicating a 46% increase. Between the years 2015–2017, the number of female victims decreased by 21% to 294,784. As shown in *Figure 4,* while the majority of the crime victims are Turkish nationals, the percentage of foreign-born victims increased sig-

Figure 3 The Number of Victims and Complainants Within the New Cases Brought at the Criminal Courts, 2009–2017

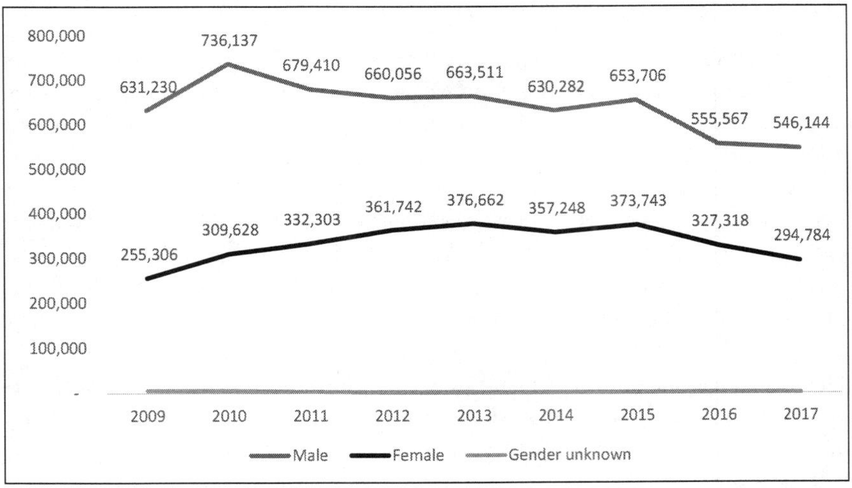

Source: Data taken from Ministry of Justice, General Directorate of Judicial Record and Statistics 2011; 2012a; 2012b; 2013; 2014; 2015; 2016; 2017; 2018.

95 *Sözüer & Topçuoğlu* 2014, pp.384–385.

96 Ministry of Justice, General Directorate of Judicial Record and Statistics 2008; 2009; 2010.

Figure 4 The Number of Victims and Complainants Within the New Cases Brought at the Criminal Courts 2009–2017, Category: by Nationality

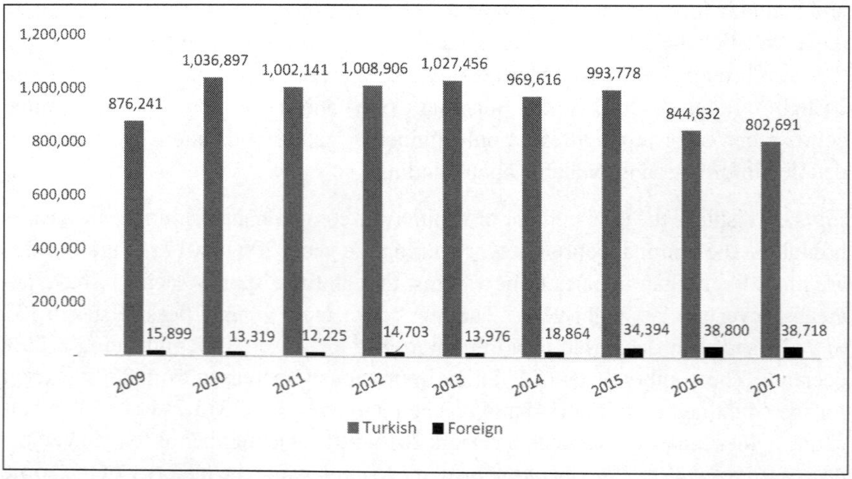

Source: Data taken from Ministry of Justice 2011; 2012a; 2012b; 2013; 2014; 2015; 2016; 2017; 2018.

nificantly after 2013. Indeed, the number of foreign victims almost tripled from 13,976 persons in 2013 to 38,718 in 2017. Unfortunately, no further information is available either on the type of crime or the country of origin of the victims.

In addition to police and judicial data, there is also information on specific types of victims in Turkey, such as victims of human trafficking. As mentioned earlier, as part of the new initiatives taken in Turkey to counter human trafficking, a new specialized institution, the General Directorate of Migration Management, has been established within the Ministry of Interior.[97] The General Directorate has a specific department for the protection of trafficked persons. This department is responsible for the coordination of counter-trafficking initiatives and currently publishes statistics on victims of human trafficking. *Figure 5* displays the number of trafficked persons identified each year since 2010. In total, Turkish authorities have been able to identify 1,730 victims of human trafficking between the years 2005–2017.[98] The majority of the group is constituted by sexually exploited young women aged between 18 and 25 who originate mainly from countries of the former Soviet Union.[99] Three specialized shelters were opened to assist trafficked persons.[100]

97 *Ersan* 2013, pp. 99–104; Ministry of Foreign Affairs 2018b; Ministry of the Interior, General Directorate of Security 2018.

98 Ministry of the Interior, General Directorate of Migration Management 2017, p. 89.

99 *Dündar & Özer* 2012, pp.24–25; *Ersan* 2013, p. 101; Human Resource Development Foundation 2007, pp. 227–228.

100 *Ersan* 2013, p. 101.

Figure 5 Victims of Human Trafficking, 2010–2017

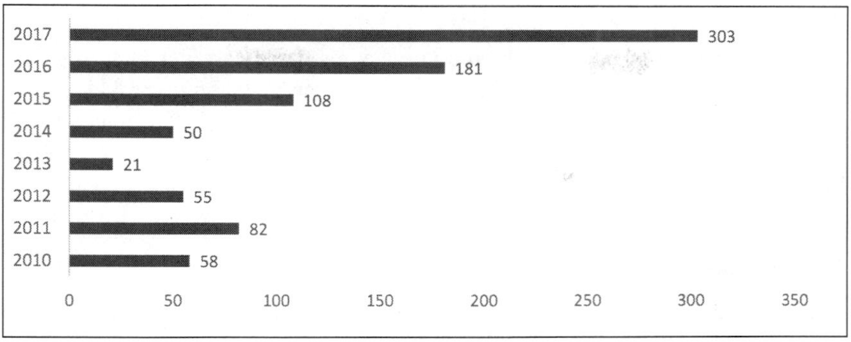

Source: Data taken from Ministry of the Interior, General Directorate of Migration Management 2018b.

As mentioned above, Turkey does not conduct regular victimisation surveys. Unfortunately, given the lack of police and gendarmerie data on crime victims (particularly adults), victimisation surveys would be of great importance. Despite the lack of nation-wide surveys, a study conducted as part of the International Crime Victim Survey (ICVS) in 2005 revealed significant findings with regard to the prevalence of victimisation as well as the extent of unreported cases.[101] Based on a sample of 1,242 people aged 16 or over (mean age 34.1 years) who were randomly drawn from households in Istanbul, the study examined both five-year and one-year victimisation rates for nine different types of crimes: car theft, theft from a car, burglary, attempted burglary, robbery, assault/threat, theft, consumer fraud, bribery. The findings of the study indicated that when compared to victimisation rates for other crimes, five-year victimisation rates for burglary were highest in Istanbul. When compared to the findings obtained in other European cities that participated in the ICVS, these rates were the highest. However, amongst those respondents whose house was burglarized, only 57.4% of the victims reported the crime to the police. Contrary to the victimisation rate for burglary, the reporting rate was found to be the lowest when compared to other European cities. The study's findings also pointed out that one-year victimisation rates for violent crimes such as robbery and assault/threat at the individual level were 1.1% and 0.7% respectively. Compared to other European cities, the latter rate was the lowest whereas the rate for robbery was in the middle of the scale. However, reporting rates for both types of crime were almost the lowest in Europe.[102] Overall, the study's findings highlight the importance of conducting such surveys, as victim reporting rates depend on the type of crime (ranging from 1.2% for bribery to 95.1% for car theft) and, amongst all nine types of

---

101 *Jahic & Akdaş Mitrani* 2007; 2010.

102 *Jahic & Akdaş Mitrani* 2007; 2010.

crimes, suggest that more than half of the crime victimisations in Istanbul were not reported to the police.

Given the scarcity of information on crime victims based on official statistics, the remainder of this section will focus on empirical research findings to provide a more detailed picture of victimisation in Turkey. In doing so, rather than cover all types of victimisation, the main focus will be on certain types of victimisation experienced by women, children and elderly people.

4.1 Women as Victims

Women may be victims of various types of crime; however, this part will mainly focus on women who are exposed to violence. Violence against women is defined by the UN as

> any act of gender-based violence that results in, or is likely to result in, physical, sexual, or mental harm or suffering to women, including threats of such acts, coercion or arbitrary deprivation of liberty, whether occurring in public or in private life.[103]

Violence against women is a widespread phenomenon, as indicated by a systematic review and meta-analysis of evidence based on representative population-based surveys carried out until 2011 in more than 80 countries.[104] The findings estimate that the global, lifetime prevalence of experiencing either physical and/or sexual violence is around 35% (i.e., 1 in 3 women).[105] As is the case throughout the world, violence against women is very common and attracts a significant amount of public and academic attention in Turkey.

Given the lack of official data on women's exposure to violence,[106] it is important to review empirical research findings based on victimological studies. A systematic review of studies published in peer-reviewed journals between 2000 and 2015 revealed 34 primary studies on the prevalence and risk factors for domestic violence against women aged between 15 and 59 in Turkey.[107] This review meta-analysed all the retrieved studies on the prevalence of different types of violence throughout marriage. The results indicate that while the prevalence rate for general violence throughout marriage was 57.2%, this rate was 33.8% for physical violence, 43.5% for verbal violence, 33.7% for emotional violence, 26.8% for economic violence and

---

[103] United Nations 1993.

[104] WHO 2013.

[105] WHO 2013.

[106] Since official police statistics are not available to the public, many NGOs try to compile their own statistics based on criminal cases reported in the media. However, due to questionable methodology and statistical inconsistencies, the results are not mentioned here.

[107] *Keser Özcan, Günaydın & Çitil* 2016.

12.3% for sexual violence.[108] However, this systematic review had two important limitations. First, although the aim was to review research findings on the prevalence rate of intimate partner violence in Turkey, the inclusion criteria were too broad to include studies based on representative as well as non-representative samples. Second, since the search was limited to published journal articles, a number of important studies on violence against women carried out at the national level with representative samples, but which were published either as a book or a research report, were excluded. Another systematic review of journal articles examining all types of intimate partner violence (IPV) against women in Turkey published between 2000 and 2010 revealed 22 studies on the prevalence of IPV against women.[109] However, once again, the majority of the studies included in this review were not based on random probability sampling and, therefore, the representativeness of the samples and the retrieved prevalence rates are questionable.

Given the significance of the topic in Turkey and the acceleration of the women's movement since the 1980s, a significant number of national studies have been carried out on all types of violence against women in Turkey.[110] The most recent, nationwide survey was conducted in 2012–2014, using a weighted, stratified and multi-staged cluster sampling technique.[111] Face-to-face interviews were conducted with 7,462 women aged between 15–59 years. The results of this study indicate that 36% of married or previously married women in Turkey reported having been exposed to physical violence by their husbands or intimate partners (8% in the last 12 months). The lifetime prevalence rate for physical violence was highest in the Central Anatolian region (43%) and lowest in the Eastern Black Sea region (27%).[112] Lifetime prevalence rates for sexual violence, emotional violence and economic violence/abuse were respectively 12%, 44% and 30% for married or previously married women.[113] The analyses based on all women indicate that 14% of women have experienced physical violence by people other than their husbands and intimate partners since the age of 15. This rate was 3% for sexual violence. The perpetrators of physical violence were mainly fathers (43%), followed by mothers (23%), older brothers (18%), father-in-law (8%), mother-in-law (8%) and brother-in-law (5%).[114] In contrast, the perpetrators of sexual violence were mainly strangers (56%), followed

---

108 *Keser Özcan, Günaydın & Çitil* 2016.

109 *Güvenç, Akyüz & Cesario* 2014.

110 *Altınay & Arat* 2007; 2009; *Ergöçmen, Yüksel-Kaptanoğlu & Jansen* 2013; *Şenol & Yıldız* 2013; Prime Ministry, Institution of Family Research 1995; *Yüksel-Kaptanoğlu, Türkyılmaz & Heise* 2012; Ministry of Family and Social Policies and Hacettepe University Institute of Population Studies 2015.

111 Ministry of Family and Social Policies 2014.

112 Ministry of Family and Social Policies 2014, p. 7.

113 Ministry of Family and Social Policies 2014, pp. 8–9.

114 Ministry of Family and Social Policies 2014, p. 16.

by male relatives (17%), boyfriends (13%) and work colleagues (12%).[115] Prevalence of childhood sexual abuse (before age 15) was 9%: perpetrators were mainly strangers (38%), followed by male relatives (29%) and acquaintances (15%).[116] The findings of this nationwide study also point out a very significant fact regarding the unreported numbers of intimate partner violence in Turkey. Overall, the majority of women (89%) who experienced either physical or sexual violence did not report it to any institution or organisation. Only 7% of the women reported it to the police and 1% to the gendarmerie.[117] This fact alone significantly shows both the limitations of official data and the importance of conducting victimisation surveys to understand female victimisation experiences.

4.2 Children as Victims

Empirical victimological research on children in Turkey focus largely on bullying and peer victimisation at schools. However, due to both the significance of the topic and limited space, this part will mainly focus on research studies carried out in Turkey on child sexual abuse and exploitation. At this point, given the scarcity of official data on child sexual victimisation, it is especially important to mention one systematic review on child sexual abuse and exploitation in Turkey which was conducted as part of the Council of Europe's "ONE in FIVE"[118] campaign (with the International Children's Centre).[119] This study systematically reviewed all empirical research studies on child sexual abuse and exploitation published between the years 2002–2013 in Turkey.[120] A review of 49 retrieved studies indicated that empirical research studies in Turkey mainly focus on child sexual abuse, and that no single study examined child pornography and trafficking. This important review also indicates that the vast majority of the studies lack essential methodological qualities such as representative samples, an adequate sample size, reliability and validity of measurement, adequacy of the research design and statistical techniques used.[121]

Overall, this review identifies only three prevalence studies on child sexual abuse in Turkey. One study examined the prevalence of sexual abuse in 1,955 female students (mean age 16.3 years) based on a representative sample randomly drawn

---

115 Ministry of Family and Social Policies 2014, p. 16.

116 Ministry of Family and Social Policies 2014, p. 17.

117 Ministry of Family and Social Policies 2014, pp. 25–26.

118 The name of the campaign refers to the research findings which indicate that one in every five children in Europe is likely to be the victim of one form of sexual violence; see *Lalor & McElvaney* 2008; *Uslu & Kapçı* 2014, p. 1.

119 *Uslu & Kapçı* 2014.

120 *Uslu & Kapçı* 2014.

121 *Uslu & Kapçı* 2014, pp. 9–10.

from the 9th through to 11th grades in Istanbul in 2000.[122] The instrument used was the international version of the Health Behaviour in School Age Children (HSBC) 1997/1998 survey.[123] Within this study, sexual abuse was defined as "unwanted sexual experience (touching and intercourse)", incest as "sexual abuse performed by a person(s) who is (are) an immediate family member (father, brother, grandfather, etc.)" and sexual assault as "intercourse with penetration."[124] Students who reported any of these behaviours were counted as sexually abused. The findings of the study indicated that overall, 13.4% of the female students had a history of sexual abuse and 4.9% reported that they have been forced to have sexual intercourse. An examination of the relationship between the victims and the perpetrators of sexual abuse pointed out that while 32% of the victims refused to respond to this question, in the majority of the remainder cases, victims were sexually abused by a stranger (50%), followed by boyfriend (14.8%), friend (13.6), relative (10.7%) or acquaintance (8.9%). Three female students (1.8%) reported that they have experienced incest at the hands of an immediate family member.[125] Finally, in 93% of the cases, the perpetrator was reported as male.

Another study examined the prevalence and correlates of school violence and sexual abuse experienced at school in 5,031 students based on a representative sample randomly drawn from the 6th through to 8th grades in Tokat in 2010/2011.[126] The Turkish translation of the International Child Abuse Screening Tool-Children's version (ICAST-C), which was developed by the International Society for the Prevention of Child Abuse and Neglect (ISPCAN), was the main instrument used.[127] The findings of the study indicated that the prevalence rate was 57% for physical violence and 6.4% for sexual abuse. Boys were more likely than girls to experience both physical violence (66.6% for boys vs. 47.1% for girls) and sexual abuse (7.9% for boys vs. 4.8% for girls). Both physical violence and sexual abuse at school was significantly more prevalent in the town centre than in the city centre (physical violence: 62% in town centre vs. 54.5% in city centre; sexual abuse: 8.3% in town centre vs. 7.6% in city centre).[128]

Finally, one study examined the prevalence of childhood sexual abuse in 1,262 university students (mean age 21 years) based on a sample drawn from seven univer-

---

122 *Alikaşifoğlu, Erginöz, Ercan, Albayrak-Kaymak, Uysal & İlter* 2006.

123 *Currie, Hurrelmann, Settertobulte, Smith & Todo* 2000.

124 *Alikaşifoğlu et al.* 2006, p. 250.

125 *Alikaşifoğlu et al.* 2006, pp. 251–252.

126 *Yıldırım, Karataş, Yılmaz, Çetin & Senel* 2013.

127 *Zolotor, Runyan, Dunne, Jain, Peturs, Ramirez, Volkova, Deb, Lidchi, Muhammad & Isaeva* 2009.

128 *Yıldırım et al.* 2013, pp. 387–388.

sities in Istanbul, İzmir, Ankara and Aydın.[129] Childhood sexual abuse (CSA) was measured using five items from the sexual abuse factor of the Childhood Trauma Questionnaire.[130] The findings of the study indicated that overall 28.1% of the students had experienced at least one form of sexual abuse during childhood. While there was no gender difference in the total CSA score, girls were more likely than boys to report that someone tried to touch them or made them touch themselves in a sexual way (26% vs. 19.8%) and that they were sexually abused (9% vs. 5.5%).[131]

4.3 Elderly People as Victims

The most common types of victimisation experienced by elderly people include abuse and neglect. Based on the definition developed by Action on Elder Abuse (UK) in 1995, the WHO-CIG (World Health Organization-Centre for Interdisciplinary Gerontology) defines elder abuse as "a single or repeated act or lack of appropriate action, occurring within any relationship where there is an expectation of trust which causes harm or distress to an older person."[132] Elder abuse can take various forms such as physical, psychological, economic or sexual, and might have serious consequences for individuals including serious physical injuries and death. While it is estimated that 15.7% of people aged 60 years and older are exposed to abuse, these prevalence rates are regarded as underestimates of actual rates since many cases of elder abuse take place behind closed doors and hence are not reported.[133] Overall, the academic interest in the victimisation experiences of elderly people is relatively new in many countries, and the situation is no different in Turkey.[134] Relatively few empirical studies focus on elder victimisation in Turkey. However, as is the case in many countries, Turkey's population is aging. The population of people aged 65 or over is currently 7,163,354 (8.7%), and is expected to more than double and reach 16,373,969 (16%) people in 2040.[135] Hence, even if not now, it is expected that victimisation experiences of the elderly population will be more likely to capture researchers' interest in the near future.

A recent systematic review of the published literature until July 2014 on abuse and neglect of elderly people in Turkey initially yielded 34 studies on the victimisation

---

[129] *Eskin, Kaynak-Demir & Demir* 2005.

[130] For the original instrument, see *Bernstein, Fink, Handelsman, Foote, Lovejoy, Wenzel, Sapareto & Ruggiero* 1994; for the psychometric test of the Turkish translation, see *Aslan & Alpaslan* 1999.

[131] *Eskin, Kaynak-Demir & Demir* 2005, pp. 189–190.

[132] WHO 2008, p. 1.

[133] WHO 2018.

[134] *Doerner ve Lab* 2012, p. 294; *Uysal* 2002.

[135] TurkStat 2018c.

of elderly people.[136] A vast majority of the relevant studies, however, were excluded from the systematic review since they were either review articles or case studies.[137] Overall, only four empirical studies were included in the systematic review. These studies were published between the years 1996–2012.

One study examined the prevalence rate of elderly abuse in a sample of 113 (42.3% female) people aged 60 and over who applied for one of three residential facilities in Istanbul.[138] The findings of the study indicated that 25.7% of these elderly people had been physically abused. An examination of the physical abuse cases revealed that the perpetrator was most commonly the daughter-in-law (41.4%), followed by sons (21%), son-in-laws (17.25%) and other relatives and neighbours.[139] Family patterns are quite different in Turkey than in most Western countries, and it is very common for the elderly to stay with their son's family. The respondents in the study reported that it was the daughter-in-law whom they had the most conflict with (35%). Elderly people's abuse by daughter-in-laws in Turkey, therefore, should be considered within the context of the extended family structure.

Another study examined the prevalence and risk factors of physical and financial abuse of 550 elderly (65 years and over) people drawn from two different socioeconomic districts in Izmir.[140] The findings of this study revealed that the prevalence rate for physical abuse was 1.5% and 2% respectively for elderly individuals living in low and high socioeconomic districts.[141] Elderly people were most commonly victimised by their sons, spouses, sons-in-law, daughters-in-law, daughters and nephews.[142] While the prevalence rate for financial abuse among elderly people was 2.5% and 0.3% in low and high socioeconomic districts respectively, the prevalence rate for neglect was much higher in both districts (27.4% in low socioeconomic districts and 11.2% in high socioeconomic districts).

Finally, another study examined the prevalence and correlates of different types of elder abuse (physical, emotional/psychological, sexual, economic and neglect) in a community sample of 768 elderly people aged 65 and above (mean age 71, 48.5% female) randomly drawn using a multi-stage sampling method from Aydın, a city in western Turkey.[143] Overall, 14.2% of the respondents had experienced any form

---

136 *Lök* 2015.

137 *Lök* 2015, pp. 150.

138 *Artan* 1996.

139 *Artan* 1996, p. 55.

140 See *Keskinoğlu, Pıçakçıefe, Bilgiç, Giray, Karakuş & Uçku* 2007; *Keskinoğlu, Giray, Pıçakçıefe, Bilgiç & Uçku* 2004.

141 *Keskinoğlu et al.* 2007.

142 *Keskinoğlu et al.* 2007, p. 724.

143 See *Ergin* 2012; *Ergin, Evci-Kiraz, Saruhan, Benli, Okyay & Beşer* 2012.

of abuse and neglect within the last 12 months. For the 768 elderly people, the previous year's prevalence rates for psychological abuse, neglect, financial, physical and sexual abuse were 8.1%, 7.6%, 3.5%, 2.9% and 0.4% respectively. Perpetrators of physical abuse were mostly children (68.1%), followed by spouses (12.9%) and siblings (9.5%).[144]

5. Public and/or Media Discourses About Victims, Victims' Rights and Victimisation

As in other countries,[145] it also seems that in Turkey there are no clear and indisputable definitions of harm, offender and victim. Research on public perceptions of crime in Turkey is scarce. However, the available evidence suggests that – as in other countries – certain harmful acts, such as violent assault and property crimes (e.g., child molestation, rape, murder, robbery), are routinely recognized as serious offences, while other crimes, such as white collar crime (e.g., tax evasion, insider trading, welfare fraud, violation of labour laws), which do not target a specific victim, are regarded as less serious offences. The latter offense group receives much less media and public attention.[146]

Violent and sexual offences, especially those committed against women and children, have recently been subject to increased political and public attention in Turkey. One significant case relates to the murder of a 20-year-old female student, Özgecan Aslan, who died whilst she resisted a rape attempt by a bus driver when she was returning home in 2015.[147] The Özgecan case led to nationwide street protests that called for the heaviest penalty for the offender. The court sentenced the offender to aggravated life imprisonment without the possibility of parole. However, to prevent future victimisations, activists called for an "Özgecan Aslan Bill" which would prohibit judges from reducing the offender's sentence at their discretion for being "provoked" into the murder of a woman. In several cases of female homicide in Turkey, male offenders were able to argue that they have been provoked by the victim or that their dignity was impugned and, hence, they received a reduced sentence for their crime. In the wake of Özgecan Aslan's murder, the opposition Republican People's Party (CHP) proposed a bill, the so-called Özgecan Bill, to introduce harsher sentences for sexual offenders and to remove the ability of judges to grant sentence

---

144 *Ergin* 2012; *Ergin et al.* 2012, p. 38.

145 *Carrabine, Cox, Lee, Plummer & South* 2009, pp. 158–159.

146 *Benk, Budak, Püren & Erdem* 2015. One characteristic of white collar crimes is also the diffusion of victimisation which refers to the existence of a large number of victims who are unidentifiable or suffer only a slight loss; see *Dursun* 2010, p. 106–107.

147 The Guardian of 04.12.2015, Three Men Get Life Sentence for Murder and Attempted Rape of Student in Turkey; https://www.theguardian.com/world/2015/dec/04/three-men-life-sentence-murder-student-turkey-ozgecan-aslan [01.05.2018].

reductions. Despite the fact that more than a million people signed a petition to support the bill, it is still under consideration.[148]

Another significant case relates to the rape of a three-year-old girl in February 2018 while she was sleeping at a wedding in southern Turkey. This case sparked significant public outrage, with public discourse about crime and justice once again moving in a more punitive direction, with a broad push for zero-tolerance and the very severe punishment of sexual offenders.[149] Shortly after this tragic event, the ruling Justice and Development Party (AKP) responded to the public outrage by bringing the issue to the cabinet's agenda.[150] To work on the legislative package, a commission of six ministers was formed in February 2018. In April 2018, the government submitted a draft law which stipulated harsher sentences for child abusers.[151] According to the draft law, the upper limit of all sexual abuse crimes committed against children should be increased from 20 to 40 years.[152] The draft law also proposes that sexual offenders who abuse children who are under age 12 will be sentenced to 30 to 40 years of imprisonment and, if they use force or weapons, to life imprisonment.[153] The draft law would also enable courts to order the chemical castration of sexual offenders, based on an expert report starting three months before their release up to five years after the release.[154]

However, while violent offences committed against women and children attract significant public and media attention in Turkey, it also seems that even for very serious crimes, certain characteristics of the victims, such as age, sexual orientation (e.g., LGBTI status) or gender identity (e.g., transgender) might adversely influence public perception and attitudes towards victims of crime.[155] Furthermore, even in very similar criminal cases, public perception of the "victim" and the reaction against

---

148 Onedio of 11.02.2017, Özgecan'dan Sonra 700 Kadın Öldürüldü; 'Özgecan Yasası' ise Meclis Raflarında Bekletiliyor; https://onedio.com/haber/ozgecan-dan-sonra-700-kadin-olduruldu-ozgecan-yasasi-ise-meclis-raflarinda-bekletiliyor-755757 [09.05.2018]; T24 of 07.07.2015, CHP 1 Milyondan Fazla İmza Verilen 'Özgecan Yasası' için Kanun Teklifi Verdi; http://t24.com.tr/haber/chp-1-milyondan-fazla-imza-verilen-ozgecan-yasasi-icin-kanun-teklifi-verdi,302059 [09.05.2018].

149 The NewArab of 05.05.2018, Rape of Child in Turkey Reignites Sexual Abuse Debate; https://www.alaraby.co.uk/english/society/2018/3/5/Rape-of-child-in-Turkey-reignites-sexual-abuse-debate [15.05.2018].

150 Hurriyet Daily News of 25.02.2018, No Reduced Sentence for Sexual Offenders: Turkish Family Minister; http://www.hurriyetdailynews.com/no-reduced-sentence-for-sexual-offenders-turkish-family-minister-127890 [15.05.2018].

151 Draft Law No. 31853594-101-1545/32, 09.04.2018.

152 See Article 3 of the Draft Law No. 31853594-101-1545/32, 09.04.2018.

153 See Article 3 of the Draft Law No. 31853594-101-1545/32, 09.04.2018.

154 See Article 5 of the Draft Law No. 31853594-101-1545/32, 09.04.2018.

155 *Cingöz-Ulu, Türkoğlu & Sayılan* 2016; Çolak 2009.

the offender might also depend on certain characteristics of the victim and/or the offender. For example, in 2009, 17-year-old *Münevver Karabulut* was stabbed to death by her boyfriend and her dismembered body was left in a trash bin. Similar to the Özgecan case, her murder attracted enormous public and media attention in Turkey. A discourse analysis of media coverage of both cases, however, indicated that despite the similarities between the two murder cases (i.e., victims were young women exposed to extreme violence), the media representation of the cases showed important dissimilarities in the reconstruction of the patriarchal discourse.[156] While *Özgecan Aslan* was portrayed as an innocent victim murdered by a stranger on her way home, *Münevver Karabulut* was murdered by her boyfriend and thus did not fit to the stereotype of the "ideal victim" due to her "objectionable" lifestyle.[157]

6. Assessment and Constructive Criticism With Suggestions for Improvement

It is a fact that significant changes to the protection of victims' rights—through the regulations within the Penal Procedure Code, Child Protection Law and the Law on Probation Services—have been realized through the Turkish penal law reform of 2004–2005. In particular, regulating the rights of victims in a separate section of the Penal Procedure Code has increased interest and awareness about victim rights in the Turkish criminal justice system. The term "child victim" is now mentioned for the first time in the Child Protection Law, which has resulted in various protective and supportive measures for child victims. However, with the penal law reform of 2004–2005, the abolition of the victim's right to claim for compensation during the criminal proceedings is a backward step related to victim rights, despite the fact that many international documents are foreseen to recognize this possibility.[158] A further deficiency is that the Victim Support Services Bureaus, which were envisaged to be established under the Law on Probation Services in 2005, have not yet actively come into effect. The establishment of the Department of the Victim Rights within the Ministry of Justice in 2013 is an important step with regards to the institutionalization of the protection of victim rights. As a matter of fact, the Draft Law on Victim Rights, which is still being debated, was prepared with the initiative of this Department. With the enactment of the Draft Law on Victim Rights, it is expected that a common institutional structure regarding victims, which includes the aforementioned centres and special interrogations rooms, will be established. It should be noted that financial assistance (state compensation) for victims is envisaged by the

156 *Gürses* 2017.

157 *Gürses* 2017, pp. 544–545.

158 For example, the Council of Europe Recommendations R (85) 11 (Council of Europe 1985) and R (2006) 8 (Council of Europe 2006) related to victim rights; see *Sokullu-Akıncı & Dursun* 2016, pp. 359–360.

draft law: thou gh this is a major reform suggestion, it is also an obstructive factor that might adversely affect the enactment of the draft law because of the burden associated with its financing.

Very important progressive steps taken in Turkey over recent years include the 2015 establishment of Child Support Centres to operate as residential rehabilitation centres for child victims; the 2012 establishment of Child Monitoring Centres as special interrogation rooms in some public hospitals for child victims of sexual abuse; the 2012 establishment of VPMCs for female victims of violence (through the Law on the Protection of Family and Prevention of Violence against Women); the 2017 establishment of the judicial interview rooms in the courthouses for the interrogation of vulnerable victims such as children, victims of sexual crime and domestic violence are all. All of these measures are designed to not only avoid secondary victimisation but also to provide protection and various support services to victims of crime. However, the number of these support and monitoring centres are not adequate to cover all 81 provinces in Turkey. Currently, there are 49 VPMCs and 143 women's shelters with a total capacity of 3,444 people. Furthermore, as of December 2017, there were 65 child support centres in Turkey, which can accommodate around 1,640 children who are victims of crime, drifted into crime or would otherwise be living on the streets. Finally, as of April 2016, there were 27 Child Monitoring Centres in Turkey. Given the enormous efforts of the Ministry of Family and Social Policies, it is expected that the scope of these centres will be extended nationwide in the near future.

Of equal importance, while it is true that both the Child Protection Law and the Law on Protection of the Family and the Prevention of Violence against Women brought significant changes to protect and support child and women victims, no single evaluation study has been conducted to determine the impact of these services on children and women. Therefore, the question of whether or not the measures implemented under these laws are successful is open to debate. Despite the significance of the discipline in developing effective policy and practices for victims, a fully-fledged education in victimology in terms of theory, research and practice is absent in Turkey. A lack of understanding of the importance of the criminology discipline and the significance of sound research also affect the way official data are compiled by Turkish authorities. The scarcity and limitations of official data on crime victims (as well as on offenders) is therefore another serious handicap for researchers in Turkey. Moreover, existing empirical research in victimology is often flawed in various ways, due to issues of sampling, research design, measurement and statistical analyses. Therefore, victimological research in Turkey is currently unable to guide policy and practices. The lack of reliance on data, theory and sound empirical research findings also reveals itself through the legislative changes and their implementation. The EU accession process has been the main drive behind all the legislative changes in Turkey, and accordingly it seems that Turkey adopted many measures without understanding the theory behind them. This is perhaps most evident in the implementation of the mediation process in Turkey, which has almost nothing in common with the restorative justice idea behind it. This is mainly because the victim and the offender almost never come face-to-face in a meeting and compensation of the material damage to the victim is considered as adequate for the realization of restorative justice ideal in Turkey. Further, it also seems that the main reason behind extending the scope of mediation in recent years has been to alleviate the burden on the criminal justice system rather than to reflect a victim-oriented perspective.

In sum, despite the fact that various progressive steps have been taken over the years with regards to the rights and protection of victims, victimological education and research, though developing, remains in its infancy in Turkey. This, in turn, makes it difficult to evaluate the success of new policies and practices. In order to better analyse the functioning of the criminal justice system and to guide future policies for both victims and offenders, Turkey definitely needs reliable and more detailed data and methodologically sound empirical research.

7. Conclusions

The general interest in victims and victim rights is relatively new in Turkey. Penal law reform in 2004–2005 resulted in important changes with regards to the rights and protection of victims. Although there is currently no special law on victims, various provisions in different laws—such as the Penal Code, Penal Procedure Code, Child Protection Law, Law on Protection of the Family and Prevention of Violence against Women, Law on Probation Services and the Law on Combating Terrorism—relate to victim rights and protection in Turkey. Recently, the government proposed a draft law on victim rights. This draft law, which is expected to be passed in 2019, defines a victim as a person who directly suffers physical, mental, psychological or economic harm as a result of the commission of a crime. Moreover, it sets forth the basic principles and rights of victims and regulates specific services for victims with certain characteristics (vulnerable victim groups). The provisions on state compensation for remedying the plight of victims are also regulated for the first time in this draft law. Furthermore, the regulations on the central and provincial organization of the Victim Rights Department[159] (established under the Ministry of Justice) are also very important in terms of the establishment of the institutional infrastructure for victims and will serve to protect and develop their rights.

Several governmental and state-related institutions, in cooperation with various NGOs, deal with victim support and protection and play key roles in victimology in Turkey. The General Directorate on the Status of Women and the General Directorate of Child Services, both under the Ministry of Family and Social Policies, are

159 For the website of the Victims' Rights Department, see http://www.magdur.adalet.gov.tr [23.05.2018].

key actors concerning issues of female and child victims. VPMCs and Child Support Centres (which function under these General Directorates) are especially important for the provision of various services to female and child victims. Other key governmental actors that support and protect victims in Turkey include the Ministry of Health (through Child Monitoring Centres) especially for child victims of sexual abuse, the Ministry of Interior (through the Department for the Protection of Victims of Human Trafficking) and the Ministry of Justice (through the Department of Probation and the Department of Victim Rights). Various NGOs (e.g., Mor Çatı Women's Shelter Foundation, the Foundation for Women's Solidarity and the Human Resource Development Foundation) deal with victim support and protection in Turkey and work in close cooperation with governmental and state-related institutions.

Yet, despite these developments, victimology is still not an institutionalised discipline in Turkey. Given the status of criminology in Turkey,[160] this is not surprising. It is generally taught as a selective graduate course at some, but not all, law faculties. While there are only two text books on victimology, there is no single academic journal in Turkey which mainly focus on victimology. Official data sources on crime victims in Turkey are scarce. Police and gendarmerie data on crime victims are available only for children. An examination of available data on child victims indicates that the number of juvenile victims continuously increased (and, in fact, more than tripled) during the years between 2008 and 2016. In 2016, 158,343 children were victims of crime. While 55% (86,519) of them were male, within both genders, children aged 15–17 years had a higher victimisation risk than other age groups. According to the most recent statistics available, a majority of the children were victims of violent crimes (60% victims of assault, 12% victims of sexual crime). Unfortunately, the available data do not include more detailed information on child victims, such as the type of the relationship between the victim and the perpetrator. In contrast to police and gendarmerie data, judicial statistics are regularly published; but they reveal only the total annual number of victims and complainants within the cases at criminal courts. These data suggest that, overall, males are more likely to be victimised than women and that the disparity between male and female victimisation has decreased over the years. Judicial statistics also show that while Turkish nationals are more likely to be victimised than foreign nationals, the number of foreign victims almost tripled between the years 2013–2017. Unfortunately, no further information is available, either on the type of crime victimisation or the country of origin.

Turkey does not currently conduct regular victimisation surveys at the national level. Therefore, no such data exist in Turkey about the number and characteristics of victims or the extent of unreported victims of crime. There are, however, a number of victimisation surveys in Turkey conducted at the national level which

---

[160] See *Sözüer & Topçuoğlu* 2014.

focus on specific type of victimisation, such as violence against women. There are also numerous victimisation studies carried out at the local level. Given the scarcity of official data on victims of crime, we tried to present a picture of victimisation based on extant research findings. Due to limited space, we focused on three groups of crime victims: women, children and the elderly. An overview of empirical research findings on violence against women, child sexual abuse and exploitation and elder abuse revealed important limitations concerning extant research in Turkey. While a large number of studies focus on violence against women and child sexual abuse, very few studies examine abuse of the elderly. However, methodological drawbacks of most empirical research studies (e.g., lack of representative samples based on probability sampling, inadequacy of research design and statistical techniques used, reliable and valid measurement, etc.) make it difficult to get an accurate picture of either the actual prevalence rates or the risk factors for victimisation.

Although not all offences and all victimisations are considered as equally serious, violent offences, particularly those committed against women and children, attract significant public and media attention in Turkey. Yet, despite the fact that both public and political interest on victimisation is increasing in Turkey (as evidenced by the various progressive initiatives taken over the recent years), victimological education and research, though developing, remains in its infancy. This makes it difficult to evaluate the success of victim-related policies and practices. In order to better analyse the functioning of the criminal justice system and to guide future policies for both victims and offenders, Turkey needs reliable and detailed data and methodologically sound empirical research. Given the obvious link between research and education, we pointed out earlier the urgent need for comprehensive criminological education programmes at universities for the scientific development of the criminology discipline in terms of theory, research and practice.[161] At this point, the establishment of the first M.A. programme in Criminology and Criminal Justice in Turkey at the Faculty of Law of Istanbul University in the 2017/2018 academic year should be considered a significant step to fill this gap.[162] There is still no single department that offers a B.A. degree in criminology in Turkey, but we very much hope that this programme will help advance theory and research in Turkey and pave the way further for the institutionalisation of the criminology and victimology disciplines throughout Turkey.

---

161 See *Sözüer & Topçuoğlu* 2014.

162 *Topçuoğlu* 2017.

8. Summary in Turkish

Bu çalışma, Türkiye'de viktimoloji ile mağdurların desteklenmesi ve korunmasına dair geliştirilen politika ve yasal düzenlemelerin genel bir resmini çizmektedir. Çalışmanın *ilk bölümü*, Türkiye'ye ilişkin genel bilgi sunarken, *ikinci bölüm* bilimsel bir disiplin olarak viktimolojinin Türkiye'deki konumunu ve viktimolojik araştırmaların mevcut durumunu ele alıp mağdurların desteklenmesi ve korunması hususunda Türkiye'de aktif rol oynayan devlet kurumları ile sivil toplum kuruluşlarına değinmektedir. Çalışmanın üçüncü bölümü, Türkiye'de mağdur hakları ve mağdurların korunmasına ilişkin hukuki düzenlemelere ve yakın zamanda mağdur haklarına ilişkin getirilen kanun tasarısına değinirken; *dördüncü bölüm* mağdurlara ilişkin mevcut resmi verilere ve bu alanda gerçekleştirilen bilimsel araştırma bulgularına dayanarak Türkiye'deki mağduriyet olgusunun resmini ortaya koymaktadır. Çalışmanın *beşinci bölümü*, Türkiye'de kamu ve medyada mağdurlar ve mağduriyete ilişkin söylemleri ve mağdur algısını ele almaktadır. *Altıncı bölüm*, Türkiye'de viktimolojinin mevcut durumu, mağdur koruma politikaları, düzenlemeleri ve uygulamalarına dair genel bir değerlendirme sunarken, *en son bölüm* ise çalışmanın temel bulguları ile Türkiye'de viktimoloji ve mağdurların korunmasına ilişkin genel durumu özetleyerek çalışmayı sonlandırmaktadır.

Literature

Akço, S., Dağlı, T., İnanıcı, M.A., Kaynak, H., Oral, R., Şahin, F., Sofuoğlu, Z., & Ulukol, B. (2013): Child abuse and neglect in Turkey: professional, governmental and non-governmental achievements in improving the national child protection system. Paediatrics and International Child Health 33 (4), pp. 301–309.

Alikaşifoğlu, M., Erginöz, E., Ercan, O., Albayrak Kaymak, D., Uysal, Ö., & İlter, Ö. (2006): Sexual abuse among female high school students in Istanbul, Turkey. Child Abuse and Neglect 30, pp. 247–255.

Altınay, A.G., & Arat, Y. (2009): Violence against women in Turkey: a nationwide survey. Istanbul.

Altınay, A.G., & Arat, Y. (2007): Türkiye'de kadına yönelik şiddet [Violence against women in Turkey]. Istanbul.

Artan, T. (1996): Aile içi fiziksel yaşlı istismarı [Physical abuse of the elderly within family]. Yüksek lisans tezi. İstanbul Üniversitesi Adli Tıp Enstitüsü. Istanbul.

Aslan, S.H., & Alpaslan, Z.N. (1999): Çocukluk örselenme yaşantıları ölçeği'nin bir üniversite öğrencisi örnekleminde geçerlik, güvenirlik ve faktör yapısı [The Reliability, Validity and Factor Structure of the Childhood Trauma Questionnaire Among a Group of University Students]. Turkish Journal of Psychiatry 10, pp. 275–285.

Benk, S., Budak, T., Püren, S., & Erdem, M. (2015): Perception of tax evasion as a crime in Turkey. Journal of Money Laundering Control 18 (1), pp. 99–111.

Bernstein, D.P., Fink, I., Handelsman, I., Foote, J., Lovejoy, M., Wenzel, K., Sapareto, E., & Ruggiero, J. (1994): Initial reliability and validity of a new retrospective measure of child abuse and neglect. American Journal of Psychiatry 151 (8), pp. 1132–1136.

Carrabine, E., Cox, P., Lee, M., Plummer, K., & South, N. (2009): Criminology: A Sociological Introduction. 2nd. ed. London.

Cingöz-Ulu, B., Türkoğlu, B., & Sayılan, G. (2016): Kadın şiddet mağdurlarına yönelik tutumlarda mağdurun trans kimliğinin etkisi [The role of victim's tansgender identity on attitudes towards female victims of violence]. Türk Psikoloji Yazıları 19 [Turkish Psychological Articles] (Special Issue), pp. 94–104.

Currie, C., Hurrelmann, K., Settertobulte, W., Smith, R., & Todo, J. (2000): Health and health behaviour among young people. Health-behaviour in school-aged children, in: WHO Regional Office for Europe (ed.), A WHO cross national study (HBSC) International report. Health Policy for children and adolescents (HEPCA). Series No. 1. Copenhagen.

Çolak, Ö. (2009): Eşcinsellere yönelik nefret suçları ve toplumun bu suçlar kapsamında fail eve mağdura yönelik tutumları [Attitudes towards perpetrators and victims of hate crime against LGBT people]. Yüksek Lisans Tezi. İstanbul Üniversitesi Adli Tıp Enstitüsü. Instanbul.

Doerner, W.G., & Lab, S.P. (2012): Victimology. 6th ed. Burlington, MA.

Dursun, S. (2010): Sermaye Piyasasında Gerçeğe Aykırılıktan Doğan Suçlar [Crimes of false representation in the capital market]. İstanbul.

Dündar, T., & Özer, E. (2012): Türkiye'ye hoş! geldiniz. Türkiye'de insan ticareti sorunu sorunu [Welcome to Turkey. Human trafficking issues in Turkey]. İstanbul.

Ergin, F. (2012): Aydın merkezinde yaşlı istismar/ihmal prevalansı ve ilişkili faktörler faktörler [Prevalence and risk factors of elder abuse/neglect in Aydın city center]. 15. Ulusal Halk Sağlığı Kongresi 2-6 Ekim 2012, Bursa, Türkiye Kongre kitabı, pp. 1079–1081. Bursa.

Ergin, F., Evci-Kiraz, E.D., Saruhan, G., Benli, C., Okyay, P., & Beşer, E. (2012): Prevalence and risk factors of elder abuse and neglect in a Western city of Turkey: A community-based study. Bulletin of the Transylvania University of Brasov 5 (54), pp. 33–50.

Ergöçmen, B.A., Yüksel-Kaptanoğlu, I., & Jansen, H.A.H. (2013): Intimate partner violence and the relation between help-seeking behaviour and the severity and frequency of physical violence among women in Turkey. Violence Against Women 19, pp. 1151–1174.

Ersan, M. (2013): Addressing cross-cutting issues in human trafficking policy: recommendations for Turkey. Perceptions 18 (3), pp. 93–107.

Eskin, M., Kaynak Demir, H., & Demir, S. (2005): Same sex sexual orientation, childhood sexual abuse, and suicidal behaviour in university students in Turkey. Archives of Sexual Behaviour 34, pp. 185–195.

Gürses, F. (2017): Kadın cinayetlerinin haber söylemi: Münevver Karabulut ve Özgecan Aslan haberleri üzerine eleştirel bir değerlendirme [News discourse of femicides: a critical assessment about news of Munevver Karabulut and Özgecan Aslan]. Ankara Üniversitesi SBF Dergisi [Ankara University SBF Journal] 72 (3), pp. 541–568.

Güvenç, G., Akyüz, A., & Cesario, S.K. (2014): Intimate partner violence against women in Turkey: A synthesis of the literature. Journal of Family Violence 29, pp. 333–341.

Jahic, G., & Akdaş, A. (2007): Uluslararası suç mağdurları araştırması: İstanbul hane halkında suç mağduriyeti [International crime victim survey: crime victimisation in Istanbul households]. Tübitak Proje No: SBB 104K100. Istanbul.

Jahic, G., & Akdaş Mitrani, A.T. (2010): International crime victim survey 2005: Crime victimisation in Istanbul households. Procedia Social and Behavioural Sciences 5, pp. 190–198.

Keser Özcan, N., Günaydın, S., & Çitil, E.T. (2016): Domestic violence against women in Turkey: a systematic review and meta-analysis. Archives of Psychiatric Nursing 30, pp. 620–629.

Keskinoğlu, P., Giray, H., Pıçakçıefe, M., Bilgiç, N. & Uçku, R. (2004): Yaşlıda fiziksel, finansal örselenme ve ihmal edilme [Physical and financial abuse and neglect of the elderly]. Türk Geriatri Dergisi [Turkish Journal of Geriatrics] 7, pp. 57–61.

Keskinoğlu, P., Pıçakçıefe, M., Bilgiç, N., Giray, H., Karakuş, N., & Uçku, R. (2007): Elder abuse and neglect in two different socieconomic districts in İzmir, Turkey. International Psychogeriatrics 19 (4), pp. 719–731.

Koca, M., & Üzülmez, İ. (2017): Türk Ceza Hukuku Genel Hükümler [Turkish Penal Law General Provisions]. Ankara.

Lalor, K., & McElvaney, R. (2008): Overview of the nature and extent of child sexual abuse in Europe, in: Council of Europe (ed.), Protecting children from sexual violence – A comprehensive approach. Strasbourg, pp. 13–43.

Lök, N. (2015): Türkiye'de Yaşlı İstismarı ve İhmali: Sistematik Derleme Derleme [Elder abuse and neglect in Turkey: a systematic review]. Psikiyatride Güncel Yaklaşımlar 7 (2), pp. 149–156.

Polat, A. (2014): Viktimoloji (Mağdurbilim) [Victimology]. Ankara.

Özgenç, İ. (2017): Türk Ceza Hukuku Genel Hükümler [Turkish Penal Law General Provisions]. Ankara.

Öztürk, B., Tezcan, D., Erdem, M.R., Sırma Gezer, Ö., Saygılar Kırıt, Y.F., Özaydın, Ö, Alan Akcan, E., & Tütüncü, E.E. (2016): Nazari ve Uygulamalı Ceza Muhakemesi Hukuku [Theoretical and applied criminal procedure law]. 10th ed. Ankara.

Sokullu-Akıncı, F. & Dursun, S. (2016): Viktimoloji (Mağdurbilim) [Victimology]. Istanbul.

Sözüer, A., & Topçuoğlu, T. (2014): The status of crime and criminology in Turkey, in: M. Getos Kalac, H.-J. Albrecht & M. Kilchling (eds.), Mapping the criminological landscape of the Balkans, vol. 1. Berlin, pp. 377–400.

Sözüer, A., Baytaz, A.B., & Kelep, T. (2012): Kadına yönelik şiddet ve ayrımcılıkla ilgili bilimsel rapor [Scientific report on violence and discrimination against women], in: A. Sözüer, T. Topçuoğlu, S. Talas & R. Erbaş (eds.), II. International crime and punishment film festival, Violence and discrimination against women, Academic papers, vol. 1. Istanbul, pp. 311–334.

Şenol, D., & Yıldız, S. (2013): Kadına Yönelik Şiddet Algısı – Kadın ve Erkek Bakış Açılarıyla Açılarıyla [Perceptions on violence against women—women's and men's perspectives]. Ankara.

Tekeli, Ş. (2010): The Turkish women's movement: A brief history of success. Quaderns de la Mediterrania 14, pp. 119–123.

Topçuoğlu, T. (2017): The law faculty at Istanbul University, a partner of the MPPG, takes the lead to establish the first M.A. in criminology and criminal justice in Turkey. Balkan Criminology News 1, pp. 5–7.

Uslu, R.İ., & Kapçı, E.G. (2014): Türkiye'de çocukların cinsel sömürü ve cinsel istismarı: Son 12 yılda yayınlanan araştırmaların sistematik değerlendirmesi değerlendirmesi [Sexual exploitation and abuse of children in Turkey: systematic review of published studies within the last 12 years]. Ankara.

Yenisey, F. (2009): Turkish Criminal Procedure Code, Ceza Muhakemesi Kanunu. Istanbul; http://www.legislationline.org/documents/id/17788 [25.05.2018].

Yeşilyurt Gündüz, Z. (2004): The women's movement in Turkey: From Tanzimat towards European Union Membership. Perceptions Autumn, pp. 115–134.

Yıldırım, A., Karakaş, M., Yılmaz, R., Çetin, İ., & Şenel, İ. (2013): Prevalence and correlates of school violence and sexual abuse among adolescents in Tokat, Turkey. HealthMED 7, pp. 382–392.

Yüksel-Kaptanoğlu, I.,Türkyılmaz, A.S., & Heise, L. (2012): What puts women at risk of violence from their husbands? Findings from a large, nationally representative survey in Turkey. Journal of Interpersonal Violence 27, pp. 2743–2769.

Zolotor, A.J., Runyan, D.K., Dunne, M.P., Jain, D., Peturs, H.R., Ramirez, C., Volkova, E., Deb, S., Lidchi, V., Muhammad, T., & Isaeva, O. (2009): ISPCAN child abuse screening tool children's version (ICAST-C): Instrument development and multi-national pilot testing. Child Abuse and Neglect 33 (11), pp. 833–841.

Documents

Bar Association of Trabzon, Committee on Children's Rights (2015): Çocuk izlem merkezleri Türkiye raporu [National report on child monitoring centres]; http://web.e-baro.web.tr/uploads/61/2015/cim%20tr.pdf [14.05.2018] [in Turkish only].

Council of Europe (2006): Recommendation Rec(2006) 8 of the Committee of Ministers to Member States on assistance to crime victims; https://victimsupport.eu/activeapp/wp-content/uploads/2012/09/Recommendation-Rec20068-of-the-Committee-of-Ministries_Council-of-Europe11.pdf [23.05.2018].

Council of Europe (1999): Recommendation No. R (99) 19 of the Committee of Ministers to Member States concerning mediation in penal matters; https://www.barobirlik.org.tr/dosyalar/duyurular/hsykkanunteklifi/rec(99)19%20(1).pdf [23.05.2018].

Council of Europe (1985): Recommendation No. R (85) 11 of the Committee of Ministers to Member States on the position of the victim in the framework of criminal law and procedure; https://www.barobirlik.org.tr/dosyalar/duyurular/hsykkanunteklifi/recR(85)11e.pdf [23.05.2018].

Council of Europe Convention (2007): Protection of Children against Sexual Exploitation and Sexual Abuse; https://rm.coe.int/1680084822 [14.05.2018].

Human Resource Development Foundation (2007): Turkey, in: Human Rights Defence Centre (ed.), Combating Human Trafficking: Problems and Prospects. Athens, pp. 225–243.

International Children's Center, University of Hacettepe, Institute of Public Health & Society of Public Health Specialists (2015): Global study on sexual exploitation of children in travel and tourism. Country-specific report Turkey; https://www.ecpat.org/wp-content/uploads/2016/10/3.-SECTT-TURKEY.pdf [14.05.2018].

Ministry of Family and Social Policies (2018): Türkiye'de Kadın 2018 [Woman in Turkey 2018]. Ankara; https://kadininstatusu.aile.gov.tr/uygulamalar/turkiyede-kadin [10.04.2018] [in Turkish only].

Ministry of Family and Social Policies (2017): 2016 yılı faaliyet raporu [Annual report 2016]. Ankara; http://www.aile.gov.tr/data/58b58e4c691407119c139239/2016%20%20Faaliyet%20Raporu.pdf [19.05.2018] [in Turkish only].

Ministry of Family and Social Policies (2014): Domestic violence against women in Turkey – Summary report. Ankara.

Ministry of Family and Social Policies, General Directorate of Child Services (2018): Çocuk destek merkezleri [Child support centres]; https://cocukhizmetleri.aile.gov.tr/cocuk-destek-merkezleri [01.04.2019] [in Turkish only].

Ministry of Family and Social Policies, General Directorate on the Status of Women (2017): Şönim: Şiddet önleme ve izleme merkezleri [VPMC: Violence prevention and monitoring centres]. Ankara; https://kadininstatusu.aile.gov.tr/uploads/pages/dagitimda-olan-yayinlar/siddet-onleme-ve-izleme-merkezleri-sonim.pdf [01.04.2019].

Ministry of Family and Social Policies, General Directorate on the Status of Women (2015): Türkiye'de kadına yönelik aile içi şiddet araştırması [Research on domestic violence against women in Turkey]. Ankara [in Turkish only].

Ministry of Family and Social Policies and Hacettepe University Institute of Population Studies (2015): Türkiye'de Kadına Yönelik Aile İçi Şiddet Araştırması [Research on domestic violence against women in Turkey]. Ankara; http://www.hips.hacettepe.edu.tr/KKSA-TRAnaRaporKitap26Mart.pdf [05.04.2018] [in Turkish only].

Ministry of Foreign Affairs (2018a): Uluslararası Kuruluşlar ve İlişkilerimiz [International Organisations and Our Relations]; http://www.mfa.gov.tr/sub.tr.mfa?23a3fc26-4f3b-47dd-943e-d8934cdad97e [19.05.2018] [in Turkish only].

Ministry of Foreign Affairs (2018b): Türkiye'nin insan ticaretiyle mücadelesi [Turkey's fight against human trafficking]; http://www.mfa.gov.tr/turkiye_nin-insan-ticaretiyle-mucadelesi-.tr.mfa [14.05.2018] [in Turkish only].

Ministry of the Interior (2018): Türkiye'de mülki idare bölümleri envanteri [Data File] [Civil administration units in Turkey]; https://www.e-icisleri.gov.tr/Anasayfa/MulkiIdariBolumleri.aspx [19.05.2018] [in Turkish only].

Ministry of the Interior, General Directorate of Migration Management (2018a): Yıllara göre geçici koruma kapsamındaki Suriyeliler [The number of Syrian refugees under temporary protection by years]; http://www.goc.gov.tr/icerik6/gecici-koruma_363_378_4713_icerik [20.05.2018] [in Turkish only].

Ministry of the Interior, General Directorate of Migration Management (2018b): Victims of human trafficking; http://www.goc.gov.tr/icerik6/victims-of-human-trafficking_915_1024_4749_icerik [15.05.2018] [in Turkish only].

Ministry of the Interior, General Directorate of Migration Management (2017): 2016 Türkiye Göç Raporu [Report on migration in Turkey 2006]. Ankara [in Turkish only].

Ministry of the Interior, General Directorate of Security (2018): Türkiye'de insan ticaretiyle mücadele çalışmaları [Fighting against human trafficking in Turkey]; https://www.egm.gov.tr/Sayfalar/turkiyenin-insan-ticareti- ile-mucadele-calismalari.aspx [14.05.2018] [in Turkish only].

Ministry of Justice, General Directorate of Judicial Record and Statistics (2018): Adli İstatistikler 2017 [Judicial Statistics 2017]; http://www.adlisicil.adalet.gov.tr/istatistik_2017/istatistik2017.pdf [14.05. 2018] [in Turkish only].

Ministry of Justice, General Directorate of Judicial Record and Statistics (2017): Adli İstatistikler 2016 [Judicial Statistics 2016]; http://www.adlisicil.adalet.gov.tr/istatistik_2016/istatistik2016.pdf [14.05. 2018] [in Turkish only].

Ministry of Justice, General Directorate of Judicial Record and Statistics (2016): Adli İstatistikler 2015 [Judicial Statistics 2015] [Data File]; http://www.adlisicil.adalet.gov.tr/istatistik_2015/CEZA/26.pdf [14.05.2018] [in Turkish only].

Ministry of Justice, General Directorate of Judicial Record and Statistics (2015): Adli İstatistikler 2014 [Judicial Statistics 2014]. Ankara [in Turkish and English].

Ministry of Justice, General Directorate of Judicial Record and Statistics (2014): Adli İstatistikler 2013 [Judicial Statistics 2013]. Ankara [in Turkish and English].

Ministry of Justice, General Directorate of Judicial Record and Statistics (2013): Adli İstatistikler 2012 [Judicial Statistics 2012]. Ankara [in Turkish and English].

Ministry of Justice, General Directorate of Judicial Record and Statistics (2012b): Adli İstatistikler 2011 [Judicial Statistics 2011]. Ankara [in Turkish and English].

Ministry of Justice, General Directorate of Judicial Record and Statistics (2012a): Adli İstatistikler 2010 [Judicial Statistics 2010]. Ankara [in Turkish and English].

Ministry of Justice, General Directorate of Judicial Record and Statistics (2011): Adli İstatistikler 2009 [Judicial Statistics 2009]. Ankara [in Turkish and English].

Ministry of Justice, General Directorate of Judicial Record and Statistics (2010): Adli İstatistikler 2008 [Judicial Statistics 2008]. Ankara [in Turkish and English].

Ministry of Justice, General Directorate of Judicial Record and Statistics (2009): Adli İstatistikler 2007 [Judicial Statistics 2007]. Ankara [in Turkish and English].

Ministry of Justice, General Directorate of Judicial Record and Statistics (2008): Adli İstatistikler 2006 [Judicial Statistics 2006]. Ankara [in Turkish and English].

Ministry of Justice, General Directorate of Penal Affairs, Department of Victim Rights (2018a): Görevlerimiz [Our mission]; http://www.magdur.adalet.gov.tr/gorevlerimiz-0174 [14.05.2018] [in Turkish only].

Ministry of Justice, General Directorate of Penal Affairs, Department of Victim Rights (2018b): Adli görüşme odaları [Judicial interview rooms]; http://www.magdur.adalet.gov.tr/adli-gorusme-odalari-01542 [25.05.2018] [in Turkish only].

Ministry of Justice, General Directorate of Penal Affairs, Department of Victim Rights (2018c): Tarihçe [History]; http://www.magdur.adalet.gov.tr/tarihce-0173 [23.05.2018] [in Turkish only].

National Consortium for the Study of Terrorism and Responses to Terrorism (START) (2016): Global Terrorism Database [Data file]; https://www.start.umd.edu/gtd [20.05.2018]; cited as: START 2016.

Prime Ministry, Institution of Family Research (1998): Aile içinde ve toplumsal alanda şiddet [Violence in the family and the public sphere]. Ankara [in Turkish only].

Prime Ministry, Institution of Family Research (1995): Aile içi şiddetin sebep ve sonuçları [Causes and consequences of domestic violence]. Ankara [in Turkish only].

START, see National Consortium for the Study of Terrorism and Responses to Terrorism.

Turkish Statistical Institute (TurkStat) (2018a): Bölgesel istatistikler [Regional Statistics] [Data File]; https://biruni.tuik.gov.tr/bolgeselistatistik/tabloOlustur.do [19.05.2018] [in Turkish only]; cited as: TurkStat 2018a.

Turkish Statistical Institute (TurkStat) (2018b): Güvenlik birimlerine gelen veya getirilen çocuk istatistikleri [Statistics on children brought into security units] [Data File]; https://

biruni.tuik.gov.tr/medas/?kn=95&locale=tr [25.04.2018] [in Turkish only]; cited as: TurkStat 2018b.

Turkish Statistical Institute (TurkStat) (2018c): Nüfus projeksiyonları [Population projections] [Data File]; http://www.tuik.gov.tr/PreTablo.do?alt_id=1027 [23.05.2018] [in Turkish only]; cited as: TurkStat 2018c.

TurkStat, see Turkish Statistical Institute.

United Nations (1993): Declaration on the elimination of violence against women. New York; http://www.un.org/documents/ga/res/48/a48r104.htm [20.05.2018].

United Nations (1985): Declaration of basic principles of justice for victims of crime and abuse of power; https://www.unodc.org/pdf/compendium/compendium_2006_part_03_02.pdf [20.05.2018].

WHO (2018): Aging and life-course; http://www.who.int/ageing/projects/elder_abuse/en [26.08.2018].

WHO (2008): A global response to elder abuse and neglect: Building primary health care capacity to deal with the problem worldwide: main report. Geneva; http://www.who.int/ageing/publications/ELDER_DocAugust08.pdf [20.05.2018].

WHO, London School of Hygiene and Tropical Medicine & South African Medical Research Council (2013): Global and regional estimates of violence against women: Prevalence and health effects of intimate partner violence and non-partner sexual violence. WHO; http://www.who.int/reproductivehealth/publications/violence/9789241564625/en/ [04.04.2018].

About the Authors

Azra Adžajlić-Dedović holds a PhD in Law based on her doctoral research on criminal law and criminology. Topics of her scientific interests are victimology and crime prevention. Adžajlić-Dedović, PhD has published scientific contributions on the rule of law, domestic violence, sexual violence and rights of victims of crime. She has also contributed to policy-making and practice of victim protection by drafting national victimological policy documents, training the police, judges and prosecutors in Bosnia and Herzegovina.

E-mail address: aadzajlic@fkn.unsa

Andrea Tünde Barabás, PhD, is a Professor of Criminology at the Faculty of Law Enforcement, National University of Public Services, and the Head of the Institute of Criminal Sciences and also works at the National Institute of Criminology. Her research interests include victimology, the dimensions of insecurity, alternative sanctions, alternative solutions in criminal procedure, the reintegration of offenders and crime prevention. Over the past years, she has written over 100 articles and studies, edited five books and authored two monographs, entitled "Börtön helyett egyezség?" [Compromise: an alternative to prison? Mediation and other alternative sanctions in Europe] and "Áldozatok és Igazságszolgáltatás" [Victims and Criminal Justice].

E-mail address: barabas@okri.hu

Zoran Burić, PhD, is an assistant professor of law at the Department for Criminal Procedural Law at the Faculty of Law, University of Zagreb. Besides criminal procedural law, he also teaches courses on European Union Criminal Law and Psychiatry and Law. His primary professional interests include criminal procedure, comparative criminal justice, EU criminal law, human rights and criminal justice, psychiatry and law, and rights of victims of crime. He has been a member of several working groups of the Croatian Ministry of Justice that had the task of drafting legislation to transpose the provisions of EU law into national law.

E-mail address: zoran.buric@pravo.hr

Flaviu Ciopec has been teaching Criminal Procedure Law and Criminology at the West University of Timişoara, Romania, since 1999. For two consecutive years (2015–2016), he did scientific research at the Max-Planck-Institut in Freiburg, Germany, focused on the extended confiscation and the principles of criminal procedures topics. He has been a member of the research team in two European projects entitled INT.E.L.JUST and I.N.S.P.IR.E. at the Padua University, Italy. He has co-authored a chapter for the book "Personal participation in criminal proceedings. A comparative study of participatory safeguards and in absentia trials in Europe", which has been published in 2019 by Springer publishing.

E-mail address: flaviu.ciopec@e-uvt.ro

Sanja Ćopić, PhD, is a Senior Research Associate at the Institute of Criminological and Sociological Research, and a researcher and the President of the Executive Board of the Victimology Society of Serbia.

E-mail address: sanja.copic011@gmail.com

Selman Dursun, PhD, is an Assistant Professor of Penal and Penal Procedural Law at Istanbul University Law Faculty. He lectures on penal law and victimology to undergraduate and graduate students. His main research interests include economic crimes, white-collar crimes, victimology, dogmatic penal law and penal procedural law. He has published work in the fields of economic penal law, banking crimes, capital market crimes, property crimes, sexual crimes, grounds of justification and excuse, defence counsel in penal procedure and victimology, especially on the concept of victim precipitation and the protection of possible sexual crimes victims.

E-mail address: sdursun@istanbul.edu.tr

Katja Eman, PhD, is an Associate Professor of Criminology at the Faculty of Criminal Justice and Security of the University of Maribor. Her research interests include criminology, victimology, penology, crime prevention, and crime mapping. She has (co)authored publications on crime and criminal justice, including crime victims in general and victims of environmental crime as part of her studies in the field of green criminology.

E-mail address: katja.eman@fvv.uni-mb.si

Anna-Maria Getoš Kalac, PhD, headed the Max Planck Partner Group for Balkan Criminology from 2013 to 2019, and currently leads the Balkan Criminology Network, while lecturing as an Associate Professor at the University of Zagreb Faculty of Law. She currently also heads the Faculty's Institute of Criminal Law Sciences, Criminology and Victimology. Her interest in criminology, criminal justice, and the Balkans started back in 2001 with empirical research into terrorism, hate crimes and political violence, which then evolved into related areas such as organised crime, illegal markets, violence research and security (perception). Since 2012, she has been interconnecting the criminological research potential of the region through her *Balkan Criminology Initiative* and developing research excellence at her Faculty, primarily through engaging PhD candidates in projects of the Partner Group. Dr. Getoš Kalac heads several international and domestic research projects in Croatia and the region (ISRD3 Croatia; Balkan Homicide Study; Violence Research Lab; member of the enlarged European Sourcebook expert group and national correspondent for Croatia), while also regularly teaching victimology at University of Lausanne's School of Criminal Sciences as Professeur Invité.

E-mail address: agetos@pravo.hr

Aleksandra Gruevska-Drakulevski, PhD, is an Associate Professor of Criminology, Penology and Criminal Law at the Iustinianus Primus Faculty of Law of the Ss. Cyril and Methodius University in Skopje. Her research interests include criminology, penology, victimology, criminal law, and juvenile justice. She is an author of textbooks, manuals and more than 40 scientific articles, policy papers and other publications published in journals nationally and abroad. She also participates in the work of many national and international research projects.

E-mail address: a.gruevskadrakulevski@pf.ukim.edu.mk

Rok Hacin, PhD, is an Assistant Professor of Criminology at the Faculty of Criminal Justice and Security of the University of Maribor, Slovenia. His main research interests comprise the legitimacy of the criminal justice system, penology, violent crime, victimology and crime mapping. He has published papers on legitimacy in prisons, the development of penology in Slovenia, alternative sanctioning, crime mapping, the fear of crime, crime and penal statistics, and other criminal justice topics.

E-mail address: rok.hacin@fvv.uni-mb.si

Aleksandra Jovanović is a PhD student at the University of Montenegro Faculty of Law in Podgorica, Montenegro. She has published papers on criminology and victimology. Her doctoral dissertation deals with the suppression of money laundering and financing of terrorism in Montenegrin and European legislation and practice.

E-mail address: aleksandrajovanovic417@gmail.com

Evisa Kambellari, PhD, is an Associate Professor of Criminal Law at the University of Tirana Faculty of Law. Since 2014, she has been representing Albania in the Balkan Criminology Network that operates as a platform of criminological and criminal justice research excellence focused on the Balkan region in the framework of the Max Planck Partner Group (MPPG) for Balkan Criminology. Her research interests include victimology, criminal sentencing, crime prevention policies, cybercrime, illicit trade offences, business, and white-collar crime.

E-mail address: evisa.kambellari@fdut.edu.al

Zoran Kanduč, PhD, is a senior researcher at the Institute of Criminology at the University of Ljubljana Faculty of Law. He also lectures on criminology and victimology. His main subjects of professional interests are theoretical criminological issues, personal and structural violence, postmodern and post-socialist forms of crime, social and class control. He published numerous academic texts, including the following monographs (in Slovenian language) "Criminology: straight and deviant paths of the science of straight and deviant paths", "Beyond crime and punishment", Subjects and objects of (in)formal social control in the context of postmodern transitions", and "Politics, law, economy, and culture: criminological reflections of postmodern society and culture".

E-mail address: zoran.kanduc@pf.uni-lj.si

Ákos Kara has been working at the Hungarian Ministry of Justice since 1995 and has specialised in the codification of substantive and international criminal law. He participated in the preparation of several international and European conventions and treaties including the Statute of the ICC, CoE and UN conventions against corruption, money laundering and organised crime. He also took part in the work of GRECO and MONEYVAL. As a deputy head of department, he coordinated the codification of the new Hungarian Criminal Code, the new Act on criminal cooperation with the EU Member States. He is the Head of Department of Substantive Criminal Law Codification.

E-mail address: akos.kara.ka@gmail.com

Michael Kilchling, PhD, is a senior researcher at the Max Planck Institute for the Study of Crime, Security and Law (previously: Max Planck Institute for Foreign and International Criminal Law) in Freiburg, Germany, and lecturer at the University of Freiburg. He has been a member of several international expert groups such as the Crime Proofing Steering Group of the EU Commission, DG Justice and Home Affairs; the informal platform of experts of the European Commission on seizure, confiscation, freezing and asset recovery; the Group of Specialists on Assistance to Victims and Prevention of Victimisation at the Council of Europe; the informal group of experts of the European Commission on victims of crime; a EU twinning project in Pristina, Kosovo, for strengthening legislative drafting (as consultant on state victim compensation law); and the group of experts on victims' rights commissioned by the Council of Europe's Committee on Crime Problems which prepared the pending draft for a renewed Recommendation on the rights, services and support for victims of crime. He has also been working at the International Monetary Fund in Washington, D.C. (as visiting expert on European legislation on asset confiscation) and is connected with the Balkan Criminology Network. Dr. Kilchling's list of publications in-

includes monographs, edited volumes, journal articles, and conference papers, mostly in German and English.

E-mail address: m.kilchling@csl.mpg.de

Anna Kiss has been working at the Hungarian National Institute of Criminology since 1987. Her current research projects include the role of the victim, the role of the prosecutor, the evidence and the proofs, and the efficiency of criminal procedure. She defended her PhD thesis titled "The role of the victim in the criminal proceedings" in 2006. She has published several articles and gave presentations at conferences in Hungary and abroad.

E-mail address: kiss@okri.hu

Barbara Kraml is candidate judge at the Higher Regional Court of appeal in Vienna and a member of the Fundamental Rights Section of the Austrian Judges Association. Additionally, she represents the Austrian Federal Ministry of Justice within the European Crime Prevention Network (EUCPN) as a board member. She holds master degrees in both law and political science. She has received her doctoral degree for her thesis titled "Ungleicher Schutz sexueller Autonomie: Sexualstrafrecht als biopolitischer Schauplatz" on the development of Austrian Sexual Penal Law from the University of Vienna in 2016. She held a scholarship of the interdisciplinary research training group "Gender, Violence, and Agency in the Era of Globalization" at the University of Vienna (2010–2013), spent a research stay at Birkbeck School of Law at the University of London (2012), contributed to the UNODC research project on "Mutual Legal Assistance among ASEAN Member States" (2013–2014), and worked as university assistant at the Department for Criminal Law and Criminology at the University of Vienna (2015–2019). Her main areas of research are Austrian and European criminal law, criminal procedural law, victims' rights, legal gender studies and philosophy of law.

E-mail: barbara.kraml@justiz.gv.at

Gordana Lažetić, PhD, is a Professor of Criminal Procedure Law, Juvenile Justice and Criminology at the Iustinianus Primus Faculty of Law in Skopje. Her research interests include criminology, penology, victimology and juvenile justice. She has published more than 30 monographs, university textbooks and brochures, more than 100 articles in national and foreign journals as well as participated in over 100 conferences, scientific and applied projects.

E-mail address: gordana2206@gmail.com

Gorazd Meško, PhD, is a Professor of Criminology at the Faculty of Criminal Justice and Security, University of Maribor. He has conducted several comparative research projects in the region of South-Eastern and Eastern Europe, including the development of policing, legitimacy of policing, crime prevention, fear of crime, and crimes against the environment. He edited a special issue of the journal of Criminal Justice and Security on the fear of crime in South-Eastern Europe in 2012. His recent edited books include "Understanding and Managing Threats to the Environment in South Eastern Europe" (Springer, 2011), "Handbook on Policing in Central and Eastern Europe" (Springer, 2013), "Trust and Legitimacy in Criminal Justice: European Perspectives" (Springer, 2015), and "Criminal Justice and Security in Central and Eastern Europe" (monograph series). He has been a chair of a biennial international conference on Criminal Justice and Security in Central and Eastern Europe organised by the Faculty of Criminal Justice and Security in Ljubljana, Slovenia, since 2004.

E-mail address: gorazd.mesko@fvv.uni-mb.si

Vesna Nikolić-Ristanović, PhD, is a Full Professor at the Faculty of Special Education and Rehabilitation, University of Belgrade, Director of the Victimology Society of Serbia, a member of the European Academy of Science and Arts, a former president of the European Society of Criminology and an honorary member of the World Society of Victimology.

E-mail: vnikolicristanovic@gmail.com

Kamen Novikov is an Assistant in Penal procedure at the most prominent and oldest Law faculty in Bulgaria – the Sofia University "St. Kliment Ohridski". His research interests include penal law and penal procedure, criminal justice and crime prevention. He has published extensively in these fields. Since 2004 he has been active as a lawyer, mainly in criminal cases. He has represented clients before prosecution, investigation bodies and at almost all Bulgarian courts. He has a lot of experience not only in working with offenders but also with victims. Therefore, he is aware of the theoretical and practical problems of victimisation.

E-mail address: novkam@yahoo.com

Antony Pemberton, PhD, is Professor of Victimology at the International Victimology Institute Tilburg (INTERVICT), Tilburg University, the Netherlands, and, from the 1st of October 2019, Professor of Restorative Justice at the Leuven Institute of Criminology (LINC), KU Leuven, Belgium. He is a political scientist and a criminologist. Antony Pemberton has published over 90 articles, chapters and books on the subjects relating to victimology and restorative justice. He is currently the Action Chair of the COST-Action CA18121 "Cultures of Victimology: understanding processes of victimization across Europe", which will run from 2019 until 2023.

E-mail address: a.pemberton@uvt.nl

Urška Pirnat, MA, has been a junior researcher and assistant in criminology at the Faculty of Criminal Justice and Security of the University of Maribor since 2016. She is a doctoral student of criminal justice and security researching safety and security in urban neighbourhoods in Slovenia. As a junior researcher in the national research programme "Security and Safety in Local Communities", she is also taking part in a study on the fear of crime in Slovenia.

E-mail address: urska.pirnat@fvv.uni-mb.si

Velimir Rakočević, PhD, is a Full Professor and Dean of the Faculty of Law, University of Montenegro in Podgorica, Montenegro. He teaches criminal law, criminology, victimology and criminalistics. He is the founder and the head of a study programme on security and criminalistics at the Faculty of Law. He is also a Head of the Chair of the Criminal Law Science. He is the president of the Association for Criminology and Victimology of Montenegro. He is the author of textbooks, monographs and articles on criminal law, criminology and victimology.

E-mail address: veljorakocevic@yahoo.com

Sunčana Roksandić Vidlička, PhD, has been a member of the MPPG for Balkan Criminology since 2013 and lectures Criminal Law, Economic Criminal Law, and Transitional Justice at the University of Zagreb Faculty of Law. She is the Head of the Croatian Unit for the International Network of the UNESCO Chair in Bioethics and a member of the UNODC Anti-Corruption Academic Initiative. She is the head of the Jean Monnet Project "Advanced Seminar in EU Criminal Law and Policy". She has acted as an expert in national and international projects, especially on the implementation of the international and EU legislation in national legal orders. She has been a member of two working groups of the Croatian Ministry of Justice that drafted Criminal Law and Law on Protection of People with Mental Disabilities. Her work on the mechanisms of national and international criminal law breaching and strengthening the international human rights (particularly economic and social rights) has been published in English, Croatian and German.

E-mail: suncana.roksandic@pravo.hr

Eszter Sárik has been working at the Hungarian National Institute of Criminology since 1999, conducting research on juvenile delinquency and crime prevention. She is a member of the Balkan Criminology Network and she used to be a national representative of the European Crime Prevention network. She defended her PhD thesis entitled "Religion, Values and Youth in the Context of Criminology" in 2018. She has published several articles and given conference presentations in Hungary and abroad.

E-mail: sarik.eszter76@gmail.com

Miodrag Simović is the appointed Judge of the Constitutional Court of Bosnia and Herzegovina. He is a full professor at the Faculty of Law in Banja Luka and the Faculty of Law in East Sarajevo. Academician Miodrag Simović has contributed professionally and academically to the victim protection in Bosnia and Herzegovina with his publications and comments on the criminal procedural legislation in Bosnia and Herzegovina, especially with textbooks on Victimology (2006), International Criminal Law (2013), Juvenile Criminal Law (2013) and Criminal Proceedings – Introduction and General Provisions (2016). It is of particular importance to mention his significant role in drafting and adoption of the Law on Witness Protection Programme in Bosnia and Herzegovina, which was adopted in 2014.

E-mail address: miodrag.simovic@ustavnisud.ba

Monika Stempkowski holds master degrees in both law and psychology, which she obtained from the universities of Vienna and Urbino, Italy. During her studies, she worked in the field of juveniles' addiction prevention for several years before she concluded her education as a clinical and health psychologist at the medical university of Vienna as well as the 'Schweizer Haus Hadersdorf', a stationary treatment facility for patients suffering from drug addiction. She is also registered with the federal ministry of justice as a certified mediator. Her focus lies on the topics of divorce, inheritance and company succession. Since 2012, Monika Stempkowski has been working as a researcher at the Department of Criminal Law and Criminology at the University of Vienna in the field of criminology (chair Univ. Prof. Dr. Christian Grafl). Her research focuses on the topics of mentally ill offenders, drug crime and victimology. In her doctoral thesis, she explored the reasons possibly responsible for the decline of the recidivism rate of mentally ill offenders within the Austrian penitentiary system. Since 2018, she has been leading the research project "Successful Tertiary Prevention of Mentally Ill Offenders" which is conducted by the Austrian Association of Psychologists. She publishes articles in German and English, and she is a member of the scientific advisory board of Weisser Ring (eng. White Ring Austria), the biggest victim support organisation in Austria.

E-mail: monika.stempkowski@univie.ac.at

Viktória Szentmihályi-Soós has been working at the Hungarian Ministry of Justice since 2006, where she has specialised on the codification of procedural and international criminal law. She participated in the drafting of several EU legal acts, including the Directive on the rights of victims. She has also taken part in the work of GRECO and MONEYVAL. As a senior legal adviser, she has participated in the codification of the new Hungarian Criminal Procedure Code due to her expertise in the EU legislation. Among others, she was responsible for the chapter on victims' rights. She has also played an important role in the drafting of the new Act on criminal cooperation with the EU Member States.

Tuba Topçuoğlu, PhD, is an Assistant Professor of Criminology at the Faculty of Law, Istanbul University, and the Head of the Criminology Department. She teaches criminological theories, quantitative research methods in criminology and statistics. Her research interests include juvenile delinquency, comparative criminology, victimology, violence against women and crime prevention. She has published in the fields of criminology, juvenile delinquency, crime prevention and social policies.

E-mail address: tuba.topcuoglu@istanbul.edu.tr

Andra-Roxana Trandafir, PhD, teaches Criminology and Criminal Law at the Faculty of Law, University of Bucharest, Romania, where she is also a Vice Dean. She is a member of the Balkan Criminology Network, a co-chair of the ESC Working Group on Balkan Criminology and the Editor-in-Chief of the Balkan Criminology News. She has published several books and more than 50 articles in Romania, Germany, Italy, Slovenia, Canada and Panama.

E-mail address: andra.trandafir@drept.unibuc.ro

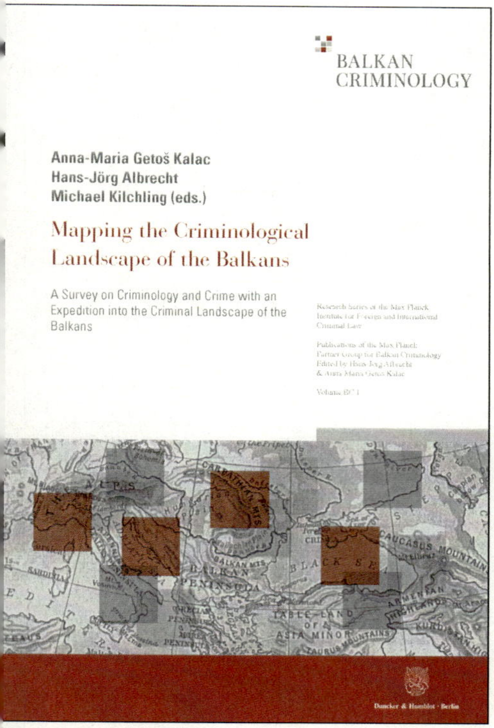
BALKAN
CRIMINOLOGY
Anna-Maria Getoš Kalac
Hans-Jörg Albrecht
Michael Kilchling (eds.)
Mapping the Criminological Landscape of the Balkans
A Survey on Criminology and Crime with an Expedition into the Criminal Landscape of the Balkans
Research Series of the Max Planck Institute for Foreign and International Criminal Law
Publications of the Max Planck Partner Group for Balkan Criminology
Edited by Hans-Jörg Albrecht & Anna-Maria Getoš Kalac
Volume BC 1
Duncker & Humblot · Berlin

BALKAN
CRIMINOLOGY
Sunčana Roksandić Vidlička
Prosecuting Serious Economic Crimes as International Crimes
A New Mandate for the ICC?
Research Series of the Max Planck Institute for Foreign and International Criminal Law
Publications of the Max Planck Partner Group for Balkan Criminology
Edited by Hans-Jörg Albrecht & Anna-Maria Getoš Kalac
Volume BC 2
Duncker & Humblot · Berlin

BALKAN
CRIMINOLOGY
Lucija Sokanović
Fraud in Criminal Law
A Normative and Criminological Analysis of Fraudulent Crime in Croatia and the Regional Context
Research Series of the Max Planck Institute for Foreign and International Criminal Law
Publications of the Max Planck Partner Group for Balkan Criminology
Edited by Hans-Jörg Albrecht & Anna-Maria Getoš Kalac
Duncker & Humblot · Berlin

BALKAN
CRIMINOLOGY
Filip Vojta
Imprisonment for International Crimes
An Interdisciplinary Analysis of the ICTY Sentence Enforcement Practice
Research Series of the Max Planck Institute for Foreign and International Criminal Law
Publications of the Max Planck Partner Group for Balkan Criminology
Edited by Hans-Jörg Albrecht & Anna-Maria Getoš Kalac
Volume BC 5
Duncker & Humblot · Berlin

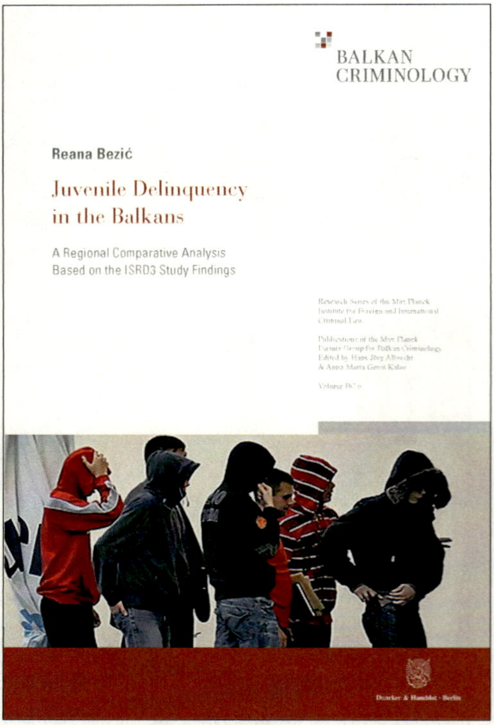

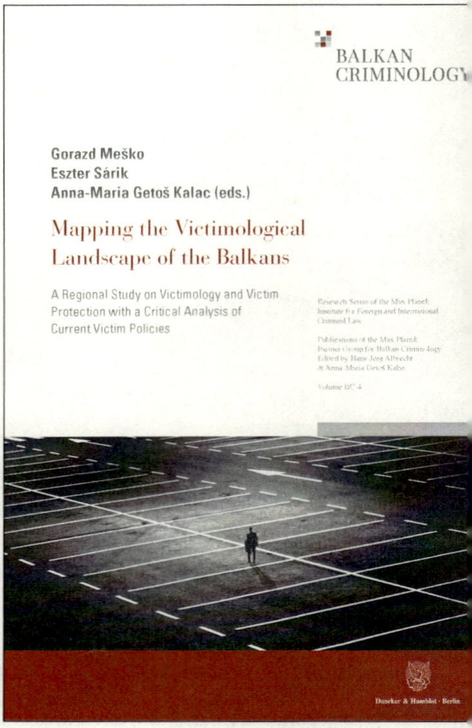

Further titles of the BALKAN CRIMINOLOGY publication series in preparation.